Foundations of Drama

Foundations of Drama

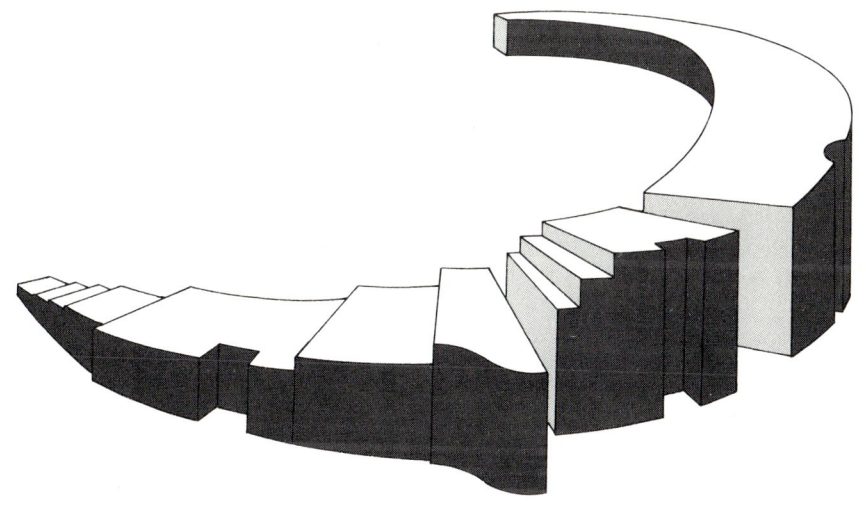

C. J. Gianakaris *Western Michigan University*

HOUGHTON MIFFLIN COMPANY / BOSTON
Altanta   Dallas   Geneva, Ill.   Hopewell, N.J.   Palo Alto   London

"Medea" from *Three Great Plays of Euripides* as translated by Rex Warner. Copyright © 1958 by Rex Warner. Reprinted by arrangement with the New American Library, Inc., New York.

"Twelfth Night" from *The New Cambridge Edition of Shakespeare,* edited by W. A. Neilson and C. J. Hill. By permission of Houghton Mifflin Company, Boston, Mass.

"An Enemy of the People" from the book *Ghosts; An Enemy of the People; The Warriors at Helgeland* by Henrik Ibsen. Translated by R. Farquarson Sharp. Everyman's Library Edition. Published by E. P. Dutton & Co., Inc., and used with their permission.

"A Touch of the Poet" reprinted by permission of Yale University Press. Copyright © 1957 by Carlotta Monterey O'Neill.

The Crucible by Arthur Miller. Copyright 1952, 1953 by Arthur Miller. All rights reserved. Reprinted by permission of the Viking Press, Inc.

"Dream Deferred" copyright 1951 by Langston Hughes. Reprinted from *The Panther and The Lash,* by Langston Hughes, by permission of Alfred A. Knopf, Inc.

"A Raisin in the Sun" by Lorraine Hansberry. Copyright © 1958, 1959, 1966 by Robert Nemiroff as Executor of the Estate of Lorraine Hansberry. Reprinted by permission of Random House, Inc.

Copyright © 1975 by Houghton Mifflin Company. All rights reserved. No part of this work may be reproduced or transmitted in any form or by any means, electronic or mechanical, including photocopying and recording, or by any information storage or retrieval system, without permission in writing from the publisher.

Printed in the U.S.A.

Library of Congress Catalog Card Number: 74-11953

ISBN: 0-395-18611-0

CONTENTS

    Preface   vii
    Overview of Drama   3

MEDEA   *Euripides*   18
    Introduction 12   *Preview* 16   *Postview* 52

TWELFTH NIGHT   *William Shakespeare*   59
    Introduction 54   *Preview* 57   *Postview* 114

AN ENEMY OF THE PEOPLE   *Henrik Ibsen*   119
    Introduction 115   *Preview* 118   *Postview* 192

A TOUCH OF THE POET   *Eugene O'Neill*   198
    Introduction 194   *Preview* 197   *Postview* 268

THE CRUCIBLE   *Arthur Miller*   274
    Introduction 270   *Preview* 272   *Postview* 357

A RAISIN IN THE SUN   *Lorraine Hansberry*   363
    Introduction 359   *Preview* 360   *Postview* 430

    Catalogue of Resources   433
    Index of Key Terms and Definitions   435

PREFACE

Foundations of Drama is a comprehensive textbook about drama. It contains six plays representing some of the most significant drama in Western literature. And it contains commentary, questions, and glosses to clarify for readers *what* a playwright communicates through his play (theme), *how* he communicates ideas through dramatic structure, and *why* a play is aesthetically worth reading.

The six plays included in *Foundations of Drama* offer readers the dramatic expression of different eras and different national cultures as well as a varied sampling of dramatic structures. This diversity does not obstruct, however, the relevance of the plays' themes to today's readers. Euripides' classical Greek drama *Medea* remains one of the strongest statements there is about the closeness of love to hate. *Twelfth Night,* one of Shakespeare's best comedies, shows the confusion all lovers make of identity and projection, and it is just as funny now as it was on the Elizabethan stage in England. Henrik Ibsen's *An Enemy of the People* illustrates a tragic confrontation of idealistic ends with political means, a perennial dilemma in society. *A Touch of the Poet* by Eugene O'Neill depicts the conflict within any person who finds his life falling short of his aspirations for it. Arthur Miller's *The Crucible* uses the social pressures in old Salem Village to study personal conduct when expediency contradicts moral right. *A Raisin in the Sun* by Lorraine Hansberry portrays a black family attempting to wrest human necessities, such as food, shelter, and the chance to achieve dreams, from a hostile society.

To demonstrate the relevance of these themes to readers and to explain the place of theme, structure, and staging techniques in drama, *Foundations of Drama* offers its readers commentary and special guidance. The "Overview of Drama" presents and explains terms and concepts fundamental to the nature of drama and its production. The "Introduction" to each play describes the playwright's particular national and cultural background along with the play's central themes and aesthetic techniques. Also preceding the text of each play is a series of questions called "Preview: Structure" that point readers to crucial structural characteristics to note while reading. At the end of each play is a series of questions called "Postview: Theme" that help readers to achieve a synthesis of the play's theme and structure. In addition to the preview and the postview guides, *Foundations of Drama* provides extensive marginal notes made up of questions and facts that increase readers' attention to what the playwright is saying and how he is saying it. These notes are available precisely where readers need them—in the margin alongside the related dialogue.

By referring to the marginal notes and to the previews and postviews, students can teach themselves about the play's inner workings and meaning. Consequently instructors can expect students to come to class well equipped to discuss the plays.

Foundations of Drama has other features to help readers in purely practical ways. Wide margins furnish students with space to take notes. For theater classes this space can also be used for blocking instructions. The photographs in the text show the six dramatists, specific productions of their plays, and features of theater stages. At the end of the text there is a resource list of books, essays, recordings, and films for each of the six plays and also an index of vital terms and definitions.

The thorough examination of six plays in *Foundations of Drama* makes it easier to read other plays with sensitivity and understanding. And with the help of the guide materials in *Foundations of Drama,* readers can become better observers at live theater productions.

Foundations of Drama

OVERVIEW OF DRAMA

Students who first approach dramatic literature must ask the same questions they would ask of any unknown phenomenon. What is the best method of definition? What are its constituent parts? How does it work, that is, how is it set in motion, or what must occur and be present? Why is it valued? How is it unique?

Overview of Drama examines each of these questions in turn because they are fundamental and valid and deserve answers. In doing so, basic literary definitions will be given while suggesting the ways drama also satisfies non-literary, psychic needs of audiences. *What* drama is made of is treated first, next, *how* it operates, and finally, *why* it is worth continuing close attention. After reading Overview of Drama, one should be better prepared to read analytically and intelligently the plays that follow.

The reader of plays quickly senses that they were not intended simply to be studied in a classroom. To experience a drama completely, a reader must also see and hear a staged production. The principal objective of this book is to assist students in developing critical capabilities for reading drama. A later section will touch upon some production dimensions of a play. For that reason, we will first concentrate on the complicated task of defining drama.

In Western civilization, the dramatic form seems to have first evolved into its now-familiar shape among the great Greek playwrights of the fifth and sixth centuries before Christ. One of the most respected tragedies of that epoch is included here, Euripides' *Medea*. That work is a sample of the classical dramatic format—a format which already incorporated the basic design of much subsequent drama. Even in antiquity, historians and theorists sought to define the essential spirit of drama. Aristotle, one of the earliest Greek observers to attempt to codify systematically the bases of literature, describes drama as "imitated human action." In his study, *The Poetics* (left to us in a fragmentary version), he generalizes that tragedy—the sole significant form of drama at that time—is made up of six elements: plot, characters, verbal expression, thought, visual adornment, and song. Although not all critics accept his scheme in every detail, it does furnish the foundations of most later theories. Consequently, we are well advised to take Aristotle's elemental but provocative remarks as our own first step in comprehending drama.

More precisely, the word "imitated" in Aristotle's discussion denotes a portrayal by actors who pretend to be human characters in a story to be communicated to an audience. Put another way, we may consider a play a story (the *what* of a play) *in motion* (the *how* of a play). Focusing on these simplified definitions, there are three components in the "story" element—theme, plot, and action—and in the "motion" element—characters, language, and kinetic movement. We shall consider theme, plot, and action first.

Not unexpectedly, plays begin as ideas of man's existence in the mind of the playwright. The sources of his inspiration are his observations of the world around him transmuted through his unique mentality and artistic talent. Particularly relevant to the sensitive observer are those central roles man plays in the complicated flow of life. At every turn he finds himself enmeshed in social relations with his peers, in spiritual tangles with metaphysical forces which seem to govern the universe, and in personal quests to clarify his individual identity through his values. The possible variations in these fundamental human experiences cannot be measured, since no two persons lead identical lives. Yet, in any play, the dramatist fastens on one central idea, an abstract concept, which reflects his observations about these human roles. He then proceeds to make his notion concrete in the fashion suggested by Aristotle, presenting his idea through characters who perform actions which constitute the plot. The organizational core within each play is its *theme,* and its episodes and characters should direct the audience to that theme.

Because no one can exist in a vacuum—cut off from all other human beings, the natural environment, his own thoughts—one's entire life is a series of social and personal interactions. Consequently, most dramatists are concerned with a character's struggle against restrictions on his freedom of action imposed by outside forces or ingrained codes of conduct. The characters which inspire the keenest interest are those who represent the onlookers metaphorically, striking back at oppressive structures in life, such as social institutions, spiritual tenets, or inner psychological inhibitions. A touch of the rebel resides in each of us, and a drama allows us to act out our defensive instincts vicariously in opposing what we consider unreasonable limitations placed on us. In fact, the desire to revolt emerges as one general theme in the six plays in this book; they bear witness to the power of the dissenting spirit.

Medea is a fascinating case in point. Medea's moral standards are firm, and she acknowledges love and responsibility for her children. But she is placed in an impossible bind when her personal integrity is tested by her husband Jason when he abandons her. Her choices are to continue abiding by society's mores—being obedient to the husband who spurns her—or to allow her psyche its due by rejecting Jason and the codes of the community. Early in the play, Medea chooses to support her own interests over those of society. The play's theme, then, becomes the wronged victim who responds by avenging herself, here by killing her innocent offspring in righteous rage. Similarly, in Miller's *The Crucible,* Proctor is trapped between his conscience and relentless pressures from the community. Miller's theme may be seen as the struggle to maintain one's individual values in the face of immense social pressures. We will try to determine each playwright's precise theme in the six plays in this book.

Plot is the organizing pattern used by the author to convey theme. More specifically, plot is planned sequence of interrelated actions which, growing out of conflict between vying forces, reach a moment of high tension and then are somehow resolved. We say that conflict generates the action of the story. A moment's thought confirms the logic because, without contending forces or points of view, no tension can be created; and without tension a story falls flat. Conflict, the interplay of one strength upon another, may be physical—the town's harassment of Dr. Stockmann in *An Enemy of the People*—or psychological—Walter's conscience pangs in *A Raisin in the Sun*. In either case, a confrontation of wills must propel the plot forward.

Action is required to move the plot and to retain the interest of an audience; few persons would enjoy sitting through a play which had none. We could even redefine a play as "action revolving around a conflict." Refining this idea still further, we experience action in those scenes which develop, and later resolve, the central conflict in the plot. We might say that the arrangement of action *is* the structure of the play. Of course there is no single, invariable design for planning scenes. Still, a basic movement underlies most conventional drama: a situation is established; a conflict evolves from that situation; the conflict leads to a crucial moment when circumstances and tension reach their peak; a decision is made or an event takes place which removes the conflicting agents; and then through the resolution of the conflict, a new equilibrium is created.

Sometimes this overall scheme is described as *rising action, crisis,* and *falling action*. It is easy enough to express the rising-falling pattern as the growth and waning of friction—hence tension—as a plot develops. According to this dynamic scheme, the play's rising action includes what is needed by an audience to become involved in the characters and their dilemmas. In the rising action we receive information—sometimes called *exposition*—concerning the situation and characters. During the rising action of a play the conflicting issues enter into view, thickening the story line in what are called *complications* or *development*.

The significance of the terms *crisis* or *climax* is evident. As the plot becomes more tangled, the conflict eventually attains a high pitch. In both serious and humorous drama, the crisis occurs when events can move forward no further. At that moment, some event takes place to break the logjam of conflicting wills and forces, thereby releasing the acute tension. As the logjam forms, we ask ourselves: What will happen? In *An Enemy of the People,* how will Dr. Stockmann react to the stubborn townspeople at the public meeting? Will he give in to them or continue to oppose them? Obviously suspense and tension are at their peak during moments of crisis.

Falling action includes the *resolution,* those events or decisions which relieve the tension of events. The resolution can be comic, as when a character reveals himself to be the long-sought heir, lover, or benefactor. In a serious play, the crisis may be relieved through some disastrous act, leading to a tragic outcome. But in all cases, the pent-up tensions are released.

Another useful term in this connection is *denouement,* that part of a resolution in which secondary details are considered and clarified. *Twelfth Night,* for instance, contains a clear denouement. Once the crisis is resolved by Sebastian's timely arrival near the end of the play, Duke Orsino looks upon Cesario—now shown to be a girl, Viola—with different eyes. Since his beloved Cesario is a woman, Orsino's strong affection can be channeled naturally. This post resolution section promises a marriage between Orsino and Viola. Here, too, the roughly treated Malvolio is soothed by Olivia to bring about a happy equilibrium in the near future—precisely the happy ending expected in comedy.

Before moving beyond this structural blueprint—rising action, crisis, resolution and denouement, falling action—we must observe that not every play adheres to such a clear-cut design. These terms and the elements they describe originate in the "well-made play," a type of drama perfected in the last century.

Shaping the action in a balanced and complete way was the prime objective of the author of the "well-made play." But some types of drama deliberately subvert the traditional "balanced plot" in achieving some other goal. All the same, knowledge of an idealized structure with perfect balance, unity, and completeness is a great aid in approaching any kind of drama. Exposition, development, crisis, resolution, and denouement are valuable measuring sticks for identifying a dramatist's methods. We will allude frequently to these critical terms as we consider each of the plays in this book.

How Drama Works

As indicated earlier, a play is more than words printed on a page; it is analogous to a blueprint which the skilled artist translates into a concrete form. Each stage direction must be transformed through the acting medium into physical movement, spoken word, and character identification, Put another way, the play text leads to *two* "hows" of drama: first is the literary dimension revealed in the written dialogue; second is the production inherent in printed words of the text. The principal goal is to understand drama as a literary phenomenon. Yet because a play must be recognized as an art of character in motion to enact its story, we must also discuss how a performance proceeds from the author's written words.

Taking the literary factors first, we find Aristotle's definition of a play as "imitated human action" still valid. If the structure of a play is to provide the development of a human predicament, we also need some human agents on stage to carry out the action in the plot. Playwrights project their themes through the deeds of *characters,* the drama's human counterparts who stand in for us, the readers and viewers. Just as the story of a play is identifiable as something that can take place in life, so do the figures in the plot reflect true-to-life persons with whom we can identify. It is important for a playwright to round out his characters sufficiently for us to understand them, even if we do not condone what they do.

All characters in the theater are symbolic figures. For certain roles in a plot, the character need not be developed extensively. What each figure stands for within the story line, however, must be made clear to the audience. The better dramatists, like those represented in this book, are skilled in creating motivation for their characters, to help audiences understand why someone behaves as he does. In Ibsen's *An Enemy of the People* the opening scene presents important plot exposition. Dr. Stockmann has suspected the town's spas to be infected and is awaiting confirmation from an impartial medical laboratory report. Even more significant, the opening scene provides essential character attributes. Dr. Stockmann's gregarious nature is established and his genuine concern for the health of the community is revealed in his determination to close down the baths for repairs, even though the baths were his idea in the first place. Without revealing Stockmann's altruism at the outset, we would wonder about financial or hidden personal reasons for his actions. Ibsen's character building, however, is psychologically solid and we can empathize with Dr. Stockmann. In a way, Stockmann stands for us at our best—desiring to right a wrong and serve society, despite the animosity which might result. Like us, too, he is very human and makes errors.

Ordinarily one of the characters is appreciated more fully than the others, because we might identify more closely with him. When that figure is the key character in the action, we call him the *protagonist*. When the protagonist is provided with an adversary in the story, that rival is called an *antagonist*. In plays where both a protagonist and antagonist are evident, they constitute the opposing factions of the play's central conflict. Moreover, to help audiences evaluate events in a play, dramatists often create a perceptive observer, called the *raisonneur*. His comments on the action can be trusted, particularly when he is the author's spokesman on stage. The nurse in *Medea* exhibits keen insights regarding the situation, and her remarks provide an accurate index to the events. Thus she fully qualifies as a raisonneur. The *chorus* is related to the observing function of the raisonneur. Prominent in ancient Greek drama but still evident in plays written today, ordinary members of a community act as choral figures, and they respond to events just like any typical person. As a result they cannot be trusted completely, unlike raisonneurs. The chorus represents the perceptions and motivations of the general community; and as stand-ins for society and us, they are susceptible to dubious logic and faulty observation. The Corinthian women in *Medea* speak for the community at large in their reactions to the shifting situations in Euripides' play. In each of the plays in this book, we shall discover a variety of choral characters and raisonneurs. They both help us develop a stable point of view regarding the issues in the play.

In a play *language* is the verbal expression of the characters to advance the plot. The play texts printed in this book are the words written by the playwright to be spoken aloud in a performance by his characters. At the same time, the characters' words have literary significance. Through the dramatist's written speeches we will understand the nature of the characters and of the story line. The more effective the language is, the better our chances to realize the author's intentions.

The interchange of spoken lines among characters is called *dialogue,* through which we gain a perspective on the story. We conclude what is happening and to whom solely on the basis of the logic of the language.

When the playwright wishes to make known the innermost feelings of a character, he can write a *soliloquy* for that figure—that is, dialogue spoken aloud but not directed to any other person in the play. A soliloquy is a theatrical technique which allows an audience access to a character's most private thought. A hilarious soliloquy in *Twelfth Night* highlights the fifth scene of Act II, when Malvolio fantasizes about himself as a nobleman. Due to such passages, a reader can laugh at Malvolio because his thoughts and motives are revealed to us.

Unlike fiction, drama shows the incidents in a play through the *movement* of characters. Readers must deduce what a given character is doing at any moment principally on the basis of dialogue. Sometimes, however, we are provided detailed accounts of a character's nature and his deeds on stage in *stage directions*, those descriptive statements by the author which usually are set off to distinguish them from actual lines of the play. Miller's *The Crucible* includes a considerable amount of stage directions. For the most part, a dramatist keeps instructions for stage movements to a minimum, which allows for more latitude when staging a play.

Up to now we have discussed how a play operates on a literary basis. When a play is performed, other matters also become crucial. Even in performance, however, the actors and director must begin with the printed words of the script, because a thorough understanding of the text is mandatory to reach a valid, unified approach to its production. Good performers consequently are first good readers.

Character depiction, for example, is as essential in the performance of a play as it is for comprehending any work of literature. An actor must first read the play to identify the nature and motives of his character and then must act to create that character on stage. His sources are the printed dialogue and his interpretation of the role in the overall story line. Once he has a firm concept about the personality of the figure he is playing, the actor develops his role by means of personalized movements, gestures, and facial expressions, as well as by speaking the lines. Ultimately an actor must convey to the audience the attitude, motivation, and general personality of his character.

A director lends an overall unifying design to the performance of drama. He oversees the entire production, and it is his interpretation of the play which determines how it will be executed. Also the director sees that the individual characters are compatible with one another. Moreover, it is his responsibility to study the play's text to visualize the action of the plot as it will be acted out in movements. He must decide where the characters should stand on stage at every moment, and how they should move and gesture to reinforce the dialogue. Such preliminary planning for the physical presence of the actors on stage is called *blocking* a play. As each decision is reached concerning positions and motions of the characters for a scene, the director notes the blocking scheme on the script itself, adjacent to the dialogue involved.

Finally, the director must approve the settings (i.e., backdrops and props) developed by the set designer, the characters' clothes designed by the costumer, the colors and lighting patterns planned by the lighting technician, and any special sound effects or music. Many creative people contribute ideas and talents to the finished product, but it is the director who is responsible for the success or failure of a production.

How then does a play work? Drama operates on several levels concurrently, but they all stem from the dialogue. From the dialogue readers can deduce plot, character, and action. From the script the performers physically will enact plot, build live, moving, and talking characters on the stage, and implement movement and gesture patterns to give the play action. Through our analyses of the plays in this book we can create in our minds personal "productions" based on the dramatic illusions we find within the dialogue.

Why We Need Drama

The most complex issue associated with drama is *why* it has been and remains a successful, irreplaceable artistic form in man's culture. The fact that plays have been written and performed for over two thousand years suggests that drama satisfies its audiences in a manner not matched by other artistic expressions. The reasons why drama is invaluable lie within what it is and how it works. We will view drama from a wide perspective, fitting it into the culture and history of the world at large. We shall consider three points: (1) why plays are able to explore raw human experiences to give them clearer meaning; (2) why in some important ways drama supersedes other art forms in its powers to express; and (3) why drama as literature offers readers unique benefits unavailable even in a play's performance.

Actual events in the world contain the same ingredients found in plays: personal or national conflict, confrontation, warfare, love, hate, jealousy—all the pleasures and tensions inherent in man's universe.

But simple reporting of real world happenings is not the primary role of drama. It is what drama does with and to life's experiences which invests plays with value. In the most elemental sense, drama proceeds in two stages. First, a selective process is involved. The observant dramatist considers the fleeting actions that compose our everyday lives, and he chooses those issues from our existence that he believes are worth looking at more closely. Second, a crucial shaping process is undertaken. Using the events from human existence as his raw material, the playwright molds self-contained units called plays which have structure and set perimeters. Plays thus become posed pictures of our lives. But because they are limited in the themes they portray and because they are focused by the dramatist's art, plays permit an audience to consider, unhurriedly, the crucial issues of life with far greater ease. According to the universality of its subject, the dramatic model which results can accommodate and clarify the separate life experiences of each onlooker. The importance of such a clarification cannot be overestimated. Man wishes to comprehend in an intellectual fashion the meaning of life's happenings. Otherwise his placement on earth cannot be rationalized within a logical system. All philosophy, religion, psychology, science, literature—indeed all areas of human knowledge—grow out of man's need to discover a rational scheme for the universe.

In many ways, then, a play is a complex symbol that captures some facet of life and then *re*-presents it within a figurative framework. Once put into dramatic terms, that in life which is formless, abstract, and conjectural becomes clarified through concrete, representative characters involved in recognizable, representative deeds. Through drama idea is given a material form.

Arthur Miller's *The Crucible* suggests the interpretive evaluation of life. The Salem witch trials of the late 1600s are historically verifiable facts. Innocent persons were charged with witchcraft on flimsy evidence, and many were executed or completely ostracized. Miller uses these historical events to probe the distorted human nature evidenced at that time. Miller's theme is the psychology of fear and he incorporates it in his play's characters, particularly in Proctor.

Beside intellectually learning about life there is a second, related impulse basic in mankind—that is, knowing life through the senses and emotions. The need to capture vital truths about experiences in ritual play-acting always has been a primitive instinct in men. Practically speaking, the moment is frozen in a make believe design so that it can be repeated whenever desired. Religious beliefs are made permanent by way of ceremonies that give graphic, physical shape to divine words. In ancient times, ritual sacrifice along with other religious displays of faith was conducted through established gestures, incantations, and movements which constituted a scenario for the participants. Each figure played his assigned role, from priest to sacrificial martyr. Current versions of religious rites include the masses and communion services found in many churches. Nor is it accidental that after a long dormant period throughout much of the Middle Ages, the play form was re-born during church ceremonies within acted representations of the Bible. Similarly, in civic functions basic forms of drama appear daily. Consider for instance such different ceremonies as inaugurating presidents, calling judicial courts to order, initiating fraternity pledges, or crowning homecoming queens. To repeat a set of words and movements which were passed down from earlier generations creates a bond, a sense of human community, which transcends time and space. Participants thus are connected with all who preceded them in the repeated roles.

Of the six plays found in this book, *Medea* is the most distinctly designed. Based on legends from the prehistorical mind of man, the Medea story probably is fictional. But Euripides did not see Medea simply as one special person who turned savage when disappointed in love. Like his fellow Greek writers, Euripides sensed a larger pattern of human behavior inherent in Medea's hideous murders. Medea's rebellion celebrates the desperate possibilities of the human spirit when driven beyond its normal tolerance. Though we do not excuse Medea for her slayings, we understand her better from the play than from studying a psychiatrist's case or all the books of law ever written. Evidently, then, both on an intellectual and emotive level drama can show us a life in a way not possible through conventional means of expression.

Since literature seeks to express and clarify existence by way of symbols, images, and illusions, we must distinguish between the characteristics of drama and the other literary arts.

By definition, all literature begins with the written word. Reading the words of the writer is the common denominator, instead of listening as with music or looking as with the visual arts. Prose fiction is most direct in its method; it tells the reader what he should know through the narrative voice chosen by the author. Characters are developed through the novelist's descriptions, and a symbolic story line evolves from the narrative. But in every instance, the reader is *told*, not shown. Poetry is more flexible because the words and their component sounds and syllables project the poet's expression. Yet like fiction, poetry is a literary form that ends once the reader has read the poem. One difference between novels and poetry is that in verse the poet fully utilizes language, demanding more effort from readers in opening themselves to word and image associations than the more literal technique of fiction.

Plays use some of the same tactics as poems and prose fiction. For instance, the written word initiates the dramatic process, although in a play's text the author no longer speaks in his own voice. Instead, he speaks through *all* his characters. There also are some dissimilarities. Unlike the other literary modes, drama is a cooperative experience, both in terms of producing and of observing the finished play: actors and directors develop the character and story from the dialogue, the set designer erects an appropriate visual setting for the play, the costume designer must imagine and then execute proper clothing for the characters. Also, there are "special effects" people, musicians, and stage managers. Whereas a poem or novel is limited to the author's printed words and his reader—an audience of one—drama is a hybrid art form, using the skills of many people simultaneously, to communicate to an audience of many viewers at a time.

More pertinent to the theater-goer is the sense of community he shares with others in the audience. Whereas a poem or novel is an individual experience (between the author's words and the reader's mind), a play allows each member of the audience to respond personally *and* jointly. Connections are made between the actors (through association and identification) and the people in the audience; this does not occur in any other literary format. In this respect the dramatic idiom transcends other literary forms. We can cheer Stockmann in *An Enemy of the People* for his valiant fight against the questionable elements of society, although few of us would repeat his actions in person in our own lives.

Finally, we are reminded that the main goal of this book is to develop effective reading skills for drama. It is evident that we value the playwright's manuscript as the blueprint for any performance of that play. Beyond that, studying the author's words permits a serious analysis of the range of meanings built into them. Because his text holds the potential action and characterization within it, and because drama is an exceedingly complex form, we should read the dialogue carefully. A play in performance verbalizes the lines and makes necessary movements according to a set pace, moving the plot through time toward its prearranged conclusion. A play in reading does not have a time limitation. The lines can be read, considered, talked about, and then re-read until they have been exhausted of all meaningful possibilities.

Without having to keep his senses alert during a play's production, the reader has the opportunity to pick out the specific play constituents we discussed earlier. Therefore he can detail the precise steps taken by the dramatist to bring about plot and character revelation. The result will be a profile of the drama and of the author's methods. Meanwhile, too, a student need not be restricted by the interpretation of any given production. Using his own imagination, he can mentally recreate his own version of the text. The reader never is limited to a single conception of drama; only his own imaginative powers limit his understanding and pleasure.

The Overview of Drama is meant to acquaint students with useful dramatic terms and to suggest the range of meanings and methods represented by the dramatic form. In the final analysis, each play must be evaluated to decide its effectiveness in portraying its subject. Each time the viewer judges a play a success in expressing one perspective of life, he proves that drama still stimulates the feelings and engages our minds, no matter what era we live in.

INTRODUCTION
MEDEA

Medea IS BEST APPROACHED by asking the same three questions discussed in the Overview of Drama. (1) We will want to know what *Medea* is about—what kind of play it is, its theme, its story. (2) We will need to understand how Euripides structured his ideas—how the classical Greek dramatic pattern affected his writing style. And (3) we shall look at *Medea* to determine why it has something to say to us today, just as it satisfied ancient audiences living within a radically different lifestyle from our own.

Euripides' *Medea,* the oldest play in this book, was first performed about 431 B.C. Consequently it represents one of the earliest structured forms of drama in Western civilization. The plays of ancient Greece ushered in *classical drama,* the first great era of dramatic production and literature known to man. Only several dozen ancient Greek and Roman plays remain for us to enjoy in modern times. Yet, the influence of those precursory dramas is inestimable in terms of subsequent themes and dramatic structures used in the theater.

What

Like other dramas written by Euripides' fellow Greek tragedians, Sophocles and Aeschylus, *Medea* concerned itself with the foremost issue of that age—to explore man's position in a cosmic hierarchy overseen by unpredictable gods. As we shall observe later, Greek drama evolved from religious rituals. Most civic and cultural institutions in fact took into account the demands of divine will, that is, the power of the gods. To the citizen of fifth-century Greece, the gods were numerous in number and individualized in interests. To an extraordinary extent, Greek gods involved themselves in the lives of mortals, either bringing them good fortune or ill. Although the gods themselves frequently visited men and women to satisfy human-like longings and express mortal emotions (i.e., sensual desire, jealousy, hatred, and so on), what ultimately remained totally unknowable were the motives of the gods. This was an integral part of most tragedies. In play after play, the boundaries dividing human will and divine will were underscored. What was man's relationship with the governing deities? What were his responsibilities to his fellow man? How far could he impose his personal will on those about him? All such matters intersected with each other to include every predicament known in man's life. Euripides' *Medea* was no exception, for it dealt with the limits of marital love, presenting a conflict between Jason's personal expediency and Medea's personal honor.

Like most ancient Greek tragedies, *Medea* was derived from a legend concerning past mythical figures. Underlying the action of the play was the lore connected with Jason and his pursuit of the Golden Fleece. The mythical Jason was son of King Aeson of Iolcus who had been deposed by his half-brother Pelias.

Secretly Jason was sent off to Mount Pelion to be raised by Chiron, a wise centaur. Upon reaching manhood, Jason returned to Iolcus to claim his rightful throne. Pelias, however, had been forewarned by a prophet that his challenger would arrive in court with one sandal missing, exactly as Jason had. As a ploy, therefore, Pelias swore that he would relinquish the crown to Jason if he succeeded in obtaining the Golden Fleece—the religiously revered wool from the ram worshipped in Colchis. Such as task seemed impossible, and Pelias felt secure in the bargain. But Jason accepted the conditions, built a ship named the Argo, and collected a crew called the Argonauts to accompany him on his dangerous expedition.

It is here that Medea herself entered the tale. Daughter of King Aeëtes of Colchis and granddaughter of Helios the sun god, Medea possessed magical powers. Also, because Colchis was far from Greece at the eastern edge of the Black Sea, Medea was considered an alien sorceress and thus a frightening figure in Greek folklore. The Golden Fleece, which also contained magical powers, was guarded diligently by King Aeëtes by means of a giant serpent. Aeëtes clearly was unwilling to give up the fleece. Thus, when Jason arrived in Colchis, Aeëtes sent him on numerous impossible tasks to divert him from the fleece. But because she loved Jason so passionately, Medea helped him through all his trials and eventually helped him seize the Golden Fleece; she then fled with him from Colchis. To assure their safe escape, Medea even killed her own brother Absyrtus to delay their pursuers. Once the lovers returned to Iolcus, Medea used her magic to trick Pelias' own daughters into slaying their father, after the king broke his word to Jason concerning the Golden Fleece and returning the throne. Forced to flee Iolcus as a result of the king's death, Jason and Medea, now married, arrived in Corinth as exiles with their two children. Euripides' play *Medea* picks up the tale at this point in the action.

Although most previous drama is concerned with deities and ruling statesmen Euripides fashioned *Medea* on the theme of love. He mostly ignored the fact that Jason and Medea are of royal birth. This play also centers on the psychology of a husband-wife relationship gone wrong. After their arduous struggle to retrieve the Golden Fleece and then being chased from each's homeland, Jason is prepared to abandon Medea for a new bride, the daughter of King Creon and princess of Corinth. From Jason's point of view, it is a practical match, because both he and Medea were considered aliens in Corinth. Through a marriage alliance within the royal household, Jason would assure himself—and possibly his children—a secure, comfortable future. Medea however judged the new match as an outright betrayal by Jason. Thus she took her place among the many aggrieved noblewomen in Greek legend, such as Electra, Clytemnestra, and Antigone.

The story of Euripides' play was familiar to his audience. His main task therefore was to compose dramatic action which would underscore the conflicting wills while moving the plot toward a catastrophe already determined by the myth. The opening episodes of the play review the past and present circumstances as witnessed by Medea's nurse and the Corinthian chorus. Medea's entrance and raging lament establish her dangerous frame of mind, leading to the formation of her plans for a hideous revenge on Jason. From that point on, we watch Medea successfully implement her strategies, step by step. At the end of the play is a spectacular scene of her escape from the now grief-crazed Jason. In large measure Euripides' *Medea* is a modern psychological study of husband and wife pursuing quite contrary goals. The intrusion of the gods is minimal here for the primary emphasis is on man's determination of his own fate through actions chosen to satisfy his will. In *Medea,* Jason chooses to leave Medea for another woman and security, while Medea decides to revenge herself on the thankless Jason by destroying that which he held most dear, their sons.

Because the conflict between Medea and Jason was known by the audience, Euripides did not need to construct a complex play. The scenes involving travel, intrigue for the fleece, and the lovers' escape from their former homelands fell outside the perimeters of the play. As a result, *Medea* has a straightforward episodic shape, as Medea progresses toward and attains her aim.

Greek drama was stylized on the basis of the history and nature of the Greek theater. Like modern drama cultivated from the Middle Ages to the present, classical drama was religious in origin. Growing out of worship of Dionysus, the fertility god, Greek drama began as unstructured choral chants, *dithyrambs,* which were sung as part of a ritual dance. It is thought that eventually the leader of the celebrants separated from the others, thereby producing a chanted dialogue between him and the remaining chorus members. Eventually a second and then a third chorister split off from the chorus to serve as the three chief role-takers in the evolving enactments of fables.

With the growth of formalized dialogue, plot, and characterization the chorus declined in importance. Nevertheless, it was structurally integrated into the performances. As the number of choristers declined from nearly fifty to about a dozen their impromptu chanting and unpatterned dancing were set down in permanent form as written dialogue and choreographed movements. As a result, the words and gestures of the protagonists and the chorus were codified as Greek drama developed. Finally, the written play script contained a detailed blueprint for the dramatist's entire conception.

When Greek drama reached its peak of excellence in the fifth century B.C., its plots drew on traditional tales concerning famed individuals and families whose lives were touched by divine will. By using large masks with exaggerated expressions painted on them, the three players portrayed all the roles vital to the story. The masks also permitted men to play the parts of women, for it was the custom of classical drama that no women took part in the play performances. Because the three actors alone took all the key parts, of course no more than three main characters could appear at the same time. Meanwhile, the chorus came to represent the typical citizens of the society involved in the plot. The chorus watched the events and reacted to the deeds they witnessed as would ordinary members of a community. They also provided a listening ear for the protagonists who would ask questions of the chorus and speak out their thoughts to which the chorus responded. When the chorus had lines to deliver, we believe they were spoken by the choral leader, the *coryphaeus.* Yet sometimes it is apparent that a response sung in unison by the entire chorus is indicated by the text. At any rate, the chorus performed an important function by standing in for society and us, witnessing the fate being determined for the play's protagonists.

In light of the standard dramatic conventions (all-male actors, masked performers, and symbolic, singing chorus figures), it is understandable that Greek drama should be highly stylized. Under these conditions, no audience could ever believe that it was watching actual events. There are additional factors contributing to the nonrealistic quality of the plays. The tragedies were performed outdoors in the daytime in large theater arenas, usually seating more than fifteen thousand spectators. To be heard and seen by all those in attendance, the actors relied on artificial, oversized masks and on padded, flowing costumes and elevated shoes. Their dialogue, written in verse form, was declaimed vigorously, while their gestures were exaggerated so that everyone in the audience could see and hear everything. The illustrations shown here indicate the typical apparel of an actor.

During the great decades of Greek drama, nearly a dozen theaters existed throughout the Grecian peninsula, with the best known one located in Athens. Ordinarily, the theater (or *theatron,* "seeing-place") was constructed on the side of a mountain, so that the tiers of seats could be built into the side in a semicircular shape, as the photographs show (see pages 16–17). Before the rows stood a large flat circular area called the *orchestra* ("dancing area"), where the chorus performed its dancing formations. An altar dedicated to the god Dionysus stood in the center of the orchestra, reminding everyone of the religious nature of the play. On the far side of the orchestra from where the spectators sat was a shallow single-story building, the *skene,* in which props were stored and costume changes made by the actors during the performances. The main action of the play took place directly before the skene (which thus served as the "scene" of the action) on a low platform called the *proskenion.* Three doorways opened into the skene from the front side to serve as entrances and exits for the play's chief protagonists. Since many dramas were set in front of palaces or in public streets before houses (as in *Medea*), the facade of the skene was flexible. Meanwhile, the chorus stood and performed in the orchestra space, entering and leaving by way of an aisle, the *parados,* located on either side of the skene.

Once drama had been formalized in terms of a permanent script of dialogue and patterned dancing and movements, it became an integral part of important religious festivals. Plays held a central role in semiannual holidays early each spring and early summer in honor of the fertility deities. Usually a week in duration, these celebrations included sporting events and other kinds of entertainment. But the highlight was the play competitions held the final three days. Three playwrights would be chosen to produce their works, each having one day in which to stage three tragedies and one brief, comical after-piece called a *satyr.* The three tragedies given each day did not portray a continuous sequence of action, although the same characters sometimes would appear in more than one. The first play each day began during the morning to allow sufficient time to complete all four plays before nightfall. At the end of the third day of performances, a panel of judges selected by civic leaders (who also partially subsidized the festivities) voted for the best play of the competition. To win was an honor, and playwrights took a serious attitude toward the productions. The winner was awarded a sum of money and the prestigious laurel wreath.

Why

As suggested in the Introduction to *Medea,* by the time Euripides wrote his play Greek drama had developed to a sophisticated degree. A careful reading of *Medea* will suggest why this play in particular has remained successful and

The theater at Epidaurus, built about 330 B.C.

pertinent. Euripides developed in *Medea* identifiable human beings circumscribed by their unbridled passions. The unrequited love epitomized by the wronged Medea would touch the hearts of many attending the play's production. But simultaneously, Jason's desire to do well by his offspring would strike a sympathetic chord in other viewers because of man's traditional role as head of the family. The collision of two such powerful wills provided the ideal conflict to spark the tragedy of the play—a fact borne out by the numerous play and opera versions of the Medea story in later eras.

Euripides' greatest achievement with *Medea* was tapping the psychological roots of human nature in his characterizations of Medea and Jason. The actions and temperaments of those two figures determined their lives' paths. Greek audiences, like us today, recognized the direct bearing of that lesson on their own lives; human beings would have to take some responsibility too, after all, for the outcome of their deeds.

PREVIEW: STRUCTURE

The prologue section which begins Greek plays provides basic information about the circumstances of the plot and the characters involved—that is, plot and character *exposition*. *Medea* is no exception. Euripides furnishes all the essential facts we need to understand the story. As you study *Medea*, therefore, it will be valuable to keep the following questions in mind and to try to answer them.

1. How is the audience offered an intimate perspective on the situation?
2. What vital facts are established about the past adventures of the protagonists?

A modern production in the theater at Epidaurus

3. How do the opening lines set the tone of the play? Is it lighthearted or comical?

The conventional dramatic structure involves growth of tension through *conflict* within the *development* or *complication* of the plot.

4. What and how is the first complication introduced into the situation?
5. How does Euripides compound the sense of Medea's frustration and anxiety early in *Medea*?
6. Whose arrival goads Medea into taking overt, immediate action? (See ll. 271 ff.) Why?
7. How does the extended argument between Medea and Jason (ll. 446 ff.) develop the play further?
8. Whose entrance allows Medea to finally put her vengeful plan into effect? Why?

As explained in the Overview, the *climax* in the plot is reached when the complications become so profuse and irreconcilable that matters can progress no further.

9. What is the precise nature of Medea's revenge? How many stages are involved?
10. Is there a separate climax in each stage of Medea's revenge? Where do they come in the play?

MEDEA 17

Once the crucial decisions are made and deeds accomplished at the climax, events must fall into place in a given manner according to the choices made —the *resolution*.

11. How does Euripides inform the audience that Medea comprehends fully the horror of the resolution she brings about? (See 11. 1002 ff. and 1. 1078.)
12. In playing what important role does the chorus help us grasp the full effects of the resolution?

In the *denouement* of the play—when one is given—the final details of the plot are "wrapped up," completing the new situation brought about by the resolution.

13. What glimpse of the new situation is given after Medea's revenge? (See 11. 1317 ff.)
14. Why might a play like *Medea* help us resolve certain personal frictions of our own?
15. What advantages does seeing a play have over actually experiencing similar predicaments?

MEDEA

Euripides

translated by Rex Warner

CHARACTERS

Medea, *princess of Colchis and wife of*
Jason, *son of Aeson, king of Iolcus*
Two children of Medea and Jason
Creon, *king of Corinth*
Aegeus, *king of Athens*
Nurse to Medea
Tutor to Medea's children
Messenger
Chorus of Corinthian Women

SCENE: *In front of Medea's house in Corinth. Enter from the house Medea's nurse.*

Jason, Medea, and their children have been living in Corinth as exiles since fleeing, first Colchis, then Iolcus. No stage props were used. Most scenes in Greek drama took place before palaces or houses, and the central doorway of the *skene* was the main entrance. Audiences quickly deduced exact locales from the dialogue, if they did not already know the story well.

NURSE
How I wish the Argo never had reached the land
Of Colchis, skimming through the blue Symplegades,
Nor ever had fallen in the glades of Pelion
The smitten fir-tree to furnish oars for the hands
Of heroes who in Pelias' name attempted
The Golden Fleece! For then my mistress Medea

The Symplegades, or "Clashing Rocks," stood at the entrance to the Black Sea. To pass them took great courage and skill, a feat successfully undertaken by the Argonauts on their way to and from Colchis.

Would not have sailed for the towers of the land of Iolcus,
Her heart on fire with passionate love for Jason;
Nor would she have persuaded the daughters of Pelias
To kill their father, and now be living here 10
In Corinth with her husband and children. She gave
Pleasure to the people of her land of exile,
And she herself helped Jason in every way.
This is indeed the greatest salvation of all—
For the wife not to stand apart from the husband. 15
But now there's hatred everywhere, Love is diseased.
For, deserting his own children and my mistress,
Jason has taken a royal wife to his bed,
The daughter of the ruler of this land, Creon.
And poor Medea is slighted, and cries aloud on the 20
Vows they made to each other, the right hands clasped
In eternal promise. She calls upon the gods to witness
What sort of return Jason has made to her love.
She lies without food and gives herself up to suffering,
Wasting away every moment of the day in tears. 25
So it has gone since she knew herself slighted by him.
Not stirring an eye, not moving her face from the ground,
No more than either a rock or surging sea water
She listens when she is given friendly advice.
Except that sometimes she twists back her white neck and 30
Moans to herself, calling out on her father's name,
And her land, and her home betrayed when she came away with
A man who now is determined to dishonor her.
Poor creature, she has discovered by her sufferings
What it means to one not to have lost one's own country. 35
She has turned from the children and does not like to see them.
I am afraid she may think of some dreadful thing,
For her heart is violent. She will never put up with
The treatment she is getting. I know and fear her
Lest she may sharpen a sword and thrust to the heart, 40
Stealing into the palace where the bed is made,
Or even kill the king and the new-wedded groom,
And thus bring a greater misfortune on herself.
She's a strange woman. I know it won't be easy
To make an enemy of her and come off best. 45
But here the children come. They have finished playing.
They have no thought at all of their mother's trouble.
Indeed it is not usual for the young to grieve.

Enter from the right the slave who is the tutor to Medea's two small children. The children follow him.

TUTOR
You old retainer of my mistress' household,
Why are you standing here all alone in front of the 50
Gates and moaning to yourself over your misfortune?
Medea could not wish you to leave her alone.

NURSE
Old man, and guardian of the children of Jason,
If one is a good servant, it's a terrible thing
When one's master's luck is out; it goes to one's heart. 55
So I myself have got into such a state of grief

That a longing stole over me to come outside here
And tell the earth and air of my mistress' sorrows.

TUTOR
Has the poor lady not yet given up her crying?

NURSE
Given up? She's at the start, not halfway through her tears.

TUTOR
Poor fool—if I may call my mistress such a name—
How ignorant she is of trouble more to come.

NURSE
What do you mean, old man? You needn't fear to speak.

TUTOR
Nothing. I take back the words which I used just now.

NURSE
Don't, by your beard, hide this from me, your fellow-servant.
If need be, I'll keep quiet about what you tell me.

TUTOR
I heard a person saying, while I myself seemed
Not to be paying attention, when I was at the place
Where the old draught-players sit, by the holy fountain,
That Creon, ruler of the land, intends to drive
These children and their mother in exile from Corinth.
But whether what he said is really true or not
I do not know. I pray that it may not be true.

NURSE
And will Jason put up with it that his children
Should suffer so, though he's no friend to their mother?

TUTOR
Old ties give place to new ones. As for Jason, he
No longer has a feeling for this house of ours.

NURSE
It's black indeed for us, when we add new to old
Sorrows before even the present sky has cleared.

TUTOR
But you be silent, and keep all this to yourself.
It is not the right time to tell our mistress of it.

NURSE
Do you hear, children, what a father he is to you?
I wish he were dead—but no, he is still my master.
Yet certainly he has proved unkind to his dear ones.

TUTOR
What's strange in that? Have you only just discovered
That everyone loves himself more than his neighbor?
Some have good reason, others get something out of it.
So Jason neglects his children for the new bride.

NURSE
Go indoors, children. That will be the best thing.
And you, keep them to themselves as much as possible.
Don't bring them near their mother in her angry mood.
For I've seen her already blazing her eyes at them

How does Euripides heighten both the suspense and agony of the unhappy situation here?

"By your beard" is a mild oath.

"Draughts" is another term for the game of checkers.

How might the Tutor's information, if proven true, serve to precipitate action in the play? The complications of the plot mount in number and seriousness.

Does Euripides inspire much sympathy for Jason at this point in the drama? "House" in this context means Medea's entire household, her family, and her family's reputation.

The Nurse's faithfulness to Jason indicates her sense of loyalty to the whole family.

What kind of an attitude toward life does the Tutor display?

How does Euripides hint of impending doom in remarks such as these throughout the tragedy?

As though she meant some mischief and I am sure that
She'll not stop raging until she has struck at someone.
May it be an enemy and not a friend she hurts! 95

Medea is heard inside the house.

MEDEA
Ah, wretch! Ah, lost in my sufferings,
I wish, I wish I might die.

NURSE
What did I say, dear children? Your mother
Frets her heart and frets it to anger.
Run away quickly into the house, 100
And keep well out of her sight.
Don't go anywhere near, but be careful
Of the wildness and bitter nature
Of that proud mind.
Go now! Run quickly indoors. 105
It is clear that she soon will put lightning
In that cloud of her cries that is rising
With a passion increasing. O, what will she do,
Proud-hearted and not to be checked on her course,
A soul bitten into with wrong? 110

The Tutor takes the children into the house.

MEDEA
Ah, I have suffered
What should be wept for bitterly. I hate you,
Children of a hateful mother. I curse you
And your father. Let the whole house crash.

NURSE
Ah, I pity you, you poor creature. 115
How can your children share in their father's
Wickedness? Why do you hate them? Oh children,
How much I fear that something may happen!
Great people's tempers are terrible, always
Having their own way, seldom checked, 120
Dangerous they shift from mood to mood.
How much better to have been accustomed
To live on equal terms with one's neighbors.
I would like to be safe and grow old in a 125
Humble way. What is moderate sounds best,
Also in practice is best for everyone.
Greatness brings no profit to people.
God indeed, when in anger, brings
Greater ruin to great men's houses. 130

Enter, on the right, a Chorus of Corinthian women. They have come to inquire about Medea and to attempt to console her.

CHORUS
I heard the voice, I heard the cry
Of Colchis' wretched daughter.
Tell me, mother, is she not yet

MEDEA 21

At rest? Within the double gates
Of the court I heard her cry. I am sorry   135
For the sorrow of this home. O, say, what has happened?

NURSE
There is no home. It's over and done with.   140
Her husband holds fast to his royal wedding,
While she, my mistress, cries out her eyes
There in her room, and takes no warmth from
Any word of any friend.

MEDEA
Oh, I wish
That lightning from heaven would split my head open.
Oh, what use have I now for life?   145
I would find my release in death
And leave hateful existence behind me.

Medea's longing for an escape from her dilemma is echoed throughout the play.

CHORUS
O God and Earth and Heaven!
Did you hear what a cry was that
Which the sad wife sings?   150
Poor foolish one, why should you long.
For that appalling rest?
The final end of death comes fast.
No need to pray for that.
Suppose your man gives honor   155
To another woman's bed.
It often happens. Don't be hurt.
God will be your friend in this.
You must not waste away
Grieving too much for him who shared your bed.

The Chorus offers ordinary reactions to the situation, questioning the prudence of Medea's grief-stricken request for instant death to remove her from her misery. Do they seem concerned here with Jason's infidelity to Medea?

MEDEA
Great Themis, lady Artemis, behold   160
The things I suffer, though I made him promise,
My hateful husband. I pray that I may see him,
Him and his bride and all their palace shattered
For the wrong they dare to do me without cause.   165
Oh, my father! Oh, my country! In what dishonor
I left you, killing my own brother for it.

See the Introduction for the precise nature of Medea's "dishonor."

NURSE
Do you hear what she says, and how she cries
Oh Themis, the goddess of Promises, and on Zeus,
Whom we believe to be the Keeper of Oaths?   170
Of this I am sure, that no small thing
Will appease my mistress' anger.

Does Medea's wrath involve the gods in any way? How?

CHORUS
Will she come into our presence?
Will she listen when we are speaking
To the words we say?   175
I wish she might relax her rage
And temper of her heart.
My willingness to help will never
Be wanting to my friends.
But go inside and bring her   180

Here the Chorus role evidently is spoken by one of the twelve or so members, because of the singular subject form.

Out of the house to us,
And speak kindly to her: hurry,
Before she wrongs her own.
This passion of hers moves to something great.

NURSE
I will, but I doubt if I'll manage
To win my mistress over. 185
But still I'll attempt it to please you.
Such a look she will flash on her servants
If any comes near with a message,
Like a lioness guarding her cubs.
It is right, I think, to consider 190
Both stupid and lacking in foresight
Those poets of old who wrote songs
For revels and dinners and banquets,
Pleasant sounds for men living at ease;
But none of them all has discovered 195
How to put to an end with their singing
Or musical instruments grief,
Bitter grief, from which death and disaster
Cheat the hopes of a house. Yet how good
If music could cure men of this! But why raise 200
To no purpose the voice at a banquet? For *there* is
Already abundance of pleasure for men
With a joy of its own.

The Nurse goes into the house.

CHORUS
I heard a shriek that is laden with sorrow.
Shrilling out her hard grief she cries out 205
Upon him who betrayed both her bed and her marriage.
Wronged, she calls on the gods,
On the justice of Zeus, the oath sworn,
Which brought her away
To the opposite shore of the Greeks 210
Through the gloomy salt straits to the gateway
Of the salty unlimited sea.

Medea, attended by servants, comes out of the house.

MEDEA
Women of Corinth, I have come outside to you
Lest you should be indignant with me; for I know
That many people are overproud, some when alone, 215
And others when in company. And those who live
Quietly, as I do, get a bad reputation.
For a just judgment is not evident in the eyes
When a man at first sight hates another, before 220
Learning his character, being in no way injured;

---

195 The Nurse provides a homespun observation regarding the difficulty of overcoming great sorrow in life.

205 Consider how Euripides weaves a pattern of frustration and dejection by the use of sorrow, grief, betrayed, wronged, and gloomy.

210 What is the Chorus alluding to when mentioning "the opposite shore of the Greeks"?

Until now, we knew Medea's character through descriptions given by others—such as the Nurse, the Tutor, and the Chorus. Now, how will we be able to judge her?

215 Why is the alien Medea choosing her words so carefully in these first remarks to the Corinthian women?

MEDEA 23

And a foreigner especially must adapt himself.
I'd not approve of even a fellow-countryman
Who by pride and want of manners offends his neighbors.
But on me this thing has fallen so unexpectedly, 225
It has broken my heart. I am finished. I let go
All my life's joy. My friends, I only want to die.
It was everything to me to think well of one man,
And he, my own husband, has turned out wholly vile.
Of all things which are living and can form a judgment 230
We women are the most unfortunate creatures.
Firstly, with an excess of wealth it is required
For us to buy a husband and take for our bodies
A master; for not to take one is even worse.
And now the question is serious whether we take 235
A good or bad one; for there is no easy escape
For a woman, nor can she say no to her marriage.
She arrives among new modes of behavior and manners,
And needs prophetic power, unless she has learned at home,
How best to manage him who shares the bed with her. 240
And if we work out all this well and carefully,
And the husband lives with us and lightly bears his yoke,
Then life is enviable. If not, I'd rather die.
A man, when he's tired of the company in his home,
Goes out of the house and puts an end to his boredom 245
And turns to a friend or companion of his own age.
But we are forced to keep our eyes on one alone.
What they say of us is that we have a peaceful time
Living at home, while they do the fighting in war.
How wrong they are! I would very much rather stand 250
Three times in the front of battle than bear one child.
Yet what applies to me does not apply to you.
You have a country. Your family home is here.
You enjoy life and the company of your friends.
But I am deserted, a refugee, thought nothing of 255
By my husband—something he won in a foreign land.
I have no mother or brother, nor any relation
With whom I can take refuge in this sea of woe.
This much then is the service I would beg from you:
If I can find the means or devise any scheme 260
To pay my husband back for what he has done to me—
Him and his father-in-law and the girl who married him—
Just to keep silent. For in other ways a woman
Is full of fear, defenseless, dreads the sight of cold
Steel; but, when once she is wronged in the matter of love, 265
No other soul can hold so many thoughts of blood.

CHORUS
This I will promise. You are in the right, Medea,
In paying your husband back. I am not surprised at you
For being sad.
But look! I see our King Creon
Approaching. He will tell us of some new plan. 270

Enter, from the right, Creon, with attendants.

CREON
You, with that angry look, so set against your husband,

This explicit profeminist passage was quoted by English suffragettes earlier this century when opening their meetings.

What irony is there in Medea's diatribe concerning maligned women (ll. 230–51)?

Medea points out (ll. 253 ff.) that her predicament goes beyond being rejected by her husband. What compounds her distress?

In ancient Greece, the name "Creon" was synonymous with "king." Consequently, this Creon is not the same Creon as found in several other Greek tragedies.

Medea, I order you to leave my territories
An exile, and take along with you your two children,
And not to waste time doing it. It is my decree,
And I will see it done. I will not return home
Until you are cast from the boundaries of my land.

MEDEA
Oh, this is the end for me. I am utterly lost.
Now I am in the full force of the storm of hate
And have no harbor from ruin to reach easily.
Yet still, in spite of it all, I'll ask the question:
What is your reason, Creon, for banishing me?

CREON
I am afraid of you—why should I dissemble it?—
Afraid that you may injure my daughter mortally.
Many things accumulate to support my feeling.
You are a clever woman, versed in evil arts,
And are angry at having lost your husband's love.
I hear that you are threatening, so they tell me,
To do something against my daughter and Jason
And me, too. I shall take my precautions first.
I tell you, I prefer to earn your hatred now
Than to be soft-hearted and afterward regret it.

MEDEA
This is not the first time, Creon. Often previously
Through being considered clever I have suffered much.
A person of sense ought never to have his children
Brought up to be more clever than the average.
For, apart from cleverness bringing them no profit,
It will make them objects of envy and ill-will.
If you put new ideas before the eyes of fools
They'll think you foolish and worthless into the bargain;
And if you are thought superior to those who have
Some reputation for learning, you will become hated.
I have some knowledge myself of how this happens;
For being clever, I find that some will envy me,
Others object to me. Yet all my cleverness
Is not so much.
            Well, then, are you frightened, Creon,
That I should harm you? There is no need. It is not
My way to transgress the authority of a king.
How have you injured me? You gave your daughter away
To the man you wanted. Oh, certainly I hate
My husband, but you, I think, have acted wisely,
Nor do I grudge it you that your affairs go well.
May the marriage be a lucky one! Only let me
Live in this land. For even though I have been wronged,
I will not raise my voice, but submit to my betters.

CREON
What you say sounds gentle enough. Still in my heart
I greatly dread that you are plotting some evil,
And therefore I trust you even less than before.
A sharp-tempered woman, or, for that matter, a man,
Is easier to deal with than the clever type
Who holds her tongue. No. You must go. No need for more

Creon's abrupt command to leave confirms Medea's apprehension of being an alien in Corinth.

Note Creon's candor in responding to Medea. Do you believe that his guilty feelings have anything to do with his decision, also?

Medea's grandfather was the sun god Helius (or Helios), which meant that she had inherited supernatural powers.

How does Euripides characterize Creon here? What specific character traits can you identify?

This passage reflects an attitude found in many parts of the world in all epochs: to enjoy good fortune of any kind also means to be on guard for envy which as a consequence is aroused in others.

Does Medea truly mean to be reconciled with Creon, or does she have other ulterior objectives in mind? What character attribute is revealed here in Medea?

Does Creon take Medea's words at face value? What does this tell us about his own ability to judge people and situations?

Speeches. The thing is fixed. By no manner of means
Shall you, an enemy of mine, stay in my country.

MEDEA
I beg you. By your knees, by your new-wedded girl.

CREON
Your words are wasted. You will never persuade me.

MEDEA
Will you drive me out, and give no heed to my prayers?

CREON
I will, for I love my family more than you.

MEDEA
O my country! How bitterly now I remember you!

CREON
I love my country too—next after my children.

MEDEA
Oh what an evil to men is passionate love!

CREON
That would depend on the luck that goes along with it.

MEDEA
O God, do not forget who is the cause of this!

CREON
Go. It is no use. Spare me the pain of forcing you.

MEDEA
I'm spared no pain. I lack no pain to be spared me.

CREON
Then you'll be removed by force by one of my men.

MEDEA
No, Creon, not that! But do listen, I beg you.

CREON
Woman, you seem to want to create a disturbance.

MEDEA
I *will* go into exile. *This* is not what I beg for.

CREON
Why then this violence and clinging to my hand?

MEDEA
Allow me to remain here just for this one day,
So I may consider where to live in my exile,
And look for support for my children, since their father
Chooses to make no kind of provision for them.
Have pity on them! You have children of your own.
It is natural for you to look kindly on them.
For myself I do not mind if I go into exile.
It is the children being in trouble that I mind.

CREON
There is nothing tyrannical about my nature,
And by showing mercy I have often been the loser.
Even now I know that I am making a mistake.
All the same you shall have your will. But this I tell you,

---

325 In lines 324 through 339, Euripides provides an excellent passage of stichomythia, i.e., dialogue comprised of line-by-line interchange between characters to produce a fast-moving, clipped narrative effect.

330

In Greek drama luck also can be defined as fortune or fate.

335 Creon displays his resolve when he intends to call guards to remove Medea forcibly.

Medea tries to implore Creon by wringing his hand, a gesture that also keeps him from calling in the guards.

340

345 What psychology does Medea use to gain a one-day reprieve from Creon?

Why do Creon's words (ll. 348 ff.) help make him a more human character?

350

That if the light of heaven tomorrow shall see you,
You and your children in the confines of my land,
You die. This word I have spoken is firmly fixed.
But now, if you must stay, stay for this day alone.   355
For in it you can do none of the things I fear.

Exit Creon with his attendants.

CHORUS
Oh, unfortunate one! Oh, cruel!
Where will you turn? Who will help you?
What house or what land to preserve you   360
From ill can you find?
Medea, a god has thrown suffering
Upon you in waves of despair.

MEDEA
Things have gone badly every way. No doubt of that
But not these things this far, and don't imagine so.   365
There are still trials to come for the new-wedded pair,
And for their relations pain that will mean something.
Do you think that I would ever have fawned on that man
Unless I had some end to gain or profit in it?
I would not even have spoken or touched him with my hands.   370
But he has got to such a pitch of foolishness
That, though he could have made nothing of all my plans
By exiling me, he has given me this one day
To stay here, and in this I will make dead bodies
Of three of my enemies—father, the girl, and my husband.   375
I have many ways of death which I might suit to them,
And do not know, friends, which one to take in hand;
Whether to set fire underneath their bridal mansion,
Or sharpen a sword and thrust it to the heart,
Stealing into the palace where the bed is made.   380
There is just one obstacle to this. If I am caught
Breaking into the house and scheming against it,
I shall die, and give my enemies cause for laughter.
It is best to go by the straight road, the one in which
I am most skilled, and make away with them by poison.   385
So be it then.
And now suppose them dead. What town will receive me?
What friend will offer me a refuge in his land,
Or the guaranty of his house and save my own life?
There is none. So I must wait a little time yet,
And if some sure defense should then appear for me,   390
In craft and silence I will set about this murder.
But if my fate should drive me on without help,
Even though death is certain, I will take the sword
Myself and kill, and steadfastly advance to crime.
It shall not be—I swear it by her, my mistress,   395
Whom most I honor and have chosen as partner,
Hecate, who dwells in the recesses of my hearth—
That any man shall be glad to have injured me.
Bitter I will make their marriage for them and mournful,
Bitter the alliance and the driving me out of the land.   400
Ah, come, Medea, in your plotting and scheming

What part of Medea's reputation has Creon already heard about, evidently?

Logically, it seems that the Chorus's emotional lament (ll. 358 ff.) was sung in unison by all its members.

How does this passage reveal how mercenary Medea can be when dealing with others?

With the simple words in line 386, Medea announces her resolution to kill her enemies. But once she has murdered them, what problem must she still face?

Hecate was a Greek goddess associated with sorcery and witchcraft.

Why is Medea reviewing all the facets of her grudge at this particular point in the action?

Leave nothing untried of all those things which you know.
Go forward to the dreadful act. The test has come
For resolution. You see how you are treated. Never
Shall you be mocked by Jason's Corinthian wedding, 405
Whose father was noble, whose grandfather Helius.
You have the skill. What is more, you were born a woman,
And women, though most helpless in doing good deeds,
Are of every evil the cleverest of contrivers.

CHORUS
Flow backward to your sources, sacred rivers, 410
And let the world's great order be reversed.
It is the thoughts of *men* that are deceitful, 415
Their pledges that are loose.

Story shall now turn my condition to a fair one,
Women are paid their due.
No more shall evil-sounding fame be theirs. 420

Cease now, you muses of the ancient singers,
To tell the tale of my unfaithfulness;
For not on us did Phoebus, lord of music,
Bestow the lyre's divine 425
Power, for otherwise I should have sung an answer
To the other sex. Long time
Has much to tell of us, and much of them. 430

You sailed away from your father's home,
With a heart on fire you passed
The double rocks of the sea.
And now in a foreign country 435
You have lost your rest in a widowed bed,
And are driven forth, a refugee
In dishonor from the land.

Good faith has gone, and no more remains
In great Greece a sense of shame. 440
It has flown away to the sky.
No father's house for a haven
Is at hand for you now, and another queen
Of your bed has dispossessed you and
Is mistress of your home. 445

Enter Jason, with attendants.

JASON
This is not the first occasion that I have noticed
How hopeless it is to deal with a stubborn temper.
For, with reasonable submission to our ruler's will,
You might have lived in this land and kept your home.
As it is you are going to be exiled for your loose speaking. 450
Not that I mind myself. You are free to continue
Telling everyone that Jason is a worthless man.
But as to your talk about the king, consider
Yourself most lucky that exile is your punishment.
I, for my part, have always tried to calm down 455

The Chorus is aroused by Medea to pick up her polemics against men. Her psychology was to deliberately criticize womankind in lines 407–409 in order to provoke the disagreement of the female chorus. These stanzas seem to have been composed for singing by the chorus at large.

As the complications accumulate, Jason's arrival signifies one of the peaks of conflict.

How does Euripides make it evident that Jason has completely washed his hands of Medea?

The anger of the king, and wished you to remain.
But you will not give up your folly, continually
Speaking ill of him, and so you are going to be banished.
All the same, and in spite of your conduct, I'll not desert
My friends, but have come to make some provision for you, 460
So that you and the children may not be penniless
Or in need of anything in exile. Certainly
Exile brings many troubles with it. And even
If you hate me, I cannot think badly of you.

MEDEA
O coward in every way—that is what I call you, 465
With bitterest reproach for your lack of manliness,
You have come, you, my worst enemy, have come to me!
It is not an example of overconfidence
Or of boldness thus to look your friends in the face, 470
Friends you have injured—no, it is the worst of all
Human diseases, shamelessness. But you did well
To come, for I can speak ill of you and lighten
My heart, and you will suffer while you are listening.
And first I will begin from what happened first. 475
I saved your life, and every Greek knows I saved it,
Who was a shipmate of yours aboard the Argo,
When you were sent to control the bulls that breathed fire
And yoke them, and when you would sow that deadly field.
Also that snake, who encircled with his many folds 480
The Golden Fleece and guarded it and never slept,
I killed, and so gave you the safety of the light.
And I myself betrayed my father and my home,
And came with you to Pelias' land of Iolcus.
And then, showing more willingness to help than wisdom, 485
I killed him, Pelias, with a most dreadful death
At his own daughters' hands, and took away your fear.
This is how I behaved to you, you wretched man,
And you forsook me, took another bride to bed,
Though you had children; for, if that had not been, 490
You would have had an excuse for another wedding.
Faith in your word has gone. Indeed, I cannot tell
Whether you think the gods whose names you swore by then
Have ceased to rule and that new standards are set up,
Since you must know you have broken your word to me. 495
O my right hand, and the knees which you often clasped
In supplication, how senselessly I am treated
By this bad man, and how my hopes have missed their mark!
Come, I will share my thoughts as though you were a friend—
You! Can I think that you would ever treat me well? 500
But I will do it, and these questions will make you
Appear the baser. Where am I to go? To my father's?
Him I betrayed and his land when I came with you.
To Pelias' wretched daughters? What a fine welcome
They would prepare for me who murdered their father! 505
For this is my position—hated by my friends
At home, I have, in kindness to you, made enemies
Of others whom there was no need to have injured.
And how happy among Greek women you have made me

Does Jason truthfully desire Medea to stay in Corinth? Does he have the welfare of either Medea or his sons in mind? What does this statement reveal about Jason's character?

One of Medea's arguing tactics is to impugn the manliness and honesty of her errant husband.

Medea explicitly documents the incidents in Jason's past trials when she assisted and saved him.

In antiquity, a barren wife could be returned to her family and a new wife taken because bearing children was an expected part of the marriage contract.

Medea argues that Jason broke the vows made before the gods. Thus he is sinning in a religious as well as moral sense.

On your side for all this! A distinguished husband 510
I have—for breaking promises. When in misery
I am cast out of the land and go into exile,
Quite without friends and all alone with my children,
That will be a fine shame for the new-wedded groom,
For his children to wander as beggars and she who saved him. 515
O God, you have given to mortals a sure method
Of telling the gold that is pure from the counterfeit;
Why is there no mark engraved upon men's bodies,
By which we could know the true ones from the false ones?

CHORUS
It is a strange form of anger, difficult to cure, 520
When two friends turn upon each other in hatred.

> How does the Chorus serve the drama at this moment?

JASON
As for me, it seems I must be no bad speaker.
But, like a man who has a good grip of the tiller,
Reef up his sail, and so run away from under
This mouthing tempest, women, of your bitter tongue. 525
Since you insist on building up your kindness to me,
My view is that Cypris was alone responsible
Of men and gods for the preserving of my life.

> Cypris is another name for Aphrodite, goddess of love and beauty.

You are clever enough—but really I need not enter
Into the story of how it was love's inescapable 530
Power that compelled you to keep my person safe.

> Observe Jason's version of Medea's earlier assistance to him. On what does he base his argument?

On this I will not go into too much detail.
In so far as you helped me, you did well enough.
But on this question of saving me, I can prove
You have certainly got from me more than you gave. 535
Firstly, instead of living among barbarians,
You inhabit a Greek land and understand our ways,
How to live by law instead of the sweet will of force.
And all the Greeks considered you a clever woman.
You were honored for it; while, if you were living at 540
The ends of the earth, nobody would have heard of you.
For my part, rather than stores of gold in my house
Or power to sing even sweeter songs than Orpheus,
I'd choose the fate that made me a distinguished man.
There is my reply to your story of my labors. 545

> Orpheus was the greatest poet and musician in Greek mythology, able to move rocks and trees with his playing. He accompanied Jason on the Argo, helping the Argonauts resist the lure of the Sirens through his music.

Remember it was you who started the argument.
Next for your attack on my wedding with the princess:
Here I will prove that, first, it was a clever move,
Secondly, a wise one, and, finally, that I made it
In your best interests and the children's. Please keep calm. 550
When I arrived here from the land of Iolcus,
Involved, as I was, in every kind of difficulty,
What luckier chance could I have come across than this,
An exile to marry the daughter of the king?

> What stage direction to the actors is indicated in line 550?

It was not—the point that seems to upset you—that I 555
Grew tired of your bed and felt the need of a new bride;
Nor with any wish to outdo your number of children.
We have enough already. I am quite content.
But—this was the main reason—that we might live well,
And not be short of anything. I know that all 560

> For Jason, the new match with Creon's daughter does represent good fortune since he and his sons—as well as Medea—also are foreigners living in Corinth at the pleasure of Creon.
>
> What is Jason's psychological intent in trying to explain his actions to Medea?

A man's friends leave him stone-cold if he becomes poor.
Also that I might bring my children up worthily
Of my position, and, by producing more of them
To be brothers of yours, we would draw the families
Together and all be happy. You need no children. 565
And it pays me to do good to those I have now
By having others. Do you think this a bad plan?
You wouldn't if the love question hadn't upset you.
But you women have got into such a state of mind
That, if your life at night is good, you think you have 570
Everything; but, if in that quarter things go wrong.
You will consider your best and truest interests
Most hateful. It would have been better far for men
To have got their children in some other way, and women
Not to have existed. Then life would have been good. 575

Jason offers a man's logic in this part of his argument. What explicitly is he claiming about Medea's grievances?

CHORUS
Jason, though you have made this speech of yours look well,
Still I think, even though others do not agree,
You have betrayed your wife and are acting badly.

One needs to be reminded that the chorus in *Medea* is made up of Medea's women neighbors, i.e., housewives, etc.

MEDEA
Surely in many ways I hold different views
From others, for I think that the plausible speaker 580
Who is a villain deserves the greatest punishment.
Confident in his tongue's power to adorn evil,
He stops at nothing. Yet he is not really wise.
As in your case. There is no need to put on the airs
Of a clever speaker, for one word will lay you flat. 585
If you were not a coward, you would not have married
Behind my back, but discussed it with me first.

Does Medea accept Jason's rationale?

JASON
And you, no doubt, would have furthered the proposal,
If I had told you of it, you who even now
Are incapable of controlling your bitter temper. 590

MEDEA
It was not that. No, you thought it was not respectable
As you got on in years to have a foreign wife.

Medea reveals again how sensitive she is as an alien.

JASON
Make sure of this: it was not because of a woman
I made the royal alliance in which I now live,
But, as I said before, I wished to preserve you 595
And breed a royal progeny to be brothers
To the children I have now, a sure defense to us.

MEDEA
Let me have no happy future that brings pain with it,
Or prosperity which is upsetting to the mind!

Is Medea prepared to pay Jason's price simply for the possibility of security in the future?

JASON
Change your ideas of what you want, and show more sense. 600
Do not consider painful what is good for you,
Nor, when you are lucky, think yourself unfortunate.

MEDEA
You can insult me. You have somewhere to turn to.
But I shall go from this land into exile, friendless.

JASON
It was what you chose yourself. Don't blame others for it. 605

MEDEA
And how did I choose it? Did I betray my husband?

JASON
You called down wicked curses on the king's family.

MEDEA
A curse, that is what I am become to your house too.

JASON
I do not propose to go into all the rest of it;
But, if you wish for the children or for yourself 610
In exile to have some of my money to help you,
Say so, for I am prepared to give with open hand,
Or to provide you with introductions to my friends
Who will treat you well. You are a fool if you do not
Accept this. Cease your anger and you will profit. 615

How does Jason's use of the word "profit" prove precisely right both in terms of logic and word imagery in this passage?

MEDEA
I shall never accept the favors of friends of yours,
Nor take a thing from you, so you need not offer it.
There is no benefit in the gifts of a bad man.

JASON
Then, in any case, I call the gods to witness that
I wish to help you and the children in every way, 620
But you refuse what is good for you. Obstinately
You push away your friends. You are sure to suffer for it.

Why does Jason believe he has morally exonerated himself?

MEDEA
Go! No doubt you hanker for your virginal bride,
And are guilty of lingering too long out of her house.
Enjoy your wedding. But perhaps—with the help of God— 625
You will make the kind of marriage that you will regret.

Jason goes out with his attendants.

CHORUS
When love is in excess
It brings a man no honor
Nor any worthiness.
But if in moderation Cypris comes, 630
There is no other power at all so gracious.
O goddess, never on me let loose the unerring
Shaft of your bow in the poison of desire.

The Chorus voices the sentiments of conservative commoners who work hard to avoid trouble.

Let my heart be wise. 635
It is the gods' best gift.
On me let mighty Cypris
Inflict no wordy wars or restless anger
To urge my passion to a different love.
But with discernment may she guide women's weddings, 640
Honoring most what is peaceful in the bed.

O country and home,
Never, never may I be without you,
Living the hopeless life, 645

32 EURIPIDES

Hard to pass through and painful,
Most pitiable of all.
Let death first lay me low and death
Free me from this daylight.
There is no sorrow above 650
The loss of a native land.

I have seen it myself,
Do not tell of a secondhand story.
Neither city nor friend 655
Pitied you when you suffered
The worst of sufferings.
O let him die ungraced whose heart
Will not reward his friends, 660
Who cannot open an honest mind
No friend will he be of mine.

Enter Aegeus, king of Athens, an old friend of Medea.

AEGEUS
Medea, greeting! This is the best introduction
Of which men know for conversation between friends.

MEDEA
Greeting to you too, Aegeus, son of King Pandion. 665
Where have you come from to visit this country's soil?

AEGEUS
I have just left the ancient oracle of Phoebus.

MEDEA
And why did you go to earth's prophetic center?

AEGEUS
I went to inquire how children might be born to me.

MEDEA
Is it so? Your life still up to this point is childless? 670

AEGEUS
Yes. By the fate of some power we have no children.

MEDEA
Have you a wife, or is there none to share your bed?

AEGEUS
There is. Yes, I am joined to my wife in marriage.

MEDEA
And what did Phoebus say to you about children?

AEGEUS
Words too wise for a mere man to guess their meaning. 675

MEDEA
It is proper for me to be told the god's reply?

AEGEUS
It is. For sure what is needed is cleverness.

MEDEA
Then what was his message? Tell me, if I may hear.

Who has won the sympathy and support of the Chorus at this point, Jason or Medea?

Pandion, before being deposed, had been king of Athens in Greek myths. He fled to Megara, married the princess, and later became king.

Phoebus is another name for the Greek god Apollo whose shrine was at Delphi, where prophecies were spoken through the oracles.

Lines 667 through 707 represent a form of dialogue called *stichomythia*, i.e., dialogue in single, alternate lines. What is its value in drama and at this particular point in *Medea*?

The Delphic oracles received enigmatic word messages from Apollo which often had to be interpreted by priests or priestesses.

MEDEA 33

AEGEUS
I am not to loosen the hanging foot of the wine-skin . . .

MEDEA
Until you have done something, or reached some country? 680

AEGEUS
Until I return again to my hearth and house.

MEDEA
And for what purpose have you journeyed to this land?

AEGEUS
There is a man called Pittheus, king of Troezen.

MEDEA
A son of Pelops, they say, a most righteous man.

AEGEUS
With him I wish to discuss the reply of the god. 685

MEDEA
Yes. He is wise and experienced in such matters.

AEGEUS
And to me also the dearest of all my spear-friends.

MEDEA
Well, I hope you have good luck, and achieve your will.

AEGEUS
But why this downcast eye of yours, and this pale cheek?

MEDEA
O Aegeus, my husband has been the worst of all to me. 690

AEGEUS
What do you mean? Say clearly what has caused this grief.

MEDEA
Jason wrongs me, though I have never injured him.

AEGEUS
What has he done? Tell me about it in clearer words.

MEDEA
He has taken a wife to his house, supplanting me.

AEGEUS
Surely he would not dare to do a thing like that. 695

MEDEA
Be sure he has. Once dear, I now am slighted by him.

AEGEUS
Did he fall in love? Or is he tired of your love?

MEDEA
He was greatly in love, this traitor to his friends.

AEGEUS
Then let him go, if, as you say, he is so bad.

MEDEA
A passionate love—for an alliance with the king. 700

AEGEUS
And who gave him his wife? Tell me the rest of it.

MEDEA
It was Creon, he who rules this land of Corinth.

Wine usually was carried in animal skins during long journeys.

Pittheus also was grandfather of Theseus, the mythical founder of Athens.

How does King Aegeus' reaction to Medea's tale of sorrow affect our own opinion of her complaints? Would he have any other reason to dislike Jason?

34   EURIPIDES

AEGEUS
Indeed, Medea, your grief was understandable.

MEDEA
I am ruined. And there is more to come: I am banished.

AEGEUS
Banished? By whom? Here you tell me of a new wrong.   705

MEDEA
Creon drives me an exile from the land of Corinth.

AEGEUS
Does Jason consent? I cannot approve of this.

MEDEA
He pretends not to, but he will put up with it.
Ah, Aegeus, I beg and beseech you, by your beard
And by your knees I am making myself your suppliant,   710
Have pity on me, have pity on your poor friend,
And do not let me go into exile desolate,
But receive me in your land and at your very hearth.
So may your love, with God's help, lead to the bearing
Of children, and so may you yourself die happy.   715
You do not know what a chance you have come on here.
I will end your childlessness, and I will make you able
To beget children. The drugs I know can do this.

AEGEUS
For many reasons, woman, I am anxious to do
This favor for you. First, for the sake of the gods,   720
And then for the birth of children which you promise,
For in that respect I am entirely at my wits' end.
But this is my position: if you reach my land,
I, being in my rights, will try to befriend you.
But this much I must warn you of beforehand: 725
I shall not agree to take you out of this country;
But if you by yourself can reach my house, then you
Shall stay there safely. To none will I give you up
But from this land you must make your escape yourself,
For I do not wish to incur blame from my friends.   730

MEDEA
It shall be so. But, if I might have a pledge from you
For this, then I would have from you all I desire.

AEGEUS
Do you not trust me? What is it rankles with you?

MEDEA
I trust you, yes. But the house of Pelias hates me,
And so does Creon. If you are bound by this oath,   735
When they try to drag me from your land, you will not
Abandon me; but if our pact is only words,
With no oath to the gods, you will be lightly armed,
Unable to resist their summons. I am weak,
While they have wealth to help them and a royal house.   740

AEGEUS
You show much foresight for such negotiations.
Well, if you will have it so, I will not refuse.
For, both on my side this will be the safest way

Gradually we sense that Medea is gaining a powerful ally in Aegeus to oppose Creon and Jason.

Why does Medea especially desire Aegeus' friendship?

How does Medea show herself to be a master of human psychology?

In the bargain he agrees to, why is Aegeus so insistent that Medea escape from Corinth by her own means before he will offer her sanctuary in Athens?

Why would Medea be especially sensitive regarding the oaths men take? (See, for instance, ll. 746–47, also.)

To have some excuse to put forward to your enemies,
And for you it is more certain. You may name the gods. 745

MEDEA
Swear by the plain of Earth, and Helius, father
Of my father, and name together all the gods . . .

AEGEUS
That I will act or not act in what way? Speak.

MEDEA
That you yourself will never cast me from your land,
Nor, if any of my enemies should demand me, 750
Will you, in your life, willingly hand me over.

AEGEUS
I swear by the Earth, by the holy light of Helius,
By all the gods, I will abide by this you say.

> This time, Medea makes certain that the oath taken by Aegeus is binding. It is clear that he too takes oaths seriously. (See l. 755.)

MEDEA
Enough. And, if you fail, what shall happen to you?

AEGEUS
What comes to those who have no regard for heaven. 755

MEDEA
Go on your way. Farewell. For I am satisfied.
And I will reach your city as soon as I can,
Having done the deed I have to do and gained my end.

Aegeus goes out.

CHORUS
May Hermes, god of travelers,
Escort you, Aegeus, to your home! 760
And may you have the things you wish
So eagerly; for you
Appear to me to be a generous man.

MEDEA
God, and God's daughter, justice, and light of Helius!
Now, friends, has come the time of my triumph over 765
My enemies, and now my foot is on the road.
Now I am confident they will pay the penalty.
For this man, Aegeus, has been like a harbor to me
In all my plans just where I was most distressed.
To him I can fasten the cable of my safety 770
When I have reached the town and fortress of Pallas.
And now I shall tell to you the whole of my plan.
Listen to these words that are not spoken idly.
I shall send one of my servants to find Jason
And request him to come once more into my sight. 775
And when he comes, the words I'll say will be soft ones.
I'll say that I agree with him, that I approve
The royal wedding he has made, betraying me.
I'll say it was profitable, an excellent idea.
But I shall beg that my children may remain here: 780
Not that I would leave in a country that hates me
Children of mine to feel their enemies' insults,
But that by a trick I may kill the king's daughter.
For I will send the children with gifts in their hands
To carry to the bride, so as not to be banished— 785

> Medea means Athens here, where the holy shrines of Athena, or Pallas, stood.
>
> Beginning here, Medea details her plans for destroying her enemies. Although the Chorus surrounds her and listens, Medea essentially is delivering a modified soliloquy through which she expresses every innermost thought.

A finely woven dress and a golden diadem.
And if she takes them and wears them upon her skin
She and all who touch the girl will die in agony;
Such poison will I lay upon the gifts I send.
But there, however, I must leave that account paid. 790
I weep to think of what a deed I have to do
Next after that; for I shall kill my own children.
My children, there is none who can give them safety.
And when I have ruined the whole of Jason's house,
I shall leave the land and flee from the murder of my 795
Dear children, and I shall have done a dreadful deed.
For it is not bearable to be mocked by enemies.
So it must happen. What profit have I in life?
I have no land, no home, no refuge from my pain.
My mistake was made the time I left behind me 800
My father's house, and trusted the words of a Greek,
Who, with heaven's help, will pay me the price for that.
For those children he had from me he will never
See alive again, nor will he on his new bride
Beget another child, for she is to be forced 805
To die a most terrible death by these my poisons.
Let no one think me a weak one, feeble-spirited,
A stay-at-home, but rather just the opposite,
One who can hurt my enemies and help my friends;
For the lives of such persons are most remembered. 810

CHORUS
Since you have shared the knowledge of your plan with us,
I both wish to help you and support the normal
Ways of mankind, and tell you not to do this thing.

MEDEA
I can do no other thing. It is understandable
For you to speak thus. You have not suffered as I have. 815

CHORUS
But can you have the heart to kill your flesh and blood?

MEDEA
Yes, for this is the best way to wound my husband.

CHORUS
And you, too. Of women you will be most unhappy.

MEDEA
So it must be. No compromise is possible.

She turns to the Nurse.

Go, you, at once, and tell Jason to come to me. 820
You I employ on all affairs of greatest trust.
Say nothing of these decisions which I have made,
If you love your mistress, if you were born a woman.

CHORUS
From of old the children of Erechtheus are
Splendid, the sons of blessed gods. They dwell 825
In Athens' holy and unconquered land,
Where famous Wisdom feeds them and they pass gaily
Always through that most brilliant air where once, they say, 830

The precise nature of Medea's poisons is not made clear among the ancient accounts. One view holds that the poison passes from the gifts to the person simply by touch, leading to prompt, painful death. Another opinion was that the poison took the form of a gel which burst into flames upon touching the victim's skin. In either case, death would be agonizing and certain.

Can you explain the dilemma of the Chorus at this moment in the plot?

What psychological tool is Medea using to win the total cooperation of the Nurse?

The mythical Erechtheus was a king of Athens who slew his own offspring as commanded by the Delphic Oracle. As a consequence, he managed to preserve Athens in a battle and his martyred children ascended to the skies as

---

MEDEA   37

That golden Harmony gave birth to the nine
Pure Muses of Pieria.

And beside the sweet flow of Cephisus' stream, 835
Where Cypris sailed, they say, to draw the water,
And mild soft breezes breathed along her path,
And on her hair were flung the sweet-smelling garlands 840
Of flowers of roses by the Lovers, the companions
Of Wisdom, her escort, the helpers of men
In every kind of excellence. 845

How then can these holy rivers
Or this holy land love you,
Or the city find you a home,
You, who will kill your children,
You, not pure with the rest? 850
O think of the blow at your children
And think of the blood that you shed.
O, over and over I beg you,
By your knees I beg you do not
Be the murderess of your babes! 855

O where will you find the courage
Or the skill of hand and heart,
When you set yourself to attempt
A deed so dreadful to do?
How, when you look upon them, 860
Can you tearlessly hold the decision
For murder? You will not be able,
When your children fall down and implore you,
You will not be able to dip
Steadfast your hand in their blood. 865

Enter Jason with attendants.

JASON
I have come at your request. Indeed, although you are
Bitter against me, this you shall have: I will listen
To what new thing you want, woman, to get from me.

MEDEA
Jason, I beg you to be forgiving toward me
For what I said. It is natural for you to bear with 870
My temper, since we have had much love together.
I have talked with myself about this and I have
Reproached myself. "Fool" I said, "why am I so mad?
Why am I set against those who have planned wisely?
Why make myself an enemy of the authorities 875
And of my husband, who does the best thing for me
By marrying royalty and having children who
Will be as brothers to my own? What is wrong with me?
Let me give up anger, for the gods are kind to me.
Have I not children, and do I not know that we 880
In exile from our country must be short of friends?"
When I considered this I saw that I had shown
Great lack of sense, and that my anger was foolish.
Now I agree with you. I think that you are wise
In having this other wife as well as me, and I 885

---

a constellation. Cephisus is a river in the Attican region. Throughout the ensuing choral passage, the purity of Medea's intended haven in Athens is contrasted to her own impending contamination by her children's blood.

What is the dramatic purpose of the Chorus's closing stanza?

How do her words help to characterize Medea?

Was mad. I should have helped you in these plans of yours,
Have joined in the wedding, stood by the marriage bed,
Have taken pleasure in attendance on your bride.
But we women are what we are—perhaps a little
Worthless; and you men must not be like us in this, 890
Nor be foolish in return when we are foolish.
Now, I give in, and admit that then I was wrong.
I have come to a better understanding now.

She turns toward the house.

Children, come here, my children, come outdoors to us!
Welcome your father with me, and say goodbye to him, 895
And with your mother, who just now was his enemy,
Join again in making friends with him who loves us.

Enter the children, attended by the Tutor.

We have made peace, and all our anger is over.
Take hold of his right hand—O God, I am thinking
Of something which may happen in the secret future. 900
O children, will you just so, after a long life,
Hold out your loving arms at the grave? O children,
How ready to cry I am, how full of foreboding!
I am ending at last this quarrel with your father,
And, look my soft eyes have suddenly filled with tears. 905

CHORUS
And the pale tears have started also in my eyes.
O may the trouble not grow worse than now it is!

JASON
I approve of what you say. And I cannot blame you
Even for what you said before. It is natural
For a woman to be wild with her husband when he 910
Goes in for secret love. But now your mind has turned
To better reasoning. In the end you have come to
The right decision, like the clever woman you are.
And of you, children, your father is taking care.
He has made, with God's help, ample provision for you. 915
For I think that a time will come when you will be
The leading people in Corinth with your brothers.
You must grow up. As to the future, your father
And those of the gods who love him will deal with that.
I want to see you, when you have become young men, 920
Healthy and strong, better men than my enemies.
Medea, why are your eyes all wet with pale tears?
Why is your cheek so white and turned away from me?
Are not these words of mine pleasing for you to hear?

MEDEA
It is nothing. I was thinking about these children. 925

JASON
You must be cheerful. I shall look after them well.

MEDEA
I will be. It is not that I distrust your words,
But a woman is a frail thing, prone to crying.

Sidebar questions:

Without stage directions, what clues in the dialogue concern the motions of the actors?

What are two very different possible reasons for her to weep at this moment?

What facet in Jason's nature comes to light in lines 908–11?

Jason refers here to the children he and the princess will beget in the future.

MEDEA 39

JASON
But why then should you grieve so much for these children?

MEDEA
I am their mother. When you prayed that they might live   930
I felt unhappy to think that these things will be.
But come, I have said something of the things I meant
To say to you, and now I will tell you the rest.
Since it is the king's will to banish me from here—
And for me, too, I know that this is the best thing,   935
Not to be in your way by living here or in
The king's way, since they think me ill-disposed to them—
I then am going into exile from this land;
But do you, so that you may have the care of them,
Beg Creon that the children may not be banished.   940

Does Medea actually mean what she says? If not, why does she speak these lines?

JASON
I doubt if I'll succeed, but still I'll attempt it.

MEDEA
Then you must tell your wife to beg from her father
That the children may be reprieved from banishment.

JASON
I will, and with her I shall certainly succeed.

MEDEA
If she is like the rest of us women, you will.   945
And I, too, will take a hand with you in this business,
For I will send her some gifts which are far fairer,
I am sure of it, than those which now are in fashion,
A finely woven dress and a golden diadem,
And the children shall present them. Quick, let one of you   950
Servants bring here to me that beautiful dress.

One of her attendants goes into the house.

She will be happy not in one way, but in a hundred,
Having so fine a man as you to share her bed,
And with this beautiful dress which Helius of old,
My father's father, bestowed on his descendants.   955

How might the audience be alerted to the possibility that magic is associated with the dress?

Enter attendant carrying the poisoned dress and diadem.

There, children, take these wedding presents in your hands.
Take them to the royal princess, the happy bride,
And give them to her. She will not think little of them.

The implied stage directions in line 956 are evident. How would they be implemented during a performance?

JASON
No, don't be foolish, and empty your hands of these.
Do you think the palace is short of dresses to wear?   960
Do you think there is no gold there? Keep them, don't give them
Away. If my wife considers me of any value,
She will think more of me than money, I am sure of it.

Explain the grim irony in Jason's seemingly considerate suggestion to Medea.

MEDEA
No, let me have my way. They say the gods themselves
Are moved by gifts, and gold does more with men than words.   965
Hers is the luck, her fortune that which god blesses;
She is young and a princess; but for my children's reprieve
I would give my very life, and not gold only.
Go children, go together to that rich palace,

Greek gods, much like mortal beings, could be influenced by opulent gifts, as Medea comments.

Be suppliants to the new wife of your father,
My lady, beg her not to let you be banished.
And give her the dress—for this is of great importance,
That she should take the gift into her hand from yours.
Go, quick as you can. And bring your mother good news
By your success of those things which she longs to gain.

Jason goes out with his attendants, followed by the Tutor and the children carrying the poisoned gifts.

CHORUS
Now there is no hope left for the children's lives.
Now there is none. They are walking already to murder.
The bride, poor bride, will accept the curse of the gold,
Will accept the bright diadem.
Around her yellow hair she will set that dress
Of death with her own hands.

The grace and the perfume and glow of the golden robe
Will charm her to put them upon her and wear the wreath,
And now her wedding will be with the dead below,
Into such a trap she will fall,
Poor thing, into such a fate of death and never
Escape from under that curse.

You, too, O wretched bridegroom, making your match with kings,
You do not see that you bring
Destruction on your children and on her,
Your wife, a fearful death.
Poor soul, what a fall is yours!
In your grief, too, I weep, mother of little children,
You who will murder your own,
In vengeance for the loss of married love
Which Jason has betrayed
As he lives with another wife.

Enter the Tutor with the children.

TUTOR
Mistress, I tell you that these children are reprieved,
And the royal bride has been pleased to take in her hands
Your gifts. In that quarter the children are secure.
But come,
Why do you stand confused when you are fortunate?
Why have you turned round with your cheek away from me?
Are not these words of mine pleasing for you to hear?

MEDEA
Oh! I am lost!

TUTOR
That word is not in harmony with my tidings.

MEDEA
I am lost, I am lost!

TUTOR
Am I in ignorance telling you
Of some disaster, and not the good news I thought?

MEDEA   41

MEDEA
You have told what you have told. I do not blame you.

TUTOR
Why then this downcast eye, and this weeping of tears?

MEDEA
Oh, I am forced to weep, old man. The gods and I,
I in a kind of madness, have contrived all this.

TUTOR
Courage! You, too, will be brought home by your children. 1015

MEDEA
Ah, before that happens I shall bring others home.

TUTOR
Others before you have been parted from their children.
Mortals must bear in resignation their ill luck.

MEDEA
That is what I shall do. But go inside the house,
And do for the children your usual daily work. 1020

The Tutor goes into the house. Medea turns to her children.

O children, O my children, you have a city,
You have a home, and you can leave me behind you,
And without your mother you may live there forever.
But I am going into exile to another land
Before I have seen you happy and taken pleasure in you, 1025
Before I have dressed your brides and made your marriage beds
And held up the torch at the ceremony of wedding.
Oh, what a wretch I am in this my self-willed thought!
What was the purpose, children, for which I reared you?
For all my travail and wearing myself away? 1030
They were sterile, those pains I had in the bearing of you.
Oh surely once the hopes in you I had, poor me,
Were high ones: you would look after me in old age,
And when I died would deck me well with your own hands;
A thing which all would have done. Oh but now it is gone, 1035
That lovely thought. For, once I am left without you,
Sad will be the life I'll lead and sorrowful for me.
And you will never see your mother again with
Your dear eyes, gone to another mode of living.
Why, children, do you look upon me with your eyes? 1040
Why do you smile so sweetly that last smile of all?
Oh, Oh, what can I do? My spirit has gone from me,
Friends, when I saw that bright look in the children's eyes.
I cannot bear to do it. I renounce my plans
I had before. I'll take my children away from 1045
This land. Why should I hurt their father with the pain
They feel, and suffer twice as much of pain myself?
No, no, I will not do it. I renounce my plans.
Ah, what is wrong with me? Do I want to let go
My enemies unhurt and be laughed at for it? 1050
I must face this thing. Oh, but what a weak woman
Even to admit to my mind these soft arguments.
Children, go into the house. And he whom laws forbids
To stand in attendance at my sacrifices,

Medea refers to the belief at that time that no mortal acted without the encouragement of one of the many gods.

What is foreshadowed in line 1016?

For a short while, beginning about here, Medea's resolve is temporarily weakened.

To the Greeks, it was important to follow proper religious burial rites, since failure of a spirit to depart correctly doomed it to perpetual unrest.

Most drama builds in gestures for the actors by way of dialogue, as in line 1040.

What powerful element in Medea's character restrains her from aborting her murderous intent in lines 1049–52 and in lines 1059–61?

42 EURIPIDES

Let him see to it. I shall not mar my handiwork. 1055
Oh! Oh!
Do not, O my heart, you must not do these things!
Poor heart, let them go, have pity upon the children.
If they live with you in Athens they will cheer you.
No! By Hell's avenging furies it shall not be—
This shall never be, that I should suffer my children 1060
To be the prey of my enemies' insolence.
Every way is it fixed. The bride will not escape.
No, the diadem is now upon her head, and she, 1065
The royal princess, is dying in the dress, I know it.
But—for it is the most dreadful of roads for me
To tread, and them I shall send on a more dreadful still—
I wish to speak to the children.

How does Euripides increase the suspense and pathos of his tale even more?

She calls the children to her.

    Come, children, give
Me your hands, give your mother your hands to kiss them. 1070
Oh the dear hands, and O how dear are these lips to me,
And the generous eyes and the bearing of my children!
I wish you happiness, but not here in this world.
What is here your father took. Oh how good to hold you!
How delicate the skin, how sweet the breath of children! 1075
Go, go! I am no longer able, no longer
To look upon you. I am overcome by sorrow.

The children go into the house.

I know indeed what evil I intend to do,
But stronger than all my afterthoughts is my fury,
Fury that brings upon mortals the greatest evils. 1080

Could this passage mark the *climax* of the play? Why? How does Euripides keep our interest high throughout those passages?

She goes out to the right, toward the royal palace.

CHORUS
Often before
I have gone through more subtle reasons,
And have come upon questionings greater
Than a woman should strive to search out.
But we too have a goddess to help us 1085
And accompany us into wisdom.
Not all of us. Still you will find
Among many women a few,
And our sex is not without learning.
This I say, that those who have never 1090
Had children, who know nothing of it,
In happiness have the advantage
Over those who are parents.
The childless, who never discover
Whether children turn out as a good thing 1095
Or as something to cause pain, are spared
Many troubles in lacking this knowledge.
And those who have in their homes
The sweet presence of children, I see that their lives
Are all wasted away by their worries. 1100
First they must think how to bring them up well and

What is the thematic function of lines 1081–115?

MEDEA 43

How to leave them something to live on.
And then after this whether all their toil
Is for those who will turn out good or bad,
Is still an unanswered question.
And of one more trouble, the last of all,   1105
That is common to mortals I tell.
For suppose you have found them enough for their living,
Suppose that the children have grown into youth
And have turned out good, still, if God so wills it,
Death will away with your children's bodies,
And carry them off into Hades.   1110
What is our profit, then, that for the sake of
Children the gods should pile upon mortals
After all else
This most terrible grief of all?   1115

Hades was the underworld, home of the dead.

Enter Medea, from the spectators' right.

MEDEA
Friends, I can tell you that for long I have waited
For the event. I stare toward the place from where
The news will come. And now, see one of Jason's servants
Is on his way here, and that labored breath of his
Shows he has tidings for us, and evil tidings.   1120

What structural function is explained in lines 1116–18?

Enter, also from the right, the Messenger.

MESSENGER
Medea, you who have done such a dreadful thing,
So outrageous, run for your life, take what you can,
A ship to bear you hence or chariot on land.

MEDEA
And what is the reason deserves such flight as this?

MESSENGER
She is dead, only just now, the royal princess,
And Creon dead, too, her father, by your poisons.

MEDEA
The finest words you have spoken. Now and hereafter
I shall count you among my benefactors and friends.

MESSENGER
What! Are you right in the mind? Are you not mad,
Woman? The house of the king is outraged by you.   1130
Do you enjoy it? Not afraid of such doings?

MEDEA
To what you say I on my side have something too
To say in answer. Do not be in a hurry, friend,
But speak. How did they die? You will delight me twice
As much again if you say they died in agony.   1135

What other quality of Medea's nature is revealed here?

MESSENGER
When those two children, born of you, had entered in,
Their father with them, and passed into the bride's house,
We were pleased, we slaves who were distressed by your wrongs.
All through the house we were talking of but one thing,
How you and your husband had made up your quarrel.   1140
Some kissed the children's hands and some their yellow hair,

In antiquity, slaves usually were captives of defeated foreign lands. Then they became servants to their captors.

And I myself was so full of my joy that I
Followed the children into the women's quarters.
Our mistress, whom we honor now instead of you,
Before she noticed that your two children were there, 1145
Was keeping her eye fixed eagerly on Jason.
Afterwards, however, she covered up her eyes,
Her cheek paled, and she turned herself away from him,
So disgusted was she at the children's coming there.
But your husband tried to end the girl's bad temper, 1150
And said "You must not look unkindly on your friends.
Cease to be angry. Turn your head to me again.
Have as your friends the same ones as your husband has.
And take these gifts, and beg your father to reprieve
These children from their exile. Do it for my sake." 1155
She, when she saw the dress, could not restrain herself.
She agreed with all her husband said, and before
He and the children had gone far from the palace,
She took the gorgeous robe and dressed herself in it,
And put the golden crown around her curly locks, 1160
And arranged the set of the hair in a shining mirror,
And smiled at the lifeless image of herself in it.
Then she rose from her chair and walked about the room,
With her gleaming feet stepping most soft and delicate,
All overjoyed with the present. Often and often 1165
She would stretch her foot out straight and look along it.
But after it was a fearful thing to see.
The color of her face changed, and she staggered back,
She ran, and her legs trembled, and she only just
Managed to reach a chair without falling flat down. 1170
An aged woman servant who, I take it, thought
This was some seizure of Pan or another god,
Cried out "God bless us," but that was before she saw
The white foam breaking through her lips and her rolling
The pupils of her eyes and her face all bloodless. 1175
Then she raised a different cry from that "God bless us,"
A huge shriek, and the women ran, one to the king,
One to the newly wedded husband to tell him
What had happened to his bride; and with frequent sound
The whole of the palace rang as they were running. 1180
One walking quickly round the course of a race-track
Would now have turned the bend and be close to the goal,
When she, poor girl, opened her shut and speechless eye,
And with a terrible groan she came to herself.
For a twofold pain was moving up against her. 1185
The wreath of gold that was resting around her head
Let forth a fearful stream of all-devouring fire,
And the finely woven dress your children gave to her,
Was fastening on the unhappy girl's fine flesh.
She leapt up from the chair, and all on fire she ran, 1190
Shaking her hair now this way and now that, trying
To hurl the diadem away; but fixedly
The gold preserved its grip, and, when she shook her hair,
Then more and twice as fiercely the fire blazed out.
Till, beaten by her fate, she fell down to the ground, 1195
Hard to be recognized except by a parent.

1145 What fact about the princess' feelings for Jason becomes evident in lines 1144–46?

1155 What finally wins over the princess to the side of the children? Is it love for Jason alone?

Pan was a mythical god known for producing sudden fear among human beings.

The exact nature of the poison Medea used is not clear, but it took the form of a corrosive that burned the flesh like fire.

Neither the setting of her eyes was plain to see,
Nor the shapeliness of her face. From the top of
Her head there oozed out blood and fire mixed together.
Like the drops on pine-bark, so the flesh from her bones   1200
Dropped away, torn by the hidden fang of the poison.
It was a fearful sight; and terror held us all
From touching the corpse. We had learned from what had
    happened.
But her wretched father, knowing nothing of the event,
Came suddenly to the house, and fell upon the corpse,   1205
And at once cried out and folded his arms about her,
And kissed her and spoke to her, saying, "O my poor child,
What heavenly power has so shamefully destroyed you?
And who has set me here like an ancient sepulcher,
Deprived of you? O let me die with you, my child!"   1210
And when he had made an end of his wailing and crying,
Then the old man wished to raise himself to his feet;
But, as the ivy clings to the twigs of the laurel,
So he stuck to the fine dress, and he struggled fearfully.
For he was trying to lift himself to his knee,   1215
And she was pulling him down, and when he tugged hard
He would be ripping his aged flesh from his bones.
At last his life was quenched, and the unhappy man
Gave up the ghost, no longer could hold up his head.
There they lie close, the daughter and the old father,   1220
Dead bodies, an event he prayed for in his tears.
As for your interests, I will say nothing of them,
For you will find your own escape from punishment.
Our human life I think and have thought a shadow,
And I do not fear to say that those who are held   1225
Wise among men and who search the reasons of things
Are those who bring the most sorrow on themselves.
For of mortals there is no one who is happy.
If wealth flows in upon one, one may be perhaps
Luckier than one's neighbor, but still not happy.   1230

exit

CHORUS
Heaven, it seems, on this day has fastened many
Evils on Jason, and Jason has deserved them.
Poor girl, the daughter of Creon, how I pity you
And your misfortunes, you who have gone quite away
To the house of Hades because of marrying Jason.   1235

MEDEA
Women, my task is fixed: as quickly as I may
To kill my children, and start away from this land,
And not, by wasting time, to suffer my children
To be slain by another hand less kindly to them.
Force every way will have it they must die, and since   1240
This must be so, then I, their mother, shall kill them.
Oh, arm yourself in steel, my heart! Do not hang back
From doing this fearful and necessary wrong.
Oh, come, my hand, poor wretched hand, and take the sword,
Take it, step forward to this bitter starting point,   1245
And do not be a coward, do not think of them,

> What distinction does the chorus draw in the fates of the princess and of Jason?

> From this point on, Medea absolutely cannot turn back. Why? What part of the play's structure does this passage represent, in terms provided in the Overview of Drama?

> Is Medea aware of the evil act she is about to commit? What explicit stage direction does Euripides furnish in lines 1244–45?

Judith Anderson in John Gielgud's production of Medea, *New York, 1947*

How sweet they are, and how you are their mother. Just for
This one short day be forgetful of your children,
Afterward weep; for even though you will kill them,
They were very dear—Oh, I am an unhappy woman!   1250

With a cry she rushes into the house.

CHORUS
O Earth, and the far shining
Ray of the Sun, look down, look down upon
This poor lost woman, look, before she raises
The hand of murder against her flesh and blood.
Yours was the golden birth from which   1255
She sprang, and now I fear divine
Blood may be shed by men.
O heavenly light, hold back her hand,
Check her, and drive from out the house
The bloody Fury raised by fiends of Hell.   1260
Vain waste, your care of children;
Was it in vain you bore the babes you loved,
After you passed the inhospitable strait
Between the dark blue rocks, Symplegades?
O wretched one, how has it come,   1265
This heavy anger on your heart,
This cruel bloody mind?
For God from mortals asks a stern

> Note that the Chorus begs the sun god to stop Medea. Why is such an appeal appropriate?

> Classical drama is filled with episodes involving the Furies (or Erinyes, in Greek), mythical female divinities of retribution. They were invoked by curses and called upon to punish those guilty of unavenged crimes.

MEDEA   47

Price for the stain of kindred blood
In like disaster falling on their homes. 1270

A cry from one of the children is heard.

CHORUS
Do you hear the cry, do you hear the children's cry?
O you hard heart, O woman fated for evil!

ONE OF THE CHILDREN *(from within)*
What can I do and how escape my mother's hands?

ANOTHER CHILD *(from within)*
O my dear brother, I cannot tell. We are lost.

CHORUS
Shall I enter the house? Oh, surely I should 1275
Defend the children from murder.

A CHILD *(from within)*
O help us, in God's name, for now we need your help.
Now, now we are close to it. We are trapped by the sword.

CHORUS
O your heart must have been made of rock or steel,
You who can kill 1280
With your own hand the fruit of your own womb.
Of one alone I have heard, one woman alone
Of those of old who laid her hands on her children,
Ino, sent mad by heaven when the wife of Zeus
Drove her out from her home and made her wander; 1285
And because of the wicked shedding of blood
Of her own children she threw
Herself, poor wretch, into the sea and stepped away
Over the sea-cliff to die with her two children.
What horror more can be? O women's love, 1290
So full of trouble,
How many evils have you caused already!

Enter Jason, with attendants.

JASON
You women, standing close in front of this dwelling,
Is she, Medea, she who did this dreadful deed,
Still in the house, or has she run away in flight? 1295
For she will have to hide herself beneath the earth,
Or raise herself on wings into the height of air,
If she wishes to escape the royal vengeance.
Does she imagine that, having killed our rulers,
She will herself escape uninjured from this house? 1300
But I am thinking not so much of her as for
The children—her the king's friends will make to suffer
For what she did. So I have come to save the lives
Of my boys, in case the royal house should harm them
While taking vengeance for their mother's wicked deed. 1305

CHORUS
O Jason, if you but knew how deeply you are
Involved in sorrow, you would not have spoken so.

JASON
What is it? That she is planning to kill me also?

Notice how Euripides creates a sense of horror as the children are slain, even without showing the deed on stage.

In mythology, Ino was chased into the sea when the arch-goddess Hera, wife of Zeus, out of jealousy maddened Ino's husband, Athamas. There may be confusion in this line, however, since another legend speaks of Io, a priestess beloved of Zeus, who in the shape of a white cow is forced to wander all over the world by vengeful, jealous Hera.

What does Euripides emphasize about Jason's character in lines 1301–05?

48 EURIPIDES

CHORUS
Your children are dead, and by their own mother's hand.

JASON
What! That is it? O woman, you have destroyed me! 1310

What is significant and ironic in Jason's words (l. 1310) that his children's deaths are his own destruction?

CHORUS
You must make up your mind your children are no more.

JASON
Where did she kill them? Was it here or in the house?

CHORUS
Open the gates and there you will see them murdered.

JASON
Quick as you can unlock the doors, men, and undo
The fastenings and let me see this double evil, 1315
My children dead and her—Oh her I will repay.

The spectacle of the chariot and the murdered boys exemplifies the eccyclema—*a machine or device used to show a scene previously concealed from view. Here it is a tableau showing the horrors of the tragedy without depicting the killings themselves.*

His attendants rush to the door. Medea appears above the house in a chariot drawn by dragons. She has the dead bodies of her children with her.

MEDEA
Why do you batter these gates and try to unbar them,
Seeking the corpses and for me who did the deed?
You may cease your trouble, and, if you have need of me,
Speak, if you wish. You will never touch me with your hand, 1320
Such a chariot has Helius, my father's father,
Given me to defend me from my enemies.

The magical flying chariot drawn by dragons is a typical deus ex machina. *Literally this means god of the machine, because some deity would be lowered mechanically onto the play area of the theater to resolve arbitrarily the dilemma of the protagonist. Therefore, the resolution and denouement do not evolve naturally from the action; instead, they reflect the approval of the gods. Otherwise here it can be deduced that Medea could not possibly have escaped safely from Corinth. In contemporary drama, a* deus ex machina *is any device used to help the hero out of an impossible situation.*

JASON
You hateful thing, you woman most utterly loathed
By the gods and me and by all the race of mankind,
You who have had the heart to raise a sword against 1325
Your children, you, their mother, and left me childless—
You have done this, and do you still look at the sun
And at the earth, after these most fearful doings?
I wish you dead. Now I see it plain, though at that time
I did not, when I took you from your foreign home 1330
And brought you to a Greek house, you, an evil thing,
A traitress to your father and your native land.
The gods hurled the avenging curse of yours on me.
For your own brother you slew at your own hearthside,
And then came aboard that beautiful ship, the Argo. 1335
And that was your beginning. When you were married
To me, your husband, and had borne children to me,
For the sake of pleasure in the bed you killed them.
There is no Greek woman who would have dared such deeds,
Out of all those whom I passed over and chose you 1340
To marry instead, a bitter destructive match,
A monster, not a woman, having a nature
Wilder than that of Scylla in the Tuscan sea.
Ah! no, not if I had ten thousand words of shame
Could I sting you. You are naturally so brazen. 1345
Go, worker in evil, stained with your children's blood.
For me remains to cry aloud upon my fate,
Who will get no pleasure from my newly wedded love,
And the boys whom I begot and brought up, never
Shall I speak to them alive. Oh, my life is over! 1350

Jason interprets his fate in a very special way, wherein he suffers divine revenge really meant for Medea. How can he construct a theory, such as expressed in lines 1329 ff.? What does this tell us about Jason as a person?

Scylla in mythology like Medea fell in love with a foreigner, King Minos, leading her to betray her father and city. The gods later transformed her into a monster, stationing her in the Straits of Messina where she fed on mariners passing through.

MEDEA
Long would be the answer which I might have made to
These words of yours, if Zeus the father did not know
How I have treated you and what you did to me.
No, it was not to be that you should scorn my love, 1355
And pleasantly live your life through, laughing at me;
Nor would the princess, nor he who offered the match,
Creon, drive me away without paying for it.
So now you may call me a monster, if you wish,
A Scylla housed in the caves of the Tuscan sea.
I too, as I had to, have taken hold of your heart. 1360

JASON
You feel the pain yourself. You share in my sorrow.

MEDEA
Yes, and my grief is gain when you cannot mock it.

JASON
O children, what a wicked mother she was to you!

MEDEA
They died from a disease they caught from their father.

JASON
I tell you it was not my hand that destroyed them. 1365

MEDEA
But it was your insolence, and your virgin wedding.

JASON
And just for the sake of that you chose to kill them.

MEDEA
Is love so small a pain, do you think, for a woman?

JASON
For a wise one, certainly. But you are wholly evil.

MEDEA
The children are dead. I say this to make you suffer. 1370

JASON
The children, I think, will bring down curses on you.

MEDEA
The gods know who was the author of this sorrow.

JASON
Yes, the gods know indeed, they know your loathsome heart.

MEDEA
Hate me. But I tire of your barking bitterness.

JASON
And I of yours. It is easier to leave you. 1375

MEDEA
How then? What shall I do? I long to leave you too.

JASON
Give me the bodies to bury and to mourn them.

MEDEA
No, that I will not. I will bury them myself,
Bearing them to Hera's temple on the promontory;
So that no enemy may evilly treat them 1380

> Why is stychomythic dialogue structurally valuable at this moment in the resolution?

> Who wins in this exchange of tirades?

> As principal Olympian goddess and Zeus' wife, Hera was among the most

50 EURIPIDES

By tearing up their grave. In this land of Corinth
I shall establish a holy feast and sacrifice
Each year for ever to atone for the blood guilt.
And I myself go to the land of Erechtheus
To dwell in Aegeus' house, the son of Pandion. 1385
While you, as is right, will die without distinction,
Struck on the head by a piece of the Argo's timber,
And you will have seen the bitter end of my love.

JASON
May a Fury for the children's sake destroy you,
And justice, Requitor of blood. 1390

MEDEA
What heavenly power lends an ear
To a breaker of oaths, a deceiver?

JASON
Oh, I hate you, murderess of children.

MEDEA
Go to your palace. Bury your bride.

JASON
I go, with two children to mourn for. 1395

MEDEA
Not yet do you feel it. Wait for the future.

JASON
Oh, children I loved!

MEDEA
I loved them, you did not.

JASON
You loved them, and killed them.

MEDEA
To make you feel pain.

JASON
Oh, wretch that I am, how I long
To kiss the dear lips of my children! 1400

MEDEA
Now you would speak to them, now you would kiss them.
Then you rejected them.

JASON
Let me, I beg you,
Touch my boys' delicate flesh.

MEDEA
I will not. Your words are all wasted.

JASON
O God, do you hear it, this persecution, 1405
These my sufferings from this hateful
Woman, this monster, murderess of children?
Still what I can do that I will do:
I will lament and cry upon heaven,
Calling the gods to bear me witness 1410
How you have killed my boys and prevent me from
Touching their bodies or giving them burial.

---

powerful deities known to the Greeks. Her cult was so strong that no one dared insult it by profaning her temples or idols.

Medea fastens on what she believes will cause Jason the most anguish. To a warrior such as Jason, an inauspicious death would be anathema. According to legend, Jason did indeed die after being struck on the head by a rotting timber of the Argo. These details about the new circumstances which result from Medea's murders are a part of the play's denouement.

Does Medea's scorn lessen throughout this final interchange with Jason?

How has Euripides developed Jason as a character, in light of the earlier haughty man he was?

Cherubini's opera of Medea *starring Maria Callas, Epidaurus Festival, 1962*

I wish I had never begot them to see them
Afterward slaughtered by you.

CHORUS
Zeus in Olympus is the overseer
Of many doings. Many things the gods
Achieve beyond our judgment. What we thought
Is not confirmed and what we thought not god
Contrives. And so it happens in this story.

Curtain

Just as the play had opened with the wish to alter past events, so too it closes with Jason's pained lament (ll. 1413–14).

1415 Zeus was the mightiest of all the Greek gods and, ultimately, all verdicts about justice would be settled by him. The Chorus declares, therefore, that man cannot know all the facts and judge —only the gods can.

POSTVIEW: THEME

As indicated in the Overview of Drama, the theme of a literary work is its central idea. Most themes of plays involve conflicts which result from the collision of the chief protagonists' will. Now that you have read the drama, review *Medea* and find the key elements which make up the theme by focusing on the following questions.

1. What is the basic conflict in *Medea?*
2. What is the basis for each argument as stated directly in lines 465 ff. and 520 ff.?

Often, conflict is built up by friction between the protagonist and other lesser antagonists.

3. What are some specific forces (or persons) opposing Medea in the drama?

4. What is their connection to the major antagonism of the play?

In light of their many crucial points of disagreement, Medea and Jason might be described as participants in a "battle of the sexes."

5. Is the sole basis of conflict that between man and woman, between wife and husband, or between alien and native?
6. How does Jason's disagreement with Medea entail broader thematic issues concerning the individual in conflict with society? Concerning the individual in conflict with another person? Concerning the individual divided within himself?
7. What parallels might be drawn between Medea's plight and that of a woman in our present day male-oriented society?
8. Is Jason the stereotype of the male chauvinist talked about so much in recent years?
9. Why would a production of *Medea* be especially effective in investigating the issues of male bias in today's world? Would the concept of the double standard enter in? Where?

INTRODUCTION
TWELFTH NIGHT

William Shakespeare

WILLIAM SHAKESPEARE was the foremost writer in the English language. Immensely popular in his own lifetime, he neither wrote over the heads of his audiences nor underestimated their ability to comprehend drama. In his plays he perfected an unmatched skill in creating character and developing story, based on an understanding of human psychology and an empathy with all humanity.

Shakespeare was born in 1564 in Stratford-upon-Avon, England, son of John Shakespeare, a glove-maker who later became the mayor of the town. Nothing in Shakespeare's youth hinted at the spectacular career to follow. Married when only eighteen to Ann Hathaway, a woman eight years his senior, Shakespeare had three children—though no sons survived long enough to perpetuate the family name. His exact activities during his twenties are uncertain, but one legend declares that he taught school for at least some of those years. When his name surfaces again on public records a few years later in 1592, he already has gained some renown as an actor, poet, and respected dramatist in London.

Shakespeare did not concentrate on any one type of play form. The thirty-eight plays he is said to have written include tragedies (such as *Hamlet, Romeo and Juliet, Macbeth, Antony and Cleopatra*), comedies (such as *A Midsummer Night's Dream, Much Ado About Nothing, As You Like It, The Tempest*), and everything in between—including dramas constructed from historical accounts of England's past. He also became part owner of a theater troupe and managed to make a very good living—a feat never before achieved in theatrical business ventures. By around 1611, Shakespeare had retired from the theater and was living comfortably in his home town where he died on April 23, 1616. Fortunately, two of Shakespeare's business associates gathered together his manuscripts and randomly published play texts. They were able to compile, edit, and publish Shakespeare's then-known dramatic works in 1623 in a volume known as the First Folio edition of Shakespeare's plays. Most of Shakespeare's play texts which we read today derive directly from the First Folio.

In Shakespeare's time, the theater had certain standards within which he was to continue his own career. For example, during at least half of his writing years he knew that his works would be performed outdoors during late morning or early afternoon. During the last quarter of the sixteenth century, the first theater structures were built in England; they had roofed circular or squared galleries for the patrons, but the interior courtyards on which the stage itself stood were open to the elements. Therefore Shakespeare could not rely on artificial lighting. Only when indoor theaters became popular later in the 1600s could dramatists design their plays to be produced in all weather conditions and with artificial illumination. Nor were stage props used very much. Shakespeare's plays included many short scenes set in different locations. Rather than remove and replace scenery backdrops to denote the site changes, Shakespeare made certain that the dialogue opening new scenes mentioned the shift of action. (The second scene of our play's first act clearly illustrates the method used.) In addition, in Shakespeare's era, women never performed on stage; all the women's roles were played by trained young men whose voices were light in timber. And the fact that in *Twelfth Night* the female character Viola was pretending to be a boy (Cesario) produced an extra layer of ironic fun for the audience.

Even the traditional seating arrangements in the theaters influenced the plays. The least expensive tickets allowed patrons to stand on the ground around the three sides of the stage which protruded into the courtyard. Ordinarily, the average citizen bought that type of admission—hence their nickname the "groundlings." Of the lower stratum of society, they expected tales and jokes geared to them. On the other hand, whereas the majority of middle-class people sat in the more comfortable galleries (see the illustrations of the theaters' configurations), a few wealthier spectators paid extra for the privilege of sitting on stage, near the edges, on stools. Shakespeare accommodated them all, by providing noble characters speaking brilliantly and wittily, average burgher-type figures speaking in ordinary speech patterns, and lower-class servant and fool characters talking in appropriate farcical and frequently ribald fashion.

Twelfth Night has remained one of Shakespeare's best-loved comedies. It has been performed regularly since about 1600; and still today it is frequently revived. Its main topic, love, is treated in a variety of comical ways. Shakespeare suggests that though love makes people act irrationally and can cause many problems, it is a laughable and pleasant matter. Well aware of the class distinctions among his Elizabethan spectators, Shakespeare fashioned a love style

The Swan Theater of London, a contemporary of the Globe, about 1596.

suitable for the varying levels of the characters in the drama. The aristocrats in Orsino's circles speak the articulate, educated language of upper-class society. At the other extreme, there is the boisterous Sir Toby Belch and flirtatious Maria who speak, shout, and drunkenly sing just like common people. Similarly, the jokes made at the expense of the frustrated Duke and Viola are of an innocent but ironical nature. But the laughter produced by Maria's fake love letter results from the obscene implications of the enigmatic initials which so puzzle Malvolio (Act II, scene v).

Shakespeare's audiences also were used to mass confusion on stage when disguises were used in comedies to evoke mistaken identities. The charming Viola transforms herself into a lad (Cesario), only to find herself in love with her master; yet she is forced to court Olivia on his behalf—thereby to earn Olivia's unsought love for her male incarnation. Conveniently, Shakespeare produces a male version of Viola in her twin brother Sebastian, so that the mismatched pairs of lovers ultimately can be straightened out. With the antics and songs of Feste and the raucous Sir Toby, it is clear why viewers were happy and satisfied. And in their satisfaction and laughter lies sufficient reason for Shakespeare to have subtitled *Twelfth Night* "What You Will." There is something in it for everybody.

The Globe Theater, with orchestra and proscenium filled.

PREVIEW: STRUCTURE

During the opening scenes of a play, the purpose of exposition is to lay the groundwork for *who* is doing *what* in the story. Without such fundamental knowledge, the audience can neither identify with the participants in the plot nor follow the unfolding action. In *Twelfth Night* Shakespeare supplies ample information to allow us to enter the world of the play.

1. At the play's opening, who is the master of the household and what is he doing during scene one?
2. What does his behavior reveal about the situation?
3. What are Viola's circumstances when we first meet her in the second scene?
4. Where does scene three take place? What kind of characters are Sir Toby Belch, Sir Andrew Aguecheek, Maria, and Malvolio?
5. How do Shakespeare's names for Sir Toby, Aguecheek, and Malvolio suggest each's character?

From the exposition it can be determined that two major levels of action exist in *Twelfth Night:* first, the frustrated loves of the aristocrats Orsino, Olivia, and Viola; and second, the farcical trickery of Maria and Sir Toby directed toward Aguecheek and Malvolio. Complications therefore develop on both planes.

6. Why does Orsino send Cesario to woo Olivia for him? How does it cause Cesario/Viola special problems?
7. How does Viola's disguise as a man lead to complications for Olivia?
8. How does Sir Toby keep Aguecheek courting Olivia in Act III, scene ii?
9. What trickery does Malvolio's spoilsport manner lead Maria to plot in Act II, scene iii?
10. What is the comic importance of Maria's forged letter in the farcical subplot?

The action of the main and secondary plots gains in momentum, confusion, and fun as the play develops, until crisis situations are reached.

11. How do the two duel encounters between Sir Andrew and Cesario differ, and why?
12. How does Antonio's "good deed" in helping Cesario during the first duel lead to anxious moments later for Viola?
13. Why does Sebastian's arrival in Ilyrium and his first meeting with Olivia also mean trouble for Viola later?
14. What is Orsino's predicament in scene one of Act V, when he hears of Cesario's alleged misdeeds from Antonio, Olivia, and then Sir Toby?
15. How does the garden scene ending Act II lead to Malvolio's desperate (but comical) situation of Act III, scene iv, when he is locked up in the dark?

By the last act of *Twelfth Night,* all reason in the events seems lost: Olivia thinks she suffers from a reluctant husband, Orsino believes his friend Cesario has betrayed him to woo Olivia for himself, Antonio thinks Cesario is Sebastian and thus an ungrateful rogue, and Malvolio desperately seeks to prove he is sane. Clearly, a striking resolution is needed to solve the dilemmas.

16. Why does the timely arrival of Sebastian (Act V, scene i) furnish the key to the puzzles for Orsino, Olivia, Viola, and Antonio?
17. Which marriage matches eventually result after Sebastian and Viola have clarified and proven their true identities?
18. How has Malvolio's humiliation led to still another marriage in the secondary plot?

When a denouement is used by a dramatist, it appears as a continuation and completion of the resolution—that is, the plot is amplified and clarified, with an added look forward into the future.

19. What important social celebration marks the end of dissension and the start of harmonious relationships?
20. How does Shakespeare imply that even Malvolio will be welcomed back into the social community at the end of the play?

TWELFTH NIGHT
OR
WHAT YOU WILL

William Shakespeare

DRAMATIS PERSONÆ

Orsino, *Duke of Illyria*
Sebastian, *brother to Viola*
Antonio, *a sea captain, friend
 to Sebastian*
A Sea Captain, *friend to Viola*
Valentine ⎫ *gentlemen attending*
Curio ⎭ *on the Duke*
Sir Toby Belch, *uncle to Olivia*
Sir Andrew Aguecheek
Malvolio, *Steward to Olivia*
Fabian ⎫ *servants to*
Feste, *a clown,* ⎭ *Olivia*
Olivia, *a rich countess*
Viola
Maria, *Olivia's woman*

Lords, Priests, Sailors, Officers, Musicians, and other Attendants

SCENE: *A city in Illyria, and the sea-coast near it.*

ACT I

SCENE I   *A room in the Duke's palace.*

Enter Orsino, Duke of Illyria, Curio, and other Lords (Musicians attending).

DUKE If music be the food of love, play on!
Give me excess of it, that surfeiting,
The appetite may sicken, and so die.
That strain again! It had a dying fall.
O, it came o'er my ear like the sweet sound   5
That breathes upon a bank of violets,
Stealing and giving odour. Enough! no more!
'Tis not so sweet now as it was before.
O spirit of love, how quick and fresh art thou,
That, notwithstanding thy capacity   10
Receiveth as the sea, nought enters there,
Of what validity and pitch soe'er,
But falls into abatement and low price
Even in a minute! So full of shapes is fancy
That it alone is high fantastical.   15

CURIO Will you go hunt, my lord?

DUKE   What, Curio?

CURIO The hart.

DUKE Why, so I do, the noblest that I have.
O, when mine eyes did see Olivia first,
Methought she purg'd the air of pestilence!   20

In the Elizabethan age, when Shakespeare wrote his plays, theaters used few stage props or elaborate costumes. To denote the Duke's palace, attending court servants and gentlemen would stand near Orsino. He probably would wear a special headpiece or distinctive clothing to set him off in rank from those around him.

Here, *dying fall* means a "fading cadence" in the music. The Musicians, playing recorders and lutes, are performing at their master's request ("play on!"). But soon, Orsino has had enough of the sweet and somber music ("Enough! no more!"). What does the Duke's sudden shift in mood tell about his character? In line 9, how does Orsino's phrase "spirit of love" inform the audience of the drama's theme?

Point out here some *puns,* that is, the deliberate substitution of a word for another which it resembles in sound, sometimes for humorous purposes. Shakespeare was a master of punning, and there are innumerable puns in his earlier plays. Why do you think puns were so popular then?

That instant was I turn'd into a hart;
And my desires, like fell and cruel hounds,
E'er since pursue me.

Enter Valentine.

How now! what news from her?

VALENTINE So please my lord, I might not be admitted,
But from her handmaid do return this answer: 25
The element itself, till seven years' heat,
Shall not behold her face at ample view;
But, like a cloistress, she will veiled walk,
And water once a day her chamber round
With eye-offending brine: all this to season 30
A brother's dead love, which she would keep fresh
And lasting in her sad remembrance.

DUKE O, she that hath a heart of that fine frame
To pay this debt of love but to a brother,
How will she love when the rich golden shaft 35
Hath kill'd the flock of all affections else
That live in her; when liver, brain, and heart,
These sovereign thrones, are all suppli'd, and fill'd
Her sweet perfections with one self king!
Away before me to sweet beds of flowers; 40
Love-thoughts lie rich when canopi'd with bowers. *(exeunt)*

SCENE II *The sea-coast.*

Enter Viola, a Captain, and Sailors.

VIOLA What country, friends, is this?

SEA CAPTAIN This is Illyria, lady.

VIOLA And what should I do in Illyria?
My brother he is in Elysium.
Perchance he is not drown'd. What think you, sailors? 5

SEA CAPTAIN It is perchance that you yourself were saved.

VIOLA O my poor brother! and so perchance may he be.

SEA CAPTAIN True, madam; and, to comfort you with chance,
Assure yourself, after our ship did split,
When you and those poor number sav'd with you 10
Hung on our driving boat, I saw your brother,
Most provident in peril, bind himself,
Courage and hope both teaching him the practice,
To a strong mast that liv'd upon the sea;
Where, like [Arion] on the dolphin's back, 15
I saw him hold acquaintance with the waves
So long as I could see.

VIOLA For saying so, there's gold.
Mine own escape unfoldeth to my hope,
Whereto thy speech serves for authority, 20
The like of him. Know'st thou this country?

SEA CAPTAIN Ay, madam, well; for I was bred and born
Not three hours' travel from this very place.

In line 21 and following, the allusion is to Actaeon, who, upon seeing Diana naked, was changed into a *hart* (a male deer) and killed by his own hounds. Why would such a parallel fit Orsino's predicament with Olivia?

The cause for Orsino's frustrated love is now evident. In remembrance of her brother's death, what has Olivia vowed to do?

The *liver* was considered by Elizabethans to be the seat of passion in a human being.

How does Orsino's reaction to Olivia's stubborn resistance suggest a form of infatuation rather than love?

Because stage props were minimal in Elizabethan productions, Shakespeare ordinarily offers clues regarding locations within the dialogue opening each scene. How can we identify the setting of scene ii as along the shore of a sea?

perchance means "by chance."

Arion, an ancient Greek poet, allegedly was saved from drowning by dolphins who rode him on their backs because they liked his singing and playing of the lyre.

Here is another stage direction within the dialogue. What action is indicated by "There's gold"?

60   WILLIAM SHAKESPEARE

VIOLA Who governs here?

SEA CAPTAIN A noble duke, in nature as in name. 25

VIOLA What is his name?

SEA CAPTAIN Orsino.

VIOLA Orsino! I have heard my father name him.
He was a bachelor then.

SEA CAPTAIN And so is now, or was so very late; 30
For but a month ago I went from hence,
And then 'twas fresh in murmur—as, you know,
What great ones do the less will prattle of—
That he did seek the love of fair Olivia.

VIOLA What's she? 35

SEA CAPTAIN A virtuous maid, the daughter of a count
That died some twelvemonth since, then leaving her
In the protection of his son, her brother,
Who shortly also died; for whose dear love,
They say, she hath abjur'd the [company 40
And sight] of men.

VIOLA   O that I serv'd that lady,
And might not be delivered to the world,
Till I had made mine own occasion mellow,
What my estate is!

That is, Viola wants to keep her true situation and identity unknown until a suitable time.

SEA CAPTAIN   That were hard to compass,
Because she will admit no kind of suit, 45
No, not the Duke's.

VIOLA There is a fair behaviour in thee, captain;
And though that nature with a beauteous wall
Doth oft close in pollution, yet of thee
I will believe thou hast a mind that suits 50
With this thy fair and outward character.
I prithee, and I'll pay thee bounteously,
Conceal me what I am, and be my aid
For such disguise as haply shall become
The form of my intent. I'll serve this duke. 55
Thou shalt present me as an eunuch to him.
It may be worth thy pains, for I can sing
And speak to him in many sorts of music
That will allow me very worth his service.
What else may hap, to time I will commit, 60
Only shape thou thy silence to my wit.

I prithee means "I pray you."

How does Viola propose to live in the Duke's court undetected as a woman? (A eunuch here means a boy singer, from the Italian castrotto—boys castrated so that they could maintain their light singing voices.)

SEA CAPTAIN Be you his eunuch, and your mute I'll be.
When my tongue blabs, then let mine eyes not see.

VIOLA I thank thee. Lead me on. *(exeunt)*

SCENE III   *A room in Olivia's house.*

Enter Sir Toby Belch and Maria.

SIR TOBY What a plague means my niece, to take the death of her brother thus? I am sure care's an enemy to life.

How do Sir Toby Belch's first lines connect the scene to earlier plot information and inform us of the new scene's location?

TWELFTH NIGHT   **61**

MARIA By my troth, Sir Toby, you must come in earlier o' nights. Your cousin, my lady, takes great exceptions to your ill hours.

SIR TOBY Why, let her except before excepted. 5

MARIA Ay, but you must confine yourself within the modest limits of order.

SIR TOBY Confine! I'll confine myself no finer than I am. These clothes are good enough to drink in, and so be these boots too; an they be not, let them hang themselves in their own straps. 10

MARIA That quaffing and drinking will undo you. I heard my lady talk of it yesterday, and of a foolish knight that you brought in one night here to be her wooer.

SIR TOBY Who? Sir Andrew Aguecheek?

MARIA Ay, he. 15

SIR TOBY He's as tall a man as any's in Illyria.

MARIA What's that to th' purpose?

SIR TOBY Why, he has three thousand ducats a year.

MARIA Ay, but he'll have but a year in all these ducats. He's a very fool and a prodigal. 20

SIR TOBY Fie, that you'll say so! He plays o' the viol-de-gamboys, and speaks three or four languages word for word without book, and hath all the good gifts of nature.

MARIA He hath indeed, almost natural; for besides that he's a fool, he's a great quarreller; and but that he hath the gift of a coward to allay the gust he hath in quarrelling, 'tis thought among the prudent he would quickly have the gift of a grave. 27

SIR TOBY By this hand, they are scoundrels and substractors that say so of him. Who are they?

MARIA They that add, moreover, he's drunk nightly in your company. 30

SIR TOBY With drinking healths to my niece. I'll drink to her as long as there is a passage in my throat and drink in Illyria. He's a coward and a coystrill that will not drink to my niece till his brains turn o' th' toe like a parish-top. What, wench! *Castiliano vulgo!* for here comes Sir Andrew Agueface. 35

Enter Sir Andrew Aguecheek.

SIR ANDREW Sir Toby Belch! How now, Sir Toby Belch!

SIR TOBY Sweet Sir Andrew!

SIR ANDREW Bless you, fair shrew.

MARIA And you too, sir.

SIR TOBY Accost, Sir Andrew, accost. 40

SIR ANDREW What's that?

SIR TOBY My niece's chambermaid.

SIR ANDREW Good Mistress Accost, I desire better acquaintance.

MARIA My name is Mary, sir.

By my troth means "on my word."

except before excepted is a bit of legal phrasing, used by Sir Toby to bluff his way out of the accusations against him. What, apparently, has been his way of living while in Olivia's home, according to Maria's lines?

an here means "if."

Here *tall* means "fine" or "brave."

Ducats are any of a variety of gold coins once widely used in European countries.

A *viol-de-gamboys* was a bass viol, similar to the modern cello.

What character portrait of Sir Andrew Aguecheek emerges from the discussion between Sir Toby and Maria?

A *coystrill* is a knave.

What does Sir Toby's distortion of Aguecheek's name (l. 35) indicate about his respect for Sir Andrew?

By *accost*, Sir Toby means that Sir Andrew should make up to Maria. But Sir Andrew misunderstands. How does his blunder cause a comic incident?

SIR ANDREW Good Mistress Mary Accost,— 45

SIR TOBY You mistake, knight. "Accost" is front her, board her, woo her, assail her.

SIR ANDREW By my troth, I would not undertake her in this company. Is that the meaning of "accost"?

MARIA Fare you well, gentlemen. 50

SIR TOBY An thou let part so, Sir Andrew, would thou mightst never draw sword again.

SIR ANDREW An you part so, mistress, I would I might never draw sword again. Fair lady, do you think you have fools in hand?

MARIA Sir, I have not you by th' hand. 55

SIR ANDREW Marry, but you shall have; and here's my hand.

MARIA Now, sir, "thought is free." I pray you, bring your hand to th'butt'ry-bar and let it drink.

SIR ANDREW Wherefore, sweetheart? What's your metaphor?

MARIA It's dry, sir. 60

SIR ANDREW Why, I think so. I am not such an ass but I can keep my hand dry. But what's your jest?

MARIA A dry jest, sir.

SIR ANDREW Are you full of them?

MARIA Ay, sir, I have them at my fingers' ends. Marry, now I let go your hand, I am barren. *(exit)* 66

SIR TOBY O knight, thou lack'st a cup of canary. When did I see thee so put down?

SIR ANDREW Never in your life, I think, unless you see canary put me down. Methinks sometimes I have no more wit than a Christian or an ordinary man has; but I am a great eater of beef and I believe that does harm to my wit. 72

SIR TOBY No question.

SIR ANDREW An I thought that, I'd forswear it. I'll ride home to-morrow, Sir Toby. 75

SIR TOBY *Pourquoi,* my dear knight?

SIR ANDREW What is *"pourquoi"*? Do or not do? I would I had bestowed that time in the tongues that I have in fencing, dancing, and bear-baiting. O, had I but followed the arts!

SIR TOBY Then hadst thou had an excellent head of hair. 80

SIR ANDREW Why, would that have mended my hair?

SIR TOBY Past question; for thou seest it will not [curl by] nature.

SIR ANDREW But it becomes me well enough, does't not?

SIR TOBY Excellent; it hangs like flax on a distaff, and I hope to see a housewife take thee between her legs, and spin it off. 85

SIR ANDREW Faith, I'll home to-morrow, Sir Toby. Your niece will not be seen, or if she be, it's four to one she'll none of me. The Count himself here hard by wooes her.

Sir Toby fails in his attempt to clarify the meaning of *accost,* leading to what accidental comic punning?

Toby's reference to Andrew's never drawing sword is, of course, another scurrilous joke.

Both visual and verbal comedy ensue here as Maria seeks to try Sir Andrew's mettle by flirting with him. For example, she takes his hand (l. 55) and places it suggestively on her bosom, hinting that he should return her advances. But in his stupidity (l. 59), Aguecheek fails to pick up Maria's hints. Her answer to Aguecheek's query (l. 59) emerges as a pun, i.e., "It's dry," meaning that he lacks the needed amorous spirit. What other puns can you locate in this scene?

A *canary* was a sweet wine from the Canary Islands.

Pourquoi means "why," in French. Does Sir Andrew's knowledge of language (l. 22) extend to even this elementary term?

Allusions to scanty hair in most of Shakespeare's comedies involve the coarse meaning of hair loss due to syphilis and similar diseases.

Very likely Sir Toby's off-color jokes here would be lost on the slow-witted Aguecheek.

TWELFTH NIGHT 63

SIR TOBY She'll none o' th' Count. She'll not match above her degree, neither in estate, years nor wit; I have heard her swear't. Tut, there's life in't, man. 91

SIR ANDREW I'll stay a month longer. I am a fellow o' the strangest mind i' th' world; I delight in masques and revels sometimes altogether.

SIR TOBY Art thou good at these kickshawses, knight? 95

SIR ANDREW As any man in Illyria, whatsoever he be, under the degree of my betters; and yet I will not compare with an old man.

SIR TOBY What is thy excellence in a galliard, knight?

SIR ANDREW Faith, I can cut a caper.

SIR TOBY And I can cut the mutton to't. 100

SIR ANDREW And I think I have the back-trick simply as strong as any man in Illyria.

SIR TOBY Wherefore are these things hid? Wherefore have these gifts a curtain before 'em? Are they like to take dust, like Mistress Mall's picture? Why dost thou not go to church in a galliard and come home in a coranto? My very walk should be a jig. I would not so much as make water but in a sink-a-pace. What dost thou mean? Is it a world to hide virtues in? I did think, by the excellent constitution of thy leg, it was form'd under the star of a galliard. 109

SIR ANDREW Ay, 'tis strong, and it does indifferent well in a damn'd colour'd stock. Shall we [set] about some revels?

SIR TOBY What shall we do else? Were we not born under Taurus?

SIR ANDREW Taurus! That's sides and heart.

SIR TOBY No, sir, it is legs and thighs. Let me see thee caper. Ha! Higher! Ha, ha! Excellent! *(exeunt)* 115

SCENE IV   *A room in the Duke's palace.*

Enter Valentine and Viola in man's attire.

VALENTINE If the Duke continue these favours towards you, Cesario, you are like to be much advanc'd. He hath known you but three days, and already you are no stranger.

VIOLA You either fear his humour or my negligence, that you call in question the continuance of his love. Is he inconstant, sir, in his favours? 6

VALENTINE No, believe me.

Enter Duke, Curio, and Attendants.

VIOLA I thank you. Here comes the Count.

DUKE Who saw Cesario, ho?

VIOLA On your attendance, my lord; here. 10

DUKE Stand you a while aloof. Cesario,
Thou know'st no less but all. I have unclasp'd
To thee the book even of my secret soul;
Therefore, good youth, address thy gait unto her,
Be not deni'd access, stand at her doors, 15

---

there's life in't means "there is still hope."

kickshawses are trifles—from the French *quelque chose*, some such thing.

A *galliard* is a lively dance.

Sir Toby playfully puns on *caper* and *mutton*, since mutton often is served with caper sauce.

A *coranto* is a fast dance.

A *sink-a-pace*, or *cinque pace*, is a five-step dance.

When Sir Toby sets Aguecheek off on a high-stepping dance to end the third scene, what do we realize about his manipulation of Sir Andrew?

Valentine's brief discourse with Viola, who now is disguised as Cesario, reveals important plot exposition. How long has Viola been serving in Orsino's court? What impression has she made on the Duke?

Like most Elizabethan playwrights, Shakespeare enjoyed ribald word play. The Duke's instructions to Viola/Cesario here are loaded with coarse allusions, i.e., *gait* (l. 14), *doors* (l. 15), and *foot shall grow* (l. 16)—all describ-

And tell them, there thy fixed foot shall grow
Till thou have audience.

VIOLA   Sure, my noble lord,
If she be so abandon'd to her sorrow
As it is spoke, she never will admit me.

DUKE Be clamorous and leap all civil bounds   20
Rather than make unprofited return.

VIOLA Say I do speak with her, my lord, what then?

DUKE O, then unfold the passion of my love,
Surprise her with discourse of my dear faith.
It shall become thee well to act my woes.   25
She will attend it better in thy youth
Than in a nuncio's of more grave aspect.

VIOLA I think not so, my lord.

DUKE   Dear lad, believe it
For they shall yet belie thy happy years,
That say thou art a man. Diana's lip   30
Is not more smooth and rubious; thy small pipe
Is as the maiden's organ, shrill and sound;
And all is semblative a woman's part.
I know thy constellation is right apt
For this affair. Some four or five attend him,—   35
All, if you will; for I myself am best
When least in company. Prosper well in this,
And thou shalt live as freely as thy lord,
To call his fortunes thine.

VIOLA   I'll do my best
To woo your lady,—*(aside)* yet, a barful strife!   40
Whoe'er I woo, myself would be his wife. *(exeunt)*

SCENE V *A room in Olivia's house.*

Enter Maria and Clown.

MARIA Nay, either tell me where thou hast been, or I will not open my lips so wide as a bristle may enter, in way of thy excuse. My lady will hang thee for thy absence.

CLOWN Let her hang me! He that is well hang'd in this world needs to fear no colours.   5

MARIA Make that good.

CLOWN He shall see none to fear.

MARIA A good lenten answer. I can tell thee where that saying was born, of "I fear no colours."

CLOWN Where, good Mistress Mary?   10

MARIA In the wars; and that may you be bold to say in your foolery.

CLOWN Well, God give them wisdom that have it; and those that are fools, let them use their talents.

MARIA Yet you will be hang'd for being so long absent; or, to be turn'd away, is not that as good as a hanging to you?   15

---

ing a sexual venture. The careful reader will find many other such sexual allusions in Shakespeare's plays.

A *nuncio* is a messenger.

What accidental, ironic pun is made by the Duke here?

Why is Viola/Cesario less than enthusiastic about wooing Olivia for Orsino?

The locations of these short scenes can be determined by whose servants and followers appear on stage. Thus, Maria's presence would signify Olivia's household.

colours means "flags" (i.e., foes), with added puns on "collars," the hangman's noose, and "cholers," bodily biles once thought to cause anger.

lenten here means "skimpy," as during Lent.

TWELFTH NIGHT   65

CLOWN Many a good hanging prevents a bad marriage; and, for turning away, let summer bear it out.

MARIA You are resolute, then?

CLOWN Not so, neither; but I am resolv'd on two points.

MARIA That if one break, the other will hold; or, if both break, your gaskins fall. 21

There are several puns on points: *first, as counts, and second, as laces to hold up the* gaskins, *or trousers.*

CLOWN Apt, in good faith; very apt. Well, go thy way. If Sir Toby would leave drinking, thou wert as witty a piece of Eve's flesh as any in Illyria.

MARIA Peace, you rogue, no more o' that. Here comes my lady. Make your excuse wisely, you were best. *(exit)* 26

Enter Lady Olivia [and retinue] with Malvolio.

CLOWN Wit, an't be thy will, put me into good fooling! Those wits, that think they have thee, do very oft prove fools; and I, that am sure I lack thee, may pass for a wise man; for what says Quinapalus? "Better a witty fool than a foolish wit."—God bless thee, lady! 30

Quinapalus is a name made up by Feste, the clown.

OLIVIA Take the fool away.

CLOWN Do you not hear, fellows? Take away the lady.

OLIVIA Go to, you're a dry fool, I'll no more of you; besides, you grow dishonest. 34

CLOWN Two faults, madonna, that drink and good counsel will amend; for give the dry fool drink, then is the fool not dry: bid the dishonest man mend himself; if he mend, he is no longer dishonest; if he cannot, let the botcher mend him. Anything that's mended is but patch'd; virtue that transgresses is but patch'd with sin, and sin that amends is but patch'd with virtue. If that this simple syllogism will serve, so; if it will not, what remedy? As there is no true cuckold but calamity, so beauty's a flower. The lady bade take away the fool; therefore, I say again, take her away.

A botcher *is a mender of old clothes.*

A cuckold *is a husband whose wife has been unfaithful to him.*

OLIVIA Sir, I bade them take away you. 44

CLOWN Misprision in the highest degree! Lady, *"cucullus non facit monachum"*; that's as much to say as I wear not motley in my brain. Good madonna, give me leave to prove you a fool.

A misprision *is a mistake.*

Feste's Latin phrase means that the cowl does not make the monk.

OLIVIA Can you do it?

CLOWN Dexteriously, good madonna.

OLIVIA Make your proof. 50

CLOWN I must catechise you for it, madonna. Good my mouse of virtue, answer me.

OLIVIA Well, sir, for want of other idleness, I'll bide your proof.

CLOWN Good madonna, why mournest thou?

OLIVIA Good fool, for my brother's death. 55

CLOWN I think his soul is in hell, madonna.

OLIVIA I know his soul is in heaven, fool.

CLOWN The more fool, madonna, to mourn for your brother's soul being in heaven. Take away the fool, gentlemen. 59

Aside from winning his mistress's forgiveness, why else does Feste undertake this playful contest of wits with Olivia?

OLIVIA What think you of this fool, Malvolio? Doth he not mend?

MALVOLIO Yes, and shall do till the pangs of death shake him. Infirmity, that decays the wise, doth ever make the better fool.

CLOWN God send you, sir, a speedy infirmity, for the better increasing your folly! Sir Toby will be sworn that I am no fox, but he will not pass his word for twopence that you are no fool. 65

OLIVIA How say you to that, Malvolio?

MALVOLIO I marvel your ladyship takes delight in such a barren rascal. I saw him put down the other day with an ordinary fool that has no more brain than a stone. Look you now, he's out of his guard already. Unless you laugh and minister occasion to him, he is gagg'd. I protest, I take these wise men that crow so at these set kind of fools no better than the fools' zanies. 72

OLIVIA O, you are sick of self-love, Malvolio, and taste with a distemper'd appetite. To be generous, guiltless, and of free disposition, is to take those things for bird-bolts that you deem cannon-bullets. There is no slander in an allow'd fool, though he do nothing but rail; nor no railing in a known discreet man, though he do nothing but reprove. 78

CLOWN Now Mercury endue thee with leasing, for thou speak'st well of fools!

Re-enter Maria.

MARIA Madam, there is at the gate a young gentleman much desires to speak with you.

OLIVIA From the Count Orsino, is it?

MARIA I know not, madam. 'Tis a fair young man, and well attended. 85

OLIVIA Who of my people hold him in delay?

MARIA Sir Toby, madam, your kinsman.

OLIVIA Fetch him off, I pray you. He speaks nothing but madman; fie on him! *(exit Maria)* Go you, Malvolio; if it be a suit from the Count, I am sick, or not at home,—what you will, to dismiss it. *(exit Malvolio)* Now you see, sir, how your fooling grows old, and people dislike it. 92

CLOWN Thou hast spoke for us, madonna, as if thy eldest son should be a fool; whose skull Jove cram with brains! for—here he comes—

Enter Sir Toby.

One of thy kin has a most weak *pia mater*. 96

OLIVIA By mine honour, half drunk. What is he at the gate, cousin?

SIR TOBY A gentleman.

OLIVIA A gentleman! What gentleman?

SIR TOBY 'Tis a gentleman here—a plague o' these pickle-herring! How now, sot! 101

CLOWN Good Sir Toby!

What qualities of Malvolio's character are brought out through his reactions to Feste's antics?

zanies are fools' assistants, thus fools themselves.

To *rail* means "to scold."

Mercury was known as the god of thieves and liars. *leasing* here means "the gift for lying."

Jove is another name for the god Jupitor.

pia mater means "brain."

TWELFTH NIGHT 67

OLIVIA Cousin, cousin, how have you come so early by this lethargy?

SIR TOBY Lechery! I defy lechery. There's one at the gate. 105

OLIVIA Ay, marry, what is he?

SIR TOBY Let him be the devil, an he will, I care not; give me faith, say I. Well, it's all one. *(exit)*

OLIVIA What's a drunken man like, fool? 109

CLOWN Like a drown'd man, a fool, and a madman. One draught above heat makes him a fool, the second mads him, and a third drowns him.

OLIVIA Go thou and seek the crowner and let him sit o' my coz, for he's in the third degree of drink, he's drown'd. Go, look after him.

A crowner *here means "coroner," that is, one who is to hold an inquest on Sir Toby and his drunkenness.*

CLOWN He is but mad yet, madonna; and the fool shall look to the madman. *(exit)* 116

Re-enter Malvolio.

MALVOLIO Madam, yond young fellow swears he will speak with you. I told him you were sick. He takes on him to understand so much, and therefore comes to speak with you. I told him you were asleep. He seems to have a foreknowledge of that too, and therefore comes to speak with you. What is to be said to him, lady? He's fortified against any denial. 122

OLIVIA Tell him he shall not speak with me.

MALVOLIO Has been told so; and he says, he'll stand at your door like a sheriff's post, and be the supporter to a bench, but he'll speak with you. 126

OLIVIA What kind o' man is he?

MALVOLIO Why, of mankind.

OLIVIA What manner of man?

In this interchange between Olivia and Malvolio, how does Shakespeare create some merry suspense?

MALVOLIO Of very ill manner. He'll speak with you, will you or no.

OLIVIA Of what personage and years is he? 131

MALVOLIO Not yet old enough for a man, nor young enough for a boy; as a squash is before 'tis a peascod, or a codling when 'tis almost an apple. 'Tis with him in standing water, between boy and man. He is very well-favour'd and he speaks very shrewishly. One would think his mother's milk were scarce out of him. 136

In l. 133, here squash *means an "unripe pea pod."*

codling *means an "unripe apple."*

standing water *means "at the turn of the tide."*

OLIVIA Let him approach. Call in my gentlewoman.

MALVOLIO Gentlewoman, my lady calls. *(exit)*

Why does Olivia now agree to see the young messenger? How does her nature become clearer through this episode?

Re-enter Maria.

OLIVIA Give me my veil. Come, throw it o'er my face. We'll once more hear Orsino's embassy. 140

Enter [Viola and Attendants].

VIOLA The honourable lady of the house, which is she?

OLIVIA Speak to me; I shall answer for her. Your will?

VIOLA Most radiant, exquisite, and unmatchable beauty,—I pray you, tell me if this be the lady of the house, for I never saw her. I would be loath to cast away my speech, for besides that it is excellently well penn'd, I have taken great pains to con it. Good beauties, let me sustain no scorn. I am very comptible, even to the least sinister usage. 148

OLIVIA Whence came you, sir?

VIOLA I can say little more than I have studied, and that question's out of my part. Good gentle one, give me modest assurance if you be the lady of the house, that I may proceed in my speech. 152

OLIVIA Are you a comedian?

VIOLA No, my profound heart; and yet, by the very fangs of malice I swear, I am not that I play. Are you the lady of the house?

OLIVIA If I do not usurp myself, I am. 156

VIOLA Most certain, if you are she, you do usurp yourself; for what is yours to bestow is not yours to reserve. But this is from my commission. I will on with my speech in your praise, and then show you the heart of my message. 160

OLIVIA Come to what is important in't. I forgive you the praise.

VIOLA Alas, I took great pains to study it, and 'tis poetical.

OLIVIA It is the more like to be feigned. I pray you, keep it in. I heard you were saucy at my gates, and allow'd your approach rather to wonder at you than to hear you. If you be not mad, be gone. If you have reason, be brief. 'Tis not that time of moon with me to make one in so skipping a dialogue. 167

MARIA Will you hoist sail, sir? Here lies your way.

VIOLA No, good swabber, I am to hull here a little longer. Some mollification for your giant, sweet lady. Tell me your mind. I am a messenger. 171

OLIVIA Sure, you have some hideous matter to deliver, when the courtesy of it is so fearful. Speak your office.

VIOLA It alone concerns your ear. I bring no overture of war, no taxation of homage. I hold the olive in my hand. My words are as full of peace as matter. 176

OLIVIA Yet you began rudely. What are you? What would you?

VIOLA The rudeness that hath appear'd in me have I learn'd from my entertainment. What I am, and what I would, are as secret as maidenhead; to your ears, divinity, to any other's, profanation. 180

OLIVIA Give us the place alone; we will hear this divinity *(exeunt Maria and Attendants)* Now, sir, what is your text?

VIOLA Most sweet lady,—

OLIVIA A comfortable doctrine, and much may be said of it. Where lies your text? 185

VIOLA In Orsino's bosom.

OLIVIA In his bosom! In what chapter of his bosom?

VIOLA To answer by the method, in the first of his heart.

OLIVIA O, I have read it; it is heresy. Have you no more to say?

What is the humor where Viola/Cesario interrupts herself at the start of the polite, gushy greeting?

comptible means "sensitive."

What playful jest does Viola/Cesario offer in line 155?

skipping means "flighty" here.

What does Maria mean by *hoist sail*?

A *swabber* is a washer of ship decks, while *hull* means "to drift or float"—all nautical expressions in keeping with Maria's metaphor of line 167.

maidenhead is a virgin's chastity.

TWELFTH NIGHT 69

VIOLA Good madam, let me see your face. 190

OLIVIA Have you any commission from your lord to negotiate with my face? You are now out of your text, but we will draw the curtain and show you the picture. Look you, sir, such a one I was—this present. Is't not well done? *(unveiling)*

VIOLA Excellently done, if God did all. 195

OLIVIA 'Tis in grain, sir; 'twill endure wind and weather.

VIOLA 'Tis beauty truly blent, whose red and white
Nature's own sweet and cunning hand laid on.
Lady, you are the cruell'st she alive
If you will lead these graces to the grave 200
And leave the world no copy.

OLIVIA O, sir, I will not be so hard-hearted; I will give out divers schedules of my beauty. It shall be inventoried, and every particle and utensil labell'd to my will: as, item, two lips, indifferent red; item, two grey eyes, with lids to them; item, one neck, one chin, and so forth. Were you sent hither to praise me? 206

VIOLA I see you what you are, you are too proud;
But, if you were the devil, you are fair.
My lord and master loves you. O, such love
Could be but recompens'd, though you were crown'd 210
The nonpareil of beauty!

OLIVIA How does he love me?

VIOLA With adorations, [with] fertile tears,
With groans that thunder love, with sighs of fire.

OLIVIA Your lord does know my mind; I cannot love him.
Yet I suppose him virtuous, know him noble; 215
Of great estate, of fresh and stainless youth,
In voices well divulg'd, free, learn'd, and valiant,
And in dimension and the shape of nature
A gracious person. But yet I cannot love him.
He might have took his answer long ago. 220

VIOLA If I did love you in my master's flame,
With such a suff'ring, such a deadly life,
In your denial I would find no sense.
I would not understand it.

OLIVIA Why, what would you?

VIOLA Make me a willow cabin at your gate, 225
And call upon my soul within the house;
Write loyal cantons of contemned love
And sing them loud even in the dead of night;
Halloo your name to the reverberate hills
And make the babbling gossip of the air 230
Cry out "Olivia!" O, you should not rest
Between the elements of air and earth,
But you should pity me!

OLIVIA You might do much.
What is your parentage?

VIOLA Above my fortunes, yet my state is well. 235
I am a gentleman.

In this pleasant bantering between Olivia and Cesario, Olivia finally agrees to remove her veil, leading Cesario to comment satirically that she is indeed beautiful, if it is genuinely her face he sees and not a creation of cosmetics.

In voices well divulg'd means that others hold Orsino "in good repute."

cantons are cantos or songs.

How does Shakespeare indicate that Olivia has become fond of Cesario?

OLIVIA   Get you to your lord.
I cannot love him. Let him send no more,—
Unless, perchance, you come to me again
To tell me how he takes it. Fare you well!
I thank you for your pains. Spend this for me.   240

VIOLA I am no fee'd post, lady. Keep your purse.   *A* post *is a messenger.*
My master, not myself, lacks recompense.
Love make his heart of flint that you shall love;
And let your fervour, like my master's, be
Plac'd in contempt! Farewell, fair cruelty. *(exit)*   245

OLIVIA "What is your parentage?"
"Above my fortunes, yet my state is well.
I am a gentleman." I'll be sworn thou art.
Thy tongue, thy face, thy limbs, actions, and spirit
Do give thee five-fold blazon. Not too fast! Soft, soft!   250   blazon *means "proof of nobility" and*
Unless the master were the man. How now!   soft *means "slow down."*
Even so quickly may one catch the plague?
Methinks I feel this youth's perfections
With an invisible and subtle stealth
To creep in at mine eyes. Well, let it be.   255
What ho, Malvolio!

Re-enter Malvolio.

MALVOLIO   Here, madam, at your service.

OLIVIA Run after that same peevish messenger,
The County's man. He left this ring behind him,   *Why does Olivia send a ring to Cesario*
Would I or not. Tell him I'll none of it.   *and make up such a story about it?*
Desire him not to flatter with his lord,   260
Nor hold him up with hopes. I'm not for him.
If that the youth will come this way to-morrow,
I'll give him reasons for't. Hie thee, Malvolio.   Hie thee *means "Get going."*

MALVOLIO Madam, I will. *(exit)*

OLIVIA I do I know not what, and fear to find   265
Mine eye too great a flatterer for my mind.
Fate, show thy force; ourselves we do not owe;
What is decreed must be, and be this so. *(exit)*

ACT II

SCENE I   *The sea-coast.*

Enter Antonio and Sebastian.

ANTONIO Will you stay no longer? Nor will you not that I go with you?

SEBASTIAN By your patience, no. My stars shine darkly over me. The malignancy of my fate might perhaps distemper yours, therefore I shall crave of you your leave that I may bear my evils alone. It were a bad recompense for your love, to lay any of them on you.   6

ANTONIO Let me yet know of you whither you are bound.

SEBASTIAN No, sooth, sir. My determinate voyage is mere ex-   *Sebastian means that it will be his*
travagancy. But I perceive in you so excellent a touch of modesty,   *destiny simply to wander.*

TWELFTH NIGHT   71

that you will not extort from me what I am willing to keep in; therefore it charges me in manners the rather to express myself. You must know of me then, Antonio, my name is Sebastian, which I call'd Roderigo. My father was that Sebastian of Messaline, whom I know you have heard of. He left behind him myself and a sister, both born in an hour. If the heavens had been pleas'd, would we had so ended! But you, sir, alter'd that; for some hour before you took me from the breach of the sea was my sister drown'd. 17

ANTONIO Alas the day!

SEBASTIAN A lady, sir, though it was said she much resembled me, was yet of many accounted beautiful; but, though I could not with such estimable wonder overfar believe that, yet thus far I will boldly publish her: she bore a mind that envy could not but call fair. She is drown'd already, sir, with salt water, though I seem to drown her remembrance again with more.

ANTONIO Pardon me, sir, your bad entertainment. 25

SEBASTIAN O good Antonio, forgive me your trouble.

ANTONIO If you will not murder me for my love, let me be your servant.

SEBASTIAN If you will not undo what you have done, that is, kill him whom you have recover'd, desire it not. Fare ye well at once. My bosom is full of kindness, and I am yet so near the manners of my mother, that upon the least occasion more mine eyes will tell tales of me. I am bound to the Count Orsino's court. Farewell. *(exit)*

ANTONIO The gentleness of all the gods go with thee!
I have many enemies in Orsino's court, 35
Else would I very shortly see thee there.
But, come what may, I do adore thee so
That danger shall seem sport, and I will go. *(exit)*

SCENE II   *A street.*

Enter Viola and Malvolio, at several doors.

MALVOLIO Were you not even now with the Countess Olivia?

VIOLA Even now, sir. On a moderate pace I have since arriv'd but hither. 3

MALVOLIO She returns this ring to you, sir. You might have saved me my pains, to have taken it away yourself. She adds, moreover, that you should put your lord into a desperate assurance she will none of him; and—one thing more—that you be never so hardy to come again in his affairs, unless it be to report your lord's taking of this. Receive it so.

VIOLA She took the ring of me. I'll none of it. 10

MALVOLIO Come, sir, you peevishly threw it to her; and her will is, it should be so return'd. If it be worth stooping for, there it lies in your eye; if not, be it his that finds it. *(exit)*

VIOLA I left no ring with her. What means this lady?
Fortune forbid my outside have not charm'd her! 15
She made good view of me; indeed, so much

How can we figure out that Sebastian's twin sister (ll. 14–15—"both born in an hour") must be Viola, whom we saw washed ashore in Act I, scene ii?

Note that Antonio secretly accompanies Sebastian out of affectionate friendship. Also, Antonio has had a run-in with Duke Orsino's men previously, so that following Sebastian is dangerous.

What stage action is communicated in Malvolio's lines?

Since Viola (disguised as Cesario) now is alone on stage, her lines constitute a *soliloquy.*

72   WILLIAM SHAKESPEARE

That [sure] methought her eyes had lost her tongue,
For she did speak in starts distractedly.
She loves me, sure. The cunning of her passion
Invites me in this churlish messenger. 20
None of my lord's ring! Why, he sent her none.
I am the man! If it be so, as 'tis,
Poor lady, she were better love a dream.

Why is dream *an apt word, in this context?*

Disguise, I see thou art a wickedness
Wherein the pregnant enemy does much. 25

pregnant is used here as resourceful.

How easy is it for the proper-false

proper-false means "handsome deceivers."

In women's waxen hearts to set their forms!
Alas, [our] frailty is the cause, not we!
For such as we are made [of], such we be.
How will this fadge? My master loves her dearly; 30

fadge means "turn out."

And I, poor monster, fond as much on him;
And she, mistaken, seems to dote on me.
What will become of this? As I am man,
My state is desperate for my master's love;
As I am woman,—now alas the day!— 35

Shakespeare makes clear not only Olivia's impending frustrated infatuation with Cesario and Orsino's fruitless pursuit of Olivia, but also what other stymied love?

What thriftless sighs shall poor Olivia breathe!
O time! thou must untangle this, not I.
It is too hard a knot for me t' untie! *(exit)*

SCENE III   *A room in Olivia's house.*

Enter Sir Toby and Sir Andrew.

SIR TOBY Approach, Sir Andrew. Not to be a-bed after midnight is to be up betimes; and *"deliculo surgere,"* thou know'st,—

deliculo surgere means "to rise early is most healthful."

SIR ANDREW Nay, by my troth, I know not; but I know, to be up late is to be up late. 4

SIR TOBY A false conclusion. I hate it as an unfill'd can. To be up after midnight and to go to bed then, is early; so that to go to bed after midnight is to go to bed betimes. Does not our lives consist of the four elements?

SIR ANDREW Faith, so they say; but I think it rather consists of eating and drinking. 10

SIR TOBY Thou'rt a scholar; let us therefore eat and drink. Marian, I say! a stoup of wine!

A stoup *is a cup.*

Enter Clown.

SIR ANDREW Here comes the fool, i' faith.

CLOWN How now, my hearts! Did you never see the picture of "we three"? 15

As usual, the Clown offers witty *repartee. Here,* we three *is the name of a picture of two asses or fools, with the spectator making the third.*

SIR TOBY Welcome, ass. Now let's have a catch.

The word catch *(l. 16) means a "song round."*

SIR ANDREW By my troth, the fool has an excellent breast. I had rather than forty shillings I had such a leg, and so sweet a breath to sing, as the fool has. In sooth, thou wast in very gracious fooling last night, when thou spok'st of Pigrogromitus, of the Vapians passing

line 17, breast *means "voice."*

TWELFTH NIGHT   73

the equinoctial of Queubus. 'Twas very good, i' faith. I sent thee sixpence for thy leman. Hadst it? 22

CLOWN I did impeticos thy gratillity; for Malvolio's nose is no whipstock. My lady has a white hand, and the Mermidons are no bottle-ale houses. 25

SIR ANDREW Excellent! Why, this is the best fooling, when all is done. Now, a song.

SIR TOBY Come on; there is sixpence for you. Let's have a song.

SIR ANDREW There's a testril of me too. If one knight give a—

CLOWN Would you have a love-song, or a song of good life? 30

SIR TOBY A love-song, a love-song.

SIR ANDREW Ay, ay. I care not for good life.

CLOWN (*sings*)

> O mistress mine, where are you roaming?
> O, stay and hear, your true love's coming,
>   That can sing both high and low. 35
> Trip no further, pretty sweeting;
> Journeys end in lovers meeting,
>   Every wise man's son doth know.

SIR ANDREW Excellent good, i' faith.

SIR TOBY Good, good. 40

CLOWN (*sings*)

> What is love? 'Tis not hereafter.
> Present mirth hath present laughter;
>   What's to come is still unsure.
> In delay there lies no plenty;
> Then come kiss me, sweet and twenty, 45
>   Youth's a stuff will not endure.

SIR ANDREW A mellifluous voice, as I am true knight.

SIR TOBY A contagious breath.

SIR ANDREW Very sweet and contagious, i' faith. 49

SIR TOBY To hear by the nose, it is dulcet in contagion. But shall we make the welkin dance indeed? Shall we rouse the night-owl in a catch that will draw three souls out of one weaver? Shall we do that?

SIR ANDREW An you love me, let's do't. I am dog at a catch.

CLOWN By'r lady, sir, and some dogs will catch well.

SIR ANDREW Most certain. Let our catch be, "Thou knave." 55

CLOWN "Hold thy peace, thou knave," knight? I shall be constrain'd in't to call thee knave, knight.

SIR ANDREW 'Tis not the first time I have constrained one to call me knave. Begin, fool. It begins, "Hold thy peace."

CLOWN I shall never begin if I hold my peace. 60

SIR ANDREW Good, i' faith. Come, begin. (*catch sung*)

Enter Maria.

Sir Andrew has believed the gibberish tales Sir Toby had told him about Pigrogromitus and the rest.

leman means "sweetheart."

impeticos thy gratillity is Feste's nonsensical way of saying pocket thy gratuity (or tip).

Mermidons were followers of Achilles.

A *testril* is sixpence.

In what way is the Clown's song a comment on the play?

A *contagious breath* means "a catchy song."

welkin means "sky."

74 WILLIAM SHAKESPEARE

MARIA What a caterwauling do you keep here! If my lady have not call'd up her steward Malvolio and bid him turn you out of doors, never trust me. 64

SIR TOBY My lady's a Cataian, we are politicians, Malvolio's a Peg-a-Ramsey, and "Three merry men be we." Am not I consanguineous? Am I not of her blood? Tilly-vally. Lady! *(sings)* "There dwelt a man in Babylon, lady, lady!"

CLOWN Beshrew me, the knight's in admirable fooling. 69

SIR ANDREW Ay, he does well enough if he be dispos'd, and so do I too. He does it with a better grace, but I do it more natural.

SIR TOBY *(sings)* "O, the twelfth day of December,"—

MARIA For the love o' God, peace! 73

Enter Malvolio.

MALVOLIO My masters, are you mad, or what are you? Have you no wit, manners, nor honesty, but to gabble like tinkers at this time of night? Do ye make an alehouse of my lady's house, that ye squeak out your coziers' catches without any mitigation or remorse of voice? Is there no respect of place, persons, nor time in you?

SIR TOBY We did keep time, sir, in our catches. Sneck up! 79

MALVOLIO Sir Toby, I must be round with you. My lady bade me tell you that, though she harbours you as her kinsman, she's nothing alli'd to your disorders. If you can separate yourself and your misdemeanours, you are welcome to the house; if not, an it would please you to take leave of her, she is very willing to bid you farewell. 85

SIR TOBY "Farewell, dear heart, since I must needs be gone."

MARIA Nay, good Sir Toby.

CLOWN "His eyes do show his days are almost done."

MALVOLIO Is't even so?

SIR TOBY "But I will never die." 90

CLOWN Sir Toby, there you lie.

MALVOLIO This is much credit to you.

SIR TOBY "Shall I bid him go?"

CLOWN "What an if you do?"

SIR TOBY "Shall I bid him go, and spare not?" 95

CLOWN "O no, no, no, no, you dare not."

SIR TOBY Out o' tune, sir! Ye lie. Art any more than a steward? Dost thou think, because thou art virtuous, there shall be no more cakes and ale? 99

CLOWN Yes, by Saint Anne, and ginger shall be hot i' th' mouth too.

SIR TOBY Thou'rt i' th' right. Go, sir, rub your chain with crumbs. A stoup of wine, Maria!

MALVOLIO Mistress Mary, if you priz'd my lady's favour at anything more than contempt, you would not give means for this uncivil rule. She shall know of it, by this hand. *(exit)* 105

TWELFTH NIGHT 75

MARIA Go shake your ears.

SIR ANDREW 'Twere as good a deed as to drink when a man's a-hungry, to challenge him the field, and then to break promise with him and make a fool of him. 109

SIR TOBY Do't, knight. I'll write thee a challenge, or I'll deliver thy indignation to him by word of mouth.

MARIA Sweet Sir Toby, be patient for to-night. Since the youth of the Count's was to-day with my lady, she is much out of quiet. For Monsieur Malvolio, let me alone with him. If I do not gull him into a nayword, and make him a common recreation, do not think I have wit enough to lie straight in my bed. I know I can do it. 116

To gull *a person means to trick him. Why are Maria, Sir Toby, and Sir Andrew so angered by Malvolio's demands that they keep still? What is Malvolio's exact function in Olivia's household—is he a member of the family, for instance?*

SIR TOBY Possess us, possess us. Tell us something of him.

MARIA Marry, sir, sometimes he is a kind of puritan.

SIR ANDREW O, if I thought that, I'd beat him like a dog!

SIR TOBY What, for being a puritan? Thy exquisite reason, dear knight? 121

SIR ANDREW I have no exquisite reason for't, but I have reason good enough.

In Shakespeare's time, Puritans were considered religious fanatics and spoilsports by most English citizens. Consequently, Puritans were ridiculed. Paradoxically, they came to rule England for a period during the seventeenth century. What picture of Malvolio's character emerges from the descriptions given here?

MARIA The devil a puritan that he is, or anything constantly, but a time-pleaser; an affection'd ass, that cons state without book and utters it by great swarths; the best persuaded of himself, so cramm'd, as he thinks, with excellencies, that it is his grounds of faith that all that look on him love him; and on that vice in him will my revenge find notable cause to work. 129

SIR TOBY What wilt thou do?

MARIA I will drop in his way some obscure epistles of love; wherein, by the colour of his beard, the shape of his leg, the manner of his gait, the expressure of his eye, forehead, and complexion, he shall find himself most feelingly personated. I can write very like my lady your niece. On a forgotten matter we can hardly make distinction of our hands. 136

epistles of love means "love letters."

hands, here, means "handwriting."

SIR TOBY Excellent! I smell a device.

SIR ANDREW I have't in my nose too.

SIR TOBY He shall think, by the letters that thou wilt drop, that they come from my niece, and that she's in love with him. 140

MARIA My purpose is, indeed, a horse of that colour.

SIR ANDREW And your horse now would make him an ass.

MARIA Ass, I doubt not.

SIR ANDREW O, 'twill be admirable! 144

MARIA Sport royal, I warrant you. I know my physic will work with him. I will plant you two, and let the fool make a third, where he shall find the letter. Observe his construction of it. For this night, to bed, and dream on the event. Farewell. *(exit)*

A physic *is a medicine used as a cathartic. Here Maria intends to rid Malvolio of what character ailments?*

SIR TOBY Good night, Penthesilea.

SIR ANDREW Before me, she's a good wench. 150

Penthesilea was Queen of the Amazons.

WILLIAM SHAKESPEARE

SIR TOBY She's a beagle, true-bred, and one that adores me. What o' that?

SIR ANDREW I was ador'd once too.

SIR TOBY Let's to bed, knight. Thou hadst need send for more money. 155

SIR ANDREW If I cannot recover your niece, I am a foul way out.

SIR TOBY Send for money, knight. If thou hast her not i' the end, call me cut.

SIR ANDREW If I do not, never trust me, take it how you will. 159

SIR TOBY Come, come, I'll burn some sack; 'tis too late to go to bed now. Come, knight; come, knight. *(exeunt)*

sack was a popular Spanish wine.

SCENE IV *A room in the Duke's palace.*

Enter Duke, Viola, Curio, and others.

DUKE Give me some music. Now,—good morrow, friends,—
Now, good Cesario, but that piece of song,
That old and antique song we heard last night.
Methought it did relieve my passion much,
More than light airs and recollected terms 5
Of these most brisk and giddy-paced times.
Come, but one verse.

What do the Duke's repeated requests for music to soothe his love agony over Olivia tell us about his character, confirming our first impressions of him from Act I, scene i?

CURIO He is not here, so please your lordship, that should sing it.

DUKE Who was it? 9

CURIO Feste, the jester, my lord; a fool that the lady Olivia's father took much delight in. He is about the house.

DUKE Seek him out, and play the tune the while.
(exit Curio) (music plays)
Come hither, boy. If ever thou shalt love,
In the sweet pangs of it remember me;
For such as I am all true lovers are, 15
Unstaid and skittish in all motions else,
Save in the constant image of the creature
That is belov'd. How dost thou like this tune?

What are the elements for ironic humor in this chat about love between the Duke and the disguised Viola?

VIOLA It gives a very echo to the seat
Where Love is thron'd.

DUKE   Thou dost speak masterly 20
My life upon't, young though thou art, thine eye
Hath stay'd upon some favour that it loves.
Hath it not, boy?

VIOLA   A little, by your favour.

DUKE What kind of woman is't?

VIOLA   Of your complexion.

DUKE She is not worth thee, then. What years, i' faith? 25

VIOLA About your years, my lord.

TWELFTH NIGHT 77

DUKE Too old, by heaven. Let still the woman take
An elder than herself; so wears she to him,
So sways she level in her husband's heart.
For, boy, however we do praise ourselves, 30
Our fancies are more giddy and unfirm,
More longing, wavering, sooner lost and worn,
Than women's are.

VIOLA   I think it well, my lord.

DUKE Then let thy love be younger than thyself,
Or thy affection cannot hold the bent. 35
For women are as roses, whose fair flower
Being once display'd, doth fall that very hour.

VIOLA And so they are; alas, that they are so!
To die, even when they to perfection grow!

Shakespeare's audiences would have an extra laugh at his pun on the term To die, *which could also mean "to have sexual intercourse."*

Re-enter Curio and Clown.

DUKE O, fellow, come, the song we had last night. 40
Mark it, Cesario, it is old and plain.
The spinsters and the knitters in the sun
And the free maids that weave their thread with bones
Do use to chant it. It is silly sooth,
And dallies with the innocence of love, 45
Like the old age.

bones *means "bobbins made of bone."*

CLOWN Are you ready, sir?

DUKE Ay; prithee, sing. *(music)*

Song

  [**CLOWN**] Come away, come away, death,
    And in sad cypress let me be laid. 50
  Fly away, fly away, breath;
    I am slain by a fair cruel maid.
  My shroud of white, stuck all with yew,
      O, prepare it!
  My part of death, no one so true 55
      Did share it.

  Not a flower, not a flower sweet,
    On my black coffin let there be strown.
  Not a friend, not a friend greet
    My poor corpse, where my bones shall be thrown. 60
  A thousand thousand sighs to save,
      Lay me, O, where
  Sad true lover never find my grave,
      To weep there!

My part . . . share it *means something like "No truer lover ever died than I."*

DUKE There's for thy pains. 65

CLOWN No pains, sir; I take pleasure in singing, sir.

DUKE I'll pay thy pleasure then.

CLOWN Truly, sir, and pleasure will be paid, one time or another.

DUKE Give me now leave to leave thee. 69

What stage action is indicated by the Duke in line 65?

78 WILLIAM SHAKESPEARE

CLOWN Now, the melancholy god protect thee, and the tailor make thy doublet of changeable taffeta, for thy mind is a very opal. I would have men of such constancy put to sea, that their business might be everything and their intent everywhere; for that's it that always makes a good voyage of nothing. Farewell. *(exit)*

DUKE Let all the rest give place. *(Curio and Attendants retire.)*
       Once more, Cesario,   75
Get thee to yond same sovereign cruelty.
Tell her, my love, more noble than the world,
Prizes not quantity of dirty lands.
The parts that fortune hath bestow'd upon her,
Tell her, I hold as giddily as fortune;   80
But 'tis that miracle and queen of gems
That nature pranks her in attracts my soul.

VIOLA But if she cannot love you, sir?

DUKE [I] cannot be so answer'd.

VIOLA   Sooth, but you must.
Say that some lady, as perhaps there is,   85
Hath for your love as great a pang of heart
As you have for Olivia. You cannot love her.
You tell her so. Must she not then be answer'd?

DUKE There is no woman's sides
Can bide the beating of so strong a passion   90
As love doth give my heart; no woman's heart
So big, to hold so much. They lack retention.
Alas, their love may be call'd appetite,
No motion of the liver, but the palate,
That suffer surfeit, cloyment, and revolt;   95
But mine is all as hungry as the sea,
And can digest as much. Make no compare
Between that love a woman can bear me
And that I owe Olivia.

VIOLA   Ay, but I know—

DUKE What dost thou know?   100

VIOLA Too well what love women to men may owe;
In faith, they are as true of heart as we.
My father had a daughter lov'd a man,
As it might be, perhaps, were I a woman,
I should your lordship

DUKE   And what's her history?   105

VIOLA A blank, my lord. She never told her love.
But let concealment, like a worm i' the bud,
Feed on her damask cheek. She pin'd in thought,
And with a green and yellow melancholy
She sat, like Patience on a monument,   110
Smiling at grief. Was not this love indeed?
We men may say more, swear more; but indeed

Why is Feste's allusion to the *melancholy god* appropriate when speaking to Orsino? What does *melancholy* mean? (See also l. 109.)

pranks here signifies "adorns."

What opportunities for humor occur in these ambiguous lines by Cesario in light of our knowledge that "he" is Viola in disguise?

Patience here refers to a statue signifying the virtue of patience. *monument* in this context means "tomb."

TWELFTH NIGHT   79

Our shows are more than will, for still we prove
Much in our vows, but little in our love.

DUKE But died thy sister of her love, my boy? 115

VIOLA I am all the daughters of my father's house,
And all the brothers too;—and yet I know not.
Sir, shall I to this lady?

Why is Viola so vague here about any of her father's sons or daughters who might yet be living?

DUKE   Ay, that's the theme.
To her in haste. Give her this jewel. Say
My love can give no place, bide no denay. *(exeunt)* 120

SCENE V *Olivia's garden.*

Enter Sir Toby, Sir Andrew, and Fabian.

SIR TOBY Come thy ways, Signior Fabian.

FABIAN Nay, I'll come. If I lose a scruple of this sport, let me be boil'd to death with melancholy.

SIR TOBY Wouldst thou not be glad to have the niggardly rascally sheep-biter come by some notable shame? 5

A sheep-biter is a vicious dog. Who are they referring to? Why are these three fellows in such a gay mood?

FABIAN I would exult, man. You know, he brought me out o' favour with my lady about a bear-baiting here.

SIR TOBY To anger him we'll have the bear again, and we will fool him black and blue. Shall we not, Sir Andrew?

SIR ANDREW An we do not, it is pity of our lives. 10

bear-baiting was a very popular sport of that time. A bear would be chained to a stake set in the center of an outdoor arena, where it would be attacked, or baited, by wild dogs, most of which would be killed by the bear before it tired and finally succumbed.

Enter Maria.

SIR TOBY Here comes the little villain. How now, my metal of India!

MARIA Get ye all three into the box-tree; Malvolio's coming down this walk. He has been yonder i' the sun practising behaviour to his own shadow this half hour. Observe him, for the love of mockery, for I know this letter will make a contemplative idiot of him. Close, in the name of jesting! Lie thou there [*throws down a letter*], for here comes the trout that must be caught with tickling. *(exit)*

Sir Toby means "gold" or "precious object," in referring to Maria. Why is he particularly pleased with her at this point in the plot?

Enter Malvolio.

MALVOLIO 'Tis but fortune. All is fortune. Maria once told me she did affect me; and I have heard herself come thus near, that, should she fancy, it should be one of my complexion. Besides, she uses me with a more exalted respect than any one else that follows her. What should I think on't? 22

One method for catching trout was thought to be to stroke or tickle it in the water until it went into a trance.

SIR TOBY Here's an overweening rogue!

FABIAN O, peace! Contemplation makes a rare turkey-cock of him. How he jets under his advanc'd plumes! 25

There has been some difference in interpreting the antecedents for "she" (l. 18), "herself" (l. 19), "she" (l. 20), "she" (l. 20), and "her" (l. 21). But the sense of the passage makes it probable that Malvolio already believes Olivia loves him, even before the episode of Maria's trick letter.

jets means "struts."

SIR ANDREW 'S light, I could so beat the rogue!

SIR TOBY Peace, I say.

MALVOLIO To be Count Malvolio!

SIR TOBY Ah, rogue!

Why should Malvolio's allusion to himself as a count so upset the others?

SIR ANDREW Pistol him, pistol him. 30

SIR TOBY Peace, peace!

80   WILLIAM SHAKESPEARE

MALVOLIO There is example for't. The lady of the Strachy married the yeoman of the wardrobe.

SIR ANDREW Fie on him, Jezebel! 34

FABIAN O, peace! now he's deeply in. Look how imagination blows him.

MALVOLIO Having been three months married to her, sitting in my state,—

SIR TOBY O, for a stone-bow, to hit him in the eye! 39

MALVOLIO Calling my officers about me, in my branch'd velvet gown, having come from a day-bed, where I have left Olivia sleeping,—

SIR TOBY Fire and brimstone!

FABIAN O, peace, peace! 44

MALVOLIO And then to have the humour of state; and after a demure travel of regard, telling them I know my place as I would they should do theirs, to ask for my kinsman Toby,—

SIR TOBY Bolts and shackles!

FABIAN O peace, peace, peace! Now, now. 49

MALVOLIO Seven of my people, with an obedient start, make out for him. I frown the while, and perchance wind up my watch, or play with my—some rich jewel. Toby approaches, curtsies there to me,—

SIR TOBY Shall this fellow live?

FABIAN Though our silence be drawn from us with cars, yet peace.

MALVOLIO I extend my hand to him thus, quenching my familiar smile with an austere regard of control,— 56

SIR TOBY And does not Toby take you a blow o' the lips then?

MALVOLIO Saying, "Cousin Toby, my fortunes, having cast me on your niece, give me this prerogative of speech,"—

SIR TOBY What, what? 60

MALVOLIO "You must amend your drunkenness."

SIR TOBY Out, scab!

FABIAN Nay, patience, or we break the sinews of our plot.

MALVOLIO "Besides, you waste the treasure of your time with a foolish knight,"— 65

SIR ANDREW That's me, I warrant you.

MALVOLIO "One Sir Andrew,"—

SIR ANDREW I knew 'twas I; for many do call me fool.

MALVOLIO What employment have we here? *(taking up the letter)*

FABIAN Now is the woodcock near the gin. 70

SIR TOBY O, peace, and the spirit of humours intimate reading aloud to him!

MALVOLIO By my life, this is my lady's hand. These be her very C's, her U's, and her T's; and thus makes she her great P's. It is, in contempt of question, her hand. 75

The Lady Strachy probably married below her station, giving Malvolio a precedent for his own situation.

In this daydream of Malvolio's, what is Olivia's relationship to him?

Here, *peace* means "keep quiet," for fear of revealing the presence of the secret onlookers.

Why would Toby be Malvolio's *kinsman* according to this fantasy?

What is so comic about Malvolio's image of Sir Toby curtsying to him? Why would Sir Toby be so upset by that image?

In this context, *employment* means "business."

Woodcocks traditionally were considered to be stupid birds. A *gin* is a snare.

Malvolio (Maurice Evans) in the garden, from the 1940 Broadway production of Twelfth Night.

SIR ANDREW Her C's, her U's, and her T's: why that?

MALVOLIO (*reads*) "To the unknown belov'd, this and my good wishes":—her very phrases! By your leave, wax. Soft! And the impressure her Lucrece, with which she uses to seal. 'Tis my lady. To whom should this be?   80

The obscene implications of the initials are clear enough to everyone except Malvolio and Sir Andrew.

In legend *Lucrece* was considered a very chaste woman.

FABIAN This wins him, liver and all.

MALVOLIO (*reads*)
"Jove knows I love;
   But who?
Lips, do not move;
No man must know."   85
"No man must know." What follows? The numbers alter'd! "No man must know!" If this should be thee, Malvolio?

SIR TOBY Marry, hang thee, brock!

A *brock* is a badger.

MALVOLIO (*reads*)
"I may command where I adore;
   But silence, like a Lucrece knife,   90
With bloodless stroke my heart doth gore.
   M, O, A, I, doth sway my life."

FABIAN A fustian riddle!

Here, *fustian* means "overly ornate" or "ridiculous."

SIR TOBY Excellent wench, say I.   94

82   WILLIAM SHAKESPEARE

MALVOLIO "M, O, A, I, doth sway my life." Nay, but first, let me see, let me see, let me see.

FABIAN What dish o' poison has she dress'd him!

SIR TOBY And with what wing the [staniel] checks at it!

MALVOLIO "I may command where I adore." Why, she may command me. I serve her. She is my lady. Why, this is evident to any formal capacity, there is no obstruction in this. And the end,—what should that alphabetical position portend? If I could make that resemble something in me!— Softly! M, O, A, I,—

SIR TOBY O, ay, make up that. He is now at a cold scent.

FABIAN Sowter will cry upon't for all this, though it be as rank as a fox.

MALVOLIO M,—Malvolio; M,—why, that begins my name.

FABIAN Did not I say he would work it out? The cur is excellent at faults.

MALVOLIO M,—but then there is no consonancy in the sequel. That suffers under probation. A should follow, but O does.

FABIAN And O shall end, I hope.

SIR TOBY Ay, or I'll cudgel him, and make him cry O!

MALVOLIO And then I comes behind.

FABIAN Ay, an you had an eye behind you, you might see more detraction at your heels than fortunes before you.

MALVOLIO M, O, A, I; this simulation is not as the former. And yet, to crush this a little, it would bow to me, for every one of these letters are in my name. Soft! here follows prose.

(reads) "If this fall into thy hand, revolve. In my stars I am above thee, but be not afraid of greatness. Some are [born] great, some achieve greatness, and some have greatness thrust upon 'em. Thy Fates open their hands, let thy blood and spirit embrace them; and, to inure thyself to what thou art like to be, cast thy humble slough and appear fresh. Be opposite with a kinsman, surly with servants; let thy tongue tang arguments of state; put thyself into the trick of singularity: she thus advises thee that sighs for thee. Remember who commended thy yellow stockings, and wish'd to see thee ever cross-garter'd. I say, remember. Go to, thou art made if thou desir'st to be so; if not, let me see thee a steward still, the fellow of servants, and not worthy to touch Fortune's fingers. Farewell. She that would alter services with thee,

THE FORTUNATE UNHAPPY."

Daylight and champaign discovers not more. This is open. I will be proud, I will read politic authors, I will baffle Sir Toby, I will wash off gross acquaintance, I will be point-device the very man. I do not now fool myself, to let imagination jade me; for every reason excites to this, that my lady loves me. She did commend my yellow stockings of late, she did praise my leg being cross-garter'd; and in this she manifests herself to my love, and with a kind of injunction drives me to these habits of her liking. I thank my stars I am happy. I will be strange, stout, in yellow stockings, and cross-garter'd, even

---

Why would Malvolio's lengthy puzzlement with the key letters "M," "O," "A," and "I" make audiences laugh?

A *staniel* is an untrained falcon. Sir Toby means that Malvolio is slow and haphazard in swooping down on the objective—here the meaning of the letter.

sowter is a stupid hound.

rank, here, is to have a strong, offensive smell—thus a rank fox should be easy for a hound to track.

cudgel means "beat."

Why would sentiments like these found in the letter especially appeal to a person like Malvolio?

champaign means "open country."

point-device means "precisely" here.

Do you believe Olivia actually ever praised such items of clothes on Malvolio? Why?

stout means "haughty."

TWELFTH NIGHT 83

with the swiftness of putting on. Jove and my stars be praised! Here is yet a postscript. 144

(reads) "Thou canst not choose but know who I am. If thou entertain'st my love, let it appear in thy smiling. Thy smiles become thee well; therefore in my presence still smile, dear my sweet, I prithee."

Jove, I thank thee. I will smile; I will do everything that thou wilt have me. *(exit)* 150

FABIAN I will not give my part of this sport for a pension of thousands to be paid from the Sophy.

SIR TOBY I could marry this wench for this device—

SIR ANDREW So could I too.

SIR TOBY And ask no other dowry with her but such another jest.

Re-enter Maria.

SIR ANDREW Nor I neither. 156

FABIAN Here comes my noble gull-catcher.

SIR TOBY Wilt thou set thy foot o' my neck?

SIR ANDREW Or o' mine either?

SIR TOBY Shall I play my freedom at tray-trip, and become thy bond-slave? 161

SIR ANDREW I' faith, or I either?

SIR TOBY Why, thou hast put him in such a dream, that when the image of it leaves him he must run mad.

MARIA Nay, but say true. Does it work upon him? 165

SIR TOBY Like aqua-vitæ with a midwife.

MARIA If you will then see the fruits of the sport, mark his first approach before my lady. He will come to her in yellow stockings, and 'tis a colour she abhors, and cross-garter'd, a fashion she detests; and he will smile upon her, which will now be so unsuitable to her disposition, being addicted to a melancholy as she is, that it cannot but turn him into a notable contempt. If you will see it, follow me.

SIR TOBY To the gates of Tartar, thou most excellent devil of wit!

SIR ANDREW I'll make one too. *(exeunt)* 175

In light of his established personality, why would a smiling—or leering—Malvolio offer cause for laughter in Olivia's court and among the audience?

The Sophy *signifies the Shah of Persia, a very wealthy ruler.*

A tray-trip *is a game played with dice.*

aqua-vitae is alcohol or any spirits.

Tartar, or Tartarus, is a classical term for Hell.

ACT III

SCENE I *Olivia's garden.*

Enter Viola and Clown (with a tabor).

VIOLA Save thee, friend, and thy music! Dost thou live by thy tabor?

CLOWN No, sir, I live by the church.

VIOLA Art thou a churchman?

CLOWN No such matter, sir. I do live by the church; for I do live at my house, and my house doth stand by the church. 5

A tabor *is a small drum.*

VIOLA So thou mayst say, the king lies by a beggar, if a beggar dwells near him; or, the church stands by thy tabor, if thy tabor stand by the church.

CLOWN You have said, sir. To see this age! A sentence is but a chev'ril glove to a good wit. How quickly the wrong side may be turn'd outward! 11

> A *chev'ril glove* is a kid glove.

VIOLA Nay, that's certain. They that dally nicely with words may quickly make them wanton.

CLOWN I would, therefore, my sister had had no name, sir.

VIOLA Why, man? 15

CLOWN Why, sir, her name's a word, and to dally with that word might make my sister wanton. But, indeed, words are very rascals since bonds disgrac'd them.

VIOLA Thy reason, man? 19

CLOWN Troth, sir, I can yield you none without words; and words are grown so false, I am loath to prove reason with them.

VIOLA I warrant thou art a merry fellow and car'st for nothing.

CLOWN Not so, sir, I do care for something; but in my conscience, sir, I do not care for you. If that be to care for nothing, sir, I would it would make you invisible. 25

VIOLA Art not thou the Lady Olivia's fool?

CLOWN No, indeed, sir; the Lady Olivia has no folly. She will keep no fool, sir, till she be married; and fools are as like husbands as pilchards are to herrings, the husband's the bigger. I am indeed not her fool, but her corrupter of words. 30

> *pilchards* are fish, like herring.

VIOLA I saw thee late at the Count Orsino's.

CLOWN Foolery, sir, does walk about the orb like the sun, it shines everywhere. I would be sorry, sir, but the fool should be as oft with your master as with my mistress. I think I saw your wisdom there.

> What was Feste doing earlier at Orsino's court?

VIOLA Nay, an thou pass upon me, I'll no more with thee. Hold, there's expenses for thee.

> To *pass upon* means to "make jokes."

CLOWN Now Jove, in his next commodity of hair, send thee a beard!

VIOLA By my troth, I'll tell thee, I am almost sick for one,—(aside) though I would not have it grow on my chin. Is thy lady within?

CLOWN Would not a pair of these have bred, sir? 40

VIOLA Yes, being kept together and put to use.

CLOWN I would play Lord Pandarus of Phrygia, sir, to bring a Cressida to this Troilus.

VIOLA I understand you, sir. 'Tis well begg'd. 44

CLOWN The matter, I hope, is not great, sir, begging but a beggar. Cressida was a beggar. My lady is within, sir. I will construe to them whence you come. Who you are and what you would are out of my welkin—I might say "element," but the word is overworn. *(exit)*

> Feste hints that if the coin (tip) Cesario had given him were doubled, then the pieces of money might metaphorically mate to produce more results for Cesario, i.e., Feste playing the part of Pandarus, a go-between, in helping Cesario see Olivia. (Cressida was desired by the youth Troilus in ancient Greek legend.)

VIOLA This fellow is wise enough to play the fool,
And to do that well craves a kind of wit. 50
He must observe their mood on whom he jests,

> Shakespeare's fools traditionally provided his plays with penetrating insights into the proceedings of the plots. Indeed, fools also were kept around courts for their special brand of "wisdom."

TWELFTH NIGHT 85

The quality of persons, and the time,
And, like the haggard, check at every feather   *A haggard is an untrained hawk.*
That comes before his eye. This is a practice
As full of labour as a wise man's art;   55
For folly that he wisely shows is fit,
But wise men, folly-fall'n, quite taint their wit.

Enter Sir Toby and Sir Andrew.

SIR TOBY Save you, gentleman.

VIOLA And you, sir.

SIR ANDREW *Dieu vous garde, monsieur.*   60   Aguecheek's French expression means "God keep you, sir," while Viola's response means "and you, too; [I am] your servant."

VIOLA *Et vous aussi; votre serviteur.*

SIR ANDREW I hope, sir, you are; and I am yours.

SIR TOBY Will you encounter the house? My niece is desirous you should enter, if your trade be to her.   64

VIOLA I am bound to your niece, sir; I mean, she is the list of my voyage.

SIR TOBY Taste your legs, sir; put them to motion.

VIOLA My legs do better understand me, sir, than I understand what you mean by bidding me taste my legs.

SIR TOBY I mean, to go, sir, to enter.   70

VIOLA I will answer you with [gait] and entrance. But we are prevented.

Enter Olivia and Gentlewoman.

Most excellent accomplish'd lady, the heavens rain odours on you!

SIR ANDREW That youth's a rare courtier. "Rain odours"; well.

VIOLA My matter hath no voice, lady, but to your own most pregnant and vouchsafed ear.   76   *By* pregnant *Cesario means "ready."*

SIR ANDREW "Odours," "pregnant," and "vouchsafed"; I'll get 'em all three all ready.   *What does Aguecheek evidently intend to do with the three expressions he has heard Viola/Cesario use?*

OLIVIA Let the garden door be shut, and leave me to hearing. *(exeunt all but Olivia and Viola)* Give me your hand, sir.   80

VIOLA My duty, madam, and most humble service.

OLIVIA What is your name?

VIOLA Cesario is your servant's name, fair princess.

OLIVIA My servant, sir! 'Twas never merry world
Since lowly feigning was call'd compliment.   85
You're servant to the Count Orsino, youth.

VIOLA And he is yours, and his must needs be yours.
Your servant's servant is your servant, madam.

OLIVIA For him, I think not on him. For his thoughts,
Would they were blanks, rather than fill'd with me!   90

VIOLA Madam, I come to whet your gentle thoughts.
On his behalf.

86   WILLIAM SHAKESPEARE

OLIVIA   O, by your leave, I pray you,
I bade you never speak again of him;
But, would you undertake another suit,
I had rather hear you to solicit that
Than music from the spheres.

VIOLA   Dear lady,—

OLIVIA Give me leave, beseech you. I did send,
After the last enchantment you did here,
A ring in chase of you; so did I abuse
Myself, my servant, and, I fear me, you.
Under your hard construction must I sit,
To force that on you, in a shameful cunning,
Which you knew none of yours. What might you think?
Have you not set mine honour at the stake
And baited it with all th' unmuzzled thoughts
That tyrannous heart can think? To one of your receiving
Enough is shown. A cypress, not a bosom,
Hides my heart. So, let me hear you speak.

VIOLA I pity you.

OLIVIA   That's a degree to love.

VIOLA No, not a grize; for 'tis a vulgar proof,
That very oft we pity enemies.

OLIVIA Why, then, methinks 'tis time to smile again.
O world, how apt the poor are to be proud!
If one should be a prey, how much the better
To fall before the lion than the wolf! *(clock strikes)*
The clock upbraids me with the waste of time.
Be not afraid, good youth, I will not have you;
And yet, when wit and youth is come to harvest,
Your wife is like to reap a proper man.
There lies your way, due west.

VIOLA Then westward-ho! Grace and good disposition
Attend your ladyship!
You'll nothing, madam, to my lord by me?

OLIVIA Stay!
I prithee, tell me what thou think'st of me.

VIOLA That you do think you are not what you are.

OLIVIA If I think so, I think the same of you.

VIOLA Then think you right. I am not what I am.

OLIVIA I would you were as I would have you be!

VIOLA Would it be better, madam, than I am?
I wish it might, for now I am your fool.

OLIVIA O, what a deal of scorn looks beautiful
In the contempt and anger of his lip!
A murd'rous guilt shows not itself more soon
Than love that would seem hid. Love's night is noon.
Cesario, by the roses of the spring,
By maidhood, honour, truth, and everything,

---

95   Olivia rejects all further consideration of Orsino's suit. Instead, she encourages the charming youth to woo on his own behalf. Despite her own warm feelings for Orsino, can it be said that Viola slights her promise to woo Olivia on behalf of the Duke? How do we know? What does this reveal about Viola's honesty and trustworthiness?

100

105 By *receiving*, Olivia means Cesario's "intelligence."

cypress is thin crepe.

Why does Viola pity Olivia here?

110 A *grize* is a step, while *vulgar proof* means "common experience."

115

120

125

Explain the basis for the repeated joking in lines 128, 130, and 144 ff.

130

135

Olivia (Sophie Stewart), left, and Viola (Helen Hayes), from the 1940 Broadway production of Twelfth Night.

I love thee so, that, maugre all thy pride,
Nor wit nor reason can my passion hide.
Do not extort thy reasons from this clause,
For that I woo, thou therefore hast no cause;
But rather reason thus with reason fetter,
Love sought is good, but given unsought is better.

VIOLA By innocence I swear, and by my youth,
I have one heart, one bosom, and one truth,
And that no woman has; nor never none
Shall mistress be of it, save I alone.
And so adieu, good madam; nevermore
Will I my master's tears to you deplore.

OLIVIA Yet come again; for thou perhaps mayst move
That heart, which now abhors, to like his love. *(exeunt)*

maugre is a distorted English version of the French word *malgré*, "in spite of."

What psychology is Olivia using to assure Cesario's eventual return?

SCENE II   *A room in Olivia's house.*

Enter Sir Toby, Sir Andrew, and Fabian.

SIR ANDREW No, faith, I'll not stay a jot longer.

SIR TOBY Thy reason, dear venom, give thy reason.

FABIAN You must needs yield your reason, Sir Andrew.

88   WILLIAM SHAKESPEARE

SIR ANDREW Marry, I saw your niece do more favours to the Count's serving-man than ever she bestow'd upon me. I saw't i' th' orchard.

SIR TOBY Did she see thee the while, old boy? Tell me that.

SIR ANDREW As plain as I see you now.

FABIAN This was a great argument of love in her toward you.

SIR ANDREW 'Slight, will you make an ass o' me?

FABIAN I will prove it legitimate, sir, upon the oaths of judgement and reason.

SIR TOBY And they have been grand-jurymen since before Noah was a sailor.

FABIAN She did show favour to the youth in your sight only to exasperate you, to awake your dormouse valour, to put fire in your heart, and brimstone in your liver. You should then have accosted her; and with some excellent jests, fire-new from the mint, you should have bang'd the youth into dumbness. This was look'd for at your hand, and this was balk'd. The double gilt of this opportunity you let time wash off, and you are now sailed into the north of my lady's opinion, where you will hang like an icicle on a Dutchman's beard, unless you do redeem it by some laudable attempt either of valour or policy.

SIR ANDREW An't be any way, it must be with valour; for policy I hate. I had a lief be a Brownist as a politician.

SIR TOBY Why, then, build me thy fortunes upon the basis of valour. Challenge me the Count's youth to fight with him; hurt him in eleven places; my niece shall take note of it; and assure thyself, there is no love-broker in the world can more prevail in man's commendation with woman than report of valour.

FABIAN There is no way but this, Sir Andrew.

SIR ANDREW Will either of you bear me a challenge to him?

SIR TOBY Go, write it in a martial hand. Be curst and brief. It is no matter how witty, so it be eloquent and full of invention. Taunt him with the license of ink. If thou thou'st him some thrice, it shall not be amiss; and as many lies as will lie in thy sheet of paper, although the sheet were big enough for the bed of Ware in England, set 'em down. Go about it. Let there be gall enough in thy ink. Though thou write with a goose-pen, no matter. About it.

SIR ANDREW Where shall I find you?

SIR TOBY We'll call thee at the cubiculo. Go. *(exit Sir Andrew)*

FABIAN This is a dear manikin to you, Sir Toby.

SIR TOBY I have been dear to him, lad, some two thousand strong, or so.

FABIAN We shall have a rare letter from him. But you'll not deliver't?

SIR TOBY Never trust me, then; and by all means stir on the youth to an answer. I think oxen and wainropes cannot hale them together. For Andrew, if he were open'd and you find so much blood in his liver as will clog the foot of a flea, I'll eat the rest of the anatomy.

Why is Andrew ready to give up his courtship of Olivia?

'Slight is a contraction for "by God's light," a mild oath.

Why are Sir Toby and Fabian so eager to maintain Sir Andrew's hopes to win Olivia? Does Aguecheek seem to catch on?

What are Fabian and Toby setting up Andrew for?

A *Brownist* was a member of a sect of Independents in religion, later to evolve into Congregationalists.

The *bed of Ware* was a famous twelve-foot-square bed located in an inn at Ware.

cubiculo means his "apartment."

How does Fabian's allusion to Aguecheek as Sir Toby's *manikin* help to confirm our understanding of Sir Andrew as a dupe?

wainropes are cartropes.

Why does there seem to be no appar-

TWELFTH NIGHT 89

FABIAN And his opposite, the youth, bears in his visage no great presage of cruelty.　　51

Enter Maria.

SIR TOBY Look, where the youngest wren of mine comes.

MARIA If you desire the spleen, and will laugh yourselves into stitches, follow me. Yond gull Malvolio is turned heathen, a very renegado; for there is no Christian that means to be saved by believing rightly can ever believe such impossible passages of grossness. He's in yellow stockings.　　57

SIR TOBY And cross-garter'd?

MARIA Most villainously; like a pedant that keeps a school i' th' church. I have dogg'd him like his murderer. He does obey every point of the letter that I dropp'd to betray him. He does smile his face into more lines than is in the new map with the augmentation of the Indies. You have not seen such a thing as 'tis. I can hardly forbear hurling things at him. I know my lady will strike him. If she do, he'll smile and take't for a great favour.　　65

SIR TOBY Come, bring us, bring us where he is. *(exeunt)*

SCENE III　　*A street.*

Enter Sebastian and Antonio.

SEBASTIAN I would not by my will have troubled you;
But, since you make your pleasure of your pains,
I will no further chide you.

ANTONIO I could not stay behind you. My desire,
More sharp than filed steel, did spur me forth,　　5
And not all love to see you, though so much
As might have drawn one to a longer voyage,
But jealousy what might befall your travel,
Being skilless in these parts; which to a stranger,
Unguided and unfriended, often prove　　10
Rough and unhospitable. My willing love,
The rather by these arguments of fear,
Set forth in your pursuit.

SEBASTIAN　　　　　My kind Antonio,
I can no other answer make but thanks,
And thanks, and ever [thanks. Too] oft good turns　　15
Are shuffl'd off with such uncurrent pay;
But, were my worth as is my conscience firm,
You should find better dealing. What's to do?
Shall we go see the reliques of this town?

ANTONIO To-morrow, sir. Best first go see your lodging.　　20

SEBASTIAN I am not weary, and 'tis long to night.
I pray you, let us satisfy our eyes
With the memorials and the things of fame
That do renown this city

ANTONIO　　　　　Would you'd pardon me.
I do not without danger walk these streets.　　25
Once, in a sea-fight, 'gainst the Count his galleys

---

ent reason for worry that either Aguecheek or Cesario will come to harm in the duel trick?

spleen means a "laughing fit."

Ribbon garters were crisscrossed up men's legs to hold up their stockings, according to courtly fashion of the time.

Maria here alludes to a map of about 1599 which showed more of the East Indies than previous maps.

By *jealousy* Antonio means "suspicion" or "concern for."

uncurrent means "worthless."

reliques are points of interest.

90　　WILLIAM SHAKESPEARE

I did some service; of such note indeed,
That were I ta'en here it would scarce be answer'd.

SEBASTIAN Belike you slew great number of his people?

ANTONIO Th' offence is not of such a bloody nature, 30
Albeit the quality of the time and quarrel
Might well have given us bloody argument.
It might have since been answer'd in repaying
What we took from them, which, for traffic's sake,
Most of our city did; only myself stood out, 35
For which, if I be lapsed in this place,
I shall pay dear.

SEBASTIAN   Do not then walk too open.

ANTONIO It doth not fit me. Hold, sir, here's my purse.
In the south suburbs, at the Elephant
Is best to lodge. I will bespeak our diet, 40
Whiles you beguile the time and feed your knowledge
With viewing of the town. There shall you have me.

SEBASTIAN Why I your purse?

ANTONIO Haply your eye shall light upon some toy
You have desire to purchase; and your store, 45
I think, is not for idle markets, sir.

SEBASTIAN I'll be your purse-bearer and leave you
For an hour.

ANTONIO   To th' Elephant.

SEBASTIAN   I do remember. *(exeunt)*

> Do we detect any signs of foreshadowing in Antonio's explanation for not wanting to tour the city openly? What kind of clues?

> The *Elephant* evidently is an inn. Antonio will go there to settle sleeping and eating arrangements while Sebastian takes a tour of Illyria.

> Antonio implies that he trusts Sebastian's judgment not to make trivial purchases.

SCENE IV *Olivia's garden.*

Enter Olivia and Maria.

OLIVIA *(aside)* I have sent after him; he says he'll come.
How shall I feast him? What bestow of him?
For youth is bought more oft than begg'd or borrow'd.
I speak too loud.—
Where is Malvolio? He is sad and civil, 5
And suits well for a servant with my fortunes.
What is Malvolio?

MARIA He's coming, madam, but in very strange manner. He is, sure, possess'd, madam.

OLIVIA Why, what's the matter? Does he rave? 10

MARIA No, madam, he does nothing but smile. Your ladyship were best to have some guard about you, if he come; for, sure, the man is tainted in's wits.

OLIVIA Go call him hither.

Enter Malvolio.

                    I am as mad as he, 15
If sad and merry madness equal be.
How now, Malvolio!

MALVOLIO Sweet lady, ho, ho.

> Here is an example of an *aside*, a device frequently used in Elizabethan drama, in which a character speaks his mind aloud to the audience without other figures on stage hearing.

> How does Shakespeare prepare both Olivia and the audience for Malvolio's alteration in personality? To be *possess'd* means to be insane because possessed with spirits.

TWELFTH NIGHT 91

OLIVIA Smil'st thou?
I sent for thee upon a sad occasion. 20

MALVOLIO Sad, lady? I could be sad. This does make some obstruction in the blood, this cross-gartering; but what of that? If it please the eye of one, it is with me as the very true sonnet is, "Please one, and please all." 24

[**OLIVIA**] Why, how dost thou, man? What is the matter with thee?

MALVOLIO Not black in my mind, though yellow in my legs. It did come to his hands, and commands shall be executed. I think we do know the sweet Roman hand.

What does Malvolio mean by the sweet Roman hand?

OLIVIA Wilt thou go to bed, Malvolio?

MALVOLIO To bed! Ay, sweet heart, and I'll come to thee. 30

OLIVIA God comfort thee! Why dost thou smile so and kiss thy hand so oft?

MARIA How do you, Malvolio?

MALVOLIO At your request! Yes. Nightingales answer daws. 34

MARIA Why appear you with this ridiculous boldness before my lady?

MALVOLIO "Be not afraid of greatness": 'twas well writ.

In lines 37, 39, and following, what does Malvolio mean for those phrases set off with quotation marks?

OLIVIA What mean'st thou by that, Malvolio?

MALVOLIO "Some are born great,"—

OLIVIA Ha! 40

MALVOLIO "Some achieve greatness,"—

OLIVIA What say'st thou?

MALVOLIO "And some have greatness thrust upon them."

OLIVIA Heaven restore thee!

MALVOLIO "Remember who commended thy yellow stockings,"—

OLIVIA Thy yellow stockings! 46

MALVOLIO "And wish'd to see thee cross-garter'd."

OLIVIA Cross-garter'd!

MALVOLIO "Go to, thou art made, if thou desir'st to be so";—

OLIVIA Am I made? 50

MALVOLIO "If not, let me see thee a servant still."

OLIVIA Why, this is very midsummer madness.

A common Elizabethan notion was that insane behavior was prevalent around midsummer's eve.

Enter Servant.

SERVANT Madam, the young gentleman of the Count Orsino's is return'd. I could hardly entreat him back. He attends your ladyship's pleasure. 55

OLIVIA I'll come to him. *(exit Servant)* Good Maria, let this fellow be look'd to. Where's my cousin Toby? Let some of my people have a special care of him. I would not have him miscarry for the half of my dowry. *(exeunt [Olivia and Maria])* 59

By miscarry *Olivia means to "suffer harm."*

92   WILLIAM SHAKESPEARE

MALVOLIO O, ho! do you come near me now? No worse man than Sir Toby to look to me! This concurs directly with the letter. She sends him on purpose, that I may appear stubborn to him, for she incites me to that in the letter. "Cast thy humble slough," says she; "be opposite with a kinsman, surly with servants; let thy tongue tang with arguments of state; put thyself into the trick of singularity"; and consequently sets down the manner how; as, a sad face, a reverend carriage, a slow tongue, in the habit of some sir of note, and so forth. I have lim'd her; but it is Jove's doing, and Jove make me thankful! And when she went away now, "Let this fellow be looked to"; "fellow!" not Malvolio, nor after my degree, but "fellow." Why, everything adheres together, that no dram of a scruple, no scruple of a scruple, no obstacle, no incredulous or unsafe circumstance—What can be said? Nothing that can be can come between me and the full prospect of my hopes. Well, Jove, not I, is the doer of this, and he is to be thanked. 75

Re-enter Maria, with Sir Toby and Fabian.

SIR TOBY Which way is he, in the name of sanctity? If all the devils of hell be drawn in little, and Legion himself possess'd him, yet I'll speak to him.

FABIAN Here he is, here he is. How is't with you, sir? How is't with you, man? 80

MALVOLIO Go off; I discard you. Let me enjoy my private. Go off.

MARIA Lo, how hollow the fiend speaks within him! Did not I tell you? Sir Toby, my lady prays you to have a care of him.

MALVOLIO Ah, ha! Does she so? 84

SIR TOBY Go to, go to; peace, peace. We must deal gently with him. Let me alone. How do you, Malvolio? How is't with you? What, man, defy the devil! Consider, he's an enemy to mankind.

MALVOLIO Do you know what you say?

MARIA La you, an you speak ill of the devil, how he takes it at heart! Pray God he be not bewitch'd! 90

FABIAN Carry his water to the wise woman.

MARIA Marry, and it shall be done to-morrow morning if I live. My lady would not lose him for more than I'll say.

MALVOLIO How now, mistress!

MARIA O Lord! 95

SIR TOBY Prithee, hold thy peace; this is not the way. Do you not see you move him? Let me alone with him.

FABIAN No way but gentleness; gently, gently. The fiend is rough, and will not be roughly us'd.

SIR TOBY Why, how now, my bawcock! How dost thou, chuck?

MALVOLIO Sir! 101

SIR TOBY Ay, "Biddy, come with me." What, man, 'tis not for gravity to play at cherry-pit with Satan. Hang him, foul collier!

MARIA Get him to say his prayers, good Sir Toby, get him to pray.

MALVOLIO My prayers, minx! 105

By *lim'd* he means that he has "caught" Olivia. How has Malvolio's total misunderstanding of the situation brought out his foolish pride?

The *Legion* was a troop of fiends who possessed a man, as referred to in the New Testament (Mark 5:9).

Why do Sir Toby and the others poke fun at Malvolio?

To bring a madman back to sanity, it was thought necessary in Shakespeare's time to rid the afflicted person of the devilish spirit which had invaded his body and, hence, possessed him.

Fabian suggests that a urine specimen from Malvolio be taken to a doctor or herb woman for diagnosis.

bawcock means "fine fellow."

cherry-pit is a children's game. How are the others treating Malvolio and how does comedy result?

TWELFTH NIGHT

MARIA No, I warrant you, he will not hear of godliness.

MALVOLIO Go, hang yourselves all! You are idle shallow things; I am not of your element. You shall know more hereafter. *(exit)*

SIR TOBY Is't possible?

FABIAN If this were played upon a stage now, I could condemn it as an improbable fiction. 111

SIR TOBY His very genius hath taken the infection of the device, man.

MARIA Nay, pursue him now, lest the device take air and taint.

FABIAN Why, we shall make him mad indeed. 115

MARIA The house will be the quieter.

SIR TOBY Come, we'll have him in a dark room and bound. My niece is already in the belief that he's mad. We may carry it thus, for our pleasure and his penance, till our very pastime, tired out of breath, prompt us to have mercy on him; at which time we will bring the device to the bar and crown thee for a finder of madmen. But see, but see. 122

At the time, the insane were treated by being held in dark rooms where the evil spirits that supposedly had invaded their bodies could be driven out. During Act IV, scene ii, such a "remedy" is being used on Malvolio.

Enter Sir Andrew.

FABIAN More matter for a May morning.

SIR ANDREW Here's the challenge, read it. I warrant there's vinegar and pepper in't. 125

there's vinegar and pepper in't means that the letter challenging Cesario to a duel is bitter (nasty) and hot (insulting).

FABIAN Is't so saucy?

SIR ANDREW Ay, is't, I warrant him. Do but read.

SIR TOBY Give me. *(reads)* "Youth whatsoever thou art, thou art but a scurvy fellow."

FABIAN Good, and valiant. 130

SIR TOBY *(reads)* "Wonder not, nor admire not in thy mind, why I do call thee so, for I will show thee no reason for't."

To admire here means to be "amazed."

FABIAN A good note. That keeps you from the blow of the law.

SIR TOBY *(reads)* "Thou com'st to the lady Olivia, and in my sight she uses thee kindly. But thou liest in thy throat; that is not the matter I challenge thee for." 136

Thou liest in thy throat was a standard insult and challenge of the day, meaning "you are a liar and a rogue."

FABIAN Very brief, and to exceeding good sense—less.

SIR TOBY *(reads)* "I will waylay thee going home; where if it be thy chance to kill me,"—

FABIAN Good. 140

SIR TOBY *(reads)* "Thou kill'st me like a rogue and a villain."

FABIAN Still you keep o' th' windy side of the law; good.

SIR TOBY *(reads)* "Fare thee well, and God have mercy upon one of our souls! He may have mercy upon mine; but my hope is better, and so look to thyself. Thy friend, as thou usest him, and thy sworn enemy, 146

       Andrew Aguecheek."

If this letter move him not, his legs cannot. I'll give't him.

MARIA You may have very fit occasion for't. He is now in some commerce with my lady, and will by and by depart. 150

SIR TOBY Go, Sir Andrew, scout me for him at the corner of the orchard like a bum-baily. So soon as ever thou seest him, draw; and, as thou draw'st, swear horrible; for it comes to pass oft that a terrible oath, with a swaggering accent sharply twang'd off, gives manhood more approbation than ever proof itself would have earn'd him. Away! 156

SIR ANDREW Nay, let me alone for swearing. *(exit)*

SIR TOBY Now will not I deliver his letter; for the behaviour of the young gentleman gives him out to be of good capacity and breeding; his employment between his lord and my niece confirms no less; therefore this letter, being so excellently ignorant, will breed no terror in the youth; he will find it comes from a clodpole. But, sir, I will deliver his challenge by word of mouth, set upon Aguecheek a notable report of valour, and drive the gentleman, as I know his youth will aptly receive it, into a most hideous opinion of his rage, skill, fury, and impetuosity. This will so fright them both that they will kill one another by the look, like cockatrices. 167

Re-enter Olivia with Viola.

FABIAN Here he comes with your niece. Give them way till he take leave, and presently after him.

SIR TOBY I will meditate the while upon some horrid message for a challenge. *(exeunt Sir Toby, Fabian, and Maria)* 171

OLIVIA I have said too much unto a heart of stone,
And laid mine honour too unchary on't.
There's something in me that reproves my fault;
But such a headstrong potent fault it is 175
That it but mocks reproof.

VIOLA With the same 'haviour that your passion bears
Goes on my master's grief.

OLIVIA Here, wear this jewel for me; 'tis my picture.
Refuse it not; it hath no tongue to vex you; 180
And I beseech you come again to-morrow.
What shall you ask of me that I'll deny,
That honour sav'd may upon asking give?

VIOLA Nothing but this,—your true love for my master.

OLIVIA How with mine honour may I give him that 185
Which I have given to you?

VIOLA   I will acquit you.

OLIVIA Well, come again to-morrow. Fare thee well!
A fiend like thee might bear my soul to hell. *(exit)*

Re-enter Sir Toby and Fabian.

SIR TOBY Gentleman, God save thee!

VIOLA And you, sir. 190

SIR TOBY That defence thou hast, betake thee to't. Of what nature the wrongs are thou hast done him, I know not; but thy intercepter,

commerce is business.

A *bum-baily* was a petty sheriff's officer who arrested debtors.

A *clodpole* means a "dunce."

A *cockatrice* was a fabled dragon-like creature whose mere glance would kill. What new trick does Toby Belch cook up involving Aguecheek and Cesario?

By the instructions given in the dialogue, it is obvious that Olivia is giving Cesario a locket containing a miniature portrait of her—a common love gift of the time.

Olivia's lines mean that her infatuation with Cesario has left her powerless to resist whatever he might suggest.

full of despite, bloody as the hunter, attends thee at the orchard-end. Dismount thy tuck, be yare in thy preparation, for thy assailant is quick, skilful, and deadly. 195

Dismount thy tuck is a grandiose way to say "Draw your sword," while *yare* here means "quick."

VIOLA You mistake, sir, I am sure. No man hath any quarrel to me. My remembrance is very free and clear from any image of offence done to any man. 198

SIR TOBY You'll find it otherwise, I assure you; therefore, if you hold your life at any price, betake you to your guard; for your opposite hath in him what youth, strength, skill, and wrath can furnish man withal. 202

VIOLA I pray you, sir, what is he?

SIR TOBY He is knight, dubb'd with unhatch'd rapier and on carpet consideration; but he is a devil in private brawl. Souls and bodies hath he divorc'd three; and his incensement at this moment is so implacable, that satisfaction can be none but by pangs of death and sepulchre. Hob, nob, is his word; give't or take't. 208

In publicizing Aguecheek's fighting ability, Sir Toby enjoys some private fun by alluding to Sir Andrew's sword as *unhatch'd* ("unhacked," or "unused") and calling him *on carpet consideration* (a "carpet knight" was one dubbed for paying money to the sovereign, rather than for his fighting valor).

VIOLA I will return again into the house and desire some conduct of the lady. I am no fighter. I have heard of some kind of men that put quarrels purposely on others, to taste their valour. Belike this is a man of that quirk. 212

SIR TOBY Sir, no; his indignation derives itself out of a very competent injury; therefore, get you on and give him his desire. Back you shall not to the house, unless you undertake that with me which with as much safety you might answer him; therefore, on, or strip your sword stark naked; for meddle you must, that's certain, or forswear to wear iron about you. 218

Toby means that Cesario must fight or else be considered a coward thereafter.

VIOLA This is as uncivil as strange. I beseech you, do me this courteous office, as to know of the knight what my offence to him is. It is something of my negligence, nothing of my purpose. 221

SIR TOBY I will do so. Signor Fabian, stay you by this gentleman till my return. *(exit)*

VIOLA Pray you, sir, do you know of this matter?

FABIAN I know the knight is incens'd against you, even to a mortal arbitrement, but nothing of the circumstance more. 226

arbitrement is trial.

VIOLA I beseech you, what manner of man is he?

FABIAN Nothing of that wonderful promise, to read him by his form, as you are like to find him in the proof of his valour. He is, indeed, sir, the most skilful, bloody, and fatal opposite that you could possibly have found in any part of Illyria. Will you walk towards him? I will make your peace with him if I can. 232

How do we know that Fabian is part of the duel plot, too?

VIOLA I shall be much bound to you for't. I am one that had rather go with sir priest than sir knight. I care not who knows so much of my mettle. *(exeunt)* 235

Re-enter Sir Toby, with Sir Andrew.

SIR TOBY Why, man, he's a very devil; I have not seen such a firago. I had a pass with him, rapier, scabbard, and all, and he gives me the stuck in with such a mortal motion, that it is inevitable; and on the answer, he pays you as surely as your feet hits the ground they step on. They say he has been fencer to the Sophy. 240

A *firago* here means a "tough fighter."

SIR ANDREW Pox on't, I'll not meddle with him.

SIR TOBY Ay, but he will not now be pacified. Fabian can scarce hold him yonder.

SIR ANDREW Plague on't, an I thought he had been valiant and so cunning in fence, I'd have seen him damn'd ere I'd have challeng'd him. Let him let the matter slip, and I'll give him my horse, grey Capilet. 247

SIR TOBY I'll make the motion. Stand here; make a good show on't. This shall end without the perdition of souls. *(aside)* Marry, I'll ride your horse as well as I ride you. 250

Re-enter Fabian and Viola.

(to Fabian) I have his horse to take up the quarrel.
I have persuaded him the youth's a devil.

FABIAN He is as horribly conceited of him; and pants and looks pale, as if a bear were at his heels. 254

SIR TOBY *(to Viola)* There's no remedy, sir; he will fight with you for's oath sake. Marry, he hath better bethought him of his quarrel, and he finds that now scarce to be worth talking of; therefore draw, for the supportance of his vow. He protests he will not hurt you.

VIOLA *(aside)* Pray God defend me! A little thing would make me tell them how much I lack of a man. 260

FABIAN Give ground, if you see him furious.

SIR TOBY Come, Sir Andrew, there's no remedy; the gentleman will, for his honour's sake, have one bout with you. He cannot by the duello avoid it; but he has promised me, as he is a gentleman and a soldier, he will not hurt you. Come on; to't. 265

SIR ANDREW Pray God, he keep his oath!

Enter Antonio.

VIOLA I do assure you, 'tis against my will. *(They draw.)*

ANTONIO Put up your sword. If this young gentleman
Have done offence, I take the fault on me;
If you offend him, I for him defy you. 270

SIR TOBY You, sir! Why, what are you?

ANTONIO One, sir, that for his love dares yet do more
Than you have heard him brag to you he will.

SIR TOBY Nay, if you be an undertaker, I am for you. *(They draw.)*

Enter Officers.

FABIAN O good Sir Toby, hold! Here come the officers. 275

SIR TOBY I'll be with you anon.

VIOLA Pray, sir, put your sword up, if you please.

SIR ANDREW Marry, will I, sir; and, for that I promis'd you, I'll be as good as my word. He will bear you easily and reins well.

1. OFFICER This is the man; do thy office. 280

2. OFFICER Antonio, I arrest thee at the suit of Count Orsino.

ANTONIO You do mistake me, sir.

How might the humor in this situation be conveyed through actions and gestures on stage by Viola and Aguecheek?
Notice what Sir Andrew is now prepared to do to have Cesario call off the fight.

The *duello* is the code of dueling.

It is clear that Antonio is drawn into the confusion.
What mistake has he made?

Here, *undertaker* means "meddler."

TWELFTH NIGHT

1. OFFICER No, sir, no jot. I know your favour well,
Though now you have no sea-cap on your head.
Take him away; he knows I know him well. 285

ANTONIO I must obey. *(to Viola)* This comes with seeking you.
But there's no remedy; I shall answer it.
What will you do, now my necessity
Makes me to ask you for my purse? It grieves me
Much more for what I cannot do for you 290
Than what befalls myself. You stand amaz'd,
But be of comfort.

2. OFFICER Come, sir, away.

ANTONIO I must entreat of you some of that money.

VIOLA What money, sir? 295
For the fair kindness you have show'd me here,
And, part, being prompted by your present trouble,
Out of my lean and low ability
I'll lend you something. My having is not much.
I'll make division of my present with you. 300
Hold, there's half my coffer.

ANTONIO Will you deny me now?
Is't possible that my deserts to you
Can lack persuasion? Do not tempt my misery,
Lest that it make me so unsound a man
As to upbraid you with those kindnesses 305
That I have done for you.

VIOLA I know of none,
Nor know I you by voice or any feature.
I hate ingratitude more in a man
Than lying, vainness, babbling, drunkenness,
Or any taint of vice whose strong corruption 310
Inhabits our frail blood.

ANTONIO O heavens themselves!

2. OFFICER Come, sir, I pray you, go.

ANTONIO Let me speak a little. This youth that you see here
I snatch'd one half out of the jaws of death,
Reliev'd him with such sanctity of love, 315
And to his image, which methought did promise
Most venerable worth, did I devotion.

1. OFFICER What's that to us? The time goes by; away!

ANTONIO But, O, how vile an idol proves this god!
Thou hast, Sebastian, done good feature shame. 320
In nature there's no blemish but the mind;
None can be call'd deform'd but the unkind.
Virtue is beauty, but the beauteous evil
Are empty trunks o'erflourish'd by the devil.

1. OFFICER The man grows mad; away with him! 325
Come, come, sir.

ANTONIO Lead me on. *(exit [with Officers])*

VIOLA Methinks his words do from such passion fly
That he believes himself; so do not I.

In Elizabethan times and later, those arrested were expected to pay for their own board and conveniences while in jail, if they were not able to post bail and gain freedom.

Aside from allowing Antonio to air his disgust with Viola—whom he believes to be Sebastian—what expository function is served by his angry outburst?

unkind in this context means "unnatural."

98 WILLIAM SHAKESPEARE

Prove true, imagination, O, prove true, 330
That I, dear brother, he now ta'en for you!

SIR TOBY Come hither, knight; come hither, Fabian; we'll whisper o'er a couplet or two of most sage saws.

VIOLA He nam'd Sebastian. I my brother know
Yet living in my glass; even such and so 335
In favour was my brother, and he went
Still in this fashion, colour, ornament,
For him I imitate. O, if it prove,
Tempests are kind and salt waves fresh in love. *(exit)*

> Viola means that Antonio addressed her by Sebastian's name, and that she realizes she looks like her brother.
>
> *if it prove* [true]

SIR TOBY A very dishonest paltry boy, and more a coward than a hare. His dishonesty appears in leaving his friend here in necessity and denying him; and, for his cowardship, ask Fabian. 342

FABIAN A coward, a most devout coward, religious in it.

SIR ANDREW 'Slid, I'll after him again and beat him.

SIR TOBY Do; cuff him soundly, but never draw thy sword. 345

> *'Slid* means "by God's eyelid," another popular oath from Shakespeare's day.

SIR ANDREW An I do not,—

FABIAN Come, let's see the event.

SIR TOBY I dare lay any money 'twill be nothing yet. *(exeunt)*

> Toby still does not believe in Sir Andrew's fighting prowess.

ACT IV

SCENE I *Before Olivia's house.*

Enter Sebastian and Clown.

CLOWN Will you make me believe that I am not sent for you?

> What new confusion arises?

SEBASTIAN Go to, go to, thou art a foolish fellow; let me be clear of thee.

CLOWN Well held out, i' faith! No, I do not know you; nor I am not sent to you by my lady, to bid you come speak with her; nor your name is not Master Cesario; nor this is not my nose neither. Nothing that is so is so. 7

> What are the comic possibilities in terms of stage behavior when Feste mistakes Sebastian for Cesario.

SEBASTIAN I prithee, vent thy folly somewhere else.
Thou know'st not me.

CLOWN Vent my folly! He has heard that word of some great man and now applies it to a fool. Vent my folly! I am afraid this great lubber, the world, will prove a cockney. I prithee now, ungird thy strangeness and tell me what I shall vent to my lady. Shall I vent to her that thou art coming? 14

> *cockney* means a "fop" or a "court pretender."

SEBASTIAN I prithee, foolish Greek, depart from me.
There's money for thee. If you tarry longer,
I shall give worse payment.

> In this context, *Greek* means a "merry companion."
>
> What does Sebastian imply by *worse payment*?

CLOWN By my troth, thou hast an open hand. These wise men that give fools money get themselves a good report—after fourteen years' purchase. 20

Enter Sir Andrew, Sir Toby, and Fabian.

SIR ANDREW Now, sir, have I met you again? There's for you.

TWELFTH NIGHT 99

SEBASTIAN Why, there's for thee, and there, and there.
Are all the people mad?

SIR TOBY Hold, sir, or I'll throw your dagger o'er the house.   25

CLOWN This will I tell my lady straight. I would not be in some of your coats for two pence. *(exit)*

SIR TOBY Come on, sir. Hold!

SIR ANDREW Nay, let him alone. I'll go another way to work with him. I'll have an action of battery against him, if there be any law in Illyria. Though I struck him first, yet it's no matter for that.   31

SEBASTIAN Let go thy hand.

SIR TOBY Come, sir, I will not let you go. Come, my young soldier, put up your iron; you are well flesh'd. Come on.

SEBASTIAN I will be free from thee. What wouldst thou now?   35
If thou dar'st tempt me further, draw thy sword.

SIR TOBY What, what? Nay, then I must have an ounce or two of this malapert blood from you.

Enter Olivia.

OLIVIA Hold, Toby! On thy life I charge thee, hold!

SIR TOBY Madam—   40

OLIVIA Will it be ever thus? Ungracious wretch,
Fit for the mountains and the barbarous caves,
Where manners ne'er were preach'd! Out of my sight!
Be not offended, dear Cesario.
Rudesby, be gone! *(exeunt Sir Toby, Sir Andrew, and Fabian)*
    I prithee, gentle friend,   45
Let thy fair wisdom, not thy passion, sway
In this uncivil and unjust extent
Against thy peace. Go with me to my house,
And hear thou there how many fruitless pranks
This ruffian hath botch'd up, that thou thereby   50
Mayst smile at this. Thou shalt not choose but go.
Do not deny. Beshrew his soul for me,
He started one poor heart of mine in thee.

SEBASTIAN What relish is in this? How runs the stream?
Or I am mad, or else this is a dream.   55
Let fancy still my sense in Lethe steep.
If it be thus to dream, still let me sleep!

OLIVIA Nay, come, I prithee. Would thou'dst be rul'd by me!

SEBASTIAN Madam, I will.

OLIVIA   O, say so, and so be! *(exeunt)*

SCENE II. *Olivia's house.*

Enter Maria and Clown.

MARIA Nay, I prithee, put on this gown and this beard. Make him believe thou art Sir Topas the curate. Do it quickly; I'll call Sir Toby the whilst. *(exit)*   3

What would account for Sir Toby's eagerness to engage Sebastian in combat?

How does Aguecheek here prove his cowardice beyond any doubt?

What stage actions are indicated through the dialogue in lines 32–36?

Rudesby means "ruffian."

extent means "attack."

relish here signifies "meaning."

In mythology *Lethe* is the river of forgetfulness. Is Sebastian unhappy with all the surprises associated with Olivia? How do we know?

Without separate stage directions, readers and viewers can tell exactly

100   WILLIAM SHAKESPEARE

CLOWN Well, I'll put it on, and I will dissemble myself in't; and I would I were the first that ever dissembled in such a gown. I am not tall enough to become the function well, nor lean enough to be thought a good student; but to be said an honest man and a good housekeeper goes as fairly as to say a careful man and a great scholar. The competitors enter.

Enter Sir Toby (and Maria).

SIR TOBY Jove bless thee, master Parson. 10

CLOWN *Bonos dies,* Sir Toby: for, as the old hermit of Prague, that never saw pen and ink, very wittily said to a niece of King Gorboduc, "That that is is"; so I, being master Parson, am master Parson; for, what is "that" but "that," and "is" but "is"?

SIR TOBY To him, Sir Topas. 15

CLOWN What, ho, I say! Peace in this prison!

SIR TOBY The knave counterfeits well; a good knave.

MALVOLIO *(within)* Who calls there?

CLOWN Sir Topas the curate, who comes to visit Malvolio the lunatic.

MALVOLIO Sir Topas, Sir Topas, good Sir Topas, go to my lady. 20

CLOWN Out, hyperbolical fiend! How vexest thou this man! Talkest thou nothing but of ladies?

SIR TOBY Well said, Master Parson.

MALVOLIO Sir Topas, never was man thus wronged. Good Sir Topas, do not think I am mad. They have laid me here in hideous darkness. 26

CLOWN Fie, thou dishonest Satan! I call thee by the most modest terms, for I am one of those gentle ones that will use the devil himself with courtesy. Say'st thou that house is dark?

MALVOLIO As hell, Sir Topas. 30

CLOWN Why, it hath bay windows transparent as barricadoes, and the clerestories toward the south north are as lustrous as ebony; and yet complainest thou of obstruction? 33

MALVOLIO I am not mad, Sir Topas. I say to you, this house is dark.

CLOWN Madman, thou errest. I say, there is no darkness but ignorance, in which thou art more puzzl'd than the Egyptians in their fog.

MALVOLIO I say, this house is dark as ignorance, though ignorance were as dark as hell; and I say, there was never man thus abus'd. I am no more mad than you are. Make the trial of it in any constant question. 40

CLOWN What is the opinion of Pythagoras concerning wild fowl?

MALVOLIO That the soul of our grandam might haply inhabit a bird.

CLOWN What think'st thou of his opinion?

MALVOLIO I think nobly of the soul, and no way approve his opinion. 45

CLOWN Fare thee well. Remain thou still in darkness. Thou shalt hold th' opinion of Pythagoras ere I will allow of thy wits, and fear to

---

what is happening because of the details offered in the dialogue.

Here, *competitors* means his "confederates" in the trickery.

Bonos dies means "good day."

Gorboduc was a legendary British king.

Whom is Feste addressing, and why?

Note that Malvolio is being held in a dark room and, therefore, he cannot see the faces of those speaking to him. Thus, Feste can get away with pretending to be Sir Topas the churchman.

clerestories are windows placed high up in the wall.

Moses set a three-day fog upon the Egyptians, according to Exodus.

constant here means "logical." How does Malvolio propose to prove his sanity for Sir Topas?

TWELFTH NIGHT 101

kill a woodcock lest thou dispossess the soul of thy grandam. Fare thee well.

MALVOLIO Sir Topas, Sir Topas! 50

SIR TOBY My most exquisite Sir Topas!

CLOWN Nay, I am for all waters.

Line 52 means "I can assume any role."

MALVOLIO Thou mightst have done this without thy beard and gown. He sees thee not. 54

SIR TOBY To him in thine own voice, and bring me word how thou find'st him. I would we were well rid of this knavery. If he may be conveniently deliver'd, I would he were, for I am now so far in offence with my niece that I cannot pursue with any safety this sport to the upshot. Come by and by to my chamber. *(exit [with Maria])*

How has Sir Toby's trickery of Malvolio backfired on him?

Why does Toby end his teasing of Malvolio? What earlier episode proved Toby's dilemma?

CLOWN *(singing)* "Hey, Robin, jolly Robin, 60
  Tell me how thy lady does."

MALVOLIO Fool!

CLOWN "My lady is unkind, perdy."

MALVOLIO Fool!

CLOWN "Alas, why is she so?" 65

MALVOLIO Fool, I say!

CLOWN "She loves another"—Who calls, ha?

MALVOLIO Good fool, as ever thou wilt deserve well at my hand, help me to a candle, and pen, ink, and paper. As I am a gentleman, I will live to be thankful to thee for't. 70

CLOWN Master Malvolio?

MALVOLIO Ay, good fool.

CLOWN Alas, sir, how fell you besides your five wits?

MALVOLIO Fool, there was never man so notoriously abus'd. I am as well in my wits, fool, as thou art. 75

CLOWN But as well? Then you are mad indeed, if you be no better in your wits than a fool.

MALVOLIO They have here propertied me, keep me in darkness, send ministers to me, asses, and do all they can to face me out of my wits. 80

They have here propertied me means that he "has been treated as a tool."

CLOWN Advise you what you say; the minister is here. Malvolio, Malvolio, thy wits the heavens restore! Endeavour thyself to sleep, and leave thy vain bibble babble.

MALVOLIO Sir Topas! 84

CLOWN Maintain no words with him, good fellow. Who, I, sir? Not I, sir. God buy you, good Sir Topas. Marry, amen. I will, sir, I will.

During this interchange between Feste and Malvolio, Feste is able to change his voice back and forth to reassume the role of Sir Topas at will, because of the darkness. Thus he carries on a dialogue with himself as two different characters.

God buy you means "God be with you."

MALVOLIO Fool, fool, fool, I say!

CLOWN Alas, sir, be patient. What say you, sir? I am shent for speaking to you.

MALVOLIO Good fool, help me to some light and some paper. I tell thee, I am as well in my wits as any man in Illyria. 91

CLOWN Well-a-day that you were, sir!

102 WILLIAM SHAKESPEARE

MALVOLIO By this hand, I am. Good fool, some ink, paper, and light; and convey what I will set down to my lady. It shall advantage thee more than ever the bearing of letter did.   95

CLOWN I will help you to't. But tell me true, are you not mad indeed, or do you but counterfeit?

MALVOLIO Believe me, I am not. I tell thee true.

CLOWN Nay, I'll ne'er believe a madman till I see his brains. I will fetch you light and paper and ink.   100

MALVOLIO Fool, I'll requite it in the highest degree.
I prithee, be gone.

CLOWN (*singing*) I am gone, sir,
    And anon, sir,
I'll be with you again,   105
    In a trice,
    Like to the old Vice,
Your need to sustain;

Who, with dagger of lath,
In his rage and his wrath,   110
    Cries, ah, ha! to the devil,
    Like a mad lad.
Pare thy nails, dad.
    Adieu, goodman devil. (*exit*)

Feste sings about the old Vice, *the standard Fool of Morality play tradition, who wore a wooden dagger which he would use in trying to pare the Devil's fingernails.*

SCENE III *Olivia's garden.*

Enter Sebastian.

SEBASTIAN This is the air, that is the glorious sun,
This pearl she gave me, I do feel't and see't;
And though 'tis wonder that enwraps me thus,
Yet 'tis not madness. Where's Antonio, then?
I could not find him at the Elephant;   5
Yet there he was, and there I found this credit,
That he did range the town to seek me out.
His counsel now might do me golden service;
For though my soul disputes well with my sense,
That this may be some error, but no madness,   10
Yet doth this accident and flood of fortune
So far exceed all instance, all discourse,
That I am ready to distrust mine eyes
And wrangle with my reason that persuades me
To any other trust but that I am mad   15
Or else the lady's mad; yet, if 'twere so,
She could not sway her house, command her followers,
Take and give back affairs and their dispatch
With such a smooth, discreet, and stable bearing
As I perceive she does. There's something in't   20
That is deceivable. But here the lady comes.

How do the facts of Sebastian's situation contradict what he sees in Ilyrium?

Enter Olivia and Priest.

OLIVIA Blame not this haste of mine. If you mean well,
Now go with me and with this holy man
Into the chantry by; there, before him,

A chantry *was a private chapel.*

TWELFTH NIGHT 103

And underneath that consecrated roof, 25
Plight me the full assurance of your faith,
That my most jealous and too doubtful soul
May live at peace. He shall conceal it
Whiles you are willing it shall come to note,
What time we will our celebration keep 30
According to my birth. What do you say?

To *plight* one's faith, or troth (l. 26) is a sworn intention of marriage; it was considered an irrevocable bond.

Whiles here means "until."

SEBASTIAN I'll follow this good man, and go with you;
And, having sworn truth, ever will be true.

OLIVIA Then lead the way, good father; and heavens so shine
That they may fairly note this act of mine! *(exeunt)* 35

ACT V

SCENE I *Before Olivia's house.*

Enter Clown and Fabian.

FABIAN Now, as thou lov'st me, let me see his letter.

CLOWN Good Master Fabian, grant me another request.

FABIAN Anything.

CLOWN Do not desire to see this letter. 4

FABIAN This is to give a dog and in recompense desire my dog again.

Whose letter are the two fools talking about?

Enter Duke, Viola, Curio, and Lords.

DUKE Belong you to the Lady Olivia, friends?

CLOWN Ay, sir! we are some of her trappings.

DUKE I know thee well; how dost thou, my good fellow?

CLOWN Truly, sir, the better for my foes and the worse for my friends. 10

DUKE Just the contrary; the better for thy friends.

CLOWN No, sir, the worse.

DUKE How can that be? 14

CLOWN Marry, sir, they praise me and make an ass of me. Now my foes tell me plainly I am an ass; so that by my foes, sir, I profit in the knowledge of myself, and by my friends I am abused; so that, conclusions to be as kisses, if your four negatives make your two affirmatives, why then, the worse for my friends and the better for my foes.

What is Feste's comic logic in declaring a foe is better for him than a friend?

DUKE Why, this is excellent. 20

CLOWN By my troth, sir, no; though it please you to be one of my friends.

DUKE Thou shalt not be the worse for me. There's gold.

CLOWN But that it would be double-dealing, sir, 25
I would you could make it another.

Note the countless ways Feste has to wheedle tips from all comers.

DUKE O, you give me ill counsel.

104 WILLIAM SHAKESPEARE

CLOWN Put your grace in your pocket, sir, for this once, and let your flesh and blood obey it. 29

DUKE Well, I will be so much a sinner, to be a double-dealer. There's another.

CLOWN Primo, secundo, tertio, is a good play; and the old saying is, the third pays for all. The triplex, sir, is a good tripping measure; or the bells of Saint Bennet, sir, may put you in mind; one, two, three.

Presumably in line 31 Feste is alluding to throws of dice, e.g., one, two, three.

DUKE You can fool no more money out of me at this throw. If you will let your lady know I am here to speak with her, and bring her along with you, it may awake my bounty further. 37

CLOWN Marry, sir, lullaby to your bounty till I come again. I go, sir, but I would not have you to think that my desire of having is the sin of covetousness; but, as you say, sir, let your bounty take a nap, I will awake it anon. *(exit)* 41

Enter Antonio and Officers.

VIOLA Here comes the man, sir, that did rescue me.

DUKE That face of his I do remember well,
Yet, when I saw it last, it was besmear'd
As black as Vulcan in the smoke of war. 45
A bawbling vessel was he captain of,
For shallow draught and bulk unprizable,
With which such scatheful grapple did he make
With the most noble bottom of our fleet,
That very envy and the tongue of loss 50
Cri'd fame and honour on him. What's the matter?

bawbling is trifling.

What kind of fighter was Antonio?

1. OFFICER Orsino, this is that Antonio
That took the *Phœnix* and her fraught from Candy,
And this is he that did the *Tiger* board,
When your young nephew Titus lost his leg. 55
Here in the streets, desperate of shame and state,
In private brabble did we apprehend him.

Candy was a term used for Candia, or Crete.

brabble means a "brawl."

VIOLA He did me kindness, sir, drew on my side,
But in conclusion put strange speech upon me.
I know not what 'twas but distraction. 60

DUKE Notable pirate! Thou salt-water thief!
What foolish boldness brought thee to their mercies
Whom thou, in terms so bloody and so dear,
Hast made thine enemies?

By dear, the Duke implies "dangerous."

ANTONIO   Orsino, noble sir,
Be pleas'd that I shake off these names you give me 65
Antonio never yet was thief or pirate,
Though I confess, on base and ground enough,
Orsino's enemy. A witchcraft drew me hither.
That most ingrateful boy there by your side,
From the rude sea's enrag'd and foamy mouth 70
Did I redeem. A wreck past hope he was.
His life I gave him, and did thereto add
My love, without retention or restraint,
All his in dedication. For his sake
Did I expose myself, pure of his love, 75

What is the effect of Antonio's long speech on the opinions of others regarding Cesario/Viola's character?

TWELFTH NIGHT 105

Into the danger of this adverse town;
Drew to defend him when he was beset;
Where being apprehended, his false cunning,
Not meaning to partake with me in danger,
Taught him to face me out of his acquaintance, 80
And grew a twenty years removed thing
While one would wink; deni'd me mine own purse,
Which I had recommended to his use
Not half an hour before.

VIOLA   How can this be?

DUKE When came he to this town? 85

ANTONIO To-day, my lord; and for three months before,
No int'rim, not a minute's vacancy,
Both day and night did we keep company.

Enter Olivia and Attendants.

DUKE Here comes the countess; now heaven walks on earth.
But for thee, fellow; fellow, thy words are madness. 90
Three months this youth hath tended upon me;
But more of that anon. Take him aside.

Why does Orsino feel secure in ignoring Antonio's story about Cesario having been with Antonio?

OLIVIA What would my lord, but that he may not have,
Wherein Olivia may seem serviceable?
Cesario, you do not keep promise with me. 95

What does Olivia refer to in line 95?

VIOLA Madam!

DUKE Gracious Olivia,—

OLIVIA What do you say, Cesario? Good my lord,—

VIOLA My lord would speak; my duty hushes me.

OLIVIA If it be aught to the old tune, my lord,
It is as fat and fulsome to mine ear 100
As howling after music.

DUKE   Still so cruel!

OLIVIA Still so constant, lord.

DUKE What, to perverseness? You uncivil lady,
To whose ingrate and unauspicious altars 105
My soul the faithfull'st off'rings have breath'd out
That e'er devotion tender'd! What shall I do?

OLIVIA Even what it please my lord, that shall become him.

DUKE Why should I not, had I the heart to do it,
Like to th' Egyptian thief at point of death, 110
Kill what I love?—a savage jealousy
That sometime savours nobly. But hear me this:
Since you to non-regardance cast my faith,
And that I partly know the instrument
That screws me from my true place in your favour, 115
Live you the marble-breasted tyrant still;
But this your minion, whom I know you love,
And whom, by heaven I swear, I tender dearly,
Him will I tear out of that cruel eye,
Where he sits crowned in his master's spite. 120

The Duke, angered by Olivia's persistent rebuffs, threatens to slay her—as did the *Egyptian thief* in Heliodorus' story in *Ethiopica*—rather than allow anyone else to have her. But then he turns his anger on Cesario, now known as his rival for Olivia's love.

Come, boy, with me; my thoughts are ripe in mischief.
I'll sacrifice the lamb that I do love,
To spite a raven's heart within a dove.

VIOLA And I, most jocund, apt, and willingly,
To do you rest, a thousand deaths would die.   125

OLIVIA Where goes Cesario?

VIOLA   After him I love
More than I love these eyes, more than my life,
More, by all mores, than e'er I shall love wife.
If I do feign, you witnesses above
Punish my life for tainting of my love!   130

OLIVIA Ay me, detested! How am I beguil'd!

VIOLA Who does beguile you? Who does do you wrong?

OLIVIA Hast thou forgot thyself? Is it so long?
Call forth the holy father.

DUKE   Come, away!

OLIVIA Whither, my lord? Cesario, husband, stay.   135

DUKE Husband!

OLIVIA   Ay, husband! Can he that deny?

DUKE Her husband, sirrah!

VIOLA   No, my lord, not I.

OLIVIA Alas, it is the baseness of thy fear
That makes thee strangle thy propriety.
Fear not, Cesario; take thy fortunes up.   140
Be that thou know'st thou art, and then thou art
As great as that thou fear'st.

Enter Priest.

                O, welcome, father!
Father, I charge thee by thy reverence
Here to unfold, though lately we intended
To keep in darkness what occasion now   145
Reveals before 'tis ripe, what thou dost know
Hath newly pass'd between this youth and me.

PRIEST A contract of eternal bond of love,
Confirm'd by mutual joinder of your hands,
Attested by the holy close of lips,   150
Strength'ned by interchangement of your rings;
And all the ceremony of this compact
Seal'd in my function, by my testimony;
Since when, my watch hath told me, toward my grave
I have travell'd but two hours.   155

DUKE O thou dissembling cub! What wilt thou be
When time hath sow'd a grizzle on thy case?
Or will not else thy craft so quickly grow,
That thine own trip shall be thine overthrow?
Farewell, and take her; but direct thy feet   160
Where thou and I henceforth may never meet.

How does Olivia interpret Cesario's decision to stay with Orsino rather than go off with her?

What does Olivia encourage Cesario to do (ll. 140 ff) after she has made public their marriage contract?

grizzle means "gray hair," and *case* means "skin."

What is particularly painful for Viola in Orsino's denunciation and exile of Cesario?

TWELFTH NIGHT 107

VIOLA My lord, I do protest—

OLIVIA   O, do not swear!
Hold little faith, though thou hast too much fear.

Enter Sir Andrew.

SIR ANDREW For the love of God, a surgeon!
Send one presently to Sir Toby.   165

OLIVIA What's the matter?

SIR ANDREW Has broke my head across and has given Sir Toby a bloody coxcomb too. For the love of God, your help! I had rather than forty pound I were at home.

OLIVIA Who has done this, Sir Andrew?   170

SIR ANDREW The Count's gentleman, one Cesario. We took him for a coward, but he's the very devil incardinate.

DUKE My gentleman, Cesario?

SIR ANDREW 'Od's lifelings, here he is! You broke my head for nothing; and that that I did, I was set on to do't by Sir Toby.   175

VIOLA Why do you speak to me? I never hurt you.
You drew your sword upon me without cause;
But I bespake you fair, and hurt you not.

Enter Sir Toby and Clown.

SIR ANDREW If a bloody coxcomb be a hurt, you have hurt me. I think you set nothing by a bloody coxcomb. Here comes Sir Toby halting. You shall hear more; but if he had not been in drink, he would have tickl'd you othergates than he did.   182

DUKE How now, gentleman! How is't with you?

SIR TOBY That's all one. Has hurt me, and there's th' end on't. Sot, didst see Dick surgeon, sot?   185

CLOWN O, he's drunk, Sir Toby, an hour agone.
His eyes were set at eight i' th' morning.

SIR TOBY Then he's a rogue, and a passy measures [pavin]. I hate a drunken rogue.

OLIVIA Away with him! Who hath made this havoc with them?   190

SIR ANDREW I'll help you, Sir Toby, because we'll be dress'd together.

SIR TOBY Will you help?—an ass-head and a coxcomb and a knave, a thin-fac'd knave, a gull!

OLIVIA Get him to bed, and let his hurt be look'd to. *(exeunt Clown, Fabian, Sir Toby, and Sir Andrew)*   196

Enter Sebastian.

SEBASTIAN I am sorry, madam, I have hurt your kinsman;
But, had it been the brother of my blood,
I must have done no less with wit and safety.
You throw a strange regard upon me, and by that
I do perceive it hath offended you.   200
Pardon me, sweet one, even for the vows
We made each other but so late ago.

Why is the play at a climax when Toby and Feste join the others here?

To indicate the beatings they got from Sebastian (whom they mistook for the meek, mild Cesario), how would Sir Toby and Sir Andrew look on stage?

In line 182, *othergates* means "otherwise."

passy measures pavin is a measured Italian dance.

What reaction among those on stage would result from Sebastian's entrance here?

Why does Olivia "throw a strange regard" on Sebastian here?

108   WILLIAM SHAKESPEARE

DUKE One face, one voice, one habit, and two persons,
A natural perspective, that is and is not!

SEBASTIAN Antonio, O my dear Antonio! 205
How have the hours rack'd and tortur'd me,
Since I have lost thee!

A natural perspective is an optical illusion produced by nature.

ANTONIO Sebastian are you?

SEBASTIAN   Fear'st thou that, Antonio?

Fear'st here means "Doubtest."

ANTONIO How have you made division of yourself?
An apple, cleft in two, is not more twin 210
Than these two creatures. Which is Sebastian?

OLIVIA Most wonderful!

SEBASTIAN Do I stand there? I never had a brother,
Nor can there be that deity in my nature,
Of here and everywhere. I had a sister, 215
Whom the blind waves and surges have devour'd.
Of charity, what kin are you to me?
What countryman? What name? What parentage?

Why would Sebastian quiz the twin "fellow" standing before him at this moment?

VIOLA Of Messaline; Sebastian was my father;
Such a Sebastian was my brother too; 220
So went he suited to his watery tomb.
If spirits can assume both form and suit
You come to fright us.

SEBASTIAN   A spirit I am indeed;
But am in that dimension grossly clad
Which from the womb I did participate. 225
Were you a woman, as the rest goes even,
I should my tears let fall upon your cheek,
And say, "Thrice welcome, drowned Viola!"

In line 223 and following, Sebastian means that he is not a spirit but wears a mortal's flesh and blood.

VIOLA My father had a mole upon his brow.

SEBASTIAN And so had mine. 230

VIOLA And died that day when Viola from her birth
Had numb'red thirteen years.

SEBASTIAN O, that record is lively in my soul!
He finished indeed his mortal act
That day that made my sister thirteen years. 235

VIOLA If nothing lets to make us happy both
But this my masculine usurp'd attire,
Do not embrace me till each circumstance
Of place, time, fortune, do cohere and jump
That I am Viola; which to confirm, 240
I'll bring you to a captain in this town,
Where lie my maiden weeds; by whose gentle help
I was preserv'd to serve this noble count.
All the occurrence of my fortune since
Hath been between this lady and this lord. 245

lets means "prevents" here.

weeds are clothes.

SEBASTIAN *(to Olivia)* So comes it, lady, you have been mistook;
But nature to her bias drew in that.
You would have been contracted to a maid;
Nor are you therein, by my life, deceiv'd,
You are betroth'd both to a maid and man. 250

Viola (Helen Hayes), left, and Sebastian (Alex Courtney), right, from the 1940 Broadway production, Twelfth Night.

DUKE Be not amaz'd, right noble is his blood.
If this be so, as yet the glass seems true,   By *glass,* Orsino means a "mirror."
I shall have share in this most happy wreck.
(to Viola) Boy, thou hast said to me a thousand times
Thou never shouldst love woman like to me.   255

VIOLA And all those sayings will I over-swear;   *over-swear* means "to swear over
And all those swearings keep as true in soul   again."
As doth that orbed continent the fire   The *orbed continent* is the sphere of
That severs day from night.   the sun.

DUKE   Give me thy hand.
And let me see thee in thy woman's weeds.   260

VIOLA The captain that did bring me first on shore
Hath my maid's garments. He upon some action
Is now in durance, at Malvolio's suit,
A gentleman, and follower of my lady's.

OLIVIA He shall enlarge him; fetch Malvolio hither   265
And yet, alas, now I remember me,
They say, poor gentleman, he's much distract.

Re-enter Clown with a letter, and Fabian.

A most extracting frenzy of mine own
From my remembrance clearly banish'd his.
How does he, sirrah?   270

110   WILLIAM SHAKESPEARE

CLOWN Truly, madam, he holds Belzebub at the stave's end as well as a man in his case may do. Has here writ a letter to you. I should have given 't you to-day morning, but as a madman's epistles are no gospels, so it skills not much when they are deliver'd.

Belzebub is an agent of the Devil.

What is the effect of delaying the reading of Malvolio's letter?

OLIVIA Open 't and read it. 275

CLOWN Look then to be well edified when the fool delivers the madman. *(shouts)* "By the Lord, madam,"—

OLIVIA How now, art thou mad?

CLOWN No, madam, I do but read madness. An your ladyship will have it as it ought to be, you must allow Vox. 280

Vox, Latin for "voice," here probably means more specifically an appropriate loud voice.

OLIVIA Prithee, read i' thy right wits.

CLOWN So I do, madonna; but to read his right wits is to read thus; therefore perpend, my princess, and give ear.

perpend means "consider."

OLIVIA Read it you, sirrah. *(to Fabian)* 284

FABIAN *(reads)* "By the Lord, madam, you wrong me, and the world shall know it. Though you have put me into darkness and given your drunken cousin rule over me, yet have I the benefit of my senses as well as your ladyship. I have your own letter that induced me to the semblance I put on; with the which I doubt not but to do myself much right, or you much shame. Think of me as you please. I leave my duty a little unthought of and speak out of my injury.
    The Madly-us'd Malvolio." 292

OLIVIA Did he write this?

CLOWN Ay, madam.

DUKE This savours not much of distraction. 295

OLIVIA See him deliver'd, Fabian; bring him hither. *(exit Fabian)*
My lord, so please you, these things further thought on,
To think me as well a sister as a wife,
One day shall crown th' alliance on't, so please you,
Here at my house and at my proper cost. 300

proper means "own."

DUKE Madam, I am most apt 't embrace your offer.
(to Viola) Your master quits you; and for your service done him,
So much against the mettle of your sex,
So far beneath your soft and tender breeding,
And since you call'd me master for so long, 305
Here is my hand. You shall from this time be
Your master's mistress.

To quit means to "release."

What does Orsino actually mean by these playful lines addressed to Viola?

OLIVIA   A sister! You are she.

Enter Malvolio (and Fabian).

DUKE Is this the madman?

OLIVIA   Ay, my lord, this same.
How now, Malvolio!

MALVOLIO   Madam, you have done me wrong,
Notorious wrong.

OLIVIA   Have I, Malvolio? No. 310

MALVOLIO Lady, you have. Pray you, peruse that letter;
You must not now deny it is your hand.

Write from it, if you can, in hand or phrase;
Or say 'tis not your seal, not your invention.
You can say none of this. Well, grant it then   315
And tell me, in the modesty of honour,
Why you have given me such clear lights of favour,
Bade me come smiling and cross-garter'd to you,
To put on yellow stockings and to frown
Upon Sir Toby and the lighter people;   320
And, acting this in an obedient hope,
Why have you suffer'd me to be imprison'd,
Kept in a dark house, visited by the priest,
And made the most notorious geck and gull
That e'er invention play'd on? Tell me why.   325

OLIVIA Alas, Malvolio, this is not my writing,
Though, I confess, much like the character;
But out of question 'tis Maria's hand.
And now I do bethink me, it was she
First told thou wast mad. Then cam'st in smiling,   330
And in such forms which here were presuppos'd
Upon thee in the letter. Prithee, be content.
This practice hath most shrewdly pass'd upon thee;
But when we know the grounds and authors of it,
Thou shalt be both the plaintiff and the judge   335
Of thine own cause.

FABIAN   Good Madam, hear me speak,
And let no quarrel nor no brawl to come
Taint the condition of this present hour,
Which I have wond'red at. In hope it shall not
Most freely I confess, myself and Toby   340
Set this device against Malvolio here,
Upon some stubborn and uncourteous parts
We had conceiv'd against him. Maria writ
The letter at Sir Toby's great importance,
In recompense whereof he hath married her.   345
How with a sportful malice it was follow'd
May rather pluck on laughter than revenge,
If that the injuries be justly weigh'd
That have on both sides pass'd.

OLIVIA Alas, poor fool, how have they baffl'd thee! 350

CLOWN Why, "some are born great, some achieve greatness, and some have greatness thrown upon them." I was one, sir, in this interlude; one Sir Topas, sir; but that's all one. "By the Lord, fool, I am not mad." But do you remember? "Madam, why laugh you at such a barren rascal? An you smile not, he's gagg'd." And thus the whirligig of time brings in his revenges.   356

MALVOLIO I'll be reveng'd on the whole pack of you. *(exit)*

OLIVIA He hath been most notoriously abus'd.

DUKE Pursue him, and entreat him to a peace;
He hath not told us of the captain yet.   360
When that is known and golden time convents,
A solemn combination shall be made
Of our dear souls. Meantime, sweet sister,

In lines 312–15, Malvolio insists that Olivia cannot deny that the handwriting on the letter is hers, even if she were to copy it over and aim for a different hand.

geck and gull are fool and dupe.

Still another confusion is cleared up during this part of the play's resolution.

Why is it wise now for Fabian to confess the trickery?

importance means "pleading request."

Where have we heard these lines before (ll. 351 ff) and why would they provoke laughter now?

Is Malvolio satisfied with the clarification of events?

convents means "suits."

112   WILLIAM SHAKESPEARE

From the 1968 production, Your Own Thing, *based on Shakespeare's* Twelfth Night.

We will not part from hence. Cesario, come;
For so you shall be, while you are a man; 365
But when in other habits you are seen,
Orsino's mistress and his fancy's queen. *(exeunt [all, except Clown])*

CLOWN *(sings)*
When that I was and a little tiny boy,
   With hey, ho, the wind and the rain,
A foolish thing was but a toy, 370
   For the rain it raineth every day.

But when I came to man's estate,
   With hey, ho, &c.
Gainst knaves and thieves men shut their gate,
   For the rain, &c. 375

But when I came, alas! to wive,
   With hey, ho, &c.
By swaggering could I never thrive,
   For the rain, &c.

But when I came unto my beds, 380
   With hey, ho, &c.

With hey, ho, &c. indicates that the refrain should be repeated as printed before.

TWELFTH NIGHT   113

With toss-pots still had drunken heads,
  For the rain, &c.

A great while ago the world begun,
  With hey, ho, &c.
But that's all one, our play is done,
  And we'll strive to please you every day. *(exit)*   385

Why is Feste's song with its particular lyrics an appropriate ending for *Twelfth Night*?

POSTVIEW: THEME

A play is built around a central subject—its theme. Shakespeare masterfully develops both the chief and secondary plots of *Twelfth Night* from a single key theme.

1. What theme emerges from the opening scene?
2. What would be the effect on the audience if music were used at the beginning of the play? Should we seriously consider Duke Orsino's laments about love? Why?
3. How does the first scene set the comic mood for the entire play?
4. What kind of "love" is depicted in Maria's bold testing of Aguecheek's manliness in Act I, scene iii?

Throughout the play, Shakespeare develops different versions of the theme for the two interrelated plots.

5. What variations of unrequited love are found among Orsino, Olivia, and Viola? Are the problems insurmountable, or are the dilemmas light in spirit?
6. On the second plane, how is Malvolio also made a victim of unrequited love—one that results in an entirely different comic tone?
7. How does *Twelfth Night,* a comedy about love, differ substantially from *Medea,* a tragedy also concerning love?

Traditionally, a comic play portrays a situation filled with misunderstandings which eventually will be clarified and resolved. A new harmony among the characters occurs at play's end, after the disruptive elements of plot and character have been made ineffective.

8. Why would marriages prove particularly effective to denote a new union and harmony in any given community?
9. Do the multiple marriages which occur at the conclusion of *Twelfth Night* confirm new, peaceful circumstances in both main plots?
10. How is Malvolio's "self-love" (Olivia uses this phrase concerning Malvolio in Act I, scene v) also brought within proper restraints at the conclusion?

The expression "Twelfth Night" derives from the twelve days of reveling used to celebrate Christmas. The twelfth night following Christmas Day, on January 6th, marks the Epiphany in the Christian calendar and thus the conclusion of the formal Christmas holidays.

11. How apt is the title *Twelfth Night* to describe the spirit of the drama?

INTRODUCTION
AN ENEMY OF THE PEOPLE

Henrik Ibsen

HENRIK IBSEN'S PLAYS are more contemporary in manner than drama written by previous authors. It is for good reason that he is called the father of modern drama. In terms of subject matter and theatrical techniques, Ibsen struck out in new directions to help create a drama that was timely and effective for the last half of the nineteenth century. No play he wrote is more pertinent to his times than *An Enemy of the People* (1882).

Norwegian by birth, Ibsen (1828–1906) lived during pivotal years when social and industrial revolutions were sweeping Europe. Old class systems were being challenged; at the same time, the equalitarian thrust of political thought gave revived emphasis to the worth of each individual. Within such an atmosphere, Ibsen, along with other intellectual leaders, argued for personal rights. The antagonists were those monolithic structures which constituted the power hierarchy of every nation's society—government, church, industry, big business, and all other giant bureaucracies. They were seen as oppressive forces which suppressed individual initiative. In Ibsen's opinion, conservative Norway moved too slowly toward a more democratic societal reform. As a result, he chose to live much of his adult life in self-exile, elsewhere in Europe. Yet Ibsen's plays were about his fellow Norwegians, and his plots dramatically revealed the issues of man in society.

After an early period in his writing career when he wrote romanticized plays, Ibsen focused on the conflict between assertive individuals and the society of which they were a part. He touched upon numerous topics which were, until then, unmentionable in public. *A Doll's House* (1879) and *Hedda Gabler* (1890) dramatized the restricted roles allowed women in a society ruled by men. In *Ghosts* (1881), he detailed the devastating aftereffects of venereal disease, thereby shocking his fellow countrymen. But it is in *An Enemy of the People* that Ibsen most directly pits a protagonist against the impinging forces of a self-seeking, hypocritical society.

Nearly all Ibsen's later plays fit within the general categories of drama of ideas, social drama, or problem plays. Each type of play has a theme concerning some segment of life. In social drama, the conflict which the protagonist encounters is a product of some social problem, and the dramatic structure focuses on the issues from different perspectives. *An Enemy of the People* is concerned with the callous pragmatism of commercial interests as they are challenged by one person's insistence on ethical choices. Few absolute solutions to dilemmas are given in most problem or social plays, because the dramatist first seeks to examine all sides by dramatizing and clarifying the problem situation. Readers of *An Enemy of the People,* therefore, can be forgiven for not finding a clear-cut answer to Dr. Stockmann's predicament.

Ibsen also earned the title of father of modern drama by virtue of another accomplishment—he raised the technique of dramatic *realism* to a refined state. Realism is a literary mode which depicts the surface appearance of the world objectively. No arbitrary patterns are superimposed on the stage, because everyday life itself, claim writers of realism, presents a series of interesting stories—once an audience sees them by developing a sharp eye for detail. Such drama seeks to reproduce a part of life as accurately as possible. The characters are commonplace figures, and the story is taken from ordinary events in life. As a result, realism accurately portrays such elements as speech, dress, and setting. Fantasy has small part in such drama, as might be expected, when emphasis is placed on duplicating surface details.

An Enemy of the People, for instance, is filled with speech idiosyncrasies to help establish the separate identities and personalities of the characters. Thomas Stockmann's prissiness, for example, contrasts with his brother's gregariousness. Aslaksen shows himself to be a coward, while Hovstad by the end of the play has shown himself to be superficial and hypocritical.

In addition, to offer an accurate version of life-like events, playwrights of realism usually specify the stage settings required. Most scenes from realistic drama are set indoors where replicas of actual rooms—frequently, living rooms—can easily be constructed. By Ibsen's era, the proscenium stage was well-established, with audiences sitting in a darkened theater facing a recessed stage area which could be cut off from view with curtains whenever needed. Such a theater allows for totally different stage conventions than found in earlier periods of drama—such as in classical Greece and in Shakespeare's time. The nineteenth-century "box set" arrangement (see the accompanying photograph) worked well for the stylistic needs of realistic plays. The three walls forming the backdrop of the recessed stage room could be fashioned like an ordinary room, while the fourth wall between the stage and the audience was imaginary, permitting playgoers to look in on the lives and actions being portrayed. Because surface details are so vital in realistic plays, readers of those dramas must read the stage directions thoroughly, to better visualize the set according to the author's intentions.

Beneath the realistic mode in drama lies a broad philosophical assumption: there is sufficient subject material for a play in true-to-life people and events. Authors do not need to make up artificial stories and characters; instead, they need only to draw them from real life. Most of Ibsen's plays were built around identifiable human beings and current social issues. Like other realists, he believed in a modified teaching function for the stage. He used his plays to show the lives of ordinary individuals, with the hope that his audiences would recognize and thereby comprehend themselves. All dramatic elements—dialogue, setting, plot, and characterization—were directed toward creating this illusion of true life. And although he realized that one could change one's life, Ibsen would not set down any particular prescription for self-improvement—it was more important to present the problems in life than to offer solutions.

Ibsen explores the tension between one's individual will and one's duties to peers. In *An Enemy of the People,* he juxtaposes personal wants with sacrificial demands made on us by the community around us. Like Dr. Stockmann, we become caught in a dilemma. The greater good for the whole may penalize us as individuals. Or, what is advantageous to us personally may result in harm to society. As a man of science, Dr. Stockmann only wants to determine the absolute facts concerning a critical health situation. After that, he expects the civic officials to implement any needed corrective measures. Stockmann's responsibilities, he believes, cease with the presentation of objective information. However, the community leaders look at the scientific facts in terms of the economic cost to the local society. Their "truth" about a resulting economic disaster is as real to them as Stockmann's scientific medical report is to him. The result is a sharp conflict between two sets of priorities, pitting one well-intentioned individual against his fellow townspeople.

In our own lives today, we see evidence of the same antagonisms in such areas as freedom of the press, conscientious objectors, and ecological controls. Ibsen addresses himself to a pattern of conflict in *An Enemy of the People* which serves as an example for men of all eras faced with issues placing individual rights in opposition to broader societal demands. The conflicting design is an eternal one. Thus Ibsen's play represents universal implications which derive from a specific situation portrayed realistically.

PREVIEW: STRUCTURE

Exposition, the offering of basic information about the situations and persons involved, can be found throughout conventionally organized drama. Yet the playwright recognizes that, at the beginning of his play, he must provide enough background to allow his audiences to understand what is going on.

1. What does the opening scene tell us about Stockmann's social class, as described in Ibsen's own stage directions? How does such a specific description suggest the strengths of drama of *realism*? (See the introduction to *An Enemy of the People*.)
2. What can we deduce about the nature of the Stockmann family, based on their attitudes and treatment of friends who enter and leave casually throughout Act I? Are they a gloomy family? Cheery? Shy?
3. How does Ibsen characterize the Stockmann brothers as polar opposites with respect to personality and politics?
4. How does the audience learn that the town Baths are the economic mainstay of the community and that Dr. Stockmann is the chief medical officer of those Baths?

The development of a plot through complications can overlap the expository elements of a play. In *An Enemy of the People* we sense conflicting factors from the very beginning.

5. How does potential (and real) friction derive from the differing importance placed on the Baths by the doctor, the Mayor, and the middle-class leadership?
6. In the development, what part is played by the letter which Stockmann is awaiting for during the first half of Act I?
7. Why do Hovstad and Aslaksen ally themselves with the doctor once the contents of the letter are made known?

The growing conflict between the doctor and the Mayor reaches an early peak in Act II.

8. What is the precise nature of their disagreement?
9. By the end of the second act, which marks the near completion of the first escalation of tension in the play, where are the battle lines drawn and between whom?

The development of the plot enters a second stage in Act III.

10. How does the Mayor's arrival in the newspaper offices alter the events of the play?
11. How does Aslaksen's and Hovstad's change in attitude toward Dr. Stockmann in Act III reflect the new situation induced by the Mayor's visit?
12. By the end of this act, what new set of alliances is established?

Act III, with the confrontation between the doctor and the Mayor, provides a form of dramatic crisis. But Act IV contains the more definitive climax during the town meeting called by the doctor.

13. How do the doctor's opponents muzzle him within traditionally accepted rules of procedures for public meetings?
14. How does Ibsen characterize the townspeople listening to the speeches?
15. Why do the doctor's pronouncements constitute the true climax of the play,

once he is allowed to speak? Is there any chance to turn back after he has announced his new-found "truth"? Why?

Dr. Stockmann's declarations at the assembly mark the ultimate turning point in the action, thus giving the resolution.

16. How do the results of the doctor's revelations affect his position as medical head of the Baths? As a respected member of the community? As a practicing physician in the town?
17. At the end of the town meeting, what are the polarizations in the community with respect to Stockmann?

Although not all plays provide an identifiable denouement (i.e., the post-section of a plot which clarifies the situation resulting from the resolution), this play does.

18. What last opportunities are offered the doctor, and by whom, to salvage some positive public esteem for himself and his family?
19. What is the doctor's final decision regarding his future in the town?

AN ENEMY OF THE PEOPLE

Henrik Ibsen

translated by R. Farquharson Sharp

DRAMATIS PERSONÆ

Dr. Thomas Stockmann, *Medical Officer of the Municipal Baths.*
Mrs. Stockmann, *his wife.*
Petra, *their daughter, a teacher.*
Ejlif ⎫ *their sons (aged 13 and 10*
Morton ⎭ *respectively).*
Peter Stockmann, *the Doctor's elder brother; Mayor of the Town and Chief Constable, Chairman of the Baths' Committee, etc., etc.*
Morten Kiil, *a tanner (Mrs. Stockmann's adoptive father).*
Hovstad, *editor of the "People's Messenger."*
Billing, *sub-editor.*
Captain Horster.
Aslaksen, *a printer.*
Men of various conditions and occupations, some few women, and a troop of schoolboys—*the audience at a public meeting.*

The action takes place in a coast town in southern Norway.

ACT I

SCENE—*Dr. Stockmann's sitting room. It is evening. The room is plainly but neatly appointed and furnished. In the right-hand wall are two doors; the farther leads out to the hall, the nearer to the doctor's study. In the*

As explained in the introduction to this play, realistic drama recreates on stage the appearance of people and life as

left-hand wall, opposite the door leading to the hall, is a door leading to the other rooms occupied by the family. In the middle of the same wall stands the stove, and, further forward, a couch with a looking-glass hanging over it and an oval table in front of it. On the table, a lighted lamp, with a lampshade. At the back of the room, an open door leads to the dining-room. Billing is seen sitting at the dining table, on which a lamp is burning. He has a napkin tucked under his chin, and Mrs. Stockmann is standing by the table handing him a large plate-full of roast beef. The other places at the table are empty, and the table somewhat in disorder, a meal having evidently recently been finished.

MRS. STOCKMANN You see, if you come an hour late, Mr. Billing, you have to put up with cold meat.

BILLING *(as he eats)* It is uncommonly good, thank you—remarkably good.

MRS. STOCKMANN My husband makes such a point of having his meals punctually, you know—

BILLING That doesn't affect me a bit. Indeed, I almost think I enjoy a meal all the better when I can sit down and eat all by myself and undisturbed.

MRS. STOCKMANN Oh well, as long as you are enjoying it—. *(turns to the hall door, listening)* I expect that is Mr. Hovstad coming too.

BILLING Very likely.

Peter Stockmann comes in. He wears an overcoat and his official hat, and carries a stick.

PETER STOCKMANN Good evening, Katherine.

MRS. STOCKMANN *(coming forward into the sitting-room)* Ah, good evening—is it you? How good of you to come up and see us!

PETER STOCKMANN I happened to be passing, and so—*(looks into the dining-room).* But you have company with you, I see.

MRS. STOCKMANN *(a little embarrassed)* Oh, no—it was quite by chance he came in. *(hurriedly)* Won't you come in and have something, too?

PETER STOCKMANN I! No, thank you. Good gracious—hot meat at night! Not with my digestion.

MRS. STOCKMANN Oh, but just once in a way—

PETER STOCKMANN No, no, my dear lady; I stick to my tea and bread and butter. It is much more wholesome in the long run—and a little more economical, too.

MRS. STOCKMANN *(smiling)* Now you mustn't think that Thomas and I are spendthrifts.

PETER STOCKMANN Not you, my dear; I would never think that of you. *(points to the Doctor's study)* Is he not at home?

MRS. STOCKMANN No, he went out for a little turn after supper—he and the boys.

PETER STOCKMANN I doubt if that is a wise thing to do. *(listens)* I fancy I hear him coming now.

MRS. STOCKMANN No, I don't think it is he. *(a knock is heard at the*

---

they exist in the actual world. In these stage directions Ibsen sets his scene realistically. The interior of a typical middle-class home is required for purposes of Ibsen's story.

What mood is established for the Stockmann household through the initial interchange between Billing and Mrs. Stockmann? Is it forbidding? Cheery?

Does Peter Stockmann's lifestyle clash with that of his brother's family? In what specific ways do they conflict?

door) Come in! *(Hovstad comes in from the hall)* Oh, it is you, Mr. Hovstad!

HOVSTAD Yes, I hope you will forgive me, but I was delayed at the printer's. Good evening, Mr. Mayor.

PETER STOCKMANN *(bowing a little distantly)* Good evening. You have come on business, no doubt.

HOVSTAD Partly. It's about an article for the paper.

PETER STOCKMANN So I imagined. I hear my brother has become a prolific contributor to the "People's Messenger."

HOVSTAD Yes, he is good enough to write in the "People's Messenger" when he has any home truths to tell.

> Through such hinting remarks, Ibsen tells us that there is some friction between the Stockmann brothers. What will Peter's tone of voice be like in these lines?

MRS. STOCKMANN *(to Hovstad)* But won't you—? *(Points to the dining-room)*

PETER STOCKMANN Quite so, quite so. I don't blame him in the least, as a writer, for addressing himself to the quarters where he will find the readiest sympathy. And, besides that, I personally have no reason to bear any ill will to your paper, Mr. Hovstad.

HOVSTAD I quite agree with you.

PETER STOCKMANN Taking one thing with another, there is an excellent spirit of toleration in the town—an admirable municipal spirit. And it all springs from the fact of our having a great common interest to unite us—an interest that is in an equally high degree the concern of every right-minded citizen—

HOVSTAD The Baths, yes.

PETER STOCKMANN Exactly—our fine, new, handsome Baths. Mark my words, Mr. Hovstad—the Baths will become the focus of our municipal life! Not a doubt of it!

MRS. STOCKMANN That is just what Thomas says.

> The Baths are alluded to very early in the play. What is their significance, according to the characters at this point?

PETER STOCKMANN Think how extraordinarily the place has developed within the last year or two! Money has been flowing in, and there is some life and some business doing in the town. Houses and landed property are rising in value every day.

HOVSTAD And unemployment is diminishing.

PETER STOCKMANN Yes, that is another thing. The burden of the poor rates has been lightened, to the great relief of the propertied classes; and that relief will be even greater if only we get a really good summer this year, and lots of visitors—plenty of invalids, who will make the Baths talked about.

> How do Peter Stockmann and Hovstad regard the Baths?

HOVSTAD And there is a good prospect of that, I hear.

PETER STOCKMANN It looks very promising. Enquiries about apartments and that sort of thing are reaching us every day.

HOVSTAD Well, the doctor's article will come in very suitably.

PETER STOCKMANN Has he been writing something just lately?

HOVSTAD This is something he wrote in the winter; a recommendation of the Baths—an account of the excellent sanitary conditions here. But I held the article over, temporarily.

PETER STOCKMANN Ah,—some little difficulty about it, I suppose?

AN ENEMY OF THE PEOPLE

HOVSTAD No, not at all; I thought it would be better to wait till the spring, because it is just at this time that people begin to think seriously about their summer quarters.

PETER STOCKMANN Quite right; you were perfectly right, Mr. Hovstad.

HOVSTAD Yes, Thomas is really indefatigable when it is a question of the Baths.

PETER STOCKMANN Well—remember, he is the Medical Officer to the Baths.

HOVSTAD Yes, and what is more, they owe their existence to him.

PETER STOCKMANN To him? Indeed! It is true I have heard from time to time that some people are of that opinion. At the same time I must say I imagined that I took a modest part in the enterprise.

MRS. STOCKMANN Yes, that is what Thomas is always saying.

HOVSTAD But who denies it, Mr. Stockmann? You set the thing going and made a practical concern of it; we all know that. I only meant that the idea of it came first from the doctor.

PETER STOCKMANN Oh, ideas—yes! My brother has had plenty of them in his time—unfortunately. But when it is a question of putting an idea into practical shape, you have to apply to a man of different mettle, Mr. Hovstad. And I certainly should have thought that in this house at least—

MRS. STOCKMANN My dear Peter—

HOVSTAD How can you think that—?

MRS. STOCKMANN Won't you go in and have something, Mr. Hovstad? My husband is sure to be back directly.

HOVSTAD Thank you, perhaps just a morsel. *(goes into the dining-room)*

PETER STOCKMANN *(lowering his voice a little)* It is a curious thing that these farmers' sons never seem to lose their want of tact.

MRS. STOCKMANN Surely it is not worth bothering about! Cannot you and Thomas share the credit as brothers?

PETER STOCKMANN I should have thought so; but apparently some people are not satisfied with a share.

MRS. STOCKMANN What nonsense! You and Thomas get on so capitally together. *(listens)* There he is at last, I think. *(goes out and opens the door leading to the hall)*

DR. STOCKMANN *(laughing and talking outside)* Look here—here is another guest for you, Katherine. Isn't that jolly! Come in, Captain Horster; hang your coat up on this peg. Ah, you don't wear an overcoat. Just think, Katherine; I met him in the street and could hardly persuade him to come up! *(Captain Horster comes into the room and greets Mrs. Stockmann. He is followed by Dr. Stockmann.)* Come along in, boys. They are ravenously hungry again, you know. Come along, Captain Horster; you must have a slice of beef. *(Pushes Horster into the dining-room. Ejlif and Morten go in after them.)*

MRS. STOCKMANN But, Thomas, don't you see—?

How do Hovstad and Peter Stockmann consider Dr. Stockmann's keen interest in the Baths? What is each's view? How is characterization furthered for each man here?

Is Peter Stockmann jealous of his brother? Why?

What kind of person does Peter perceive himself to be, as contrasted to the doctor?

In just this one speech, how does Ibsen characterize Dr. Stockmann? What kind of a person is he?

DR. STOCKMANN *(turning in the doorway)* Oh, is it you, Peter? *(shakes hands with him)* Now that is very delightful.

PETER STOCKMANN Unfortunately I must go in a moment—

DR. STOCKMANN Rubbish! There is some toddy just coming in. You haven't forgotten the toddy, Katherine?

MRS. STOCKMANN Of course not; the water is boiling now. *(goes into the dining-room)*

PETER STOCKMANN Toddy too!

DR. STOCKMANN Yes, sit down and we will have it comfortably.

PETER STOCKMANN Thanks, I never care about an evening's drinking.

DR. STOCKMANN But this isn't an evening's drinking.

PETER STOCKMANN It seems to me—. *(looks towards the dining-room)* It is extraordinary how they can put away all that food.

Ibsen effectively contrasts the opposite temperaments of the brothers in the following interchange.

DR. STOCKMANN *(rubbing his hands)* Yes, isn't it splendid to see young people eat? They have always got an appetite, you know! That's as it should be. Lots of food—to build up their strength! They are the people who are going to stir up the fermenting forces of the future, Peter.

PETER STOCKMANN May I ask what they will find here to "stir up," as you put it?

DR. STOCKMANN Ah, you must ask the young people that—when the time comes. We shan't be able to see it, of course. That stands to reason—two old fogies, like us—

PETER STOCKMANN Really, really! I must say that is an extremely odd expression to—

How is the audience's impression of Peter's character reinforced by his objection to Dr. Stockmann's choice of words?

DR. STOCKMANN Oh, you mustn't take me too literally, Peter. I am so heartily happy and contented, you know. I think it is such an extraordinary piece of good fortune to be in the middle of all this growing, germinating life. It is a splendid time to live in! It is as if a whole new world were being created around one.

PETER STOCKMANN Do you really think so?

DR. STOCKMANN Ah, naturally you can't appreciate it as keenly as I. You have lived all your life in these surroundings, and your impressions have got blunted. But I, who have been buried all these years in my little corner up north, almost without ever seeing a stranger who might bring new ideas with him—well, in my case it has just the same effect as if I had been transported into the middle of a crowded city.

In keeping with the influence of realism in literature (see the introduction to this play), Ibsen here provides psychological roots for Dr. Stockmann's zeal for life. What are some important factors in his earlier life for us to remember?

PETER STOCKMANN Oh, a city—!

DR. STOCKMANN I know, I know; it is all cramped enough here, compared with many other places. But there is life here—there is promise—there are innumerable things to work for and fight for; and that is the main thing. *(calls)* Katherine, hasn't the postman been here?

MRS. STOCKMANN *(from the dining-room)* No.

Note the first mention of an awaited letter.

DR. STOCKMANN And then to be comfortably off, Peter! That is

AN ENEMY OF THE PEOPLE

something one learns to value, when one has been on the brink of starvation, as we have.

PETER STOCKMANN Oh, surely—

DR. STOCKMANN Indeed I can assure you we have often been very hard put to it, up there. And now to be able to live like a lord! To-day, for instance, we had roast beef for dinner—and, what is more, for supper too. Won't you come and have a little bit? Or let me show it to you, at any rate? Come here—

PETER STOCKMANN No, no—not for worlds!

DR. STOCKMANN Well, but just come here then. Do you see, we have got a table-cover?

What additional character details concerning Peter are found here to reinforce the reader's opinion about him?

PETER STOCKMANN Yes, I noticed it.

DR. STOCKMANN And we have got a lamp-shade too. Do you see? All out of Katherine's savings! It makes the room so cosy. Don't you think so? Just stand here for a moment—no, no, not there—just here, that's it! Look now, when you get the light on it altogether—I really think it looks very nice, doesn't it?

PETER STOCKMANN Oh, if you can afford luxuries of this kind—

DR. STOCKMANN Yes, I can afford it now. Katherine tells me I earn almost as much as we spend.

PETER STOCKMANN Almost—yes!

DR. STOCKMANN But a scientific man must live in a little bit of style. I am quite sure an ordinary civil servant spends more in a year than I do.

PETER STOCKMANN I daresay. A civil servant—a man in a well-paid position—

DR. STOCKMANN Well, any ordinary merchant, then! A man in that position spends two or thee times as much as—

PETER STOCKMANN It just depends on circumstances.

DR. STOCKMANN At all events I assure you I don't waste money unprofitably. But I can't find it in my heart to deny myself the pleasure of entertaining my friends. I need that sort of thing, you know. I have lived for so long shut out of it all, that it is a necessity of life to me to mix with young, eager, ambitious men, men of liberal and active minds; and that describes every one of those fellows who are enjoying their supper in there. I wish you knew more of Hovstad—

Here Stockmann clarifies his fundamental perspective on life.

PETER STOCKMANN By the way, Hovstad was telling me he was going to print another article of yours.

DR. STOCKMANN An article of mine?

PETER STOCKMANN Yes, about the Baths. An article you wrote in the winter.

DR. STOCKMANN Oh, that one! No, I don't intend that to appear just for the present.

PETER STOCKMANN Why not? It seems to me that this would be the most opportune moment.

DR. STOCKMANN Yes, very likely—under normal conditions. *(crosses the room)*

PETER STOCKMANN *(following him with his eyes)* Is there anything abnormal about the present conditions?

> How does Ibsen project Peter's cautious and suspicious nature here?

DR. STOCKMANN *(standing still)* To tell you the truth, Peter, I can't say just at this moment—at all events not to-night. There may be much that is very abnormal about the present conditions—and it is possible there may be nothing abnormal about them at all. It is quite possible it may be merely my imagination.

PETER STOCKMANN I must say it all sounds most mysterious. Is there something going on that I am to be kept in ignorance of? I should have imagined that I, as Chairman of the governing body of the Baths—

DR. STOCKMANN And I should have imagined that I— Oh, come, don't let us fly out at one another, Peter.

PETER STOCKMANN Heaven forbid! I am not in the habit of flying out at people, as you call it. But I am entitled to request most emphatically that all arrangements shall be made in a business-like manner, through the proper channels, and shall be dealt with by the legally constituted authorities. I can allow no going behind our backs by any roundabout means.

> Peter expounds on his rigid expectations of the community. What kind of a mayor would he be to work under?

DR. STOCKMANN Have I ever at any time tried to go behind your backs!

PETER STOCKMANN You have an ingrained tendency to take your own way, at all events; and that is almost equally inadmissible in a well ordered community. The individual ought undoubtedly to acquiesce in subordinating himself to the community—or, to speak more accurately, to the authorities who have the care of the community's welfare.

> Peter Stockmann here sees his brother as a troublemaker, thus preparing the audience for the confrontation lying ahead.

DR. STOCKMANN Very likely. But what the deuce has all this got to do with me?

PETER STOCKMANN That is exactly what you never appear to be willing to learn, my dear Thomas. But, mark my words, some day you will have to suffer for it—sooner or later. Now I have told you. Good-bye.

> Later, Peter's forewarning will be recalled for its ironic accuracy.

DR. STOCKMANN Have you taken leave of your senses? You are on the wrong scent altogether.

PETER STOCKMANN I am not usually that. You must excuse me now if I—*(calls into the dining-room)*. Good night, Katherine. Good night, gentlemen. *(goes out)*

MRS. STOCKMANN *(coming from the dining-room)* Has he gone?

DR. STOCKMANN Yes, and in such a bad temper.

MRS. STOCKMANN But, dear Thomas, what have you been doing to him again?

DR. STOCKMANN Nothing at all. And, anyhow, he can't oblige me to make my report before the proper time.

MRS. STOCKMANN What have you got to make a report to him about?

DR. STOCKMANN Hm! Leave that to me, Katherine.—It is an extraordinary thing that the postman doesn't come.

Hovstad, Billing and Horster have got up from the table and come into the sitting-room. Ejlif and Morten come in after them.

BILLING (*stretching himself*) Ah!—one feels a new man after a meal like that.

HOVSTAD The mayor wasn't in a very sweet temper to-night, then.

DR. STOCKMANN It is his stomach; he has a wretched digestion.

HOVSTAD I rather think it was us two of the "People's Messenger" that he couldn't digest.

MRS. STOCKMANN I thought you came out of it pretty well with him.

HOVSTAD Oh yes; but it isn't anything more than a sort of truce.

BILLING That is just what it is! That word sums up the situation.

DR. STOCKMANN We must remember that Peter is a lonely man, poor chap. He has no home comforts of any kind; nothing but everlasting business. And all that infernal weak tea wash that he pours into himself! Now then, my boys, bring chairs up to the table. Aren't we going to have that toddy, Katherine?

MRS. STOCKMANN (*going into the dining-room*) I am just getting it.

DR. STOCKMANN Sit down here on the couch beside me, Captain Horster. We so seldom see you—. Please sit down, my friends. (*They sit down at the table. Mrs. Stockmann brings a tray, with a spirit-lamp, glasses, bottles, etc., upon it.*)

MRS. STOCKMANN There you are! This is arrack, and this is rum, and this one is the brandy. Now every one must help themselves.

DR. STOCKMANN (*taking a glass*) We will. (*They all mix themselves some toddy.*) And let us have the cigars. Ejlif, you know where the box is. And you, Morten, can fetch my pipe. (*The two boys go into the room on the right.*) I have a suspicion that Ejlif pockets a cigar now and then!—but I take no notice of it. (*calls out*) And my smoking-cap too, Morten. Katherine, you can tell him where I left it. Ah, he has got it. (*The boys bring the various things.*) Now, my friends. I stick to my pipe, you know. This one has seen plenty of bad weather with me up north. (*touches glasses with them*) Your good health! Ah, it is good to be sitting snug and warm here.

MRS. STOCKMANN (*who sits knitting*) Do you sail soon, Captain Horster?

HORSTER I expect to be ready to sail next week.

MRS. STOCKMANN I suppose you are going to America?

HORSTER Yes, that is the plan.

MRS. STOCKMANN Then you won't be able to take part in the coming election.

HORSTER Is there going to be an election?

BILLING Didn't you know?

HORSTER No, I don't mix myself up with those things.

BILLING But do you not take an interest in public affairs?

Obviously, the awaited letter is very important to the doctor.

Here, Dr. Stockmann's assessment of his brother's temperament is far kinder than Peter's is of his brother.

How does the bringing in of after-dinner drinks and tobacco reinforce the mood in the Stockmann home at the beginning of the play?

How does Ibsen insert more exposition here? In what ways might this factor account for Peter's touchiness concerning the smooth running of city affairs?

HORSTER No, I don't know anything about politics.

BILLING All the same, one ought to vote, at any rate.

HORSTER Even if one doesn't know anyting about what is going on?

BILLING Doesn't know! What do you mean by that? A community is like a ship; every one ought to be prepared to take the helm.

HORSTER May be that is all very well on shore; but on board ship it wouldn't work.

HOVSTAD It is astonishing how little most sailors care about what goes on on shore.

BILLING Very extraordinary.

DR. STOCKMANN Sailors are like birds of passage; they feel equally at home in any latitude. And that is only an additional reason for our being all the more keen, Hovstad. Is there to be anything of public interest in tomorrow's "Messenger"?

HOVSTAD Nothing about municipal affairs. But the day after tomorrow I was thinking of printing your article—

DR. STOCKMANN Ah, devil take it—my article! Look here, that must wait a bit.

HOVSTAD Really? We had just got convenient space for it, and I thought it was just the opportune moment—

DR. STOCKMANN Yes, yes, very likely you are right; but it must wait all the same. I will explain to you later. *(Petra comes in from the hall, in hat and cloak and with a bundle of exercise books under her arm.)*

PETRA Good evening.

DR. STOCKMANN Good evening, Petra; come along. *(Mutual greetings; Petra takes off her things and puts them down on a chair by the door.)*

PETRA And you have all been sitting here enjoying yourselves, while I have been out slaving!

DR. STOCKMANN Well, come and enjoy yourself too!

BILLING May I mix a glass for you?

PETRA *(coming to the table)* Thanks, I would rather do it; you always mix it too strong. But I forgot, father—I have a letter for you. *(goes to the chair where she has laid her things)*

DR. STOCKMANN A letter? From whom?

PETRA *(looking in her coat pocket)* The postman gave it to me just as I was going out—

DR. STOCKMANN *(getting up and going to her)* And you only give it to me now!

PETRA I really had not time to run up again. There it is!

DR. STOCKMANN *(seizing the letter)* Let's see, let's see, child! *(looks at the address)* Yes, that's all right!

MRS. STOCKMANN Is it the one you have been expecting so anxiously, Thomas?

DR. STOCKMANN Yes, it is. I must go to my room now and—. Where shall I get a light, Katherine? Is there no lamp in my room again?

Why has Ibsen kept Stockmann (and us) waiting so long for this letter? What kind of device does the letter become among the basic components of drama?

MRS. STOCKMANN Yes, your lamp is all ready lit on your desk.

DR. STOCKMANN Good, good. Excuse me for a moment— *(goes into his study)*

PETRA What do you suppose it is, mother?

MRS. STOCKMANN I don't know; for the last day or two he has always been asking if the postman has not been.

BILLING Probably some country patient.

PETRA Poor old dad!—he will overwork himself soon. *(mixes a glass for herself)* There, that will taste good!

HOVSTAD Have you been teaching in the evening school again to-day?

PETRA *(sipping from her glass)* Two hours.

BILLING And four hours of school in the morning—

PETRA Five hours.

MRS. STOCKMANN And you have still got exercises to correct, I see.

PETRA A whole heap, yes.

HORSTER You are pretty full up with work too, it seems to me.

PETRA Yes—but that is good. One is so delightfully tired after it.

BILLING Do you like that?

PETRA Yes, because one sleeps so well then.

MORTEN You must be dreadfully wicked, Petra.

PETRA Wicked?

MORTEN Yes, because you work so much. Mr. Rörlund says work is a punishment for our sins.

EJLIF Pooh, what a duffer you are, to believe a thing like that!

MRS. STOCKMANN Come, come, Ejlif!

BILLING *(laughing)* That's capital!

HOVSTAD Don't you want to work as hard as that, Morten?

MORTEN No, indeed I don't.

HOVSTAD What do you want to be, then?

MORTEN I should like best to be a Viking.

EJLIF You would have to be a pagan then.

MORTEN Well, I could become a pagan, couldn't I?

BILLING I agree with you, Morten! My sentiments, exactly.

MRS. STOCKMANN *(signalling to him)* I am sure that is not true, Mr. Billing.

BILLING Yes, I swear it is! I am a pagan, and I am proud of it. Believe me, before long we shall all be pagans.

MORTEN And then shall be allowed to do anything we like?

BILLING Well, you see, Morten—.

MRS. STOCKMANN You must go to your room now, boys; I am sure you have some lessons to learn for to-morrow.

By now, the audience will have deduced that there is some connection between the long-awaited letter, Stockmann's article for the "Messenger," and the city's Baths.

Another attribute of realism is shown in the casual dialogue exchanged between Petra, her brothers, and the visitors—i.e., ordinary language used to chat aimlessly, much as in real life when friends get together.

What are some long-range ramifications of Billing's pleading on behalf of pagan behavior? Why does Mrs. Stockmann try to turn the conversation away from these matters?

EJLIF I should like so much to stay a little longer—

MRS. STOCKMANN No, no; away you go, both of you.

The boys say good night and go into the room on the left.

HOVSTAD Do you really think it can do the boys any harm to hear such things?

MRS. STOCKMANN I don't know; but I don't like it.

PETRA But you know, mother, I think you really are wrong about it.

MRS. STOCKMANN Maybe, but I don't like it—not in our own home.

PETRA There is so much falsehood both at home and at school. At home one must not speak, and at school we have to stand and tell lies to the children.

HORSTER Tell lies?

PETRA Yes, don't you suppose we have to teach them all sorts of things that we don't believe?

BILLING That is perfectly true.

PETRA If only I had the means I would start a school of my own, and it would be conducted on very different lines.

BILLING Oh, bother the means—!

HORSTER Well if you are thinking of that, Miss Stockmann, I shall be delighted to provide you with a school-room. The great big old house my father left me is standing almost empty; there is an immense dining-room downstairs—

PETRA (*laughing*) Thank you very much; but I am afraid nothing will come of it.

HOVSTAD No, Miss Petra is much more likely to take to journalism, I expect. By the way, have you had time to do anything with that English story you promised to translate for us?

PETRA No, not yet; but you shall have it in good time.

Dr. Stockmann comes in from his room with an open letter in his hand.

DR. STOCKMANN (*waving the letter*) Well, now the town will have something new to talk about, I can tell you!

BILLING Something new?

MRS. STOCKMANN What is this?

DR. STOCKMANN A great discovery, Katherine.

HOVSTAD Really?

MRS. STOCKMANN A discovery of yours?

DR. STOCKMANN A discovery of mine. (*walks up and down*) Just let them come saying, as usual, that it is all fancy and a crazy man's imagination! But they will be careful what they say this time, I can tell you!

PETRA But, father, tell us what it is.

DR. STOCKMANN Yes, yes—only give me time, and you shall know all about it. If only I had Peter here now! It just shows how we men

> How does Petra's stand represent the modern liberated viewpoint? Ultimately, we will discover that holding such beliefs will be held against Petra.

> At the end of the play, Petra's early dream will be recalled for its devastating irony.

> Captain Horster's offer to loan out his big house with an "immense dining-room" will be vital to the plot of the play later.

> Ibsen subtly conveys a sensitivity on Dr. Stockmann's part concerning his reputation among certain townspeople, including his brother the Mayor.

AN ENEMY OF THE PEOPLE 129

can go about forming our judgments, when in reality we are as blind as any moles—

HOVSTAD What are you driving at, Doctor?

DR. STOCKMANN *(standing still by the table)* Isn't it the universal opinion that our town is a healthy spot?

HOVSTAD Certainly.

DR. STOCKMANN Quite an unusually healthy spot, in fact—a place that deserves to be recommended in the warmest possible manner either for invalids or for people who are well—

MRS. STOCKMANN Yes, but my dear Thomas—

DR. STOCKMANN And we have been recommending it and praising it—I have written and written, both in the "Messenger" and in pamphlets—

HOVSTAD Well, what then?

DR. STOCKMANN And the Baths—we have called them the "main artery of the town's life-blood," the "nerve-centre of our town," and the devil knows what else—

BILLING "The town's pulsating heart" was the expression I once used on an important occasion—

DR. STOCKMANN Quite so. Well, do you know what they really are, these great, splendid, much praised Baths, that have cost so much money—do you know what they are?

HOVSTAD No, what are they?

MRS. STOCKMANN Yes, what are they?

DR. STOCKMANN The whole place is a pesthouse!

PETRA The Baths, father?

MRS. STOCKMANN *(at the same time)* Our Baths!

HOVSTAD But, Doctor—

BILLING Absolutely incredible!

DR. STOCKMANN The whole Bath establishment is a whited, poisoned sepulchre, I tell you—the gravest possible danger to the public health! All the nastiness up at Mölledal, all that stinking filth, is infecting the water in the conduit-pipes leading to the reservoir; and the same cursed, filthy poison oozes out on the shore too—

HORSTER Where the bathing-place is?

DR. STOCKMANN Just there.

HOVSTAD How do you come to be so certain of all this, Doctor?

DR. STOCKMANN I have investigated the matter most conscientiously. For a long time past I have suspected something of the kind. Last year we had some very strange cases of illness among the visitors—typhoid cases, and cases of gastric fever—

MRS. STOCKMANN Yes, that is quite true.

DR. STOCKMANN At the time, we supposed the visitors had been infected before they came; but later on, in the winter, I began to have a different opinion; and so I set myself to examine the water, as well as I could.

Here Ibsen presents one of the basic issues of the play: the fallibility of the vast majority. How does this point stand out?

Stockmann's surprise announcement instantly injects a powerful complicating factor in the action.

MRS. STOCKMANN Then that is what you have been so busy with?

DR. STOCKMANN Indeed I have been busy, Katherine. But here I had none of the necessary scientific apparatus; so I sent samples, both of the drinking-water and of the sea-water, up to the University, to have an accurate analysis made by a chemist.

HOVSTAD And have you got that?

DR. STOCKMANN (showing him the letter) Here it is! It proves the presence of decomposing organic matter in the water—it is full of infusoria. The water is absolutely dangerous to use, either internally or externally.

MRS. STOCKMANN What a mercy you discovered it in time.

DR. STOCKMANN You may well say so.

HOVSTAD And what do you propose to do now, Doctor?

DR. STOCKMANN To see the matter put right—naturally.

HOVSTAD Can that be done?

DR. STOCKMANN It must be done. Otherwise the Baths will be absolutely useless and wasted. But we need not anticipate that; I have a very clear idea what we shall have to do.

MRS. STOCKMANN But why have you kept this all so secret, dear?

DR. STOCKMANN Do you suppose I was going to run about the town gossiping about it, before I had absolute proof? No, thank you. I am not such a fool.

PETRA Still, you might have told us—

DR. STOCKMANN Not a living soul. But to-morrow you may run round to the old Badger—

MRS. STOCKMANN Oh, Thomas! Thomas!

DR. STOCKMANN Well, to your grandfather, then. The old boy will have something to be astonished at! I know he thinks I am cracked—and there are lots of other people think so too, I have noticed. But now these good folks shall see—they shall just see—! (walks about, rubbing his hands) There will be a nice upset in the town, Katherine; you can't imagine what it will be. All the conduit-pipes will have to be relaid.

HOVSTAD (getting up) All the conduit-pipes—?

DR. STOCKMANN Yes, of course. The intake is too low down; it will have to be lifted to a position much higher up.

PETRA Then you were right after all.

DR. STOCKMANN Ah, you remember, Petra—I wrote opposing the plans before the work was begun. But at that time no one would listen to me. Well, I am going to let them have it, now! Of course I have prepared a report for the Baths Committee; I have had it ready for a week, and was only waiting for this to come. (shows the letter) Now it shall go off at once. (goes into his room and comes back with some papers) Look at that! Four closely written sheets!—and the letter shall go with them. Give me a bit of paper, Katherine—something to wrap them up in. That will do! Now give it to—to—(stamps his foot)—what the deuce is her name?—give it to the maid, and tell her to take it at once to the Mayor.

Can one fault the doctor's approach while tracking down the illnesses associated with the Baths? Why?

Infusoria are a variety of minute, microscopic animal and vegetative organisms which result from decaying organic matter.

Stockmann responds openly and without any hesitation, strictly in light of scientific considerations.

What dimension of Dr. Stockmann's personality shows itself at this point?

Is there another motive behind Dr. Stockmann's decision to investigate the Baths? To what extent might his ego be involved in the matter of the correct placement of the conduits?

Mrs. Stockmann takes the packet and goes out through the dining-room.

PETRA What do you think uncle Peter will say, father?

DR. STOCKMANN What is there for him to say? I should think he would be very glad that such an important truth has been brought to light.

> Here, as elsewhere, the doctor misjudges his brother.

HOVSTAD Will you let me print a short note about your discovery in the "Messenger?"

DR. STOCKMANN I shall be very much obliged if you will.

HOVSTAD It is very desirable that the public should be informed of it without delay.

DR. STOCKMANN Certainly.

MRS. STOCKMANN *(coming back)* She has just gone with it.

BILLING Upon my soul, Doctor, you are going to be the foremost man in the town!

DR. STOCKMANN *(walking about happily)* Nonsense! As a matter of fact I have done nothing more than my duty. I have only made a lucky find—that's all. Still, all the same—

BILLING Hovstad, don't you think the town ought to give Dr. Stockmann some sort of testimonial?

HOVSTAD I will suggest it, anyway.

BILLING And I will speak to Aslaksen about it.

DR. STOCKMANN No, my good friends, don't let us have any of that nonsense. I won't hear of anything of the kind. And if the Baths Committee should think of voting me an increase of salary, I will not accept it. Do you hear, Katherine?—I won't accept it.

> How are Stockmann's ego and naivete underscored here?

MRS. STOCKMANN You are quite right, Thomas.

PETRA *(lifting her glass)* Your health, father!

HOVSTAD and BILLING Your health, Doctor! Good health!

HORSTER *(touches glasses with Dr. Stockmann)* I hope it will bring you nothing but good luck.

DR. STOCKMANN Thank you, thank you, my dear fellows! I feel tremendously happy! It is a splendid thing for a man to be able to feel that he has done a service to his native town and to his fellow-citizens. Hurrah, Katherine! *(He puts his arms round her and whirls her round and round, while she protests with laughing cries. They all laugh, clap their hands, and cheer the Doctor. The boys put their heads in at the door to see what is going on.)*

> Dr. Stockmann's pleased expressions at the end of Act I will return to haunt him with bitter irony.

ACT II

SCENE—*The same. The door into the dining-room is shut. It is morning. Mrs. Stockmann, with a sealed letter in her hand, comes in from the dining-room, goes to the door of the Doctor's study, and peeps in.*

MRS. STOCKMANN Are you in, Thomas?

DR. STOCKMANN *(from within his room)* Yes, I have just come in. *(comes into the room)* What is it?

MRS. STOCKMANN A letter from your brother.

DR. STOCKMANN Aha, let us see! *(opens the letter and reads)* "I return herewith the manuscript you sent me"—*(reads on in a low murmur)* Hm!—

MRS. STOCKMANN What does he say?

DR. STOCKMANN *(putting the papers in his pocket)* Oh, he only writes that he will come up here himself about midday.

MRS. STOCKMANN Well, try and remember to be at home this time.

DR. STOCKMANN That will be all right; I have got through all my morning visits.

MRS. STOCKMANN I am extremely curious to know how he takes it.

DR. STOCKMANN You will see he won't like it's having been I, and not he, that made the discovery.

MRS. STOCKMANN Aren't you a little nervous about that?

DR. STOCKMANN Oh, he really will be pleased enough, you know. But, at the same time, Peter is so confoundedly afraid of anyone's doing any service to the town except himself.

MRS. STOCKMANN I will tell you what, Thomas—you should be good natured, and share the credit of this with him. Couldn't you make out that it was he who set you on the scent of this discovery?

DR. STOCKMANN I am quite willing. If only I can get the thing set right. I—

Morten Kiil puts his head in through the door leading from the hall, looks round in an enquiring manner, and chuckles.

MORTEN KIIL *(slyly)* Is it—is it true?

MRS. STOCKMANN *(going to the door)* Father!—is it you?

DR. STOCKMANN Ah, Mr. Kiil—good morning, good morning!

MRS. STOCKMANN But come along in.

MORTEN KIIL If it is true, I will; if not, I am off.

DR. STOCKMANN If what is true?

MORTEN KIIL This tale about the water supply. Is it true?

DR. STOCKMANN Certainly it is true. But how did you come to hear it?

MORTEN KIIL *(coming in)* Petra ran in on her way to the school—

DR. STOCKMANN Did she?

MORTEN KIIL Yes; and she declares that—. I thought she was only making a fool of me, but it isn't like Petra to do that.

DR. STOCKMANN Of course not. How could you imagine such a thing!

MORTEN KIIL Oh well, it is better never to trust anybody; you may find you have been made a fool of before you know where you are. But it is really true, all the same?

DR. STOCKMANN You can depend upon it that it is true. Won't you sit down? *(settles him on the couch)* Isn't it a real bit of luck for the town—

The complications of the plot are presented at the opening of Act II. What new factors suggest that fresh ordeals lie ahead for Dr. Stockmann? Notice how the play's overall mood alters substantially throughout this act.

Note how Ibsen builds anticipation as part of the play's development.

To what extent are the brothers alike in this respect?

Why does Kiil find it difficult to believe the news about the despoiled waters?

In the Stockmann home, from a production with Florence Eldridge (left) as Mrs. Stockmann, and Frederic March (right) as Dr. Stockmann.

MORTEN KIIL (*suppressing his laughter*) A bit of luck for the town?

DR. STOCKMANN Yes, that I made the discovery in good time.

MORTEN KIIL (*as before*) Yes, yes, yes!—But I should never have thought you the sort of man to pull your own brother's leg like this!

DR. STOCKMANN Pull his leg!

MRS. STOCKMANN Really, father dear—

MORTEN KIIL (*resting his hands and his chin on the handle of his stick and winking slyly at the Doctor*) Let me see, what was the story? Some kind of beast that had got into the water-pipes, wasn't it?

DR. STOCKMANN Infusoria—yes.

MORTEN KIIL And a lot of these beasts had got in, according to Petra—a tremendous lot.

DR. STOCKMANN Certainly; hundreds of thousands of them, probably.

MORTEN KIIL But no one can see them—isn't that so?

DR. STOCKMANN Yes; you can't see them.

MORTEN KIIL (*with a quiet chuckle*) Damme—it's the finest story I have ever heard!

DR. STOCKMANN What do you mean?

What is the nature of Kiil's ridicule of the Doctor's findings and proposal? How does Kiil judge the truth of a situation? On what basis?

134   HENRIK IBSEN

MORTEN KIIL But you will never get the Mayor to believe a thing like that.

DR. STOCKMANN We shall see.

MORTEN KIIL Do you think he will be fool enough to—?

DR. STOCKMANN I hope the whole town will be fools enough.

MORTEN KIIL The whole town! Well, it wouldn't be a bad thing. It would just serve them right, and teach them a lesson. They think themselves so much cleverer than we old fellows. They hounded me out of the council; they did, I tell you—they hounded me out. Now they shall pay for it. You pull their legs too, Thomas!

DR. STOCKMANN Really, I—

MORTEN KIIL You pull their legs! *(gets up)* If you can work it so that the Mayor and his friends all swallow the same bait, I will give ten pounds to a charity—like a shot!

DR. STOCKMANN That is very kind of you.

MORTEN KIIL Yes, I haven't got much money to throw away, I can tell you; but if you can work this, I will give five pounds to a charity at Christmas.

Hovstad comes in by the hall door.

HOVSTAD Good morning! *(stops)* Oh, I beg your pardon—

DR. STOCKMANN Not at all; come in.

MORTEN KIIL *(with another chuckle)* Oho!—is he in this too?

HOVSTAD What do you mean?

DR. STOCKMANN Certainly he is.

MORTEN KIIL I might have known it! It must get into the papers. You know how to do it, Thomas! Set your wits to work. Now I must go.

DR. STOCKMANN Won't you stay a little while?

MORTEN KIIL No, I must be off now. You keep up this game for all it is worth; you won't repent it, I'm damned if you will!

He goes out; Mrs. Stockmann follows him into the hall.

DR. STOCKMANN *(laughing)* Just imagine—the old chap doesn't believe a word of all this about the water supply.

HOVSTAD Oh that was it, then?

DR. STOCKMANN Yes, that was what we were talking about. Perhaps it is the same thing that brings you here?

HOVSTAD Yes, it is. Can you spare me a few minutes, Doctor?

DR. STOCKMANN As long as you like, my dear fellow.

HOVSTAD Have you heard from the Mayor yet?

DR. STOCKMANN Not yet. He is coming here later.

HOVSTAD I have given the matter a great deal of thought since last night.

DR. STOCKMANN Well?

HOVSTAD From your point of view, as a doctor and a man of science,

---

Kiil understands the situation and the Mayor's probable response far better than the doctor. Thus Kiil is able to predict future events more accurately.

Morten Kiil's arrival introduces another dimension in the play's development. What conflict is caused between Kiil and who else?

What kind of "game" does Kiil believe Dr. Stockmann is playing now? Does the fact that new city elections are pending help to clarify the matter?

Do you think that Hovstad will treat the

AN ENEMY OF THE PEOPLE   135

this affair of the water-supply is an isolated matter. I mean, you do not realise that it involves a great many other things.

DR. STOCKMANN How, do you mean?—Let us sit down, my dear fellow. No, sit here on the couch.

(*Hovstad sits down on the couch, Dr. Stockmann on a chair on the other side of the table.*) Now then. You mean that—?

HOVSTAD You said yesterday that the pollution of the water was due to impurities in the soil.

DR. STOCKMANN Yes, unquestionably it is due to that poisonous morass up at Mölledal.

HOVSTAD Begging your pardon, doctor, I fancy it is due to quite another morass altogether.

DR. STOCKMANN What morass?

HOVSTAD The morass that the whole life of our town is built on and is rotting in.

DR. STOCKMANN What the deuce are you driving at, Hovstad?

HOVSTAD The whole of the town's interests have, little by little, got into the hands of a pack of officials.

DR. STOCKMANN Oh, come!—they are not all officials.

HOVSTAD No, but those that are not officials are at any rate the officials' friends and adherents; it is the wealthy folk, the old families in the town, that have got us entirely in their hands.

DR. STOCKMANN Yes, but after all they are men of ability and knowledge.

HOVSTAD Did they show any ability or knowledge when they laid the conduit-pipes where they are now?

DR. STOCKMANN No, of course that was a great piece of stupidity on their part. But that is going to be set right now.

HOVSTAD Do you think that will be all such plain sailing?

DR. STOCKMANN Plain sailing or no, it has got to be done, anyway.

HOVSTAD Yes, provided the press takes up the question.

DR. STOCKMANN I don't think that will be necessary, my dear fellow, I am certain my brother—

HOVSTAD Excuse me, doctor; I feel bound to tell you I am inclined to take the matter up.

DR. STOCKMANN In the paper?

HOVSTAD Yes. When I took over the "People's Messenger" my idea was to break up this ring of self-opinionated old fossils who had got hold of all the influence.

DR. STOCKMANN But you know you told me yourself what the result had been; you nearly ruined your paper.

HOVSTAD Yes, at the time we were obliged to climb down a peg or two, it is quite true; because there was a danger of the whole project of the Baths coming to nothing if they failed us. But now the scheme has been carried through, and we can dispense with these grand gentlemen.

---

water pollution as a medical and scientific problem which requires remedy? Why?

Hovstad clearly has his own reasons for supporting the doctor, quite aside from any altruism.

Is Stockmann trying to be fair in evaluating the crisis of the Baths at this moment in the plot? How can we tell?

The complications in the plot become more complex when Hovstad announces his intention to use the issue of the Baths for his own purposes. What does he propose to do regarding the paper he edits?

DR. STOCKMANN Dispense with them, yes; but we owe them a great debt of gratitude.

HOVSTAD That shall be recognised ungrudgingly. But a journalist of my democratic tendencies cannot let such an opportunity as this slip. The bubble of official infallibility must be pricked. This superstition must be destroyed, like any other.

Why could the term "opportunistic" be applicable to Hovstad here?

DR. STOCKMANN I am whole-heartedly with you in that, Mr. Hovstad; if it is a superstition, away with it!

Does it make any difference what a crusader's motives may be, as long as he advocates reform?

HOVSTAD I should be very reluctant to bring the Mayor into it, because he is your brother. But I am sure you will agree with me that truth should be the first consideration.

DR. STOCKMANN That goes without saying. *(with sudden emphasis)* Yes, but—but—

HOVSTAD You must not misjudge me. I am neither more self-interested nor more ambitious than most men.

DR. STOCKMANN My dear fellow—who suggests anything of the kind?

HOVSTAD I am of humble origin, as you know; and that has given me opportunities of knowing what is the most crying need in the humbler ranks of life. It is that they should be allowed some part in the direction of public affairs, Doctor. That is what will develop their faculties and intelligence and self respect—

How do Hovstad's theories fit in with modern ideas of participatory democracy?

DR. STOCKMANN I quite appreciate that.

HOVSTAD Yes—and in my opinion a journalist incurs a heavy responsibility if he neglects a favourable opportunity of emancipating the masses—the humble and oppressed. I know well enough that in exalted circles I shall be called an agitator, and all that sort of thing; but they may call what they like. If only my conscience doesn't reproach me, then—

DR. STOCKMANN Quite right! Quite right, Mr. Hovstad. But all the same—devil take it! *(A knock is heard at the door.)* Come in!

Dr. Stockmann is faced with a dilemma in Hovstad's determination to move the issue of Baths out of the medical arena into politics.

Aslaksen appears at the door. He is poorly but decently dressed, in black, with a slightly crumpled white neckcloth; he wears gloves and has a felt hat in his hand.

ASLAKSEN *(bowing)* Excuse my taking the liberty, Doctor—

DR. STOCKMANN *(getting up)* Ah, it is you, Aslaksen!

ASLAKSEN Yes, Doctor.

HOVSTAD *(standing up)* Is it me you want, Aslaksen?

ASLAKSEN No, I didn't know I should find you here. No, it was the Doctor I—

Dramatic irony is a condition of affairs in a play that is the reverse of what some of the participants think. What is the dramatic irony here?

DR. STOCKMANN I am quite at your service. What is it?

ASLAKSEN Is what I heard from Mr. Billing true, sir—that you mean to improve our water-supply?

DR. STOCKMANN Yes, for the Baths.

ASLAKSEN Quite so, I understand. Well, I have come to say that I will back that up by every means in my power.

HOVSTAD *(to the Doctor)* You see!

AN ENEMY OF THE PEOPLE 137

DR. STOCKMANN I shall be very grateful to you, but—

ASLAKSEN Because it may be no bad thing to have us small tradesmen at your back. We form, as it were, a compact majority in the town—if we choose. And it is always a good thing to have the majority with you, Doctor.

DR. STOCKMANN That is undeniably true; but I confess I don't see why such unusual precautions should be necessary in this case. It seems to me that such a plain, straightforward thing—

ASLAKSEN Oh, it may be very desirable, all the same. I know our local authorities so well; officials are not generally very ready to act on proposals that come from other people. That is why I think it would not be at all amiss if we made a little demonstration.

HOVSTAD That's right.

DR. STOCKMANN Demonstration, did you say? What on earth are you going to make a demonstration about?

ASLAKSEN We shall proceed with the greatest moderation, Doctor. Moderation is always my aim; it is the greatest virtue in a citizen—at least, I think so.

DR. STOCKMANN It is well known to be a characteristic of yours, Mr. Aslaksen.

ASLAKSEN Yes, I think I may pride myself on that. And this matter of the water-supply is of the greatest importance to us small tradesmen. The Baths promise to be a regular gold-mine for the town. We shall all make our living out of them, especially those of us who are householders. That is why we will back up the project as strongly as possible. And as I am at present Chairman of the Householders' Association—

DR. STOCKMANN Yes—?

ASLAKSEN And, what is more, local secretary of the Temperance Society—you know, sir, I suppose, that I am a worker in the temperance cause?

DR. STOCKMANN Of course, of course.

ASLAKSEN Well, you can understand that I come into contact with a great many people. And as I have the reputation of a temperate and law-abiding citizen—like yourself, Doctor—I have a certain influence in the town, a little bit of power, if I may be allowed to say so.

DR. STOCKMANN I know that quite well, Mr. Aslaksen.

ASLAKSEN So you see it would be an easy matter for me to set on foot some testimonial, if necessary.

DR. STOCKMANN A testimonial?

ASLAKSEN Yes, some kind of an address of thanks from the townsmen for your share in a matter of such importance to the community. I need scarcely say that it would have to be drawn up with the greatest regard to moderation, so as not to offend the authorities—who, after all, have the reins in their hands. If we pay strict attention to that, no one can take it amiss, I should think!

HOVSTAD Well, and even supposing they didn't like it—

What new element within the community has joined Dr. Stockmann?

Does Aslaksen understand the dynamics of political action any better than Dr. Stockmann? How do we know by what Aslaksen proposes?

Like Hovstad earlier, Aslaksen indirectly shows his true colors here.

Temperance groups advocate the abolishment of hard liquors. Why would Aslaksen's involvement in such a cause be perfectly suited to his character, as it has been developed so far?

to set on foot means "to get something started"

ASLAKSEN No, no, no; there must be no discourtesy to the authorities, Mr. Hovstad. It is no use falling foul of those upon whom our welfare so closely depends. I have done that in my time, and no good ever comes of it. But no one can take exception to a reasonable and frank expression of a citizen's views.

DR. STOCKMANN (shaking him by the hand) I can't tell you, dear Mr. Aslaksen, how extremely pleased I am to find such hearty support among my fellow-citizens. I am delighted—delighted! Now, you will take a small glass of sherry, eh?

ASLAKSEN No, thank you; I never drink alcohol of that kind.

DR. STOCKMANN Well, what do you say to a glass of beer, then?

ASLAKSEN Nor that either, thank you, Doctor. I never drink anything as early as this. I am going into town now to talk this over with one or two householders, and prepare the ground.

DR. STOCKMANN It is tremendously kind of you, Mr. Aslaksen; but I really cannot understand the necessity for all these precautions. It seems to me that the thing should go of itself.

ASLAKSEN The authorities are somewhat slow to move, Doctor. Far be it from me to seem to blame them—

HOVSTAD We are going to stir them up in the paper to-morrow, Aslaksen.

ASLAKSEN But not violently, I trust, Mr. Hovstad. Proceed with moderation, or you will do nothing with them. You may take my advice; I have gathered my experience in the school of life. Well, I must say good-bye, Doctor. You know now that we small tradesmen are at your back at all events, like a solid wall. You have the compact majority on your side, Doctor.

DR. STOCKMANN I am very much obliged, dear Mr. Aslaksen. (shakes hands with him) Good-bye, good-bye.

ASLAKSEN Are you going my way, towards the printing-office, Mr. Hovstad?

HOVSTAD I will come later; I have something to settle up first.

ASLAKSEN Very well. (Bows and goes out; Stockmann follows him into the hall.)

HOVSTAD (as Stockmann comes in again) Well, what do you think of that, Doctor? Don't you think it is high time we stirred a little life into all this slackness and vacillation and cowardice?

DR. STOCKMANN Are you referring to Aslaksen?

HOVSTAD Yes, I am. He is one of those who are floundering in a bog—decent enough fellow though he may be, otherwise. And most of the people here are in just the same case—see-sawing and edging first to one side and then to the other, so overcome with caution and scruple that they never dare to take any decided step.

DR. STOCKMANN Yes, but Aslaksen seemed to me so thoroughly well-intentioned.

HOVSTAD There is one thing I esteem higher than that; and that is for a man to be self-reliant and sure of himself.

DR. STOCKMANN I think you are perfectly right there.

What clues does Aslaksen offer regarding his past as a political activist? Along the political spectrum, where does he stand at the time of the play's events?

What exactly does Aslaksen mean by the "compact majority" he insists is supporting the doctor? It is a vital expression, used many times in the play.

A good deal of backbiting and hypocrisy surface at this point. Who manifests these traits, and how are they reflected?

HOVSTAD That is why I want to seize this opportunity, and try if I cannot manage to put a little virility into these well-intentioned people for once. The idol of Authority must be shattered in this town. This gross and inexcusable blunder about the water-supply must be brought home to the mind of every municipal voter.

DR. STOCKMANN Very well; if you are of opinion that it is for the good of the community, so be it. But not until I have had a talk with my brother.

HOVSTAD Anyway, I will get a leading article ready; and if the Mayor refuses to take the matter up—

DR. STOCKMANN How can you suppose such a thing possible?

HOVSTAD It is conceivable. And in that case—

DR. STOCKMANN In that case I promise you—. Look here, in that case you may print my report—every word of it.

HOVSTAD May I? Have I your word for it?

DR. STOCKMANN *(giving him the MS.)* Here it is; take it with you. It can do no harm for you to read it through, and you can give it back to me later on.

HOVSTAD Good, good! That is what I will do. And now good-bye, Doctor.

DR. STOCKMANN Good-bye, good-bye. You will see everything will run quite smoothly, Mr. Hovstad—quite smoothly.

HOVSTAD Hm!—we shall see. *(bows and goes out)*

DR. STOCKMANN *(opens the dining-room door and looks in)* Katherine! Oh, you are back, Petra?

PETRA *(coming in)* Yes, I have just come from the school.

MRS. STOCKMANN *(coming in)* Has he not been here yet?

DR. STOCKMANN Peter? No. But I have had a long talk with Hovstad. He is quite excited about my discovery. I find it has a much wider bearing than I at first imagined. And he has put his paper at my disposal if necessity should arise.

MRS. STOCKMANN Do you think it will?

DR. STOCKMANN Not for a moment. But at all events it makes me feel proud to know that I have the liberal-minded independent press on my side. Yes, and—just imagine—I have had a visit from the Chairman of the Householders' Association!

MRS. STOCKMANN Oh! What did he want?

DR. STOCKMANN To offer me his support too. They will support me in a body if it should be necessary. Katherine—do you know what I have got behind me?

MRS. STOCKMANN Behind you? No, what have you got behind you?

DR. STOCKMANN The compact majority.

MRS. STOCKMANN Really? Is that a good thing for you, Thomas?

DR. STOCKMANN I should think it was a good thing. *(walks up and down rubbing his hands)* By Jove, it's a fine thing to feel this bond of brotherhood between oneself and one's fellow citizens!

How are we to interpret the fact that Stockmann agrees to bring the issue before the community only after he speaks with his brother the Mayor?

The doctor's naivete is revealed here. Is there, in fact, a "bond of brotherhood" in what Hovstad and Aslaksen

PETRA And to be able to do so much that is good and useful, father!

DR. STOCKMANN And for one's own native town into the bargain, my child!

MRS. STOCKMANN That was a ring at the bell.

DR. STOCKMANN It must be he, then. *(A knock is heard at the door.)* Come in!

PETER STOCKMANN *(comes in from the hall)* Good morning.

DR. STOCKMANN Glad to see you, Peter!

MRS. STOCKMANN Good morning, Peter. How are you?

PETER STOCKMANN So so, thank you. *(to Dr. Stockmann)* I received from you yesterday, after office hours, a report dealing with the condition of the water at the Baths.

DR. STOCKMANN Yes. Have you read it?

PETER STOCKMANN Yes, I have.

DR. STOCKMANN And what have you to say to it?

PETER STOCKMANN *(with a sidelong glance)* Hm!—

MRS. STOCKMANN Come along, Petra. *(She and Petra go into the room on the left.)*

PETER STOCKMANN *(after a pause)* Was it necessary to make all these investigations behind my back?

DR. STOCKMANN Yes, because until I was absolutely certain about it—

PETER STOCKMANN Then you mean that you are absolutely certain now?

DR. STOCKMANN Surely you are convinced of that.

PETER STOCKMANN Is it your intention to bring this document before the Baths Committee as a sort of official communication?

DR. STOCKMANN Certainly. Something must be done in the matter—and that quickly.

PETER STOCKMANN As usual, you employ violent expressions in your report. You say, among other things, that what we offer visitors in our Baths is a permanent supply of poison.

DR. STOCKMANN Well, can you describe it any other way, Peter? Just think—water that is poisonous, whether you drink it or bathe in it! And this we offer to the poor sick folk who come to us trustfully and pay us at an exorbitant rate to be made well again!

PETER STOCKMANN And your reasoning leads you to this conclusion, that we must build a sewer to draw off the alleged impurities from Mölledal and must re-lay the water-conduits.

DR. STOCKMANN Yes. Do you see any other way out of it? I don't.

PETER STOCKMANN I made a pretext this morning to go and see the town engineer, and, as if only half seriously, broached the subject of these proposals as a thing we might perhaps have to take under consideration some time later on.

DR. STOCKMANN Some time later on!

---

have proposed? Have they misrepresented the situation, or has Dr. Stockmann simply misinterpreted them?

What does Peter imply when he states that he received the report "after office hours"?

Why should we expect the Mayor to be displeased by the report?

The fact that the Mayor went first to a civil engineer to determine cost, rather than to a health expert, illuminates his character. Why?

PETER STOCKMANN He smiled at what he considered to be my extravagance, naturally. Have you taken the trouble to consider what your proposed alterations would cost? According to the information I obtained, the expenses would probably mount up to fifteen or twenty thousand pounds.

DR. STOCKMANN Would it cost so much?

PETER STOCKMANN Yes; and the worst part of it would be that the work would take at least two years.

DR. STOCKMANN Two years? Two whole years?

PETER STOCKMANN At least. And what are we to do with the Baths in the meantime? Close them? Indeed we should be obliged to. And do you suppose any one would come near the place after it had got about that the water was dangerous?

Here, for the first time, the full impact of the play's theme is expressed: is monetary gain to supersede concern for human life?

DR. STOCKMANN Yes but, Peter, that is what it is.

PETER STOCKMANN And all this at this juncture—just as the Baths are beginning to be known. There are other towns in the neighbourhood with qualifications to attract visitors for bathing purposes. Don't you suppose they would immediately strain every nerve to divert the entire stream of strangers to themselves? Unquestionably they would; and then where should we be? We should probably have to abandon the whole thing, which has cost us so much money—and then you would have ruined your native town.

The Mayor's biased diagnosis of affairs places the brunt of blame and cost on his brother's shoulders.

DR. STOCKMANN I—should have ruined—!

PETER STOCKMANN It is simply and solely through the Baths that the town has before it any future worth mentioning. You know that just as well as I.

DR. STOCKMANN But what do you think ought to be done, then?

PETER STOCKMANN Your report has not convinced me that the condition of the water at the Baths is as bad as you represent it to be.

DR. STOCKMANN I tell you it is even worse!—or at all events it will be in summer, when the warm weather comes.

PETER STOCKMANN As I said, I believe you exaggerate the matter considerably. A capable physician ought to know what measures to take—he ought to be capable of preventing injurious influences or of remedying them if they become obviously persistent.

How does the Mayor start to undermine his brother's credibility as a medical man?

DR. STOCKMANN Well? What more?

PETER STOCKMANN The water supply for the Baths is now an established fact, and in consequence must be treated as such. But probably the Committee, at its discretion, will not be disinclined to consider the question of how far it might be possible to introduce certain improvements consistently with a reasonable expenditure.

How would one translate into more direct words the Mayor's political double talk here? Analyze what he genuinely means *as contrasted to what he* says.

DR. STOCKMANN And do you suppose that I will have anything to do with such a piece of trickery as that?

PETER STOCKMANN Trickery!!

DR. STOCKMANN Yes, it would be a trick—a fraud, a lie, a downright crime towards the public, towards the whole community!

PETER STOCKMANN I have not, as I remarked before, been able to convince myself that there is actually any imminent danger.

DR. STOCKMANN You have! It is impossible that you should not be convinced. I know I have represented the facts absolutely truthfully and fairly. And you know it very well, Peter, only you won't acknowledge it. It was owing to your action that both the Baths and the water-conduits were built where they are; and that is what you won't acknowledge—that damnable blunder of yours. Pooh!—do you suppose I don't see through you?

PETER STOCKMANN And even if that were true? If I perhaps guard my reputation somewhat anxiously, it is in the interests of the town. Without moral authority I am powerless to direct public affairs as seems, to my judgment, to be best for the common good. And on that account—and for various other reasons too—it appears to me to be a matter of importance that your report should not be delivered to the Committee. In the interests of the public, you must withhold it. Then, later on, I will raise the question and we will do our best, privately; but nothing of this unfortunate affair—not a single word of it—must come to the ears of the public.

This is an important admission on Peter's part because it indicates his line of self-protective thinking. How does he view the concept of a public leader?

DR. STOCKMANN I am afraid you will not be able to prevent that now, my dear Peter.

PETER STOCKMANN It must and shall be prevented.

Peter Stockmann's use of the term "privately" makes appropriate our use of the term "white wash" to his proposal.

DR. STOCKMANN It is no use, I tell you. There are too many people that know about it.

PETER STOCKMANN That know about it? Who? Surely you don't mean those fellows on the "People's Messenger"?

DR. STOCKMANN Yes, they know. The liberal-minded independent press is going to see that you do your duty.

The doctor evidently has taken the newspapermen at their word. What does this tell us of Ibsen's characterization of Dr. Stockmann?

PETER STOCKMANN (*after a short pause*) You are an extraordinarily independent man, Thomas. Have you given no thought to the consequences this may have for yourself?

DR. STOCKMANN Consequences?—for me?

PETER STOCKMANN For you and yours, yes.

DR. STOCKMANN What the deuce do you mean?

In your opinion, has the doctor thoroughly analyzed the situation? Why?

PETER STOCKMANN I believe I have always behaved in a brotherly way to you—have always been ready to oblige or to help you?

DR. STOCKMANN Yes, you have, and I am grateful to you for it.

PETER STOCKMANN There is no need. Indeed, to some extent I was forced to do so—for my own sake. I always hoped that, if I helped to improve your financial position, I should be able to keep some check on you.

DR. STOCKMANN What!! Then it was only for your own sake—!

PETER STOCKMANN Up to a certain point, yes. It is painful for a man in an official position to have his nearest relative compromising himself time after time.

DR. STOCKMANN And do you consider that I do that?

PETER STOCKMANN Yes, unfortunately, you do, without even being aware of it. You have a restless, pugnacious, rebellious disposition. And then there is that disastrous propensity of yours to want to write about every sort of possible and impossible thing. The moment an idea comes into your head, you must needs go and write a newspaper article or a whole pamphlet about it.

DR. STOCKMANN Well, but is it not the duty of a citizen to let the public share in any new ideas he may have?

PETER STOCKMANN Oh, the public doesn't require any new ideas. The public is best served by the good, old-established ideas it already has.

DR. STOCKMANN And that is your honest opinion?

PETER STOCKMANN Yes, and for once I must talk frankly to you. Hitherto I have tried to avoid doing so, because I know how irritable you are; but now I must tell you the truth, Thomas. You have no conception what an amount of harm you do yourself by your impetuosity. You complain of the authorities, you even complain of the government—you are always pulling them to pieces; you insist that you have been neglected and persecuted. But what else can such a cantankerous man as you expect?

DR. STOCKMANN What next! Cantankerous, am I?

PETER STOCKMANN Yes, Thomas, you are an extremely cantankerous man to work with—I know that to my cost. You disregard everything that you ought to have consideration for. You seem completely to forget that it is me you have to thank for your appointment here as medical officer of the Baths—

Aside from the economic factors, what other more personal issues are at stake in this confrontation between the brothers? Had we been forewarned of this possibility earlier? Where?

DR. STOCKMANN I was entitled to it as a matter of course!—I and nobody else! I was the first person to see that the town could be made into a flourishing watering-place, and I was the only one who saw it at that time. I had to fight single-handed in support of the idea for many years; and I wrote and wrote—

PETER STOCKMANN Undoubtedly. But things were not ripe for the scheme then—though, of course, you could not judge of that in your out-of-the-way corner up north. But as soon as the opportune moment came I—and the others—took the matter into our hands—

DR. STOCKMANN Yes, and made this mess of all my beautiful plan. It is pretty obvious now what clever fellows you were!

PETER STOCKMANN To my mind the whole thing only seems to mean that you are seeking another outlet for your combativeness. You want to pick a quarrel with your superiors—an old habit of yours. You cannot put up with any authority over you. You look askance at anyone who occupies a superior official position; you regard him as a personal enemy, and then any stick is good enough to beat him with. But now I have called your attention to the fact that the town's interests are at stake—and, incidently, my own too. And therefore I must tell you, Thomas, that you will find me inexorable with regard to what I am about to require you to do.

Do you think the Mayor's arguments are fair and accurate? Why?

DR. STOCKMANN And what is that?

PETER STOCKMANN As you have been so indiscreet as to speak of this delicate matter to outsiders, despite the fact that you ought to have treated it as entirely official and confidential, it is obviously impossible to hush it up now. All sorts of rumours will get about directly, and everybody who has a grudge against us will take care to embellish these rumours. So it will be necessary for you to refute them publicly.

DR. STOCKMANN I! How? I don't understand.

PETER STOCKMANN What we shall expect is that, after making further investigations, you will come to the conclusion that the matter is not by any means as dangerous or as critical as you imagined in the first instance.

DR. STOCKMANN Oho!—so that is what you expect!

PETER STOCKMANN And, what is more, we shall expect you to make public profession of your confidence in the Committee and in their readiness to consider fully and conscientiously what steps may be necessary to remedy any possible defects.

DR. STOCKMANN But you will never be able to do that by patching and tinkering at it—never! Take my word for it, Peter; I mean what I say, as deliberately and emphatically as possible.

PETER STOCKMANN As an officer under the Committee, you have no right to any individual opinion.

According to Peter, how does one define and circumscribe an individual's rights? According to the Doctor?

DR. STOCKMANN *(amazed)* No right?

PETER STOCKMANN In your official capacity, no. As a private person, it is quite another matter. But as a subordinate member of the staff of the Baths, you have no right to express any opinion which runs contrary to that of your superiors.

DR. STOCKMANN This is too much! I, a doctor, a man of science, have no right to—!

PETER STOCKMANN The matter in hand is not simply a scientific one. It is a complicated matter, and has its economic as well as its technical side.

The Mayor keeps moving the discussion back to the economic factors. Is there any evidence that Dr. Stockmann had given thought to the financial dimension of the crisis?

DR. STOCKMANN I don't care what it is! I intend to be free to express my opinion on any subject under the sun.

PETER STOCKMANN As you please—but not on any subject concerning the Baths. That we forbid.

DR. STOCKMANN *(shouting)* You forbid—! You! A pack of—

PETER STOCKMANN I forbid it—I, your chief; and if I forbid it, you have to obey.

DR. STOCKMANN *(controlling himself)* Peter—if you were not my brother—

PETRA *(throwing open the door)* Father, you shan't stand this!

MRS. STOCKMANN *(coming in after her)* Petra, Petra!

PETER STOCKMANN Oh, so you have been eavesdropping.

MRS. STOCKMANN You were talking so loud, we couldn't help—

PETRA Yes, I was listening,

PETER STOCKMANN Well, after all, I am very glad—

Note the contrast in behavior (and attitudes) between Petra and her mother.

DR. STOCKMANN *(going up to him)* You were saying something about forbidding and obeying?

PETER STOCKMANN You obliged me to take that tone with you.

AN ENEMY OF THE PEOPLE 145

DR. STOCKMANN And so I am to give myself the lie, publicly?

PETER STOCKMANN We consider it absolutely necessary that you should make some such public statement as I have asked for.

DR. STOCKMANN And if I do not—obey?

PETER STOCKMANN Then we shall publish a statement ourselves to reassure the public.

DR. STOCKMANN Very well; but in that case I shall use my pen against you. I stick to what I have said; I will show that I am right and that you are wrong. And what will you do then?

PETER STOCKMANN Then I shall not be able to prevent your being dismissed.

DR. STOCKMANN What—?

PETRA Father—dismissed!

MRS. STOCKMANN Dismissed!

PETER STOCKMANN Dismissed from the staff of the Baths. I shall be obliged to propose that you shall immediately be given notice, and shall not be allowed any further participation in the Baths' affairs.

DR. STOCKMANN You would dare to do that!

PETER STOCKMANN It is you that are playing the daring game.

PETRA Uncle, that is a shameful way to treat a man like father!

MRS. STOCKMANN Do hold your tongue, Petra!

PETER STOCKMANN *(looking at Petra)* Oh, so we volunteer our opinions already, do we? Of course. *(to Mrs. Stockmann)* Katherine, I imagine you are the most sensible person in this house. Use any influence you may have over your husband, and make him see what this will entail for his family as well as—

DR. STOCKMANN My family is my own concern and nobody else's!

PETER STOCKMANN —for his own family, as I was saying, as well as for the town he lives in.

DR. STOCKMANN It is I who have the real good of the town at heart! I want to lay bare the defects that sooner or later must come to the light of day. I will show whether I love my native town.

PETER STOCKMANN You, who in your blind obstinacy want to cut off the most important source of the town's welfare?

DR. STOCKMANN The source is poisoned, man! Are you mad? We are making our living by retailing filth and corruption! The whole of our flourishing municipal life derives its sustenance from a lie!

PETER STOCKMANN All imagination—or something even worse. The man who can throw out such offensive insinuations about his native town must be an enemy to our community.

DR. STOCKMANN *(going up to him)* Do you dare to—!

MRS. STOCKMANN *(throwing herself between them)* Thomas!

PETRA *(catching her father by the arm)* Don't lose your temper, father!

PETER STOCKMANN I will not expose myself to violence. Now you have had a warning; so reflect on what you owe to yourself and your family. Good-bye. *(goes out)*

to give oneself the lie means "to admit one's errors."

Evidently, Dr. Stockmann insists on viewing the situation strictly on the basis of ethics.

Peter Stockmann is able to induce cooperation (or submission) due to what factor?

What doctrine does Peter Stockmann advocate that Katherine teach her husband?

The credibility gap said to exist in contemporary times between government and citizens clearly has antecedents in earlier history.

Note how the term "enemy" of the masses begins to be heard in the play.

DR. STOCKMANN *(walking up and down)* Am I to put up with such treatment as this? In my own house, Katherine! What do you think of that!

MRS. STOCKMANN Indeed it is both shameful and absurd, Thomas—

PETRA If only I could give uncle a piece of my mind—

DR. STOCKMANN It is my own fault. I ought to have flown out at him long ago!—shown my teeth!—bitten! To hear him call me an enemy to our community! Me! I shall not take that lying down, upon my soul!

MRS. STOCKMANN But, dear Thomas, your brother has power on his side—

DR. STOCKMANN Yes, but I have right on mine, I tell you.

MRS. STOCKMANN Oh yes, right—right. What is the use of having right on your side if you have not got might?

PETRA Oh, mother!—how can you say such a thing!

DR. STOCKMANN Do you imagine that in a free country it is no use having right on your side? You are absurd, Katherine. Besides, haven't I got the liberal-minded, independent press to lead the way, and the compact majority behind me? That is might enough, I should think!

MRS. STOCKMANN But, good heavens, Thomas, you don't mean to—?

DR. STOCKMANN Don't mean to what?

MRS. STOCKMANN To set yourself up in opposition to your brother.

DR. STOCKMANN In God's name, what else do you suppose I should do but take my stand on right and truth?

PETRA Yes, I was just going to say that.

MRS. STOCKMANN But it won't do you any earthly good. If they won't do it, they won't.

DR. STOCKMANN Oho, Katherine! Just give me time, and you will see how I will carry the war into their camp.

MRS. STOCKMANN Yes, you carry the war into their camp, and you get your dismissal—that is what you will do.

DR. STOCKMANN In any case I shall have done my duty towards the public—towards the community. I, who am called its enemy!

MRS. STOCKMANN But towards your family, Thomas? Towards your own home! Do you think that is doing your duty towards those you have to provide for?

PETRA Ah, don't think always first of us, mother.

MRS. STOCKMANN Oh, it is easy for you to talk; you are able to shift for yourself, if need be. But remember the boys, Thomas; and think a little too of yourself, and of me—

DR. STOCKMANN I think you are out of your senses, Katherine! If I were to be such a miserable coward as to go on my knees to Peter and his damned crew, do you suppose I should ever know an hour's peace of mind all my life afterwards?

MRS. STOCKMANN I don't know anything about that; but God pre-

---

Mrs. Stockmann introduces the power/right dichotomy which later will find expression in Dr. Stockmann's pronouncements about his home community in Act IV.

How does the doctor's political innocence show itself once more at this point?

Mrs. Stockmann's basic character is revealed in interchanges such as this. How can one best describe her approach to life?

Petra most resembles which of her parents? In what ways? Is her type of young person still in evidence today? Illustrate.

Stockmann does not declare that his acts are totally altruistic. Beyond the good of the community, he seeks peace of mind and conscience as well. Is his wife impressed by that argument?

AN ENEMY OF THE PEOPLE

serve us from the peace of mind we shall have, all the same, if you go on defying him! You will find yourself again without the means of subsistence, with no income to count upon. I should think we had had enough of that in the old days. Remember that, Thomas; think what that means.

DR. STOCKMANN *(collecting himself with a struggle and clenching his fists)* And this is what this slavery can bring upon a free, honourable man! Isn't it horrible, Katherine?

MRS. STOCKMANN Yes, it is sinful to treat you so, it is perfectly true. But, good heavens, one has to put up with so much injustice in this world.—There are the boys, Thomas! Look at them! What is to become of them? Oh, no, no, you can never have the heart—.

Ejlif and Morten have come in while she was speaking, with their school books in their hands.

DR. STOCKMANN The boys—! *(recovers himself suddenly)* No, even if the whole world goes to pieces, I will never bow my neck to this yoke! *(goes towards his room)*

MRS. STOCKMANN *(following him)* Thomas—what are you going to do!

DR. STOCKMANN *(at his door)* I mean to have the right to look my sons in the face when they are grown men. *(goes into his room)*

MRS. STOCKMANN *(bursting into tears)* God help us all!

PETRA Father is splendid! He will not give in.

The boys look on in amazement; Petra signs to them not to speak.

ACT III

SCENE—*The editorial office of the "People's Messenger." The entrance door is on the left-hand side of the back wall; on the right-hand side is another door with glass panels through which the printing-room can be seen. Another door in the right-hand wall. In the middle of the room is a large table covered with papers, newspapers and books. In the foreground on the left a window, before which stands a desk and a high stool. There are a couple of easy chairs by the table, and other chairs standing along the wall. The room is dingy and uncomfortable; the furniture is old, the chairs stained and torn. In the printing-room the compositors are seen at work, and a printer is working a hand-press. Hovstad is sitting at the desk, writing. Billing comes in from the right with Dr. Stockmann's manuscript in his hand.*

BILLING Well, I must say!

HOVSTAD *(still writing)* Have you read it through?

BILLING *(laying the MS. on the desk)* Yes, indeed I have.

HOVSTAD Don't you think the Doctor hits them pretty hard?

BILLING Hard? Bless my soul, he's crushing! Every word falls like—how shall I put it?—like the blow of a sledgehammer.

HOVSTAD Yes, but they are not the people to throw up the sponge at the first blow.

Are there other motives involved as well? What is the difference between a man of principle and a zealot?

How is Mrs. Stockmann like a chorus figure?

Why does this moment seem especially appropriate for ending the act?

At this point in the play, how does Billing's attitude toward society compare with the Mayor's?

148 HENRIK IBSEN

BILLING That is true; and for that reason we must strike blow upon blow until the whole of this aristocracy tumbles to pieces. As I sat in there reading this, I almost seemed to see a revolution in being.

HOVSTAD *(turning round)* Hush!—Speak so that Aslaksen cannot hear you.

BILLING *(lowering his voice)* Aslaksen is a chicken-hearted chap, a coward; there is nothing of the man in him. But this time you will insist on your own way, won't you? You will put the Doctor's article in?

HOVSTAD Yes, and if the Mayor doesn't like it—

BILLING That will be the devil of a nuisance.

HOVSTAD Well, fortunately we can turn the situation to good account, whatever happens. If the Mayor will not fall in with the Doctor's project, he will have all the small tradesmen down on him—the whole of the Householders' Association and the rest of them. And if he does fall in with it, he will fall out with the whole crowd of large shareholders in the Baths, who up to now have been his most valuable supporters—

BILLING Yes, because they will certainly have to fork out a pretty penny—

HOVSTAD Yes, you may be sure they will. And in this way the ring will be broken up, you see, and then in every issue of the paper we will enlighten the public on the Mayor's incapability on one point and another, and make it clear that all the positions of trust in the town, the whole control of municipal affairs, ought to be put in the hands of the Liberals.

Does the welfare of the town itself mean very much to these self-styled liberal newspapermen?

BILLING That is perfectly true! I see it coming—I see it coming; we are on the threshold of a revolution!

A knock is heard at the door.

HOVSTAD Hush! *(calls out)* Come in! *(Dr. Stockmann comes in by the street door. Hovstad goes to meet him.)* Ah, it is you, Doctor! Well?

DR. STOCKMANN You may set to work and print it, Mr. Hovstad!

HOVSTAD Has it come to that, then?

BILLING Hurrah!

DR. STOCKMANN Yes, print away. Undoubtedly it has come to that. Now they must take what they get. There is going to be a fight in the town, Mr. Billing!

How has Dr. Stockmann's temperament changed here? Can we trace this change to any specific prior episode? Which?

BILLING War to the knife, I hope! We will get our knives to their throats, Doctor!

DR. STOCKMANN This article is only a beginning. I have already got four or five more sketched out in my head. Where is Aslaksen?

BILLING *(calls into the printing-room)* Aslaksen, just come here for a minute!

HOVSTAD Four or five articles, did you say? On the same subject?

DR. STOCKMANN No—far from it, my dear fellow. No, they are about quite another matter. But they all spring from the question of the

Stockmann's intentions now have widened to include additional reforms

water-supply and the drainage. One thing leads to another, you know. It is like beginning to pull down an old house, exactly.

BILLING Upon my soul, it's true; you find you are not done till you have pulled all the old rubbish down.

ASLAKSEN (coming in) Pulled down? You are not thinking of pulling down the Baths surely, Doctor?

HOVSTAD Far from it, don't be afraid.

DR. STOCKMANN No, we meant something quite different. Well, what do you think of my article, Mr. Hovstad?

HOVSTAD I think it is simply a masterpiece—

DR. STOCKMANN Do you really think so? Well, I am very pleased, very pleased.

HOVSTAD It is so clear and intelligible. One need have no special knowledge to understand the bearing of it. You will have every enlightened man on your side.

ASLAKSEN And every prudent man too, I hope?

BILLING The prudent and the imprudent—almost the whole town.

ASLAKSEN In that case we may venture to print it.

DR. STOCKMANN I should think so!

HOVSTAD We will put it in to-morrow morning.

DR. STOCKMANN Of course—you must not lose a single day. What I wanted to ask you, Mr. Aslaksen, was if you would supervise the printing of it yourself.

ASLAKSEN With pleasure.

DR. STOCKMANN Take care of it as if it were a treasure! No misprints—every word is important. I will look in again a little later; perhaps you will be able to let me see a proof. I can't tell you how eager I am to see it in print, and see it burst upon the public—

BILLING Burst upon them—yes, like a flash of lightning!

DR. STOCKMANN —and to have it submitted to the judgment of my intelligent fellow-townsmen. You cannot imagine what I have gone through to-day. I have been threatened first with one thing and then with another; they have tried to rob me of my most elementary rights as a man—

BILLING What! Your rights as a man!

DR. STOCKMANN —they have tried to degrade me, to make a coward of me, to force me to put personal interests before my most sacred convictions—

BILLING That is too much—I'm damned if it isn't.

HOVSTAD Oh, you mustn't be surprised at anything from that quarter.

DR. STOCKMANN Well, they will get the worst of it with me; they may assure themselves of that. I shall consider the "People's Messenger" my sheet-anchor now, and every single day I will bombard them with one article after another, like bomb-shells—

in the town. Can we deduce the nature of the other articles he plans to write? What will they deal with?

Why should Hovstad be so gratified by Stockmann's report, at least for the time being?

There is an interesting, subtle interplay between Aslaksen and Hovstad throughout this first half of the drama. Can we sense the basis for the friction?

The irony of the doctor's expectations with his fellow townspeople will become painfully clear in Act IV.

150   HENRIK IBSEN

ASLAKSEN Yes, but—

BILLING Hurrah!—it is war, it is war!

DR. STOCKMANN I shall smite them to the ground—I shall crush them—I shall break down all their defences, before the eyes of the honest public! That is what I shall do!

ASLAKSEN Yes, but in moderation, Doctor—proceed with moderation—

BILLING Not a bit of it, not a bit of it! Don't spare the dynamite!

DR. STOCKMANN Because it is not merely a question of water-supply and drains now, you know. No—it is the whole of our social life that we have got to purify and disinfect—

BILLING Spoken like a deliverer!

DR. STOCKMANN All the incapables must be turned out, you understand—and that in every walk of life! Endless vistas have opened themselves to my mind's eye to-day. I cannot see it all quite clearly yet, but I shall in time. Young and vigorous standard-bearers—those are what we need and must seek, my friends; we must have new men in command at all our outposts.

BILLING Hear, hear!

DR. STOCKMANN We only need to stand by one another, and it will all be perfectly easy. The revolution will be launched like a ship that runs smoothly off the stocks. Don't you think so?

HOVSTAD For my part I think we have now a prospect of getting the municipal authority into the hands where it should lie.

ASLAKSEN And if only we proceed with moderation, I cannot imagine that there will be any risk.

DR. STOCKMANN Who the devil cares whether there is any risk or not! What I am doing, I am doing in the name of truth and for the sake of my conscience.

HOVSTAD You are a man who deserves to be supported, Doctor.

ASLAKSEN Yes, there is no denying that the Doctor is a true friend to the town—a real friend to the community, that he is.

BILLING Take my word for it, Aslaksen, Dr. Stockmann is a friend of the people.

ASLAKSEN I fancy the Householders' Association will make use of that expression before long.

DR. STOCKMANN (*affected, grasps their hands*) Thank you, thank you, my dear staunch friends. It is very refreshing to me to hear you say that; my brother called me something quite different. By Jove, he shall have it back, with interest! But now I must be off to see a poor devil—. I will come back, as I said. Keep a very careful eye on the manuscript, Aslaksen, and don't for worlds leave out any of my notes of exclamation! Rather put one or two more in! Capital, capital! Well, good-bye for the present—good-bye, good-bye!

They show him to the door, and bow him out.

HOVSTAD He may prove an invaluably useful man to us.

Dr. Stockmann's personality has been "radicalized," according to contemporary terminology. From the earlier actions of the play, what evidence allows us to see this potential in his character?

The irony grows as Billing suggests that the doctor is some sort of messiah for the people. Watch for the name he later pins on the doctor, during the open town assembly.

How does Ibsen develop the plot by having Aslaksen join in here?

AN ENEMY OF THE PEOPLE

ASLAKSEN Yes, so long as he confines himself to this matter of the Baths. But if goes farther afield, I don't think it would be advisable to follow him.

HOVSTAD Hm!—that all depends—

BILLING You are so infernally timid, Aslaksen!

ASLAKSEN Timid? Yes, when it is a question of the local authorities, I am timid, Mr. Billing; it is a lesson I have learnt in the school of experience, let me tell you. But try me in higher politics, in matters that concern the government itself, and then see if I am timid.

BILLING No, you aren't, I admit. But this is simply contradicting yourself.

ASLAKSEN I am a man with a conscience, and that is the whole matter. If you attack the government, you don't do the community any harm, anyway; those fellows pay no attention to attacks, you see—they go on just as they are, in spite of them. But *local* authorities are different; they *can* be turned out, and then perhaps you may get an ignorant lot into office who may do irreparable harm to the householders and everybody else.

> Aslaksen's view about the role and function of governmental bureaucracies is a popular one. Can we isolate its main features?

HOVSTAD But what of the education of citizens by self government—don't you attach any importance to that?

ASLAKSEN When a man has interests of his own to protect, he cannot think of everything, Mr. Hovstad.

> Aslaksen's conscience clearly has its limits.

HOVSTAD Then I hope I shall never have interests of my own to protect!

BILLING Hear, hear!

ASLAKSEN *(with a smile)* Hm! *(points to the desk)* Mr. Sheriff Stensgaard was your predecessor at that editorial desk.

BILLING *(spitting)* Bah! That turncoat.

HOVSTAD I am not a weathercock—and never will be.

> Hovstad's denial will echo with irony within a short time. What is a weathercock, and why is it an appropriate term to apply to Hovstad?

ASLAKSEN A politician should never be too certain of anything, Mr. Hovstad. And as for you, Mr. Billing, I should think it is time for you to be taking in a reef or two in your sails, seeing that you are applying for the post of secretary to the Bench.

BILLING I—!

HOVSTAD Are you, Billing?

BILLING Well, yes—but you must clearly understand I am only doing it to annoy the bigwigs.

> Did Hovstad know about Billing's desire to seek public office? Why would this information demand our reassessment of Billing as a character?

ASLAKSEN Anyhow, it is no business of mine. But if I am to be accused of timidity and of inconsistency in my principles, this is what I want to point out: my political past is an open book. I have never changed, except perhaps to become a little more moderate, you see. My heart is still with the people; but I don't deny that my reason has a certain bias towards the authorities—the local ones, I mean. *(goes into the printing-room)*

BILLING Oughtn't we try and get rid of him, Hovstad?

HOVSTAD Do you know anyone else who will advance the money for our paper and printing bill?

> Evidently Hovstad and Billing are tied to Aslaksen out of necessity, not from unified political thinking.

HENRIK IBSEN

BILLING It is an infernal nuisance that we don't possess some capital to trade on.

HOVSTAD *(sitting down at his desk)* Yes, if we only had that, then—

BILLING Suppose you were to apply to Dr. Stockmann?

HOVSTAD *(turning over some papers)* What is the use? He has got nothing.

BILLING No, but he has got a warm man in the background, old Morten Kiil—"the Badger," as they call him.

HOVSTAD *(writing)* Are you so sure *he* has got anything?

BILLING Good Lord, of course he has! And some of it must come to the Stockmanns. Most probably he will do something for the children, at all events.

HOVSTAD *(turning half round)* Are you counting on that?

BILLING Counting on it? Of course I am not counting on anything.

HOVSTAD That is right. And I should not count on the secretaryship to the Bench either, if I were you; for I can assure you—you won't get it.

BILLING Do you think I am not quite aware of that? My object is precisely *not* to get it. A slight of that kind stimulates a man's fighting power—it is like getting a supply of fresh bile—and I am sure one needs that badly enough in a hole-and-corner place like this, where it is so seldom anything happens to stir one up.

HOVSTAD *(writing)* Quite so, quite so.

BILLING Ah, I shall be heard of yet!—Now I shall go and write the appeal to the Householders' Association. *(goes into the room on the right)*

HOVSTAD *(sitting at his desk, biting his penholder, says slowly)* Hm!—that's it, is it. *(A knock is heard.)* Come in! *(Petra comes in by the outer door. Hovstad gets up.)* What, you!—here?

PETRA Yes, you must forgive me—

HOVSTAD *(pulling a chair forward)* Won't you sit down?

PETRA No, thank you; I must go again in a moment.

HOVSTAD Have you come with a message from your father, by any chance?

PETRA No, I have come on my own account. *(takes a book out of her coat pocket)* Here is the English story.

HOVSTAD Why have you brought it back?

PETRA Because I am not going to translate it.

HOVSTAD But you promised me faithfully—

PETRA Yes, but then I had not read it. I don't suppose you have read it either?

HOVSTAD No, you know quite well I don't understand English; but—

PETRA Quite so. That is why I wanted to tell you that you must find something else. *(lays the book on the table)* You can't use this for the "People's Messenger."

Hovstad admits that he is relatively powerless without money. Thus, in his proposed revolution, he would symbolize the nonmonied outsider seeking to pull down the wealthy power holders. How does this opposition compare with other civil revolutions in recent years?

Is Billing believable in his rationalizations? Why?

For many years "bile" was thought to be those special body fluids which induced anger and a bad temper.

AN ENEMY OF THE PEOPLE 153

HOVSTAD Why not?

PETRA Because it conflicts with all your opinions.

HOVSTAD Oh, for that matter—

PETRA You don't understand me. The burden of this story is that there is a supernatural power that looks after the so-called good people in this world and makes everything happen for the best in their case—while all the so-called bad people are punished.

HOVSTAD Well, but that is all right. That is just what our readers want.

PETRA And are you going to be the one to give it to them? For myself, I do not believe a word of it. You know quite well that things do not happen so in reality.

HOVSTAD You are perfectly right; but an editor cannot always act as he would prefer. He is often obliged to bow to the wishes of the public in unimportant matters. Politics are the most important thing in life—for a newspaper, anyway; and if I want to carry my public with me on the path that leads to liberty and progress, I must not frighten them away. If they find a moral tale of this sort in the serial at the bottom of the page, they will be all the more ready to read what is printed above it; they feel more secure, as it were.

PETRA For shame! You would never go and set a snare like that for your readers; you are not a spider!

HOVSTAD (smiling) Thank you for having such a good opinion of me. No; as a matter of fact that is Billing's idea and not mine.

PETRA Billing's!

HOVSTAD Yes; anyway he propounded that theory here one day. And it is Billing who is so anxious to have that story in the paper; I don't know anything about the book.

PETRA But how can Billing, with his emancipated views—

HOVSTAD Oh, Billing is a many-sided man. He is applying for the post of secretary of the Bench, too, I hear.

PETRA I don't believe it, Mr. Hovstad. How could he possibly bring himself to do such a thing?

HOVSTAD Ah, you must ask him that.

PETRA I should never have thought it of him.

HOVSTAD (looking more closely at her) No? Does it really surprise you so much?

PETRA Yes. Or perhaps not altogether. Really, I don't quite know—

HOVSTAD We journalists are not much worth, Miss Stockmann.

PETRA Do you really mean that?

HOVSTAD I think so sometimes.

PETRA Yes, in the ordinary affairs of everyday life, perhaps; I can understand that. But now, when you have taken a weighty matter in hand—

HOVSTAD This matter of your father's, you mean?

How does this scene show Petra's development as a consistent figure throughout the play?

Describe what Hovstad means in his explanation to Petra about running a newspaper. How do his actions here prejudice his actions later in the play?

Who has a more realistic outlook on life—Hovstad or Petra? Why?

154 HENRIK IBSEN

PETRA Exactly. It seems to me that now you must feel you are a man worth more than most.

HOVSTAD Yes, to-day I do feel something of that sort.

PETRA Of course you do, don't you? It is a splendid vocation you have chosen—to smooth the way for the march of unappreciated truths, and new and courageous lines of thought. If it were nothing more than because you stand fearlessly in the open and take up the cause of an injured man—

In contemporary terms, Petra might be referred to as a crusader on the basis of her doctrinaire position.

HOVSTAD Especially when that injured man is—ahem!—I don't rightly know how to—

PETRA When that man is so upright and so honest, you mean?

HOVSTAD (more gently) Especially when he is your father, I meant.

PETRA (suddenly checked) That?

HOVSTAD Yes, Petra—Miss Petra.

PETRA Is it *that,* that is first and foremost with you? Not the matter itself? Not the truth?—not my father's big generous heart?

HOVSTAD Certainly—of course—that too.

Ibsen reverts to the central theme of the play, that is, what one's priorities in life are to be—the self or others first.

PETRA No, thank you; you have betrayed yourself, Mr. Hovstad, and now I shall never trust you again in anything.

HOVSTAD Can you really take it so amiss in me that it is mostly for your sake—?

PETRA What I am angry with you for, is for not having been honest with my father. You talked to him as if the truth and the good of the community were what lay nearest to your heart. You have made fools of both my father and me. You are not the man you made yourself out to be. And for that I shall never forgive you—never!

HOVSTAD You ought not to speak so bitterly, Miss Petra—least of all now.

PETRA Why not now, especially?

HOVSTAD Because your father cannot do without my help.

PETRA (looking him up and down) Are you that sort of man too? For shame!

Petra's blunt talk serves to flush out Hovstad from his verbal defenses.

HOVSTAD No, no, I am not. This came upon me so unexpectedly—you must believe that.

PETRA I know what to believe. Good-bye.

ASLAKSEN (coming from the printing-room, hurriedly and with an air of mystery) Damnation, Hovstad!— (sees Petra) Oh, this is awkward—

PETRA There is the book; you must give it to some one else. (goes towards the door)

HOVSTAD (following her) But, Miss Stockmann—

PETRA Good-bye. (goes out)

ASLAKSEN I say—Mr. Hovstad—

HOVSTAD Well, well!—what is it?

ASLAKSEN The Mayor is outside in the printing-room.

AN ENEMY OF THE PEOPLE 155

HOVSTAD The Mayor, did you say?

ASLAKSEN Yes, he wants to speak to you. He came in by the back door—didn't want to be seen, you understand.

HOVSTAD What can he want? Wait a bit—I will go myself. *(goes to the door of the printing-room, opens it, bows and invites Peter Stockmann in)* Just see, Aslaksen, that no one—

ASLAKSEN Quite so. *(goes into the printing-room)*

PETER STOCKMANN You did not expect to see me here, Mr. Hovstad?

HOVSTAD No, I confess I did not.

PETER STOCKMANN *(looking round)* You are very snug in here—very nice indeed.

HOVSTAD Oh—

PETER STOCKMANN And here I come, without any notice, to take up your time!

HOVSTAD By all means, Mr. Mayor. I am at your service. But let me relieve you of your— *(takes Stockmann's hat and stick and puts them on a chair)* Won't you sit down?

PETER STOCKMANN *(sitting down by the table)* Thank you. *(Hovstad sits down.)* I have had an extremely annoying experience to-day, Mr. Hovstad.

HOVSTAD Really? Ah well, I expect with all the various business you have to attend to—

PETER STOCKMANN The Medical Officer of the Baths is responsible for what happened to-day.

HOVSTAD Indeed? The Doctor?

PETER STOCKMANN He has addressed a kind of report to the Baths Committee on the subject of certain supposed defects in the Baths.

HOVSTAD Has he indeed?

PETER STOCKMANN Yes—has he not told you? I thought he said—

HOVSTAD Ah, yes—it is true he did mention something about—

ASLAKSEN *(coming from the printing-room)* I ought to have that copy—

HOVSTAD *(angrily)* Ahem!—there it is on the desk.

ASLAKSEN *(taking it)* Right.

PETER STOCKMANN But look there—that is the thing I was speaking of!

ASLAKSEN Yes, that is the Doctor's article, Mr. Mayor.

HOVSTAD Oh, is *that* what you were speaking about?

PETER STOCKMANN Yes, that is it. What do you think of it?

HOVSTAD Oh, I am only a layman—and I have only taken a very cursory glance at it.

PETER STOCKMANN But are you going to print it?

HOVSTAD I cannot very well refuse a distinguished man—

ASLAKSEN I have nothing to do with editing the paper, Mr. Mayor—

The Mayor's arrival makes the newspapermen anxious. Why?

How does Hovstad's ingratiating manner with the Mayor now compare with his earlier revolutionary charges against the city fathers?

By using the expression "supposed defects in the Baths," the Mayor suggests the position he intends to take regarding the doctor's medical report.

Why must Hovstad admit that he is aware of the doctor's article and intends to print it?

156 HENRIK IBSEN

PETER STOCKMANN I understand.

ASLAKSEN I merely print what is put into my hands.

PETER STOCKMANN Quite so.

ASLAKSEN And so I must— *(moves off towards the printing-room)*

PETER STOCKMANN No, but wait a moment, Mr. Aslaksen. You will allow me, Mr. Hovstad?

HOVSTAD If you please, Mr. Mayor.

PETER STOCKMANN You are a discreet and thoughtful man, Mr. Aslaksen.

ASLAKSEN I am delighted to hear you think so, sir.

PETER STOCKMANN And a man of very considerable influence.

ASLAKSEN Chiefly among the small tradesmen, sir.

PETER STOCKMANN The small tax-payers are the majority—here as everywhere else.

ASLAKSEN That is true.

PETER STOCKMANN And I have no doubt you know the general trend of opinion among them, don't you?

ASLAKSEN Yes I think I may say I do, Mr. Mayor.

PETER STOCKMANN Yes. Well since there is such a praiseworthy spirit of self-sacrifice among the less wealthy citizens of our town—

ASLAKSEN What?

HOVSTAD Self-sacrifice?

PETER STOCKMANN It is pleasing evidence of a public-spirited feeling, extremely pleasing evidence. I might almost say I hardly expected it. But you have a closer knowledge of public opinion than I.

ASLAKSEN But, Mr. Mayor—

PETER STOCKMANN And indeed it is no small sacrifice that the town is going to make.

HOVSTAD The town?

ASLAKSEN But I don't understand. Is it the Baths—?

PETER STOCKMANN At a provisional estimate, the alterations that the Medical Officer asserts to be desirable will cost somewhere about twenty thousand pounds

ASLAKSEN This is a lot of money, but—

PETER STOCKMANN Of course it will be necessary to raise a municipal loan.

HOVSTAD *(getting up)* Surely you never mean that the town must pay—?

ASLAKSEN Do you mean that it must come out of the municipal funds?—out of the ill-filled pockets of the small tradesmen?

PETER STOCKMANN Well, my dear Mr. Aslaksen, where else is the money to come from?

ASLAKSEN The gentlemen who own the Baths ought to provide that.

> Why does the Mayor begin his pressure tactics on Aslaksen first? Has Ibsen prepared us well for this scene? How?

> Through brilliant use of psychology, the Mayor will now shift full responsibility for resolving the problem of the Baths onto the common citizens, not the town leaders.

> The term "self-sacrifice" results in what kind of reaction from Hovstad and Aslaksen? Why is the term ironic?

> Why would the Mayor say that Hovstad knows "public opinion" better than he does?

AN ENEMY OF THE PEOPLE   157

PETER STOCKMANN The proprietors of the Baths are not in a position to incur any further expense.

ASLAKSEN Is that absolutely certain, Mr. Mayor.

PETER STOCKMANN I have satisfied myself that it is so. If the town wants these very extensive alterations, it will have to pay for them.

How does this passage illustrate a selective use of information to suit one's political ends?

ASLAKSEN But, damn it all!—I beg your pardon—this is quite another matter, Mr. Hovstad!

HOVSTAD It is, indeed.

PETER STOCKMANN The most fatal part of it is that we shall be obliged to shut the Baths for a couple of years.

HOVSTAD Shut them? Shut them altogether?

ASLAKSEN For two years?

PETER STOCKMANN Yes, the work will take as long as that—at least.

ASLAKSEN I'm damned if we will stand that, Mr. Mayor! What are we householders to live upon in the meantime?

PETER STOCKMANN Unfortunately that is an extremely difficult question to answer, Mr. Aslaksen. But what would you have us do? Do you suppose we shall have a single visitor in the town, if we go about proclaiming that our water is polluted, that we are living over a plague spot, that the entire town—

What is the psychological basis of the Mayor's argument?

ASLAKSEN And the whole thing is merely imagination?

PETER STOCKMANN With the best will in the world, I have not been able to come to any other conclusion.

ASLAKSEN Well then I must say it is absolutely unjustifiable of Dr. Stockmann—I beg your pardon, Mr. Mayor—

PETER STOCKMANN What you say is lamentably true, Mr. Aslaksen. My brother has unfortunately always been a headstrong man.

ASLAKSEN After this, do you mean to give him your support, Mr. Hovstad?

HOVSTAD Can you suppose for a moment that I—?

PETER STOCKMANN I have drawn up a short *résumé* of the situation as it appears from a reasonable man's point of view. In it I have indicated how certain possible defects might suitably be remedied without out-running the resources of the Baths Committee.

It seems that the Mayor has correctly foreseen the results of his talk with the crusaders. How does Ibsen let us know so?

HOVSTAD Have you got it with you, Mr. Mayor.

PETER STOCKMANN (*fumbling in his pocket*) Yes, I brought it with me in case you should—

ASLAKSEN Good Lord, there he is!

PETER STOCKMANN Who? My brother?

HOVSTAD Where? Where?

ASLAKSEN He has just gone through the printing-room.

PETER STOCKMANN How unlucky! I don't want to meet him here, and I had still several things to speak to you about.

HOVSTAD (*pointing to the door on the right*) Go in there for the present.

PETER STOCKMANN But—?

HOVSTAD You will only find Billing in there.

ASLAKSEN Quick, quick, Mr. Mayor—he is just coming.

PETER STOCKMANN Yes, very well; but see that you get rid of him quickly. *(goes out through the door on the right, which Aslaksen opens for him and shuts after him)*

HOVSTAD Pretend to be doing something, Aslaksen.

Sits down and writes. Aslaksen begins foraging among a heap of newspapers that are lying on a chair.

DR. STOCKMANN *(coming in from the printing-room)* Here I am again. *(puts down his hat and stick)*

HOVSTAD *(writing)* Already, Doctor? Hurry up with what we were speaking about, Aslaksen. We are very pressed for time to-day.

DR. STOCKMANN *(to Aslaksen)* No proof for me to see yet, I hear.

ASLAKSEN *(without turning round)* You couldn't expect it yet, Doctor.

DR. STOCKMANN No, no; but I am impatient, as you can understand. I shall not know a moment's peace of mind till I see it in print.

HOVSTAD Hm!—It will take a good while yet, won't it, Aslaksen?

ASLAKSEN Yes, I am almost afraid it will.

DR. STOCKMANN All right, my dear friends; I will come back. I do not mind coming back twice if necessary. A matter of such great importance—the welfare of the town at stake—it is no time to shirk trouble. *(is just going, but stops and comes back)* Look here—there is one thing more I want to speak to you about.

HOVSTAD Excuse me, but could it not wait till some other time?

DR. STOCKMANN I can tell you in half a dozen words. It is only this. When my article is read to-morrow and it is realised that I have been quietly working the whole winter for the welfare of the town—

HOVSTAD Yes but, Doctor—

DR. STOCKMANN I know what you are going to say. You don't see how on earth it was any more than my duty—my obvious duty as a citizen. Of course it wasn't; I know that as well as you. But my fellow citizens, you know—! Good Lord, think of all the good souls who think so highly of me—!

ASLAKSEN Yes, our townsfolk have had a very high opinion of you so far, Doctor.

DR. STOCKMANN Yes, and that is just why I am afraid they—. Well, this is the point; when this reaches them, especially the poorer classes, and sounds in their ears like a summons to take the town's affairs into their own hands for the future—

HOVSTAD *(getting up)* Ahem! Doctor, I won't conceal from you the fact—

DR. STOCKMANN Ah!—I knew there was something in the wind! But I won't hear a word of it. If anything of that sort is being set on foot—

HOVSTAD Of what sort?

DR. STOCKMANN Well, whatever it is—whether it is a demonstration

Why would the Mayor not wish his brother to know he has been talking with the town newspaper publishers? What does this reveal about Peter Stockmann's character?

Why do Hovstad and Aslaksen pretend to be busy when Dr. Stockmann makes his surprise return visit?

There are some elements here for grim humor as the former zealots now attempt to put off Dr. Stockmann.

As usual, the naive doctor is wrong in his expectations from the community.

AN ENEMY OF THE PEOPLE   159

in my honour, or a banquet, or a subscription list for some presentation to me—whatever it is, you most promise me solemnly and faithfully to put a stop to it. You too, Mr. Aslaksen; do you understand?

HOVSTAD You must forgive me, Doctor, but sooner or later we must tell you the plain truth—

He is interrupted by the entrance of Mrs. Stockmann, who comes in from the street door.

MRS. STOCKMANN *(seeing her husband)* Just as I thought!

HOVSTAD *(going towards her)* You too, Mrs. Stockmann?

DR. STOCKMANN What on earth do *you* want here, Katherine?

MRS. STOCKMANN I should think you know very well what I want.

HOVSTAD Won't you sit down? Or perhaps—

MRS. STOCKMANN No, thank you; don't trouble. And you must not be offended at my coming to fetch my husband; I am the mother of three children, you know.

DR. STOCKMANN Nonsense!—we know all about that.

MRS. STOCKMANN Well, one would not give you credit for much thought for your wife and children to-day; if you had had that, you would not have gone and dragged us all into misfortune.

DR. STOCKMANN Are you out of your senses, Katherine! Because a man has a wife and children, is he not to be allowed to proclaim the truth—is he not to be allowed to be an actively useful citizen—is he not to be allowed to do a service to his native town!

MRS. STOCKMANN Yes, Thomas—in reason.

ASLAKSEN Just what I say. Moderation in everything.

MRS. STOCKMANN And that is why you wrong us, Mr. Hovstad, in enticing my husband away from his home and making a dupe of him in all this.

HOVSTAD I certainly am making a dupe of no one—

DR. STOCKMANN Making a dupe of me! Do you suppose *I* should allow myself to be duped!

MRS. STOCKMANN It is just what you do. I know quite well you have more brains than anyone in the town, but you are extremely easily duped, Thomas. *(to Hovstad)* Please realise that he loses his post at the Baths if you print what he has written—

ASLAKSEN What!

HOVSTAD Look here, Doctor—

DR. STOCKMANN *(laughing)* Ha—ha!—just let them try! No, no—they will take good care not to. I have got the compact majority behind me, let me tell you!

MRS. STOCKMANN Yes, that is just the worst of it—your having any such horrid thing behind you.

DR. STOCKMANN Rubbish, Katherine!—Go home and look after your house and leave me to look after the community. How can you be so afraid, when I am so confident and happy? *(walks up and down,*

What is the dramatic effect of Mrs. Stockmann's sudden entrance?

How has Mrs. Stockmann changed here? What has caused this change in her?

Why is Aslaksen's remark about "moderation" ironic in view of his earlier comments in the play?

Sharp irony emerges in Dr. Stockmann's instruction to his wife.

160 HENRIK IBSEN

rubbing his hands) Truth and the People will win the fight, you may be certain! I see the whole of the broad-minded middle class marching like a victorious army—! *(stops beside a chair)* What the deuce is that lying there?

ASLAKSEN Good Lord!

HOVSTAD Ahem!

DR. STOCKMANN Here we have the topmost pinnacle of authority! *(takes the Mayor's official hat carefully between his finger-tips and holds it up in the air)*

MRS. STOCKMANN The Mayor's hat!

DR. STOCKMANN And here is the staff of office too. How in the name of all that's wonderful—?

HOVSTAD Well, you see—

DR. STOCKMANN Oh, I understand. He has been here trying to talk you over. Ha—ha!—he made rather a mistake there! And as soon as he caught sight of me in the printing-room—. *(bursts out laughing)* Did he run away, Mr. Aslaksen?

ASLAKSEN *(hurriedly)* Yes, he ran away, Doctor.

DR. STOCKMANN Ran away without his stick or his—. Fiddlesticks! Peter doesn't run away and leave his belongings behind him. But what the deuce have you done with him? Ah!—in there, of course. Now you shall see, Katherine!

MRS. STOCKMANN Thomas—please don't—!

ASLAKSEN Don't be rash, Doctor.

Dr. Stockmann has put on the Mayor's hat and taken his stick in his hand. He goes up to the door, opens it, and stands with his hand to his hat at the salute. Peter Stockmann comes in, red with anger. Billing follows him.

PETER STOCKMANN What does this tomfoolery mean?

DR. STOCKMANN Be respectful, my good Peter. I am the chief authority in the town now. *(walks up and down)*

MRS. STOCKMANN *(almost in tears)* Really, Thomas!

PETER STOCKMANN *(following him about)* Give me my hat and stick.

DR. STOCKMANN *(in the same tone as before)* If you are chief constable, let me tell you that I am the Mayor—I am the master of the whole town, please understand!

PETER STOCKMANN Take off my hat, I tell you. Remember it is part of an official uniform.

DR. STOCKMANN Pooh! Do you think the newly awakened lion-hearted people are going to be frightened by an official hat? There is going to be a revolution in the town to-morrow, let me tell you. You thought you could turn me out; but now I shall turn you out—turn you out of all your various offices. Do you think I cannot? Listen to me. I have triumphant social forces behind me. Hovstad and Billing will thunder in the "People's Messenger," and Aslaksen will take the field at the head of the whole Householders' Association—

ASLAKSEN That I won't, Doctor.

DR. STOCKMANN Of course you will—

Ibsen indicates stage directions in the dialogue, as Dr. Stockmann notices the Mayor's hat and cane, forgotten in his hurried departure from the room.

How does this episode reveal the doctor's naivete?

More stage directions are indicated in the dialogue, as Dr. Stockmann points to the next room where his brother indeed is hiding from him.

Why does Dr. Stockmann's imitation of him anger the Mayor?

What is ironic about the term "thunder"? How can "thunder" be considered a pun?

PETER STOCKMANN Ah!—may I ask then if Mr. Hovstad intends to join this agitation.

HOVSTAD No, Mr. Mayor.

ASLAKSEN No, Mr. Hovstad is not such a fool as to go and ruin his paper and himself for the sake of an imaginary grievance.

DR. STOCKMANN (*looking round him*) What does this mean?

HOVSTAD You have represented your case in a false light, Doctor, and therefore I am unable to give you my support.

BILLING And after what the Mayor was so kind as to tell me just now, I—

DR. STOCKMANN A false light! Leave that part of it to me. Only print my article; I am quite capable of defending it.

HOVSTAD I am not going to print it. I cannot and will not and dare not print it.

DR. STOCKMANN You dare not? What nonsense!—you are the editor; and an editor controls his paper, I suppose!

ASLAKSEN No, it is the subscribers, Doctor.

PETER STOCKMANN Fortunately, yes.

ASLAKSEN It is public opinion—the enlightened public—householders and people of that kind; they control the newspapers.

DR. STOCKMANN (*composedly*) And I have all these influences against me?

ASLAKSEN Yes, you have. It would mean the absolute ruin of the community if your article were to appear.

DR. STOCKMANN Indeed.

PETER STOCKMANN My hat and stick, if you please.

Dr. Stockmann takes off the hat and lays it on the table with the stick. Peter Stockmann takes them up. Your authority as mayor has come to an untimely end.

DR. STOCKMANN We have not got to the end yet. (*to Hovstad*) Then it is quite impossible for you to print my article in the "People's Messenger"?

HOVSTAD Quite impossible—out of regard for your family as well.

MRS. STOCKMANN You need not concern yourself about his family, thank you, Mr. Hovstad.

PETER STOCKMANN (*taking a paper from his pocket*) It will be sufficient, for the guidance of the public, if this appears. It is an official statement. May I trouble you?

HOVSTAD (*taking the paper*) Certainly; I will see that it is printed.

DR. STOCKMANN But not mine. Do you imagine that you can silence me and stifle the truth! You will not find it so easy as you suppose. Mr. Aslaksen, kindly take my manuscript at once and print it as a pamphlet—at my expense. I will have four hundred copies—no, five—six hundred.

ASLAKSEN If you offered me its weight in gold, I could not lend my

---

The dam bursts as the doctor's supposed allies abandon him abruptly.

Aslaksen's reference to the pollution as "an imaginary grievance" suggests the hard line being taken by the doctor's opponents.

Note that the theme of "not daring" because of public opinion begins to appear regularly from here on.

What stage in the play's development seems concluded here, with Dr. Stockmann's question?

How do Aslaksen, Hovstad, and the

In the newspaper office, from a 1927 production of An Enemy of the People *at New York's Hamden Theater.*

press for any such purpose, Doctor. It would be flying in the face of public opinion. You will not get it printed anywhere in the town.

DR. STOCKMANN Then give it back to me.

HOVSTAD *(giving him the MS.)* Here it is.

DR. STOCKMANN *(taking his hat and stick)* It shall be made public all the same. I will read it out at a mass meeting of the townspeople. All my fellow-citizens shall hear the voice of truth!

PETER STOCKMANN You will not find any public body in the town that will give you the use of their hall for such a purpose.

ASLAKSEN Not a single one, I am certain.

BILLING No, I'm damned if you will find one.

MRS. STOCKMANN But this is too shameful! Why should every one turn against you like that?

DR. STOCKMANN *(angrily)* I will tell you why. It is because all the men in this town are old women—like you; they all think of nothing but their families, and never of the community.

MRS. STOCKMANN *(putting her arm into his)* Then I will show them that an an old woman can be a man for once. I am going to stand by you, Thomas!

DR. STOCKMANN Bravely said, Katherine! It shall be made public—as I am a living soul! If I can't hire a hall, I shall hire a drum, and parade the town with it and read it at every street-corner.

PETER STOCKMANN You are surely not such an arrant fool as that!

DR. STOCKMANN Yes, I am.

ASLAKSEN You won't find a single man in the whole town to go with you.

BILLING No, I'm damned if you will.

Mayor undertake a process of censorship?

Only the doctor's immediate family is left to support him, as Act III ends.

MRS. STOCKMANN Don't give in, Thomas. I will tell the boys to go with you.

DR. STOCKMANN That is a splendid idea!

MRS. STOCKMANN Morten will be delighted; and Ejlif will do whatever he does.

DR. STOCKMANN Yes, and Petra!—and you too, Katherine!

MRS. STOCKMANN No, I won't do that; but I will stand at the window and watch you, that's what I will do.

DR. STOCKMANN *(puts his arms round her and kisses her)* Thank you, my dear! Now you and I are going to try a fall, my fine gentlemen! I am going to see whether a pack of cowards can succeed in gagging a patriot who wants to purify society! *(He and his wife go out by the street door.)*

"To try a fall" suggests that the doctor will be competing with his opponents as in a sport, with each side trying to score points on the other.

PETER STOCKMANN *(shaking his head seriously)* Now he has sent *her* out of her senses, too.

ACT IV

SCENE—*A big old-fashioned room in Captain Horster's house. At the back folding-doors, which are standing open, lead to an ante-room. Three windows in the left-hand wall. In the middle of the opposite wall a platform has been erected. On this is a small table with two candles, a water-bottle and glass, and a bell. The room is lit by lamps placed between the windows. In the foreground on the left there is a table with candles and a chair. To the right is a door and some chairs standing near it. The room is nearly filled with a crowd of townspeople of all sorts, a few women and schoolboys being amongst them. People are still streaming in from the back, and the room is soon filled.*

Ibsen's opening stage instructions create the excitement of the impending showdown. How do the scenic arrangements suggest a sense of community ritual with judging witnesses?

1ST CITIZEN *(meeting another)* Hullo, Lamstad! You here too?

2ND CITIZEN I go to every public meeting, I do.

3RD CITIZEN Brought your whistle too, I expect!

2ND CITIZEN I should think so. Haven't you?

3RD CITIZEN Rather! And old Evensen said he was going to bring a cow-horn, he did.

2ND CITIZEN Good old Evensen! *(laughter among the crowd)*

4TH CITIZEN *(coming up to them)* I say, tell me what is going on here to-night.

2ND CITIZEN Dr. Stockmann is going to deliver an address attacking the Mayor.

4TH CITIZEN But the Mayor is his brother.

1ST CITIZEN That doesn't matter; Dr. Stockmann's not the chap to be afraid.

3RD CITIZEN But he is in the wrong; it said so in the "People's Messenger."

2ND CITIZEN Yes, I expect he must be in the wrong this time, because neither the Householders' Association nor the Citizens' Club would lend him their hall for his meeting.

1ST CITIZEN He couldn't even get the loan of the hall at the Baths.

2ND CITIZEN No, I should think not.

A MAN IN ANOTHER PART OF THE CROWD I say—who are we to back up in this?

ANOTHER MAN *(beside him)* Watch Aslaksen, and do as he does.

BILLING *(pushing his way through the crowd, with a writing-case under his arm)* Excuse me, gentlemen—do you mind letting me through? I am reporting for the "People's Messenger." Thank you very much!

He sits down at the table on the left.

A WORKMAN Who was that?

SECOND WORKMAN Don't you know him? It's Billing, who writes for Aslaksen's paper.

Captain Horster brings in Mrs. Stockmann and Petra through the door on the right. Ejlif and Morten follow them in.

HORSTER I thought you might all sit here; you can slip out easily from here, if things get too lively.

MRS. STOCKMANN Do you think there will be a disturbance?

HORSTER One can never tell—with such a crowd. But sit down, and don't be uneasy.

MRS. STOCKMANN *(sitting down)* It was extremely kind of you to offer my husband the room.

HORSTER Well, if nobody else would—

PETRA *(who has sat down beside her mother)* And it was a plucky thing to do, Captain Horster.

HORSTER Oh, it is not such a great matter as all that.

Hovstad and Aslaksen make their way through the crowd.

ASLAKSEN *(going up to Horster)* Has the Doctor not come yet?

HORSTER He is waiting in the next room. *(movement in the crowd by the door at the back)*

HOVSTAD Look—here comes the Mayor!

BILLING Yes, I'm damned if he hasn't come after all!

Peter Stockmann makes his way gradually through the crowd, bows courteously, and takes up a position by the wall on the left. Shortly afterwards Dr. Stockmann comes in by the right-hand door. He is dressed in a black frock-coat, with a white tie. There is a little feeble applause, which is hushed down. Silence is obtained.

DR. STOCKMANN *(in an undertone)* How do you feel, Katherine?

MRS. STOCKMANN All right, thank you. *(lowering her voice)* Be sure not to lose your temper, Thomas.

DR. STOCKMANN Oh, I know how to control myself. *(looks at his watch, steps on to the platform, and bows)* It is a quarter past—so I will begin. *(takes his MS. out of his pocket)*

ASLAKSEN I think we ought to elect a chairman first.

DR. STOCKMANN No, it is quite unnecessary.

Ibsen presents typical citizen reactions to the situation through this dialogue. What seems to be the general inclination of the crowd before a single word is uttered from the speaker's platform? How similar are they to a chorus?

The tension mounts in anticipation of the doctor's speech. How does the seating of Mrs. Stockmann and her family add to an audience's anxiety?

Ibsen's stage directions provide a visual equivalent of the conflicts of will. How does Ibsen create the impression of a contest between two opponents?

Aslaksen's suggestion marks the first tactical move in the battle of wits. What is the result of his proposal that a

AN ENEMY OF THE PEOPLE 165

SOME OF THE CROWD Yes—yes!

PETER STOCKMANN I certainly think too that we ought to have a chairman.

DR. STOCKMANN But I have called this meeting to deliver a lecture, Peter.

PETER STOCKMANN Dr. Stockmann's lecture may possibly lead to a considerable conflict of opinion.

VOICES IN THE CROWD A chairman! A chairman!

HOVSTAD The general wish of the meeting seems to be that a chairman should be elected.

DR. STOCKMANN (*restraining himself*) Very well—let the meeting have its way.

ASLAKSEN Will the Mayor be good enough to undertake the task?

THREE MEN (*clapping their hands*) Bravo! Bravo!

PETER STOCKMANN For various reasons, which you will easily understand, I must beg to be excused. But fortunately we have amongst us a man who I think will be acceptable to you all. I refer to the President of the Householders' Association, Mr. Aslaksen.

SEVERAL VOICES Yes—Aslaksen! Bravo Aslaksen!

Dr. Stockmann takes up his MS. and walks up and down the platform.

ASLAKSEN Since my fellow-citizens choose to entrust me with this duty, I cannot refuse.

Loud applause. Aslaksen mounts the platform.

BILLING (*writing*) "Mr. Aslaksen was elected with enthusiasm."

ASLAKSEN And now, as I am in this position, I should like to say a few brief words. I am a quiet and peaceable man, who believes in discreet moderation, and—and—in moderate discretion. All my friends can bear witness to that.

SEVERAL VOICES That's right! That's right, Aslaksen!

ASLAKSEN I have learnt in the school of life and experience that moderation is the most valuable virtue a citizen can possess—

PETER STOCKMANN Hear, hear!

ASLAKSEN —And moreover that discretion and moderation are what enable a man to be of most service to the community. I would therefore suggest to our esteemed fellow-citizen, who has called this meeting, that he should strive to keep strictly within the bounds of moderation.

A MAN BY THE DOOR Three cheers for the Moderation Society!

A VOICE Shame!

SEVERAL VOICES Sh!—Sh!

ASLAKSEN No interruptions, gentlemen, please! Does anyone wish to make any remarks?

PETER STOCKMANN Mr. Chairman.

ASLAKSEN The Mayor will address the meeting.

---

chairman be chosen? To whose advantage is it?

These stage directions convey the image of Dr. Stockmann as a caged animal, trapped by the cunning manipulators at the session. How is this effect attained?

Where have we heard Aslaksen expound on "moderation" earlier?

The plans of Dr. Stockmann's opponents begin to become evident now. Why would the Mayor's speech be more effective by coming first?

PETER STOCKMANN In consideration of the close relationship in which, as you all know, I stand to the present Medical Officer of the Baths, I should have preferred not to speak this evening. But my official position with regard to the Baths and my solicitude for the vital interests of the town compel me to bring forward a motion. I venture to presume that there is not a single one of our citizens present who considers it desirable that unreliable and exaggerated accounts of the sanitary condition of the Baths and the town should be spread abroad.

SEVERAL VOICES No, no! Certainly not! We protest against it!

PETER STOCKMANN Therefore I should like to propose that the meeting should not permit the Medical Officer either to read or to comment on his proposed lecture.

How is the right of free speech treated here?

DR. STOCKMANN *(impatiently)* Not permit—! What the devil—!

MRS. STOCKMANN *(coughing)* Ahem!—ahem!

DR. STOCKMANN *(collecting himself)* Very well. Go ahead!

PETER STOCKMANN In my communication to the "People's Messenger," I have put the essential facts before the public in such a way that every fair-minded citizen can easily form his own opinion. From it you will see that the main result of the Medical Officer's proposals—apart from their constituting a vote of censure on the leading men of the town—would be to saddle the ratepayers with an unnecessary expenditure of at least some thousands of pounds.

Sounds of disapproval among the audience, and some cat-calls.

ASLAKSEN *(ringing his bell)* Silence, please, gentlemen! I beg to support the Mayor's motion. I quite agree with him that there is something behind this agitation started by the Doctor. He talks about the Baths; but it is a revolution he is aiming at—he wants to get the administration of the town put into new hands. No one doubts the honesty of the Doctor's intentions—no one will suggest that there can be any two opinions as to that. I myself am a believer in self-government for the people, provided it does not fall too heavily on the ratepayers. But that would be the case here; and that is why I will see Dr. Stockmann damned—I beg your pardon—before I go with him in the matter. You can pay too dearly for a thing sometimes; that is my opinion.

In what kind of doubletalk does Aslaksen indulge himself? Is his reasoning sound?

How do these arguments pertain to current ecological issues, where corrective measures cost a great deal of money?

Loud applause on all sides.

HOVSTAD I, too, feel called upon to explain my position. Dr. Stockmann's agitation appeared to be gaining a certain amount of sympathy at first, so I supported it as impartially as I could. But presently we had reason to suspect that we had allowed ourselves to be misled by misrepresentation of the state of affairs—

DR. STOCKMANN Misrepresentation—!

HOVSTAD Well, let us say a not entirely truthworthy representation. The Mayor's statement has proved that. I hope no one here has any doubt as to my liberal principles; the attitude of the "People's Messenger" towards important political questions is well known to every one. But the advice of experienced and thoughtful men has convinced me that in purely local matters a newspaper ought to proceed with a certain caution.

AN ENEMY OF THE PEOPLE   167

The town meeting, from the Hamden Theater production of 1927.

ASLAKSEN I entirely agree with the speaker.

HOVSTAD And, in the matter before us, it is now an undoubted fact that Dr. Stockmann has public opinion against him. Now, what is an editor's first and most obvious duty, gentlemen? Is it not to work in harmony with his readers? Has he not received a sort of tacit mandate to work persistently and assiduously for the welfare of those whose opinions he represents? Or is it possible I am mistaken in that?

VOICES FROM THE CROWD No, no! You are quite right!

HOVSTAD It has cost me a severe struggle to break with a man in whose house I have been lately a frequent guest—a man who till to-day has been able to pride himself on the undivided goodwill of his fellow-citizens—a man whose only, or at all events whose essential, failing is that he is swayed by his heart rather than his head.

> Why is it ironic for Hovstad to condemn the doctor's emotionalism now? Had it disturbed Hovstad earlier when they were allied?

A FEW SCATTERED VOICES That is true! Bravo, Stockmann!

HOVSTAD But my duty to the community obliged me to break with him. And there is another consideration that impels me to oppose him, and, as far as possible, to arrest him on the perilous course he has adopted; that is, consideration for his family—

> Note the ironic use of the term "duty" by Hovstad.

DR. STOCKMANN Please stick to the water-supply and drainage!

HOVSTAD —consideration, I repeat, for his wife and his children for whom he has made no provision.

MORTEN Is that us, mother?

MRS. STOCKMANN Hush!

ASLAKSEN I will now put the Mayor's proposition to the vote.

> Who has won the first round in this bout?

168 HENRIK IBSEN

DR. STOCKMANN There is no necessity! To-night I have no intention of dealing with all that filth down at the Baths. No; I have something quite different to say to you.

PETER STOCKMANN *(aside)* What is coming now?

A DRUNKEN MAN *(by the entrance door)* I am a ratepayer! And therefore I have a right to speak too! And my entire—firm—inconceivable opinion is—

A NUMBER OF VOICES Be quiet, at the back there!

OTHERS He is drunk! Turn him out! *(They turn him out.)*

DR. STOCKMANN Am I allowed to speak?

ASLAKSEN *(ringing his bell)* Dr. Stockmann will address the meeting.

Why does Aslaksen now feel it is safe to permit Dr. Stockmann to speak?

DR. STOCKMANN I should like to have seen anyone, a few days ago, dare to attempt to silence me as has been done to-night! I would have defended my sacred rights as a man, like a lion! But now it is all one to me; I have something of even weightier importance to say to you. *(The crowd presses nearer to him, Morten Kiil conspicuous among them.)*

Again, Ibsen's stage directions emphasize the tension of the moment.

DR. STOCKMANN *(continuing)* I have thought and pondered a great deal, these last few days—pondered over such a variety of things that in the end my head seemed too full to hold them—

PETER STOCKMANN *(with a cough)* Ahem!

DR. STOCKMANN —but I got them clear in my mind at last, and then I saw the whole situation lucidly. And that is why I am standing here to-night. I have a great revelation to make to you, my fellow-citizens! I will impart to you a discovery of a far wider scope than the trifling matter that our water-supply is poisoned and our medicinal Baths are standing on pestiferous soil.

How does Dr. Stockmann use psychology to keep the attention of the crowd? Is it done consciously?

A NUMBER OF VOICES *(shouting)* Don't talk about the Baths! We won't hear you! None of that!

DR. STOCKMANN I have already told you that what I want to speak about is the great discovery I have made lately—the discovery that all the sources of our *moral* life are poisoned and that the whole fabric of our civic community is founded on the pestiferous soil of falsehood.

VOICES OF DISCONCERTED CITIZENS What is that he says?

PETER STOCKMANN Such an insinuation—!

ASLAKSEN *(with his hand on his bell)* I call upon the speaker to moderate his language.

DR. STOCKMANN I have always loved my native town as a man only can love the home of his youthful days. I was not old when I went away from here; and exile, longing and memories cast as it were an additional halo over both the town and its inhabitants. *(some clapping and applause)* And there I stayed, for many years, in a horrible hole far away up north. When I came into contact with some of the people that lived scattered about among the rocks, I often thought it would have been of more service to the poor half-starved creature if a veterinary doctor had been sent up there, instead of a man like me. *(murmurs among the crowd)*

AN ENEMY OF THE PEOPLE 169

BILLING *(laying down his pen)* I'm damned if I have ever heard—!

HOVSTAD It is an insult to a respectable population!

DR. STOCKMANN Wait a bit! I do not think anyone will charge me with having forgotten my native town up there. I was like one of the eider-ducks brooding on its nest, and what I hatched was—the plans for these Baths. *(applause and protests)* And then when fate at last decreed for me the great happiness of coming home again—I assure you, gentlemen, I thought I had nothing more in the world to wish for. Or rather, there was one thing I wished for—eagerly, untiringly, ardently—and that was to be able to be of service to my native town and the good of the community.

PETER STOCKMANN *(looking at the ceiling)* You chose a strange way of doing it—ahem!

DR. STOCKMANN And so, with my eyes blinded to the real facts, I revelled in happiness. But yesterday morning—no, to be precise, it was yesterday afternoon—the eyes of my mind were opened wide, and the first thing I realised was the colossal stupidity of the authorities—. *(Uproar, shouts and laughter. Mrs. Stockmann coughs persistently.)*

> In these and succeeding assertions made by the doctor at the meeting, note the almost futile lashing out of a man muzzled by procedural convention.
> Why does Mrs. Stockmann frequently cough?

PETER STOCKMANN Mr. Chairman!

ASLAKSEN *(ringing his bell)* By virtue of my authority—!

DR. STOCKMANN It is a petty thing to catch me up on a word, Mr. Aslaksen. What I mean is only that I got scent of the unbelievable piggishness our leading men had been responsible for down at the Baths. I can't stand leading men at any price!—I have had enough of such people in my time. They are like billy-goats in a young plantation; they do mischief everywhere. They stand in a free man's way, whichever way he turns, and what I should like best should be to see them exterminated like any other vermin—. *(uproar)*

PETER STOCKMANN Mr. Chairman, can we allow such expressions to pass?

ASLAKSEN *(with his hand on his bell)* Doctor—!

DR. STOCKMANN I cannot understand how it is that I have only now acquired a clear conception of what these gentry are, when I had almost daily before my eyes in this town such an excellent specimen of them—my brother Peter—slow-witted and hide-bound in prejudice—. *(Laughter, uproar and hisses. Mrs. Stockmann sits coughing assiduously. Aslaksen rings his bell violently.)*

> Although the doctor had hoped to convey his ideas to the townspeople, his means have veered to an extreme that is opposite to those purposes—he has now resorted to personal insult. Has he anything to lose at this point?

THE DRUNKEN MAN *(who has got in again)* Is it me he is talking about? My name's Petersen, all right—but devil take me if I—

ANGRY VOICES Turn out that drunken man! Turn him out. *(He is turned out again.)*

PETER STOCKMANN Who was that person?

1ST CITIZEN I don't know who he is, Mr. Mayor.

2ND CITIZEN He doesn't belong here.

3RD CITIZEN I expect he is a navvy from over at— *(The rest is inaudible.)*

ASLAKSEN He had obviously had too much beer.—Proceed, Doctor; but please strive to be moderate in your language.

> "Navvy," a British term, denotes a common laborer employed to construct railroads, canals, and other similar projects.

170 HENRIK IBSEN

DR. STOCKMANN Very well, gentlemen, I will say no more about our leading men. And if anyone imagines, from what I have just said, that my object is to attack these people this evening, he is wrong—absolutely wide of the mark. For I cherish the comforting conviction that these parasites—all these venerable relics of a dying school of thought—are most admirably paving the way for their own extinction; they need no doctor's help to hasten their end. Nor is it folk of that kind who constitute the most pressing danger to the community. It is not they who are most instrumental in poisoning the sources of our moral life and infecting the ground on which we stand. It is not they who are the most dangerous enemies of truth and freedom amongst us.

SHOUTS FROM ALL SIDES Who then? Who is it? Name! Name!

DR. STOCKMANN You may depend upon it I shall name them! That is precisely the great discovery I made yesterday. *(raises his voice)* The most dangerous enemy of truth and freedom amongst us is the compact majority—yes, the damned compact Liberal majority—that is it! Now you know! *(Tremendous uproar. Most of the crowd are shouting, stamping and hissing. Some of the older men among them exchange stolen glances and seem to be enjoying themselves. Mrs. Stockmann gets up, looking anxious. Ejlif and Morten advance threateningly upon some schoolboys who are playing pranks. Aslaksen rings his bell and begs for silence. Hovstad and Billing both talk at once, but are inaudible. At last quiet is restored.)*

ASLAKSEN As chairman, I call upon the speaker to withdraw the ill-considered expressions he has just used.

DR. STOCKMANN Never, Mr. Aslaksen! It is the majority in our community that denies me my freedom and seeks to prevent my speaking the truth.

HOVSTAD The majority always has right on its side.

BILLING And truth too, by God!

DR. STOCKMANN The majority *never* has right on its side. Never, I say! That is one of these social lies against which an independent, intelligent man must wage war. Who is it that constitute the majority of the population in a country? Is it the clever folk or the stupid? I don't imagine you will dispute the fact that at present the stupid people are in an absolutely overwhelming majority all the world over. But, good Lord!—you can never pretend that it is right that the stupid folk should govern the clever ones! *(uproar and cries)* Oh, yes—you can shout me down, I know! but you cannot answer me. The majority has *might* on its side—unfortunately; but *right* it has *not*. I am in the right—I and a few other scattered individuals. The minority is always in the right. *(renewed uproar)*

HOVSTAD Aha!—so Dr. Stockmann has become an aristocrat since the day before yesterday!

DR. STOCKMANN I have already said that I don't intend to waste a word on the puny, narrow-chested, short-winded crew whom we are leaving astern. Pulsating life no longer concerns itself with them. I am thinking of the few, the scattered few amongst us, who have absorbed new and vigorous truths. Such men stand, as it were, at the outposts, so far ahead that the compact majority has not yet been able to come up with them; and there they are fighting for truths that

---

As Dr. Stockmann warms up to his subject, he increases his audience's anticipation. What does he promise to reveal?

The doctor drops his bombshell.

Where before in the drama have we heard voiced the fundamental conflict between the rights of the individual and of society as a whole?

Dr. Stockmann's anger and frustration have driven him to an extreme conclusion regarding where the "right" resides in society. Where has his train of thought led him?

are too newly-born into the world of consciousness to have any considerable number of people on their side as yet.

HOVSTAD So the Doctor is a revolutionary now!

DR. STOCKMANN Good heavens—of course I am, Mr. Hovstad! I propose to raise a revolution against the lie that the majority has the monopoly of the truth. What sort of truths are they that the majority usually supports? They are truths that are of such advanced age that they are beginning to break up. And if a truth is as old as that, it is also in a fair way to become a lie, gentlemen. *(laughter and mocking cries)* Yes, believe me or not, as you like; but truths are by no means as long-lived as Methuselah—as some folk imagine. A normally constituted truth lives, let us say, as a rule seventeen or eighteen, or at most twenty years; seldom longer. But truths as aged as that are always worn frightfully thin, and nevertheless it is only then that the majority recognises them and recommends them to the community as wholesome moral nourishment. There is no great nutritive value in that sort of fare, I can assure you; and, as a doctor, I ought to know. These "majority truths" are like last year's cured meat—like rancid, tainted ham; and they are the origin of the moral scurvy that is rampant in our communities.

ASLAKSEN It appears to me that the speaker is wandering a long way from his subject.

PETER STOCKMANN I quite agree with the Chairman.

DR. STOCKMANN Have you gone clean out of your senses, Peter? I am sticking as closely to my subject as I can; for my subject is precisely this, that it is the masses, the majority—this infernal compact majority—that poisons the sources of our moral life and infects the ground we stand on.

HOVSTAD And all this because the great, broadminded majority of the people is prudent enough to show deference only to well-ascertained and well-approved truths?

DR. STOCKMANN Ah, my good Mr. Hovstad, don't talk nonsense about well-ascertained truths! The truths of which the masses now approve are the very truths that the fighters at the outposts held to in the days of our grandfathers. We fighters at the outposts nowadays no longer approve of them; and I do not believe there is any other well-ascertained truth except this, that no community can live a healthy life if it is nourished only on such old marrowless truths.

HOVSTAD But instead of standing there using vague generalities, it would be interesting if you would tell us what these old marrowless truths are, that we are nourished on.

Applause from many quarters.

DR. STOCKMANN Oh, I could give you a whole string of such abominations; but to begin with I will confine myself to one well-approved truth, which at bottom is a foul lie, but upon which nevertheless Mr. Hovstad and the "People's Messenger" and all the "Messenger's" supporters are nourished.

HOVSTAD And that is—?

DR. STOCKMANN That is, the doctrine you have inherited from your forefathers and proclaim thoughtlessly far and wide—the doctrine that the public, the crowd, the masses, are the essential part of the

---

Hovstad's accusation is ironic in light of his previously stated position about the need for a revolution.

How does Hovstad's reply about "well-approved truths" inadvertently reveal his method of using only those facts which will suit his purposes?

What has happened to Stockmann's earlier avowal to help the citizens of his hometown?

population—that they constitute the People—that the common folk, the ignorant and incomplete element in the community, have the same right to pronounce judgment and to approve, to direct and to govern, as the isolated, intellectually superior personalities in it.

BILLING Well, damn me if ever I—

HOVSTAD (*at the same time, shouting out*) Fellow-citizens, take good note of that!

A NUMBER OF VOICES (*angrily*) Oho!—we are not the People! Only the superior folk are to govern, are they!

A WORKMAN Turn the fellow out, for talking such rubbish!

ANOTHER Out with him!

ANOTHER (*calling out*) Blow your horn, Evensen!

A horn is blown loudly, amidst hisses and an angry uproar.

DR. STOCKMANN (*when the noise has somewhat abated*) Be reasonable! Can't you stand hearing the voice of truth for once? I don't in the least expect you to agree with me all at once; but I must say I did expect Mr. Hovstad to admit I was right, when he had recovered his composure a little. He claims to be a freethinker—

VOICES (*in murmurs of astonishment*) Freethinker, did he say? Is Hovstad a freethinker?

HOVSTAD (*shouting*) Prove it, Dr. Stockmann! When have I said so in print?

DR. STOCKMANN (*reflecting*) No, confound it, you are right!—you have never had the courage to. Well, I won't put you in a hole, Mr. Hovstad. Let us say it is I that am the freethinker, then. I am going to prove to you, scientifically, that the "People's Messenger" leads you by the nose in a shameful manner when it tells you that you—that the common people, the crowd, the masses, are the real essence of the People. That is only a newspaper lie, I tell you! The common people are nothing more than the raw material of which a People is made. (*groans, laughter and uproar*) Well, isn't that the case. Isn't there an enormous difference between a well-bred and an ill-bred strain of animals? Take, for instance, a common barn-door hen. What sort of eating do you get from a shrivelled up old scrag of a fowl like that? Not much, do you! And what sort of eggs does it lay? A fairly good crow or a raven can lay pretty nearly as good an egg. But take a well-bred Spanish or Japanese hen, or a good pheasant or a turkey—then you will see the difference. Or take the case of dogs, with whom we humans are on such intimate terms. Think first of an ordinary common cur—I mean one of the horrible, coarse-haired, low-bred curs that do nothing but run about the streets and befoul the walls of the houses. Compare one of these curs with a poodle whose sires for many generations have been bred in a gentleman's house, where they have had the best of food and had the opportunity of hearing soft voices and music. Do you not think that the poodle's brain is developed to quite a different degree from that of the cur? Of course it is. It is puppies of well-bred poodles like that, that showmen train to do incredibly clever tricks—things that a common cur could never learn to do even if it stood on its head. (*uproar and mocking cries*)

A CITIZEN (*calls out*) Are you going to make out we are dogs, now?

There are some who prefer to drown out an opposing point of view rather than to hear it. How does Ibsen show this? What instances of this phenomenon have we witnessed in our own time?

How has the title of the newspaper now assumed an ironic connotation?

Do you think such an argument would be accepted by those attending this town meeting? Why?

ANOTHER CITIZEN We are not animals, Doctor!

DR. STOCKMANN Yes but, bless my soul, we *are,* my friend! It is true we are the finest animals anyone could wish for; but, even amongst us, exceptionally fine animals are rare. There is a tremendous difference between poodle-men and cur-men. And the amusing part of it is that Mr. Hovstad quite agrees with me as long as it is a question of four-footed animals—

HOVSTAD Yes, it is true enough as far as they are concerned.

DR. STOCKMANN Very well. But as soon as I extend the principle and apply it to two-legged animals, Mr. Hovstad stops short. He no longer dares to think independently, or to pursue his ideas to their logical conclusion; so he turns the whole theory upside down and proclaims in the "People's Messenger" that it is the barn-door hens and street curs that are the finest specimens in the menagerie. But that is always the way, as long as a man retains the traces of common origin and has not worked his way up to intellectual distinction.

HOVSTAD I lay no claim to any sort of distinction. I am the son of humble countryfolk, and I am proud that the stock I came from is rooted deep among the common people he insults.

Stockmann's arguments permit his opponents, such as Hovstad, to score points by getting the sympathy of the crowd. How does Hovstad turn the arguments to his advantage?

VOICES Bravo, Hovstad! Bravo! Bravo!

DR. STOCKMANN The kind of common people I mean are not only to be found low down in the social scale; they crawl and swarm all around us—even in the highest social positions. You have only to look at your own fine, distinguished Mayor! My brother Peter is every bit as plebeian as anyone that walks in two shoes—(*laughter and hisses*)

PETER STOCKMANN I protest against personal allusions of this kind.

DR. STOCKMANN (*imperturbably*)—and that, not because he is, like myself, descended from some old rascal of a pirate from Pomerania or thereabouts—because that is who we are descended from—

PETER STOCKMANN An absurd legend. I deny it!

Why would Peter Stockmann resist any suggestion impugning his forefathers?

DR. STOCKMANN —but because he thinks what his superiors think and holds the same opinions as they. People who do that are, intellectually speaking, common people; and that is why my magnificent brother Peter is in reality so very far from any distinction—and consequently also so far from being liberal-minded.

PETER STOCKMANN Mr. Chairman—!

HOVSTAD So it is only the distinguished men that are liberal-minded in this country? We are learning something quite new! (*laughter*)

DR. STOCKMANN Yes, that is part of my new discovery too. And another part of it is that broad-mindedness is almost precisely the same thing as morality. That is why I maintain that it is absolutely inexcusable in the "People's Messenger" to proclaim, day in and day out, the false doctrine that it is the masses, the crowd, the compact majority, that have the monopoly of broad-mindedness and morality—and that vice and corruption and every kind of intellectual depravity are the result of culture, just as all the filth that is draining into our Baths is the result of the tanneries up at Mölledal! (*Uproar and interruptions. Dr. Stockmann is undisturbed, and goes on, carried*

According to the doctor's theories, which segment of society alone is suited to be truly liberal and moral?

away by his ardour, with a smile.) And yet this same "People's Messenger" can go on preaching that the masses ought to be elevated to higher conditions of life! But, bless my soul, if the "Messenger's" teaching is to be depended upon, this very raising up the masses would mean nothing more or less than setting them straightway upon the paths of depravity! Happily the theory that culture demoralises is only an old falsehood that our forefathers believed in and we have inherited. No, it is ignorance, poverty, ugly conditions of life that do the devil's work! In a house which does not get aired and swept every day—my wife Katherine maintains that the floor ought to be scrubbed as well, but that is a debatable question—in such a house, let me tell you, people will lose within two or three years the power of thinking or acting in a moral manner. Lack of oxygen weakens the conscience. And there must be a plentiful lack of oxygen in very many houses in this town, I should think, judging from the fact that the whole compact majority can be unconscientious enough to wish to build the town's prosperity on a quagmire of falsehood and deceit.

ASLAKSEN We cannot allow such a grave accusation to be flung at a citizen community.

A CITIZEN I move that the Chairman direct the speaker to sit down.

VOICES (*angrily*) Hear, hear! Quite right! Make him sit down!

DR. STOCKMANN (*losing his self-control*) Then I will go and shout the truth at every street corner! I will write it in other towns' newspapers! The whole country shall know what is going on here!

HOVSTAD It almost seems as if Dr. Stockmann's intention were to ruin the town.

DR. STOCKMANN Yes, my native town is so dear to me that I would rather ruin it than see it flourishing upon a lie.

ASLAKSEN This is really serious. (*Uproar and catcalls. Mrs. Stockmann coughs, but to no purpose; her husband does not listen to her any longer.*)

HOVSTAD (*shouting above the din*) A man must be a public enemy to wish to ruin a whole community!

DR. STOCKMANN (*with growing fervour*) What does the destruction of a community matter, if it lives on lies! It ought to be razed to the ground, I tell you! All who live by lies ought to be exterminated like vermin! You will end by infecting the whole country; you will bring about such a state of things that the whole country will deserve to be ruined. And if things come to that pass, I shall say from the bottom of my heart: Let the whole country perish, let all these people be exterminated!

VOICES FROM THE CROWD That is talking like an out-and-out enemy of the people!

BILLING There sounded the voice of the people, by all that's holy!

THE WHOLE CROWD (*shouting*) Yes, yes! He is an enemy of the people! He hates his country! He hates his own people!

ASLAKSEN Both as a citizen and as an individual, I am profoundly disturbed by what we have had to listen to. Dr. Stockmann has shown himself in a light I should never have dreamed of. I am unhappily obliged to subscribe to the opinion which I have just

The doctor's line of inquiry touches upon a matter which remains controversial today—the instinctive anti-intellectualism among many ordinary citizens. Can you recall any illustrations in today's world?

At this point, the crux of the doctor's conflict is his decision to pursue one of two undesirable alternatives.

From here on, the chant "enemy of the people" dominates the assembly, much to the disbelief of the well-intentioned Dr. Stockmann.

AN ENEMY OF THE PEOPLE   175

heard my estimable fellow-citizens utter; and I propose that we should give expression to that opinion in a resolution. I propose a resolution as follows: "This meeting declares that it considers Dr. Thomas Stockmann, Medical Officer of the Baths, to be an enemy of the people." (*A storm of cheers and applause. A number of men surround the Doctor and hiss him. Mrs. Stockmann and Petra have got up from their seats. Morten and Ejlif are fighting the other schoolboys for hissing; some of their elders separate them.*)

DR. STOCKMANN (*to the men who are hissing him*) Oh, you fools! I tell you that—

ASLAKSEN (*ringing his bell*) We cannot hear you now, Doctor. A formal vote is about to be taken; but, out of regard for personal feelings, it shall be by ballot and not verbal. Have you any clean paper, Mr. Billing?

BILLING I have both blue and white here.

ASLAKSEN (*going to him*) That will do nicely; we shall get on more quickly that way. Cut it up into small strips—yes, that's it. (*to the meeting*) Blue means no; white means yes. I will come round myself and collect votes. (*Peter Stockmann leaves the hall. Aslaksen and one or two others go round the room with the slips of paper in their hats.*)

1ST CITIZEN (*to Hovstad*) I say, what has come to the Doctor? What are we to think of it?

HOVSTAD Oh, you know how headstrong he is.

2ND CITIZEN (*to Billing*) Billing, you go to their house—have you ever noticed if the fellow drinks?

BILLING Well I'm hanged if I know what to say. There are always spirits on the table when you go.

3RD CITIZEN I rather think he goes quite off his head sometimes.

1ST CITIZEN I wonder if there is any madness in his family?

BILLING I shouldn't wonder if there were.

4TH CITIZEN No, it is nothing more than sheer malice; he wants to get even with somebody for something or other.

BILLING Well certainly he suggested a raise in his salary on one occasion lately, and did not get it.

THE CITIZENS (*together*) Ah!—then it is easy to understand how it is!

THE DRUNKEN MAN (*who has got amongst the audience again*) I want a blue one, I do! And I want a white one too!

VOICES It's that drunken chap again! Turn him out!

MORTEN KIIL (*going up to Dr. Stockmann*) Well, Stockmann, do you see what these monkey tricks of yours lead to?

DR. STOCKMANN I have done my duty.

MORTEN KIIL What was that you said about the tanneries at Mölledal?

DR. STOCKMANN You heard well enough. I said they were the source of all the filth.

MORTEN KIIL My tannery too?

DR. STOCKMANN Unfortunately your tannery is by far the worst.

It is now clear how important the chairmanship of the assembly has been for presenting only one side of the issue.

Billing's comment seems ironic when we recall that he formerly had dined in Stockmann's home with much pleasure.

The citizens seem quick to understand someone's actions when explained in terms of money.

MORTEN KIIL Are you going to put that in the papers?

DR. STOCKMANN I shall conceal nothing.

MORTEN KIIL That may cost you dear, Stockmann. (*goes out*)

A STOUT MAN (*going up to Captain Horster, without taking any notice of the ladies*) Well, Captain, so you lend your house to enemies of the people?

HORSTER I imagine I can do what I like with my own possessions, Mr. Vik.

> Like others, Mr. Vik uses his money as a cudgel to intimidate and retaliate. What does he imply here?

THE STOUT MAN Then you can have no objection to my doing the same with mine.

HORSTER What do you mean, sir?

THE STOUT MAN You shall hear from me in the morning. (*turns his back on him and moves off*)

PETRA Was that not your owner, Captain Horster?

HORSTER Yes, that was Mr. Vik the ship-owner.

ASLAKSEN (*with the voting-papers in his hands, gets up on to the platform and rings his bell*) Gentlemen, allow me to announce the result. By the votes of every one here except one person—

A YOUNG MAN That is the drunk chap!

ASLAKSEN By the votes of every one here except a tipsy man, this meeting of citizens declares Dr. Thomas Stockmann to be an enemy of the people. (*shouts and applause*) Three cheers for our ancient and honourable citizen community! (*renewed applause*) Three cheers for our able and energetic Mayor, who has so loyally suppressed the promptings of family feeling! (*cheers*) The meeting is dissolved. (*gets down*)

BILLING Three cheers for the Chairman!

THE WHOLE CROWD Three cheers for Aslaksen! Hurrah!

> In Act II, Billing and Hovstad had harsh criticism for Aslaksen; but here they praise him.

DR. STOCKMANN My hat and coat, Petra! Captain, have you room on your ship for passengers to the New World?

HORSTER For you and yours we will make room, Doctor.

DR. STOCKMANN (*as Petra helps him into his coat*) Good. Come, Katherine! Come, boys!

MRS. STOCKMANN (*in an undertone*) Thomas, dear, let us go out by the back way.

DR. STOCKMANN No back ways for me, Katherine. (*raising his voice*) You will hear more of this enemy of the people, before he shakes the dust off his shoes upon you! I am not so forgiving as a certain Person; I do not say: "I forgive you, for ye know not what ye do."

ASLAKSEN (*shouting*) That is a blasphemous comparison, Dr. Stockmann!

BILLING It is, by God! It's dreadful for an earnest man to listen to.

A COARSE VOICE Threatens us now, does he!

OTHER VOICES (*excitedly*) Let's go and break his windows! Duck him in the fjord!

ANOTHER VOICE Blow your horn, Evensen! Pip, pip!

AN ENEMY OF THE PEOPLE

Horn-blowing, hisses, and wild cries. Dr. Stockmann goes out through the hall with his family, Horster elbowing a way for them.

THE WHOLE CROWD (*howling after them as they go*) Enemy of the People! Enemy of the People!

BILLING (*as he puts his papers together*) Well, I'm damned if I go and drink toddy with the Stockmanns tonight!

The crowd press towards the exit. The uproar continues outside; shouts of "Enemy of the People!" are heard from without.

> How has Ibsen indicated that Act IV should end in complete chaos and uneasiness?

ACT V

Scene—Dr. Stockmann's study. Bookcases, and cabinets containing specimens, line the walls. At the back is a door leading to the hall; in the foreground on the left, a door leading to the sitting-room. In the right-hand wall are two windows, of which all the panes are broken. The Doctor's desk, littered with books and papers, stands in the middle of the room, which is in disorder. It is morning. Dr. Stockmann in dressing-gown, slippers and a smoking-cap, is bending down and raking with an umbrella under one of the cabinets. After a little while he rakes out a stone.

DR. STOCKMANN (*calling through the open sitting-room door*) Katherine, I have found another one.

MRS. STOCKMANN (*from the sitting-room*) Oh, you will find a lot more yet, I expect.

DR. STOCKMANN (*adding the stone to a heap of others on the table*) I shall treasure these stones as relics. Ejlif and Morten shall look at them every day, and when they are grown up they shall inherit them as heirlooms. (*rakes about under a bookcase*) Hasn't—what the deuce is her name?—the girl, you know—hasn't she been to fetch the glazier yet?

MRS. STOCKMANN (*coming in*) Yes, but he said he didn't know if he would be able to come to-day.

DR. STOCKMANN You will see he won't dare to come.

MRS. STOCKMANN Well, that is just what Randine thought—that he didn't dare to, on account of the neighbours. (*calls into the sitting-room*) What is it you want, Randine? Give it to me. (*goes in, and comes out again directly*) Here is a letter for you, Thomas.

DR. STOCKMANN Let me see it (*opens and reads it*) Ah!—of course.

MRS. STOCKMANN Who is it from?

DR. STOCKMANN From the landlord. Notice to quit.

MRS. STOCKMANN Is it possible? Such a nice man—

DR. STOCKMANN (*looking at the letter*) Does not dare do otherwise, he says. Doesn't like doing it, but dare not do otherwise—on account of his fellow-citizens—out of regard for public opinion. Is in a dependent position—dare not offend certain influential men—

MRS. STOCKMANN There, you see, Thomas!

DR. STOCKMANN Yes, yes, I see well enough; the whole lot of them in the town are cowards; not a man among them dares do anything

> A Biblical passage (John viii, 3-11) about the throwing of stones may come to mind at this point.

> A new verbal theme starts in the final act—the Stockmanns' acquaintances "dare not" show them any friendship or consideration, out of fear of what other townspeople might say.

for fear of the others. (*throws the letter on to the table*) But it doesn't matter to us, Katherine. We are going to sail away to the New World, and—

MRS. STOCKMANN But, Thomas, are you sure we are well advised to take this step?

DR. STOCKMANN Are you suggesting that I should stay here, where they have pilloried me as an enemy of the people—branded me—broken my windows! And just look here, Katherine—they have torn a great rent in my black trousers too!

MRS. STOCKMANN Oh, dear!—and they are the best pair you have got!

DR. STOCKMANN You should never wear your best trousers when you go out to fight for freedom and truth. It is not that I care so much about the trousers, you know; you can always sew them up again for me. But that the common herd should dare to make this attack on me, as if they were my equals—that is what I cannot, for the life of me, swallow!

MRS. STOCKMANN There is no doubt they have behaved very ill to you, Thomas; but is that sufficient reason for our leaving our native country for good and all?

DR. STOCKMANN If we went to another town, do you suppose we should not find the common people just as insolent as they are here? Depend upon it, there is not much to choose between them. Oh, well, let the curs snap—that is not the worst part of it. The worst is that, from one end of this country to the other, every man is the slave of his Party. Although, as far as that goes, I daresay it is not much better in the free West either; the compact majority, and liberal public opinion, and all that infernal old bag of tricks are probably rampant there too. But there things are done on a larger scale, you see. They may kill you, but they won't put you to death by slow torture. They don't squeeze a free man's soul in a vice, as they do here. And, if need be, one can live in solitude. (*walks up and down*) If only I knew where there was a virgin forest or a small South Sea island for sale, cheap—

MRS. STOCKMANN But think of the boys, Thomas!

DR. STOCKMANN (*standing still*) What a strange woman you are, Katherine! Would you prefer to have the boys grow up in a society like this? You saw for yourself last night that half the population are out of their minds; and if the other half have not lost their senses, it is because they are mere brutes, with no sense to lose.

MRS. STOCKMANN But, Thomas dear, the imprudent things you said had something to do with it, you know.

DR. STOCKMANN Well, isn't what I said perfectly true? Don't they turn every idea topsy-turvy? Don't they make a regular hotch-potch of right and wrong? Don't they say that the things I know are true, are lies? The craziest part of it is the fact of these "liberals," men of full age, going about in crowds imagining that they are the broad-minded party! Did you ever hear anything like it, Katherine!

MRS. STOCKMANN Yes, yes, it's mad enough of them, certainly; but—(*Petra comes in from the sitting-room.*) Back from school already?

Which of Stockmann's statements—"to sail away to the New World" or to stay "where they have pilloried" him—agrees best with his earlier theories about individual courage?

What does Stockmann mean about not wearing one's best clothes when entering a battle for freedom and truth?

Stockmann's initial reaction is to leave the insensitive society that has so abused him. How does his wife serve as a sounding board for his point of view?

Ibsen touches on the issue of men living unknowingly with illusions, a topic he examines in greater depth in other plays, such as *The Wild Duck*.

AN ENEMY OF THE PEOPLE

PETRA Yes. I have been given notice of dismissal.

MRS. STOCKMANN Dismissal!

DR. STOCKMANN You too?

PETRA Mrs. Busk gave me my notice; so I thought it was best to go at once.

DR. STOCKMANN You were perfectly right, too!

MRS. STOCKMANN Who would have thought Mrs. Busk was a woman like that!

PETRA Mrs. Busk isn't a bit like that, mother; I saw quite plainly how it hurt her to do it. But she didn't dare do otherwise, she said; and so I got my notice.

DR. STOCKMANN (*laughing and rubbing his hands*) She didn't dare do otherwise, either! It's delicious!

MRS. STOCKMANN Well, after the dreadful scenes last night—

PETRA It was not only that. Just listen to this, father!

DR. STOCKMANN Well?

PETRA Mrs. Busk showed me no less than three letters she received this morning—

DR. STOCKMANN Anonymous, I suppose?

> What are the full ramifications of the letters being anonymous?

PETRA Yes.

DR. STOCKMANN Yes, because they didn't dare to risk signing their names, Katherine!

PETRA And two of them were to the effect that a man, who has been our guest here, was declaring last night at the Club that my views on various subjects are extremely emancipated—

DR. STOCKMANN You did not deny that, I hope?

PETRA No, you know I wouldn't. Mrs. Busk's own views are tolerably emancipated, when we are alone together; but now that this report about me is being spread, she dare not keep me on any longer.

MRS. STOCKMANN And some one who had been a guest of ours! That shows you the return you get for your hospitality, Thomas!

DR. STOCKMANN We won't live in such a disgusting hole any longer. Pack up as quickly as you can, Katherine; the sooner we get away, the better.

MRS. STOCKMANN Be quiet—I think I hear someone in the hall. See who it is, Petra.

PETRA (*opening the door*) Oh, it's you Captain Horster! Do come in.

HORSTER (*coming in*) Good morning. I thought I would just come in and see how you were.

DR. STOCKMANN (*shaking his hand*) Thanks—that is really kind of you.

MRS. STOCKMANN And thank you, too, for helping us through the crowd, Captain Horster.

PETRA How did you manage to get home again?

HORSTER Oh, somehow or other. I am fairly strong, and there is more sound than fury about these folks.

DR. STOCKMANN Yes, isn't their swinish cowardice astonishing? Look here, I will show you something! There are all the stones they have thrown through my windows. Just look at them! I'm hanged if there are more than two decently large bits of hardstone in the whole heap; the rest are nothing but gravel—wretched little things. And yet they stood out there bawling and swearing that they would do me some violence; but as for *doing* anything—you don't see much of that in this town.

> What parallel might be drawn between Stockmann's description of the stones as bits of gravel and his earlier pronouncements on the value of the commoner?

HORSTER Just as well for you this time, doctor!

DR. STOCKMANN True enough. But it makes one angry all the same; because if some day it should be a question of a national fight in real earnest, you will see that public opinion will be in favour of taking to one's heels, and the compact majority will turn tail like a flock of sheep, Captain Horster. That is what is so mournful to think of; it gives me so much concern, that—. No, devil take it, it is ridiculous to care about it! They have called me an enemy of the people, so an enemy of the people let me be!

MRS. STOCKMANN You will never be that, Thomas.

DR. STOCKMANN Don't swear to that, Katherine. To be called an ugly name may have the same effect as a pin-scratch in the lung. And that hateful name—I can't get quit of it. It is sticking here in the pit of my stomach, eating into me like a corrosive acid. And no magnesia will remove it.

> Magnesia is a remedy for stomach upset.

PETRA Bah!—you should only laugh at them, father.

HORSTER They will change their minds some day, Doctor.

MRS. STOCKMANN Yes, Thomas, as sure as you are standing here.

DR. STOCKMANN Perhaps, when it is too late. Much good may it do them! They may wallow in their filth then and rue the day when they drove a patriot into exile. When do you sail, Captain Horster?

HORSTER Hm!—that was just what I had come to speak about—

DR. STOCKMANN Why, has anything gone wrong with the ship?

HORSTER No; but what has happened is that I am not to sail in it.

PETRA Do you mean that you have been dismissed from your command?

HORSTER (*smiling*) Yes, that's just it.

PETRA You too.

MRS. STOCKMANN There, you see, Thomas!

> Mrs. Stockmann's fears are valid after all.

DR. STOCKMANN And that for the truth's sake! Oh, if I had thought such a thing possible—

HORSTER You mustn't take it to heart; I shall be sure to find a job with some ship-owner or other, elsewhere.

DR. STOCKMANN And that is this man Vik—a wealthy man, independent of everyone and everything—! Shame on him!

HORSTER He is quite an excellent fellow otherwise; he told me himself he would willingly have kept me on, if only he had dared—

DR. STOCKMANN But he didn't dare? No, of course not.

HORSTER It is not such an easy matter, he said, for a party man—

DR. STOCKMANN The worthy man spoke the truth. A party is like a sausage machine; it mashes up all sorts of heads together into the same mincemeat—fatheads and blockheads, all in one mash!

MRS. STOCKMANN Come, come, Thomas dear!

PETRA (*to Horster*) If only you had not come home with us, things might not have come to this pass.

HORSTER I do not regret it.

PETRA (*holding out her hand to him*) Thank you for that!

HORSTER (*to Dr. Stockmann*) And so what I came to say was that if you are determined to go away, I have thought of another plan—

DR. STOCKMANN That's splendid!—if only we can get away at once.

MRS. STOCKMANN Hush!—wasn't that someone knocking?

PETRA That is uncle, surely.

DR. STOCKMANN Aha! (*calls out*) Come in!

MRS. STOCKMANN Dear Thomas, promise me definitely—.

Peter Stockmann comes in from the hall.

PETER STOCKMANN Oh, you are engaged. In that case, I will—.

DR. STOCKMANN No, no, come in.

PETER STOCKMANN But I wanted to speak to you alone.

MRS. STOCKMANN We will go into the sitting-room in the meanwhile.

HORSTER And I will look in again later.

DR. STOCKMANN No, go in there with them, Captain Horster; I want to hear more about—.

HORSTER Very well, I will wait, then. (*He follows Mrs. Stockmann and Petra into the sitting-room.*)

DR. STOCKMANN I daresay you find it rather draughty here to-day. Put your hat on.

PETER STOCKMANN Thank you, if I may. (*does so*) I think I caught cold last night; I stood and shivered—

DR. STOCKMANN Really? I found it warm enough.

PETER STOCKMANN I regret that it was not in my power to prevent those excesses last night.

DR. STOCKMANN Have you anything particular to say to me besides that?

PETER STOCKMANN (*taking a big letter from his pocket*) I have this document for you, from the Baths Committee.

DR. STOCKMANN My dismissal?

PETER STOCKMANN Yes, dating from to-day. (*lays the letter on the table*) It gives us pain to do it; but, to speak frankly, we dared not do otherwise on account of public opinion.

Horster, alone of Stockmann's friends, has "dared" to remain true to the besieged family. What qualities visible in him from the beginning of the play help explain his loyalty? Does his occupation and his attitude toward politics have anything to do with this?

Even at an awkward moment such as this, the doctor manages to make some slight jokes based on the situation. What are some?

By now, the audience is alert to the grand irony when Peter Stockmann also takes refuge behind the excuse that he dare not contradict public opinion by retaining the doctor in his governmental capacity.

DR. STOCKMANN (*smiling*) Dared not? I seem to have heard that word before, to-day.

PETER STOCKMANN I must beg you to understand your position clearly. For the future you must not count on any practice whatever in the town.

DR. STOCKMANN Devil take the practice! But why are you so sure of that?

PETER STOCKMANN The Householders' Association is circulating a list from house to house. All right-minded citizens are being called upon to give up employing you; and I can assure you that not a single head of a family will risk refusing his signature. They simply dare not.

DR. STOCKMANN No, no; I don't doubt it. But what then?

PETER STOCKMANN If I might advise you, it would be best to leave the place for a little while—

DR. STOCKMANN Yes, the propriety of leaving the place *has* occurred to me.

PETER STOCKMANN Good. And then, when you have had six months to think things over, if, after mature consideration, you can persuade yourself to write a few words of regret, acknowledging your error—

DR. STOCKMANN I might have my appointment restored to me, do you mean?

PETER STOCKMANN Perhaps. It is not at all impossible.

DR. STOCKMANN But what about public opinion, then? Surely you would not dare to do it on account of public feeling.

PETER STOCKMANN Public opinion is an extremely mutable thing. And, to be quite candid with you, it is a matter of great importance to us to have some admission of that sort from you in writing.

Why has Peter Stockmann gone to his brother's home?

DR. STOCKMANN Oh, that's what you are after, is it! I will just trouble you to remember what I said to you lately about foxy tricks of that sort!

PETER STOCKMANN Your position was quite different then. At that time you had reason to suppose you had the whole town at your back—

DR. STOCKMANN Yes, and now I feel I have the whole town *on* my back—(*flaring up*). I would not do it if I had the devil and his dam on my back—! Never—never, I tell you!

PETER STOCKMANN A man with a family has no right to behave as you do. You have no right to do it, Thomas.

Here the "devil and his dam" means that not even the devil and his mother together could pressure Stockmann into writing a retraction as asked by his brother.

DR. STOCKMANN I have no right! There is only one single thing in the world a free man has no right to do. Do you know what that is?

PETER STOCKMANN No.

DR. STOCKMANN Of course you don't, but I will tell you. A free man has no right to soil himself with filth; he has no right to behave in a way that would justify his spitting in his own face.

PETER STOCKMANN This sort of thing sounds extremely plausible, of

AN ENEMY OF THE PEOPLE   183

course; and if there were no other explanation for your obstinacy—. But as it happens that there is.

DR. STOCKMANN What do you mean?

PETER STOCKMANN You understand very well what I mean. But, as your brother and as a man of discretion, I advise you not to build too much upon expectations and prospects that may so very easily fail you.

DR. STOCKMANN What in the world is all this about?

PETER STOCKMANN Do you really ask me to believe that you are ignorant of the terms of Mr. Kiil's will?

DR. STOCKMANN I know that the small amount he possesses is to go to an institution for indigent old workpeople. How does that concern me?

PETER STOCKMANN In the first place, it is by no means a small amount that is in question. Mr. Kiil is a fairly wealthy man.

DR. STOCKMANN I had no notion of that!

PETER STOCKMANN Hm!—hadn't you really? Then I suppose you had no notion, either, that a considerable portion of his wealth will come to your children, you and your wife having a life-rent of the capital. Has he never told you so?

Leave it to Peter Stockmann to know about the financial arrangements of everyone in the town! Why is it appropriate that the Mayor serve as a possible version of a deus ex machina *for his brother's family?*

DR. STOCKMANN Never, on my honour! Quite the reverse; he has consistently done nothing but fume at being so unconscionably heavily taxed. But are you perfectly certain of this, Peter?

PETER STOCKMANN I have it from an absolutely reliable source.

DR. STOCKMANN Then, thank God, Katherine is provided for—and the children too! I must tell her this at once—(*calls out*) Katherine, Katherine!

PETER STOCKMANN (*restraining him*) Hush, don't say a word yet!

MRS. STOCKMANN (*opening the door*) What is the matter?

DR. STOCKMANN Oh, nothing, nothing; you can go back. (*She shuts the door. Dr. Stockmann walks up and down in his excitement.*) Provided for!—Just think of it, we are all provided for! And for life! What a blessed feeling it is to know one is provided for!

Is Stockmann immune from worrying about security for his family? How do we know?

PETER STOCKMANN Yes, but that is just exactly what you are not. Mr. Kiil can alter his will any day he likes.

DR. STOCKMANN But he won't do that, my dear Peter. The "Badger" is much too delighted at my attack on you and your wise friends.

PETER STOCKMANN (*starts and looks intently at him*) Ah, that throws a light on various things.

DR. STOCKMANN What things?

PETER STOCKMANN I see that the whole thing was a combined manœuvre on your part and his. These violent, reckless attacks that you have made against the leading men of the town, under the pretence that it was in the name of truth—

Because of his own deviousness, the Mayor imagines the worst of others in their relationships, as here.

DR. STOCKMANN What about them?

PETER STOCKMANN I see that they were nothing else than the stipulated price for that vindictive old man's will.

DR. STOCKMANN (*almost speechless*) Peter—you are the most disgusting plebeian I have ever met in all my life.

PETER STOCKMANN All is over between us. Your dismissal is irrevocable—we have a weapon against you now. (*goes out*)

DR. STOCKMANN For shame! For shame! (*calls out*) Katherine, you must have the floor scrubbed after him! Let—what's her name —devil take it, the girl who has always got soot on her nose—

MRS. STOCKMANN (*in the sitting-room*) Hush, Thomas, be quiet!

PETRA (*coming to the door*) Father, grandfather is here, asking if he may speak to you alone.

DR. STOCKMANN Certainly he may. (*going to the door*) Come in, Mr. Kiil. (*Morten Kiil comes in. Dr. Stockmann shuts the door after him.*) What can I do for you? Won't you sit down?

MORTEN KIIL I won't sit. (*looks around*) You look very comfortable here to-day, Thomas.

DR. STOCKMANN Yes, don't we!

MORTEN KIIL Very comfortable—plenty of fresh air. I should think you have got enough to-day of that oxygen you were talking about yesterday. Your conscience must be in splendid order to-day, I should think.

DR. STOCKMANN It is.

MORTEN KIIL So I should think. (*taps his chest*) Do you know what I have got here?

DR. STOCKMANN A good conscience, too, I hope.

MORTEN KIIL Bah!—No, it is something better than that. (*He takes a thick pocket-book from his breast-pocket, opens it, and displays a packet of papers.*)

DR. STOCKMANN (*looking at him in astonishment*) Shares in the Baths?

MORTEN KIIL They were not difficult to get to-day.

DR. STOCKMANN And you have been buying—?

MORTEN KIIL As many as I could pay for.

DR. STOCKMANN But, my dear Mr. Kiil—consider the state of the Baths' affairs!

MORTEN KIIL If you behave like a reasonable man, you can soon set the Baths on their feet again.

DR. STOCKMANN Well, you can see for yourself that I have done all I can, but—. They are all mad in this town!

MORTEN KIIL You said yesterday that the worst of this pollution came from my tannery. If that is true, then my grandfather and my father before me, and I myself, for many years past, have been poisoning the town like three destroying angels. Do you think I am going to sit quiet under that reproach?

DR. STOCKMANN Unfortunately I am afraid you will have to.

MORTEN KIIL No, thank you. I am jealous of my name and reputation. They call me "the Badger," I am told. A badger is a kind of pig, I believe; but I am not going to give them the right to call me that. I mean to live and die a clean man.

The Mayor's completely cynical attitude is evident here; now that he believes he no longer needs the doctor to clean up the affair, he dismisses him outright for good.

Kiil offers the pragmatist's view concerning anyone's scruples.

Does Kiil value his conscience very highly? How do we know?

How else might Kiil have removed the stigma of being called a polluter and poisoner?

AN ENEMY OF THE PEOPLE

DR. STOCKMANN And how are you going to set about it?

MORTEN KIIL You shall cleanse me, Thomas.

DR. STOCKMANN I!

MORTEN KIIL Do you know what money I have brought these shares with? No, of course you can't know—but I will tell you. It is the money that Katherine and Petra and the boys will have when I am gone. Because I have been able to save a little bit after all, you know.

DR. STOCKMANN (*flaring up*) And you have gone and taken Katherine's money for *this*!

MORTEN KIIL Yes, the whole of the money is invested in the Baths now. And now I just want to see whether you are quite stark, staring mad, Thomas! If you still make out that these animals and other nasty things of that sort come from my tannery, it will be exactly as if you were to flay broad strips of skin from Katherine's body, and Petra's, and the boys'; and no decent man would do that—unless he were mad.

> Kiil's arrangements place Stockmann in a terrific bind, as both of them acknowledge. What exactly has Kiil done with his daughter's inheritance money?

DR. STOCKMANN (*walking up and down*) Yes, but I *am* mad; I *am* mad!

MORTEN KIIL You cannot be so absurdly mad as all that, when it is a question of your wife and children.

DR. STOCKMANN (*standing still in front of him*) Why couldn't you consult me about it, before you went and bought all that trash?

MORTEN KIIL What is done cannot be undone.

DR. STOCKMANN (*walks about uneasily*) If only I were not so certain about it—! But I am absolutely convinced that I am right.

MORTEN KIIL (*weighing the pocket-book in his hand*) If you stick to your mad idea, this won't be worth much, you know. (*puts the pocket-book in his pocket*)

DR. STOCKMANN But, hang it all! it might be possible for science to discover some prophylactic, I should think—or some antidote of some kind—

MORTEN KIIL To kill these animals, do you mean?

DR. STOCKMANN Yes, or to make them innocuous.

MORTEN KIIL Couldn't you try some rat's-bane?

DR. STOCKMANN Don't talk nonsense! They all say it is only imagination, you know. Well, let it go at that! Let them have their own way about it! Haven't the ignorant, narrow-minded curs reviled me as an enemy of the people?—and haven't they been ready to tear the clothes off my back too?

> Stockmann is momentarily tempted to make what decision?

MORTEN KIIL And broken all your windows to pieces!

DR. STOCKMANN And then there is my duty to my family. I must talk it over with Katherine; she is great on those things.

MORTEN KIIL That is right; be guided by a reasonable woman's advice.

DR. STOCKMANN (*advancing towards him*) To think you could do such a preposterous thing! Risking Katherine's money in this way, and putting me in such a horribly painful dilemma! When I look at you, I think I see the devil himself—.

> How is the doctor's response to Kiil similar to Peter's response to the doctor?

MORTEN KIIL Then I had better go. But I must have an answer from you before two o'clock—yes or no. If it is no, the shares go to a charity, and that this very day.

DR. STOCKMANN And what does Katherine get?

MORTEN KIIL Not a halfpenny. (*The door leading to the hall opens, and Hovstad and Aslaksen make their appearance.*) Look at those two!

DR. STOCKMANN (*staring at them*) What the devil!—have *you* actually the face to come into my house?

HOVSTAD Certainly.

ASLAKSEN We have something to say to you, you see.

MORTEN KIIL (*in a whisper*) Yes or no—before two o'clock.

ASLAKSEN (*glancing at Hovstad*) Aha! (*Morten Kiil goes out.*)

DR. STOCKMANN Well, what do you want with me? Be brief.

HOVSTAD I can quite understand that you are annoyed with us for our attitude at the meeting yesterday—

DR. STOCKMANN Attitude, do you call it? Yes, it was a charming attitude! I call it weak, womanish—damnably shameful!

HOVSTAD Call it what you like, we could not do otherwise.

DR. STOCKMANN You *dared* not do otherwise—isn't that it?

HOVSTAD Well, if you like to put it that way.

ASLAKSEN But why did you not let us have word of it beforehand!—just a hint to Mr. Hovstad or to me?

DR. STOCKMANN A hint? Of what?

ASLAKSEN Of what was behind it all.

DR. STOCKMANN I don't understand you in the least.

ASLAKSEN (*with a confidential nod*) Oh yes, you do, Dr. Stockmann.

HOVSTAD It is no good making a mystery of it any longer.

DR. STOCKMANN (*looking first at one of them and then at the other*) What the devil do you both mean?

ASLAKSEN May I ask if your father-in-law is not going round the town buying up all the shares in the Baths?

DR. STOCKMANN Yes, he has been buying Baths shares to-day; but—

ASLAKSEN It would have been more prudent to get some one else to do it—some one less nearly related to you.

HOVSTAD And you should not have let your name appear in the affair. There was no need for anyone to know that the attack on the Baths came from you. You ought to have consulted me, Dr. Stockmann.

DR. STOCKMANN (*looks in front of him; then a light seems to dawn on him and he says in amazement:*) Are such things conceivable? Are such things possible?

ASLAKSEN (*with a smile*) Evidently they are. But it is better to use a little *finesse*, you know.

HOVSTAD And it is much better to have several persons in a thing

---

There is a form of symmetry here, since in Act IV the same people who entered Stockmann's house in the first act have returned for their own purposes. What is the dramatic function of the return of these characters?

What have Aslaksen and Hovstad concluded about Stockmann's announcement concerning the Baths and Kiil's subsequent purchase of the stocks?

Why have Stockmann's enemies come to him now?

AN ENEMY OF THE PEOPLE   187

of that sort; because the responsibility of each individual is lessened, when there are others with him.

DR. STOCKMANN (*composedly*) Come to the point, gentlemen. What do you want?

ASLAKSEN Perhaps Mr. Hovstad had better—

HOVSTAD No, you tell him, Aslaksen.

ASLAKSEN Well, the fact is that, now we know the bearings of the whole affair, we think we might venture to put the "People's Messenger" at your disposal.

DR. STOCKMANN Do you dare do that now? What about public opinion? Are you not afraid of a storm breaking upon our heads?

HOVSTAD We will try to weather it.

Only when what commodity is at stake will Hovstad and Aslaksen risk offending the townspeople?

ASLAKSEN And you must be ready to go off quickly on a new tack, Doctor. As soon as your invective has done its work—

DR. STOCKMANN Do you mean, as soon as my father-in-law and I have got hold of the shares at a low figure?

HOVSTAD Your reasons for wishing to get the control of the Baths are mainly scientific, I take it.

DR. STOCKMANN Of course; it was for scientific reasons that I persuaded the old "Badger" to stand in with me in the matter. So we will tinker at the conduit-pipes a little, and dig up a little bit of the shore, and it shan't cost the town a sixpence. That will be all right —eh?

Stockmann is baiting his visitors. Does he actually intend to carry out what he describes?

HOVSTAD I think so—if you have the "People's Messenger" behind you.

ASLAKSEN The Press is a power in a free community, Doctor.

DR. STOCKMANN Quite so. And so is public opinion. And you, Mr. Aslaksen—I suppose you will be answerable for the Householders' Association?

ASLAKSEN Yes, and for the Temperance Society. You may rely on that.

DR. STOCKMANN But, gentlemen—I really am ashamed to ask the question—but, what return do you—?

HOVSTAD We should prefer to help you without any return whatever, believe me. But the "People's Messenger" is in rather a shaky condition; it doesn't go really well; and I should be very unwilling to suspend the paper now, when there is so much work to do here in the political way.

Is Hovstad's offer entirely ethical? Why?

DR. STOCKMANN Quite so; that would be a great trial to such a friend of the people as you are. (*flares up*) But I am an enemy of the people, remember! (*walks about the room*) Where have I put my stick? Where the devil is my stick?

HOVSTAD What's that?

ASLAKSEN Surely you never mean—?

DR. STOCKMANN (*standing still*) And suppose I don't give you a single penny of all I get out of it? Money is not very easy to get out of us rich folk, please to remember!

HOVSTAD And you please to remember that this affair of the shares can be represented in two ways!

DR. STOCKMANN Yes, and you are just the man to do it. If I don't come to the rescue of the "People's Messenger," you will certainly take an evil view of the affair; you will hunt me down, I can well imagine—pursue me—try to throttle me as a dog does a hare.

HOVSTAD It is a natural law; every animal must fight for its own livelihood.

ASLAKSEN And get its food where it can, you know.

DR. STOCKMANN (*walking about the room*) Then you go and look for yours in the gutter; because I am going to show you which is the strongest animal of us three! (*finds an umbrella and brandishes it above his head*) Ah, now—!

HOVSTAD You are surely not going to use violence!

ASLAKSEN Take care what you are doing with that umbrella.

DR. STOCKMANN Out of the window with you, Mr. Hovstad!

HOVSTAD (*edging to the door*) Are you quite mad!

DR. STOCKMANN Out of the window, Mr. Aslaksen! Jump, I tell you! You will have to do it, sooner or later.

ASLAKSEN (*running round the writing-table*) Moderation, Doctor—I am a delicate man—I can stand so little—(*calls out*) help, help!

Mrs. Stockmann, Petra and Horster come in from the sitting-room.

MRS. STOCKMANN Good gracious, Thomas! What is happening?

DR. STOCKMANN (*brandishing the umbrella*) Jump out, I tell you! Out into the gutter!

HOVSTAD An assault on an unoffending man! I call you to witness, Captain Horster. (*hurries out through the hall*)

ASLAKSEN (*irresolutely*) If only I knew the way about here—. (*steals out through the sitting-room*)

MRS. STOCKMANN (*holding her husband back*) Control yourself, Thomas!

DR. STOCKMANN (*throwing down the umbrella*) Upon my soul, they have escaped after all.

MRS. STOCKMANN What did they want you to do?

DR. STOCKMANN I will tell you later on; I have something else to think about now. (*goes to the table and writes something on a calling-card*) Look there, Katherine; what is written there?

MRS. STOCKMANN Three big *Noes*; what does that mean?

DR. STOCKMANN I will tell you that too, later on. (*holds out the card to Petra*) There, Petra; tell sooty-face to run over to the "Badger's" with that, as quick as she can. Hurry up! (*Petra takes the card and goes out to the hall.*)

DR. STOCKMANN Well, I think I have had a visit from every one of the devil's messengers to-day! But now I am going to sharpen my pen till they can feel its point; I shall dip it in venom and gall; I shall hurl my inkpot at their heads!

By this time, Stockmann completely understands how the minds of his former friends operate.

What do the newspapermen imply they will do if Stockmann refuses to go along with their proposal?

What is the significance of Stockmann's note to Kiil?

MRS. STOCKMANN Yes, but we are going away, you know, Thomas.

Petra comes back.

DR. STOCKMANN Well?

PETRA She has gone with it.

DR. STOCKMANN Good.—Going away, did you say? No, I'll be hanged if we are going away! We are going to stay where we are, Katherine!

PETRA Stay here?

MRS. STOCKMANN Here, in the town?

DR. STOCKMANN Yes, here. This is the field of battle—this is where the fight will be. This is where I shall triumph! As soon as I have had my trousers sewn up I shall go out and look for another house. We must have a roof over our heads for the winter.

HORSTER That you shall have in my house.

DR. STOCKMANN Can I?

HORSTER Yes, quite well. I have plenty of room, and I am almost never at home.

MRS. STOCKMANN How good of you, Captain Horster!

PETRA Thank you!

DR. STOCKMANN (*grasping his hand*) Thank you, thank you! That is one trouble over! Now I can set to work in earnest at once. There is an endless amount of things to look through here, Katherine! Luckily I shall have all my time at my disposal; because I have been dismissed from the Baths, you know.

MRS. STOCKMANN (*with a sigh*) Oh yes, I expected that.

DR. STOCKMANN And they want to take my practice away from me too. Let them! I have got the poor people to fall back upon, anyway—those that don't pay anything; and, after all, they need me most, too. But, by Jove, they will have to listen to me; I shall preach to them in season and out of season, as it says somewhere.

MRS. STOCKMANN But, dear Thomas, I should have thought events had showed you what use it is to preach.

DR. STOCKMANN You are really ridiculous, Katherine. Do you want me to let myself be beaten off the field by public opinion and the compact majority and all that devilry? No, thank you! And what I want to do is so simple and clear and straightforward. I only want to drum into the heads of these curs the fact that the liberals are the most insidious enemies of freedom—that party programmes strangle every young and vigorous truth—that considerations of expediency turn morality and justice upside down—and that they will end by making life here unbearable. Don't you think, Captain Horster, that I ought to be able to make people understand that?

HORSTER Very likely; I don't know much about such things myself.

DR. STOCKMANN Well, look here—I will explain! It is the party leaders that must be exterminated. A party leader is like a wolf, you see—like a voracious wolf. He requires a certain number of smaller victims to prey upon every year, if he is to live. Just look at Hovstad

---

Stockmann now has nothing else to lose, and he is prepared to fight on his home grounds.

Has Mrs. Stockmann changed her position much during the play? How do we measure her attitudes?

and Aslaksen! How many smaller victims have they not put an end to—or to any rate maimed and mangled until they are fit for nothing except to be householders or subscribers to the "People's Messenger"! (*sits down on the edge of the table*) Come here, Katherine—look how beautifully the sun shines to-day! And this lovely spring air I am drinking in!

MRS. STOCKMANN Yes, if only we could live on sunshine and spring air, Thomas.

As before, through Mrs. Stockmann's reservations, Ibsen makes available opposing views concerning Stockmann's decisions.

DR. STOCKMANN Oh, you will have to pinch and save a bit—then we shall get along. That gives me very little concern. What is much worse is that I know of no one who is liberal-minded and high-minded enough to venture to take up my work after me.

PETRA Don't think about that, father; you have plenty of time before you.—Hullo, here are the boys already!

Ejlif and Morten come in from the sitting-room.

MRS. STOCKMANN Have you got a holiday?

MORTEN No; but we were fighting with the other boys between lessons—

The reason behind the boys' fights is obvious.

EJLIF That isn't true; it was the other boys were fighting with us.

MORTEN Well, and then Mr. Rörlund said we had better stay at home for a day or two.

DR. STOCKMANN (*snapping his fingers and getting up from the table*) I have it! I have it, by Jove! You shall never set foot in the school again!

THE BOYS No more school!

MRS. STOCKMANN But, Thomas—

DR. STOCKMANN Never, I say. I will educate you myself; that is to say, you shan't learn a blessed thing—

MORTEN Hooray!

DR. STOCKMANN —but I will make liberal-minded and high-minded men of you. You must help me with that, Petra.

PETRA Yes, father, you may be sure I will.

DR. STOCKMANN And my school shall be in the room where they insulted me and called me an enemy of the people. But we are too few as we are; I must have at least twelve boys to begin with.

What are some purposes of the doctor's school?

MRS. STOCKMANN You will certainly never get them in this town.

DR. STOCKMANN We shall. (*to the boys*) Don't you know any street urchins—regular ragamuffins—?

MORTEN Yes, father, I know lots!

DR. STOCKMANN That's capital! Bring me some specimens of them. I am going to experiment with curs, just for once; there may be some exceptional heads amongst them.

MORTEN And what are we going to do, when you have made liberal-minded and high-minded men of us?

DR. STOCKMANN Then you shall drive all the wolves out of the country, my boys!

What does Stockmann mean by driving "all the wolves out of the country"?

AN ENEMY OF THE PEOPLE 191

Ejlif looks rather doubtful about it; Morten jumps about crying "Hurrah!"

MRS. STOCKMANN Let us hope it won't be the wolves that will drive you out of the country, Thomas.

DR. STOCKMANN Are you out of your mind, Katherine? Drive me out! Now—when I am the strongest man in the town!

MRS. STOCKMANN The strongest—now?

DR. STOCKMANN Yes, and I will go so far as to say that now I am the strongest man in the whole world.

MORTEN I say!

DR. STOCKMANN (*lowering his voice*) Hush! You mustn't say anything about it yet; but I have made a great discovery.

MRS. STOCKMANN Another one?

DR. STOCKMANN Yes. (*gathers them round him, and says confidentially*) It is this, let me tell you—that the strongest man in the world is he who stands most alone.

MRS. STOCKMANN (*smiling and shaking her head*) Oh, Thomas, Thomas!

PETRA (*encouragingly, as she grasps her father's hands*) Father!

Stockmann's last declaration makes sense only when considered in the context of the arguments he had voiced at the town meeting and after.

The theme of *An Enemy of the People* is reflected in the title, and it surfaces continually in the play.

POSTVIEW: THEME

1. As briefly as possible, state the basic theme of the play.
2. Why are Dr. Stockmann and his brother the perfect exponents of two alternative ideals central to the theme?
3. How does the play's title echo the theme?

To solidify the theme, Ibsen uses the town Baths as a focal point for exploring the issues at stake.

4. Why are the Baths effective in generating the psychological and philosophical tug-of-war involved?
5. What are the *real* issues: sanitation, ethics, economics, or personality conflicts?
6. Is there anyone besides the doctor who believes the issue of the Baths is strictly a moral matter? Who?
7. Is Dr. Stockmann altruistically motivated in wanting to expose the poisoning of the Baths, or has he some secondary, perhaps subconscious, personal considerations in mind? If so, what might they be?
8. Why is Peter Stockmann so sensitive concerning the well-being of the Baths?

In order to maintain his rights and self-respect, Dr. Stockmann is forced into becoming a rebel against the Establishment of his home town. But in that dissenting role, he discovers acute difficulties.

9. What position does the doctor find himself forced to defend at the town assembly in Act IV?
10. Is his position wholly tenable in the eyes of an objective audience? Why?

11. Does Ibsen portray Dr. Stockmann's revolt against the ruling system as imprudent in theory? In its expression? Why?
12. Among the characters, who could be considered Ibsen's spokesman—the raisonneur? Why?
13. How does Ibsen imply through the play's conclusion that there is no easy answer in life for separating one's personal rights from one's duty to his society?
14. In what ways is this play an example of a "drama of ideas"? (See the introduction to the play.)

INTRODUCTION
A TOUCH OF THE POET

Eugene O'Neill

THE NAME OF EUGENE O'NEILL is significant in American drama. First, he wrote an impressive array of plays, nearly fifty, many of which are now considered masterpieces. Among O'Neill's finest dramatic efforts are *The Emperor Jones* (1920), *The Hairy Ape* (1922), *Desire Under the Elms* (1925), *Strange Interlude* (1928), *Mourning Becomes Electra* (1931), *Ah, Wilderness!* (1933), *The Iceman Cometh* (1939), *Long Day's Journey into Night* (1956), and *A Touch of the Poet* (1957). Second, O'Neill's success in the theater established him as America's *first* premium playwright: his plays earned him four Pulitzer Prizes, and in 1936 he received the Nobel Prize for literature. O'Neill marked the coming to maturity of drama in the United States, leaving behind a legacy of plays written in a wide range of dramatic idioms.

O'Neill (1888–1953) was the second of three sons born to the famed actor James O'Neill. Although he was born in a hotel room in New York City and sometimes travelled with his theatrical father, Eugene and his one surviving older brother nonetheless had an Irish-Catholic upbringing in strict parochial schools and in an upper-middle-class home. Beneath the façade of conventional family life, however, seethed an excruciating tangle of frustrations and tensions. His mother accidently had become a drug addict because of a physician's miscalculation; meanwhile, James O'Neill became a heavy drinker and a chronic penny-pincher. In his plays, O'Neill was to dramatize the festering love-hate relationships he knew first-hand among father, mother, brother, and self. Most clearly depicting his family's psychological turmoil is *Long Day's Journey into Night,* a lacerating masterpiece first produced posthumously in 1956.

O'Neill's plays reflect his early years of wanderlust when he left Princeton without a degree, sailed the seas as a sailor and reporter, recuperated in a hospital for tuberculosis, and lived a nomadic life in Greenwich Village. Married first while quite young, O'Neill was married twice again during his lifetime. Eventually he was drawn tightly and irrevocably to the theater. He took a course in playwriting at Harvard and worked with the experimental Provincetown Players in Massachusetts. It was there that his first dramatic efforts were performed.

The Catholic schools O'Neill attended failed to confirm him in the Christian faith, and he emerged as an agnostic. Yet, because of a deep concern for the soul, O'Neill mirrors in his plays a mind in quest of spiritual values. His characters manifest the ruthless self-exploration of their inner beings by men and women struggling against fate, as expresssed by the psychological emphasis on environment and biological heredity. O'Neill believed what Freud wrote and considered himself an expert in the theories of psychoanalysis.

O'Neill's chief preoccupation in his dramas—mankind's trapped status in a friendless universe—predates the great human anguish communicated by existential thinkers and artists. In a letter in 1929 regarding his play *Dynamo,* O'Neill stated that all artists must isolate and treat the malady of the modern world, that is, "the death of the old God and the failure of science and materialism" to provide us with any new, satisfying system or religion.

No single theatrical technique dominated O'Neill's plays. He continued to experiment with the forms available to the stage. In *Long Day's Journey into Night* he displayed a mastery of *representationalism,* that is, dramatization and staging techniques that emphasize the illusion that reality is being shown on stage. According to the methods of representationalism, settings are made to appear precisely like the objects they represent. Yet O'Neill's plays also ranged in opposite directions, into the avant-garde. Dramas like *The Hairy Ape* and *Desire Under the Elms* are examples of *expressionism,* in which the external appearance of objects is distorted deliberately to portray those objects as they are *felt* by the artist and his characters, rather than to recreate a photographically valid version of things. In very imaginative plays, O'Neill successfully fused the attributes of naturalistic and symbolic dramatic architecture and techniques.

A Touch of the Poet was the last full-length play O'Neill finished. Written during the period of 1939–40, it was published posthumously in 1957 and produced on Broadway the following year. Like the uncompleted *More Stately Mansions, A Touch of the Poet* was part of a projected cycle of at least nine plays O'Neill had contemplated to dramatize the history of the United States from 1775 to the 1920s. The focal point in these works was to have been the succeeding generations of an Irish-American family torn in two directions by lust for wealth and by high spiritual idealism. *A Touch of the Poet,* for example, is set in 1828, in a tavern outside Boston. The proprietor, Cornelius (Con) Melody, has emigrated from Ireland to America where, snubbed by Yankee aristocrats, he

A rehearsal of the 1958 Broadway production, A Touch of the Poet. *In the foreground, the stage manager keeps track of the action. Sara (Kim Stanley) stands to the left of Con (Eric Portman).*

lives in a dream world where he recites Byron to maintain a "touch of the poet" in his soul. O'Neill envisioned that later plays in the series would pursue the troubled fortunes of Melody's heirs, as in *More Stately Mansions.* But O'Neill never completed his enterprise. Instead, he destroyed the manuscripts he had worked on, because he felt they were inferior.

In his proposed series, O'Neill had not intended to revert to period drama simply for the sake of experimentation. All his plays probe man's search for values in life. And that search crosses all time boundaries, to account for mankind of all epochs. In the sketchy notes comprising *Fragmentary Work Diary* (1929), O'Neill wrote: "No matter in what period of American history [a] play is laid, [it] must remain a modern psychological drama—nothing to do with period except to use it as a mash. . . ." O'Neill depicts the human spirit, welded by fate to a mundane earthly existence, as the emblem of all sensitive persons striving to know and better themselves. It is Con Melody in *A Touch of the Poet* who epitomizes frustrated man in an unfriendly environment which encases him. Whether to face up to the spiritual pain in actual life, then, or to soften the truth about oneself with illusions becomes the primary question underlying most of O'Neill's plays.

A Touch of the Poet is not one of O'Neill's most innovative plays. In delivering needed exposition, for instance, the play is wholly conventional.

PREVIEW: STRUCTURE

1. What appears to be the functional purpose of Jamie Cregan during the opening episode?
2. Why is Jamie's account of Con Melody's nature so vital to the audience?
3. What do we learn from our first glimpse about the characters of Sara and Nora?

O'Neill uses a daring device in developing the complications of his plot.

4. What role does Simon Harford play in the lives of the Melody family?
5. What kind of person is Simon?
6. How do we learn about Simon? About his mother Deborah Harford? About his father Henry Harford?
7. How does Melody's complex personality lead to further complications when Mrs. Harford arrives, seeking her son?
8. How does the anonymous letter to the Harfords concerning Simon's whereabouts function to advance the play's development?

O'Neill creates tension leading to a crisis during Melody's private discourse with his daughter.

9. What is the topic of Melody's talk with Sara?
10. How does his approach to her alert her (and us) to be ready for greater conflict in the proceedings?

In the action, the climax arises when Gadsby arrives.

11. What is the nature of Gadsby's visit on behalf of the Harfords?
12. How does the audience come to realize that money, as such, is not Con Melody's primary goal in life? What is most important to him?
13. When do we witness the high point of the physical action of the play?
14. How does Gadsby's mission precipitate resolving actions by Melody? By Sara?
15. What is at stake for Melody? For Sara? For the senior Harfords? For Simon?

In revealing the resolution to the play's crises, O'Neill surprises the audience by not showing the physical actions on stage.

16. How does O'Neill build up suspense regarding the outcome of the play's complications?
17. What constitutes the resolution for Sara? For Melody?
18. What was the determining factor during the melee at the Harford estate that altered Melody's entire concept of himself?
19. How does Jamie Cregan function in these late episodes of the play?

With Melody's new-found direction in life, a denouement emerges at play's end.

20. What confirms for the audience Melody's significant decision to change his objectives in life?
21. How does Nora respond to the new situation with Melody?
22. How is Sara's reaction different from her mother's? Why?
23. What can be expected in regard to Melody's future behavior?

A TOUCH OF THE POET

Eugene O'Neill

CHARACTERS

Mickey Maloy
Jamie Cregan
Sara Melody
Nora Melody
Cornelius Melody
Deborah (*Mrs. Henry Harford*)
Dan Roche
Paddy O'Dowd
Patch Riley
Nicholas Gadsby

SCENES

Act One
Dining room of Melody's Tavern morning of July 27, 1828.

Act Two
The same, later that morning.

Act Three
The same, that evening.

Act Four
The same, that night.

ACT I

SCENE—*The dining room of Melody's Tavern, in a village a few miles from Boston. The tavern is over a hundred years old. It had once been prosperous, a breakfast stop for the stagecoach, but the stage line had been discontinued and for some years now the tavern has fallen upon neglected days.*

The dining room and barroom were once a single spacious room, low-ceilinged, with heavy oak beams and paneled walls—the taproom of the tavern in its prosperous days, now divided into two rooms by a flimsy partition, the barroom being off left. The partition is painted to imitate the old paneled walls but this only makes it more of an eyesore.

At left front, two steps lead up to a closed door opening on a flight of stairs to the floor above. Farther back is the door to the bar. Between these doors hangs a large mirror. Beyond the bar door a small cabinet is fastened to the wall. At rear are four windows. Between the middle two is the street door. At right front is another door, open, giving on a hallway and the main stairway to the second floor, and leading to the kitchen. Farther front at right, there is a high schoolmaster's desk with a stool.

In the foreground are two tables. One, with four chairs, at left center; a larger one, seating six, at right center. At left and right, rear, are two more tables, identical with the ones at right center. All these tables are set with white tablecloths, etc., except the small ones in the foreground at left.

Note that all the events of the play take place in a single day. By compressing the events, O'Neill focuses the play's tension.

From the description of the setting, O'Neill wants us to recognize what facts concerning Melody's Tavern?

It is around nine in the morning of July 27, 1828. Sunlight shines in through the windows at rear.

Mickey Maloy sits at the table at left front, facing right. He is glancing through a newspaper. Maloy is twenty-six, with a sturdy physique and an amiable, cunning face, his mouth usually set in a half-leering grin.

Jamie Cregan peers around the half-open door to the bar. Seeing Maloy, he comes in. As obviously Irish as Maloy, he is middle-aged, tall, with a lantern-jawed face. There is a scar of a saber cut over one cheekbone. He is dressed neatly but in old, worn clothes. His eyes are bloodshot, his manner sickly, but he grins as he greets Maloy sardonically.

CREGAN God bless all here—even the barkeep.

MALOY *(with an answering grin)* Top o' the mornin'.

CREGAN Top o' me head. *(He puts his hand to his head and groans.)* Be the saints, there's a blacksmith at work on it!

MALOY Small wonder. You'd the divil's own load when you left at two this mornin'.

CREGAN I must have. I don't remember leaving. *(He sits at right of table.)* Faix, you're takin' it aisy.

MALOY There's no trade this time o'day.

CREGAN It was a great temptation, when I saw no one in the bar, to make off with a bottle. A hair av the dog is what I need, but I've divil a penny in my pantaloons.

MALOY Have one on the house. *(He goes to the cupboard and takes out a decanter of whiskey and a glass.)*

CREGAN Thank you kindly. Sure, the good Samaritan was a crool haythen beside you.

MALOY *(putting the decanter and glass before him)* It's the same you was drinking last night—his private dew. He keeps it here for emergencies when he don't want to go in the bar.

CREGAN *(pours out a big drink)* Lave it to Con never to be caught dry. *(raising his glass)* Your health and inclinations—if they're virtuous! *(He drinks and sighs with relief.)* God bless you, Whiskey, it's you can rouse the dead! Con hasn't been down yet for his morning's morning?

MALOY No. He won't be till later.

CREGAN It's like a miracle, me meeting him again. I came to these parts looking for work. It's only by accident I heard talk of a Con Melody and come here to see was it him. Until last night, I'd not seen hide nor hair of him since the war with the French in Spain—after the battle of Salamanca in '12. I was corporal in the Seventh Dragoons and he was major. *(proudly)* I got this cut from a saber at Talavera, bad luck to it!—serving under him. He was a captain then.

MALOY So you told me last night.

CREGAN *(with a quick glance at him)* Did I now? I must have said more than my prayers, with the lashings of whiskey in me.

MALOY *(with a grin)* More than your prayers is the truth. *(Cregan glances at him uneasily. Maloy pushes the decanter toward him.)* Take another taste.

Here and throughout the play, O'Neill conveys the strong Irish brogue of Melody and his patrons by use of transliterated spelling in the dialogue.

CREGAN I don't like sponging. Sure, my credit ought to be good in this shebeen! Ain't I his cousin?

MALOY You're forgettin' what himself told you last night as he went up to bed. You could have all the whiskey you could pour down you, but not a penny's worth of credit. This house, he axed you to remember, only gives credit to gentlemen.

CREGAN Divil mend him!

MALOY *(with a chuckle)* You kept thinking about his insults after he'd gone out, getting madder and madder.

CREGAN God pity him, that's like him. He hasn't changed much. *(He pours out a drink and gulps it down—with a cautious look at Maloy.)* If I was mad at Con, and me blind drunk, I must have told you a power of lies.

MALOY *(winks slyly)* Maybe they wasn't lies.

CREGAN If I said any wrong of Con Melody—

MALOY Arrah, are you afraid I'll gab what you said to him? I won't, you can take my oath.

CREGAN *(his face clearing)* Tell me what I said and I'll tell you if it was lies.

MALOY You said his father wasn't of the quality of Galway like he makes out, but a thievin' shebeen keeper who got rich by moneylendin' and squeezin' tenants and every manner of trick. And when he'd enough he married, and bought an estate with a pack of hounds and set up as one of the gentry. He'd hardly got settled when his wife died givin' birth to Con.

CREGAN There's no lie there.

MALOY You said none of the gentry would speak to auld Melody, but he had a tough hide and didn't heed them. He made up his mind he'd bring Con up a true gentleman, so he packed him off to Dublin to school, and after that to the College with sloos of money to prove himself the equal of any gentleman's son. But Con found, while there was plenty to drink on him and borrow money, there was few didn't sneer behind his back at his pretensions.

CREGAN That's the truth, too. But Con wiped the sneer off their mugs when he called one av thim out and put a bullet in his hip. That was his first duel. It gave his pride the taste for revenge and after that he was always lookin' for an excuse to challenge someone.

MALOY He's done a power av boastin' about his duels, but I thought he was lyin'.

CREGAN There's no lie in it. It was that brought disgrace on him in the end, right after he'd been promoted to major. He got caught by a Spanish noble making love to his wife, just after the battle of Salamanca, and there was a duel and Con killed him. The scandal was hushed up but Con had to resign from the army. If it wasn't for his fine record for bravery in battle, they'd have court-martialed him. *(then guiltily)* But I'm sayin' more than my prayers again.

MALOY It's no news about his women. You'd think, to hear him when he's drunk, there wasn't one could resist him in Portugal and Spain.

200 EUGENE O'NEILL

Shebeen is an Irish-Scottish term for a place where liquor is sold without a license.

How does O'Neill introduce needed background exposition concerning Con Melody?

Why was Melody so often drawn into duels?

What caused the abrupt end of Melody's flamboyant military career, according to Cregan?

CREGAN If you'd seen him then, you wouldn't wonder. He was as strong as an ox, and on a thoroughbred horse, in his uniform, there wasn't a handsomer man in the army. And he had the chance he wanted in Portugal and Spain where a British officer was welcome in the gentry's houses. At home, the only women he'd known was whores. *(He adds hastily.)* Except Nora, I mean. *(lowering his voice)* Tell me, has he done any rampagin' wid women here?

MALOY He hasn't. The damned Yankee gentry won't let him come near them, and he considers the few Irish around here to be scum beneath his notice. But once in a while there'll be some Yankee stops overnight wid his wife or daughter and then you'd laugh to see Con, if he thinks she's gentry, sidlin' up to her, playin' the great gentleman and makin' compliments, and then boasting afterward he could have them in bed if he'd had a chance at it, for all their modern Yankee airs.

CREGAN And maybe he could. If you'd known him in the auld days, you'd nivir doubt any boast he makes about fightin' and women, and gamblin' or any kind av craziness. There nivir was a madder divil.

MALOY *(lowering his voice)* Speakin' av Nora, you nivir mentioned her last night, but I know all about it without you telling me. I used to have my room here, and there's nights he's madder drunk than most when he throws it in her face he had to marry her because —Mind you, I'm not saying anything against poor Nora. A sweeter woman never lived. And I know you know all about it.

CREGAN *(reluctantly)* I do. Wasn't I raised on his estate?

MALOY He tells her it was the priests tricked him into marrying her. He hates priests.

CREGAN He's a liar, then. He may like to blame it on them but it's little Con Melody cared what they said. Nothing ever made him do anything, except himself. He married her because he'd fallen in love with her, but he was ashamed of her in his pride at the same time because her folks were only ignorant peasants on his estate, as poor as poor. Nora was as pretty a girl as you'd find in a year's travel, and he'd come to be bitter lonely, with no woman's company but the whores was helpin' him ruin the estate. *(He shrugs his shoulders.)* Well, anyways, he married her and then went off to the war, and left her alone in the castle to have her child, and nivir saw her again till he was sent home from Spain. Then he raised what money he still was able, and took her and Sara here to America where no one would know him.

MALOY *(thinking this over for a moment)* It's hard for me to believe he ever loved her. I've seen the way he treats her now. Well, thank you for telling me, and I take my oath I'll nivir breathe a word of it—for Nora's sake, not his.

CREGAN *(grimly)* You'd better kape quiet for fear of him, too. If he's one-half the man he was, he could bate the lights out of the two av us.

MALOY He's strong as a bull still for all the whiskey he's drunk. *(He pushes the bottle toward Cregan.)* Have another taste. *(Cregan pours out a drink.)* Drink hearty.

Cregan's reminiscences about Melody's past behavior provide vital characteristics which will make Con's conduct later both understandable and predictable.

The basis for Con and Nora's uneasy marriage is made known to us, due to Cregan's gossip.

CREGAN Long life. (*He drinks. Malloy puts the decanter and glass back on the cupboard. A girl's voice is heard from the hall at right. Cregan jumps up—hastily.*) That's Sara, isn't it? I'll get out. She'll likely blame me for Con getting so drunk last night. I'll be back after Con is down. (*He goes out. Maloy starts to go in the bar, as if he too wanted to avoid Sara. Then he sits down defiantly.*)

MALOY Be damned if I'll run from her. (*He takes up the paper as Sara Melody comes in from the hall at right.*)

Sara is twenty, an exceedingly pretty girl with a mass of black hair, fair skin with rosy cheeks, and beautiful, deep-blue eyes. There is a curious blending in her of what are commonly considered aristocratic and peasant characteristics. She has a fine forehead. Her nose is thin and straight. She has small ears set close to her well-shaped head, and a slender neck. Her mouth, on the other hand, has a touch of coarseness and sensuality and her jaw is too heavy. Her figure is strong and graceful, with full, firm breasts and hips, and a slender waist. But she has large feet and broad, ugly hands with stubby fingers. Her voice is soft and musical, but her speech has at times a self-conscious, stilted quality about it, due to her restraining a tendency to lapse into brogue. Her everyday working dress is of cheap material, but she wears it in a way that gives a pleasing effect of beauty unadorned.

> How do Sara's looks and mannerisms suggest her kinship to Con Melody?

SARA (*with a glance at Maloy, sarcastically*) I'm sorry to interrupt you when you're so busy, but have you your bar book ready for me to look over?

MALOY (*surlily*) I have, I put it on your desk.

SARA Thank you. (*She turns her back on him, sits at the desk, takes a small account book from it, and begins checking figures.*)

MALOY (*watches her over his paper*) If it's profits you're looking for, you won't find them—not with all the drinks himself's been treating to. (*She ignores this. He becomes resentful.*) You've got your airs of a grand lady this morning, I see. There's no talkin' to you since you've been playin' nurse to the young Yankee upstairs. (*She makes herself ignore this, too.*) Well, you've had your cap set for him ever since he came to live by the lake, and now's your chance, when he's here sick and too weak to defend himself.

SARA (*turns on him—with quiet anger*) I warn you to mind your own business, Mickey, or I'll tell my father of your impudence. He'll teach you to keep your place, and God help you.

MALOY (*doesn't believe this threat but is frightened by the possibility*) Arrah, don't try to scare me. I know you'd never carry tales to him. (*placatingly*) Can't you take a bit of teasing, Sara?

SARA (*turns back to her figuring*) Leave Simon out of your teasing.

MALOY Oho, he's Simon to you now, is he? Well, well. (*He gives her a cunning glance.*) Maybe, if you'd come down from your high horse, I could tell you some news.

SARA You're worse than an old woman for gossip. I don't want to hear it.

MALOY When you was upstairs at the back taking him his breakfast, there was a grand carriage with a nigger coachman stopped at the corner and a Yankee lady got out and came in here. I was sweeping and Nora was scrubbing the kitchen. (*Sara has turned to him, all

> Sara's striving to upgrade herself socially is revealed in these next few lines. All that she does later is a result of this thirst for social acceptance by the Harfords and other aristocrats.

202 EUGENE O'NEILL

attention now.) She asked me what road would take her near the lake—

SARA *(starts)* Ah.

MALOY So I told her, but she didn't go. She kept looking around, and said she'd like a cup of tea, and where was the waitress. I knew she must be connected someway with Harford or why would she want to go to the lake, where no one's ever lived but him. She didn't want tea at all, but only an excuse to stay.

SARA *(resentfully)* So she asked for the waitress, did she? I hope you told her I'm the owner's daughter, too.

MALOY I did. I don't like Yankee airs any more than you. I was short with her. I said you was out for a walk, and the tavern wasn't open yet, anyway. So she went out and drove off.

SARA *(worriedly now)* I hope you didn't insult her with your bad manners. What did she look like, Mickey?

MALOY Pretty, if you like that kind. A pale, delicate wisp of a thing with big eyes.

SARA That fits what he's said of his mother. How old was she?

MALOY It's hard to tell, but she's too young for his mother, I'd swear. Around thirty, I'd say. Maybe it's his sister.

SARA He hasn't a sister.

MALOY *(grinning)* Then maybe she's an old sweetheart looking for you to scratch your eyes out.

SARA He's never had a sweetheart.

MALOY *(mockingly)* Is that what he tells you, and you believe him? Faix, you must be in love!

SARA *(angrily)* Will you mind your own business? I'm not such a fool! *(worried again)* Maybe you ought to have told her he's here sick to save her the drive in the hot sun and the walk through the woods for nothing.

MALOY Why would I tell her, when she never mentioned him?

SARA Yes, it's her own fault. But— Well, there's no use thinking of it now—or bothering my head about her, anyway, whoever she was. *(She begins checking figures again. Her mother appears in the doorway at right.)*

Nora Melody is forty, but years of overwork and worry have made her look much older. She must have been as pretty as a girl as Sara is now. She still has the beautiful eyes her daughter has inherited. But she has become too worn out to take care of her appearance. Her black hair, streaked with gray, straggles in untidy wisps about her face. Her body is dumpy, with sagging breasts, and her old clothes are like a bag covering it, tied around the middle. Her red hands are knotted by rheumatism. Cracked working shoes, run down at the heel, are on her bare feet. Yet in spite of her slovenly appearance there is a spirit which shines through and makes her lovable, a simple sweetness and charm, something gentle and sad and, somehow, dauntless.

MALOY *(jumps to his feet, his face lighting up with affection)* God bless you, Nora, you're the one I was waitin' to see. Will you keep an eye on the bar while I run to the store for a bit av 'baccy?

SARA (*sharply*) Don't do it, Mother.

NORA (*smiles—her voice is soft, with a rich brogue*) Why wouldn't I? "Don't do it, Mother."

<small>Nora, unlike Sara, is unashamed of her Irish brogue.</small>

MALOY Thank you, Nora. (*He goes to the door at rear and opens it, burning for a parting shot at Sara.*) And the back o' my hand to you, your Ladyship! (*He goes out, closing the door.*)

SARA You shouldn't encourage his laziness. He's always looking for excuses to shirk.

NORA Ah, nivir mind, he's a good lad. (*She lowers herself painfully on the nearest chair at the rear of the table at center front.*) Bad cess to the rheumatism. It has me destroyed this mornin'.

<small>What is the contrast, immediately noticeable, between the temperaments of mother and daughter?</small>

SARA (*Still checking figures in the book—gives her mother an impatient but at the same time worried glance. Her habitual manner toward her is one of mingled love and pity and exasperation.*) I've told you a hundred times to see the doctor.

NORA We've no money for doctors. They're bad luck anyway. They bring death with them. (*A pause. Nora sighs.*) Your father will be down soon. I've some fine fresh eggs for his breakfast.

SARA (*Her face becomes hard and bitter.*) He won't want them.

NORA (*defensively*) You mean he'd a drop too much taken last night? Well, small blame to him, he hasn't seen Jamie since—

<small>How does O'Neill make certain that there will be sufficient exposition to follow the plot development? Does his method seem effective or contrived? Why?</small>

SARA Last night? What night hasn't he?

NORA Ah, don't be hard on him. (*a pause—worriedly*) Neilan sent round a note to me about his bill. He says we'll have to settle by the end of the week or we'll get no more groceries. (*with a sigh*) I can't blame him. How we'll manage, I dunno. There's the intrist on the mortgage due the first. But that I've saved, God be thanked.

SARA (*exasperatedly*) If you'd only let me take charge of the money.

NORA (*with a flare of spirit*) I won't. It'd mean you and himself would be at each other's throats from dawn to dark. It's bad enough between you as it is.

SARA Why didn't you pay Neilan the end of last week? You told me you had the money put aside.

NORA So I did. But Dickinson was tormentin' your father with his feed bill for the mare.

SARA (*angrily*) I might have known! The mare comes first, if she takes the bread out of our mouths! The grand gentleman must have his thoroughbred to ride out in state!

NORA (*defensively*) Where's the harm? She's his greatest pride. He'd be heartbroken if he had to sell her.

<small>An important characteristic of Nora—her defense of Con's actions—is apparent here.</small>

SARA Oh, yes, I know well he cares more for a horse than for us!

NORA Don't be saying that. He has great love for you, even if you do be provokin' him all the time.

SARA Great love for me! Arrah, God pity you, Mother!

NORA (*sharply*) Don't put on the brogue, now. You know how he hates to hear you. And I do, too. There's no excuse not to cure

204 EUGENE O'NEILL

yourself. Didn't he send you to school so you could talk like a gentleman's daughter?

SARA *(resentfully, but more careful of her speech)* If he did, I wasn't there long.

NORA It was you insisted on leavin'.

SARA Because if he hadn't the pride or love for you not to live on your slaving your heart out, I had that pride and love!

NORA *(tenderly)* I know, Acushla. I know.

SARA *(with bitter scorn)* We can't afford a waitress, but he can afford to keep a thoroughbred mare to prance around on and show himself off! And he can afford a barkeep when, if he had any decency, he'd do his part and tend the bar himself.

NORA *(indignantly)* Him, a gentleman, tend bar!

SARA A gentleman! Och, Mother, it's all right for the two of us, out of our own pride, to pretend to the world we believe that lie, but it's crazy for you to pretend to me.

NORA *(stubbornly)* It's no lie. He *is* a gentleman. Wasn't he born rich in a castle on a grand estate and educated in college, and wasn't he an officer in the Duke of Wellington's army—

SARA All right, Mother. You can humor his craziness, but he'll never make me pretend to him I don't know the truth.

NORA Don't talk as if you hated him. You ought to be shamed—

SARA I do hate him for the way he treats you. I heard him again last night, raking up the past, and blaming his ruin on his having to marry you.

NORA *(protests miserably)* It was the drink talkin', not him.

SARA *(exasperated)* It's you ought to be ashamed, for not having more pride! You bear all his insults as meek as a lamb! You keep on slaving for him when it's that has made you old before your time! *(angrily)* You can't much longer, I tell you! He's getting worse. You'll have to leave him.

NORA *(aroused)* I'll never! Howld your prate!

SARA You'd leave him today, if you had any pride!

NORA I've pride in my love for him! I've loved him since the day I set eyes on him, and I'll love him till the day I die! *(with a strange superior scorn)* It's little you know of love, and you never will, for there's the same divil of pride in you that's in him, and it'll kape you from ivir givin' all of yourself, and that's what love is—

SARA I could give all of myself if I wanted to, but—

NORA If! Wanted to! Faix, it proves how little of love you know when you prate about if's and want-to's. It's when you don't give a thought for all the if's and want-to's in the world! It's when, if all the fires of hell was between you, you'd walk in them gladly to be with him, and sing with joy at your own burnin', if only his kiss was on your mouth! That's love, and I'm proud I've known the great sorrow and joy of it!

Even sending his daughter to school was part of Con's campaign to achieve higher social status for the family's name.

"Acushla," an Irish term of endearment usually applied to a child, means (roughly) "darling."

Nora has a special concept of "love." What are its essential features?

SARA *(cannot help being impressed—looks at her mother with wondering respect)* You're a strange woman, Mother. *(She kisses her impulsively.)* And a grand woman! *(defiant again, with an arrogant toss of her head)* I'll love—but I'll love where it'll gain me freedom and not put me in slavery for life.

NORA There's no slavery in it when you love! *(Suddenly her exultant expression crumbles and she breaks down.)* For the love of God, don't take the pride of my love from me, Sara, for without it what am I at all but an ugly, fat woman gettin' old and sick!

SARA *(puts her arm around her—soothingly)* Hush, Mother. Don't mind me. *(briskly, to distract her mother's mind)* I've got to finish the bar book. Mickey can't put two and two together without making five. *(She goes to the desk and begins checking figures again.)*

NORA *(dries her eyes—after a pause she sighs worriedly)* I'm worried about your father. Father Flynn stopped me on the road yesterday and tould me I'd better warn him not to sneer at the Irish around here and call thim scum, or he'll get in trouble. Most of thim is in a rage at him because he's come out against Jackson and the Democrats and says he'll vote with the Yankees for Quincy Adams.

> Does it appear that Melody ever went out of his way to cultivate friendships when he moved to America? How do we know?

SARA *(contemptuously)* Faith, they can't see a joke, then, for it's a great joke to hear him shout against mob rule, like one of the Yankee gentry, when you know what he came from. And after the way the Yanks swindled him when he came here, getting him to buy this inn by telling him a new coach line was going to stop here. *(She laughs with bitter scorn.)* Oh, he's the easiest fool ever came to America! It's that I hold against him as much as anything, that when he came here the chance was before him to make himself all his lies pretended to be. He had education above most Yanks, and he had money enough to start him, and this is a country where you can rise as high as you like, and no one but the fools who envy you care what you rose from, once you've the money and the power goes with it. *(passionately)* Oh, if I was a man with the chance he had, there wouldn't be a dream I'd not make come true! *(She looks at her mother, who is staring at the floor dejectedly and hasn't been listening. She is exasperated for a second—then she smiles pityingly.)* You're a fine one to talk to, Mother. Wake up. What's worrying you now?

> How has Melody approached the problem of assimilation into American culture?

NORA Father Flynn tould me again I'd be damned in hell for lettin' your father make a haythen of me and bring you up a haythen, too.

SARA *(with an arrogant toss of her head)* Let Father Flynn mind his own business, and not frighten you with fairy tales about hell.

NORA It's true, just the same.

> Alienated in the New World because of financial and social friction, the Melodys also have severed their past religious ties.

SARA True, me foot! You ought to tell the good Father we aren't the ignorant shanty scum he's used to dealing with. *(She changes the subject abruptly—closing Mickey's bar book.)* There. That's done. *(She puts the book in the desk.)* I'll take a walk to the store and have a talk with Neilan. Maybe I can blarney him to let the bill go another month.

NORA *(gratefully)* Oh, you can. Sure, you can charm a bird out of a tree when you want to. But I don't like you beggin' to a Yankee. It's all right for me but I know how you hate it.

> Traditionally, sociologists have discerned two patterns of cultural assimilation: (1) a denial of one's ethnic identity and the acceptance of a majority identity—here, that of the Yankee; or (2) identification with one's ethnic roots in order to develop a base of power within the pluralistic society in the United States. Is it clear which path Sara will follow? Nora? Melody? Why, in each instance?

SARA *(puts her arms around her mother—tenderly)* I don't mind at all, if

I can save you a bit of the worry that's killing you. *(She kisses her.)* I'll change to my Sunday dress so I can make a good impression.

NORA *(with a teasing smile)* I'm thinkin' it isn't on Neilan alone you want to make an impression. You've changed to your Sunday best a lot lately.

SARA *(coquettishly)* Aren't you the sly one! Well, maybe you're right.

NORA How was he when you took him his breakfast?

SARA Hungry, and that's a good sign. He had no fever last night. Oh, he's on the road to recovery now, and it won't be long before he'll be back in his cabin by the lake.

NORA I'll never get it clear in my head what he's been doing there the past year, living like a tramp or a tinker, and him a rich gentleman's son.

SARA *(with a tender smile)* Oh, he isn't like his kind, or like anyone else at all. He's a born dreamer with a raft of great dreams, and he's very serious about them. I've told you before he wanted to get away from his father's business, where he worked for a year after he graduated from Harvard College, because he didn't like being in trade, even if it is a great company that trades with the whole world in its own ships.

NORA *(approvingly)* That's the way a true gentleman would feel—

SARA He wanted to prove his independence by living alone in the wilds, and build his own cabin, and do all the work, and support himself simply, and feel one with Nature, and think great thoughts about what life means, and write a book about how the world can be changed so people won't be greedy to own money and land and get the best of each other but will be content with little and live in peace and freedom together, and it will be like heaven on earth. *(She laughs fondly—and a bit derisively.)* I can't remember all of it. It seems crazy to me, when I think of what people are like. He hasn't written any of it yet, anyway—only the notes for it. *(She smiles coquettishly.)* All he's written the last few months are love poems.

NORA That's since you began to take long walks by the lake. *(She smiles.)* It's you are the sly one.

SARA *(laughing)* Well, why shouldn't I take walks on our own property? *(Her tone changes to a sneer.)* The land our great gentleman was swindled into buying when he came here with grand ideas of owning an American estate!—a bit of farm land no one would work any more, and the rest all wilderness! You couldn't give it away.

NORA *(soothingly)* Hush, now. *(changing the subject)* Well, it's easy to tell young Master Harford has a touch av the poet in him—*(She adds before she thinks.)* the same as your father.

SARA *(scornfully)* God help you, Mother! Do you think Father's a poet because he shows off reciting Lord Byron?

NORA *(with an uneasy glance at the door at left front)* Whist, now. Himself will be down any moment. *(changing the subject)* I can see the Harford lad is falling in love with you.

SARA *(Her face lights up triumphantly.)* Falling? He's fallen head over heels. He's so timid, he hasn't told me yet, but I'll get him to soon.

The women are talking about Simon Harford, the wealthy Yankee youth recuperating upstairs over the tavern. Although he never personally appears on stage, his unseen presence is a significant counterpart to Melody's brand of idealistic dreaming. Note that Simon writes poetry, a parallel to Con's reciting of Byron's poems repeatedly throughout the drama.

Nora explicitly aligns her husband with young Harford because each has "a touch av the poet." What exactly is the significance of this? Is the "touch" the same for everyone, or is it different for each one?

A TOUCH OF THE POET

NORA I know you're in love with him.

SARA *(simply)* I am, Mother. *(She adds quickly.)* But not too much. I'll not let love make me any man's slave. I want to love him just enough so I can marry him without cheating him, or myself. *(determinedly)* For I'm going to marry him, Mother. It's my chance to rise in the world and nothing will keep me from it.

NORA *(admiringly)* Musha, but you've boastful talk! What about his fine Yankee family? His father'll likely cut him off widout a penny if he marries a girl who's poor and Irish.

SARA He may at first, but when I've proved what a good wife I'll be—He can't keep Simon from marrying me. I know that. Simon doesn't care what his father thinks. It's only his mother I'm afraid of. I can tell she's had great influence over him. She must be a queer creature, from all he's told me. She's very strange in her ways. She never goes out at all but stays home in their mansion, reading books, or in her garden. *(She pauses.)* Did you notice a carriage stop here this morning, Mother?

NORA *(preoccupied—uneasily)* Don't count your chickens before they're hatched. Young Harford seems a dacent lad. But maybe it's not marriage he's after.

SARA *(angrily)* I won't have you wronging him, Mother. He has no thought— *(bitterly)* I suppose you're bound to suspect— *(She bites her words back, ashamed.)* Forgive me, Mother. But it's wrong of you to think badly of Simon. *(She smiles.)* You don't know him. Faith, if it came to seducing, it'd be me that'd have to do it. He's that respectful you'd think I was a holy image. It's only in his poems, and in the diary he keeps— I had a peek in it one day I went to tidy up the cabin for him. He's terribly ashamed of his sinful inclinations and the insult they are to my purity. *(She laughs tenderly.)*

NORA *(smiling, but a bit shocked)* Don't talk so bould. I don't know if it's right, you to be in his room so much, even if he is sick. There's power av talk about the two av you already.

SARA Let there be, for all I care! Or all Simon cares, either. When it comes to not letting others rule him, he's got a will of his own behind his gentleness. Just as behind his poetry and dreams I feel he has it in him to do anything he wants. So even if his father cuts him off, with me to help him we'll get on in the world. For I'm no fool, either.

NORA Glory be to God, you have the fine opinion av yourself!

SARA *(laughing)* Haven't I, though! *(then bitterly)* I've had need to have, to hold my head up, slaving as a waitress and chambermaid so my father can get drunk every night like a gentleman!

The door at left front is slowly opened and Cornelius Melody appears in the doorway above the two steps. He and Sara stare at each other. She stiffens into hostility and her mouth sets in scorn. For a second his eyes waver and he looks guilty. Then his face becomes expressionless. He descends the steps and bows—pleasantly.

MELODY Good morning, Sara.

SARA *(curtly)* Good morning. *(then, ignoring him)* I'm going up and change my dress, Mother. *(She goes out right.)*

What motivates Sara's love for Harford in the early part of the drama?

Does Simon's mother also appear to have a "touch"?

The audience is aware of the irony in Sara's defense of her lover, while she cannot understand at all Nora's defense of Con.

O'Neill's specific stage directions convey the meaning of the action at any given moment. What kind of antagonism is established here by looks alone, for instance?

Cornelius Melody is forty-five, tall, broad-shouldered, deep-chested, and powerful, with long muscular arms, big feet, and large hairy hands. His heavy-boned body is still firm, erect, and soldierly. Beyond shaky nerves, it shows no effects of hard drinking. It has a bull-like, impervious strength, a tough peasant vitality. It is his face that reveals the ravages of dissipation—a ruined face, which was once extraordinarily handsome in a reckless, arrogant fashion. It is still handsome—the face of an embittered Byronic hero, with a finely chiseled nose over a domineering, sensual mouth set in disdain, pale, hollow-cheeked, framed by thick, curly iron-gray hair. There is a look of wrecked distinction about it, of brooding, humiliated pride. His bloodshot gray eyes have an insulting cold stare which anticipates insult. His manner is that of a polished gentleman. Too much so. He overdoes it and one soon feels that he is overplaying a role which has become more real than his real self to him. But in spite of this, there is something formidable and impressive about him. He is dressed with foppish elegance in old, expensive, finely tailored clothes of the style worn by English aristocracy in Peninsular War days.

> O'Neill's description of Con Melody confirms the earlier hearsay that he always is pretending to be something that he is not. To what does he aspire? Does Melody have a problem with assimilation?

MELODY *(advancing into the room—bows formally to his wife)* Good morning, Nora. *(His tone condescends. It addresses a person of inferior station.)*

> How do Melody's gestures and dialogue confirm the visual impression made by his appearance?

NORA *(stumbles to her feet—timidly)* Good mornin', Con. I'll get your breakfast.

MELODY No. Thank you. I want nothing now.

NORA *(coming toward him)* You look pale. Are you sick, Con, darlin'?

MELODY No.

NORA *(puts a timid hand on his arm)* Come and sit down. *(He moves his arm away with instinctive revulsion and goes to the table at center front, and sits in the chair she had occupied. Nora hovers round him.)* I'll wet a cloth in cold water to put round your head.

MELODY No! I desire nothing—except a little peace in which to read the news. *(He picks up the paper and holds it so it hides his face from her.)*

NORA *(meekly)* I'll lave you in peace. *(She starts to go to the door at right but turns to stare at him worriedly again. Keeping the paper before his face with his left hand, he reaches out with his right and pours a glass of water from the carafe on the table. Although he cannot see his wife, he is nervously conscious of her. His hand trembles so violently that when he attempts to raise the glass to his lips the water sloshes over his hand and he sets the glass back on the table with a bang. He lowers the paper and explodes nervously.)*

MELODY For God's sake, stop your staring!

NORA I— I was thinkin' you'd feel better if you'd a bit av food in you.

MELODY I told you once—! *(controlling his temper)* I am not hungry, Nora. *(He raises the paper again. She sighs, her hands fiddling with her apron. A pause.)*

NORA *(dully)* Maybe it's a hair av the dog you're needin'.

MELODY *(As if this were something he had been waiting to hear, his expression loses some of its nervous strain. But he replies virtuously.)* No, damn the liquor. Upon my conscience, I've about made up my mind I'll have no more of it. Besides, it's a bit early in the day.

A TOUCH OF THE POET

NORA If it'll give you an appetite—

MELODY To tell the truth, my stomach is out of sorts. *(He licks his lips.)* Perhaps a drop wouldn't come amiss. *(Nora gets the decanter and glass from the cupboard and sets them before him. She stands gazing at him with a resigned sadness. Melody, his eyes on the paper, is again acutely conscious of her. His nerves cannot stand it. He throws his paper down and bursts out in bitter anger.)* Well? I know what you're thinking! Why haven't you the courage to say it for once? By God, I'd have more respect for you! I hate the damned meek of this earth! By the rock of Cashel, I sometimes believe you have always deliberately encouraged me to— It's the one point of superiority you can lay claim to, isn't it?

NORA *(bewilderedly—on the verge of tears)* I don't— It's your comfort— I can't bear to see you—

MELODY *(His expression changes and a look of real affection comes into his eyes. He reaches out a shaking hand to pat her shoulder with an odd, guilty tenderness. He says quietly and with genuine contrition.)* Forgive me, Nora. That was unpardonable. *(Her face lights up. Abruptly he is ashamed of being ashamed. He looks away and grabs the decanter. Despite his trembling hand he manages to pour a drink and get it to his mouth and drain it. Then he sinks back in his chair and stares at the table, waiting for the liquor to take effect. After a pause he sighs with relief.)* I confess I needed that as medicine. I begin to feel more myself. *(He pours out another big drink and this time his hand is steadier, and he downs it without much difficulty. He smacks his lips.)* By the Immortal, I may have sunk to keeping an inn but at least I've a conscience in my trade. I keep liquor a gentleman can drink. *(He starts looking over the paper again—scowls at something—disdainfully, emphasizing his misquote of the line from Byron.)* "There shall he rot—Ambition's dishonored fool!" The paper is full of the latest swindling lies of that idol of the riffraff, Andrew Jackson. Contemptible, drunken scoundrel! But he will be the next President, I predict, for all we others can do to prevent. There is a cursed destiny in these decadent times. Everywhere the scum rises to the top. *(His eyes fasten on the date and suddenly he strikes the table with his fist.)* Today is the 27th! By God, and I would have forgotten!

NORA Forgot what?

MELODY The anniversary of Talavera!

NORA *(hastily)* Oh, ain't I stupid not to remember.

MELODY *(bitterly)* I had forgotten myself and no wonder. It's a far cry from this dunghill on which I rot to that glorious day when the Duke of Wellington—Lord Wellesley, then—did me honor before all the army to commend my bravery. *(He glances around the room with loathing.)* A far cry, indeed! It would be better to forget!

NORA *(rallying him)* No, no, you mustn't. You've never missed celebratin' it and you won't today. I'll have a special dinner for you like I've always had.

MELODY *(with a quick change of manner—eagerly)* Good, Nora. I'll invite Jamie Cregan. It's a stroke of fortune he is here. He served under me at Talavera, as you know. A brave soldier, if he isn't a gentleman. You can place him on my right hand. And we'll have

---

How are character and plot exposition effectively conveyed in a conversation like this? What do we learn about Con and Nora?

The *rock of Cashel* in Irish antiquity was a church or sacred building surrounded by a circular wall.

Here is the first of Con's many recitations from the poet Byron, an English contemporary who snubbed his nose at his homeland when involved in social scandal and who roamed Europe in exile.

How are Jackson and Melody alike?

Talavera, a city in central Spain, was the site of an important battle in which the British and Spanish defeated the French in 1809.

Does Melody want these cronies for their wit, or simply to serve as an audience for him?

Patch Riley to make music, and O'Dowd and Roche. If they are rabble, they're full of droll humor at times. But put them over there. *(He points to the table at left front.)* I may tolerate their presence out of charity, but I'll not sink to dining at the same table.

NORA I'll get your uniform from the trunk, and you'll wear it for dinner like you've done each year.

MELODY Yes, I must confess I still welcome an excuse to wear it. It makes me feel at least the ghost of the man I was then.

> What part does Melody's old uniform play in his life now?

NORA You're so handsome in it still, no woman could take her eyes off you.

MELODY *(with a pleased smile)* I'm afraid you've blarney on your tongue this morning, Nora. *(then boastfully)* But it's true, in those days in Portugal and Spain— *(He stops a little shamefacedly, but Nora gives no sign of offense. He takes her hand and pats it gently—avoiding her eyes.)* You have the kindest heart in the world, Nora. And I— *(His voice breaks.)*

> Does Nora also have a "a touch of the poet"?

NORA *(instantly on the verge of grateful tears)* Ah, who wouldn't, Con darlin', when you—*(She brushes a hand across her eyes—hastily.)* I'll go to the store and get something tasty. *(Her face drops as she remembers.)* But, God help us, where's the money?

MELODY *(stiffens—haughtily)* Money? Since when has my credit not been good?

NORA *(hurriedly)* Don't fret, now. I'll manage. *(He returns to his newspaper, disdaining further interest in money matters.)*

MELODY Ha. I see work on the railroad at Baltimore is progressing. *(lowering his paper)* By the Eternal, if I had not been a credulous gull and let the thieving Yankees swindle me of all I had when we came here, that's how I would invest my funds now. And I'd become rich. This country, with its immense territory cannot depend solely on creeping canal boats, as shortsighted fools would have us believe. We must have railroads. Then you will see how quickly America will become rich and great! *(His expression changes to one of bitter hatred.)* Great enough to crush England in the next war between them, which I know is inevitable! Would I could live to celebrate that victory! If I have one regret for the past—and there are few things in it that do not call for bitter regret—it is that I shed my blood for a country that thanked me with disgrace. But I will be avenged. This country—my country, now—will drive the English from the face of the earth their shameless perfidy has dishonored!

> Melody associates himself with the new American nation which will pay back those countries or persons who do not sufficiently appreciate him. How is this at odds with his attitude toward his fellow Irish-Americans?

NORA Glory be to God for that! And we'll free Ireland!

MELODY *(contemptuously)* Ireland? What benefit would freedom be to her unless she could be freed from the Irish? *(then irritably)* But why do I discuss such things with you?

> Does Nora understand Melody's figurative identification of himself with America? Why is that not surprising?

NORA *(humbly)* I know. I'm ignorant.

MELODY Yet I tried my best to educate you, after we came to America—until I saw it was hopeless.

NORA You did, surely. And I tried, too, but—

MELODY You won't even cure yourself of that damned peasant's brogue. And your daughter is becoming as bad.

A TOUCH OF THE POET

NORA She only puts on the brogue to tease you. She can speak as fine as any lady in the land if she wants.

MELODY (*is not listening—sunk in bitter brooding*) But, in God's name, who am I to reproach anyone with anything? Why don't you tell me to examine my own conduct?

> Con's sudden shift in mood from arrogance to bitter self-reproach also is part of his Byronic posing.

NORA You know I'd never.

MELODY (*stares at her—again he is moved—quietly*) No. I know you would not, Nora. (*He looks away—after a pause.*) I owe you an apology for what happened last night.

NORA Don't think of it.

MELODY (*with assumed casualness*) Faith, I'd a drink too many, talking over old times with Jamie Cregan.

NORA I know.

MELODY I am afraid I may have— The thought of old times— I become bitter. But you understand, it was the liquor talking, if I said anything to wound you.

NORA I know it.

MELODY (*deeply moved, puts his arm around her*) You're a sweet, kind woman, Nora—too kind. (*He kisses her.*)

NORA (*with blissful happiness*) Ah, Con darlin', what do I care what you say when the black thoughts are on you? Sure, don't you know I love you?

> In this episode, we see several sides of Con and we can reach some conclusions about his character. Where in this section do we have evidence of his insecurity? Of his alienation? Of his pride?

MELODY (*A sudden revulsion of feeling convulses his face. He bursts out with disgust, pushing her away from him.*) For God's sake, why don't you wash your hair? It turns my stomach with its stink of onions and stew! (*He reaches for the decanter and shakingly pours a drink. Nora looks as if he had struck her.*)

NORA (*dully*) I do be washin' it often to plaze you. But when you're standin' over the stove all day, you can't help—

MELODY Forgive me, Nora. Forget I said that. My nerves are on edge. You'd better leave me alone.

NORA (*her face brightening a little*) Will you ate your breakfast now? I've fine fresh eggs—

MELODY (*grasping at this chance to get rid of her—impatiently*) Yes! In a while. Fifteen minutes, say. But leave me alone now. (*She goes out right. Melody drains his drink. Then he gets up and paces back and forth, his hands clasped behind him. The third drink begins to work and his face becomes arrogantly self-assured. He catches his reflection in the mirror on the wall at left and stops before it. He brushes a sleeve fastidiously, adjusts the set of his coat, and surveys himself.*) Thank God, I still bear the unmistakable stamp of an officer and a gentleman. And so I will remain to the end, in spite of all fate can do to crush my spirit! (*He squares his shoulders defiantly. He stares into his eyes in the glass and recites from Byron's "Childe Harold," as if it were an incantation by which he summons pride to justify his life to himself.*)

> Is Melody's continual pose a matter of dreaming about and planning for a more gratifying future? Or is it a form of self-delusion growing out of pride or out of a sense of inferiority?

"I have not loved the World, nor the World me;
I have not flattered its rank breath, nor bowed
To its idolatries a patient knee,

212 EUGENE O'NEILL

> Nor coined my cheek to smiles,—nor cried aloud
> In worship of an echo: in the crowd
> They could not deem me one of such—I stood
> Among them, but not of them . . ."

(*He pauses, then repeats.*) "Among them, but not of them." By the Eternal, that expresses it! Thank God for you, Lord Byron—poet and nobleman who made of his disdain immortal music! (*Sara appears in the doorway at right. She has changed to her Sunday dress, a becoming blue that brings out the color of her eyes. She draws back for a moment—then stands watching him contemptuously. Melody senses her presence. He starts and turns quickly away from the mirror. For a second his expression is guilty and confused, but he immediately assumes an air of gentlemanly urbanity and bows to her.*) Ah, it's you, my dear. Are you going for a morning stroll? You've a beautiful day for it. It will bring fresh roses to your cheeks.

> *Evidently Con Melody sees Byron's words as relevant to himself. In what ways, perhaps?*

> *What is the function of the mirror throughout the drama? What is its thematic relevance?*

SARA I don't know about roses, but it will bring a blush of shame to my cheeks. I have to beg Neilan to give us another month's credit, because you made Mother pay the feed bill for your fine thoroughbred mare! (*He gives no sign he hears this. She adds scathingly.*) I hope you saw something in the mirror you could admire!

MELODY (*in a light tone*) Faith, I suppose I must have looked a vain peacock, preening himself, but you can blame the bad light in my room. One cannot make a decent toilet in that dingy hole in the wall.

SARA You have the best room in the house, that we ought to rent to guests.

MELODY Oh, I've no complaints. I was merely explaining my seeming vanity.

SARA Seeming!

MELODY (*keeping his tone light*) Faith, Sara, you must have risen the wrong side of the bed this morning, but it takes two to make a quarrel and I don't feel quarrelsome. Quite the contrary. I was about to tell you how exceedingly charming and pretty you look, my dear.

SARA (*with a mocking, awkward, servant's curtsy—in broad brogue*) Oh, thank ye, yer Honor.

MELODY Every day you resemble your mother more, as she looked when I first knew her.

SARA Musha, but it's you have the blarneyin' tongue, God forgive you!

MELODY (*in spite of himself, this gets under his skin—angrily*) Be quiet! How dare you talk to me like a common, ignorant— You're my daughter, damn you. (*He controls himself and forces a laugh.*) A fair hit! You're a great tease, Sara. I shouldn't let you score so easily. Your mother warned me you only did it to provoke me. (*Unconsciously he reaches out for the decanter on the table—then pulls his hand back.*)

SARA (*contemptuously—without brogue now*) Go on and drink. Surely you're not ashamed before me, after all these years.

MELODY (*haughtily*) Ashamed? I don't understand you. A gentleman drinks as he pleases—provided he can hold his liquor as he should.

SARA A gentleman!

MELODY *(pleasantly again)* I hesitated because I had made a good resolve to be abstemious today. But if you insist—*(He pours a drink—a small one—his hand quite steady now.)* To your happiness, my dear. *(She stares at him scornfully. He goes on graciously.)* Will you do me the favor to sit down? I have wanted a quiet chat with you for some time. *(He holds out a chair for her at rear of table at center.)*

SARA *(eyes him suspiciously—then sits down)* What is it you want?

MELODY *(with a playfully paternal manner)* Your happiness, my dear, and what I wish to discuss means happiness to you, unless I have grown blind. How is our patient, young Simon Harford, this morning?

> This dialogue between Sara and her father provides one of the central conflicts in the play.

SARA *(curtly)* He's better.

MELODY I am delighted to hear it. *(gallantly)* How could he help but be with such a charming nurse? *(She stares at him coldly. He goes on.)* Let us be frank. Young Simon is in love with you. I can see that with half an eye—and, of course, you know it. And you return his love, I surmise.

SARA Surmise whatever you please.

MELODY Meaning you do love him? I am glad, Sara. *(He becomes sentimentally romantic.)* Requited love is the greatest blessing life can bestow on us poor mortals and first love is the most blessed of all. As Lord Byron has it *(He recites.)*

> "But sweeter still than this, than these, than all,
> Is first and passionate Love–it stands alone,
> Like Adam's recollection of his fall . . ."

SARA *(interrupts him rudely)* Was it to listen to you recite Byron—?

MELODY *(concealing discomfiture and resentment—pleasantly)* No. What I was leading up to is that you have my blessing, if that means anything to you. Young Harford is, I am convinced, an estimable youth. I have enjoyed my talks with him. It has been a privilege to be able to converse with a cultured gentleman again. True, he is a bit on the sober side for one so young, but by way of compensation, there is a romantic touch of the poet behind his Yankee phlegm.

SARA It's fine you approve of him!

MELODY In your interest I have had some enquiries made about his family.

SARA *(angered—with taunting brogue)* Have you, indade? Musha, that's cute av you! Was it auld Patch Riley, the Piper, made them? Or was it Dan Roche or Paddy O'Dowd, or some other drunken sponge—

MELODY *(as if he hadn't heard—condescendingly)* I find his people will pass muster.

SARA Oh, do you? That's nice!

MELODY Apparently, his father is a gentleman—that is, by Yankee standards, insofar as one in trade can lay claim to the title. But as I've become an American citizen myself, I suppose it would be downright snobbery to hold to old-world standards.

> Despite their general antagonism, Melody concedes his approval of a potential match between Simon Harford and his daughter. Why?

214 EUGENE O'NEILL

SARA Yes, wouldn't it be!

MELODY Though it is difficult at times for my pride to remember I am no longer the master of Melody Castle and an estate of three thousand acres of as fine pasture and woodlands as you'd find in the whole United Kingdom, with my stable of hunters, and—

SARA (bitterly) Well, you've a beautiful thoroughbred mare now, at least—to prove you're still a gentleman!

MELODY (stung into defiant anger) Yes, I've the mare! And by God, I'll keep her if I have to starve myself so she may eat.

SARA You mean, make Mother slave to keep her for you, even if she has to starve!

MELODY (controls his anger—and ignores this) But what was I saying? Oh, yes, young Simon's family. His father will pass muster, but it's through his mother, I believe, he comes by his really good blood. My information is, she springs from generations of well-bred gentlefolk.

The irony of this exchange would not go unnoticed by an audience.

SARA It would be a great pride to her, I'm sure, to know you found her suitable!

MELODY I suppose I may expect the young man to request an interview with me as soon as he is up and about again?

SARA To declare his honorable intentions and ask you for my hand, is that what you mean?

MELODY Naturally. He is a man of honor. And there are certain financial arrangements Simon's father or his legal representative will wish to discuss with me. The amount of your settlement has to be agreed upon.

A settlement, or dowry, once was a mandatory part of any marriage contract—the bride's father would give money or property to the groom.

SARA (stares at him as if she could not believe her ears) My settlement! Simon's father! God pity you—!

MELODY (firmly) Your settlement, certainly. You did not think, I hope, that I would give you away without a penny to your name as if you were some poverty stricken peasant's daughter? Please remember I have my own position to maintain. Of course, it is a bit difficult at present. I am temporarily hard pressed. But perhaps a mortgage on the inn—

SARA It's mortgaged to the hilt already, as you very well know.

MELODY If nothing else, I can always give my note at hand for whatever amount—

SARA You can give it, sure enough! But who'll take it?

MELODY Between gentlemen, these matters can always be arranged.

Sara's hard-headed pragmatism concerning money contrasts sharply with Melody's fantasies.

SARA God help you, it must be a wonderful thing to live in a fairy tale where only dreams are real to you. (then sharply) But you needn't waste your dreams worrying about my affairs. I'll thank you not to interfere. Attend to your drinking and leave me alone. (He gives no indication that he has heard a word she has said. She stares at him and a look almost of fear comes into her eyes. She bursts out with a bitter exasperation in which there is a strong undercurrent of entreaty.) Father! Will you never let yourself wake up—not even now when you're sober, or nearly? Is it stark mad you've gone, so you can't tell any more what's dead and a lie, and what's the living truth?

Why does Sara seem to encourage her father to drink?

A TOUCH OF THE POET   215

MELODY (*His face is convulsed by a spasm of pain as if something vital had been stabbed in him—with a cry of tortured appeal.*) Sara! (*But instantly his pain is transformed into rage. He half rises from his chair threateningly.*) Be quiet, damn you! How dare you—! (*She shrinks away and rises to her feet. He forces control on himself and sinks back in his chair, his hands gripping the arms.*)

The street door at rear is flung open and Dan Roche, Paddy O'Dowd, and Patch Riley attempt to pile in together and get jammed for a moment in the doorway. They all have hangovers, and Roche is talking boisterously. Dan Roche is middle-aged, squat, bowlegged, with a potbelly and short arms lumpy with muscle. His face is flat with a big mouth, protruding ears, and red-rimmed little pig's eyes. He is dressed in dirty, patched clothes. Paddy O'Dowd is thin, round-shouldered, flat-chested, with a pimply complexion, bulgy eyes, and a droopy mouth. His manner is oily and fawning, that of a born sponger and parasite. His clothes are those of a cheap sport. Patch Riley is an old man with a thatch of dirty white hair. His washed-out blue eyes have a wandering, half-witted expression. His skinny body is clothed in rags and there is nothing under his tattered coat but his bare skin. His mouth is sunken in, toothless. He carries an Irish bagpipe under his arm.

> What is the dramatic effect of having Melody's cronies break in on the action at this moment?

ROCHE (*His back is half turned as he harangues O'Dowd and Riley, and he does not see Melody and Sara.*) And I says, it's Andy Jackson will put you in your place, and all the slave-drivin' Yankee skinflints like you! Take your damned job, I says, and—

O'DOWD (*warningly, his eyes on Melody*) Whist! Whist! Hold your prate! (*Roche whirls around to face Melody and his aggressiveness oozes from him, changing to hangdog apprehension. For Melody has sprung to his feet, his eyes blazing with an anger which is increased by the glance of contempt Sara cast from him to the three men. O'Dowd avoids Melody's eyes, busies himself in closing the door. Patch Riley stands gazing at Sara with a dreamy, admiring look, lost in a world of his own fancy, oblivious to what is going on.*)

> What does it mean when Sara looks with contempt from Melody to his cronies who barge onto the stage?

ROCHE (*placatingly*) Good mornin' to ye, Major.

O'DOWD (*fawning*) Good mornin', yer Honor.

> Note that Melody's friends know and play the games to humor his pretensions.

MELODY How dare you come tramping in here in that manner! Have you mistaken this inn for the sort of dirty shebeen you were used to in the old country where the pigs ran in and out the door?

O'DOWD We ask pardon, yer Honor.

MELODY (*to Roche—an impressive menace in his tone*) You, Paddy. Didn't I forbid you ever to mention that scoundrel Jackson's name in my house or I'd horsewhip the hide off your back? (*He takes a threatening step toward him.*) Perhaps you think I cannot carry out that threat.

ROCHE (*backs away frightenedly*) No, no, Major. I forgot— Good mornin' to ye, Miss.

O'DOWD Good mornin', Miss Sara. (*She ignores them. Patch Riley is still gazing at her with dreamy admiration, having heard nothing, his hat still on his head. O'Dowd officiously snatches it off for him—rebukingly.*) Where's your wits, Patch? Didn't ye hear his Honor?

RILEY (*unheeding—addresses Sara*) Sure it's you, God bless you, looks

216 EUGENE O'NEILL

like a fairy princess as beautiful as a rose in the mornin' dew. I'll raise a tune for you. *(He starts to arrange his pipes.)*

SARA *(curtly)* I want none of your tunes. *(Then, seeing the look of wondering hurt in the old man's eyes, she adds kindly.)* That's sweet of you, Patch. I know you'd raise a beautiful tune, but I have to go out. *(Consoled, the old man smiles at her gratefully.)*

MELODY Into the bar, all of you, where you belong! I told you not to use this entrance! *(with disdainful tolerance)* I suppose it's a free drink you're after. Well, no one can say of me that I turned away anyone I knew thirsty from my door.

O'DOWD Thank ye, yer Honor. Come along, Dan. *(He takes Riley's arm.)* Come on, Patch. *(The three go into the bar and O'Dowd closes the door behind them.)*

SARA *(in derisive brogue)* Sure, it's well trained you've got the poor retainers on your American estate to respect the master! *(Then as he ignores her and casts a furtive glance at the door to the bar, running his tongue over his dry lips, she says acidly, with no trace of brogue.)* Don't let me keep you from joining the gentlemen! *(She turns her back on him and goes out the street door at rear.)*

MELODY *(His face is again convulsed by a spasm of pain—pleadingly.)* Sara!

Nora enters from the hall at right, carrying a tray with toast, eggs, bacon, and tea. She arranges his breakfast on the table at front center, bustling garrulously.

NORA Have I kept you waitin'? The divil was in the toast. One lot burned black as a naygur when my back was turned. But the bacon is crisp, and the eggs not too soft, the way you like them. Come and sit down now. *(Melody does not seem to hear her. She looks at him worriedly.)* What's up with you, Con? Don't you hear me?

O'DOWD *(pokes his head in the door from the bar)* Mickey won't believe you said we could have a drink, yer Honor, unless ye tell him.

MELODY *(licking his lips)* I'm coming. *(He goes to the bar door.)*

NORA Con! Have this in your stomach first! It'll all get cauld.

MELODY *(without turning to her—in his condescendingly polite tone)* I find I am not the least hungry, Nora. I regret your having gone to so much trouble. *(He goes into the bar, closing the door behind him. Nora slumps on a chair at the rear of the table and stares at the breakfast with a pitiful helplessness. She begins to sob quietly.)*

Curtain

Why do the old Irish rowdies play up to Melody, despite any personal feelings they may have for him?

What is Nora's main objective in life?

ACT II

SCENE—*Same as Act I. About half an hour has elapsed. The barroom door opens and Melody comes in. He has had two more drinks and still no breakfast, but this has had no outward effect except that his face is paler and his manner more disdainful. He turns to give orders to the spongers in the bar.*

MELODY Remember what I say. None of your loud brawling. And you, Riley, keep your bagpipe silent, or out you go. I wish to be alone in quiet for a while with my memories. When Corporal Cregan returns, Mickey, send him in to me. He, at least, knows Talavera is not the name of a new brand of whiskey. *(He shuts the door contemptuously on Mickey's "Yes, Major" and the obedient murmur of the others. He sits at rear of the table at left front. At first, he poses to himself, striking an attitude—a Byronic hero, noble, embittered, disdainful, defying his tragic fate, brooding over past glories. But he has no audience and he cannot keep it up. His shoulders sag and he stares at the table top, hopelessness and defeat bringing a trace of real tragedy to his ruined, handsome face.)*

The street door is opened and Sara enters. He does not hear the click of the latch, or notice her as she comes forward. Fresh from the humiliation of cajoling the storekeeper to extend more credit, her eyes are bitter. At sight of her father they become more so. She moves toward the door at right, determined to ignore him, but something unusual in his attitude strikes her and she stops to regard him searchingly. She starts to say something bitter—stops—finally, in spite of herself, she asks with a trace of genuine pity in her voice.

SARA What's wrong with you, Father? Are you really sick or is it just— *(He starts guiltily, ashamed of being caught in such a weak mood.)*

MELODY *(gets to his feet politely and bows)* I beg your pardon, my dear. I did not hear you come in. *(with a deprecating smile)* Faith, I was far away in spirit, lost in memories of a glorious battle in Spain, nineteen years ago today.

SARA *(Her face hardens.)* Oh. It's the anniversary of Talavera, is it? Well, I know what that means—a great day for the spongers and a bad day for this inn!

MELODY *(coldly)* I don't understand you. Of course I shall honor the occasion.

SARA You needn't tell me. I remember the other celebrations—and this year, now Jamie Cregan has appeared, you've an excuse to make it worse.

MELODY Naturally, an old comrade in arms will be doubly welcome—

SARA Well, I'll say this much. From the little I've seen of him, I'd rather have free whiskey go down his gullet than the others'. He's a relation, too.

MELODY *(stiffly)* Merely a distant cousin. That has no bearing. It's because Corporal Cregan fought by my side—

SARA I suppose you've given orders to poor Mother to cook a grand feast for you, as usual, and you'll wear your beautiful uniform, and I'll have the honor of waiting on table. Well, I'll do it just this once more for Mother's sake, or she'd have to, but it'll be the last time. *(She turns her back on him and goes to the door at right.)* You'll be pleased to learn your daughter had almost to beg on her knees to Neilan before he'd let us have another month's credit. He made it plain it was to Mother he gave it because he pities her for the husband she's got. But what do you care about that, as long as you and your fine thoroughbred mare can live in style! *(Melody is shaken for a second. He glances toward the bar as if he longed to return there to escape her. Then he gets hold of himself. His face becomes expressionless. He sits in the same chair and picks up the paper, ignoring her. She starts to go out just as her mother appears in the doorway. Nora is carrying a glass of milk.)*

218 EUGENE O'NEILL

O'Neill's stage directions confirm our suspicions as to why Melody must surround himself with comrades. Why?

Why does Melody insist that Sara acknowledge Cregan simply as a corporal and only secondly as a distant cousin?

NORA Here's the milk the doctor ordered for the young gentleman. It's time for it, and I knew you'd be going upstairs.

SARA *(takes the milk)* Thank you, Mother. *(She nods scornfully toward her father.)* I've just been telling him I begged another month's credit from Neilan, so he needn't worry.

NORA Ah, thank God for that. Neilan's a kind man.

MELODY *(explodes)* Damn his kindness! By the Eternal, if he'd refused, I'd have—! *(He controls himself, meeting Sara's contemptuous eyes. He goes on quietly, a bitter, sneering antagonism underneath.)* Don't let me detain you, my dear. Take his milk to our Yankee guest, as your mother suggests. Don't miss any chance to play the ministering angel. *(vindictively)* Faith, the poor young devil hasn't a chance to escape with you two scheming peasants laying snares to trap him!

SARA That's a lie! And leave Mother out of your insults!

MELODY And if all other tricks fail, there's always one last trick to get him through his honor!

SARA *(tensely)* What trick do you mean? *(Nora grabs her arm.)*

NORA Hould your prate, now! Why can't you leave him be? It's your fault, for provoking him.

SARA *(quietly)* All right, Mother. I'll leave him to look in the mirror, like he loves to, and remember what he said, and be proud of himself. *(Melody winces. Sara goes out right.)*

MELODY *(after a pause—shakenly)* I— She mistook my meaning— It's as you said. She goads me into losing my temper, and I say things—

NORA *(sadly)* I know what made you say it. You think maybe she's like I was, and you can't help remembering my sin with you.

MELODY *(guiltily vehement)* No! No! I tell you she mistook my meaning, and now you— *(then exasperatedly)* Damn your priests' prating about your sin! *(with a strange, scornful vanity)* To hear you tell it, you'd think it was you who seduced me! That's likely, isn't it? —remembering the man I was then!

NORA I remember well. Sure, you was that handsome, no woman could resist you. And you are still.

MELODY *(pleased)* None of your blarney, Nora. *(with Byronic gloom)* I am but a ghost haunting a ruin. *(then gallantly but without looking at her)* And how about you in those days? Weren't you the prettiest girl in all Ireland? *(scornfully)* And be damned to your lying, pious shame! You had no shame then, I remember. It was love and joy and glory in you and you were proud!

NORA *(her eyes shining)* I'm still proud and will be to the day I die!

MELODY *(gives her an approving look which turns to distaste at her appearance—looks away irritably)* Why do you bring up the past? I do not wish to discuss it.

NORA *(after a pause—timidly)* All the same, you shouldn't talk to Sara as if you thought she'd be up to anything to catch young Harford.

MELODY I did not think that! She is my daughter—

NORA She is surely. And he's a dacent lad. *(She smiles a bit*

What does Melody imply about Sara's methods for getting young Harford to marry her? Why is Melody especially sensitive on this point?

A TOUCH OF THE POET

scornfully.) Sure, from all she's told me, he's that shy he's never dared even to kiss her hand!

MELODY (*with more than a little contempt*) I can well believe it. When it comes to making love the Yankees are clumsy, fish-blooded louts. They lack savoir-faire. They have no romantic fire! They know nothing of women. (*He snorts disdainfully.*) By the Eternal, when I was his age— (*then quickly*) Not that I don't approve of young Harford, mind you. He is a gentleman. When he asks me for Sara's hand I will gladly give my consent, provided his father and I can agree on the amount of her settlement.

NORA (*hastily*) Ah, there's no need to think of that yet. (*then lapsing into her own dream*) Yes, she'll be happy because she loves him dearly, a lot more than she admits. And it'll give her a chance to rise in the world. We'll see the day when she'll live in a grand mansion, dressed in silks and satins, and riding in a carriage with coachman and footman.

MELODY I desire that as much as you do, Nora. I'm done—finished —no future but the past. But my daughter has the looks, the brains —ambition, youth— She can go far. (*then sneeringly*) That is, if she can remember she's a gentlewoman and stop acting like a bog-trotting peasant wench! (*He hears Sara returning downstairs.*) She's coming back. (*He gets up—bitterly.*) As the sight of me seems to irritate her, I'll go in the bar for a while. I've had my fill of her insults for one morning. (*He opens the bar door. There is a chorus of eager, thirsty welcome from inside. He goes in, closing the door. Sara enters from right. Her face is flushed and her eyes full of dreamy happiness.*)

NORA (*rebukingly*) Himself went in the bar to be out of reach of your tongue. A fine thing! Aren't you ashamed you haven't enough feeling not to torment him, when you know it's the anniversary—

SARA All right, Mother. Let him take what joy he can out of the day. I'll even help you get his uniform out of the trunk in the attic and brush and clean it for you.

NORA Ah, God bless you, that's the way— (*then, astonished at this unexpected docility*) Glory be, but you've changed all of a sudden. What's happened to you?

SARA I'm so happy now—I can't feel bitter against anyone. (*She hesitates—then shyly.*) Simon kissed me. (*Having said this, she goes on triumphantly.*) He got his courage up at last, but it was me made him. I was freshening up his pillows and leaning over him, and he couldn't help it, if he was human. (*She laughs tenderly.*) And then you'd have laughed to see him. He near sank through the bed with shame at his boldness. He began apologizing as if he was afraid I'd be so insulted I'd never speak to him again.

NORA (*teasingly*) And what did you do? I'll wager you wasn't as brazen as you pretend.

SARA (*ruefully*) It's true, Mother. He made me as bashful as he was. I felt a great fool.

NORA And was that all? Sure, kissing is easy. Didn't he ask you if you'd marry—?

SARA No. (*quickly*) But it was my fault he didn't. He was trying to be brave enough. All he needed was a word of encouragement. But I

The learning that Melody does have is shown in his use of "savoir-faire," a French expression which means "know how."

220 EUGENE O'NEILL

stood there, dumb as a calf, and when I did speak it was to say I had to come and help you, and the end was I ran from the room, blushing as red as a beet— *(She comes to her mother. Nora puts her arms around her. Sara hides her face on her shoulder, on the verge of tears.)* Oh, Mother, ain't it crazy to be such a fool?

NORA Well, then you're in love—

SARA *(breaking away from her—angrily)* That's just it! I'm too much in love and I don't want to be! I won't let my heart rule my head and make a slave of me! *(Suddenly she smiles confidently.)* Ah well, he loves me as much, and more, I know that, and the next time I'll keep my wits. *(She laughs happily.)* You can consider it as good as done, Mother. I'm Mrs. Simon Harford, at your pleasure. *(She makes a sweeping bow.)*

NORA *(smiling)* Arrah, none of your airs and graces with me! Help me, now, like you promised, and we'll get your father's uniform out of the trunk. It won't break your back in the attic, like it does me.

SARA *(gaily puts her arm around her mother's waist)* Come along then.

NORA *(as they go out right)* I disremember which trunk—and you'll have to help me find the key.

There is a pause. Then the bar door is opened and Melody enters again in the same manner as he did at the beginning of the act. There is the same sound of voices from the bar but this time Melody gives no parting orders but simply shuts the door behind him. He scowls with disgust.

MELODY Cursed ignorant cattle. *(then with a real, lonely yearning)* I wish Jamie Cregan would come. *(bitterly)* Driven from pillar to post in my own home! Everywhere ignorance—or the scorn of my own daughter! *(then defiantly)* But by the Eternal God, no power on earth, nor in hell itself, can break me! *(His eyes are drawn irresistibly to the mirror. He moves in front of it, seeking the satisfying reassurance of his reflection there. What follows is an exact repetition of his scene before the mirror in Act One. There is the same squaring of his shoulders, arrogant lifting of his head, and then the favorite quote from Byron, recited aloud to his own image.)*

> "I have not loved the World, nor the World me;
> I have not flattered its rank breath, nor bowed
> To its idolatries a patient knee,
> Nor coined my cheek to smiles,—nor cried aloud
> In the worship of an echo; in the crowd
> They could not deem me one of such—I stood
> Among them, but not of them . . ."

He stands staring in the mirror and does not hear the latch of the street door click. The door opens and Deborah (Mrs. Henry Harford), Simon's mother, enters, closing the door quietly behind her. Melody continues to be too absorbed to notice anything. For a moment, blinded by the sudden change from the bright glare of the street, she does not see him. When she does, she stares incredulously. Then she smiles with an amused and mocking relish.

Deborah is forty-one, but looks to be no more than thirty. She is small, a little over five feet tall, with a fragile, youthful figure. One would never suspect that she is the middle-aged mother of two grown sons. Her face is beautiful—that is, it is beautiful from the standpoint of the artist with an

---

The contrast between mother and daughter on how much to let yourself go in a love relationship is not as great as it appears. What proof do we have that Sara also is subject to the pull of love, as was Nora?

A TOUCH OF THE POET   221

eye for bone structure and unusual character. It is small, with high cheekbones, wedge-shaped, narrowing from a broad forehead to a square chin, framed by thick, wavy, red-brown hair. The nose is delicate and thin, a trifle aquiline. The mouth, with full lips and even, white teeth, is too large for her face. So are the long-lashed, green-flecked brown eyes, under heavy, angular brows. These would appear large in any face, but in hers they seem enormous and are made more startling by the pallor of her complexion. She has tiny, high-arched feet and thin, tapering hands. Her slender, fragile body is dressed in white with calculated simplicity. About her whole personality is a curious atmosphere of deliberate detachment, the studied aloofness of an ironically amused spectator. Something perversely assertive about it too, as if she consciously carried her originality to the point of whimsical eccentricity._

> O'Neill describes Mrs. Harford in great detail. Though approximately the same age as Nora, Deborah Harford is far different from Melody's wife in appearance and bearing. What is the symbolic contrast in their different looks?

DEBORAH I beg your pardon. _(Melody jumps and whirls around. For a moment his face has an absurdly startled, stupid look. He is shamed and humiliated and furious at being caught for the second time in one morning before the mirror. His revenge is to draw himself up haughtily and survey her insolently from head to toe. But at once, seeing she is attractive and a lady, his manner changes. Opportunity beckons and he is confident of himself, put upon his mettle. He bows, a gracious, gallant gentleman. There is seductive charm in his welcoming smile and in his voice.)_

MELODY Good morning, Mademoiselle. It is an honor to welcome you to this unworthy inn. _(He draws out a chair at rear of the larger table in the foreground—bowing again.)_ If I may presume. You will find it comfortable here, away from the glare of the street.

> In the following conversation, look for specific words and phrases that raise Con's speech to a more formal level. If he were speaking to Nora, what words might he use?

DEBORAH _(Regards him for a second puzzledly. She is impressed in spite of herself by his bearing and distinguished, handsome face.)_ Thank you. _(She comes forward. Melody makes a gallant show of holding her chair and helping her be seated. He takes in all her points with sensual appreciation. It is the same sort of pleasure a lover of horseflesh would have in the appearance of a thoroughbred horse. Meanwhile he speaks with caressing courtesy.)_

MELODY Mademoiselle— _(He sees her wedding ring.)_ Pray forgive me, I see it is Madame— Permit me to say again, how great an honor I will esteem it to be of any service. _(He manages, as he turns away, as if by accident to brush his hand against her shoulder. She is startled and caught off guard. She shrinks and looks up at him. Their eyes meet and at the nakedly physical appraisement she sees in his, a fascinated fear suddenly seizes her. But at once she is reassured as he shifts his gaze, satisfied by her reactions to his first attack, and hastens to apologize.)_ I beg your pardon, Madame. I am afraid my manners have grown clumsy with disuse. It is not often a lady comes here now. This inn, like myself, has fallen upon unlucky days.

DEBORAH _(curtly ignoring this)_ I presume you are the innkeeper, Melody?

MELODY _(a flash of anger in his eyes—arrogantly)_ I am _Major_ Cornelius Melody, one time of His Majesty's Seventh Dragoons, at your service. _(He bows with chill formality.)_

DEBORAH _(is now an amused spectator again—apologetically)_ Oh. Then it is I who owe you an apology, Major Melody.

MELODY _(encouraged—gallantly)_ No, no, dear lady, the fault is mine. I

> Deborah Harford's presence has set off Melody on a ritual of courtesy and flirtation as he had practiced it during his heyday as a gallant. Her reac-

should not have taken offense. *(with the air of one frankly admitting a praiseworthy weakness)* Faith, I may as well confess my besetting weakness is that of all gentlemen who have known better days. I have a pride unduly sensitive to any fancied slight.

DEBORAH *(playing up to him now)* I assure you sir, there was no intention on my part to slight you.

MELODY *(His eyes again catch hers and hold them—his tone insinuatingly caressing.)* You are as gracious as you are beautiful, Madame. *(Deborah's amusement is gone. She is again confused and, in spite of herself, frightened and fascinated. Melody proceeds with his attack, full of confidence now, the successful seducer of old. His voice takes on a calculated melancholy cadence. He becomes a romantic, tragic figure, appealing for a woman's understanding and loving compassion.)* I am a poor fool, Madame. I would be both wiser and happier if I could reconcile myself to being the proprietor of a tawdry tavern, if I could abjure pride and forget the past. Today of all days it is hard to forget, for it is the anniversary of the battle of Talavera. The most memorable day of my life, Madame. It was on that glorious field I had the honor to be commended for my bravery by the great Duke of Wellington, himself—Sir Arthur Wellesley, then. So I am sure you can find it in your heart to forgive— *(his tone more caressing)* One so beautiful must understand the hearts of men full well, since so many must have given their hearts to you. *(A coarse passion comes into his voice.)* Yes, I'll wager my all against a penny that even among the fish-blooded Yankees there's not a man whose heart doesn't catch flame from your beauty! *(He puts his hand over one of her hands on the table and stares into her eyes ardently.)* As mine does now!

DEBORAH *(Feeling herself borne down weakly by the sheer force of his physical strength, struggles to release her hand. She stammers, with an attempt at lightness.)* Is this—what the Irish call blarney, sir?

MELODY *(with a fierce, lustful sincerity)* No! I take my oath by the living God, I would charge a square of Napoleon's Old Guard singlehanded for one kiss of your lips. *(He bends lower, while his eyes hold hers. For a second it seems he will kiss her and she cannot help herself. Then abruptly the smell of whiskey on his breath brings her to herself, shaken with disgust and coldly angry. She snatches her hand from his and speaks with withering contempt.)*

DEBORAH Pah! You reek of whiskey! You are drunk, sir! You are insolent and disgusting! I do not wonder your inn enjoys such meager patronage, if you regale all your guests of my sex with this absurd performance! *(Melody straightens up with a jerk, taking a step back as though he had been slapped in the face. Deborah rises to her feet, ignoring him disdainfully. At this moment Sara and her mother enter through the doorway at right. They take in the scene at a glance. Melody and Deborah do not notice their entrance.)*

NORA *(half under her breath)* Oh, God help us!

SARA *(Guesses at once this must be the woman Mickey had told her about. She hurries toward them quickly, trying to hide her apprehension and anger and shame at what she knows must have happened.)* What is it, Father? What does the lady wish? *(Her arrival is a further blow for Melody, seething now in a fury of humiliated pride. Deborah turns to face Sara.)*

---

tions to his role playing, however, bear watching.

Does Melody really expect to seduce Deborah, or does he have some other motivation?

Deborah Harford has seen through Melody's routine and appropriately labels it as an "absurd performance" not to be believed.

A TOUCH OF THE POET

DEBORAH *(coolly self-possessed—pleasantly)* I came here to see you, Miss Melody, hoping you might know the present whereabouts of my son, Simon. *(This is a bombshell for Melody.)*

MELODY *(blurts out with no apology in his tone but angrily, as if she had intentionally made a fool of him)* You're his mother? In God's name, Madame, why didn't you say so!

DEBORAH *(ignoring him—to Sara)* I've been out to his hermit's cabin, only to find the hermit flown.

SARA *(stammers)* He's here, Mrs. Harford—upstairs in bed. He's been sick—

DEBORAH Sick? You don't mean seriously?

SARA *(recovering a little from her confusion)* Oh, he's over it now, or almost. It was only a spell of chills and fever he caught from the damp of the lake. I found him shivering and shaking and made him come here where there's a doctor handy and someone to nurse him.

DEBORAH *(pleasantly)* The someone being you, Miss Melody?

SARA Yes, me and—my mother and I.

DEBORAH *(graciously)* I am deeply grateful to you and your mother for your kindness.

NORA *(who has remained in the background, now comes forward—with her sweet, friendy smile)* Och, don't be thankin' us, ma'am. Sure, your son is a gentle, fine lad, and we all have great fondness for him. He'd be welcome here if he never paid a penney— *(She stops embarrassedly, catching a disapproving glance from Sara. Deborah is repelled by Nora's slovenly appearance, but she feels her simple charm and gentleness, and returns her smile.)*

Why does Nora not fit into the genteel exchanges under way at this point?

SARA *(with embarrassed stiffness)* This is my mother, Mrs. Harford. *(Deborah inclines her head graciously. Nora instinctively bobs in a peasant's curtsy to one of the gentry. Melody, snubbed and seething, glares at her.)*

NORA I'm pleased to make your acquaintance, ma'am.

MELODY Nora! For the love of God, stop—*(Suddenly he is able to become the polished gentleman again—considerately and even a trifle condescendingly.)* I am sure Mrs. Harford is waiting to be taken to her son. Am I not right, Madame? *(Deborah is so taken aback by his effrontery that for a moment she is speechless. She replies coldly, obviously doing so only becaue she does not wish to create further embarrassment.)*

DEBORAH That is true, sir. *(She turns her back on him.)* If you will be so kind, Miss Melody. I've wasted so much of the morning and I have to return to the city. I have only time for a short visit—

SARA Just come with me, Mrs. Harford. *(She goes to the door at right, and steps aside to let Deborah precede her.)* What a pleasant surprise this will be for Simon. He'd have written you he was sick, but he didn't want to worry you. *(She follows Deborah into the hall.)*

MELODY Damned fool of a woman! If I'd known— No, be damned if I regret! Cursed Yankee upstart! *(with a sneer)* But she didn't fool me with her insulted airs! I've known too many women— *(in a rage)* "Absurd performance," was it? God damn her!

NORA *(timidly)* Don't be cursing her and tormenting yourself. She

224 EUGENE O'NEILL

seems a kind lady. She won't hold it against you, when she stops to think, knowing you didn't know who she is.

MELODY *(tensely)* Be quiet!

NORA Forget it now, do, for Sara's sake. Sure, you wouldn't want anything to come between her and the lad. *(He is silent. She goes on comfortingly.)* Go on up to your room now and you'll find something to take your mind off. Sara and I have your uniform brushed and laid out on the bed.

MELODY *(harshly)* Put it back in the trunk! I don't want it to remind me— *(with humiliated rage again)* By the Eternal, I'll wager she believed what I told her of Talavera and the Great Duke honoring me was a drunken liar's boast!

NORA No, she'd never, Con. She couldn't.

MELODY *(seized by an idea)* Well, seeing would be believing, eh, my fine lady? Yes, by God, that will prove to her— *(He turns to Nora, his self-confidence partly restored.)* Thank you for reminding me of my duty to Sara. You are right. I do owe it to her interests to forget my anger and make a formal apology to Simon's mother for our little misunderstanding. *(He smiles condescendingly.)* Faith, as a gentleman, I should grant it is a pretty woman's privilege to be always right even when she is wrong. *(He goes to the door at extreme left front and opens it.)* If the lady should come back, kindly keep her here on some excuse until I return. *(This is a command. He disappears, closing the door behind him.)*

NORA *(sighs)* Ah well, it's all right. He'll be on his best behavior now, and he'll feel proud again in his uniform.

She sits at the end of center table right and relaxes wearily. A moment later Sara enters quickly from right and comes to her.

SARA Where's Father?

NORA I got him to go up and put on his uniform. It'll console him.

SARA *(bitterly)* Console *him?* It's me ought to be consoled for having such a great fool for a father!

NORA Hush now! How could he know who—?

SARA *(with a sudden reversal of feeling—almost vindictively)* Yes, it serves her right. I suppose she thinks she's such a great lady anyone in America would pay her respect. Well, she knows better now. And she didn't act as insulted as she might. Maybe she liked it, for all her pretenses. *(again with an abrupt reversal of feeling)* Ah, how can I talk such craziness! Him and his drunken love-making! Well, he got put in his place, and aren't I glad! He won't forget in a hurry how she snubbed him, as if he was no better than dirt under her feet!

NORA She didn't. She had the sense to see he'd been drinking and not to mind him.

SARA *(dully)* Maybe. But isn't that bad enough? What woman would want her son to marry the daughter of a man like—*(She breaks down.)* Oh, Mother, I was feeling so happy and sure of Simon, and now— Why did she have to come today? If she'd waited till tomorrow, even, I'd have got him to ask me to marry him, and once he'd done that no power on earth could change him.

What is Melody's plan for retaliating against Mrs. Harford's snubs?

When Sara thinks like her father, she feels that Mrs. Harford pretends to be offended, implying that Mrs. Harford is playing a false role in the world, too.

How does Nora's view of events differ from Sara's?

A TOUCH OF THE POET 225

NORA If he loves you no power can change him, anyway. *(proudly)* Don't I know! *(reassuringly)* She's his mother, and she loves him and she'll want him to be happy, and she'll see he loves you. What makes you think she'll try to change him?

SARA Because she hates me, Mother—for one reason.

NORA She doesn't. She couldn't.

SARA She does. Oh, she acted as nice as nice, but she didn't fool me. She's the kind would be polite to the hangman, and her on the scaffold. *(She lowers her voice.)* It isn't just to pay Simon a visit she came. It's because Simon's father got a letter telling him about us, and he showed it to her.

NORA Who did a dirty trick like that?

SARA It wasn't signed, she said. I suppose someone around here that hates Father—and who doesn't?

NORA Bad luck to the blackguard, whoever it was!

SARA She said she'd come to warn Simon his father is wild with anger and he's gone to see his lawyer—But that doesn't worry me. It's only her influence I'm afraid of.

NORA How do you know about the letter?

SARA *(avoiding her eyes)* I sneaked back to listen outside the door.

NORA Shame on you! You should have more pride!

SARA I was ashamed, Mother, after a moment or two, and I came away. *(then defiantly)* No, I'm not ashamed. I wanted to learn what tricks she might be up to, so I'll be able to fight them. I'm not ashamed at all. I'll do anthing to keep him. *(lowering her voice)* She started talking the second she got in the door. She had only a few minutes because she has to be home before dinner so her husband won't suspect she came here. He's forbidden her to see Simon ever since Simon came out here to live.

NORA Well, doesn't her coming against her husband's orders show she's on Simon's side?

SARA Yes, but it doesn't show she wants him to marry me. *(impatiently)* Don't be so simple, Mother. Wouldn't she tell Simon that anyway, even if the truth was her husband sent her to do all she could to get him away from me?

NORA Don't look for trouble before it comes. Wait and see, now. Maybe you'll find—

SARA I'll find what I said, Mother—that she hates me. *(bitterly)* Even if she came here with good intentions, she wouldn't have them now, after our great gentleman has insulted her. Thank God, if he's putting on his uniform, he'll be hours before the mirror, and she'll be gone before he can make a fool of himself again. *(Nora starts to tell her the truth—then thinks better of it. Sara goes on, changing her tone.)* But I'd like her to see him in his uniform, at that, if he was sober. She'd find she couldn't look down on him— *(exasperatedly)* Och! I'm as crazy as he is. As if she hadn't the brains to see through him.

NORA *(wearily)* Leave him be, for the love of God.

SARA *(after a pause—defiantly)* Let her try whatever game she likes. I

> Why does the unsigned letter, which alerts Simon's parents to Sara's involvement with their son, serve as a complicating factor during the development of the plot?

226 EUGENE O'NEILL

have brains too, she'll discover. *(then uneasily)* Only, like Simon's told me, I feel she's strange and queer behind her lady's airs, and it'll be hard to tell what she's really up to. *(They both hear a sound from upstairs.)* That's her, now. She didn't waste much time. Well, I'm ready for her. Go in the kitchen, will you, Mother? I want to give her the chance to have it out with me alone. *(Nora gets up—then, remembering Melody's orders, glances toward the door at left front uneasily and hesitates. Sara says urgently.)* Don't you hear me? Hurry Mother! *(Nora sighs and goes out quickly, right. Sara sits at rear of the center table and waits, drawing herself up in an unconscious imitation of her father's grand manner. Deborah appears in the doorway at right. There is nothing in her expression to betray any emotion resulting from her interview with her son. She smiles pleasantly at Sara, who rises graciously from her chair.)*

DEBORAH *(coming to her)* I am glad to find you here, Miss Melody. It gives me another opportunity to express my gratitude for your kindness to my son during his illness.

SARA Thank you, Mrs. Harford. My mother and I have been only too happy to do all we could. *(She adds defiantly.)* We are very fond of Simon.

DEBORAH *(a glint of secret amusement in her eyes)* Yes, I feel you are. And he has told me how fond he is of you. *(Her manner becomes reflective. She speaks rapidly in a remote, detached way, lowering her voice unconsciously as if she were thinking aloud to herself.)* This is the first time I have seen Simon since he left home to seek self-emancipation at the breast of Nature. I find him not so greatly changed as I had been led to expect from his letters. Of course, it is some time since he has written. I had thought his implacably honest discovery that the poetry he hoped the pure freedom of Nature would inspire him to write is, after all, but a crude imitation of Lord Byron's would have more bitterly depressed his spirit. *(She smiles.)* But evidently he has found a new romantic dream by way of recompense. As I might have known he would. Simon is an inveterate dreamer—a weakness he inherited from me, I'm afraid, although I must admit the Harfords have been great dreamers, too, in their way. Even my husband has a dream—a conservative, material dream, naturally. I have just been reminding Simon that his father is rigidly unforgiving when his dream is flouted, and very practical in his methods of defending it. *(She smiles again.)* My warning was the mechanical gesture of a mother's duty, merely. I realized it would have no effect. He did not listen to what I said. For that matter, neither did I. *(She laughs a little detached laugh, as if she were secretly amused.)*

SARA *(stares at her, unable to decide what is behind all this and how she should react—with an undercurrent of resentment)* I don't think Simon imitates Lord Byron. I hate Lord Byron's poetry. And I know there's a true poet in Simon.

DEBORAH *(vaguely surprised—speaks rapidly again)* Oh, in feeling, of course. It is natural you should admire that in him—now. But I warn you it is a quality difficult for a woman to keep on admiring in a Harford, judging from what I know of the family history. Simon's greatgrandfather, Jonathan Harford, had it. He was killed at Bunker Hill, but I suspect the War for Independence was merely a symbolic opportunity for him. His was a personal war, I am sure—for pure

---

O'Neill wanted his audiences to be certain of the resemblances between Sara and her father, despite their outward antagonism.

What special kind of "Nature" does Deborah mean here?

In this section of the dialogue, Mrs. Harford clearly focuses the nature of the "dreams," or hopes, held by her family. Thus, although neither her husband nor son ever appear on stage, the audience knows precisely what each is like.

freedom. Simon's grandfather, Evan Harford, had the quality too. A fanatic in the cause of pure freedom, he became scornful of our Revolution. It made too many compromises with the ideal to free him. He went to France and became a rabid Jacobin, a worshiper of Robespierre. He would have liked to have gone to the guillotine with his incorruptible Redeemer, but he was too unimportant. They simply forgot to kill him. He came home and lived in a little temple of Liberty he had built in a corner of what is now my garden. It is still there. I remember him well. A dry, gentle, cruel, indomitable, futile old idealist who used frequently to wear his old uniform of the French Republican National Guard. He died wearing it. But the point is, you can have no idea what revengeful hate the Harford pursuit of freedom imposed upon the women who shared their lives. The three daughters-in-law of Jonathan, Evan's half-sisters, had to make a large, greedy fortune out of privateering and the Northwest trade, and finally were even driven to embrace the profits of the slave trade—as a triumphant climax, you understand, of their long battle to escape the enslavement of freedom by enslaving it. Evan's wife, of course, was drawn into this conflict, and became their tool and accomplice. They even attempted to own me, but I managed to escape because there was so little of me in the flesh that aged, greedy fingers could clutch. I am sorry they are dead and cannot know you. They would approve of you, I think. They would see that you are strong and ambitious and determined to take what you want. They would have smiled like senile, hungry serpents and welcomed you into their coils. *(She laughs.)* Evil old witches! Detestable, but I could not help admiring them—pitying them, too—in the end. We had a bond in common. They idolized Napoleon. They used to say he was the only man they would ever have married. And I used to dream I was Josephine—even after my marriage, I'm afraid. The Sisters, as everyone called them, and all of the family accompanied my husband and me on our honeymoon—to Paris to witness the Emperor's coronation. *(She pauses, smiling at her memories.)*

SARA *(Against her will, has become a bit hypnotized by Deborah's rapid, low, musical flow of words, as she strains to grasp the implication for her. She speaks in a low, confidential tone herself, smiling naturally.)* I've always admired him too. It's one of the things I've held against my father, that he fought against him and not for him.

DEBORAH *(starts, as if awakening—with a pleasant smile)* Well, Miss Melody, this is tiresome of me to stand here giving you a discourse on Harford family history. I don't know what you must think of me—but doubtless Simon has told you I am a bit eccentric at times. *(She glances at Sara's face—amusedly.)* Ah, I can see he has. Then I am sure you will make allowances. I really do not know what inspired me—except perhaps, that I wish to be fair and warn you, too.

SARA *(stiffens)* Warn me about what, Mrs. Harford?

DEBORAH Why, that the Harfords never part with their dreams even when they deny them. They cannot. That is the family curse. For example, this book Simon plans to write to denounce the evil of greed and possessive ambition, and uphold the virtue of freeing oneself from the lust for power and saving our souls by being content with little. I cannot imagine you taking that seriously. *(She again *flashes a glance at Sara.*) I see you do not. Neither do I. I do not even believe Simon will ever write this book on paper. But I warn you it is already written on his conscience and— (*She stops with a little disdaining laugh.*) I begin to resemble Cassandra with all my warnings. And I continue to stand here boring you with words. (*She holds out her hand graciously.*) Goodbye, Miss Melody.

SARA (*takes her hand mechanically*) Goodbye, Mrs. Harford. (*Deborah starts for the door at rear. Sara follows her, her expression confused, suspicious, and at the same time hopeful. Suddenly she blurts out impulsively.*) Mrs. Harford, I—

DEBORAH (*turns on her, pleasantly*) Yes, Miss Melody?

But her eyes have become blank and expressionless and discourage any attempt at further contact.

SARA (*silenced—with stiff politeness*) Isn't there some sort of cooling drink I could get you before you go? You must be parched after walking from the road to Simon's cabin and back on this hot day.

DEBORAH Nothing, thank you. (*then talking rapidly again in her strange detached way*) Yes, I did find my walk alone in the woods a strangely overpowering experience. Frightening—but intoxicating, too. Such a wild feeling of release and fresh enslavement. I have not ventured from my garden in many years. There, Nature is tamed, constrained to obey and adorn. I had forgotten how compelling the brutal power of primitive, possessive Nature can be—when suddenly one is attacked by it. (*She smiles.*) It has been a most confusing morning for a tired, middle-aged matron, but I flatter myself I have preserved a philosophic poise, or should I say, pose, as well as may be. Nevertheless, it will be a relief to return to my garden and books and meditations and listen indifferently again while the footsteps of life pass and recede along the street beyond the high wall. I shall never venture forth again to do my duty. It is a noble occupation, no doubt, for those who can presume they know what their duty to others is; but I— (*She laughs.*) Mercy, here I am chattering on again. (*She turns to the door.*) Cato will be provoked at me for keeping him waiting. I've already caused his beloved horses to be half-devoured by flies. Cato is our black coachman. He also is fond of Simon, although since Simon became emancipated he has embarrassed Cato acutely by shaking his hand whenever they meet. Cato was always a self-possessed free man even when he was a slave. It astonishes him that Simon has to prove that he—I mean Simon—is free. (*She smiles.*) Goodbye again, Miss Melody. This time I really am going. (*Sara opens the door for her. She walks past Sara into the street, turns left, and, passing before the two windows, disappears. Sara closes the door and comes back slowly to the head of the table at center. She stands thinking, her expression puzzled, apprehensive, and resentful. Nora appears in the doorway at right.*)

NORA God forgive you, Sara, why did you let her go? Your father told me—

SARA I can't make her out, Mother. You'd think she didn't care, but she does care. And she hates me. I could feel it. But you can't tell— She's crazy, I think. She talked on and on as if she couldn't stop— queer blather about Simon's ancestors, and herself, and Napoleon,

---

In Greek mythology, Cassandra told prophecies fated to come true but never to be believed by others around her.

What evidence leads Sara to this conclusion?

and Nature, and her garden and freedom, and God knows what—but letting me know all the time she had a meaning behind it, and was warning and threatening me. Oh, she may be daft in some ways, but she's no fool. I know she didn't let Simon guess she'd rather have him dead than married to me. Oh, no, I'm sure she told him if he was sure he loved me and I meant his happiness— But then she'd say he ought to wait and prove he's sure—anything to give her time. She'd make him promise to wait. Yes, I'll wager that's what she's done!

NORA *(who has been watching the door at left front, preoccupied by her own worry—frightenedly)* Your father'll be down any second. I'm going out in the garden. *(She grabs Sara's arm.)* Come along with me, and give him time to get over his rage.

SARA *(shakes off her hand—exasperatedly)* Leave me be, Mother. I've enough to worry me without bothering about him. I've got to plan the best way to act when I see Simon. I've got to be as big a liar as she was. I'll have to pretend I liked her and I'd respect whatever advice she gave him. I mustn't let him see— But I won't go to him again today, Mother. You can take up his meals and his milk, if you will. Tell him I'm too busy. I want to get him anxious and afraid maybe I'm mad at him for something, that maybe his mother said something. If he once has the idea maybe he's lost me—that ought to help, don't you think, Mother?

NORA *(sees the door at left front begin to open—in a whisper)* Oh, God help me! *(She turns in panicky flight and disappears through the doorway, right.)*

The door at left front slowly opens—slowly because Melody, hearing voices in the room and hoping Deborah is there, is deliberately making a dramatic entrance. And in spite of its obviousness, it is effective. Wearing the brilliant scarlet full-dress uniform of a major in one of Wellington's dragoon regiments, he looks extraordinarily handsome and distinguished—a startling, colorful, romantic figure, possessing now a genuine quality he has not had before, the quality of the formidably strong, disdainfully fearless cavalry officer he really had been. The uniform has been preserved with the greatest care. Each button is shining and the cloth is spotless. Being in it has notably restored his self-confident arrogance. Also, he has done everything he can to freshen up his face and hide any effect of his morning's drinks. When he discovers Deborah is not in the room, he is mildly disappointed and, as always when he first confronts Sara alone, he seems to shrink back guiltily within himself. Sara's face hardens and she gives no sign of knowing he is there. He comes slowly around the table at left front, until he stands at the end of the center table facing her. She still refuses to notice him and he is forced to speak. He does so with the air of one who condescends to be amused by his own foibles.

MELODY I happened to go to my room and found you and your mother had laid out my uniform so invitingly that I could not resist the temptation to put it on at once instead of waiting until evening.

SARA *(Turns on him. In spite of herself she is so struck by his appearance that the contempt is forced back and she can only stammer a bit foolishly.)* Yes, I—I see you did. *(There is a moment's pause. She stares at him fascinatedly—then blurts out with impulsive admiration.)* You look grand and handsome, Father.

> Sara does not know for certain the particulars of Mrs. Harford's conversation with Simon. But Sara senses that Deborah has come to retrieve her son by breaking up his relationship with Sara.

> From the audience's perspective, are Sara's plans appropriate?

MELODY (*as pleased as a child*) Why, it is most kind of you to say that, my dear Sara. (*preening himself*) I flatter myself I do not look too unworthy of the man I was when I wore this uniform with honor.

SARA (*an appeal forced out of her that is both pleading and a bitter reproach*) Oh, Father, why can't you ever be the thing you can seem to be? (*A sad scorn comes into her voice.*) The man you were. I'm sorry I never knew that soldier. I think he was the only man who wasn't just a dream.

MELODY (*His face becomes a blank disguise—coldly.*) I don't understand you. (*A pause. He begins to talk in an arrogantly amused tone.*) I suspect you are still holding against me my unfortunate blunder with your future mother-in-law. I would not blame you if you did. (*He smiles.*) Faith, I did put my foot in it. (*He chuckles.*) The devil of it is, I can never get used to these Yankee ladies. I do them the honor of complimenting them with a bit of harmless flattery and, lo and behold, suddenly my lady acts as if I had insulted her. It must be their damned narrow Puritan background. They can't help seeing sin hiding under every bush, but this one need not have been alarmed. I never had an eye for skinny, pale snips of women— (*hastily*) But what I want to tell you is I am sorry it happened, Sara, and I will do my best, for the sake of your interests, to make honorable amends. I shall do the lady the honor of tendering her my humble apologies when she comes downstairs. (*with arrogant vanity*) I flatter myself she will be graciously pleased to make peace. She was not as outraged by half as her conscience made her pretend, if I am any judge of feminine frailty.

SARA (*who has been staring at him with scorn until he says this last—impulsively, with a sneer of agreement*) I'll wager she wasn't for all her airs. (*then furious at herself and him*) Ah, will you stop telling me your mad dreams! (*controlling herself—coldly*) You'll have no chance to make bad worse by trying to fascinate her with your beautiful uniform. She's gone.

MELODY (*stunned*) Gone? (*furiously*) You're lying, damn you!

SARA I'm not. She left ten minutes ago, or more.

MELODY (*before he thinks*) But I told your mother to keep her here until— (*He stops abruptly.*)

SARA So that's why Mother is so frightened. Well, it was me let her go, so don't take out your rage on poor Mother.

MELODY Rage? My dear Sara, all I feel is relief. Surely you can't believe I could have looked forward to humbling my pride, even though it would have furthered your interests.

SARA Furthered my interests by giving her another reason to laugh up her sleeve at your pretenses? (*with angry scorn, lapsing into broad brogue*) Arrah, God pity you! (*She turns her back on him and goes off, right. Melody stands gripping the back of the chair at the foot of the table in his big, powerful hands in an effort to control himself. There is a crack as the chair back snaps in half. He stares at the fragments in his hands with stupid surprise. The door to the bar is shoved open and Mickey calls in.*)

MALOY Here's Cregan back to see you, Major.

MELODY (*startled, repeats stupidly*) Cregan? (*Then his face suddenly*

Note the psychology of this moment: along with the thoroughbred mare, Melody's spotless uniform is his most direct link with the glorious past which once was his life. To wear the uniform, consequently, erases intervening time and allows him to recapture the confidence felt years earlier.

Sara's question reveals a great deal about her own need for delusions and ideals.

What does Sara do, instinctively, when she wants to hurt Melody? Why does this always upset him so much?

Why is Cregan's appearance so vital to Melody at this moment?

A TOUCH OF THE POET

lights up with pathetic eagerness and his voice is full of welcoming warmth as he calls.) Jamie! My old comrade in arms! *(As Cregan enters, he grips his hand.)* By the Powers I'm glad you're here, Jamie. *(Cregan is surprised and pleased by the warmth of his welcome. Melody draws him into the room.)* Come: Sit down. You'll join me in a drink, I know. *(He gets Cregan a glass from the cupboard. The decanter and Melody's glass are already on the table.)*

CREGAN *(admiringly)* Be God, it's the old uniform, no less, and you look as fine a figure in it as ever you did in Spain. *(He sits at right of table at left front as Melody sits at rear.)*

MELODY *(immensely pleased—deprecatingly)* Hardly, Jamie—but not a total ruin yet, I hope. I put it on in honor of the day. I see you've forgotten. For shame, you dog, not to remember Talavera.

CREGAN *(excitedly)* Talavera, is it? Where I got my saber cut. Be the mortal, I remember it, and you've a right to celebrate. You was worth any ten men in the army that day! *(Melody has shoved the decanter toward him. He pours a drink.)*

MELODY *(This compliment completely restores him to his arrogant self.)* Yes, I think I may say I did acquit myself with honor. *(patronizingly)* So, for that matter, did you. *(He pours a drink and raises his glass.)* To the day and your good health, Corporal Cregan.

CREGAN *(enthusiastically)* To the day and yourself, God bless you, Con! *(He tries to touch brims with Melody's glass, but Melody holds his glass away and draws himself up haughtily.)*

MELODY *(with cold rebuke)* I said, to the day and your good health, Corporal Cregan.

CREGAN *(For a second is angry—then he grins and mutters admiringly.)* Be God, it's you can bate the world and never let it change you! *(correcting his toast with emphasis)* To the day and yourself, *Major Melody.*

MELODY *(touches his glass to Cregan's—graciously condescending)* Drink hearty, Corporal. *(They drink.)*

Curtain

> After his earlier rebuffs, how does Melody still salvage some satisfaction?

ACT III

SCENE—*The same. The door to the bar is closed. It is around eight that evening and there are candles on the center table. Melody sits at the head of this table. In his brilliant uniform he presents more than ever an impressively colorful figure in the room, which appears smaller and dingier in the candlelight. Cregan is in the chair on his right. The other chairs at this table are unoccupied. Riley, O'Dowd, and Roche sit at the table at left front. Riley is at front, but his chair is turned sideways so he faces right. O'Dowd has the chair against the wall, facing right, with Roche across the table from him, his back to Melody. All five are drunk, Melody more so than any of them, but except for the glazed glitter in his eyes and his deathly pallor, his appearance does not betray him. He is holding his liquor like a gentleman.*

Cregan is the least drunk. O'Dowd and Roche are boisterous. The effect of the drink on Riley is merely to sink him deeper in dreams. He seems oblivious to his surroundings.

> Why should the colorfully clad Melody be placed somewhere near center stage?

232 EUGENE O'NEILL

Con (Eric Portman) at right, with patrons in Melody's Tavern.

An empty and half-empty bottle of port are on the table before Melody and Cregan, and their glasses are full. The three at the table have a decanter of whiskey.

Sara, wearing her working dress and an apron, is removing dishes and the remains of the dinner. Her face is set. She is determined to ignore them, but there is angry disgust in her eyes. Melody is arranging forks, knives, spoons, saltcellar, etc., in a plan of battle on the table before him. Cregan watches him. Patch Riley gives a few tuning-up quavers on his pipes.

MELODY Here's the river Tagus. And here, Talavera. This would be the French position on a rise of ground with the plain between our lines and theirs. Here is our redoubt with the Fourth Division and the Guards. And here's our cavalry brigade in a valley toward our left, if you'll remember, Corporal Cregan.

CREGAN *(excitedly)* Remember? Sure I see it as clear as yesterday!

RILEY *(bursts into a rollicking song, accompanying himself on the pipes, his voice the quavering ghost of a tenor but still true—to the tune of "Baltiorum")*

"She'd a pig and boneens,
She'd a bed and a dresser,
And a nate little room
For the father confessor;
With a cupboard and curtains, and something,
                      I'm towld,
That his riv'rance liked when the weather was cowld.
And it's hurroo, hurroo! Biddy O'Rafferty!"

Roche and O'Dowd roar after him, beating time on the table with their glasses—"Hurroo, hurroo! Biddy O'Rafferty!"—and laugh drunkenly. Cregan, too, joins in this chorus. Melody frowns angrily at the interruption, but at the end he smiles with lordly condescension, pleased by the irreverence of the song.

A TOUCH OF THE POET

O'DOWD (*after a cunning glance at Melody's face to see what his reaction is—derisively*) Och, lave it to the priests, divil mend thim! Ain't it so, Major?

MELODY Ay, damn them all! A song in the right spirit, Piper. Faith, I'll have you repeat it for my wife's benefit when she joins us. She still has a secret fondness for priests. And now, less noise, you blackguards. Corporal Cregan and I cannot hear each other with your brawling.

O'DOWD (*smirkingly obedient*) Quiet it is, yer Honor. Be quiet, Patch. (*He gives the old man, who is lost in dreams, a shove that almost knocks him off his chair. Riley stares at him bewilderedly. O'Dowd and Roche guffaw.*)

MELODY (*scowls at them, then turns to Cregan*) Where was I, Corporal? Oh, yes, we were waiting in the valley. We heard a trumpet from the French lines and saw them forming for the attack. An aide-de-camp galloped down the hill to us—

SARA (*who has been watching him disdainfully, reaches out to take his plate—rudely in mocking brogue*) I'll have your plate, av ye plaze, Major, before your gallant dragoons charge over it and break it.

MELODY (*holds his plate on the table with one hand so she cannot take it, and raises his glass of wine with the other—ignoring her*) Wet your lips, Corporal. Talavera was a devilish thirsty day, if you'll remember. (*He drinks.*)

CREGAN (*glances uneasily at Sara*) It was that. (*He drinks.*)

MELODY (*smacking his lips*) Good wine, Corporal. Thank God, I still have wine in my cellar fit for a gentleman.

SARA (*angrily*) Are you going to let me take your plate?

MELODY (*ignoring her*) No, I have no need to apologize for the wine. Nor for the dinner, for that matter. Nora is a good cook when she forgets her infernal parsimony and buys food that one can eat without disgust. But I do owe you an apology for the quality of the service. I have tried to teach the waitress not to snatch plates from the table as if she were feeding dogs in a kennel but she cannot learn. (*He takes his hand from the plate—to Sara.*) There. Now let me see you take it properly. (*She stares at him for a moment, speechless with anger—then snatches the plate from in front of him.*)

CREGAN (*hastily recalls Melody to the battlefield*) You were where the aide-de-camp galloped up to us, Major. It was then the French artillery opened on us. (*Sara goes out right, carrying a tray laden with plates.*)

MELODY We charged the columns on our left—here— (*He marks the tablecloth.*) that were pushing back the Guards. I'll never forget the blast of death from the French squares. And then their chasseurs and lancers were on us! By God, it's a miracle any of us came through!

CREGAN You wasn't touched except you'd a bullet through your coat, but I had this token on my cheek to remember a French saber by.

MELODY Brave days, those! By the Eternal, then one lived! Then one

> Point out three ways in which a thoroughly Irish flavor is achieved at this celebration.

> What induces Melody to risk a fight with Sara at this particular moment?

forgot! *(He stops—when he speaks again it is bitterly.)* Little did I dream then the disgrace that was to be my reward later on.

CREGAN *(consolingly)* Ah well, that's the bad luck of things. You'd have been made a colonel soon, if you'd left the Spanish woman alone and not fought that duel.

MELODY *(arrogantly threatening)* Are you presuming to question my conduct in that affair, Corporal Cregan?

CREGAN *(hastily)* Sorra a bit! Don't mind me, now.

MELODY *(stiffly)* I accept your apology. *(He drinks the rest of his wine, pours another glass, then stares moodily before him. Cregan drains his glass and refills it.)*

O'DOWD *(peering past Roche to watch Melody, leans across to Roche—in a sneering whisper)* Ain't he the lunatic, sittin' like a play-actor in his red coat, lyin' about his battles with the French!

ROCHE *(sullenly—but careful to keep his voice low)* He'd ought to be shamed he ivir wore the bloody red av England, God's curse on him!

O'DOWD Don't be wishin' him harm, for it's thirsty we'd be without him. Drink long life to him, and may he always be as big a fool as he is this night! *(He sloshes whiskey from the decanter into both their glasses.)*

ROCHE *(with a drunken leer)* Thrue for you! I'll toast him on that. *(He twists round to face Melody, holds up his glass and bawls.)* To the grandest gintleman ivir come from the shores av Ireland! Long life to you, Major!

O'DOWD Hurroo! Long life, yer Honor!

RILEY *(awakened from his dream, mechanically raises his glass)* And to all that belong to ye.

MELODY *(startled from his thoughts, becomes at once the condescending squire—smiling tolerantly)* I said, less noise, you dogs. All the same, I thank you for your toast. *(They drink. A pause. Abruptly Melody begins to recite from Byron. He reads the verse well, quietly, with a bitter eloquence.)*

> "But midst the crowd, the hum, the shock of men,
> To hear, to see, to feel, and to possess,
> And roam along, the World's tired denizen,
> With none who bless us, none whom we can bless;
> Minions of Splendour shrinking from distress!
> None that, with kindred consciousness endued,
> If we were not, would seem to smile the less,
> Of all that flattered—followed—sought, and sued;
> This is to be alone—This, this is Solitude!"

(He stops and glances from one face to another. Their expressions are all blank. He remarks with insulting derisiveness.) What? You do not understand, my lads? Well, all the better for you. So may you go on fooling yourselves that I am fooled in you. *(then with a quick change of mood, heartily)* Give us a hunting song, Patch. You've not forgotten "Modideroo," I'll be bound.

RILEY *(roused to interest immediately)* Does a duck forget wather? I'll show ye! *(He begins the preliminary quavers on his pipes.)*

Sidebar notes:

How is Melody's love for England appropriate to his current attitude?

Despite the free food and drink, Melody's friends are quick to criticize his eccentric ways. What does this reveal about their characters?

How do Byron's lines pertain to Melody's view of his own predicament in life?

O'DOWD Modideroo!

ROCHE Hurroo!

RILEY *(accompanying himself, sings with wailing melancholy the first verse that comes to his mind of an old hunting song)*

"And the fox set him down and looked about,
And many were feared to follow;
'Maybe I'm wrong,' says he, 'but I doubt
That you'll be as gay tomorrow.
For loud as you cry, and high as you ride,
And little you feel my sorrow,
I'll be free on the mountainside
While you'll lie low tomorrow.'
Oh, Modideroo, aroo, aroo!"

(Melody, excited now, beats time on the table with his glass along with Cregan, Roche, and O'Dowd, and all bellow the refrain, "Oh, Modideroo, aroo, aroo!")

MELODY *(His eyes alight, forgetting himself, a strong lilt of brogue coming into his voice.)* Ah, that brings it back clear as life! Melody Castle in the days that's gone! A wind from the south, and a sky gray with clouds—good weather for the hounds. A true Irish hunter under me that knows and loves me and would raise to a jump over hell if I gave the word! To hell with men, I say!—and women, too!—with their cowardly hearts rotten and stinking with lies and greed and treachery! Give me a horse to love and I'll cry quits to men! And then away, with the hounds in full cry, and after them! Off with divil a care for your neck, over ditches and streams and stone walls and fences, the fox doubling up the mountainside through the furze and the heather—! *(Sara has entered from right as he begins this longing invocation of old hunting days. She stands behind his chair, listening contemptuously. He suddenly feels her presence and turns his head. When he catches the sneer in her eyes, it is as if cold water were dashed in his face. He addresses her as if she were a servant.)* Well? What is it? What are you waiting for now?

SARA *(roughly, with coarse brogue)* What would I be waitin' for but for you to get through with your blather about lovin' horses, and give me a chance to finish my work? Can't you—and the other gintlemen—finish gettin' drunk in the bar and lave me clear the tables? *(O'Dowd conceals a grin behind his hand; Roche stifles a malicious guffaw.)*

CREGAN *(with an apprehensive glance at Melody, shakes his head at her admonishingly)* Now, Sara, be aisy. *(But Melody suppresses any angry reaction. He rises to his feet, a bit stiffly and carefully, and bows.)*

MELODY *(coldly)* I beg your pardon if we have interfered with your duties. *(to O'Dowd and his companions)* Into the bar, you louts!

O'DOWD The bar it is, sorr. Come, Dan. Wake up, Patch. *(He pokes the piper. He and Roche go into the bar, and Riley stumbles vaguely after them. Cregan waits for Melody.)*

MELODY Go along, Corporal. I'll join you presently. I wish to speak to my daughter.

O'Neill effectively juxtaposes the lofty sentiments of Byron (representing Melody's illusions) with the mundane Irish folk songs (representing Melody's actual status). How does O'Neill inform us through this juxtaposition that by nature Melody's personality is gruff, middle-class Irish?

CREGAN All right, Major. *(He again shakes his head at Sara, as if to say, don't provoke him. She ignores him. He goes into the bar, closing the door behind him. She stares at her father with angry disgust.)*

SARA You're drunk. If you think I'm going to stay here and listen to—

MELODY *(his face expressionless, draws out his chair at the head of the center table for her—politely)* Sit down, my dear.

SARA I won't. I have no time. Poor Mother is half dead on her feet. I have to help her. There's a pile of dishes to wash after your grand anniversary feast! *(with bitter anger)* Thank God it's over, and it's the last time you'll ever take satisfaction in having me wait on table for drunken scum like O'Dowd and—

MELODY *(quietly)* A daughter who takes satisfaction in letting even the scum see that she hates and despises her father! *(He shrugs his shoulders.)* But no matter. *(indicating the chair again)* Won't you sit down, my dear?

SARA If you ever dared face the truth, you'd hate and despise yourself! *(passionately)* All I pray to God is that someday when you're admiring yourself in the mirror something will make you see at last what you really are! That will be revenge in full for all you've done to Mother and me! *(She waits defiantly, as if expecting him to lose his temper and curse her. But Melody acts as if he had not heard her.)*

MELODY *(his face expressionless, his manner insistently bland and polite)* Sit down, my dear. I will not detain you long, and I think you will find what I have to tell you of great interest. *(She searches his face, uneasy now, feeling a threat hidden behind his cold, quiet, gentlemanly tone. She sits down and he sits at rear of table, with an empty chair separating them.)*

SARA You'd better think well before you speak, Father. I know the devil that's in you when you're quiet like this with your brain mad with drink.

MELODY I don't understand you. All I wish is to relate something which happened this afternoon.

SARA *(giving way to bitterness at her humiliation again—sneeringly)* When you went riding on you beautiful thoroughbred mare while Mother and I were sweating and suffocating in the heat of the kitchen to prepare your Lordship's banquet? Sure, I hope you didn't show off and jump your beauty over a fence into somebody's garden, like you've done before, and then have to pay damages to keep out of jail!

MELODY *(roused by mention of his pet—disdainfully)* The damned Yankee yokels should feel flattered that she deigns to set her dainty hooves in their paltry gardens! She's a truer-born, well-bred lady than any of their women—than the one who paid us a visit this morning, for example.

SARA Mrs. Harford was enough of a lady to put you in your place and make a fool of you.

MELODY *(seemingly unmoved by this taunt—calmly)* You are very simple-minded, my dear, to let yourself be taken in by such an

How does O'Neill create an expectant atmosphere in Melody's talk with Sara?

A TOUCH OF THE POET

obvious bit of clever acting. Naturally, the lady was a bit discomposed when she heard you and your mother coming, after she had just allowed me to kiss her. She had to pretend—

SARA *(eagerly)* She let you kiss her? *(then disgustedly)* It's a lie, but I don't doubt you've made yourself think it's the truth by now. *(angrily)* I'm going. I don't want to listen to the whiskey in you boasting of what never happened—as usual! *(She puts her hands on the table and starts to rise.)*

MELODY *(with a quick movement pins hers down with one of his)* Wait! *(A look of vindictive cruelty comes into his eyes—quietly.)* Why are you so jealous of the mare, I wonder? Is it because she has such slender ankles and dainty feet? *(He takes his hand away and stares at her hands—with disgust, commandingly.)* Keep your thick wrists and ugly, peasant paws off the table in my presence, if you please! They turn my stomach! I advise you never to let Simon get a good look at them—

SARA *(Instinctively jerks her hands back under the table guiltily. She stammers.)* You—you cruel devil! I knew you'd—

MELODY *(for a second is ashamed and really contrite)* Forgive me, Sara. I didn't mean—the whiskey talking—as you said. *(He adds in a forced tone, a trace of mockery in it.)* An absurd taunt, when you really have such pretty hands and feet, my dear. *(She jumps to her feet, so hurt and full of hatred her lips tremble and she cannot speak. He speaks quietly.)* Are you going? I was about to tell you of the talk I had this afternoon with young Harford. *(She stares at him in dismay. He goes on easily.)* It was after I returned from my ride. I cantered the mare by the river and she pulled up lame. So I dismounted and led her back to the barn. No one noticed my return and when I went upstairs it occurred to me I would not find again such an opportunity to have a frank chat with Harford—free from interruptions. *(He pauses, as if he expects her to be furious, but she remains tensely silent, determined not to let him know her reaction.)* I did not beat about the bush. I told him he must appreciate, as a gentleman, it was my duty as your father to demand he lay his cards on the table. I said he must realize that even before you began nursing him here and going alone to his bedroom, there was a deal of gossip about your visits to his cabin, and your walks in the woods with him. I put it to him that such an intimacy could not continue without gravely compromising your reputation.

SARA *(stunned—weakly)* God forgive you! And what did he say?

MELODY What could he say? He is a man of honor. He looked damn embarrassed and guilty for a moment, but when he found his tongue, he agreed with me most heartily. He said his mother had told him the same thing.

SARA Oh, she did, did she? I suppose she did it to find out by watching him how far—

MELODY *(coldly)* Well, why not? Naturally, it was her duty as his mother to discover all she could about you. She is a woman of the world. She would be bound to suspect that you might be his mistress.

SARA *(tensely)* Oh, would she!

> Melody retreats to personal insults, even with his own daughter. Why do his allusions to her hands and legs so unsettle Sara?

> What is ironic about Melody playing the role of the cautious father of a pretty daughter?

238   EUGENE O'NEILL

MELODY But that's beside the point. The point is, my bashful young gentleman finally blurted out that he wanted to marry you.

SARA *(forgetting her anger—eagerly)* He told you that?

MELODY Yes, and he said he had told his mother, and she had said all she wanted was his happiness but she felt in fairness to you and to himself—and I presume she also meant to both families concerned—he should test his love and yours by letting a decent interval of time elapse before your marriage. She mentioned a year, I believe.

SARA *(angrily)* Ah! Didn't I guess that would be her trick!

MELODY *(lifting his eyebrows—coldly)* Trick? In my opinion, the lady displayed more common sense and knowledge of the world than I thought she possessed. The reasons she gave him are sound and show a consideration for your good name which ought to inspire gratitude in you and not suspicion.

Why does Melody agree with Mrs. Harford's position? Doesn't he want his daughter married?

SARA Arrah, don't tell me she's made a fool of you again! A lot of consideration she has for me!

MELODY She pointed out to him that if you were the daughter of some family in their own little Yankee clique, there would be no question of a hasty marriage, and so he owed it to you—

SARA I see. She's the clever one!

MELODY Another reason was—and here your Simon stammered so embarrassedly I had trouble making him out—she warned him a sudden wedding would look damnably suspicious and start a lot of evil-minded gossip.

SARA *(tensely)* Oh, she's clever, all right! But I'll beat her.

MELODY I told him I agreed with his mother. It is obvious that were there a sudden wedding without a suitable period of betrothal, everyone would believe—

SARA I don't care what they believe! Tell me this! Did she get him to promise her he'd wait? *(before he can answer—bitterly)* But of course she did! She'd never have left till she got that out of him!

MELODY *(ignores this)* I told him I appreciated the honor he did me in asking for your hand, but he must understand that I could not commit myself until I had talked to his father and was assured the necessary financial arrangements could be concluded to our mutual satisfaction. There was the amount of settlement to be agreed upon, for instance.

SARA That dream, again! God pity you! *(She laughs helplessly and a bit hysterically.)* And God help Simon. He must have thought you'd gone out of your mind! What did he say?

MELODY He said nothing, naturally. He is well bred and he knows this is a matter he must leave to his father to discuss. There is also the equally important matter of how generous an allowance Henry Harford is willing to settle on his son. I did not mention this to Simon, of course, not wishing to embarrass him further with talk of money.

This section is crucial to understand Sara and Melody. Whereas Sara is anxious to become Simon's wife as soon as possible and at any price, Melody is willing to jeopardize the match in order to continue playing his role of "gentlemen," by insisting that everything be socially correct.

SARA Thank God for that, at least! *(She giggles hysterically.)*

A TOUCH OF THE POET 239

MELODY *(quietly)* May I ask what you find so ridiculous in an old established custom? Simon is an elder son, the heir to his father's estate. No matter what their differences in the past may have been, now that Simon has decided to marry and settle down his father will wish to do the fair thing by him. He will realize, too, that although there is no more honorable calling than that of poet and philosopher, which his son has chosen to pursue, there is no decent living to be gained by its practice. So naturally he will settle an allowance on Simon, and I shall insist it be a generous one, befitting your position as my daughter. I will tolerate no niggardly trader's haggling on his part.

> How is Melody's evaluation of a poet ironic?

SARA *(stares at him fascinatedly, on the edge of helpless, hysterical laughter)* I suppose it would never occur to you that old Harford might not think it an honor to have his son marry your daughter.

MELODY *(calmly)* No, it would never occur to me—and if it should occur to him, I would damned soon disabuse his mind. Who is he but a money-grubbing trader? I would remind him that I was born in a castle and there was a time when I possessed wealth and position, and an estate compared to which any Yankee upstart's home in this country is but a hovel stuck in a cabbage patch. I would remind him that you, my daughter, were born in a castle!

SARA *(impulsively, with a proud toss of her head)* Well, that's no more than the truth. *(then furious with herself and him)* Och, what crazy blather! *(She springs to her feet.)* I've had enough of your mad dreams!

MELODY Wait! I haven't finished yet. *(He speaks quietly, but as he goes on there is an increasing vindictiveness in his tone.)* There was another reason why I told young Harford I could not make a final decision. I wished time to reflect on a further aspect of this proposed marriage. Well, I have been reflecting, watching you and examining your conduct, without prejudice, trying to be fair to you and make every possible allowance— *(He pauses.)* Well, to be brutally frank, my dear, all I can see in you is a common, greedy, scheming, cunning peasant girl, whose only thought is money and who has shamelessly thrown herself at a young man's head because his family happens to possess a little wealth and position.

> Melody's once-held position now influences his current decisions, even when his present status disqualifies him from making the demands he does.

SARA *(trying to control herself)* I see your game, Father. I told you when you were drunk like this— But this time, I won't give you the satisfaction— *(Then she bursts out angrily.)* It's a lie! I love Simon, or I'd never—

MELODY *(as if she hadn't spoken)* So, I have about made up my mind to decline for you Simon Harford's request for your hand in marriage.

SARA *(jeers angrily now)* Oh, you have, have you? As if I cared a damn what you—!

MELODY As a gentleman, I feel I have a duty, in honor, to Simon. Such a marriage would be a tragic misalliance for him—and God knows I know the sordid tragedy of such a union.

> What emerge as Melody's priorities: loyalty to one's own family or to an indefinite idea of social status?

SARA It's Mother has had the tragedy!

MELODY I hold young Harford in too high esteem. I cannot stand by and let him commit himself irrevocably to what could only bring him disgust and bitterness, and ruin to all his dreams.

240 EUGENE O'NEILL

SARA So I'm not good enough for him, you've decided now?

MELODY That is apparent from your every act. No one, no matter how charitably inclined, could mistake you for a lady. I have tried to make you one. It was an impossible task. God Himself cannot transform a sow's ear into a silk purse!

SARA (furiously) Father!

MELODY Young Harford needs to be saved from himself. I can understand his physical infatuation. You are pretty. So was your mother pretty once. But marriage is another matter. The man who would be the ideal husband for you, from a standpoint of conduct and character, is Mickey Maloy, my bartender, and I will be happy to give him my parental blessing—

SARA Let you stop now, Father!

MELODY You and he would be congenial. You can match tongues together. He's a healthy animal. He can give you a raft of peasant brats to squeal and fight with the pigs on the mud floor of your hovel.

SARA It's the dirty hut in which your father was born and raised you're remembering, isn't it?

MELODY (Stung to fury, glares at her with hatred. His voice quivers but is deadly quiet.): Of course, if you trick Harford into getting you with child, I could not refuse my consent. (Letting go, he bangs his fist on the table.) No, by God, even then, when I remember my own experience, I'll be damned if I could with a good conscience advise him to marry you!

SARA (glaring back at him with hatred) You drunken devil! (She makes a threatening move toward him, raising her hand as if she were going to slap his face—then she controls herself and speaks with quiet, biting sarcasm.) Consent or not, I want to thank you for your kind fatherly advice on how to trick Simon. I don't think I'll need it but if the worst comes to the worst I promise you I'll remember—

MELODY (coldly, his face expressionless) I believe I have said all I wished to say to you. (He gets up and bows stiffly.) If you will excuse me, I shall join Corporal Cregan. (He goes to the bar door. Sara turns and goes quietly out right, forgetting to clear the few remaining dishes on the center table. His back turned, he does not see her go. With his hand on the knob of the bar door, he hesitates. For a second he breaks—torturedly.) Sara! (then quietly) There are things I said which I regret—even now. I—I trust you will overlook   As your mother knows, it's the liquor talking, not— I must admit that, due to my celebrating the anniversary, my brain is a bit addled by whiskey—as you said. (He waits, hoping for a word of forgiveness. Finally, he glances over his shoulder. As he discovers she is not there and has not heard him, for a second he crumbles, his soldierly erectness sags and his face falls. He looks sad and hopeless and bitter and old, his eyes wandering dully. But, as in the two preceding acts, the mirror attracts him, and as he moves from the bar door to stand before it he assumes his arrogant, Byronic pose again. He repeats in each detail his pantomime before the mirror. He speaks proudly.) Myself to the bitter end! No weakening, so help me God! (There is a knock on the street door but he does not hear it. He starts his familiar incantation quotes from Byron.)

Melody's disapproval of a sensitive man's marriage with a common girl—even if it is his own daughter—reflects the great disappointment he feels in his own life, built as it was on such an alliance.

Does Melody mean what he told Sara in this scene? How do we know?

A TOUCH OF THE POET   241

>   "I have not loved the World, nor the World me;
>   I have not flattered its rank breath, nor bowed
>   To its idolatries a patient knee . . ."

(The knock on the door is repeated more loudly. Melody starts guiltily and steps quickly away from the mirror. His embarrassment is transformed into resentful anger. He calls.) Come in, damn you! Do you expect a lackey to open the door for you? *(The door opens and Nicholas Gadsby comes in. Gadsby is in his late forties, short, stout, with a big, bald head, round, florid face, and small, blue eyes. A rigidly conservative, best-family attorney, he is stiffly correct in dress and manner, dryly portentous in speech, and extremely conscious of his professional authority and dignity. Now, however, he is venturing on unfamiliar ground and is by no means as sure of himself as his manner indicates. The unexpected vision of Melody in his uniform startles him and for a second he stands, as close to gaping as he can be, impressed by Melody's handsome distinction. Melody, in his turn, is surprised. He had not thought the intruder would be a gentleman. He unbends, although his tone is still a bit curt. He bows a bit stiffly, and Gadsby finds himself returning the bow.)* Your pardon, sir. When I called, I thought it was one of the damned riffraff mistaking the barroom door. Pray be seated, sir. *(Gadsby comes forward and takes the chair at the head of the center table, glancing at the few dirty dishes on it with distate. Melody says.)* Your pardon again, sir. We have been feasting late, which accounts for the disarray. I will summon a servant to inquire your pleasure.

GADSBY *(beginning to recover his aplomb—shortly)* Thank you, but I want nothing, sir. I came here to seek a private interview with the proprietor of this tavern, by name, Melody. *(He adds a bit hesitantly.)* Are you, by any chance, he?

MELODY *(stiffens arrogantly)* I am not, sir. But if you wish to see Major Cornelius Melody, one time of His Majesty's Seventh Dragoons, who served with honor under the Duke of Wellington in Spain, I am he.

GADSBY *(dryly)* Very well, sir. Major Melody, then.

MELODY *(does not like his tone—insolently sarcastic.)* And whom have I the honor of addressing? *(As Gadsby is about to reply, Sara enters from right, having remembered the dishes. Melody ignores her as he would a servant. Gadsby examines her carefully as she gathers up the dishes. She notices him staring at her and gives him a resentful, suspicious glance. She carries the dishes out, right, to the kitchen, but a moment later she can be seen just inside the hall at right, listening. Meanwhile, as soon as he thinks she has gone, Gadsby speaks.)*

GADSBY *(with affected casualness)* A pretty young woman. Is she your daughter, sir? I seemed to detct a resemblance—

MELODY *(angrily)* No! Do I look to you, sir, like a man who would permit his daughter to work as a waitress? Resemblance to me? You must be blind, sir. *(coldly)* I am still waiting for you to inform me who you are and why you should wish to see me.

> Why does Melody deny that the servant girl is his daughter?

GADSBY *(hands him a card—extremely nettled by Melody's manner—curtly)* My card, sir.

MELODY *(glances at the card)* Nicholas Gadsby. *(He flips it aside disdainfully.)* Attorney, eh? The devil take all your tribe, say I. I have small

242 EUGENE O'NEILL

liking for your profession, sir, and I cannot imagine what business you can have with me. The damned thieves of the law did their worst to me many years ago in Ireland. I have little left to tempt you. So I do not see— (*Suddenly an idea comes to him. He stares at Gadsby, then goes on in a more friendly tone.*) That is, unless— Do you happen by any chance to represent the father of young Simon Harford?

GADSBY (*indignant at Melody's insults to his profession—with a thinly veiled sneer*) Ah, then you were expecting— That makes things easier. We need not beat about the bush. I do represent Mr. Henry Harford, sir.

MELODY (*thawing out, in his total misunderstanding of the situation*) Then accept my apologies, sir, for my animadversions against your profession. I am afraid I may be prejudiced. In the army, we used to say we suffered more casualties from your attacks at home than the French ever inflicted. (*He sits down on the chair on Gadsby's left, at rear of table—remarking with careless pride.*) A word of explanation as to why you find me in uniform. It is the anniversary of the battle of Talavera, sir, and— [What *is* Melody's misunderstanding?]

GADSBY (*interrupts dryly*) Indeed, sir? But I must tell you my time is short. With your permission, we will proceed at once to the matter in hand.

MELODY (*controlling his angry discomfiture—coldly*) I think I can hazard a guess as to what that matter is. You have come about the settlement?

GADSBY (*misunderstanding him, replies in a tone almost openly contemptuous*) Exactly, sir. Mr. Harford was of the opinion, and I agreed with him, that a settlement would be foremost in your mind.

MELODY (*Scowls at his tone but, as he completely misunderstands Gadsby's meaning, he forces himself to bow politely.*) It does me honor, sir, that Mr. Harford appreciates he is dealing with a gentleman and has the breeding to know how these matters are properly arranged. (*Gadsby stares at him, absolutely flabbergasted by what he considers a piece of the most shameless effrontery. Melody leans toward him confidentially.*) I will be frank with you, sir. The devil of it is, this comes at a difficult time for me. Temporary, of course, but I cannot deny I am pinched at the moment—devilishly pinched. But no matter. Where my only child's happiness is at stake, I am prepared to make every possible effort. I will sign a note of hand, no matter how ruinous the interest demanded by the scoundrelly moneylenders. By the way, what amount does Mr. Harford think proper? Anything in reason—

GADSBY (*listening in utter confusion, finally gets the idea Melody is making him the butt of a joke—fuming*) I do not know what you are talking about, sir, unless you think to make a fool of me! If this is what is known as Irish wit—

MELODY (*bewildered for a second—then in a threatening tone*) Take care, sir, and watch your words or I warn you you will repent them, no matter whom you represent! No damned pettifogging dog can insult me with impunity! (*As Gadsby draws back apprehensively, he adds with insulting disdain.*) As for making a fool of you, sir, I would be the fool if I attempted to improve on God's handiwork!

GADSBY (*ignoring the insults, forces a placating tone*) I wish no quarrel

A TOUCH OF THE POET

with you, sir. I cannot for the life of me see— I fear we are dealing at cross-purposes. Will you tell me plainly what you mean by your talk of settlement?

MELODY Obviously, I mean the settlement I am prepared to make on my daughter. *(As Gadsby only looks more dumfounded, he continues sharply.)* Is not your purpose in coming here to arrange, on Mr. Harford's behalf, for the marriage of his son with my daughter?

GADSBY Marriage? Good God, no! Nothing of the kind!

MELODY *(dumfounded)* Then what have you come for?

GADSBY *(feeling he has now the upper hand—sharply)* To inform you that Mr. Henry Harford is unalterably opposed to any further relationship between his son and your daughter, whatever the nature of that relationship in the past.

MELODY *(leans forward threateningly)* By the Immortal, sir, if you dare insinuate—!

GADSBY *(Draws back again, but he is no coward and is determined to carry out his instructions)* I insinuate nothing, sir. I am here on Mr. Harford's behalf, to make you an offer. That is what I thought you were expecting when you mentioned a settlement. Mr. Harford is prepared to pay you the sum of three thousand dollars—provided, mark you, that you and your daughter sign an agreement I have drawn up which specifies that you relinquish all claims, of whatever nature. And also provided you agree to leave this part of the country at once with your family. Mr. Harford suggests it would be advisable that you go West—to Ohio, say.

MELODY *(So overcome by a rising tide of savage, humiliated fury, he can only stammer hoarsely.)* So Henry Harford does me the honor—to suggest that, does he?

GADSBY *(watching him uneasily, attempts a reasonable, persuasive tone)* Surely you could not have spoken seriously when you talked of marriage. There is such a difference in station. The idea is preposterous. If you knew Mr. Harford, you would realize he would never countenance—

MELODY *(His pent-up rage bursts out—smashing his fist on the table.)* Know him? By the Immortal God, I'll know him soon! And he'll know me! *(He springs to his feet.)* But first, you Yankee scum, I'll deal with you! *(He draws back his fist to smash Gadsby in the face, but Sara has run from the door at right and she grabs his arm. She is almost as furious as he is and there are tears of humiliated pride in her eyes.)*

SARA Father! Don't! He's only a paid lackey. Where is your pride that you'd dirty your hands on the like of him? *(While she is talking the door from the bar opens and Roche, O'Dowd, and Cregan crowd into the room. Mickey stands in the doorway. Nora follows Sara in from right.)*

> What contradictions in Sara's character emerge here?

ROCHE *(with drunken enthusiasm)* It's a fight! For the love of God, clout the damned Yankee, Major!

MELODY *(controls himself—his voice shaking)* You are right, Sara. It would be beneath me to touch such a vile lickspittle. But he won't get off scot-free. *(sharply, a commander ordering his soldiers)* Here you, Roche and O'Dowd! Get hold of him! *(They do so with enthusiasm and yank Gadsby from his chair.)*

GADSBY You drunken ruffians! Take your hands off me!

MELODY (*addressing him—in his quiet, threatening tone now*) You may tell the swindling trader, Harford, who employs you that he'll hear from me! (*to Roche and O'Dowd.*) Throw this thing out! Kick it down to the crossroads!

ROCHE Hurroo! (*He and O'Dowd run Gadsby to the door at rear. Cregan jumps ahead, grinning, and opens the door for them.*)

GADSBY (*struggling futilely as they rush him through the door*) You scoundrels! Take your hands off me! Take— (*Melody looks after them. The two women watch him, Nora frightened, Sara with a strange look of satisfied pride.*)

CREGAN (*in the doorway, looking out—laughing*) Oh, it'd do your heart good, Con, to see the way they're kicking his butt down the street! (*He comes in and shuts the door.*)

MELODY (*his rage welling again, as his mind dwells on his humiliation —starting to pace up and down*) It's with his master I have to deal, and, by the Powers, I'll deal with him! You'll come with me, Jamie. I'll want you for a witness. He'll apologize to me—more than that, he'll come back here this very night and apologize publicly to my daughter, or else he meets me in the morning! By God, I'll face him at ten paces or across a handkerchief! I'll put a bullet through him, so help me, Christ!

NORA (*breaks into a dirgelike wail*) God forgive you, Con, is it a duel again—murtherin' or gettin' murthered?

MELODY Be quiet, woman! Go back to your kitchen! Go, do you hear me! (*Nora turns obediently toward the door at right, beginning to cry.*)

SARA (*Puts an arm around her mother. She is staring at Melody apprehensively now.*) There, Mother, don't worry. Father knows that's all foolishness. He's only talking. Go on now in the kitchen and sit down and rest, Mother. (*Nora goes out right. Sara closes the door after her and comes back.*)

MELODY (*turns on her with bitter anger*) Only talking, am I? It's the first time in my life I ever heard anyone say Con Melody was a coward! It remains for my own daughter—!

SARA (*placatingly*) I didn't say that, Father. But can't you see—you're not in Ireland in the old days now. The days of duels are long past and dead, in this part of America anyway. Harford will never fight you. He—

MELODY He won't, won't he? By God, I'll make him! I'll take a whip. I'll drag him out of his house and lash him down the street for all his neighbors to see! He'll apologize, or he'll fight, or I'll brand him a craven before the world!

SARA (*frightened now*) But you'll never be let see him! His servants will keep you out! He'll have the police arrest you, and it'll be in the papers about another drunken Mick raising a crazy row! (*She appeals to Cregan.*) Tell him I'm telling the truth, Jamie. You've still got some sober sense in you. Maybe he'll listen to you.

CREGAN (*glances at Melody uneasily*) Maybe Sara's right, Major.

MELODY When I want your opinion, I'll ask for it! (*sneeringly*) Of

---

Will the manhandling of Gadsby by Melody's cronies help convince the Harfords that their opinion of Melody is wrong or will it confirm their viewpoint? Why?

How is history repeating itself, because of Melody's temperament?

The term "Mick" is a demeaning one, alluding to an Irishman.

course, if you've become such a coward you're afraid to go with me—

CREGAN (*stung*) Coward, is ut? I'll go, and be damned to you!

SARA Jamie, you fool! Oh, it's like talking to crazy men! (*She grabs her father's arm—pleadingly.*) Don't do it, Father, for the love of God! Have I ever asked you anything? Well, I ask you to heed me now! I'll beg you on my knees, if you like! Isn't it me you'd fight about, and haven't I a right to decide? You punished that lawyer for the insult. You had him thrown out of here like a tramp. Isn't that your answer to old Harford that insults him? It's for him to challenge you, if he dares, isn't it? Why can't you leave it at that and wait—

MELODY (*shaking off her hand—angrily*) You talk like a scheming peasant! It's a question of my honor!

SARA No! It's a question of my happiness, and I won't have your mad interfering—! (*desperately forcing herself to reason with him again*) Listen, Father! If you'll keep out of it, I'll show you how I'll make a fool of old Harford! Simon won't let anything his father does keep him from marrying me. His mother is the only one who might have the influence over him to come between us. She's only watching for a good excuse to turn Simon against marrying me, and if you go raising a drunken row at their house, and make a public scandal, shouting you want to murder his father, can't you see what a chance that will give her?

MELODY (*raging*) That damned, insolent Yankee bitch! She's all the more reason. Marry, did you say? You dare to think there can be any question now of your marrying the son of a man who has insulted my honor—and yours?

SARA (*defiantly*) Yes, I dare to think it! I love Simon and I'm going to marry him!

MELODY And I say you're not! If he wasn't sick, I'd— But I'll get him out of here tomorrow! I forbid you ever to see him again! If you dare disobey me I'll—! (*beginning to lose all control of himself*) If you dare defy me—for the sake of the dirty money you think you can beg from his family, if you're his wife—!

SARA (*fiercely*) You lie! (*then with quiet intensity*) Yes. I defy you or anyone who tries to come between us!

MELODY You'd sell your pride as my daughter—! (*his face convulsed by fury*) You filthy peasant slut! You whore! I'll see you dead first—! By the living God, I'd kill you myself! (*He makes a threatening move toward her.*)

SARA (*shrinks back frightenedly*) Father! (*Then she stands and faces him defiantly.*)

CREGAN (*steps between them*) Con! In the name of God! (*Melody's fit of insane fury leaves him. He stands panting for breath, shuddering with the effort to regain some sort of poise. Cregan speaks, his only thought to get him away from Sara.*) If we're going after old Harford, Major, we'd better go. That thief of a lawyer will warn him—

MELODY (*seizing on this—hoarsely*) Yes, let's go. Let's go, Jamie. Come along, Corporal. A stirrup cup, and we'll be off. If the mare wasn't lame, I'd ride alone—but we can get a rig at the livery stable.

> Sara realizes that Melody's proposed actions will affect her whole future, unlike her father who seeks simple revenge for an assumed wrong.

> The movements on stage can be visualized from the dialogue and from O'Neill's stage directions. It is evident that this episode marks one of the crisis points in the plot.

246   EUGENE O'NEILL

Don't let me forget to stop at the barn for my whip. *(By the time he finishes speaking, he has himself in hand again and his ungovernable fury has gone. There is a look of cool, menacing vengefulness in his face. He turns toward the bar door.)*

SARA *(helplessly)* Father! *(desperately, as a last, frantic threat)* You'll force me to go to Simon—and do what you said! *(If he hears this, he gives no sign of it. He strides into the bar. Cregan follows him, closing the door. Sara stares before her, the look of defiant desperation hardening on her face. The street door is flung open and O'Dowd and Roche pile in, laughing uproariously.)*

ROCHE Hurroo!

O'DOWD The army is back, Major, with the foe flying in retreat. *(He sees Melody is not there—to Sara.)* Where's himself? *(Sara appears not to see or hear him.)*

ROCHE *(after a quick glance at her)* Lave her be. He'll be in the bar. Come on. *(He goes to the bar.)*

O'DOWD *(following him, speaks over his shoulder to Sara)* You should have seen the Yank! His coachman had to help him in his rig at the corner—and Roche gave the coachman a clout too, for good measure! *(He disappears, laughing, slamming the door behind him. Nora opens the door at right and looks in cautiously. Seeing Sara alone, she comes in.)*

NORA Sara. *(She comes over to her.)* Sara. *(She takes hold of her arm—whispers uneasily.)* Where's himself?

SARA *(dully)* I couldn't stop him.

NORA I could have told you you was wastin' breath. *(with a queer pride)* The divil himself couldn't kape Con Melody from a duel! *(then mournfully)* It's like the auld times come again, and the same worry and sorrow. Even in the days before ivir I'd spoke a word to him, or done more than make him a bow when he'd ride past on his hunter, I used to lie awake and pray for him when I'd hear he was fightin' a duel in the mornin'. *(She smiles a shy, gentle smile.)* I was in love with him even then. *(Sara starts to say something bitter but what she sees in her mother's face stops her. Nora goes on, with a feeble attempt at boastful confidence.)* But I'll not worry this time, and let you not, either. There wasn't a man in Galway was his equal with a pistol, and what chance will this auld stick av a Yankee have against him? *(There is a noise of boisterous farewells from the bar and the noise of an outer door shutting. Nora starts.)* That's him leavin'! *(Her mouth pulls down pitiably. She starts for the bar with a sob.)* Ah, Con darlin', don't—! *(She stops, shaking her head helplessly.)* But what's the good? *(She sinks on a chair with a weary sigh.)*

SARA *(bitterly, aloud to herself more than to her mother)* No good. Let him go his way—and I'll go mine. *(tensely)* I won't let him destroy my life with his madness, after all the plans I've made and the dreams I've dreamed. I'll show him I can play at the game of gentleman's honor too! *(Nora has not listened. She is sunk in memories of old fears and her present worry about the duel. Sara hesitates—then, keeping her face turned away from her mother, touches her shoulder.)* I'm going upstairs to bed, Mother.

NORA *(starts—then indignantly)* To bed, is it? You can think of sleepin' when he's—

> What, exactly, does Sara threaten to do?

> What is Sara's plan now?

A TOUCH OF THE POET 247

SARA I didn't say sleep, but I can lie down and try to rest. *(still avoiding looking at her mother)* I'm dead tired, Mother.

NORA *(tenderly solicitous now, puts an arm around her)* You must be, darlin'. It's been the divil's own day for you, with all— *(with sudden remorse)* God forgive me, darlin'. I was forgettin' about you and the Harford lad. *(miserably)* Oh, God help us! *(suddenly with a flash of her strange, fierce pride in the power of love)* Never mind! If there's true love between you, you'll not let duel or anything in the world kape you from each other whatever the cost! Don't I know!

SARA *(kisses her impulsively, then looks away again)* You're going to sit up and wait down here?

NORA I am. I'd be destroyed with fear lying down in the dark. Here, the noise of them in the bar kapes up my spirits, in a way.

SARA Yes, you'd better stay here. Good night, Mother.

NORA Good night, darlin'. *(Sara goes out at right, closing the door behind her.)*

Curtain

> Why is this an ideal spot to break the action between acts? Where are we in the development of the plot and its complications?

ACT IV

SCENE—*The same. It is around midnight. The room is in darkness except for one candle on the table, center. From the bar comes the sound of Patch Riley's pipes playing a reel and the stamp of dancing feet.*

Nora sits at the foot of the table at center. She is hunched up in an old shawl, her arms crossed over her breast, hugging herself as if she were cold. She looks on the verge of collapse from physical fatigue and hours of worry. She starts as the door from the bar is opened. It is Mickey. He closes the door behind him, shutting out an uproar of music and drunken voices. He has a decanter of whiskey and a glass in his hand. He has been drinking, but is not drunk.

NORA *(eagerly)* There's news of himself?

MALOY *(putting the decanter and glass on the table)* Sorra a bit. Don't be worryin' now. Sure, it's not so late yet.

NORA *(dully)* It's aisy for you to say—

MALOY I came in to see how you was, and bring you a taste to put heart in you. *(as she shakes her head)* Oh, I know you don't indulge, but I've known you once in a while, and you need it this night. *(as she again shakes her head—with kindly bullying)* Come now, don't be stubborn. I'm the doctor and I highly recommend a drop to drive out black thoughts and rheumatism.

NORA Well—maybe—a taste, only.

MALOY That's the talkin'. *(He pours a small drink and hands it to her.)* Drink hearty, now.

NORA *(takes a sip, then puts the glass on the table and pushes it away listlessly)* I've no taste for anything. But I thank you for the thought. You're a kind lad, Mickey.

MALOY Here's news to cheer you. The word has got round among the boys, and they've all come in to wait for Cregan and himself.

> Through Nora's first question and the background sounds, O'Neill informs his audience that a period of time has passed since Melody stormed off to his duel and Sara went to her love rendezvous.

248 EUGENE O'NEILL

(with enthusiasm) There'll be more money taken over the bar than any night since this shebeen started!

NORA That's good.

MALOY If they do hate Con Melody, he's Irish, and they hate the Yanks worse. They're all hopin' he's bate the livin' lights out of Harford.

NORA *(with belligerent spirit)* And so he has, I know that!

MALOY *(grins)* That's the talk. I'm glad to see you roused from your worryin'. *(turning away)* I'd better get back. I left O'Dowd to tend bar and I'll wager he has three drinks stolen already. *(He hesitates.)* Sara's not been down?

NORA No.

MALOY *(resentfully)* It's a wonder she wouldn't have more thought for you than to lave you sit up alone.

NORA *(stiffens defensively)* I made her go to bed. She was droppin' with tiredness and destroyed with worry. She must have fallen asleep, like the young can. None of your talk against Sara, now!

MALOY *(starts an exasperated retort)* The divil take— *(He stops and grins at her with affection.)* There's no batin' you, Nora. Sure, it'd be the joy av me life to have a mother like you to fight for me—or, better still, a wife like you.

NORA *(A sweet smile of pleased coquetry lights up her drawn face.)* Arrah, save your blarney for the young girls!

MALOY The divil take young girls. You're worth a hundred av thim.

NORA *(with a toss of her head)* Get along with you!

Mickey grins with satisfaction at having cheered her up and goes in the bar, closing the door. As soon as he is gone, she sinks back into apprehensive brooding.

Sara appears silently in the doorway at right. She wears a faded old wrapper over her nightgown, slippers on her bare feet. Her hair is down over her shoulders, reaching to her waist. There is a change in her. All the bitterness and defiance have disappeared from her face. It looks gentle and calm and at the same time dreamily happy and exultant. She is much prettier than she has ever been before. She stands looking at her mother, and suddenly she becomes shy and uncertain—as if, now that she'd come this far, she had half a mind to retreat before her mother discovered her. But Nora senses her presence and looks up.

NORA *(dully)* Ah, it's you, darlin'! *(then gratefully)* Praise be, you've come at last! I'm sick with worry and I've got to the place where I can't bear waitin' alone, listenin' to drunks dancin' and celebratin'. *(Sara comes to her. Nora breaks. Tears well from her eyes.)* It's cruel, it is! There's no heart or thought for himself in divil a one av thim. *(She starts to sob, Sara hugs her and kisses her cheek gently. But she doesn't speak. It is as if she were afraid her voice would give her away. Nora stops sobbing. Her mood changes to resentment and she speaks as if Sara had spoken.)* Don't tell me not to worry. You're as bad as Mickey. The Yankee didn't apologize or your father'd been back here long since. It's a duel, that's certain, and he must have taken a room in the city so he'll be near the ground. I hope he'll sleep, but I'm feared he'll

> This gentle dialogue between Nora and Mickey is a needed relief after the rowdy scene just completed.

> Sara's wordless entrance creates tension, since her appearance tells us that something important has happened.

A TOUCH OF THE POET

stay up drinkin', and at the dawn he'll have had too much to shoot his best and maybe— *(then defiantly self-reassuringly)* Arrah, I'm the fool! It's himself can keep his head clear and his eyes sharp, no matter what he's taken! *(pushing Sara away—with nervous peevishness)* Let go of me. You've hardened not to care. I'd rather stay alone. *(She grabs Sara's hand.)* No. Don't heed me. Sit down, darlin'. *(Sara sits down on her left at rear of table. She pats her mother's hand, but remains silent, her expression dreamily happy, as if she heard Nora's words but they had no meaning for her. Nora goes on worriedly again.)* But if he's staying in the city, why hasn't he sent Jamie Cregan back for his duelin' pistols? I know he'd nivir fight with any others. *(resentful now at Melody)* Or you'd think he'd send Jamie or someone back with a word for me. He knows well how tormented I'd be waiting. *(bitterly)* Arrah, don't talk like a loon! Has he ever cared for anyone except himself and his pride? Sure, he'd never stoop to think of me, the grand gentleman in his red livery av bloody England! His pride, indade! What is it but a lie? What's in his veins, God pity him, but the blood of thievin' auld Ned Melody who kept a dirty shebeen? *(then is horrified at herself as if she had blasphemed)* No! I won't say it! I've nivir! It would break his heart if he heard me! I'm the only one in the world he knows nivir sneers at his dreams! *(working herself to rebellion again)* All the same, I won't stay here the rist of the night worryin' my heart out for a man who—it isn't only fear over the duel. It's because I'm afraid it's God's punishment, all the sorrow and trouble that's come on us, and I have the black tormint in my mind that it's the fault of the mortal sin I did with him unmarried, and the promise he made me make to leave the Church that's kept me from ever confessin' to a priest. *(She pauses—dully.)* Go to a doctor, you say, to cure the rheumatism. Sure, what's rheumatism but a pain in your body? I could bear ten of it. It's the pain of guilt in my soul. Can a doctor's medicine cure that? No, only a priest of Almighty God— *(with a roused rebellion again)* It would serve Con right if I took the chance now and broke my promise and woke up the priest to hear my confession and give me God's forgiveness that'd bring my soul peace and comfort so I wouldn't feel the three of us were damned. *(yearningly)* Oh, if I only had the courage! *(She rises suddenly from her chair—with brave defiance.)* I'll do it, so I will! I'm going to the priest's, Sara. *(She starts for the street door—gets halfway to it and stops.)*

SARA *(a strange, tenderly amused smile on her lips—teasingly)* Well, why don't you go, Mother?

NORA *(defiantly)* Ain't I goin'? *(She takes a few more steps toward the door—stops again—she mutters beatenly.)* God forgive me, I can't. What's the use pretendin'?

SARA *(as before)* No use at all, Mother. I've found that out.

NORA *(as if she hadn't heard, comes back slowly)* He'd feel I'd betrayed him and my word and my love for him—and for all his scorn, he knows my love is all he has in the world to comfort him. *(then spiritedly, with a proud toss of her head)* And it's my honor, too! It's not for his sake at all! Divil mend him, he always prates as if he had all the honor there is, but I've mine, too, as proud as his. *(She sits down in the same chair.)*

What is the dramatic effect of Nora's long, nervous monologue as contrasted with Sara's calm silence?

What characterization emerges from the shifting moods and attitudes?

How do we know now that Nora is not one-dimensional?

Melody's bondage of Nora even has extended to her spiritual life, where he has forbidden her from going to church or confession.

Sara (Kim Stanley) and Nora (Helen Hayes).

SARA *(softly)* Yes, the honor of her love to a woman. I've learned about that too, Mother.

NORA *(as if this were the first time she was really conscious of Sara speaking, and even now had not heard what she said—irritably)* So you've found your tongue, have you? Thank God. You're cold comfort, sitting silent like a statue, and me making talk to myself. *(regarding her as if she hadn't really seen her before—resentfully)* Musha but it's pleased and pretty you look, as if there wasn't a care in the world, while your poor father—

> The word *musha* is an Irish interjection, expressing surprise.

SARA *(dreamily amused, as if this no longer had any importance or connection with her)* I know it's no use telling you there won't be any duel, Mother, and it's crazy to give it a thought. You're living in Ireland long ago, like Father. But maybe you'll take Simon's word for it, if you won't mine. He said his father would be paralyzed with indignation just at the thought he'd ever fight a duel. It's against the law.

NORA *(scornfully)* Och, who cares for the law? He must be a coward. *(She looks relieved.)* Well, if the young lad said that, maybe it's true.

SARA Of course it's true, Mother.

NORA Your father'd be satisfied with Harford's apology and that'd end it.

SARA *(helplessly)* Oh, Mother! *(then quickly)* Yes, I'm sure it ended hours ago.

NORA *(intent on her hope)* And you think what's keeping him out is he and Jamie would take a power av drinks to celebrate.

SARA They'd drink, that's sure, whatever happened. *(She adds dreamily.)* But that doesn't matter now at all.

> Why is Sara not as concerned as Nora about her father's safety?

NORA *(stares at her—wonderingly)* You've a queer way of talking, as if you'd been asleep and was still half in a dream.

A TOUCH OF THE POET   251

SARA In a dream right enough, Mother, and it isn't half of me that's in it but all of me, body and soul. And it's a dream that's true, and always will be to the end of life, and I'll never wake from it.

NORA Sure, what's come over you at all?

SARA (*gets up impulsively and comes around in back of her mother's chair and slips to her knees and puts her arms about her—giving her a hug*) Joy. That's what's come over me. I'm happy, Mother. I'm happy because I know now Simon is mine, and no one can ever take him from me.

NORA (*at first her only reaction is pleased satisfaction*) God be thanked! It was a great sorrow tormentin' me that the duel would come between you. (*defiantly*) Honor or not, why should the children have their lives and their love destroyed!

SARA I was a great fool to fear his mother could turn him against me, no matter what happened.

NORA You've had a talk with the lad?

SARA I have. That's where I've been.

NORA You've been in his room ever since you went up?

SARA Almost. After I'd got upstairs it took me a while to get up my courage.

NORA (*rebukingly*) All this time—in the dead of the night!

SARA (*teasingly*) I'm his nurse, aren't I? I've a right.

NORA That's no excuse!

SARA (*her face hardening*) Excuse? I had the best in the world. Would you have me do nothing to save my happiness and my chance in life, when I thought there was danger they'd be ruined forever? Don't you want me to have love and be happy, Mother?

NORA (*melting*) I do, darlin'. I'd give my life— (*then rebuking again*) Were you the way you are, in only a nightgown and wrapper?

SARA (*gaily*) I was—and Simon liked my costume, if you don't, although he turned red as a beet when I came in.

NORA Small wonder he did! Shame on you!

SARA He was trying to read a book of poetry, but he couldn't he was that worried hoping I'd come to say goodnight, and being frightened I wouldn't. (*She laughs tenderly.*) Oh, it was the cutest thing I've ever done, Mother, not to see him at all since his mother left. He kept waiting for me and when I didn't come, he got scared to death that his kissing me this morning had made me angry. So he was wild with joy to see me—

NORA In your bare legs with only your nightgown and wrapper to cover your nakedness! Where's your modesty?

SARA (*gaily teasing*) I had it with me, Mother, though I'd tried hard to leave it behind. I got as red as he was. (*She laughs.*) Oh, Mother, it's a great joke on me. Here I'd gone to his room with my mind made up to be as bold as any street woman and tempt him because I knew his honor would make him marry me right away if— (*She laughs.*) And then all I could do was stand and gape at him and blush!

NORA Oh. *(rebukingly)* I'm glad you had the dacency to blush.

SARA It was Simon spoke first, and once he started, all he'd been holding back came out. The waiting for me, and the fear he'd had made him forget all his shyness, and he said he loved me and asked me to marry him the first day we could. Without knowing how it happened, there I was with his arms around me and mine around him and his lips on my lips and it was heaven, Mother.

NORA *(moved by the shining happiness in Sara's face)* God bless the two av you.

> Does Nora's blessing suggest a contradiction in her moral values? What does it reveal about her character?

SARA Then I was crying and telling him how afraid I'd been his mother hated me, Father's madness about the duel would give her a good chance to come between us; Simon said no one could ever come between us and his mother would never try to, now she knew he loved me, which was what she came over to find out. He said all she wanted was for him to be free to do as he pleased, and she only suggested he wait a year, she didn't make him promise. And Simon said I was foolish to think she would take the duel craziness serious. She'd only be amused at the joke it would be on his father, after he'd been so sure he could buy us off, if he had to call the police to save him.

> Simon Harford's existence off-stage is made credible as Sara relates their conversation and actions.

NORA *(aroused at the mention of police)* Call the police, is it? The coward!

SARA *(goes on, unheedingly)* Simon was terribly angry at his father for that. And at Father too when I told how he threatened he'd kill me. But we didn't talk of it much. We had better things to discuss. *(She smiles tenderly.)*

NORA *(belligerently)* A lot Con Melody cares for police, and him in a rage! Not the whole dirty force av thim will dare interfere with him!

SARA *(goes on as if she hadn't heard)* And then Simon told me how scared he'd been I didn't love him and wouldn't marry him. I was so beautiful, he said, and he wasn't handsome at all. So I kissed him and told him he was the handsomest in the world, and he is. And he said he wasn't worthy because he had so little to offer, and was a failure at what he'd hoped he could be, a poet. So I kissed him and told him he was too a poet, and always would be, and it was what I loved most about him.

> How is Sara's reaction to Simon's words similar to Nora's reaction to Melody's pose as the "poet"?

NORA The police! Let one av thim lay his dirty hand on Con Melody, and he'll knock him senseless with one blow

SARA Then Simon said how poor he was, and he'd never accept a penny from his father, even if he offered it. And I told him never mind, that if we had to live in a hut, or sleep in the grass of a field without a roof to our heads, and work our hands to the bone, or starve itself, I'd be in heaven and sing with the joy of our love! *(She looks up at her mother.)* And I meant it, Mother! I meant every word of it from the bottom of my heart!

> Why is Sara so impressed by her own words to Simon regarding money matters?

NORA *(answers vaguely from her preoccupation with the police—patting Sara's hair mechanically)* Av course you did, darlin'.

SARA But he kissed me and said it wouldn't be as bad as that, he'd been thinking and he'd had an offer from an old college friend who'd inherited a cotton mill and who wants Simon to be equal partners if he'll take complete charge of it. It's only a small mill and that's what tempts Simon. He said maybe I couldn't believe it but he knows from his experience working for his father he has the ability for trade, though he hates it, and he could easily make a living for us from this mill—just enough to be comfortable, and he'd have time over to write his book, and keep his wisdom, and never let himself become a slave to the greed for more than enough that is the curse of mankind. Then he said he was afraid maybe I'd think it was weakness in him, not wisdom, and could I be happy with enough and no more. So I kissed him and said all I wanted in life was his love, and whatever meant happiness to him would be my only ambition. *(She looks up at her mother again—exultantly.)* And I meant it, Mother! With all my heart and soul!

NORA *(as before, patting her hair)* I know, darlin'.

SARA Isn't that a joke on me, with all my crazy dreams of riches and a grand estate and me a haughty lady riding around in a carriage with coachman and footman! *(She laughs at herself.)* Wasn't I the fool to think that had any meaning at all when you're in love? You were right, Mother. I knew nothing of love, or the pride a woman can take in giving everything—the pride in her own love! I was only an ignorant, silly girl boasting, but I'm a woman now, Mother, and I know.

> What has Sara learned about love that emphasizes her similarity to her mother?

NORA *(as before, mechanically)* I'm sure you do, darlin'. *(She mutters fumingly to herself.)* Let the police try it! He'll whip them back to their kennels, the dirty curs!

SARA *(lost in her happiness)* And then we put out the light and talked about how soon we'd get married, and how happy we'd be the rest of our lives together, and we'd have children—and he forgot whatever shyness was left in the dark and said he meant all the bold things he'd written in the poems I'd seen. And I confessed that I was up to every scheme to get him, because I loved him so much there wasn't anything I wouldn't do to make sure he was mine. And all the time we were kissing each other, wild with happiness. And— *(She stops abruptly and looks down guiltily.)*

NORA *(as before)* Yes, darlin', I know.

SARA *(guiltily, keeping her eyes down)* You—know, Mother?

NORA *(abruptly comes out of her preoccupation, startled and uneasy)* I know what? What are you sayin'? Look up at me! *(She pulls Sara's head back so she can look down in her face—falteringly.)* I can see— You let him! You wicked, sinful girl!

SARA *(defiantly and proudly)* There was no letting about it, only love making the two of us!

NORA *(helplessly resigned already but feeling it her duty to rebuke)* Ain't you ashamed to boast—?

SARA No! There was no shame in it! *(proudly)* Ashamed? You know I'm not! Haven't you told me of the pride in your love? Were you ashamed?

NORA *(weakly)* I was. I was dead with shame.

SARA You were not! You were proud like me!

NORA But it's a mortal sin. God will punish you—

EUGENE O'NEILL

SARA Let Him! If He'd say to me, for every time you kiss Simon you'll have a thousand years in hell, I wouldn't care, I'd wear out my lips kissing him!

NORA *(frightenedly)* Whist, now! He might hear you.

SARA Wouldn't you have said the same—?

NORA *(distractedly)* Will you stop! Don't torment me with your sinful questions! I won't answer you!

SARA *(hugging her)* All right. Forgive me, Mother. *(a pause—smilingly)* It was Simon who felt guilty and repentant. If he'd had his way, he'd be out of bed now, and the two of us would be walking around in the night, trying to wake up someone who could marry us. But I was so drunk with love, I'd lost all thought or care about marriage. I'd got to the place where all you know or care is that you belong to love, and you can't call your soul your own any more, let alone your body, and you're proud you've given them to love. *(She pauses—then teasing lovingly.)* Sure, I've always known you're the sweetest woman in the world, Mother, but I never suspected you were a wise woman too, until I knew tonight the truth of what you said this morning, that a woman can forgive whatever the man she loves could do and still love him, because it was through him she found the love in herself; that, in one way, he doesn't count at all, because it's love, your own love, your love in him, and to keep that your pride will do anything. *(She smiles with a self-mocking happiness.)* It's love's slaves we are, Mother, not men's—and wouldn't it shame their boasting and vanity if we ever let them know our secret? *(She laughs—then suddenly looks guilty.)* But I'm talking great nonsense. I'm glad Simon can't hear me. *(She pauses. Nora is worrying and hasn't listened. Sara goes on.)* Yes, I can even understand now—a little anyway—how you can still love Father and be proud of it, in spite of what he is.

NORA *(at the mention of Melody, comes out of her brooding)* Hush, now! *(miserably)* God help us, Sara, why doesn't he come, what's happened to him?

SARA *(gets to her feet exasperatedly)* Don't be a fool, Mother. *(bitterly)* Nothing's happened except he's made a public disgrace of himself, for Simon's mother to sneer at. If she wanted revenge on him, I'm sure she's had her fill of it. Well, I don't care. He deserves it. I warned him and I begged him, and got called a peasant slut and a whore for my pains. All I hope now is that whatever happened wakes him from his lies and mad dreams so he'll have to face the truth of himself in that mirror. *(sneeringly)* But there's devil a chance he'll ever let that happen. Instead, he'll come home as drunk as two lords, boasting of his glorious victory over old Harford, whatever the truth is! *(But Nora isn't listening. She has heard the click of the latch on the street door at rear.)*

NORA *(excitedly)* Look, Sara! *(The door is opened slowly and Jamie Cregan sticks his head in cautiously to peer around the room. His face is battered, nose red and swollen, lips cut and puffed, and one eye so blackened it is almost closed. Nora's first reaction is a cry of relief.)* Praise be to the Saints, you're back, Jamie!

CREGAN *(puts a finger to his lips—cautioningly)* Whist!

NORA *(frightenedly)* Jamie! Where's himself?

How does Sara differ from her mother in religious matters?

What is the significance of Sara's discovery ("It's love's slaves we are...not men's") with respect to the drama as a whole?

What is foreshadowed by this latest reference to Con's mirror?

CREGAN (*sharply*) Whist, I'm telling you! (*in a whisper*) I've got him in a rig outside, but I had to make sure no one was here. Lock the bar door, Sara, and I'll bring him in. (*She goes and turns the key in the door, her expression contemptuous. Cregan then disappears, leaving the street door half open.*)

> Although not aware of specific details, the audience realizes that whatever Melody has done is embarrassing, because Jamie wants to be sure no outsiders are present as witnesses.

NORA Did you see Jamie's face? They've been fightin' terrible. Oh, I'm afraid, Sara.

SARA Afraid of what? It's only what I told you to expect. A crazy row—and now he's paralyzed drunk. (*Cregan appears in the doorway at rear. He is half leading, half supporting Melody. The latter moves haltingly and woodenly. But his movements do not seem those of drunkenness. It is more as if a sudden shock or stroke had shattered his coordination and left him in a stupor. His scarlet uniform is filthy and torn and pulled awry. The pallor of his face is ghastly. He has a cut over his left eye, a blue swelling on his left cheekbone, and his lips are cut and bloody. From a big raw bruise on his forehead, near the temple, trickles of dried blood run down to his jaw. Both his hands are swollen, with skinned knuckles, as are Cregan's. His eyes are empty and lifeless. He stares at his wife and daughter as if he did not recognize them.*)

NORA (*rushes and puts her arm around him*) Con, darlin'! Are you hurted bad? (*He pushes her away without looking at her. He walks dazedly to his chair at the head of the center table. Nora follows him, breaking into lamentation.*) Con, don't you know me? Oh, God help us, look at his head!

SARA Be quiet, Mother. Do you want them in the bar to know he's come home—the way he is. (*She gives her father a look of disgust.*)

CREGAN Ay, that's it, Sara. We've got to rouse him first. His pride'd nivir forgive us if we let thim see him dead bate like this. (*There is a pause. They stare at him and he stares sightlessly at the table top. Nora stands close by his side, behind the table, on his right, Sara behind her on her right, Cregan at right of Sara.*)

SARA He's drunk, isn't that all it is, Jamie?

CREGAN (*sharply*) He's not. He's not taken a drop since we left here. It's the clouts on the head he got, that's what ails him. A taste of whiskey would bring him back, if he'd only take it, but he won't.

SARA (*gives her father a puzzled, uneasy glance*) He won't?

NORA (*gets the decanter and a glass and hands them to Cregan*) Here. Try and make him.

CREGAN (*pours out a big drink and puts it before Melody—coaxingly*) Drink this now, Major, and you'll be right as rain! (*Melody does not seem to notice. His expression remains blank and dead. Cregan scratches his head puzzledly.*) He won't. That's the way he's been all the way back when I tried to persuade him. (*then irritably*) Well, if he won't, I will, be your leave. I'm needin' it bad. (*He downs the whiskey, and pours out another—to Nora and Sara.*) It's the divil's own rampage we've had.

> O'Neill builds suspense by having Melody not accept whiskey, unlike his usual self.

SARA (*quietly contemptuous, but still with the look of puzzled uneasiness at her father*) From your looks it must have been.

CREGAN (*indignantly*) You're takin' it cool enough, and you seein' the marks av the batin' we got! (*He downs his second drink—boastfully.*)

But if we're marked, there's others is marked worse and some av thim is police!

NORA God be praised! The dirty cowards!

SARA Be quiet, Mother. Tell us what happened, Jamie.

CREGAN Faix, what didn't happen? Be the rock av Cashel, I've nivir engaged in a livelier shindy! We had no trouble findin' where Harford lived. It's a grand mansion, with a big walled garden behind it, and we wint to the front door. A flunky in livery answered wid two others behind. A big black naygur one was. That pig av a lawyer must have warned Harford to expect us. Con spoke wid the airs av a lord. "Kindly inform your master," he says, "that Major Cornelius Melody, late of His Majesty's Seventh Dragoons, respectfully requests a word with him." Well, the flunky put an insolent sneer on him. "Mr. Harford won't see you," he says. I could see Con's rage risin' but he kept polite. "Tell him," he says, "if he knows what's good for him he'll see me. For if he don't, I'll come in and see him." "Ye will, will ye?" says the flunky, "I'll have you know Mr. Harford don't allow drunken Micks to come here disturbing him. The police have been informed," he says, "and you'll be arrested if you make trouble." Then he started to shut the door. "Anyway, you've come to the wrong door," he says, "the place for the loiks av you is the servants' entrance."

> Why can these actions best be reported by a messenger rather than dramatized on stage?
>
> Would your answer also explain why messengers in classical Greek drama also related violent events which occurred offstage? Why?

NORA *(angrily)* Och, the impident divil!

SARA *(In spite of herself her temper has been rising. She looks at Melody with angry scorn.):* You let Harford's servants insult you! *(then quickly)* But it serves you right! I knew what would happen! I warned you!

CREGAN Let them be damned! Kape your mouth shut, and lave me tell it, and you'll see if we let them! When he'd said that, the flunky tried to slam the door in our faces, but Con was too quick. He pushed it back on him and lept in the hall, roarin' mad, and hit the flunky a cut with his whip across his ugly mug that set him screamin' like a stuck pig!

> On the basis of her character, how can we account for Sara's ambivalent reaction to these events?

NORA *(enthusiastically)* Good for you, Con darlin'!

SARA *(humiliatedly)* Mother! Don't! *(to Melody with biting scorn)* The famous duelist—in a drunken brawl with butlers and coachmen! *(But he is staring sightlessly at the table top as if he didn't see her or know her.)*

CREGAN *(angrily, pouring himself another drink)* Shut your mouth, Sara, and don't be trying to plague him. You're wastin' breath anyway, the way he is. He doesn't know you or hear you. And don't put on lady's airs about fighting when you're the whole cause of it.

SARA *(angrily)* It's a lie! You know I tried to stop—

CREGAN *(gulps down his drink, ignoring this, and turns to Nora— enthusiastically)* Wait till you hear, Nora! *(He plunges into the midst of battle again.)* The naygur hit me a clout that had my head dizzy. He'd have had me down only Con broke the butt av the whip over his black skull and knocked him to his knees. Then the third man punched Con and I gave him a kick where it'd do him least good, and he rolled on the floor, grabbin' his guts. The naygur was in again and grabbed me, but Con came at him and knocked him down. Be

> In Cregan's narrative we can imagine other battles he shared with Melody in past wartime encounters.

A TOUCH OF THE POET

the mortal, we had the three av thim licked, and we'd have dragged auld Harford from his burrow and tanned his Yankee hide if the police hadn't come!

NORA *(furiously)* Arrah, the dirthy cowards! Always takin' sides with the rich Yanks against the poor Irish!

SARA *(more and more humiliated and angry and torn by conflicting emotions—pleadingly)* Mother! Can't you keep still?

CREGAN Four av thim wid clubs came behind us. They grabbed us before we knew it and dragged us into the street. Con broke away and hit the one that held him, and I gave one a knee in his belly. And then, glory be, there was a fight! Oh, it'd done your heart good to see himself! He was worth two men, lettin' out right and left, roarin' wid rage and cursin' like a trooper—

MELODY *(without looking up or any change in his dazed expression, suddenly speaks in a jeering mumble to himself)* Bravely done, Major Melody! The Commander of the Forces honors your exceptional gallantry! Like the glorious field of Talavera! Like the charge on the French square! Cursing like a drunken, foul-mouthed son of a thieving shebeen keeper who sprang from the filth of a peasant hovel, with pigs on the floor—with that pale Yankee bitch watching from a window, sneering with disgust!

> Melody's remarks draw the parallel between the skirmish with police and his past military escapades even more closely.
>
> Who is the "pale Yankee bitch watching from a window" during the fighting?

NORA *(frightenedly)* God preserve us, it's crazed he is!

SARA *(Stares at him startled and wondering. For a second there is angry pity in her eyes. She makes an impulsive move toward him.)* Father! *(then her face hardening)* He isn't crazed, Mother. He's come to his senses for once in his life! *(to Melody)* So she was sneering, was she? I don't blame her! I'm glad you've been taught a lesson! *(then vindictively)* But I've taught her one, too. She'll soon sneer from the wrong side of her mouth!

CREGAN *(angrily)* Will you shut your gab, Sara! Lave him be and don't heed him. It's the same crazy blather he's talked every once in a while since they brought him to—about the Harford woman—and speakin' av the pigs and his father one minute, and his pride and honor and his mare the next. *(He takes up the story again.)* Well, anyways, they was too much for us, the four av thim wid clubs. The last thing I saw before I was knocked senseless was three av thim clubbing Con. But, be the Powers, we wint down fightin' to the last for the glory av auld Ireland!

> Cregan also views fighting Yankees as one way to restore glory to Ireland and its past.

MELODY *(in a jeering mutter to himself)* Like a rumsoaked trooper, brawling before a brothel on a Saturday night, puking in the gutter!

SARA *(strickenly)* Don't, Father!

CREGAN *(indignantly to Melody)* We wasn't in condition. If we had been—but they knocked us senseless and rode us to the station and locked us up. And we'd be there yet if Harford hadn't made thim turn us loose, for he's rich and has influence. Small thanks to him! He was afraid the row would get in the paper and put shame on him. *(Melody laughs crazily and springs to his feet. He sways dizzily, clutching his head—then goes toward the door at left front.)*

NORA Con! Where are you goin'? *(She starts after him and grabs his arm. He shakes her hand off roughly as if he did not recognize her.)*

CREGAN He don't know you. Don't cross him now, Nora. Sure, he's only goin' upstairs to bed. *(wheedlingly)* You know what's best for you, don't you, Major? *(Melody feels his way gropingly through the door and disappears, leaving it open.)*

SARA *(uneasy, but consoling her mother)* Jamie's right, Mother. If he'll fall asleep, that's the best thing— *(Abruptly she is terrified.)* Oh God, maybe he'll take revenge on Simon— *(She rushes to the door and stands listening—with relief.)* No, he's gone to his room. *(She comes back—a bit ashamed.)* I'm a fool. He'd never harm a sick man, no matter— *(She takes her mother's arm—gently.)* Don't stand there, Mother. Sit down. You're tired enough—

NORA *(frightenedly)* I've never heard him talk like that in all the years—with that crazy dead look in his eyes. Oh, I'm afeered, Sara. Lave go of me. I've got to make sure he's gone to bed. *(She goes quickly to the door and disappears. Sara makes a move to follow her.)*

CREGAN *(roughly)* Stay here, unless you're a fool, Sara. He might come to all av a sudden and give you a hell av a thrashin'. Troth, you deserve one. You're to blame for what's happened. Wasn't he fightin' to revenge the insults to you? *(He sprawls on a chair at rear of the table at center.)*

SARA *(sitting down at rear of the small table at left front—angrily)* I'll thank you to mind your own business, Jamie Cregan. Just because you're a relation—

CREGAN *(harshly)* Och, to hell with your airs! *(He pours out a drink and downs it. He is becoming drunk again.)*

SARA I can revenge my own insults, and I have! I've beaten the Harfords—and he's only made a fool of himself for her to sneer at. But I've beaten her and I'll sneer last! *(She pauses, a hard, triumphant smile on her lips. It fades. She gives a little bewildered laugh.)* God forgive me, what a way to think of—I must be crazy, too.

Why is Sara alarmed to catch herself describe her love-making with Simon as a form of revenge on the Harfords?

CREGAN *(drunkenly)* Ah, don't be talkin'! Didn't the two of us lick them all! And Con's all right. He's all right, I'm sayin'! It's only the club on the head makes him quare a while. I've seen it often before. Ay, and felt it meself. I remember at a fair in the auld country I was clouted with the butt av a whip and I didn't remember a thing for hours, but they told me after I never stopped gabbin' but went around tellin' every stranger all my secrets. *(He pauses. Sara hasn't listened. He goes on uneasily.)* All the same, it's no fun listening to his mad blather about the pale bitch, as he calls her, like she was a ghost, haunting and scorning him. And his gab about his beautiful thoroughbred mare is madder still, raving what a grand, beautiful lady she is, with her slender ankles and dainty feet, sobbin' and beggin' her forgiveness and talkin' of dishonor and death— *(He shrinks superstitiously—then angrily, reaching for the decanter.)* Och, be damned to this night! *(Before he can pour a drink, Nora comes hurrying in from the door at left front.)*

NORA *(breathless and frightened)* He's come down! He pushed me away like he didn't see me. He's gone out to the barn. Go after him, Jamie.

CREGAN *(drunkenly)* I won't. He's all right. Lave him alone.

SARA *(jeeringly)* Sure, he's only gone to pay a call on his sweetheart,

A TOUCH OF THE POET 259

the mare, Mother, and hasn't he slept in her stall many a time when he was dead drunk, and she never even kicked him?

NORA *(distractedly)* Will you shut up, the two av you! I heard him openin' the closet in his room where he keeps his auld set of duelin' pistols, and he was carryin' the box when he came down—

CREGAN *(scrambles hastily to his feet)* Oh, the lunatic!

NORA He'll ride the mare back to Harford's! He'll murther someone! For the love av God, stop him, Jamie!

CREGAN *(drunkenly belligerent)* Be Christ, I'll stop him for you, Nora, pistols or no pistols! *(He walks a bit unsteadily out the door at left front.)*

SARA *(stands tensely—bursts out with a strange triumphant pride)* Then he's not beaten! *(Suddenly she is overcome by a bitter, tortured revulsion of feeling.)* Merciful God, what am I thinking? As if he hadn't done enough to destroy— *(distractedly)* Oh, the mad fool! I wish he was— *(From the yard, off left front, there is the muffled crack of a pistol shot hardly perceptible above the noise in the barroom. But Sara and Nora both hear it and stand frozen with horror. Sara babbles hysterically.)* I didn't mean it, Mother! I didn't!

> Explain the need for perfect timing as Sara's wish is interrupted by a gunshot.

NORA *(numb with fright—mumbles stupidly)* A shot!

SARA You know I didn't mean it, Mother!

NORA A shot! God help us, he's kilt Jamie!

SARA *(stammers)* No—not Jamie— *(wildly)* Oh, I can't bear waiting! I've got to know— *(She rushes to the door at left front—then stops frightenedly.)* I'm afraid to know! I'm afraid—

> How does O'Neill increase the tension to a high pitch?

NORA *(mutters stupidly)* Not Jamie? Then who else? *(She begins to tremble—in a horrified whisper.)* Sara! You think— Oh, God have mercy!

SARA Will you hush, Mother! I'm trying to hear— *(She retreats quickly into the room and backs around the table at left front until she is beside her mother.)* Someone's at the yard door. It'll be Jamie coming to tell us—

NORA It's a lie! He'd nivir. He'd nivir! *(They stand paralyzed by terror, clinging to each other, staring at the open door. There is a moment's pause in which the sound of drunken roistering in the bar seems louder. Then Melody appears in the doorway with Cregan behind him. Cregan has him by the shoulder and pushes him roughly into the room, like a bouncer handling a drunk. Cregan is shaken by the experience he has just been through and his reaction is to make him drunkenly angry at Melody. In his free hand is a dueling pistol. Melody's face is like gray wax. His body is limp, his feet drag, his eyes seem to have no sight. He appears completely possessed by a paralyzing stupor.)*

SARA *(impulsively)* Father! Oh, thank God! *(She takes one step toward him—then her expression begins to harden.)*

NORA *(sobs with relief)* Oh, praise God you're alive! Sara and me was dead with fear— *(She goes toward them.)* Con! Con, darlin'!

CREGAN *(dumps Melody down on the nearest chair at left of the small table—roughly, his voice trembling)* Let you sit still now, Con Melody, and behave like a gintleman! *(to Nora)* Here he is for ye, Nora, and you're welcome, bad luck to him! *(He moves back as Nora comes and puts her arms around Melody and hugs him tenderly.)*

NORA Oh, Con, Con, I was so afeered for you! *(He does not seem to hear or see her, but she goes on crooning to him comfortably as if he were a sick child.)*

CREGAN He was in the stable. He'd this pistol in his hand, with the mate to it on the floor beside the mare. *(He shudders and puts the pistol on the table shakenly.)* It's mad he's grown entirely! Let you take care av him now, his wife and daughter! I've had enough. I'm no damned keeper av lunatics! *(He turns toward the barroom.)*

SARA Wait, Jamie. We heard a shot. What was it?

CREGAN *(angrily)* Ask him, not me! *(then with bewildered horror)* He kilt the poor mare, the mad fool! *(Sara stares at him in stunned amazement.)* I found him on the floor with her head in his lap, and her dead. He was sobbing like a soul in hell— *(He shudders.)* Let me get away from the sight of him where there's men in their right senses laughing and singing! *(He unlocks the barroom door.)* And don't be afraid, Sara, that I'll tell the boys a word av this. I'll talk of our fight in the city only, because it's all I want to remember. *(He jerks open the door and goes in the bar, slamming the door quickly behind him. A roar of welcome is heard as the crowd greets his arrival. Sara locks the door again. She comes back to the center table, staring at Melody, an hysterical sneering grin making her lips quiver and twitch.)*

Does Con's shooting of the mare prepare us for the scenes to follow?

SARA What a fool I was to be afraid! I might know you'd never do it as long as a drink of whiskey was left in the world! So it was the mare you shot? *(She bursts into uncontrollable, hysterical laughter. It penetrates Melody's stupor and he stiffens rigidly on his chair, but his eyes remain fixed on the table top.)*

NORA Sara! Stop! For the love av God, how can you laugh—!

SARA I can't—help it, Mother. Didn't you hear—Jamie? It was the mare he shot! *(She gives way to laughter again.)*

NORA *(distractedly)* Stop it, I'm sayin'! *(Sara puts her hand over her mouth to shut off the sound of her laughing, but her shoulders still shake. Nora sinks on the chair at rear of the table. She mutters dazedly.)* Kilt his beautiful mare? He must be mad entirely.

MELODY *(suddenly speaks, without looking up, in the broadest brogue, his voice coarse and harsh)* Lave Sara laugh. Sure, who could blame her? I'm roarin' meself inside me. It's the damnedest joke a man ivir played on himself since time began. *(They stare at him. Sara's laughter stops. She is startled and repelled by his brogue. Then she stares at him suspiciously, her face hardening.)*

SARA What joke? Do you think murdering the poor mare a good joke? *(Melody stiffens for a second, but that is all. He doesn't look up or reply.)*

Why is the killing of the horse such a momentous occasion in Melody's life in view of its symbolic significance?

NORA *(frightened)* Look at the dead face on him, Sara. He's like a corpse. *(She reaches out and touches one of his hands on the table top with a furtive tenderness—pleadingly.)* Con, darlin'. Don't!

MELODY *(Looks up at her. His expression changes so that his face loses all its remaining distinction and appears vulgar and common, with a loose, leering grin on his swollen lips.)* Let you not worry, Allanah. Sure, I'm no corpse, and with a few drinks in me, I'll soon be lively enough to suit you.

A TOUCH OF THE POET

NORA *(miserably confused)* Will you listen to him, Sara—puttin' on the brogue to torment us.

SARA *(growing more uneasy but sneering)* Pay no heed to him, Mother. He's play-acting to amuse himself. If he's that cruel and shameless after what he's done—

NORA *(defensively)* No, it's the blow on the head he got fightin' the police.

MELODY *(vulgarly)* The blow, me foot! That's Jamie Cregan's blather. Sure, it'd take more than a few clubs on the head to darken my wits long. Me brains, if I have any, is clear as a bell. And I'm not puttin' on brogue to tormint you, me darlint. Nor play-actin', Sara. That was the Major's game. It's quare, surely, for the two av ye to object when I talk in me natural tongue, and yours, and don't put on airs loike the late lamented auld liar and lunatic, Major Cornelius Melody, av His Majesty's Seventh Dragoons, used to do.

NORA God save us, Sara, will you listen!

MELODY But he's dead now, and his last bit av lyin' pride is murthered and stinkin'. *(He pats Nora's hand with what seems to be genuine comforting affection.)* So let you be aisy, darlint. He'll nivir again hurt you with his sneers, and his pretindin' he's a gintleman, blatherin' about pride and honor, and his boastin' av duels in the days that's gone, and his showin' off before the Yankees, and thim laughin' at him, prancing around drunk on his beautiful thoroughbred mare— *(He gulps as if he were choking back a sob.)* For she's dead, too, poor baste.

> What decision has Melody made here concerning his life?

SARA *(This is becoming unbearable for her—tensely.)* Why—why did you kill her?

MELODY Why did the Major, you mean! Be Christ, you're stupider than I thought you, if you can't see that. Wasn't she the livin' reminder, so to spake, av all his lyin' boasts and dreams? He meant to kill her first wid one pistol, and then himself wid the other. But faix, he saw the shot that killed her had finished him, too. There wasn't much pride left in the auld lunatic, anyway, and seeing her die made an end av him. So he didn't bother shooting himself, because it'd be a mad thing to waste a good bullet on a corpse! *(He laughs coarsely.)*

> Why do these revelations serve as the climax of the drama? How is the fate of the horse connected with Melody's own life?

SARA *(tensely)* Father! Stop it!

MELODY Didn't I tell you there was a great joke in it? Well, that's the joke. *(He begins to laugh again but he chokes on a stifled sob. Suddenly his face loses the coarse, leering, brutal expression and is full of anguished grief. He speaks without brogue, not to them but aloud to himself.)* Blessed Christ, the look in her eyes by the lantern light with life ebbing out of them—wondering and sad, but still trustful, not reproaching me—with no fear in them—proud, understanding pride—loving me—she saw I was dying with her. She understood! She forgave me! *(He starts to sob but wrenches himself out of it and speaks in broad, jeering brogue.)* Begorra, if that wasn't the mad Major's ghost speakin'! But be damned to him, he won't haunt me long, if I know it! I intind to live at my ease from now on and not let the dead bother me, but enjoy life in my proper station as auld Nick Melody's son. I'll bury his Major's damned red livery av bloody England deep in the ground and he can haunt its grave if he likes, and boast to the

> Melody's unconscious shift back and forth to crude Irish brogue reflects his mental state.

262　EUGENE O'NEILL

Nora (Helen Hayes), left, Con (Eric Portman), center, and Sara (Kim Stanley), right.

lonely night av Talavera and the ladies of Spain and fightin' the French! *(with a leer)* Troth, I think the boys is right when they say he stole the uniform and he nivir fought under Wellington at all. He was a terrible liar, as I remember him.

NORA Con, darlin', don't be grievin' about the mare. Sure, you can get another. I'll manage—

SARA Mother! Hush! *(to Melody, furiously)* Father, will you stop this mad game you're playing—?

MELODY *(roughly)* Game, is it? You'll find it's no game. It was the Major played a game all his life, the crazy auld loon, and cheated only himself. But I'll be content to stay meself in the proper station I was born to, from this day on. *(with a cunning leer at Sara)* And it's meself feels it me duty to give you a bit av fatherly advice, Sara darlint, while my mind is on it. I know you've great ambition, so remember it's to hell wid honor if ye want to rise in this world. Remember the blood in your veins and be your grandfather's true descendant. There was an able man for you! Be Jaysus, he nivir felt anything beneath him that could gain him something, and for lyin' tricks to swindle the bloody fools of gintry, there wasn't his match in Ireland, and he ended up wid a grand estate, and a castle, and a pile av gold in the bank.

SARA *(distractedly)* Oh, I hate you!

NORA Sara!

MELODY *(goes on as if he hadn't heard)* I know he'd advise that to give you a first step up, darlint, you must make the young Yankee gintleman have you in his bed, and after he's had you, weep great tears

A TOUCH OF THE POET 263

and appeal to his honor to marry you and save yours. Be God, he'll nivir resist that, if I know him, for he's a young fool, full av dacency and dreams, and looney, too, wid a touch av the poet in him. Oh, it'll be aisy for you—

SARA *(goaded beyond bearing)* I'll make you stop your dirty brogue and your play-acting! *(She leans toward him and speaks with taunting vindictiveness, in broad brogue herself.)* Thank you kindly but I've already taken your wise advice, Father. I made him have me in his bed, while you was out drunk fightin' the police!

NORA *(frightenedly)* Sara! Hault your brazen tongue!

MELODY *(His body stiffens on his chair and the coarse leer vanishes from his face. It becomes his old face. His eyes fix on her in a threatening stare. He speaks slowly, with difficulty keeping his words in brogue.)* Did you now, God bless you! I might have known you'd not take any chance that the auld loon av a Major, going out to revenge an insult to you, would spoil your schemes. *(He forces a horrible grin.)* Be the living God, it's me should be proud this night that one av the Yankee gintry has stooped to be seduced by my slut av a daughter! *(Still keeping his eyes fixed on hers, he begins to rise from his chair, his right hand groping along the table top until it clutches the dueling pistol. He aims it at Sara's heart, like an automation, his eyes as cold, deadly, and merciless as they must have been in his duels of long ago. Sara is terrified but she stands unflinchingly.)*

NORA *(horror-stricken, lunges from her chair and grabs his arm)* Con! For the love av God! Would you be murthering Sara? *(A dazed look comes over his face. He grows limp and sinks back on his chair and lets the pistol slide from his fingers on the table. He draws a shuddering breath—then laughs hoarsely.)*

MELODY *(with a coarse leer)* Murtherin' Sara, is it? Are ye daft, Nora? Sure, all I want is to congratulate her!

SARA *(hopelessly)* Oh! *(She sinks down on her chair at rear of the center table and covers her face with her hands.)*

NORA *(with pitifully well-meant reassurance)* It's all right, Con. The young lad wants to marry her as soon as can be, she told me, and he did before.

MELODY Musha, but that's kind of him! Be God, we ought to be proud av our daughter, Nora. Lave it to her to get what she wants by hook or crook. And won't we be proud watchin' her rise in the world till she's a grand lady!

NORA *(simply)* We will, surely.

SARA Mother!

MELODY She'll have some trouble, rootin' out his dreams. He's set in his proud, noble ways, but she'll find the right trick! I'd lay a pound, if I had one, to a shilling she'll see the day when she'll wear fine silks and drive in a carriage wid a naygur coachman behind spankin' thoroughbreds, her nose in the air; and she'll live in a Yankee mansion, as big as a castle, on a grand estate av stately woodland and soft green meadows and a lake. *(with a leering chuckle)* Be the Saints, I'll start her on her way by making her a wedding present av the Major's place where he let her young gintleman build his cabin—the

> Sara does not appreciate the mundane Melody any better than the poseur he was earlier.

land the Yankees swindled him into buyin' for his American estate, the mad fool! *(He glances at the dueling pistol—jeeringly.)* Speakin' av the departed, may his soul roast in hell, what am I doin' wid his pistol? Be God, I don't need pistols. Me fists, or a club if it's handy, is enough. Didn't me and Jamie lick a whole regiment av police this night?

NORA *(stoutly)* You did, and if there wasn't so many av thim—

MELODY *(turns to her—grinningly)* That's the talk, darlint! Sure, there's divil a more loyal wife in the whole world— *(He pauses, staring at her—then suddenly kisses her on the lips, roughly but with a strange real tenderness.)* and I love you.

NORA *(with amazed, unthinking joy)* Oh, Con!

MELODY *(grinning again)* I've meant to tell you often, only the Major, damn him, had me under his proud thumb. *(He pulls her over and kisses her hair.)*

NORA Is it kissin' my hair—!

MELODY I am. Why wouldn't I? You have beautiful hair, God bless you! And don't remember what the Major used to tell you. The gintleman's sneers he put on is buried with him. I'll be a real husband to you, and help ye run this shebeen, instead of being a sponge. I'll fire Mickey and tend the bar myself, like my father's son ought to.

NORA You'll not! I'll nivir let you!

MELODY *(leering cunningly)* Well, I offered, remember. It's you refused. Sure, I'm not in love with work, I'll confess, and maybe you're right not to trust me too near the whiskey. *(He licks his lips.)* Be Jaysus, that reminds me. I've not had a taste for hours. I'm dyin' av thirst.

NORA *(starts to rise)* I'll get you—

MELODY *(pushes her back on her chair)* Ye'll not. I want company and singin' and dancin' and great laughter. I'll join the boys in the bar and help Cousin Jamie celebrate our wonderful shindy wid the police. *(He gets up. His old soldierly bearing is gone. He slouches and his movements are shambling and clumsy, his big hairy hands dangling at his sides. In his torn, disheveled, dirt-stained uniform, he looks like a loutish, grinning clown.)*

NORA You ought to go to bed, Con darlin', with your head hurted.

MELODY Me head? Faix, it was nivir so clear while the Major lived to torment me, makin' me tell mad lies to excuse his divilments. *(He grins.)* And I ain't tired a bit. I'm fresh as a man new born. So I'll say goodnight to you, darlint. *(He bends and kisses her. Sara has lifted her tear-stained face from her hands and is staring at him with a strange, anguished look of desperation. He leers at her.)* And you go to bed, too, Sara. Troth, you deserve a long, dreamless slape after all you've accomplished this day.

SARA Please! Oh, Father, I can't bear— Won't you be yourself again?

MELODY *(threatening her good-humoredly)* Let you kape your mouth closed, ye slut, and not talk like you was ashamed of me, your father. I'm not the Major who was too much of a gintleman to lay

---

Why does Melody's kissing of his wife and her hair confirm the transformation taking place during the resolution?

How does O'Neill's description of Melody match the psychological alteration involved in the protagonist?

A TOUCH OF THE POET

hand on you. Faix, I'll give you a box on the ear that'll teach you respect, if ye kape on trying to raise the dead! *(She stares at him, sick and desperate. He starts toward the bar door.)*

SARA *(springs to her feet)* Father! Don't go in with those drunken scum! Don't let them hear and see you! You can drink all you like here. Jamie will come and keep you company. He'll laugh and sing and help you celebrate Talavera—

MELODY *(roughly)* To hell wid Talavera! *(His eyes are fastened on the mirror. He leers into it.)* Be Jaysus, if it ain't the mirror the auld loon was always admirin' his mug in while he spouted Byron to pretend himself was a lord wid a touch av the poet— *(He strikes a pose which is a vulgar burlesque of his old before-the-mirror one and recites in mocking brogue.)*

> "I have not loved the World, nor the World me;
> I have not flatthered uts rank breath, nor bowed
> To uts idolatries a pashunt knee,
> Nor coined me cheek to smiles,—nor cried aloud
> In worship av an echo: in the crowd
> They couldn't deem me one av such—I stood
> Among thim, but not av thim . . ."

(He guffaws contemptuously.) Be Christ, if he wasn't the joke av the world, the Major. He should have been a clown in a circus. God rest his soul in the flames av tormint! *(roughly)* But to hell wid the dead. *(The noise in the bar rises to an uproar of laughter as if Jamie had just made some climactic point in his story. Melody looks away from the mirror to the bar door.)* Be God, I'm alive and in the crowd they *can* deem me one av such! I'll be among thim and av thim, too—and make up for the lonely dog's life the Major led me. *(He goes to the bar door.)*

SARA *(starts toward him—beseechingly)* Father! Don't put this final shame on yourself. You're not drunk now. There's no excuse you can give yourself. You'll be as dead to yourself after, as if you'd shot yourself along with the mare!

MELODY *(leering—with a wink at Nora)* Listen to her, Nora, reproachin' me because I'm not drunk. Troth, that's a condition soon mended. *(He puts his hand on the knob of the door.)*

SARA Father!

NORA *(has given way to such complete physical exhaustion, she hardly hears, much less comprehends what is said—dully)* Lave him alone, Sara. It's best.

MELODY *(as another roar is heard from the bar)* I'm missin' a lot av fun. Be God, I've a bit of news to tell the boys that'll make them roar the house down. The Major's passin' to his eternal rest has set me free to jine the Democrats, and I'll vote for Andy Jackson, the friend av the common men like me, God bless him! *(He grins with anticipation.)* Wait till the boys hear that! *(He starts to turn the knob.)*

SARA *(rushes to him and grabs his arm)* No! I won't let you! It's my pride, too! *(She stammers.)* Listen! Forgive me, Father! I know it's my fault—always sneering and insulting you—but I only meant the lies in it. The truth—Talavera—the Duke praising your bravery—an officer in his army—even the ladies in Spain—deep down that's

---

What has been the function of the mirror throughout the play? Is Melody's shift to the third person important? If so, why?

How have these lines changed their meaning when they are recited this time?

What do we learn about Sara's character in her pleas to Melody not to embrace permanently his new loss of illusions?

been my pride, too—that I was your daughter. So don't— I'll do anything you ask—I'll even tell Simon—that after his father's insult to you—I'm too proud to marry a Yankee coward's son!

MELODY *(Has been visibly crumbling as he listens until he appears to have no character left in which to hide and defend himself. He cries wildly and despairingly, as if he saw his last hope of escape suddenly cut off.)* Sara! For the love of God, stop—let me go—!

NORA *(dully)* Lave your poor father be. It's best. *(In a flash Melody recovers and is the leering peasant again.)*

SARA *(with bitter hopelessness)* Oh, Mother! Why couldn't you be still!

MELODY *(roughly)* Why can't you, ye mean. I warned ye what ye'd get if ye kept on interferin' and tryin' to raise the dead. *(He cuffs her on the side of the head. It is more of a playful push than a blow, but it knocks her off balance back to the end of the table at center.)*

NORA *(aroused—bewilderedly)* God forgive you, Con! *(angrily)* Don't you be hittin' Sara now. I've put up with a lot but I won't—

MELODY *(with rough good nature)* Shut up, darlint. I won't have to again. *(He grins leeringly at Sara.)* That'll teach you, me proud Sara! I know you won't try raisin' the dead any more. And let me hear no more gab out of you about not marryin' the young lad upstairs. Be Jaysus, haven't ye any honor? Ye seduced him and ye'll make an honest gentleman av him if I have to march ye both by the scruff av the neck to the nearest church. *(He chuckles—then leeringly.)* And now with your permission, ladies both, I'll join me good friends in the bar. *(He opens the door and passes into the bar, closing the door behind him. There is a roar of welcoming drunken shouts, pounding of glasses on bar and tables, then quiet as if he had raised a hand for silence, followed by his voice greeting them and ordering drinks, and other roars of acclaim mingled with the music of Riley's pipes. Sara remains standing by the side of the center table, her shoulders bowed, her head hanging, staring at the floor.)*

NORA *(overcome by physical exhaustion again, sighs)* Don't mind his giving you a slap. He's still quare in his head. But he'll sing and laugh and drink a power av whiskey and slape sound after, and tomorrow he'll be himself again—maybe.

SARA *(dully—aloud to herself rather than to her mother)* No. He'll never be. He's beaten at last and he wants to stay beaten. Well, I did my best. Though why I did, I don't know. I must have his crazy pride in me. *(She lifts her head, her face hardening—bitterly.)* I mean, the late Major Melody's pride. I mean, I did have it. Now it's dead—thank God—and I'll make a better wife for Simon. *(There is a sudden lull in the noise from the bar, as if someone had called for silence, then Melody's voice is plainly heard in the silence as he shouts a toast.)* "Here's to our next President, Andy Jackson! Hurroo for Auld Hickory, God bless him!" *(There is a drunken chorus of answering "hurroos" that shakes the walls.)*

NORA Glory be to God, cheerin' for Andy Jackson! Did you hear him, Sara?

SARA *(her face hard)* I heard someone. But it wasn't anyone I ever knew or want to know.

What is Sara finally admitting when she says that "deep down that's been my pride, too"?

The irony here is powerful, as Con Melody insists his daughter marry the man she has seduced for Simon's honor.

Considering that Andrew Jackson was the choice of the "common man," why is it remarkable that Melody drinks a toast to him?

A TOUCH OF THE POET

NORA *(as if she hadn't heard)* Ah well, that's good. They won't all be hatin' him now. *(She pauses—her tired, worn face becomes suddenly shy and tender.)* Did you hear him tellin' me he loved me, Sara? Did you see him kiss me on the mouth—and then kiss my hair? *(She gives a little, soft laugh.)* Sure, he must have gone mad altogether!

SARA *(Stares at her mother. Her face softens.)* No, Mother, I know he meant it. He'll keep on meaning it, too, Mother. He'll be free to, now. *(She smiles strangely.)* Maybe I deserved the slap for interfering.

> What kind of freedom does Sara mean here?

NORA *(preoccupied with her own thoughts)* And if he wants to kape on makin' game of everyone, puttin' on the brogue and actin' like one av thim in there— *(She nods toward the bar.)* Well, why shouldn't he if it brings him peace and company in his loneliness? God pity him, he's had to live all his life alone in the hell av pride. *(proudly)* And I'll play any game he likes and give him love in it. Haven't I always? *(She smiles.)* Sure, I have no pride at all—except that.

> How could you compare Nora's values with current feminist notions?

SARA *(stares at her—moved)* You're a strange, noble woman, Mother. I'll try and be like you. *(She comes over and hugs her—then she smiles tenderly.)* I'll wager Simon never heard the shot or anything. He was sleeping like a baby when I left him. A cannon wouldn't wake him. *(In the bar, Riley starts playing a reel on his pipes and there is the stamp of dancing feet. For a moment Sara's face becomes hard and bitter again. She tries to be mocking.)* Faith, Patch Riley don't know it but he's playing a requiem for the dead. *(Her voice trembles.)* May the hero of Talavera rest in peace! *(She breaks down and sobs, hiding her face on her mother's shoulder—bewilderedly.)* But why should I cry, Mother? Why do I mourn for him?

> Why is it appropriate that Sara refers to Riley's music-playing as a requiem for the dead?

NORA *(at once forgetting her own exhaustion, is all tender, loving help and comfort)* Don't, darlin', don't. You're destroyed with tiredness, that's all. Come on to bed, now, and I'll help you undress and tuck you in. *(trying to rouse her—in a teasing tone)* Shame on you to cry when you have love. What would the young lad think of you?

Curtain

Two main subjects are correlated in *A Touch of the Poet* to produce a central theme. Both parts derive from Con Melody's frustrated goals in life.

1. What is the theme of the drama as it concerns the Melody family?
2. How does Cregan's recounting of Melody's past in Ireland provide the needed information to understand Con's ambitions in life?
3. Why does the theme account for the intense antagonism between Melody and his daughter?
4. How are Melody and Sara alike? How are they opposite?
5. What is the symbolic purpose of Melody's expensive riding horse and his military uniform?

As another topic which contributes to the general theme of the play, O'Neill cultivates the theories of love as held by Nora and Sara.

6. What is Nora's understanding of the force of love and its relationship to personal honor?

POSTVIEW: THEME

7. How does Sara's attitude toward love and honor differ from her mother's during the first three acts?
8. Why does Sara's stance change greatly by the opening of Act IV?
9. What stands in Melody's way to show his wife the true affection he feels for her, as evidenced at the end of the drama?

A symbolic object, Melody's mirror, unifies both parts of the theme.

10. Why is the mirror such an appropriate symbol, in light of Melody's character?
11. What does Melody physically do in front of the mirror on each occasion?
12. What does the mirror permit Melody to do in his thoughts and imagination?
13. How does the last episode—of Melody declaiming into the mirror—differ from all previous occasions? What does this signify?
14. Why does Con identify with Lord Byron, the poet?
15. Why does Simon Harford also seem engrossed with Byron and his way of life?

INTRODUCTION
THE CRUCIBLE

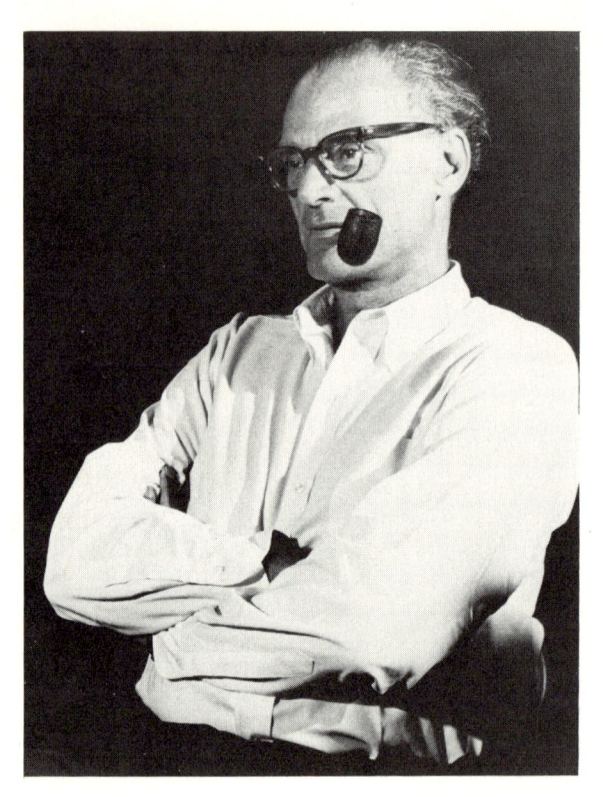

Arthur Miller

Arthur Miller has been called an heir to Ibsen. If Ibsen established the contours for realistic drama and the problem play of the nineteenth century, it is Miller who perfected these forms for the stage in mid-twentieth-century America. A series of successes marked his emergence as one of the finest American playwrights.

Born in 1915 in Manhattan, Miller grew up in a middle-class Jewish household which he reproduced in many of his dramas. He nurtured his desire to become a writer while attending the University of Michigan where he earned numerous prizes for writing plays. Miller's initial attempt at commercial theater in New York (1944) was ill-fated. But soon thereafter his *All My sons* (1947) was voted best play of that season by the Drama Critics' Circle. When he received the Pulitzer Prize in drama for *Death of a Salesman* in 1949, Miller climbed to the highest echelon of American playwrights. His other plays include *The Crucible* (1953), *A Memory of Two Mondays* (1955), *A View from the Bridge* (1955; revised in 1956), *After the Fall* (1964), *Incident at Vichy* (1964), *The Price* (1968), and a comedy, *The Creation of the World and Other Business* (1972). Also he has authored short stories, essays, poetry, a novel, and a screenplay, *The Misfits.*

Following the success of *Death of a Salesman,* Miller did an adaptation of *An Enemy of the People* in 1950. Its theme clearly attracted Miller, that is, the legal superstructure of a community can lead to a blind tyranny over its citizens instead of to a defense of personal rights. Most of Miller's plays analyze the repeated betrayal of the individual by his society and the response left him in seeking to redeem his sense of self. Regarding the nature of tragedy, as early as 1949 Miller wrote in the *New York Times:* "I think the tragic feeling is evoked in us when we are in the presence of a character who is ready to lay down his life, if need be, to secure one thing—his sense of personal dignity." For Miller, life is marked by conflicting encounters between man and his community—encounters which pit the individual's self-esteem and self-concept against the inhibiting demands of his society at large.

Miller features the common man as his tragic protagonist and, therefore, his plays are excellent examples of *domestic tragedy.* Domestic tragedy is based upon the lives of everyday, ordinary people, and it reveals a clear-cut moralistic bias. As a result, Miller's plays are serious in tone.

In *The Crucible,* Miller creates domestic tragedy by using the historical events associated with the infamous Salem witch trials in the 1690s. All the needed ingredients for provocative drama were present in the Salem affair—strong-willed individuals who refuse to accede to bureaucratic edicts. Miller shapes the incidents taken from historical accounts into a two-layered chronicle to create a period play. More particularly, he intertwines the inner conflict of John Proctor, who struggles with marital and sexual problems, and the social dilemma confronting Proctor as a result of the witch panic. Miller takes some liberties with the true historical facts concerning Proctor (who was an actual figure in the affair) and the Salem witch trials; he acknowledges his alterations in a note preceding the printed text of the play. In true history, for example, Abigail was much younger than in Miller's version. Nor, apparently, had there been any actual liaison between Proctor and Abigail. Since the deeds themselves were intriguing and exciting, Miller did not use radical theatrical techniques. Rather, he wrote *The Crucible* in the straightforward fashion of realism. The episodes occur in chronological order in the various homes of the participants Parris and Proctor, with the climactic scenes taking place in a courtroom setting and in a jail cell. And although Miller uses a dialect and syntax to suggest archaic, early American speech patterns, the play's dialogue is wholly understandable.

The Crucible has continued to be popular in succeeding decades and it is revived regularly in all parts of the world today. Miller's play includes an added contemporary dimension through its affinities with the despicable conduct of societal authorities in the Salem of the 1690s. In the prose commentaries in the play text, Miller directly refers to the McCarthy hearings of the early 1950s. The late Joseph McCarthy, then a senator from Wisconsin, had become one of the most powerful men in Washington by virtue of his flamboyant crusade to find supposed Communists in the government. McCarthy's chief instrument of power was the subcommittee, which he chaired. Federal employees first, and later artists and intellectuals in general, were summoned to testify before the subcommittee regarding their loyalty. Any taint of communistic thinking or suspicious past deeds was seized upon as "evidence" of participation in a mas-

Witchcraft hysteria victims being taken to the gallows.

ter Red conspiracy to subvert the United States Government and the country. Guilt by association and by innuendo became the rule, which ruined many lives and careers. It was this latter issue—assumed guilt without firm evidence—which Miller puts to powerful use in *The Crucible,* where personal rather than altruistic motives led to false accusations against one's neighbors.

In more recent years, the specter of McCarthyism does not haunt Miller's play to the extent it did when first produced during the 1950s. Now, readers and viewers can appreciate the even more universal pattern of an individual wrestling with both his own will and that of an irrational, self-seeking community of which he is a part.

PREVIEW: STRUCTURE

Our discussions of other plays in this book brought out some ways the playwright can provide his audience with exposition. At the beginning of *The Crucible,* Arthur Miller sets up a rapid tempo for the action of the plot and offers essential information of a straightforward nature.

1. Why might Miller's narrative commentary during the play's opening lines be useful to the play's director and cast, even though Miller's words themselves would never be heard or seen by a theater audience?
2. How does Miller immediately catapult his audiences into a tense situation?
3. What logic of the plot allows for most of the main characters to be assembled together in Parris' house, thus to provide a climactic finish to Act I?

Complications emerge from the beginning of the play, along with basic exposition.

272   THE CRUCIBLE / INTRODUCTION

4. How does Parris' close questioning of his niece Abigail in the first act advance the development of the story line *and* furnish expository background?
5. Why does the entrance of the Putnams result in a heightened sense of tension? For whom, in particular?
6. What is the basis for the evident conflict between Proctor and his wife that is revealed during the first third of Act II?
7. In Act II, how does Miller project in concrete numerical terms the seriousness of the growing conflict in Salem?

The crisis concerning the effects of the witch trials on a community level arises in Act III, where the tension reaches an acute pitch.

8. What turns out to be the chief interest of Danforth, Hathorne, and Parris in the trial proceedings—Christian faith or egoistic concerns? How do we know?
9. What exact scene, featuring the confrontation of what characters, marks the climax in the third act?
10. What are the opposing factions during this showdown?

Another personal crisis arises in the final act of Miller's play.

11. What are the factors involved in Proctor's trial of himself in his own mind?
12. In the closing act, how does Miller use Elizabeth to indicate that Proctor's ultimate decision must be his own?

Miller presents different resolutions to solve the dilemmas of the two primary plot levels of his play.

13. What is the outcome of the challenge to the court, represented by Proctor's testimony in Act III?
14. What is Proctor's personal decision regarding the confession he makes to witchcraft in the final act?
15. How does Proctor's ultimate choice affect the court's proceedings? How does it affect Proctor's own life and reputation?

A brief denouement can be seen in the concluding lines of *The Crucible*.

16. What is the effect of Proctor's resolution on the other condemned prisoners such as Rebecca Nurse? On his wife Elizabeth? On the court prosecutors?
17. How can we assume that the Salem craze has passed its peak with Proctor's rejection of a forced confession and that more rational conduct will be forthcoming on the part of the citizens—excluding Miller's post-note on the historical facts?

THE CRUCIBLE

Arthur Miller

CHARACTERS
CAST (in order of appearance)

Reverend Parris, a Puritan minister in Salem, Massachusetts
Betty Parris, the minister's daughter, aged ten
Tituba, Parris' Negro slave from Barbados
Abigail Williams, Parris' orphaned niece, aged seventeen
Susanna Walcott, friend and companion of Betty and Abigail
Mrs. Ann Putnam, a middle-aged woman of the village
Thomas Putnam, a well-to-do, hard-handed landowner, near fifty
Mercy Lewis, the Putnams' servant, aged eighteen
Mary Warren, servant to the Proctors, aged seventeen
John Proctor, a farmer in his middle thirties
Rebecca Nurse, seventy-two-year-old woman
Giles Corey, eighty-three-year-old citizen of Salem
Reverend John Hale, from neighboring town of Beverly; aged nearly forty
Elizabeth Proctor, John Proctor's wife
Francis Nurse, Rebecca Nurse's elderly husband; a landowner
Ezekiel Cheever, a local citizen
Marshal Herrick, man in his early thirties
Judge Hathorne, a Salem judge, in his sixties
Deputy Governor Danforth, a powerful administrator, in his sixties
Sarah Good, one of the women jailed during the trials
Hopkins, a guard at the jail

A NOTE ON THE HISTORICAL ACCURACY OF THIS PLAY

This play is not history in the sense in which the word is used by the academic historian. Dramatic purposes have sometimes required many characters to be fused into one; the number of girls involved in the "crying-out" has been reduced; Abigail's age has been raised; while there were several judges of almost equal authority, I have symbolized them all in Hathorne and Danforth. However, I believe that the reader will discover here the essential nature of one of the strangest and most awful chapters in human history. The fate of each character is exactly that of his historical model, and there is no one in the drama who did not play a similar—and in some cases exactly the same—role in history.

As for the characters of the persons, little is known about most of them excepting what may be surmised from a few letters, the trial record, certain broadsides written at the time, and references to their conduct in sources of varying reliability. They may therefore be taken as creations of my own, drawn to the best of my ability in conformity with their known behavior, except as indicated in the commentary I have written for this text.

There are several studies about the Salem trials: Marion L. Starkey, *The Devil in Massachusetts: An Inquiry into the Salem Witch Trials* (New York: Alfred A. Knopf, 1949) and Paul Boyer and Stephen Nissenbaum, eds., *Salem-Village Witchcraft: A Documentary Record of Local Conflict in Colonial New England* (Belmont, Cal.: Wadsworth Pub. Co., 1972).

ACT I

(AN OVERTURE)

A small upper bedroom in the home of Reverend Samuel Parris, Salem, Massachusetts, in the spring of the year 1692.

There is a narrow window at the left. Through its leaded panes the morning sunlight streams. A candle still burns near the bed, which is at the right. A chest, a chair, and a small table are the other furnishings. At the back a door opens on the landing of the stairway to the ground floor. The room gives off an air of clean spareness. The roof rafters are exposed, and the wood colors are raw and unmellowed.

As the curtain rises, Reverend Parris is discovered kneeling beside the bed, evidently in prayer. His daughter, Betty Parris, aged ten, is lying on the bed, inert.

At the time of these events Parris was in his middle forties. In history he cut a villainous path, and there is very little good to be said for him. He believed he was being persecuted wherever he went, despite his best efforts to win people and God to his side. In meeting, he felt insulted if someone rose to shut the door without first asking his permission. He was a widower with no interest in children, or talent with them. He regarded them as young adults, and until this strange crisis he, like the rest of Salem, never conceived that the children were anything but thankful for being permitted to walk straight, eyes slightly lowered, arms at the sides, and mouths shut until bidden to speak.

His house stood in the "town"—but we today would hardly call it a village. The meeting house was nearby, and from this point outward—toward the bay or inland—there were a few small-windowed, dark houses snuggling against the raw Massachusetts winter. Salem had been established hardly forty years before. To the European world the whole province was a barbaric frontier inhabited by a sect of fanatics who, nevertheless, were shipping out products of slowly increasing quantity and value.

No one can really know what their lives were like. They had no novelists—and would not have permitted anyone to read a novel if one were handy. Their creed forbade anything resembling a theater or "vain enjoyment." They did not celebrate Christmas, and a holiday from work meant only that they must concentrate even more upon prayer.

Which is not to say that nothing broke into this strict and somber way of life. When a new farmhouse was built, friends assembled to "raise the roof," and there would be special foods cooked and probably some potent cider passed around. There was a good supply of ne'er-do-wells in Salem, who dallied at the shovelboard in Bridget Bishop's tavern. Probably more than the creed, hard work kept the morals of the place from spoiling, for the people were forced to fight the land like heroes for every grain of corn, and no man had very much time for fooling around.

That there were some jokers, however, is indicated by the practice of appointing a two-man patrol whose duty was to "walk forth in the time of God's worship to take notice of such as either lye about the meeting house, without attending to the word and ordinances, or that lye at home or in the fields without giving good account thereof, and to take the names of such persons, and to present them to the magistrates, whereby they may be accordingly proceeded against." This predilection for minding other people's business was time-honored among the people of Salem, and it undoubtedly created many of the suspicions which were to feed the coming madness. It was also, in my opinion, one of the things that a John

The description of the setting conveys the unadorned quality associated with strict religious zealots. What expository significance is indicated by the burning candle in the bright morning sunlight?

Miller's commentary suggests the mood required for the events of the play. How might one describe the atmosphere in Salem at the time?

Proctor would rebel against, for the time of the armed camp had almost passed, and since the country was reasonably—although not wholly—safe, the old disciplines were beginning to rankle. But, as in all such matters, the issue was not clearcut, for danger was still a possibility, and in unity still lay the best promise of safety.

The edge of the wilderness was close by. The American continent stretched endlessly west, and it was full of mystery for them. It stood, dark and threatening, over their shoulders night and day, for out of it Indian tribes marauded from time to time, and Reverend Parris had parishioners who had lost relatives to these heathen.

The parochial snobbery of these people was partly responsible for their failure to convert the Indians. Probably they also preferred to take land from heathens rather than from fellow Christians. At any rate, very few Indians were converted, and the Salem folk believed that the virgin forest was the Devil's last preserve, his home base and the citadel of his final stand. To the best of their knowledge the American forest was the last place on earth that was not paying homage to God.

For these reasons, among others, they carried about an air of innate resistance, even of persecution. Their fathers had, of course, been persecuted in England. So now they and their church found it necessary to deny any other sect its freedom, lest their New Jerusalem be defiled and corrupted by wrong ways and deceitful ideas.

"New Jerusalem" is synonymous with the City of God, or Heaven. (See Revelation xxi, 2.)

They believed, in short, that they held in their steady hands the candle that would light the world. We have inherited this belief, and it has helped and hurt us. It helped them with the discipline it gave them. They were a dedicated folk, by and large, and they had to be to survive the life they had chosen or been born into in this country.

The proof of their belief's value to them may be taken from the opposite character of the first Jamestown settlement, farther south, in Virginia. The Englishmen who landed there were motivated mainly by a hunt for profit. They had thought to pick off the wealth of the new country and then return rich to England. They were a band of individualists, and a much more ingratiating group than the Massachusetts men. But Virginia destroyed them. Massachusetts tried to kill off the Puritans, but they combined; they set up a communal society which, in the beginning, was little more than an armed camp with an autocratic and very devoted leadership. It was, however, an autocracy by consent, for they were united from top to bottom by a commonly held ideology whose perpetuation was the reason and justification for all their sufferings. So their self-denial, their purposefulness, their suspicion of all vain pursuits, their hard-handed justice, were altogether perfect instruments for the conquest of this space so antagonistic to man.

But the people of Salem in 1692 were not quite the dedicated folk that arrived on the *Mayflower*. A vast differentiation had taken place, and in their own time a revolution had unseated the royal government and substituted a junta which was at this moment in power. The times, to their eyes, must have been out of joint, and to the common folk must have seemed as insoluble and complicated as do ours today. It is not hard to see how easily many could have been led to believe that the time of confusion had been brought upon them by deep and darkling forces. No hint of such speculation appears on the court record, but social disorder in any age breeds such mystical suspicions, and when, as in Salem, wonders are brought forth from below the social surface, it is too much to expect people to hold back very long from laying on the victims with all the force of their frustrations.

The Salem tragedy, which is about to begin in these pages, developed from a paradox. It is a paradox in whose grip we still live, and there is no prospect yet that we will discover its resolution. Simply, it was this: for good purposes, even high purposes, the people of Salem developed a theocracy, a combine of state and religious power whose function was to keep the community together, and to prevent any kind of disunity that might open it to destruction by material or ideological enemies. It was forged for a necessary purpose and accomplished that purpose. But all organization is and must be grounded on the idea of exclusion and prohibition, just as two objects cannot occupy the same space. Evidently the time came in New England when the repressions of order were heavier than seemed warranted by the dangers against which the order was organized. The witch-hunt was a perverse manifestation of the panic which set in among all classes when the balance began to turn toward greater individual freedom.

A theocracy, such as in Salem, meant that the community was governed by a priesthood which claimed divine authority for its decisions and actions.

When one rises above the individual villainy displayed, one can only pity them all, just as we shall be pitied someday. It is still impossible for man to organize his social life without repressions, and the balance has yet to be struck between order and freedom.

The witch-hunt was not, however, a mere repression. It was also, and as importantly, a long overdue opportunity for everyone so inclined to express publicly his guilt and sins, under the cover of accusations against the victims. It suddenly became possible—and patriotic and holy—for a man to say that Martha Corey had come into his bedroom at night, and that, while his wife was sleeping at his side, Martha laid herself down on his chest and "nearly suffocated him." Of course it was her spirit only, but his satisfaction at confessing himself was no lighter than if it had been Martha herself. One could not ordinarily speak such things in public.

Long-held hatreds of neighbors could now be openly expressed, and vengeance taken, despite the Bible's charitable injunctions. Land-lust which had been expressed before by constant bickering over boundaries and deeds, could now be elevated to the arena of morality; one could cry witch against one's neighbor and feel perfectly justified in the bargain. Old scores could be settled on a plane of heavenly combat between Lucifer and the Lord; suspicions and the envy of the miserable toward the happy could and did burst out in the general revenge.

Reverend Parris is praying now, and, though we cannot hear his words, a sense of his confusion hangs about him. He mumbles, then seems about to weep; then he weeps, then prays again; but his daughter does not stir on the bed.

The door opens, and his Negro slave enters. Tituba is in her forties. Parris brought her with him from Barbados, where he spent some years as a merchant before entering the ministry. She enters as one does who can no longer bear to be barred from the sight of her beloved, but she is also very frightened because her slave sense has warned her that, as always, trouble in this house eventually lands on her back.

TITUBA *(already taking a step backward)* My Betty be hearty soon?

PARRIS Out of here!

TITUBA *(backing to the door)* My Betty not goin' die . . .

PARRIS *(scrambling to his feet in a fury)* Out of my sight! *(She is gone.)* Out of my—*(He is overcome with sobs. He clamps his teeth against them and closes the door and leans against it, exhausted.)* Oh, my God! God help me! *(Quaking with fear, mumbling to himself through his sobs, he goes to the bed and gently takes Betty's hand.)* Betty. Child. Dear child. Will you wake, will you open up your eyes! Betty, little one . . .

He is bending to kneel again when his niece, Abigail Williams, seventeen, enters—a strikingly beautiful girl, an orphan, with an endless capacity for dissembling. Now she is all worry and apprehension and propriety.

ABIGAIL Uncle? *(He looks to her.)* Susanna Walcott's here from Doctor Griggs.

PARRIS Oh? Let her come, let her come.

ABIGAIL *(leaning out the door to call to Susanna, who is down the hall a few steps)* Come in, Susanna.

Susanna Walcott, a little younger than Abigail, a nervous, hurried girl, enters.

PARRIS *(eagerly)* What does the doctor say, child?

SUSANNA *(craning around Parris to get a look at Betty)* He bid me come and tell you, reverend sir, that he cannot discover no medicine for it in his books.

PARRIS Then he must search on.

SUSANNA Aye, sir, he have been searchin' his books since he left you, sir. But he bid me tell you, that you might look to unnatural things for the cause of it.

PARRIS *(his eyes going wide)* No—no. There be no unnatural cause here. Tell him I have sent for Reverend Hale of Beverly, and Mr. Hale will surely confirm that. Let him look to medicine and put out all thought of unnatural causes here. There be none.

SUSANNA Aye, sir. He bid me tell you. *(She turns to go.)*

ABIGAIL Speak nothin' of it in the village, Susanna.

PARRIS Go directly home and speak nothing of unnatural causes.

SUSANNA Aye, sir. I pray for her. *(She goes out.)*

ABIGAIL Uncle, the rumor of witchcraft is all about; I think you'd best go down and deny it yourself. The parlor's packed with people, sir. I'll sit with her.

PARRIS *(pressed, turns on her)* And what shall I say to them? That my daughter and my niece I discovered dancing like heathen in the forest?

ABIGAIL Uncle, we did dance; let you tell them I confessed it—and I'll be whipped if I must be. But they're speakin' of witchcraft. Betty's not witched.

PARRIS Abigail, I cannot go before the congregation when I know you have not opened with me. What did you do with her in the forest?

How is a sense of acute fear created within the first lines and stage movements in Act I?

A fundamental attitude of the time is reflected in the doctor's diagnosis: since he can find no medical cause for Betty's coma, then an "unnatural" reason must be involved.

What is appropriate about the woods as a locale for dancing? (See Miller's comment in his introduction.)

ABIGAIL We did dance, uncle, and when you leaped out of the bush so suddenly, Betty was frightened and then she fainted. And there's the whole of it.

PARRIS Child. Sit you down.

ABIGAIL (*quavering, as she sits*) I would never hurt Betty. I love her dearly.

PARRIS Now look you, child, your punishment will come in its time. But if you trafficked with spirits in the forest I must know it now, for surely my enemies will, and they will ruin me with it.

ABIGAIL But we never conjured spirits.

PARRIS Then why can she not move herself since midnight? This child is desperate! (*Abigail lowers her eyes.*) It must come out—my enemies will bring it out. Let me know what you done there. Abigail, do you understand that I have many enemies?

ABIGAIL I have heard of it, uncle.

PARRIS There is a faction that is sworn to drive me from my pulpit. Do you understand that?

ABIGAIL I think so, sir.

PARRIS Now then, in the midst of such disruption, my own household is discovered to be the very center of some obscene practice. Abominations are done in the forest—

ABIGAIL It were sport, uncle!

PARRIS (*pointing at Betty*) You call this sport? (*She lowers her eyes. He pleads.*) Abigail, if you know something that may help the doctor, for God's sake tell it to me. (*She is silent.*) I saw Tituba waving her arms over the fire when I came on you. Why was she doing that? And I heard a screeching and gibberish coming from her mouth. She were swaying like a dumb beast over that fire!

ABIGAIL She always sings her Barbados songs, and we dance.

PARRIS I cannot blink what I saw, Abigail, for my enemies will not blink it. I saw a dress lying on the grass.

ABIGAIL (*innocently*) A dress?

PARRIS —(*It is very hard to say.*) Aye, a dress. And I thought I saw—someone naked running through the trees!

ABIGAIL (*in terror*) No one was naked! You mistake yourself, uncle!

PARRIS (*with anger*) I saw it! (*He moves from her. Then, resolved.*) Now tell me true, Abigail. And I pray you feel the weight of truth upon you, for now my ministry's at stake, my ministry and perhaps your cousin's life. Whatever abomination you have done, give me all of it now, for I dare not be taken unaware when I go before them down there.

ABIGAIL There is nothin' more. I swear it, uncle.

PARRIS (*studies her, then nods, half convinced*) Abigail, I have fought here three long years to bend these stiff-necked people to me, and now, just now when some good respect is rising for me in the parish, you compromise my very character. I have given you a home, child, I have put clothes upon your back—now give me upright answer. Your name in the town—it is entirely white, is it not?

According to Parris, why is he in trouble with the townspeople concerning the rumors of suspected witchcraft?

What is the true source of Parris' concern? What evil was done? How is his name involved in the evil? How will these deeds affect his position in the community? Compare Parris' reaction to the challenge to his reputation with that of Peter Stockmann in *An Enemy of the People*.

Miller here uses sound logic in directing his audience toward an awareness of Abigail's questionable character.

ABIGAIL *(with an edge of resentment)* Why, I am sure it is, sir. There be no blush about my name.

PARRIS *(to the point)* Abigail, is there any other cause than you have told me, for your being discharged from Goody Proctor's service? I have heard it said, and I tell you as I heard it, that she comes so rarely to the church this year for she will not sit so close to something soiled. What signified that remark?

ABIGAIL She hates me, uncle, she must, for I would not be her slave. It's a bitter woman, a lying, cold, sniveling woman, and I will not work for such a woman!

PARRIS She may be. And yet it has troubled me that you are now seven month out of their house, and in all this time no other family has ever called for your service.

ABIGAIL They want slaves, not such as I. Let them send to Barbados for that. I will not black my face for any of them! *(with ill-concealed resentment at him)* Do you begrudge my bed, uncle?

PARRIS No—no.

ABIGAIL *(in a temper)* My name is good in the village! I will not have it said my name is soiled! Goody Proctor is a gossiping liar!

Enter Mrs. Ann Putnam. She is a twisted soul of forty-five, a death-ridden woman, haunted by dreams.

PARRIS *(as soon as the door begins to open)* No—no, I cannot have anyone. *(He sees her, and a certain deference springs into him, although his worry remains.)* Why, Goody Putnam, come in.

MRS. PUTNAM *(full of breath, shiny-eyed)* It is a marvel. It is surely a stroke of hell upon you.

PARRIS No, Goody Putnam, it is—

MRS. PUTNAM *(glancing at Betty)* How high did she fly, how high?

PARRIS No, no, she never flew—

MRS. PUTNAM *(very pleased with it)* Why, it's sure she did. Mr. Collins saw her goin' over Ingersoll's barn, and come down light as bird, he says!

PARRIS Now, look you, Goody Putnam, she never—*(enter Thomas Putnam, a well-to-do, hard-handed landowner, near fifty)* Oh, good morning, Mr. Putnam.

PUTNAM It is a providence the thing is out now! It is a providence. *(He goes directly to the bed.)*

PARRIS What's out, sir, what's—?

Mrs. Putnam goes to the bed.

PUTNAM *(looking down at Betty)* Why, her eyes is closed! Look you, Ann.

MRS. PUTNAM Why, that's strange. *(to Parris)* Ours is open.

PARRIS *(shocked)* Your Ruth is sick?

MRS. PUTNAM *(with vicious certainty)* I'd not call it sick; the Devil's touch is heavier than sick. It's death, y'know, it's death drivin' into them, forked and hoofed.

"Goody" is a variation of the term "goodwife," an archaic word used before a surname when addressing a married woman of common social rank. The male equivalent for the term is "goodman," a title of civility applied to the surname of a man below the rank of gentleman.

Mrs. Putnam represents a type of person frequently found in any community. What is she like?

PARRIS Oh, pray not! Why, how does Ruth ail?

MRS. PUTNAM She ails as she must—she never waked this morning, but her eyes open and she walks, and hears naught, sees naught, and cannot eat. Her soul is taken, surely

Parris is struck.

PUTNAM *(as though for further details)* They say you've sent for Reverend Hale of Beverly?

PARRIS *(with dwindling conviction now)* A precaution only. He has much experience in all demonic arts, and I—

MRS. PUTNAM He has indeed; and found a witch in Beverly last year, and let you remember that.

PARRIS Now, Goody Ann, they only thought that were a witch, and I am certain there be no element of witchcraft here.

PUTNAM No witchcraft! Now look you, Mr. Parris—

PARRIS Thomas, Thomas, I pray you, leap not to witchcraft. I know that you—you least of all, Thomas, would ever wish so disastrous a charge laid upon me. We cannot leap to witchcraft. They will howl me out of Salem for such corruption in my house.

> Reverend Hale is being summoned as an expert on evil spirits. How does this fact correlate with Parris' denial of any witchcraft being involved?

A word about Thomas Putnam. He was a man with many grievances, at least one of which appears justified. Some time before, his wife's brother-in-law, James Bayley, had been turned down as minister at Salem. Bayley had all the qualifications, and a two-thirds vote into the bargain, but a faction stopped his acceptance, for reasons that are not clear.

Thomas Putnam was the eldest son of the richest man in the village. He had fought the Indians at Narragansett, and was deeply interested in parish affairs. He undoubtedly felt it poor payment that the village should so blatantly disregard his candidate for one of its more important offices, especially since he regarded himself as the intellectual superior of most of the people around him.

His vindictive nature was demonstrated long before the witchcraft began. Another former Salem minister, George Burroughs, had had to borrow money to pay for his wife's funeral, and, since the parish was remiss in his salary, he was soon bankrupt. Thomas and his brother John had Burroughs jailed for debts the man did not owe. The incident is important only in that Burroughs succeeded in becoming minister where Bayley, Thomas Putnam's brother-in-law, had been rejected; the motif of resentment is clear here. Thomas Putnam felt that his own name and the honor of his family had been smirched by the village, and he meant to right matters however he could.

> Notice the differences between prose narrative and drama by comparing these long prose inserts with the regular dialogue of the play. Here, Miller *tells* his readers what he wants them to know about Putnam and his background. But in the following pages of the play, Miller *shows* his readers what Putnam is like by letting the character speak and act for himself.

Another reason to believe him a deeply embittered man was his attempt to break his father's will, which left a disproportionate amount to a stepbrother. As with every other public cause in which he tried to force his way, he failed in this.

So it is not surprising to find that so many accusations against people are in the handwriting of Thomas Putnam, or that his name is so often found as a witness corroborating the supernatural testimony, or that his daughter led the crying-out at the most opportune junctures of the trials, especially when—But we'll speak of that when we come to it.

> Through these inserted commentaries, what kind of motivation for Putnam's actions is established?

THE CRUCIBLE

PUTNAM —(*At the moment he is intent upon getting Parris, for whom he has only contempt, to move toward the abyss.*) Mr. Parris, I have taken your part in all contention here, and I would continue; but I cannot if you hold back in this. There are hurtful, vengeful spirits layin' hands on these children.

PARRIS But, Thomas, you cannot—

PUTNAM Ann! Tell Mr. Parris what you have done.

MRS. PUTNAM Reverend Parris, I have laid seven babies unbaptized in the earth. Believe me, sir, you never saw more hearty babies born. And yet, each would wither in my arms the very night of their birth. I have spoke nothin', but my heart has clamored intimations. And now, this year, my Ruth, my only— I see her turning strange. A secret child she has become this year, and shrivels like a sucking mouth were pullin' on her life too. And so I thought to send her to your Tituba—

PARRIS To Tituba! What may Tituba—?

MRS. PUTNAM Tituba knows how to speak to the dead, Mr. Parris.

PARRIS Goody Ann, it is a formidable sin to conjure up the dead!

MRS. PUTNAM I take it on my soul, but who else may surely tell us what person murdered my babies?

PARRIS (*horrified*) Woman!

MRS. PUTNAM They were murdered, Mr. Parris! And mark this proof! Mark it! Last night my Ruth were ever so close to their little spirits; I know it, sir. For how else is she struck dumb now except some power of darkness would stop her mouth? It is a marvelous sign, Mr. Parris!

PUTNAM Don't you understand it, sir? There is a murdering witch among us, bound to keep herself in the dark. (*Parris turns to Betty, a frantic terror rising in him.*) Let your names make of it what they will, you cannot blink it more.

PARRIS (*to Abigail*) Then you were conjuring spirits last night.

ABIGAIL (*whispering*) Not I, sir—Tituba and Ruth.

PARRIS (*turns now, with new fear, and goes to Betty, looks down at her, and then, gazing off*) Oh, Abigail, what proper payment for my charity! Now I am undone.

PUTNAM You are not undone! Let you take hold here. Wait for no one to charge you—declare it yourself. You have discovered witchcraft—

PARRIS In my house? In my house, Thomas? They will topple me with this! They will make of it a—

Enter Mercy Lewis, the Putnams' servant, a fat, sly, merciless girl of eighteen.

MERCY Your pardons. I only thought to see how Betty is.

PUTNAM Why aren't you home? Who's with Ruth?

MERCY Her grandma come. She's improved a little, I think—she give a powerful sneeze before.

MRS. PUTNAM Ah, there's a sign of life!

Human nature is evident here, as Putnam, whose wife has encouraged the conjuring of dead spirits, insists that Parris confess spiritual misdeeds in his household.

MERCY I'd fear no more, Goody Putnam. It were a grand sneeze; another like it will shake her wits together, I'm sure. *(She goes to the bed to look.)*

PARRIS Will you leave me now, Thomas? I would pray a while alone.

ABIGAIL Uncle, you've prayed since midnight. Why do you not go down and—

PARRIS No—no. *(to Putnam)* I have no answer for that crowd. I'll wait till Mr. Hale arrives. *(to get Mrs. Putnam to leave)* If you will, Goody Ann . . .

PUTNAM Now look you, sir. Let you strike out against the Devil, and the village will bless you for it! Come down, speak to them—pray with them. They're thirsting for your word, Mister! Surely you'll pray with them.

PARRIS *(swayed)* I'll lead them in a psalm, but let you say nothing of witchcraft yet. I will not discuss it. The cause is yet unknown. I have had enough contention since I came; I want no more.

MRS. PUTNAM Mercy, you go home to Ruth, d'y'hear?

MERCY Aye, mum.

Mrs. Putnam goes out.

PARRIS *(to Abigail)* If she starts for the window, cry for me at once.

ABIGAIL I will, uncle.

PARRIS *(to Putnam)* There is a terrible power in her arms today. *(He goes out with Putnam.)*

ABIGAIL *(with hushed trepidation)* How is Ruth sick?

MERCY It's weirdish, I know not—she seems to walk like a dead one since last night.

ABIGAIL *(turns at once and goes to Betty, and now, with fear in her voice)* Betty? *(Betty doesn't move. She shakes her.)* Now stop this! Betty! Sit up now!

Betty doesn't stir. Mercy comes over.

MERCY Have you tried beatin' her? I gave Ruth a good one and it waked her for a minute. Here, let me have her.

ABIGAIL *(holding Mercy back)* No, he'll be comin' up. Listen, now; if they be questioning us, tell them we danced—I told him as much already.

MERCY Aye. And what more?

ABIGAIL He knows Tituba conjured Ruth's sisters to come out of the grave.

MERCY And what more?

ABIGAIL He saw you naked.

MERCY *(clapping her hands together with a frightened laugh)* Oh, Jesus!

Enter Mary Warren, breathless. She is seventeen, a subservient, naive, lonely girl.

MARY WARREN What'll we do? The village is out! I just come from the

From the manner of Abigail and Mercy in trying to rouse Betty, does it seem plausible that they genuinely believe evil powers are involved in the comas of their friends? Why?

farm; the whole country's talkin' witchcraft! They'll be callin' us witches, Abby!

MERCY *(pointing and looking at Mary Warren)* She means to tell, I know it.

MARY WARREN Abby, we've got to tell. Witchery's a hangin' error, a hangin' like they done in Boston two year ago! We must tell the truth, Abby! You'll only be whipped for dancin', and the other things!

ABIGAIL Oh, *we'll* be whipped!

MARY WARREN I never done none of it, Abby. I only looked!

MERCY *(moving menacingly toward Mary)* Oh, you're a great one for lookin', aren't you, Mary Warren? What a grand peeping courage you have!

Betty, on the bed, whimpers. Abigail turns to her at once.

ABIGAIL Betty? *(She goes to Betty.)* Now, Betty, dear, wake up now. It's Abigail. *(She sits Betty up and furiously shakes her.)* I'll beat you, Betty! *(Betty whimpers.)* My, you seem improving. I talked to your papa and I told him everything. So there's nothing to—

BETTY *(darts off the bed, frightened of Abigail, and flattens herself against the wall)* I want my mama!

ABIGAIL *(with alarm, as she cautiously approaches Betty)* What ails you, Betty? Your mama's dead and buried.

BETTY I'll fly to Mama. Let me fly! *(She raises her arms as though to fly, and streaks for the window, gets one leg out.)*

ABIGAIL *(pulling her away from the window)* I told him everything; he knows now, he knows everything we—

BETTY You drank blood, Abby! You didn't tell him that!

ABIGAIL Betty, you never say that again! You will never—

BETTY You did, you did! You drank a charm to kill John Proctor's wife! You drank a charm to kill Goody Proctor!

ABIGAIL *(smashes her across the face)* Shut it! Now shut it!

BETTY *(collapsing on the bed)* Mama, Mama! *(She dissolves into sobs.)*

ABIGAIL Now look you. All of you. We danced. And Tituba conjured Ruth Putnam's dead sisters. And that is all. And mark this. Let either of you breathe a word, or the edge of a word, about the other things, and I will come to you in the black of some terrible night and I will bring a pointy reckoning that will shudder you. And you know I can do it; I saw Indians smash my dear parents' heads on the pillow next to mine, and I have seen some reddish work done at night, and I can make you wish you had never seen the sun go down! *(She goes to Betty and roughly sits her up.)* Now, you—sit up and stop this!

But Betty collapses in her hands and lies inert on the bed.

MARY WARREN *(with hysterical fright)* What's got her? *(Abigail stares in fright at Betty.)* Abby, she's going to die! It's a sin to conjure, and we—

ABIGAIL *(starting for Mary)* I say shut it, Mary Warren!

Miller increases the tension by revealing to the audience the true nature of the young girls caught up in the witch scandal. Who is the ringleader among the girls, and how do we know?

284 ARTHUR MILLER

Enter John Proctor. On seeing him, Mary Warren leaps in fright.

Proctor was a farmer in his middle thirties. He need not have been a partisan of any faction in the town, but there is evidence to suggest that he had a sharp and biting way with hypocrites. He was the kind of man—powerful of body, even-tempered, and not easily led—who cannot refuse support to partisans without drawing their deepest resentment. In Proctor's presence a fool felt his foolishness instantly—and a Proctor is always marked for calumny therefore.

But as we shall see, the steady manner he displays does not spring from an untroubled soul. He is a sinner, a sinner not only against the moral fashion of the time, but against his own vision of decent conduct. These people had no ritual for the washing away of sins. It is another trait we inherited from them, and it has helped to discipline us as well as to breed hypocrisy among us. Proctor, respected and even feared in Salem, has come to regard himself as a kind of fraud. But no hint of this has yet appeared on the surface, and as he enters from the crowded parlor below it is a man in his prime we see, with a quiet confidence and an unexpressed, hidden force. Mary Warren, his servant, can barely speak for embarrassment and fear.

Miller's discussion of Proctor, though not available to a live theater audience, can be read carefully for the clues it offers the actor playing the role of Proctor and how others would react to him in the play.

MARY WARREN Oh! I'm just going home, Mr. Proctor.

PROCTOR Be you foolish, Mary Warren? Be you deaf? I forbid you leave the house, did I not? Why shall I pay you? I am looking for you more often than my cows!

MARY WARREN I only come to see the great doings in the world.

PROCTOR I'll show you a great doin' on your arse one of these days. Now get you home; my wife is waitin' with your work! *(Trying to retain a shred of dignity, she goes slowly out.)*

MERCY LEWIS *(both afraid of him and strangely titillated)* I'd best be off. I have my Ruth to watch. Good morning, Mr. Proctor.

Mercy sidles out. Since Proctor's entrance, Abigail has stood as though on tiptoe, absorbing his presence, wide-eyed. He glances at her then goes to Betty on the bed.

ABIGAIL Gad. I'd almost forgot how strong you are, John Proctor!

PROCTOR *(looking at Abigail now, the faintest suggestion of a knowing smile on his face)* What's this mischief here?

ABIGAIL *(with a nervous laugh)* Oh, she's only gone silly somehow.

PROCTOR The road past my house is a pilgrimage to Salem all morning. The town's mumbling witchcraft.

ABIGAIL Oh, posh! *(Winningly she comes a little closer, with a confidential, wicked air.)* We were dancin' in the woods last night, and my uncle leaped in on us. She took fright, is all.

PROCTOR *(his smile widening)* Ah, you're wicked yet, aren't y'! *(A trill of expectant laughter escapes her, and she dares come closer, feverishly looking into his eyes.)* You'll be clapped in the stocks before you're twenty.

He takes a step to go, and she springs into his path.

ABIGAIL Give me a word, John. A soft word. *(Her concentrated desire destroys his smile.)*

The lines "you're wicked yet" and "That's done with" suggest what kind of a past relationship between Proctor and Abigail?

THE CRUCIBLE 285

PROCTOR No, no, Abby. That's done with.

ABIGAIL *(tauntingly)* You come five mile to see a silly girl fly? I know you better.

PROCTOR *(setting her firmly out of his path)* I come to see what mischief your uncle's brewin' now. *(with final emphasis)* Put it out of mind, Abby.

ABIGAIL *(grasping his hand before he can release her)* John—I am waitin' for you every night.

PROCTOR Abby, I never give you hope to wait for me.

ABIGAIL *(Now beginning to anger—she can't believe it.)* I have somethin' better than hope, I think!

PROCTOR Abby, you'll put it out of mind. I'll not be comin' for you more.

> What are the new complications between Proctor and Abigail?

ABIGAIL You're surely sportin' with me.

PROCTOR You know me better.

ABIGAIL I know how you clutched my back behind your house and sweated like a stallion whenever I come near! Or did I dream that? It's she put me out, you cannot pretend it were you. I saw your face when she put me out, and you loved me then and you do now!

PROCTOR Abby, that's a wild thing to say—

ABIGAIL A wild thing may say wild things. But not so wild, I think. I have seen you since she put me out; I have seen you nights.

PROCTOR I have hardly stepped off my farm this seven-month.

ABIGAIL I have a sense for heat, John, and yours has drawn me to my window, and I have seen you looking up, burning in your loneliness. Do you tell me you've never looked up at my window?

PROCTOR I may have looked up.

ABIGAIL *(now softening)* And you must. You are no wintry man. I know you, John. I *know* you. *(She is weeping.)* I cannot sleep for dreamin'; I cannot dream but I wake and walk about the house as though I'd find you comin' through some door. *(She clutches him desperately.)*

PROCTOR *(gently pressing her from him, with great sympathy but firmly)* Child—

ABIGAIL *(with a flash of anger)* How do you call me child!

PROCTOR Abby, I may think of you softly from time to time. But I will cut off my hand before I'll ever reach for you again. Wipe it out of mind. We never touched, Abby.

ABIGAIL Aye, but we did.

PROCTOR Aye, but we did not.

ABIGAIL *(with a bitter anger)* Oh, I marvel how such a strong man may let such a sickly wife be—

PROCTOR *(angered—at himself as well)* You'll speak nothin' of Elizabeth!

ABIGAIL She is blackening my name in the village! She is telling lies about me! She is a cold, sniveling woman, and you bend to her! Let her turn you like a—

PROCTOR *(shaking her)* Do you look for whippin'?

A psalm is heard being sung below.

ABIGAIL *(in tears)* I look for John Proctor that took me from my sleep and put knowledge in my heart! I never knew what pretense Salem was, I never knew the lying lessons I was taught by all these Christian women and their covenanted men! And now you bid me tear the light out of my eyes? I will not, I cannot! You loved me, John Proctor, and whatever sin it is, you love me yet! *(He turns abruptly to go out. She rushes to him.)* John, pity me, pity me!

The words "going up to Jesus" are heard in the psalm, and Betty claps her ears suddenly and whines loudly.

ABIGAIL Betty? *(She hurries to Betty, who is now sitting up and screaming. Proctor goes to Betty as Abigail is trying to pull her hands down, calling "Betty!")*

PROCTOR *(growing unnerved)* What's she doing? Girl, what ails you? Stop that wailing!

The singing has stopped in the midst of this, and now Parris rushes in.

PARRIS What happened? What are you doing to her? Betty! *(He rushes to the bed, crying, "Betty, Betty!" Mrs. Putnam enters, feverish with curiosity, and with her Thomas Putnam and Mercy Lewis. Parris, at the bed, keeps lightly slapping Betty's face, while she moans and tries to get up.)*

ABIGAIL She heard you singin' and suddenly she's up and screamin'.

MRS. PUTNAM The psalm! The psalm! She cannot bear to hear the Lord's name!

PARRIS No, God forbid. Mercy, run to the doctor! Tell him what's happened here! *(Mercy Lewis rushes out.)*

MRS. PUTNAM Mark it for a sign, mark it!

Rebecca Nurse, seventy-two, enters. She is white-haired, leaning upon her walking-stick.

PUTNAM *(pointing at the whimpering Betty)* That is a notorious sign of witchcraft afoot, Goody Nurse, a prodigious sign!

MRS. PUTNAM My mother told me that! When they cannot bear to hear the name of—

PARRIS *(trembling)* Rebecca, Rebecca, go to her, we're lost. She suddenly cannot bear to hear the Lord's—

Giles Corey, eighty-three, enters. He is knotted with muscle, canny, inquisitive, and still powerful.

REBECCA There is hard sickness here, Giles Corey, so please to keep the quiet.

GILES I've not said a word. No one here can testify I've said a word. Is she going to fly again? I hear she flies.

PUTNAM Man, be quiet now!

What do Betty's sudden actions reveal—that she does not want to hear the psalm, or that she does not want to hear any more of the conversation between Abigail and Proctor?

Everything is quiet. Rebecca walks across the room to the bed. Gentleness exudes from her. Betty is quietly whimpering, eyes shut. Rebecca simply stands over the child, who gradually quiets.

And while they are so absorbed, we may put a word in for Rebecca. Rebecca was the wife of Francis Nurse, who, from all accounts, was one of those men for whom both sides of the argument had to have respect. He was called upon to arbitrate disputes as though he were an unofficial judge, and Rebecca also enjoyed the high opinion most people had for him. By the time of the delusion, they had three hundred acres, and their children were settled in separate homesteads within the same estate. However, Francis had originally rented the land, and one theory has it that, as he gradually paid for it and raised his social status, there were those who resented his rise.

Another suggestion to explain the systematic campaign against Rebecca, and inferentially against Francis, is the land war he fought with his neighbors, one of whom was a Putnam. This squabble grew to the proportions of a battle in the woods between partisans of both sides, and it is said to have lasted for two days. As for Rebecca herself, the general opinion of her character was so high that to explain how anyone dared cry her out for a witch—and more, how adults could bring themselves to lay hands on her—we must look to the fields and boundaries of that time.

As we have seen, Thomas Putnam's man for the Salem ministry was Bayley. The Nurse clan had been in the faction that prevented Bayley's taking office. In addition, certain families allied to the Nurses by blood or friendship, and whose farms were contiguous with the Nurse farm or close to it, combined to break away from the Salem town authority and set up Topsfield, a new and independent entity whose existence was resented by old Salemites.

That the guiding hand behind the outcry was Putnam's is indicated by the fact that, as soon as it began, this Topsfield-Nurse faction absented themselves from church in protest and disbelief. It was Edward and Jonathan Putnam who signed the first complaint against Rebecca; and Thomas Putnam's little daughter was the one who fell into a fit at the hearing and pointed to Rebecca as her attacker. To top it all, Mrs. Putnam—who is now staring at the bewitched child on the bed—soon accused Rebecca's spirit of "tempting her to iniquity," a charge that had more truth in it than Mrs. Putnam could know.

> Without this background sketch of Rebecca Nurse, her function both as a mediator and as a model for behavior in the final act would not be clear.

MRS. PUTNAM *(astonished)* What have you done?

Rebecca, in thought, now leaves the bedside and sits.

PARRIS *(wondrous and relieved)* What do you make of it, Rebecca?

PUTNAM *(eagerly)* Goody Nurse, will you go to my Ruth and see if you can wake her?

REBECCA *(sitting)* I think she'll wake in time. Pray calm yourselves. I have eleven children, and I am twenty-six times a grandma, and I have seen them all through their silly seasons, and when it come on them they will run the Devil bowlegged keeping up with their mischief. I think she'll wake when she tires of it. A child's spirit is like a child, you can never catch it by running after it; you must stand still, and, for love, it will soon itself come back.

> What is Rebecca Nurse's diagnosis of the girls' ailments? Note that John Proctor agrees with her entirely.

PROCTOR Aye, that's the truth of it, Rebecca.

MRS. PUTNAM This is no silly season, Rebecca. My Ruth is bewildered, Rebecca; she cannot eat.

REBECCA Perhaps she is not hungered yet. *(to Parris)* I hope you are not decided to go in search of loose spirits, Mr. Parris. I've heard promise of that outside.

PARRIS A wide opinion's running in the parish that the Devil may be among us, and I would satisfy them that they are wrong.

PROCTOR Then let you come out and call them wrong. Did you consult the wardens before you called this minister to look for devils?

PARRIS He is not coming to look for devils!

PROCTOR Then what's he coming for?

PUTNAM There be children dyin' in the village, Mister!

PROCTOR I seen none dyin'. This society will not be a bag to swing around your head, Mr. Putnam. *(to Parris)* Did you call a meeting before you—?

PUTNAM I am sick of meetings; cannot the man turn his head without he have a meeting?

PROCTOR He may turn his head, but not to Hell!

REBECCA Pray, John, be calm. *(Pause. He defers to her.)* Mr. Parris, I think you'd best send Reverend Hale back as soon as he come. This will set us all to arguin' again in the society, and we thought to have peace this year. I think we ought rely on the doctor now, and good prayer.

MRS. PUTNAM Rebecca, the doctor's baffled!

REBECCA If so he is, then let us go to God for the cause of it. There is prodigious danger in the seeking of loose spirits. I fear it, I fear it. Let us rather blame ourselves and—

What philosophical positions are in tension in this scene?

PUTNAM How may we blame ourselves? I am one of nine sons; the Putnam seed have peopled this province. And yet I have but one child left of eight—and now she shrivels!

REBECCA I cannot fathom that.

MRS. PUTNAM *(with a growing edge of sarcasm)* But I must! You think it God's work you should never lose a child, nor grandchild either, and I bury all but one? There are wheels within wheels in this village, and fires within fires!

Why does Ann Putnam resent Rebecca Nurse?

PUTNAM *(to Parris)* When Reverend Hale comes, you will proceed to look for signs of witchcraft here.

PROCTOR *(to Putnam)* You cannot command Mr. Parris. We vote by name in this society, not by acreage.

PUTNAM I never heard you worried so on this society, Mr. Proctor. I do not think I saw you at Sabbath meeting since snow flew.

PROCTOR I have trouble enough without I come five mile to hear him preach only hellfire and bloody damnation. Take it to heart, Mr. Parris. There are many others who stay away from church these days because you hardly ever mention God any more.

Does it sound as though Parris' God is one of mercy or of judgment?

THE CRUCIBLE

PARRIS *(now aroused)* Why, that's a drastic charge!

REBECCA It's somewhat true; there are many that quail to bring their children—

PARRIS I do not preach for children, Rebecca. It is not the children who are unmindful of their obligations toward this ministry.

REBECCA Are there really those unmindful?

PARRIS I should say the better half of Salem village—

PUTNAM And more than that!

PARRIS Where is my wood? My contract provides I be supplied with all my firewood. I am waiting since November for a stick, and even in November I had to show my frostbitten hands like some London beggar!

GILES You are allowed six pound a year to buy your wood, Mr. Parris.

PARRIS I regard that six pound as part of my salary. I am paid little enough without I spend six pound on firewood.

PROCTOR Sixty, plus six for firewood—

PARRIS The salary is sixty-six pound, Mr. Proctor! I am not some preaching farmer with a book under my arm; I am a graduate of Harvard College.

GILES Aye, and well instructed in arithmetic!

PARRIS Mr. Corey, you will look far for a man of my kind at sixty pound a year! I am not used to this poverty; I left a thrifty business in the Barbados to serve the Lord. I do not fathom it, why am I persecuted here? I cannot offer one proposition but there be a howling riot of argument. I have often wondered if the Devil be in it somewhere; I cannot understand you people otherwise.

PROCTOR Mr. Parris, you are the first minister ever did demand the deed to this house—

PARRIS Man! Don't a minister deserve a house to live in?

PROCTOR To live in, yes. But to ask ownership is like you shall own the meeting house itself; the last meeting I were at you spoke so long on deeds and mortgages I thought it were an auction.

PARRIS I want a mark of confidence, is all! I am your third preacher in seven years. I do not wish to be put out like the cat whenever some majority feels the whim. You people seem not to comprehend that a minister is the Lord's man in the parish; a minister is not to be so lightly crossed and contradicted—

PUTNAM Aye!

PARRIS There is either obedience or the church will burn like Hell is burning!

PROCTOR Can you speak one minute without we land in Hell again? I am sick of Hell!

PARRIS It is not for you to say what is good for you to hear!

PROCTOR I may speak my heart, I think!

Why does Parris respond so sensitively to Proctor's words?

One of the frictions in a theocracy is shown in the backbiting which erupts in this section.

Salem was a Puritan community in which the idea of society as a theocracy was dominant. According to Puritan doctrine, God ruled in civil matters with His laws being interpreted by church authority. Life was to be lived in strict accordance with the detailed laws of God as read in the Bible and as interpreted by the ministers of the church. Why, then, does Parris insist on "obedience" from Proctor and the others?

PARRIS (*in a fury*) What, are we Quakers? We are not Quakers here yet, Mr. Proctor. And you may tell that to your followers!

PROCTOR My followers!

PARRIS (*Now he's out with it.*) There is a party in this church. I am not blind; there is a faction and a party.

PROCTOR Against you?

PUTNAM Against him and all authority!

PROCTOR Why, then I must find it and join it.

There is shock among the others.

REBECCA He does not mean that.

PUTNAM He confessed it now!

PROCTOR I mean it solemnly, Rebecca; I like not the smell of this "authority."

REBECCA No, you cannot break charity with your minister. You are another kind, John. Clasp his hand, make your peace.

PROCTOR I have a crop to sow and lumber to drag home. (*He goes angrily to the door and turns to Corey with a smile.*) What say you, Giles, let's find the party. He says there's a party.

GILES I've changed my opinion of this man, John. Mr. Parris, I beg your pardon. I never thought you had so much iron in you.

PARRIS (*surprised*) Why, thank you, Giles!

GILES It suggests to the mind what the trouble be among us all these years. (*to all*) Think on it. Wherefore is everybody suing everybody else? Think on it now, it's a deep thing, and dark as a pit. I have been six time in court this year—

PROCTOR (*familiarly, with warmth, although he knows he is approaching the edge of Giles' tolerance with this*) Is it the Devil's fault that a man cannot say you good morning without you clap him for defamation? You're old, Giles, and you're not hearin' so well as you did.

GILES (*He cannot be crossed.*) John Proctor, I have only last month collected four pound damages for you publicly sayin' I burned the roof off your house, and I—

PROCTOR (*laughing*) I never said no such thing, but I've paid you for it, so I hope I can call you deaf without charge. Now come along, Giles, and help me drag my lumber home.

PUTNAM A moment, Mr. Proctor. What lumber is that you're draggin', if I may ask you?

PROCTOR My lumber. From out my forest by the riverside.

PUTNAM Why, we are surely gone wild this year. What anarchy is this? That tract is in my bounds, it's in my bounds, Mr. Proctor.

PROCTOR In your bounds! (*indicating Rebecca*) I bought that tract from Goody Nurse's husband five months ago.

PUTNAM He had no right to sell it. It stands clear in my grandfather's will that all the land between the river and—

Quakers (members of the Society of Friends) believed that a person needed no spiritual intermediary (such as a minister or church) but could find understanding individually through "inward light" supplied by the Holy Spirit. Why does Parris attack Proctor by implying that Proctor thinks like a Quaker?

PROCTOR Your grandfather had a habit of willing land that never belonged to him, if I may say it plain.

GILES That's God's truth; he nearly willed away my north pasture but he knew I'd break his fingers before he'd set his name to it. Let's get your lumber home, John. I feel a sudden will to work coming on.

PUTNAM You load one oak of mine and you'll fight to drag it home!

GILES Aye, and we'll win too, Putnam—this fool and I. Come on! *(He turns to Proctor and starts out.)*

PUTNAM I'll have my men on you, Corey! I'll clap a writ on you!

Enter Reverend John Hale of Beverly.

Mr. Hale is nearing forty, a tight-skinned, eager-eyed intellectual. This is a beloved errand for him; on being called here to ascertain witchcraft he felt the pride of the specialist whose unique knowledge has at last been publicly called for. Like almost all men of learning, he spent a good deal of his time pondering the invisible world, especially since he had himself encountered a witch in his parish not long before. That woman, however, turned into a mere pest under his searching scrutiny, and the child she had allegedly been afflicting recovered her normal behavior after Hale had given her his kindness and a few days of rest in his own house. However, that experience never raised a doubt in his mind as to the reality of the underworld or the existence of Lucifer's many-faced lieutenants. And his belief is not to his discredit. Better minds than Hale's were—and still are—convinced that there is a society of spirits beyond our ken. One cannot help noting that one of his lines has never yet raised a laugh in any audience that has seen this play; it is his assurance that "We cannot look to superstition in this. The Devil is precise." Evidently we are not quite certain even now whether diabolism is holy and not to be scoffed at. And it is no accident that we should be so bemused.

Like Reverend Hale and the others on this stage, we conceive the Devil as a necessary part of a respectable view of cosmology. Ours is a divided empire in which certain ideas and emotions and actions are of God, and their opposites are of Lucifer. It is as impossible for most men to conceive of a morality without sin as of an earth without "sky." Since 1692 a great but superficial change has wiped out God's beard and the Devil's horns, but the world is still gripped between two diametrically opposed absolutes. The concept of unity, in which positive and negative are attributes of the same force, in which good and evil are relative, ever-changing, and always joined to the same phenomenon—such a concept is still reserved to the physical sciences and to the few who have grasped the history of ideas. When it is recalled that until the Christian era the underworld was never regarded as a hostile area, that all gods were useful and essentially friendly to man despite occasional lapses; when we see the steady and methodical inculcation into humanity of the idea of man's worthlessness—until redeemed—the necessity of the Devil may become evident as a weapon, a weapon designed and used time and time again in every age to whip men into a surrender to a particular church or church-state.

Our difficulty in believing the—for want of a better word —political inspiration of the Devil is due in great part to the fact that

---

Some playgoers have sensed a kinship between Dr. Stockmann in Ibsen's *An Enemy of the People* and Proctor in *The Crucible*—both protagonists insist on their individual rights and dignity, though society deems them fools for their stands.

"Cosmology" is a philosophy of the universe, which is viewed as integrated sectors and phenomena—all in keeping with set patterns. Miller here states that the Puritans in Salem considered the Devil to reign in one realm of the universe and God in another. Miller's interpretations on these matters, however, are not universally held, because they impress some as simplistic.

he is called up and damned not only by our social antagonists but by our own side, whatever it may be. The Catholic Church, through its Inquisition, is famous for cultivating Lucifer as the arch-fiend, but the Church's enemies relied no less upon the Old Boy to keep the human mind enthralled. Luther was himself accused of alliance with Hell, and he in turn accused his enemies. To complicate matters further, he believed that he had had contact with the Devil and had argued theology with him. I am not surprised at this, for at my own university a professor of history—a Lutheran, by the way—used to assemble his graduate students, draw the shades, and commune in the classroom with Erasmus. He was never, to my knowledge, officially scoffed at for this, the reason being that the university officials, like most of us, are the children of a history which still sucks at the Devil's teats. At this writing, only England has held back before the temptations of contemporary diabolism. In the countries of the Communist ideology, all resistance of any import is linked to the totally malign capitalist succubi, and in America any man who is not reactionary in his views is open to the charge of alliance with the Red hell. Political opposition, thereby, is given an inhumane overlay which then justifies the abrogation of all normally applied customs of civilized intercourse. A political policy is equated with moral right, and opposition to it with diabolical malevolence. Once such an equation is effectively made, society becomes a congerie of plots and counterplots, and the main role of government changes from that of the arbiter to that of the scourge of God.

The results of this process are no different now from what they ever were, except sometimes in the degree of cruelty inflicted, and not always even in that department. Normally the actions and deeds of a man were all that society felt comfortable in judging. The secret intent of an action was left to the ministers, priests, and rabbis to deal with. When diabolism rises, however, actions are the least important manifests of the true nature of a man. The Devil, as Reverend Hale said, is a wily one, and until an hour before he fell, even God thought him beautiful in Heaven.

The analogy, however, seems to falter when one considers that, while there were no witches then, there are Communists and capitalists now, and in each camp there is certain proof that spies of each side are at work undermining the other. But this is a snobbish objection and not at all warranted by the facts. I have no doubt that people *were* communing with, and even worshiping, the Devil in Salem, and if the whole truth could be known in this case, as it is in others, we should discover a regular and conventionalized propitiation of the dark spirit. One certain evidence of this is the confession of Tituba, the slave of Reverend Parris, and another is the behavior of the children who were known to have indulged in sorceries with her.

There are accounts of similar *klatsches* in Europe, where the daughters of the towns would assemble at night and, sometimes with fetishes, sometimes with a selected young man, give themselves to love, with some bastardly results. The Church, sharp-eyed as it must be when gods long dead are brought to life, condemned these orgies as witchcraft and interpreted them, rightly, as a resurgence of the Dionysiac forces it had crushed long before. Sex, sin, and the Devil were early linked, and so they continued to be in Salem, and are today. From all accounts there are no more puritanical mores in

In folklore, "succubi" are female demons, fabled to have had sexual intercourse with men in their sleep.

Miller reveals his sensitivity to self-righteous politicians who claim their political position is "right" in a religious and moral sense, while their opponents' views automatically are morally "wrong."

"Klatsch" is a German term used to designate a group of persons gathered together primarily to gossip.

the world than those enforced by the Communists in Russia, where women's fashions, for instance, are as prudent and all-covering as any American Baptist would desire. The divorce laws lay a tremendous responsibility on the father for the care of his children. Even the laxity of divorce regulations in the early years of the revolution was undoubtedly a revulsion from the nineteenth-century Victorian immobility of marriage and the consequent hypocrisy that developed from it. If for no other reasons, a state so powerful, so jealous of the uniformity of its citizens, cannot long tolerate the atomization of the family. And yet, in American eyes at least, there remains the conviction that the Russian attitude toward women is lascivious. It is the Devil working again, just as he is working within the Slav who is shocked at the very idea of a woman's disrobing herself in a burlesque show. Our opposites are always robed in sexual sin, and it is from this unconscious conviction that demonology gains both its attractive sensuality and its capacity to infuriate and frighten.

Coming into Salem now, Reverend Hale conceives of himself much as a young doctor on his first call. His painfully acquired armory of symptoms, catchwords, and diagnostic procedures are now to be put to use at last. The road from Beverly is unusually busy this morning, and he has passed a hundred rumors that make him smile at the ignorance of the yeomanry in this most precise science. He feels himself allied with the best minds of Europe—kings, philosophers, scientists, and ecclesiasts of all churches. His goal is light, goodness and its preservation, and he knows the exaltation of the blessed whose intelligence, sharpened by minute examinations of enormous tracts, is finally called upon to face what may be a bloody fight with the Fiend himself.

> For the actor playing Reverend Hale, these remarks provide crucial attitudes to be cultivated in that role.

He appears loaded down with half a dozen heavy books.

HALE Pray you, someone take these!

PARRIS *(delighted)* Mr. Hale! Oh! it's good to see you again! *(taking some books)* My, they're heavy!

HALE *(setting down his books)* They must be; they are weighted with authority.

PARRIS *(a little scared)* Well, you do come prepared!

HALE We shall need hard study if it comes to tracking down the Old Boy. *(noticing Rebecca)* You cannot be Rebecca Nurse?

REBECCA I am, sir. Do you know me?

HALE It's strange how I knew you, but I suppose you look as such a good soul should. We have all heard of your great charities in Beverly.

PARRIS Do you know this gentleman? Mr. Thomas Putnam. And his good wife Ann.

HALE Putnam! I had not expected such distinguished company, sir.

PUTNAM *(pleased)* It does not seem to help us today, Mr. Hale. We look to you to come to our house and save our child.

HALE Your child ails too?

MRS. PUTNAM Her soul, her soul seems flown away. She sleeps and yet she walks . . .

PUTNAM She cannot eat.

HALE Cannot eat! *(thinks on it. then, to Proctor and Giles Corey)* Do you men have afflicted children?

PARRIS No, no, these are farmers. John Proctor—

GILES He don't believe in witches.

PROCTOR *(to Hale)* I never spoke on witches one way or the other. Will you come, Giles?

GILES No—no, John, I think not. I have some few queer questions of my own to ask this fellow.

PROCTOR I've heard you to be a sensible man, Mr. Hale. I hope you'll leave some of it in Salem.

Proctor goes. Hale stands embarrassed for an instant.

PARRIS *(quickly)* Will you look at my daughter, sir? *(leads Hale to the bed)* She has tried to leap out the window; we discovered her this morning on the highroad, waving her arms as though she'd fly.

HALE *(narrowing his eyes)* Tries to fly.

PUTNAM She cannot bear to hear the Lord's name, Mr. Hale; that's a sure sign of witchcraft afloat.

HALE *(holding up his hands)* No, no. Now let me instruct you. We cannot look to superstition in this. The Devil is precise; the marks of his presence are definite as stone, and I must tell you all that I shall not proceed unless you are prepared to believe me if I should find no bruise of hell upon her.

PARRIS It is agreed, sir—it is agreed—we will abide by your judgment.

HALE Good then. *(He goes to the bed, looks down at Betty. To Parris.)* Now, sir, what were your first warnings of this strangeness?

PARRIS Why, sir—I discovered her—*(indicating Abigail)*—and my niece and ten or twelve of the other girls, dancing in the forest last night.

HALE *(surprised)* You permit dancing?

PARRIS No, no, it were secret—

MRS. PUTNAM *(unable to wait)* Mr. Parris's slave has knowledge of conjurin', sir.

PARRIS *(to Mrs. Putnam)* We cannot be sure of that, Goody Ann—

MRS. PUTNAM *(frightened, very softly)* I know it, sir. I sent my child —she should learn from Tituba who murdered her sisters.

REBECCA *(horrified)* Goody Ann! You sent a child to conjure up the dead?

MRS. PUTNAM Let God blame me, not you, not you, Rebecca! I'll not have you judging me any more! *(to Hale)* Is it a natural work to lose seven children before they live a day?

PARRIS Sssh!

Rebecca, with great pain, turns her face away. There is a pause.

HALE Seven dead in childbirth.

MRS. PUTNAM *(softly)* Aye. *(Her voice breaks; she looks up at him. Silence.*

Hale is impressed. Parris looks to him. He goes to his books, opens one, turns pages, then reads. All wait, avidly.)

PARRIS *(hushed)* What book is that?

MRS. PUTNAM What's there, sir?

HALE *(with a tasty love of intellectual pursuit)* Here is all the invisible world, caught, defined, and calculated. In these books the Devil stands stripped of all his brute disguises. Here are all your familiar spirits—your incubi and succubi; your witches that go by land, by air, and by sea; your wizards of the night and of the day. Have no fear now—we shall find him out if he has come among us, and I mean to crush him utterly if he has shown his face! *(He starts for the bed.)*

Readers should bear in mind Reverend Hale's total confidence at this moment, to contrast it with his growing uncertainty throughout the rest of the drama.

REBECCA Will it hurt the child, sir?

HALE I cannot tell, If she is truly in the Devil's grip we may have to rip and tear to get her free.

REBECCA I think I'll go, then. I am too old for this. *(She rises.)*

PARRIS *(striving for conviction)* Why, Rebecca, we may open up the boil of all our troubles today!

REBECCA Let us hope for that. I go to God for you, sir.

PARRIS *(with trepidation—and resentment)* I hope you do not mean to go to Satan here! *(slight pause)*

REBECCA I wish I knew. *(She goes out; they feel resentful of her note of moral superiority.)*

PUTNAM *(abruptly)* Come, Mr. Hale, let's get on. Sit you here.

GILES Mr. Hale, I have always wanted to ask a learned man—what signifies the readin' of strange books?

HALE What books?

GILES I cannot tell; she hides them.

HALE Who does this?

GILES Martha, my wife. I have waked at night many a time and found her in a corner, readin' of a book. Now what do you make of that?

HALE Why, that's not necessarily—

GILES It discomfits me! Last night—mark this—I tried and tried and could not say my prayers. And then she close her book and walks out of the house, and suddenly—mark this—I could pray again!

With Giles' innocent question concerning his wife and her "strange books," Miller adds another suspicion of spiritualism.

Old Giles must be spoken for, if only because his fate was to be so remarkable and so different from that of all the others. He was in his early eighties at this time, and was the most comical hero in the history. No man has ever been blamed for so much. If a cow was missed, the first thought was to look for her around Corey's house; a fire blazing up at night brought suspicion of arson to his door. He didn't give a hoot for public opinion, and only in his last years—after he had married Martha—did he bother much with the church. That she stopped his prayer is very probable, but he forgot to say that he'd only recently learned any prayers and it didn't take much to make him stumble over them. He was a crank and a nuisance, but withal a deeply innocent and brave man. In court, once, he was asked if it were true that he had been frightened by the strange behavior of a hog and had then said he knew it to be the Devil in an animal's shape. "What frighted you?" he was asked. He forgot everything but the word "frighted," and instantly replied, "I do not know that I ever spoke that word in my life."

HALE Ah! The stoppage of prayer—that is strange. I'll speak further on that with you.

GILES I'm not sayin' she's touched the Devil, now, but I'd admire to know what books she reads and why she hides them. She'll not answer me, y' see.

HALE Aye, we'll discuss it. *(to all)* Now mark me, if the Devil is in her you will witness some frightful wonders in this room, so please to keep your wits about you. Mr. Putnam, stand close in case she flies. Now, Betty, dear, will you sit up? *(Putnam comes in closer, ready-handed. Hale sits Betty up, but she hangs limp in his hands.)* Hmmm. *(He observes her carefully. The others watch breathlessly.)* Can you hear me? I am John Hale, minister of Beverly. I have come to help you, dear. Do you remember my two little girls in Beverly? *(She does not stir in his hands.)*

PARRIS *(in fright)* How can it be the Devil? Why would he choose my house to strike? We have all manner of licentious people in the village!

HALE What victory would the Devil have to win a soul already bad? It is the best the Devil wants, and who is better than the minister?

GILES That's deep, Mr. Parris, deep, deep!

PARRIS *(with resolution now)* Betty! Answer Mr. Hale! Betty!

HALE Does someone afflict you, child? It need not be a woman, mind you, or a man. Perhaps some bird invisible to others comes to you—perhaps a pig, a mouse, or any beast at all. Is there some figure bids you fly? *(The child remains limp in his hands. In silence he lays her back on the pillow. Now, holding out his hands toward her, he intones.)* In nomine Domini Sabaoth sui filiique ite ad infernos. *(She does not stir. He turns to Abigail, his eyes narrowing.)* Abigail, what sort of dancing were you doing with her in the forest?

ABIGAIL Why—common dancing is all.

PARRIS I think I ought to say that I—I saw a kettle in the grass where they were dancing.

ABIGAIL That were only soup.

HALE What sort of soup were in this kettle, Abigail?

ABIGAIL Why, it were beans—and lentils, I think, and—

HALE Mr. Parris, you did not notice, did you, any living thing in the kettle? A mouse, perhaps, a spider, a frog—?

PARRIS *(fearfully)* I—do believe there were some movement—in the soup.

ABIGAIL That jumped in, we never put it in!

HALE *(quickly)* What jumped in?

ABIGAIL Why, a very little frog jumped—

Hale uses this Latin sentence as a form of exorcism. The line means "In the name of the Lord of Hosts and of His Son, go thou to the infernal regions."

PARRIS A frog, Abby!

HALE *(grasping Abigail)* Abigail, it may be your cousin is dying. Did you call the Devil last night?

ABIGAIL I never called him! Tituba, Tituba . . .

PARRIS *(blanched)* She called the Devil?

HALE I should like to speak with Tituba.

PARRIS Goody Ann, will you bring her up? *(Mrs. Putnam exits.)*

HALE How did she call him?

ABIGAIL I know not—she spoke Barbados.

HALE Did you feel any strangeness when she called him? A sudden cold wind, perhaps? A trembling below the ground?

ABIGAIL I didn't see no Devil! *(shaking Betty)* Betty, wake up. Betty! Betty!

HALE You cannot evade me, Abigail. Did your cousin drink any of the brew in that kettle?

ABIGAIL She never drank it!

HALE Did you drink it?

ABIGAIL No, sir!

HALE Did Tituba ask you to drink it?

ABIGAIL She tried, but I refused.

HALE Why are you concealing? Have you sold yourself to Lucifer?

ABIGAIL I never sold myself! I'm a good girl! I'm a proper girl!

Mrs. Putnam enters with Tituba, and instantly Abigail points at Tituba.

ABIGAIL She made me do it! She made Betty do it!

TITUBA *(shocked and angry)* Abby!

ABIGAIL She makes me drink blood!

PARRIS Blood!!

MRS. PUTNAM My baby's blood?

TITUBA No, no, chicken blood. I give she chicken blood!

HALE Woman, have you enlisted these children for the Devil?

TITUBA No, no, sir, I don't truck with no Devil!

HALE Why can she not wake? Are you silencing this child?

TITUBA I love me Betty!

HALE You have sent your spirit out upon this child, have you not? Are you gathering souls for the Devil?

ABIGAIL She sends her spirit on me in church; she makes me laugh at prayer!

PARRIS She have often laughed at prayer!

ABIGAIL She comes to me every night to go and drink blood!

TITUBA You beg *me* to conjure! She beg *me* make charm—

ABIGAIL Don't lie! *(to Hale)* She comes to me while I sleep; she's always making me dream corruptions!

What type of psychology is shown by Abigail's behavior during her questioning by Hale?

Tituba's irregular dialect is meant to convey her alien, slave heritage.

TITUBA Why you say that, Abby?

ABIGAIL Sometimes I wake and find myself standing in the open doorway and not a stitch on my body! I always hear her laughing in my sleep. I hear her singing her Barbados songs and tempting me with—

TITUBA Mister Reverend, I never—

HALE *(resolved now)* Tituba, I want you to wake this child.

TITUBA I have no power on this child, sir.

HALE You most certainly do, and you will free her from it now! When did you compact with the Devil?

TITUBA I don't compact with no Devil!

PARRIS You will confess yourself or I will take you out and whip you to your death, Tituba!

PUTNAM This woman must be hanged! She must be taken and hanged!

TITUBA *(terrified, falls to her knees)* No, no, don't hang Tituba! I tell him I don't desire to work for him, sir.

PARRIS The Devil?

HALE Then you saw him! *(Tituba weeps.)* Now Tituba, I know that when we bind ourselves to Hell it is very hard to break with it. We are going to help you tear yourself free—

TITUBA *(frightened by the coming process)* Mister Reverend, I do believe somebody else be witchin' these children.

HALE Who?

TITUBA I don't know, sir, but the Devil got him numerous witches.

HALE Does he! *(It is a clue.)* Tituba, look into my eyes. Come, look into me. *(She raises her eyes to his fearfully.)* You would be a good Christian woman, would you not, Tituba?

TITUBA Aye, sir, a good Christian woman.

HALE And you love these little children?

TITUBA Oh, yes, sir, I don't desire to hurt little children.

HALE And you love God, Tituba?

TITUBA I love God with all my bein'.

HALE Now, in God's holy name—

TITUBA Bless Him. Bless Him. *(She is rocking on her knees, sobbing in terror.)*

HALE And to His glory—

TITUBA Eternal glory. Bless Him—bless God . . .

HALE Open yourself, Tituba—open yourself and let God's holy light shine on you.

TITUBA Oh, bless the Lord.

HALE When the Devil comes to you does he ever come—with another person? *(She stares up into his face.)* Perhaps another person in the village? Someone you know.

PARRIS Who came with him?

Why is this scene of Tituba's interrogation so dramatic on stage?

THE CRUCIBLE

PUTNAM Sarah Good? Did you ever see Sarah Good with him? Or Osburn?

PARRIS Was it man or woman came with him?

TITUBA Man or woman. Was—was woman.

PARRIS What woman? A woman, you said. What woman?

TITUBA It was black dark, and I—

PARRIS You could see him, why could you not see her?

TITUBA Well, they was always talking; they was always runnin' round and carryin' on—

PARRIS You mean out of Salem? Salem witches?

TITUBA I believe so, yes, sir.

Now Hale takes her hand. She is surprised.

HALE Tituba. You must have no fear to tell us who they are, do you understand? We will protect you. The Devil can never overcome a minister. You know that, do you not?

TITUBA *(kisses Hale's hand)* Aye, sir, oh, I do.

HALE You have confessed yourself to witchcraft, and that speaks a wish to come to Heaven's side. And we will bless you, Tituba.

TITUBA *(deeply relieved)* Oh, God bless you, Mr. Hale!

HALE *(with rising exaltation)* You are God's instrument put in our hands to discover the Devil's agent among us. You are selected, Tituba, you are chosen to help us cleanse our village. So speak utterly, Tituba, turn your back on him and face God—face God, Tituba, and God will protect you.

TITUBA *(joining with him)* Oh, God, protect Tituba!

HALE *(kindly)* Who came to you with the Devil? Two? Three? Four? How many?

Tituba pants, and begins rocking back and forth again, staring ahead.

TITUBA There was four. There was four.

PARRIS *(pressing in on her)* Who? Who? Their names, their names!

TITUBA *(suddenly bursting out)* Oh, how many times he bid me kill you, Mr. Parris!

PARRIS Kill me!

TITUBA *(in a fury)* He say Mr. Parris must be kill! Mr. Parris no goodly man, Mr. Parris mean man and no gentle man, and he bid me rise out of my bed and cut your throat! *(They gasp.)* But I tell him "No! I don't hate that man. I don't want kill that man." But he say, "You work for me, Tituba, and I make you free! I give you pretty dress to wear, and put you way high up in the air, and you gone fly back to Barbados!" And I say, "You lie, Devil, you lie!" And then he come one stormy night to me, and he say, "Look! I have *white* people belong to me." And I look—and there was Goody Good.

PARRIS Sarah Good!

TITUBA *(rocking and weeping)* Aye, sir, and Goody Osburn.

MRS. PUTNAM I knew it! Goody Osburn were midwife to me three

Putnam hopes to establish his version of the affair through the power of suggestion.

Remember later that it is here, with Tituba's very tentative belief, that the presence of witches in Salem is first seemingly confirmed.

How can one explain the feverish atmosphere of this episode that would so trigger Tituba and the girls into denouncing innocent townswomen as witches?

In the Parris home; Abby (Pamela Peyton-Wright) is in the foreground. From the Lincoln Center Repertory Theater production, The Crucible.

times. I begged you, Thomas, did I not? I begged him not to call Osburn because I feared her. My babies always shriveled in her hands!

HALE Take courage, you must give us all their names. How can you bear to see this child suffering? Look at her, Tituba. *(He is indicating Betty on the bed.)* Look at her God-given innocence; her soul is so tender; we must protect her, Tituba; the Devil is out and preying on her like a beast upon the flesh of the pure lamb. God will bless you for your help.

Abigail rises, staring as though inspired, and cries out.

ABIGAIL I want to open myself! *(They turn to her, startled. She is enraptured, as though in a pearly light.)* I want the light of God, I want the sweet love of Jesus! I danced for the Devil; I saw him; I wrote in his book; I go back to Jesus; I kiss His hand. I saw Sarah Good with the Devil! I saw Goody Osburn with the Devil! I saw Bridget Bishop with the Devil!

As she is speaking, Betty is rising from the bed, a fever in her eyes, and picks up the chant.

BETTY *(staring too)* I saw George Jacobs with the Devil! I saw Goody Howe with the Devil!

PARRIS She speaks! *(He rushes to embrace Betty.)* She speaks!

HALE Glory to God! It is broken, they are free!

BETTY *(calling out hysterically and with great relief)* I saw Martha Bellows with the Devil!

ABIGAIL I saw Goody Sibber with the Devil! (*It is rising to a great glee.*)

PUTNAM The marshal, I'll call the marshal!

Parris is shouting a prayer of thanksgiving.

BETTY I saw Alice Barrow with the Devil!

The curtain begins to fall.

HALE (*as Putnam goes out*) Let the marshal bring irons!

ABIGAIL I saw Goody Hawkins with the Devil!

BETTY I saw Goody Bibber with the Devil!

ABIGAIL I saw Goody Booth with the Devil!

On their ecstatic cries, the curtain falls.

ACT II

The common room of Proctor's house, eight days later.

    At the right is a door opening on the fields outside. A fireplace is at the left, and behind it a stairway leading upstairs. It is the low, dark, and rather long living room of the time. As the curtain rises, the room is empty. From above, Elizabeth is heard softly singing to the children. Presently the door opens and John Proctor enters, carrying his gun. He glances about the room as he comes toward the fireplace, then halts for an instant as he hears her singing. He continues on to the fireplace, leans the gun against the wall as he swings a pot out of the fire and smells it. Then he lifts out the ladle and tastes. He is not quite pleased. He reaches to a cupboard, takes a pinch of salt, and drops it into the pot. As he is tasting again, her footsteps are heard on the stair. He swings the pot into the fireplace and goes to a basin and washes his hands and face. Elizabeth enters.

ELIZABETH What keeps you so late? It's almost dark.

PROCTOR I were planting far out to the forest edge.

ELIZABETH Oh, you're done then.

PROCTOR Aye, the farm is seeded. The boys asleep?

ELIZABETH They will be soon. (*and she goes to the fireplace, proceeds to ladle up stew in a dish*)

PROCTOR Pray now for a fair summer.

ELIZABETH Aye.

PROCTOR Are you well today?

ELIZABETH I am. (*She brings the plate to the table, and, indicating the food*) It is a rabbit.

PROCTOR (*going to the table*) Oh, is it! In Jonathan's trap?

ELIZABETH No, she walked into the house this afternoon; I found her sittin' in the corner like she come to visit.

PROCTOR Oh, that's a good sign walkin' in.

ELIZABETH Pray God. It hurt my heart to strip her, poor rabbit. (*She sits and watches him taste it.*)

> Even in his stage directions, Miller supplies *stage business*—that is, minor physical movements by a performer, such as posture and facial expression—which clarifies the character of the figure involved. Proctor's independent will and preferences show up, for instance, when he seasons the food to suit his own taste.

PROCTOR It's well seasoned.

ELIZABETH *(blushing with pleasure)* I took great care. She's tender?

PROCTOR Aye. *(He eats. She watches him.)* I think we'll see green fields soon. It's warm as blood beneath the clods.

ELIZABETH That's well.

Proctor eats, then looks up.

PROCTOR If the crop is good I'll buy George Jacob's heifer. How would that please you?

ELIZABETH Aye, it would.

PROCTOR *(with a grin)* I mean to please you, Elizabeth.

ELIZABETH —*(It is hard to say.)* I know it, John.

He gets up, goes to her, kisses her. She receives it. With a certain disappointment, he returns to the table.

PROCTOR *(as gently as he can)* Cider?

ELIZABETH *(with a sense of reprimanding herself for having forgot)* Aye! *(She gets up and goes and pours a glass for him. He now arches his back.)*

PROCTOR This farm's a continent when you go foot by foot droppin' seeds in it.

ELIZABETH *(coming with the cider)* It must be.

PROCTOR *(drinks a long draught, then, putting the glass down)* You ought to bring some flowers in the house.

ELIZABETH Oh! I forgot! I will tomorrow.

PROCTOR It's winter in here yet. On Sunday let you come with me, and we'll walk the farm together; I never see such a load of flowers on the earth. *(With good feeling he goes and looks up at the sky through the open doorway.)* Lilacs have a purple smell. Lilac is the smell of nightfall, I think. Massachusetts is a beauty in the spring!

ELIZABETH Aye, it is.

There is a pause. She is watching him from the table as he stands there absorbing the night. It is as though she would speak but cannot. Instead, now, she takes up his plate and glass and fork and goes with them to the basin. Her back is turned to him. He turns to her and watches her. A sense of their separation rises.

PROCTOR I think you're sad again. Are you?

ELIZABETH *(She doesn't want friction, and yet she must.)* You come so late I thought you'd gone to Salem this afternoon.

PROCTOR Why? I have no business in Salem.

ELIZABETH You did speak of going, earlier this week.

PROCTOR *(He knows what she means.)* I thought better of it since.

ELIZABETH Mary Warren's there today.

PROCTOR Why'd you let her? You heard me forbid her go to Salem any more!

ELIZABETH I couldn't stop her.

> How can we deduce from this eating scene that there is marital tension in the Proctor household?

PROCTOR *(holding back a full condemnation of her)* It is a fault, it is a fault, Elizabeth—you're the mistress here, not Mary Warren.

ELIZABETH She frightened all my strength away.

PROCTOR How may that mouse frighten you, Elizabeth? You—

ELIZABETH It is a mouse no more. I forbid her go, and she raises up her chin like the daughter of a prince and says to me, "I must go to Salem, Goody Proctor; I am an official of the court!"

PROCTOR Court! What court?

ELIZABETH Aye, it is a proper court they have now. They've sent four judges out of Boston, she says, weighty magistrates of the General Court, and at the head sits the Deputy Governor of the Province.

PROCTOR *(astonished)* Why, she's mad.

ELIZABETH I would to God she were. There be fourteen people in the jail now, she says. *(Proctor simply looks at her, unable to grasp it.)* And they'll be tried, and the court have power to hang them too, she says.

PROCTOR *(scoffing, but without conviction)* Ah, they'd never hang—

ELIZABETH The Deputy Governor promise hangin' if they'll not confess, John. The town's gone wild, I think. She speak of Abigail, and I thought she were a saint, to hear her. Abigail brings the other girls into the court, and where she walks the crowd will part like the sea for Israel. And folks are brought before them, and if they scream and howl and fall to the floor—the person's clapped in the jail for bewitchin' them.

PROCTOR *(wide-eyed)* Oh, it is a black mischief.

ELIZABETH I think you must go to Salem, John. *(He turns to her.)* I think so. You must tell them it is a fraud.

PROCTOR *(thinking beyond this)* Aye, it is, it is surely.

ELIZABETH Let you go to Ezekiel Cheever—he knows you well. And tell him what she said to you last week in her uncle's house. She said it had naught to do with witchcraft, did she not?

PROCTOR *(in thought)* Aye, she did, she did. *(now, a pause)*

ELIZABETH *(quietly, fearing to anger him by prodding)* God forbid you keep that from the court, John. I think they must be told.

PROCTOR *(quietly, struggling with his thought)* Aye, they must, they must. It is a wonder they do believe her.

ELIZABETH I would go to Salem now, John—let you go tonight.

PROCTOR I'll think on it.

ELIZABETH *(with her courage now)* You cannot keep it, John.

PROCTOR *(angering)* I know I cannot keep it. I say I will think on it!

ELIZABETH *(hurt, and very coldly)* Good, then, let you think on it. *(She stands and starts to walk out of the room.)*

PROCTOR I am only wondering how I may prove what she told me, Elizabeth. If the girl's a saint now, I think it is not easy to prove she's

---

What vital information for the plot emerges to catch John Proctor unaware?

Proctor obviously has told his wife everything about Abigail's overtures to

fraud, and the town gone so silly. She told it to me in a room alone—I have no proof for it.

ELIZABETH You were alone with her?

PROCTOR *(stubbornly)* For a moment alone, aye.

ELIZABETH Why, then, it is not as you told me.

PROCTOR *(his anger rising)* For a moment, I say. The others come in soon after.

ELIZABETH *(Quietly—she has suddenly lost all faith in him.)* Do as you wish, then. *(She starts to turn.)*

PROCTOR Woman. *(She turns to him.)* I'll not have your suspicion any more.

ELIZABETH *(a little loftily)* I have no—

PROCTOR I'll not have it!

ELIZABETH Then let you not earn it.

PROCTOR *(with a violent undertone)* You doubt me yet?

ELIZABETH *(with a smile, to keep her dignity)* John, if it were not Abigail that you must go to hurt, would you falter now? I think not.

PROCTOR Now look you—

ELIZABETH I see what I see, John.

PROCTOR *(with solemn warning)* You will not judge me more, Elizabeth. I have good reason to think before I charge fraud on Abigail, and I will think on it. Let you look to your own improvement before you go to judge your husband any more. I have forgot Abigail, and—

ELIZABETH And I.

PROCTOR Spare me! You forget nothin' and forgive nothin'. Learn charity, woman. I have gone tiptoe in this house all seven month since she is gone. I have not moved from there to there without I think to please you, and still an everlasting funeral marches round your heart. I cannot speak but I am doubted, every moment judged for lies, as though I come into a court when I come into this house!

ELIZABETH John, you are not open with me. You saw her with a crowd, you said. Now you—

PROCTOR I'll plead my honesty no more, Elizabeth.

ELIZABETH *(Now she would justify herself.)* John, I am only—

PROCTOR No more! I should have roared you down when first you told me your suspicion. But I wilted, and, like a Christian, I confessed. Confessed! Some dream I had must have mistaken you for God that day. But you're not, you're not, and let you remember it! Let you look sometimes for the goodness in me, and judge me not.

ELIZABETH I do not judge you. The magistrate sits in your heart that judges you. I never thought you but a good man, John—*(with a smile)*—only somewhat bewildered.

PROCTOR *(laughing bitterly)* Oh, Elizabeth, your justice would freeze beer! *(He turns suddenly toward a sound outside. He starts for the door as*

him at Parris' house (as seen in Act I), in an effort to regain Elizabeth's trust and love. But wifely jealousy instantly revives when she learns that Proctor and Abigail had been alone together.

Now the reason becomes clear for the somber mood observed earlier in Proctor's home.

Mary Warren enters. As soon as he sees her, he goes directly to her and grabs her by the cloak, furious.) How do you go to Salem when I forbid it? Do you mock me? *(shaking her)* I'll whip you if you dare leave this house again!

Strangely, she doesn't resist him, but hangs limply by his grip.

MARY WARREN I am sick, I am sick, Mr. Proctor. Pray, pray, hurt me not. *(Her strangeness throws him off, and her evident pallor and weakness. He frees her.)* My insides are all shuddery; I am in the proceedings all day, sir.

PROCTOR *(with draining anger—his curiosity is draining it)* And what of these proceedings here? When will you proceed to keep this house, as you are paid nine pound a year to do—and my wife not wholly well?

As though to compensate, Mary Warren goes to Elizabeth with a small rag doll.

MARY WARREN I made a gift for you today, Goody Proctor. I had to sit long hours in a chair, and passed the time with sewing.

ELIZABETH *(perplexed, looking at the doll)* Why, thank you, it's a fair poppet.

MARY WARREN *(with a trembling, decayed voice)* We must all love each other now, Goody Proctor.

ELIZABETH *(amazed at her strangeness)* Aye, indeed we must.

MARY WARREN *(glancing at the room)* I'll get up early in the morning and clean the house. I must sleep now. *(She turns and starts off.)*

PROCTOR Mary. *(She halts.)* Is it true? There be fourteen women arrested?

MARY WARREN No, sir. There be thirty-nine now—*(She suddenly breaks off and sobs and sits down, exhausted.)*

ELIZABETH Why, she's weepin'! What ails you, child?

MARY WARREN Goody Osburn—will hang!

There is a shocked pause, while she sobs.

PROCTOR Hang! *(He calls into her face.)* Hang, y'say?

MARY WARREN *(through her weeping)* Aye.

PROCTOR The Deputy Governor will permit it?

MARY WARREN He sentenced her. He must. *(to ameliorate it)* But not Sarah Good. For Sarah Good confessed, y'see.

PROCTOR Confessed! To what?

MARY WARREN That she—*(in horror at the memory)*—she sometimes made a compact with Lucifer, and wrote her name in his black book—with her blood—and bound herself to torment Christians till God's thrown down—and we all must worship Hell forevermore.

Pause

PROCTOR But—surely you know what a jabberer she is. Did you tell them that?

How does Mary Warren's behavior alert Proctor and the audience that matters have become more complicated since the first act?

Notice the doll, for it bears directly on the subsequent events in this act.

What is the correlation between Mary Warren's exhausted shakiness and the news of Goody Osburn's penalty to be hanged?

MARY WARREN Mr. Proctor, in open court she near to choked us all to death.

PROCTOR How, choked you?

MARY WARREN She sent her spirit out.

ELIZABETH Oh, Mary, Mary, surely you—

MARY WARREN *(with an indignant edge)* She tried to kill me many times, Goody Proctor!

ELIZABETH Why, I never heard you mention that before.

MARY WARREN I never knew it before. I never knew anything before. When she come into the court I say to myself, I must not accuse this woman, for she sleep in ditches, and so very old and poor. But then—then she sit there, denying and denying, and I feel a misty coldness climbin' up my back, and the skin on my skull begin to creep, and I feel a clamp around my neck and I cannot breathe air; and then—*(entranced)*—I hear a voice, a screamin' voice, and it were my voice—and all at once I remembered everything she done to me!

PROCTOR Why? What did she do to you?

MARY WARREN *(like one awakened to a marvelous secret insight)* So many time, Mr. Proctor, she come to this very door, beggin' bread and a cup of cider—and mark this: whenever I turned her away empty, she *mumbled*.

ELIZABETH Mumbled! She may mumble if she's hungry.

MARY WARREN But *what* does she mumble? You must remember, Goody Proctor. Last month—a Monday, I think—she walked away, and I thought my guts would burst for two days after. Do you remember it?

ELIZABETH Why—I do, I think, but—

MARY WARREN And so I told that to Judge Hathorne, and he asks her so. "Goody Osburn," says he, "what curse do you mumble that this girl must fall sick after turning you away?" And then she replies—*(mimicking an old crone)*—"Why, your excellence, no curse at all. I only say my commandments; I hope I may say my commandments," says she!

ELIZABETH And that's an upright answer.

MARY WARREN Aye, but then Judge Hathorne say, "Recite for us your commandments!"—*(leaning avidly toward them)*—and of all the ten she could not say a single one. She never knew no commandments, and they had her in a flat lie!

PROCTOR And so condemned her?

MARY WARREN *(now a little strained, seeing his stubborn doubt)* Why, they must when she condemned herself.

PROCTOR But the proof, the proof!

MARY WARREN *(with greater impatience with him)* I told you the proof. It's hard proof, hard as rock, the judges said.

PROCTOR *(pauses an instant, then)* You will not go to court again, Mary Warren.

We must understand the "logic" used to condemn Goody Osburn to death in order to see how the witch fever could have spread in Salem. What exactly is the "hard proof" Mary Warren speaks of as having confirmed the old woman's guilt?

MARY WARREN I must tell you, sir, I will be gone every day now. I am amazed you do not see what weighty work we do.

PROCTOR What work you do! It's strange work for a Christian girl to hang old women!

MARY WARREN But, Mr. Proctor, they will not hang them if they confess. Sarah Good will only sit in jail some time—*(recalling)*—and here's a wonder for you; think on this. Goody Good is pregnant!

ELIZABETH Pregnant! Are they mad? The woman's near to sixty!

MARY WARREN They had Doctor Griggs examine her, and she's full to the brim. And smokin' a pipe all these years, and no husband either! But she's safe, thank God, for they'll not hurt the innocent child. But be that not a marvel? You must see it, sir, it's God's work we do. So I'll be gone every day for some time. I'm—I am an official of the court, they say, and I—*(She has been edging toward offstage.)*

The prohibition of hanging pregnant women will be important in later events concerning Proctor and his wife.

PROCTOR I'll official you! *(He strides to the mantel, takes down the whip hanging there.)*

MARY WARREN *(terrified, but coming erect, striving for her authority)* I'll not stand whipping any more!

ELIZABETH *(hurriedly, as Proctor approaches)* Mary, promise you'll stay at home—

MARY WARREN *(backing from him, but keeping her erect posture, striving, striving for her way)* The devil's loose in Salem, Mr. Proctor; we must discover where he's hiding!

PROCTOR I'll whip the Devil out of you! *(With whip raised he reaches out for her, and she streaks away and yells.)*

MARY WARREN *(pointing at Elizabeth)* I saved her life today!

Silence. His whip comes down.

ELIZABETH *(softly)* I am accused?

MARY WARREN *(quaking)* Somewhat mentioned. But I said I never see no sign you ever sent your spirit out to hurt no one, and seeing I do live so closely with you, they dismissed it.

ELIZABETH Who accused me?

MARY WARREN I am bound by law, I cannot tell it. *(to Proctor)* I only hope you'll not be so sarcastical no more. Four judges and the King's deputy sat to dinner with us but an hour ago. I—I would have you speak civilly to me, from this out.

From what does Mary Warren's new-found courage and pride result?

PROCTOR *(in horror, muttering in disgust at her)* Go to bed.

MARY WARREN *(with a stamp of her foot)* I'll not be ordered to bed no more, Mr. Proctor! I am eighteen and a woman, however single!

PROCTOR Do you wish to sit up? Then sit up.

MARY WARREN I wish to go to bed!

PROCTOR *(in anger)* Good night, then!

MARY WARREN Good night. *(Dissatisfied, uncertain of herself, she goes out. Wide-eyed, both, Proctor and Elizabeth stand staring.)*

ELIZABETH *(quietly)* Oh, the noose, the noose is up!

PROCTOR There'll be no noose.

ELIZABETH She wants me dead. I knew all week it would come to this!

PROCTOR (*without conviction*) They dismissed it. You heard her say—

ELIZABETH And what of tomorrow? She will cry me out until they take me!

PROCTOR Sit you down.

ELIZABETH She wants me dead, John, you know it!

PROCTOR I say sit down! (*She sits, trembling. He speaks quickly, trying to keep his wits.*) Now we must be wise, Elizabeth.

ELIZABETH (*with sarcasm, and a sense of being lost*) Oh, indeed, indeed!

PROCTOR Fear nothing. I'll find Ezekiel Cheever. I'll tell him she said it were all sport.

ELIZABETH John, with so many in the jail, more than Cheever's help is needed now, I think. Would you favor me with this? Go to Abigail.

PROCTOR (*his soul hardening as he senses . . .*) What have I to say to Abigail?

ELIZABETH (*delicately*) John—grant me this. You have a faulty understanding of young girls. There is a promise made in any bed—

PROCTOR (*striving against his anger*) What promise!

ELIZABETH Spoke or silent, a promise is surely made. And she may dote on it now—I am sure she does—and thinks to kill me, then to take my place.

Proctor's anger is rising; he cannot speak.

ELIZABETH It is her dearest hope, John, I know it. There be a thousand names; why does she call mine? There be a certain danger in calling such a name—I am no Goody Good that sleeps in ditches, nor Osburn, drunk and half-witted. She'd dare not call out such a farmer's wife but there be monstrous profit in it. She thinks to take my place, John.

PROCTOR She cannot think it! (*He knows it is true.*)

ELIZABETH (*"reasonably"*) John, have you ever shown her somewhat of contempt? She cannot pass you in the church but you will blush—

PROCTOR I may blush for my sin.

ELIZABETH I think she sees another meaning in that blush.

PROCTOR And what see you? What see you, Elizabeth?

ELIZABETH (*"conceding"*) I think you be somewhat ashamed, for I am there, and she so close.

PROCTOR When will you know me, woman? Were I stone I would have cracked for shame this seven month!

ELIZABETH Then go and tell her she's a whore. Whatever promise she may sense—break it, John, break it.

PROCTOR (*between his teeth*) Good, then. I'll go. (*He starts for his rifle.*)

ELIZABETH (*trembling, fearfully*) Oh, how unwillingly!

> Unlike those in drama of earlier eras, Miller's stage directions provide precise cues concerning the way he wishes the performers to portray their characters.

PROCTOR *(turning on her, rifle in hand)* I will curse her hotter than the oldest cinder in hell. But pray, begrudge me not my anger!

ELIZABETH Your anger! I only ask you—

PROCTOR Woman, am I so base? Do you truly think me base?

ELIZABETH I never called you base.

PROCTOR Then how do you charge me with such a promise? The promise that a stallion gives a mare I gave that girl!

ELIZABETH Then why do you anger with me when I bid you break it?

PROCTOR Because it speaks deceit, and I am honest! But I'll plead no more! I see now your spirit twists around the single error of my life, and I will never tear it free!

ELIZABETH *(crying out)* You'll tear it free—when you come to know that I will be your only wife, or no wife at all! She has an arrow in you yet, John Proctor, and you know it well!

Quite suddenly, as though from the air, a figure appears in the doorway. They start slightly. It is Mr. Hale. He is different now—drawn a little, and there is a quality of deference, even of guilt, about his manner now.

HALE Good evening.

PROCTOR *(still in his shock)* Why, Mr. Hale! Good evening to you, sir. Come in, come in.

HALE *(to Elizabeth)* I hope I do not startle you.

ELIZABETH No, no, it's only that I heard no horse—

HALE You are Goodwife Proctor.

PROCTOR Aye; Elizabeth.

HALE *(nods, then)* I hope you're not off to bed yet.

PROCTOR *(setting down his gun)* No, no. *(Hale comes further into the room. And Proctor, to explain his nervousness)* We are not used to visitors after dark, but you're welcome here. Will you sit you down, sir?

HALE I will. *(He sits.)* Let you sit, Goodwife Proctor.

She does, never letting him out of her sight. There is a pause as Hale looks about the room.

PROCTOR *(to break the silence)* Will you drink cider, Mr. Hale?

HALE No, it rebels my stomach; I have some further traveling yet tonight. Sit you down, sir. *(Proctor sits.)* I will not keep you long, but I have some business with you.

PROCTOR Business of the court?

HALE No—no, I come of my own, without the court's authority. Hear me. *(He wets his lips.)* I know not if you are aware, but your wife's name is—mentioned in the court.

PROCTOR We know it, sir. Our Mary Warren told us. We are entirely amazed.

HALE I am a stranger here, as you know. And in my ignorance I find it hard to draw a clear opinion of them that come accused before the court. And so this afternoon, and now tonight, I go from house to house—I come now from Rebecca Nurse's house and—

ELIZABETH *(shocked)* Rebecca's charged!

HALE God forbid such a one be charged. She is, however—mentioned somewhat.

ELIZABETH *(with an attempt at a laugh)* You will never believe, I hope, that Rebecca trafficked with the Devil.

HALE Woman, it is possible.

PROCTOR *(taken aback)* Surely you cannot think so.

HALE This is a strange time, Mister. No man may longer doubt the powers of the dark are gathered in monstrous attack upon this village. There is too much evidence now to deny it. You will agree, sir?

PROCTOR *(evading)* I—have no knowledge in that line. But it's hard to think so pious a woman be secretly a Devil's bitch after seventy year of such good prayer.

HALE Aye. But the Devil is a wily one, you cannot deny it. However, she is far from accused, and I know she will not be. *Pause.* I thought, sir, to put some questions as to the Christian character of this house, if you'll permit me.

PROCTOR *(coldly, resentful)* Why, we—have no fear of questions, sir.

HALE Good, then. *(He makes himself more comfortable.)* In the book of record that Mr. Parris keeps, I note that you are rarely in the church on Sabbath Day.

PROCTOR No, sir, you are mistaken.

HALE Twenty-six time in seventeen month, sir. I must call that rare. Will you tell me why you are so absent?

PROCTOR Mr. Hale, I never knew I must account to that man for I come to church or stay at home. My wife were sick this winter.

HALE So I am told. But you, Mister, why could you not come alone?

PROCTOR I surely did come when I could, and when I could not I prayed in this house.

HALE Mr. Proctor, your house is not a church; your theology must tell you that.

PROCTOR It does, sir, it does; and it tells me that a minister may pray to God without he have golden candlesticks upon the altar.

HALE What golden candlesticks?

PROCTOR Since we built the church there were pewter candlesticks upon the altar; Francis Nurse made them, y'know, and a sweeter hand never touched the metal. But Parris came, and for twenty week he preach nothin' but golden candlesticks until he had them. I labor the earth from dawn of day to blink of night, and I tell you true, when I look to heaven and see my money glaring at his elbows—it hurt my prayer, sir, it hurt my prayer. I think, sometimes, the man dreams cathedrals, not clapboard meetin' houses.

HALE *(thinks, then)* And yet, Mister, a Christian on Sabbath Day must be in church. *(pause)* Tell me—you have three children?

PROCTOR Aye. Boys.

HALE How comes it that only two are baptized?

What are the implications of Hale's investigation of the "Christian character" of Proctor and his wife?

What are the guidelines used in judging the guilt or innocence of persons accused at the trials?

Proctor's strong independence of mind regarding Parris is in direct conflict with church authority.

THE CRUCIBLE 311

PROCTOR *(starts to speak, then stops, then, as though unable to restrain this)* I like it not that Mr. Parris should lay his hand upon my baby. I see no light of God in that man. I'll not conceal it.

HALE I must say it, Mr. Proctor; that is not for you to decide. The man's ordained, therefore the light of God is in him.

PROCTOR *(flushed with resentment but trying to smile)* What's your suspicion, Mr. Hale?

HALE No, no, I have no—

PROCTOR I nailed the roof upon the church, I hung the door—

HALE Oh, did you! That's a good sign, then.

PROCTOR It may be I have been too quick to bring the man to book, but you cannot think we ever desired the destruction of religion. I think that's in your mind, is it not?

HALE *(not altogether giving way)* I—have—there is a softness in your record, sir, a softness.

ELIZABETH I think, maybe, we have been too hard with Mr. Parris. I think so. But sure we never loved the Devil here.

HALE *(Nods, deliberating this. Then, with the voice of one administering a secret test.)* Do you know your Commandments, Elizabeth?

ELIZABETH *(Without hesitation, even eagerly)* I surely do. There be no mark of blame upon my life, Mr. Hale. I am a covenanted Christian woman.

HALE And you, Mister?

PROCTOR *(a trifle unsteadily)* I—am sure I do, sir.

HALE *(glances at her open face, then at John, then)* Let you repeat them, if you will.

PROCTOR The Commandments.

HALE Aye.

PROCTOR *(looking off, beginning to sweat)* Thou shalt not kill.

HALE Aye.

PROCTOR *(counting on his fingers)* Thou shalt not steal. Thou shalt not covet thy neighbor's goods, nor make unto thee any graven image. Thou shalt not take the name of the Lord in vain; thou shalt have no other gods before me. *(with some hesitation)* Thou shalt remember the Sabbath Day and keep it holy. *(Pause. Then)* Thou shalt honor thy father and mother. Thou shalt not bear false witness. *(He is stuck. He counts back on his fingers, knowing one is missing.)* Thou shalt not make unto thee any graven image.

HALE You have said that twice, sir.

PROCTOR *(lost)* Aye. *(He is flailing for it.)*

ELIZABETH *(delicately)* Adultery, John.

PROCTOR *(as though a secret arrow had pained his heart)* Aye. *(trying to grin it away—to Hale)* You see, sir, between the two of us we do know them all. *(Hale only looks at Proctor, deep in his attempt to define this man. Proctor grows more uneasy.)* I think it be a small fault.

HALE Theology, sir, is a fortress; no crack in a fortress may be ac-

> Why is it appropriate that Proctor "forgets" this Commandment?

counted small. *(He rises; he seems worried now. He paces a little, in deep thought.)*

PROCTOR There be no love for Satan in this house, Mister.

HALE I pray it, I pray it dearly. *(He looks to both of them, an attempt at a smile on his face, but his misgivings are clear.)* Well, then—I'll bid you good night.

ELIZABETH *(unable to restrain herself)* Mr. Hale. *(He turns.)* I do think you are suspecting me somewhat? Are you not?

HALE *(obviously disturbed—and evasive)* Goody Proctor, I do not judge you. My duty is to add what I may to the godly wisdom of the court. I pray you both good health and good fortune. *(to John)* Good night, sir. *(He starts out.)*

ELIZABETH *(with a note of desperation)* I think you must tell him, John.

HALE What's that?

ELIZABETH *(restraining a call)* Will you tell him?

Slight pause. Hale looks questioningly at John.

PROCTOR *(with difficulty)* I—I have no witness and cannot prove it, except my word be taken. But I know the children's sickness had naught to do with witchcraft.

HALE *(stopped, struck)* Naught to do—?

PROCTOR Mr. Parris discovered them sportin' in the woods. They were startled and took sick.

Pause.

HALE Who told you this?

PROCTOR *(hesitates, then)* Abigail Williams.

HALE Abigail!

PROCTOR Aye.

HALE *(his eyes wide)* Abigail Williams told you it had naught to do with witchcraft!

PROCTOR She told me the day you came, sir.

HALE *(suspiciously)* Why—why did you keep this?

PROCTOR I never knew until tonight that the world is gone daft with this nonsense.

HALE Nonsense! Mister, I have myself examined Tituba, Sarah Good, and numerous others that have confessed to dealing with the Devil. They have *confessed* it.

PROCTOR And why not, if they must hang for denyin' it? There are them that will swear to anything before they'll hang; have you never thought of that?

HALE I have. I—I have indeed. *(It is his own suspicion, but he resists it. He glances at Elizabeth, then at John.)* And you—would you testify to this in court?

PROCTOR I—had not reckoned with goin' into court. But if I must I will.

HALE Do you falter here?

With Hale's interrogation, Miller creates a mood of desperation, leading to Proctor's forced announcement of the fraud perpetuated by the accusing girls at the trials.

Unlike the other "authorities" involved in the trials, Hale does recognize the coercive nature of the charges that can lead to false admissions in order to preserve one's life.

THE CRUCIBLE 313

PROCTOR I falter nothing, but I may wonder if my story will be credited in such a court. I do wonder on it, when such a steady-minded minister as you will suspicion such a woman that never lied, and cannot, and the world knows she cannot! I may falter somewhat, Mister; I am no fool.

HALE (*Quietly—it has impressed him.*) Proctor, let you open with me now, for I have a rumor that troubles me. It's said you hold no belief that there may even be witches in the world. Is that true, sir?

PROCTOR (*He knows this is critical, and is striving against his disgust with Hale and with himself for even answering.*) I know not what I have said, I may have said it. I have wondered if there be witches in the world—although I cannot believe they come among us now.

Why would the Proctors' disbelief in witches be unacceptable to Hale and to the presiding church magistrates at the trials?

HALE Then you do not believe—

PROCTOR I have no knowledge of it; the Bible speaks of witches, and I will not deny them.

HALE And you, woman?

ELIZABETH I—I cannot believe it.

HALE (*shocked*) You cannot!

PROCTOR Elizabeth, you bewilder him!

ELIZABETH (*to Hale*) I cannot think the Devil may own a woman's soul, Mr. Hale, when she keeps an upright way, as I have. I am a good woman, I know it; and if you believe I may do only good work in the world, and yet be secretly bound to Satan, then I must tell you, sir, I do not believe it.

HALE But, woman, you do believe there are witches in—

ELIZABETH If you think that I am one, then I say there are none.

HALE You surely do not fly against the Gospel, the Gospel—

PROCTOR She believe in the Gospel, every word!

ELIZABETH Question Abigail Williams about the Gospel, not myself!

Hale stares at her.

PROCTOR She do not mean to doubt the Gospel, sir, you cannot think it. This be a Christian house, sir, a Christian house.

HALE God keep you both; let the third child be quickly baptized, and go you without fail each Sunday in to Sabbath prayer; and keep a solemn, quiet way among you. I think—

What kind of advice does Hale offer here?

Giles Corey appears in doorway.

GILES John!

PROCTOR Giles! What's the matter?

GILES They take my wife.

Francis Nurse enters.

GILES And his Rebecca!

PROCTOR (*to Francis*) Rebecca's in the *jail*!

FRANCIS Aye, Cheever come and take her in his wagon. We've only now come from the jail, and they'll not even let us in to see them.

ELIZABETH They've surely gone wild now, Mr. Hale!

FRANCIS (going to Hale) Reverend Hale! Can you not speak to the Deputy Governor? I'm sure he mistakes these people—

HALE Pray calm yourself, Mr. Nurse.

FRANCIS My wife is the very brick and mortar of the church, Mr. Hale—(indicating Giles)—and Martha Corey, there cannot be a woman closer yet to God than Martha.

HALE How is Rebecca charged, Mr. Nurse?

FRANCIS (with a mocking, half-hearted laugh) For murder, she's charged! (mockingly quoting the warrant) "For the marvelous and supernatural murder of Goody Putnam's babies." What am I to do, Mr. Hale?

HALE (turns from Francis, deeply troubled, then) Believe me, Mr. Nurse, if Rebecca Nurse be tainted, then nothing's left to stop the whole green world from burning. Let you rest upon the justice of the court; the court will send her home, I know it.

FRANCIS You cannot mean she will be tried in court!

HALE (pleading) Nurse, though our hearts break, we cannot flinch; these are new times, sir. There is a misty plot afoot so subtle we should be criminal to cling to old respects and ancient friendships. I have seen too many frightful proofs in court—the Devil is alive in Salem, and we dare not quail to follow wherever the accusing finger points!

PROCTOR (angered) How may such a woman murder children?

HALE (in great pain) Man, remember, until an hour before the Devil fell, God thought him beautiful in Heaven.

GILES I never said my wife were a witch, Mr. Hale; I only said she were reading books!

HALE Mr. Corey, exactly what complaint were made on your wife?

GILES That bloody mongrel Walcott charge her. Y'see, he buy a pig of my wife four or five year ago, and the pig died soon after. So he come dancin' in for his money back. So my Martha, she says to him, "Walcott, if you haven't the wit to feed a pig properly, you'll not live to own many," she says. Now he goes to court and claims that from that day to this he cannot keep a pig alive for more than four weeks because my Martha bewitch them with her books!

Enter Ezekiel Cheever. A shocked silence.

CHEEVER Good evening to you, Proctor.

PROCTOR Why, Mr. Cheever. Good evening.

CHEEVER Good evening, all. Good evening, Mr. Hale.

PROCTOR I hope you come not on business of the court.

CHEEVER I do, Proctor, aye. I am clerk of the court now, y'know.

Enter Marshal Herrick, a man in his early thirties, who is somewhat shamefaced at the moment.

GILES It's a pity, Ezekiel, that an honest tailor might have gone to Heaven must burn in Hell. You'll burn for this, do you know it?

Note the contrast of reactions at the new turn of events between Proctor and Hale—one is a hard-headed pragmatist, and the other is an apologist for the proceedings.

CHEEVER You know yourself I must do as I'm told. You surely know that, Giles. And I'd as lief you'd not be sending me to Hell. I like not the sound of it, I tell you; I like not the sound of it. *(He fears Proctor, but starts to reach inside his coat.)* Now believe me, Proctor, how heavy be the law, all its tonnage I do carry on my back tonight. *(He takes out a warrant.)* I have a warrant for your wife.

PROCTOR *(to Hale)* You said she were not charged!

HALE I know nothin' of it. *(to Cheever)* When were she charged?

CHEEVER I am given sixteen warrant tonight, sir, and she is one.

PROCTOR Who charged her?

CHEEVER Why, Abigail Williams charge her.

PROCTOR On what proof, what proof?

CHEEVER *(looking about the room)* Mr. Proctor, I have little time. The court bid me search your house, but I like not to search a house. So will you hand me any poppets that your wife may keep here?

PROCTOR Poppets?

ELIZABETH I never kept no poppets, not since I were a girl.

CHEEVER *(embarrassed, glancing toward the mantel where sits Mary Warren's poppet)* I spy a poppet, Goody Proctor.

ELIZABETH Oh! *(going for it)* Why, this is Mary's.

CHEEVER *(shyly)* Would you please to give it to me?

ELIZABETH *(handing it to him, asks Hale)* Has the court discovered a text in poppets now?

CHEEVER *(carefully holding the poppet)* Do you keep any others in this house?

PROCTOR No, nor this one either till tonight. What signifies a poppet?

CHEEVER Why, a poppet— *(He gingerly turns the poppet over.)* —a poppet may signify— Now, woman, will you please to come with me?

PROCTOR She will not! *(to Elizabeth)* Fetch Mary here.

CHEEVER *(ineptly reaching toward Elizabeth)* No, no, I am forbid to leave her from my sight.

PROCTOR *(pushing his arm away)* You'll leave her out of sight and out of mind, Mister. Fetch Mary, Elizabeth. *(Elizabeth goes upstairs.)*

HALE What signifies a poppet, Mr. Cheever?

CHEEVER *(turning the poppet over in his hands)* Why, they say it may signify that she— *(He has lifted the poppet's skirt, and his eyes widen in astonished fear.)* Why, this, this—

PROCTOR *(reaching for the poppet)* What's there?

CHEEVER Why— *(He draws out a long needle from the poppet.)* —it is a needle! Herrick, Herrick, it is a needle!

Herrick comes toward him.

PROCTOR *(angrily, bewildered)* And what signifies a needle!

CHEEVER *(his hands shaking)* Why, this go hard with her, Proctor,

> Why is it so difficult to assign responsibility when someone claims "I must do as I'm told," as Cheever says here?

this—I had my doubts, Proctor, I had my doubts, but here's calamity. *(to Hale, showing the needle)* You see it, sir, it is a needle!

HALE Why? What meanin' has it?

CHEEVER *(wide-eyed, trembling)* The girl, the Williams girl, Abigail Williams, sir. She sat to dinner in Reverend Parris's house tonight, and without word nor warnin' she falls to the floor. Like a struck beast, he says, and screamed a scream that a bull would weep to hear. And he goes to save her, and, stuck two inches in the flesh of her belly, he draw a needle out. And demandin' of her how she come to be so stabbed, she—*(to Proctor now)*—testify it were your wife's familiar spirit pushed it in.

PROCTOR Why, she done it herself! *(to Hale)* I hope you're not takin' this for proof, Mister!

Hale, struck by the proof, is silent.

CHEEVER 'Tis hard proof! *(to Hale)* I find here a poppet Goody Proctor keeps. I have found it, sir. And in the belly of the poppet a needle's stuck. I tell you true, Proctor, I never warranted to see such proof of Hell, and I bid you obstruct me not, for I—

Enter Elizabeth with Mary Warren. Proctor, seeing Mary Warren, draws her by the arm to Hale.

PROCTOR Here now! Mary, how did this poppet come into my house?

MARY WARREN *(frightened for herself, her voice very small)* What poppet's that, sir?

PROCTOR *(impatiently, points at the doll in Cheever's hand)* This poppet, this poppet.

MARY WARREN *(evasively, looking at it)* Why, I—I think it is mine.

PROCTOR It is your poppet, is it not?

MARY WARREN *(not understanding the direction of this)* It—is, sir.

PROCTOR And how did it come into this house?

MARY WARREN *(glancing about at the avid faces)* Why—I made it in the court, sir, and—give it to Goody Proctor tonight.

PROCTOR *(to Hale)* Now, sir—do you have it?

HALE Mary Warren, a needle have been found inside this poppet.

MARY WARREN *(bewildered)* Why, I meant no harm by it, sir.

PROCTOR *(quickly)* You stuck that needle in yourself?

MARY WARREN I—I believe I did, sir, I—

PROCTOR *(to Hale)* What say you now?

HALE *(watching Mary Warren closely)* Child, you are certain this be your natural memory? May it be, perhaps, that someone conjures you even now to say this?

MARY WARREN Conjures me? Why, no, sir, I am entirely myself, I think. Let you ask Susanna Walcott—she saw me sewin' it in court. *(or better still)* Ask Abby, Abby sat beside me when I made it.

PROCTOR *(to Hale, of Cheever)* Bid him begone. Your mind is surely settled now. Bid him out, Mr. Hale.

Like the others, Cheever is caught up in the hysteria. He is totally convinced of witchcraft because of the needle and doll.

ELIZABETH What signifies a needle?

HALE Mary—you charge a cold and cruel murder on Abigail.

MARY WARREN Murder! I charge no—

HALE Abigail were stabbed tonight; a needle were found stuck into her belly—

ELIZABETH And she charges me?

HALE Aye.

ELIZABETH (*her breath knocked out*) Why—! The girl is murder! She must be ripped out of the world!

CHEEVER (*pointing at Elizabeth*) You've heard that, sir! Ripped out of the world! Herrick, you heard it!

PROCTOR (*suddenly snatching the warrant out of Cheever's hands*) Out with you.

CHEEVER Proctor, you dare not touch the warrant.

PROCTOR (*ripping the warrant*) Out with you!

CHEEVER You've ripped the Deputy Governor's warrant, man!

PROCTOR Damn the Deputy Governor! Out of my house!

HALE Now, Proctor, Proctor!

PROCTOR Get y'gone with them! You are a broken minister.

HALE Proctor, if she is innocent, the court—

PROCTOR If *she* is innocent! Why do you never wonder if Parris be innocent, or Abigail? Is the accuser always holy now? Were they born this morning as clean as God's fingers? I'll tell you what's walking Salem—vengeance is walking Salem. We are what we always were in Salem, but now the little crazy children are jangling the keys of the kingdom, and common vengeance writes the law! This warrant's vengeance! I'll not give my wife to vengeance!

ELIZABETH I'll go, John—

PROCTOR You will not go!

HERRICK I have nine men outside. You cannot keep her. The law binds me, John, I cannot budge.

PROCTOR (*to Hale, ready to break him*) Will you see her taken?

HALE Proctor, the court is just—

PROCTOR Pontius Pilate! God will not let you wash your hands of this!

ELIZABETH John—I think I must go with them. (*He cannot bear to look at her.*) Mary, there is bread enough for the morning; you will bake, in the afternoon. Help Mr. Proctor as you were his daughter—you owe me that, and much more. (*She is fighting her weeping. To Proctor*) When the children wake, speak nothing of witchcraft—it will frighten them. (*She cannot go on.*)

PROCTOR I will bring you home. I will bring you soon.

ELIZABETH Oh, John, bring me soon!

PROCTOR I will fall like an ocean on that court! Fear nothing, Elizabeth.

Proctor's critical question to Hale represents one that plagues all people who knowingly permit injustices to occur without objection.

Why is Pontius Pilate the most appropriate parallel in Proctor's mind for Hale's evasion of his moral obligations?

ELIZABETH *(with great fear)* I will fear nothing. *(She looks about the room, as though to fix it in her mind.)* Tell the children I have gone to visit someone sick.

She walks out the door, Herrick and Cheever behind her. For a moment, Proctor watches from the doorway. The clank of chain is heard.

PROCTOR Herrick! Herrick, don't chain her! *(He rushes out the door. From outside)* Damn you, man, you will not chain her! Off with them! I'll not have it! I will not have her chained!

There are other men's voices against his. Hale, in a fever of guilt and uncertainty, turns from the door to avoid the sight; Mary Warren bursts into tears and sits weeping. Giles Corey calls to Hale.

GILES And yet silent, minister? It is fraud, you know it is fraud! What keeps you, man?

Proctor is half braced, half pushed into the room by two deputies and Herrick.

PROCTOR I'll pay you, Herrick, I will surely pay you!

HERRICK *(panting)* In God's name, John, I cannot help myself. I must chain them all. Now let you keep inside this house till I am gone! *(He goes out with his deputies.)*

Proctor stands there, gulping air. Horses and a wagon creaking are heard.

HALE *(in great uncertainty)* Mr. Proctor—

PROCTOR Out of my sight!

HALE Charity, Proctor, charity. What I have heard in her favor, I will not fear to testify in court. God help me, I cannot judge her guilty or innocent—I know not. Only this consider: the world goes mad, and it profit nothing you should lay the cause to the vengeance of a little girl.

PROCTOR You are a coward! Though you be ordained in God's own tears, you are a coward now!

HALE Proctor, I cannot think God be provoked so grandly by such a petty cause. The jails are packed—our greatest judges sit in Salem now—and hangin's promised. Man, we must look to cause proportionate. Were there murder done, perhaps, and never brought to light? Abomination? Some secret blasphemy that stinks to Heaven? Think on cause, man, and let you help me to discover it. For there's your way, believe it, there is your only way, when such confusion strikes upon the world. *(He goes to Giles and Francis.)* Let you counsel among yourselves; think on your village and what may have drawn from heaven such thundering wrath upon you all. I shall pray God open up our eyes.

Hale goes out.

FRANCIS *(struck by Hale's mood)* I never heard no murder done in Salem.

PROCTOR —*(He has been reached by Hale's words.)* Leave me, Francis, leave me.

GILES *(shaken)* John—tell me, are we lost?

PROCTOR Go home now, Giles. We'll speak on it tomorrow.

Hale rationalizes his own inaction in not stopping the trials, but there is an obvious flaw in his reasoning. What is the loophole in saying, "I cannot think God be provoked so grandly by such a petty cause"?

GILES Let you think on it. We'll come early, eh?

PROCTOR Aye. Go now, Giles.

GILES Good night, then.

Giles Corey goes out. After a moment:

MARY WARREN *(in a fearful squeak of a voice)* Mr. Proctor, very likely they'll let her come home once they're given proper evidence.

PROCTOR You're coming to the court with me, Mary. You will tell it in the court.

MARY WARREN I cannot charge murder on Abigail.

PROCTOR *(moving menacingly toward her)* You will tell the court how that poppet come here and who stuck the needle in.

MARY WARREN She'll kill me for sayin' that! *(Proctor continues toward her.)* Abby'll charge lechery on you, Mr. Proctor!

PROCTOR *(halting)* She's told you!

MARY WARREN I have known it, sir. She'll ruin you with it, I know she will.

PROCTOR *(hesitating, and with deep hatred of himself)* Good. Then her saintliness is done with. *(Mary backs from him.)* We will slide together into our pit; you will tell the court what you know.

> Proctor now is resolved that the truth must be told. What does he mean when he tells Mary Warren that "we will slide together into our pit"?

MARY WARREN *(in terror)* I cannot, they'll turn on me—

Proctor strides and catches her, and she is repeating, "I cannot, I cannot!"

PROCTOR My wife will never die for me! I will bring your guts into your mouth but that goodness will not die for me!

MARY WARREN *(struggling to escape him)* I cannot do it, I cannot!

PROCTOR *(grasping her by the throat as though he would strangle her)* Make your peace with it! Now Hell and Heaven grapple on our backs, and all our old pretense is ripped away—make your peace! *(He throws her to the floor, where she sobs, "I cannot, I cannot . . ." And now, half to himself, staring, and turning to the open door.)* Peace. It is a providence, and no great change; we are only what we always were, but naked now. *(He walks as though toward a great horror, facing the open sky.)* Aye, naked! And the wind, God's icy wind, will blow!

> Why is this such an effective ending on stage for the act?

And she is over and over again sobbing, "I cannot, I cannot, I cannot," as the curtain falls.

ACT III

The vestry room of the Salem meeting house, now serving as the anteroom of the General court.

As the curtain rises, the room is empty, but for sunlight pouring through two high windows in the back wall. The room is solemn, even forbidding. Heavy beams jut out, boards of random widths make up the walls. At the right are two doors leading into the meeting house proper, where the court is being held. At the left another door leads outside.

There is a plain bench at the left, and another at the right. In the center a rather long meeting table, with stools and a considerable armchair snugged up to it.

Through the partitioning wall at the right we hear a prosecutor's voice, Judge Hathorne's, asking a question; then a woman's voice, Martha Corey's, replying.

HATHORNE'S VOICE Now, Martha Corey, there is abundant evidence in our hands to show that you have given yourself to the reading of fortunes. Do you deny it?

MARTHA COREY'S VOICE I am innocent to a witch. I know not what a witch is.

HATHORNE'S VOICE How do you know, then, that you are not a witch?

MARTHA COREY'S VOICE If I were, I would know it.

HATHORNE'S VOICE Why do you hurt these children?

MARTHA COREY'S VOICE I do not hurt them. I scorn it!

GILES' VOICE *(roaring)* I have evidence for the court!

Voices of townspeople rise in excitement.

DANFORTH'S VOICE You will keep your seat!

GILES' VOICE Thomas Putnam is reaching out for land!

DANFORTH'S VOICE Remove that man, Marshal!

GILES' VOICE You're hearing lies, lies!

A roaring goes up from the people.

HATHORNE'S VOICE Arrest him, excellency!

GILES' VOICE I have evidence. Why will you not hear my evidence?

The door opens and Giles is half carried into the vestry room by Herrick.

GILES Hands off, damn you, let me go!

HERRICK Giles, Giles!

GILES Out of my way, Herrick! I bring evidence—

HERRICK You cannot go in there, Giles; it's a court!

Enter Hale from the court.

HALE Pray be calm a moment.

GILES You, Mr. Hale, go in there and demand I speak.

HALE A moment, sir, a moment.

GILES They'll be hangin' my wife!

Judge Hathorne enters. He is in his sixties, a bitter, remorseless Salem judge.

HATHORNE How do you dare come roarin' into this court! Are you gone daft, Corey?

GILES You're not a Boston judge, Hathorne. You'll not call me daft!

Enter Deputy Governor Danforth and, behind him, Ezekiel Cheever and Parris. On his appearance, silence falls. Danforth is a grave man in his sixties, of some humor and sophistication that does not, however, interfere with an exact loyalty to his position and his cause. He comes down to Giles, who awaits his wrath.

From this brief exchange of dialogue, how do we learn that only selective evidence is desired in the court—not information which might disqualify a witness?

The judge was an ancestor of the later famous American novelist, Nathaniel Hawthorne. Hawthorne deliberately altered the spelling of his surname out of shame for his kinship with Judge Hathorne.

DANFORTH *(looking directly at Giles)* Who is this man?

PARRIS Giles Corey, sir, and a more contentious—

GILES *(to Parris)* I am asked the question, and I am old enough to answer it! *(to Danforth, who impresses him and to whom he smiles through his strain)* My name is Corey, sir, Giles Corey. I have six hundred acres, and timber in addition. It is my wife you be condemning now. *(He indicates the courtroom.)*

DANFORTH And how do you imagine to help her cause with such contemptuous riot? Now be gone. Your old age alone keeps you out of jail for this.

GILES *(beginning to plead)* They be tellin' lies about my wife, sir, I—

DANFORTH Do you take it upon yourself to determine what this court shall believe and what it shall set aside?

GILES Your Excellency, we mean no disrespect for—

DANFORTH Disrespect indeed! It is disruption, Mister. This is the highest court of the supreme government of this province, do you know it?

At the outset, Danforth establishes his imperial manner which will not permit him to be crossed by anyone.

GILES *(beginning to weep)* Your Excellency, I only said she were readin' books, sir, and they come and take her out of my house for—

DANFORTH *(mystified)* Books! What books?

GILES *(through helpless sobs)* It is my third wife, sir; I never had no wife that be so taken with books, and I thought to find the cause of it, d'y'see, but it were no witch I blamed her for. *(He is openly weeping.)* I have broke charity with the woman, I have broke charity with her. *(He covers his face, ashamed. Danforth is respectfully silent.)*

HALE Excellency, he claims hard evidence for his wife's defense. I think that in all justice you must—

DANFORTH Then let him submit his evidence in proper affidavit. You are certainly aware of our procedure here, Mr. Hale. *(to Herrick)* Clear this room.

HERRICK Come now, Giles. *(He gently pushes Corey out.)*

FRANCIS We are desperate, sir; we come here three days now and cannot be heard.

DANFORTH Who is this man?

Evidence on behalf of those accused is difficult to present to the court, adding to the frustration and tension seen in the husbands of the accused wives.

FRANCIS Francis Nurse, Your Excellency.

HALE His wife's Rebecca that were condemned this morning.

DANFORTH Indeed! I am amazed to find you in such uproar. I have only good report of your character, Mr. Nurse.

HATHORNE I think they must both be arrested in contempt, sir.

DANFORTH *(to Francis)* Let you write your plea, and in due time I will—

FRANCIS Excellency, we have proof for your eyes; God forbid you shut them to it. The girls, sir, the girls are frauds.

DANFORTH What's that?

FRANCIS We have proof of it, sir. They are all deceiving you.

Danforth is shocked, but studying Francis.

HATHORNE This is contempt, sir, contempt!

DANFORTH Peace, Judge Hathorne. Do you know who I am, Mr. Nurse?

FRANCIS I surely do, sir, and I think you must be a wise judge to be what you are.

DANFORTH And do you know that near to four hundred are in the jails from Marblehead to Lynn, and upon my signature?

FRANCIS I—

DANFORTH And seventy-two condemned to hang by that signature?

FRANCIS Excellency, I never thought to say it to such a weighty judge, but you are deceived.

Enter Giles Corey from left. All turn to see as he beckons in Mary Warren with Proctor. Mary is keeping her eyes to the ground; Proctor has her elbow as though she were near collapse.

PARRIS *(on seeing her, in shock)* Mary Warren! *(He goes directly to bend close to her face.)* What are you about here?

PROCTOR *(pressing Parris away from her with a gentle but firm motion of protectiveness)* She would speak with the Deputy Governor.

DANFORTH *(shocked by this, turns to Herrick)* Did you not tell me Mary Warren were sick in bed?

HERRICK She were, Your Honor. When I go to fetch her to the court last week, she said she were sick.

GILES She has been strivin' with her soul all week, Your Honor; she comes now to tell the truth of this to you.

DANFORTH Who is this?

PROCTOR John Proctor, sir. Elizabeth Proctor is my wife.

PARRIS Beware this man, Your Excellency, this man is mischief.

HALE *(excitedly)* I think you must hear the girl, sir, she—

DANFORTH *(who has become very interested in Mary Warren and only raises a hand toward Hale)* Peace. What would you tell us, Mary Warren?

Proctor looks at her, but she cannot speak.

PROCTOR She never saw no spirits, sir.

DANFORTH *(with great alarm and surprise, to Mary)* Never saw no spirits!

GILES *(eagerly)* Never.

PROCTOR *(reaching into his jacket)* She has signed a deposition, sir—

DANFORTH *(instantly)* No, no, I accept no depositions. *(He is rapidly calculating this; he turns from her to Proctor.)* Tell me, Mr. Proctor, have you given out this story in the village?

PROCTOR We have not.

PARRIS They've come to overthrow the court, sir! This man is—

THE CRUCIBLE 323

DANFORTH I pray you, Mr. Parris. Do you know, Mr. Proctor, that the entire contention of the state in these trials is that the voice of Heaven is speaking through the children?

PROCTOR I know that, sir.

DANFORTH *(thinks, staring at Proctor, then turns to Mary Warren)* And you, Mary Warren, how came you to cry out people for sending their spirits against you?

MARY WARREN It were pretense, sir.

DANFORTH I cannot hear you.

PROCTOR It were pretense, she says.

DANFORTH Ah? And the other girls? Susanna Walcott, and—the others? They are also pretending?

MARY WARREN Aye, sir.

DANFORTH *(wide-eyed)* Indeed. *(Pause. He is baffled by this. He turns to study Proctor's face.)*

PARRIS *(in a sweat)* Excellency, you surely cannot think to let so vile a lie be spread in open court.

DANFORTH Indeed not, but it strike hard upon me that she will dare come here with such a tale. Now, Mr. Proctor, before I decide whether I shall hear you or not, it is my duty to tell you this. We burn a hot fire here; it melts down all concealment.

PROCTOR I know that, sir.

DANFORTH Let me continue. I understand well, a husband's tenderness may drive him to extravagance in defense of a wife. Are you certain in your conscience, Mister, that your evidence is the truth?

PROCTOR It is. And you will surely know it.

DANFORTH And you thought to declare this revelation in the open court before the public?

PROCTOR I thought I would, aye—with your permission.

DANFORTH *(his eyes narrowing)* Now, sir, what is your purpose in so doing?

PROCTOR Why, I—I would free my wife, sir.

DANFORTH There lurks nowhere in your heart, nor hidden in your spirit, any desire to undermine this court?

PROCTOR *(with the faintest faltering)* Why, no, sir.

CHEEVER *(clears his throat, awakening)* I—Your Excellency.

DANFORTH Mr. Cheever.

CHEEVER I think it be my duty, sir—*(kindly, to Proctor)* You'll not deny it, John. *(to Danforth)* When we come to take his wife, he damned the court and ripped your warrant.

PARRIS Now you have it!

DANFORTH He did that, Mr. Hale?

HALE *(takes a breath)* Aye, he did.

PROCTOR It were a temper, sir. I knew not what I did.

From Danforth's deliberate and intimidating questioning, the audience learns that the prosecution is based on the testimony of the girls introduced in Act I.

Because of the importance of the girls' testimony, any refutation of it would invalidate the court proceedings. What is Danforth's primary concern, then, with Proctor's evidence: justice or keeping face? How do we know?

324   ARTHUR MILLER

DANFORTH (*studying him*) Mr. Proctor.

PROCTOR Aye, sir.

DANFORTH (*straight into his eyes*) Have you ever seen the Devil?

PROCTOR No, sir.

DANFORTH You are in all respects a Gospel Christian?

PROCTOR I am, sir.

PARRIS Such a Christian that will not come to church but once in a month!

DANFORTH (*Restrained—he is curious.*) Not come to church?

PROCTOR I—I have no love for Mr. Parris. It is no secret. But God I surely love.

CHEEVER He plow on Sunday, sir.

DANFORTH Plow on Sunday!

CHEEVER (*apologetically*) I think it be evidence, John. I am an official of the court, I cannot keep it.

PROCTOR I—I have once or twice plowed on Sunday. I have three children, sir, and until last year my land give little.

GILES You'll find other Christians that do plow on Sunday if the truth be known.

HALE Your Honor, I cannot think you may judge the man on such evidence.

DANFORTH I judge nothing. (*Pause. He keeps watching Proctor, who tries to meet his gaze.*) I tell you straight, Mister—I have seen marvels in this court. I have seen people choked before my eyes by spirits; I have seen them stuck by pins and slashed by daggers. I have until this moment not the slightest reason to suspect that the children may be deceiving me. Do you understand my meaning?

PROCTOR Excellency, does it not strike upon you that so many of these women have lived so long with such upright reputation, and—

PARRIS Do you read the Gospel, Mr. Proctor?

PROCTOR I read the Gospel.

PARRIS I think not, or you should surely know that Cain were an upright man, and yet he did kill Abel.

PROCTOR Aye, God tells us that. (*to Danforth*) But who tells us Rebecca Nurse murdered seven babies by sending out her spirit on them? It is the children only, and this one will swear she lied to you.

Danforth considers, then beckons Hathorne to him. Hathorne leans in, and he speaks in his ear. Hathorne nods.

HATHORNE Aye, she's the one.

DANFORTH Mr. Proctor, this morning, your wife send me a claim in which she states that she is pregnant now.

PROCTOR My wife pregnant!

DANFORTH There be no sign of it—we have examined her body.

How can one explain Cheever's offering any observations without being asked? How does Cheever himself defend his statements?

In these episodes, proving one's *innocence* is far more difficult than proving *guilt*.

PROCTOR But if she say she is pregnant, then she must be! That woman will never lie, Mr. Danforth.

DANFORTH She will not?

PROCTOR Never, sir, never.

DANFORTH We have thought it too convenient to be credited. However, if I should tell you now that I will let her be kept another month; and if she begin to show her natural signs, you shall have her living yet another year until she is delivered—what say you to that? *(John Proctor is struck silent.)* Come now. You say your only purpose is to save your wife. Good, then, she is saved at least this year, and a year is long. What say you, sir? It is done now. *(In conflict, Proctor glances at Francis and Giles.)* Will you drop this charge?

> Proctor's absolute certainty that his wife would never lie will prove his undoing later in this act.

PROCTOR I—I think I cannot.

DANFORTH *(now an almost imperceptible hardness in his voice)* Then your purpose is somewhat larger.

PARRIS He's come to overthrow this court, Your Honor!

PROCTOR These are my friends. Their wives are also accused—

DANFORTH *(with a sudden briskness of manner)* I judge you not, sir. I am ready to hear your evidence.

PROCTOR I come not to hurt the court; I only—

DANFORTH *(cutting him off)* Marshal, go into the court and bid Judge Stoughton and Judge Sewall declare recess for one hour. And let them go to the tavern, if they will. All witnesses and prisoners are to be kept in the building.

HERRICK Aye, sir. *(very deferentially)* If I may say it, sir, I know this man all my life. It is a good man, sir.

DANFORTH *(It is the reflection on himself he resents.)* I am sure of it, Marshal. *(Herrick nods, then goes out.)* Now, what deposition do you have for us, Mr. Proctor? And I beg you be clear, open as the sky, and honest.

PROCTOR *(as he takes out several papers)* I am no lawyer, so I'll—

DANFORTH The pure in heart need no lawyers. Proceed as you will.

> What does Danforth imply here regarding Proctor?

PROCTOR *(handing Danforth a paper)* Will you read this first, sir? It's a sort of testament. The people signing it declare their good opinion of Rebecca, and my wife, and Martha Corey. *(Danforth looks down at the paper.)*

PARRIS *(to enlist Danforth's sarcasm)* Their good opinion! *(But Danforth goes on reading, and Proctor is heartened.)*

PROCTOR These are all landholding farmers, members of the church. *(delicately, trying to point out a paragraph)* If you'll notice, sir—they've known the women many years and never saw no sign they had dealings with the Devil.

Parris nervously moves over and reads over Danforth's shoulder.

DANFORTH *(glancing down a long list)* How many names are here?

FRANCIS Ninety-one, Your Excellency.

> We already know that Danforth is impressed by numbers. Here that character trait again arises.

326 ARTHUR MILLER

PARRIS (*sweating*) These people should be summoned. (*Danforth looks up at him questioningly.*) For questioning.

FRANCIS (*trembling with anger*) Mr. Danforth, I gave them all my word no harm would come to them for signing this.

PARRIS This is a clear attack upon the court!

HALE (*to Parris, trying to contain himself*) Is every defense an attack upon the court? Can no one—?

PARRIS All innocent and Christian people are happy for the courts in Salem! These people are gloomy for it. (*to Danforth directly*) And I think you will want to know, from each and every one of them, what discontents them with you!

HATHORNE I think they ought to be examined, sir.

DANFORTH It is not necessarily an attack, I think. Yet—

FRANCIS These are all covenanted Christians, sir.

DANFORTH Then I am sure they may have nothing to fear. (*hands Cheever the paper*) Mr. Cheever, have warrants drawn for all of these—arrest for examination. (*to Proctor*) Now, Mister, what other information do you have for us? (*Francis is still standing, horrified.*) You may sit, Mr. Nurse.

What is Danforth's motive for arresting all those who signed the deposition?

FRANCIS I have brought trouble on these people; I have—

DANFORTH No, old man, you have not hurt these people if they are of good conscience. But you must understand, sir, that a person is either with this court or he must be counted against it, there be no road between. This is a sharp time, now, a precise time—we live no longer in the dusky afternoon when evil mixed itself with good and befuddled the world. Now, by God's grace, the shining sun is up, and them that fear not light will surely praise it. I hope you will be one of those. (*Mary Warren suddenly sobs.*) She's not hearty, I see.

PROCTOR No, she's not, sir. (*to Mary, bending to her, holding her hand, quietly*) Now remember what the angel Raphael said to the boy Tobias. Remember it.

MARY WARREN (*hardly audible*) Aye.

PROCTOR "Do that which is good, and no harm shall come to thee."

MARY WARREN Aye.

DANFORTH Come, man, we wait you.

Marshal Herrick returns, and takes his post at the door.

GILES John, my deposition, give him mine.

PROCTOR Aye. (*He hands Danforth another paper.*) This is Mr. Corey's deposition.

DANFORTH Oh? (*He looks down at it. Now Hathorne comes behind him and reads with him.*)

HATHORNE (*suspiciously*) What lawyer drew this, Corey?

GILES You know I never hired a lawyer in my life, Hathorne.

DANFORTH (*finishing the reading*) It is very well phrased. My compliments. Mr. Parris, if Mr. Putnam is in the court, will you bring him

THE CRUCIBLE 327

in? *(Hathorne takes the deposition, and walks to the window with it. Parris goes into the court.)* You have no legal training, Mr. Corey?

GILES *(very pleased)* I have the best, sir—I am thirty-three time in court in my life. And always plaintiff, too.

DANFORTH Oh, then you're much put-upon.

GILES I am never put-upon; I know my rights, sir, and I will have them. You know, your father tried a case of mine—might be thirty-five year ago, I think.

DANFORTH Indeed.

GILES He never spoke to you of it?

DANFORTH No, I cannot recall it.

GILES That's strange, he give me nine pound damages. He were a fair judge, your father. Y'see, I had a white mare that time, and this fellow come to borrow the mare— *(Enter Parris with Thomas Putnam. When he sees Putnam, Giles' ease goes; he is hard.)* Aye, there he is.

DANFORTH Mr. Putnam, I have here an accusation by Mr. Corey against you. He states that you coldly prompted your daughter to cry witchery upon George Jacobs that is now in jail.

PUTNAM It is a lie.

DANFORTH *(turning to Giles)* Mr. Putnam states your charge is a lie. What say you to that?

GILES *(furious, his fists clenched)* A fart on Thomas Putnam, that is what I say to that!

DANFORTH What proof do you submit for your charge, sir?

GILES My proof is there! *(pointing to the paper)* If Jacobs hangs for a witch he forfeit up his property—that's law! And there is none but Putnam with the coin to buy so great a piece. This man is killing his neighbors for their land!

DANFORTH But proof, sir, proof.

GILES *(pointing at his deposition)* The proof is there! I have it from an honest man who heard Putnam say it! The day his daughter cried out on Jacobs, he said she'd given him a fair gift of land.

> The deck is stacked against anyone who would dare impugn the validity—or motivation—of the trials.

HATHORNE And the name of this man?

GILES *(taken aback)* What name?

HATHORNE The man that give you this information.

GILES *(hesitates, then)* Why, I—I cannot give you his name.

HATHORNE And why not?

GILES *(hesitates, then bursts out)* You know well why not! He'll lay in jail if I give his name!

HATHORNE This is contempt of the court, Mr. Danforth!

DANFORTH *(to avoid that)* You will surely tell us the name.

GILES I will not give you no name. I mentioned my wife's name once and I'll burn in hell long enough for that. I stand mute.

DANFORTH In that case, I have no choice but to arrest you for contempt of this court, do you know that?

GILES This is a hearing; you cannot clap me for contempt of a hearing.

DANFORTH Oh, it is a proper lawyer! Do you wish me to declare the court in full session here? Or will you give me good reply?

GILES *(faltering)* I cannot give you no name, sir, I cannot.

DANFORTH You are a foolish old man. Mr. Cheever, begin the record. The court is now in session. I ask you, Mr. Corey—

PROCTOR *(breaking in)* Your Honor—he has the story in confidence, sir, and he—

PARRIS The Devil lives on such confidences! *(to Danforth)* Without confidences there could be no conspiracy, Your Honor!

HATHORNE I think it must be broken, sir.

DANFORTH *(to Giles)* Old man, if your informant tells the truth let him come here openly like a decent man. But if he hide in anonymity I must know why. Now sir, the government and central church demand of you the name of him who reported Mr. Thomas Putnam a common murderer.

HALE Excellency—

DANFORTH Mr. Hale.

HALE We cannot blink it more. There is a prodigious fear of this court in the country—

DANFORTH Then there is a prodigious guilt in the country. Are *you* afraid to be questioned here?

HALE I may only fear the Lord, sir, but there is fear in the country nevertheless.

DANFORTH *(angered now)* Reproach me not with the fear in the country; there is fear in the country because there is a moving plot to topple Christ in the country!

HALE But it does not follow that everyone accused is part of it.

DANFORTH No uncorrupted man may fear this court, Mr. Hale! None! *(to Giles)* You are under arrest in contempt of this court. Now sit you down and take counsel with yourself, or you will be set in the jail until you decide to answer all questions.

Giles Corey makes a rush for Putnam. Proctor lunges and holds him.

PROCTOR No, Giles!

GILES *(over Proctor's shoulder at Putnam)* I'll cut your throat, Putnam, I'll kill you yet!

PROCTOR *(forcing him into a chair)* Peace, Giles, peace. *(releasing him)* We'll prove ourselves. Now we will. *(He starts to turn to Danforth.)*

GILES Say nothin' more, John. *(pointing at Danforth)* He's only playin' you! He means to hang us all!

Mary Warren bursts into sobs.

DANFORTH This is a court of law, Mister. I'll have no effrontery here!

PROCTOR Forgive him, sir, for his old age. Peace, Giles, we'll prove it all now. *(He lifts up Mary's chin.)* You cannot weep, Mary. Remember the angel, what he say to the boy. Hold to it, now; there is

> Reverend Hale is an interesting figure, because his viewpoint regarding the trials has been changing gradually throughout the play.

your rock. *(Mary quiets. He takes out a paper, and turns to Danforth.)* This is Mary Warren's deposition. I—I would ask you remember, sir, while you read it, that until two week ago she were no different than the other children are today. *(He is speaking reasonably, restraining all his fears, his anger, his anxiety.)* You saw her scream, she howled, she swore familiar spirits choked her; she even testified that Satan, in the form of women now in jail, tried to win her soul away, and then when she refused—

DANFORTH We know all this.

PROCTOR Aye, sir. She swears now that she never saw Satan; nor any spirit, vague or clear, that Satan may have sent to hurt her. And she declares her friends are lying now.

Proctor starts to hand Danforth the deposition, and Hale comes up to Danforth in a trembling state.

HALE Excellency, a moment. I think this goes to the heart of the matter.

DANFORTH *(with deep misgivings)* It surely does.

HALE I cannot say he is an honest man; I know him little. But in all justice, sir, a claim so weighty cannot be argued by a farmer. In God's name, sir, stop here; send him home and let him come again with a lawyer—

DANFORTH *(patiently)* Now look you, Mr. Hale—

HALE Excellency, I have signed seventy-two death warrants; I am a minister of the Lord, and I dare not take a life without there be a proof so immaculate no slightest qualm of conscience may doubt it.

DANFORTH Mr. Hale, you surely do not doubt my justice.

HALE I have this morning signed away the soul of Rebecca Nurse, Your Honor. I'll not conceal it, my hand shakes yet as with a wound! I pray you, sir, *this* argument let lawyers present to you.

> Hale faces Danforth's anger for the first time. Does his speaking out at this moment, after the trials are well under way, have any effect? Would an earlier objection to the hearings have been more effective in halting the proceedings?

DANFORTH Mr. Hale, believe me; for a man of such terrible learning you are most bewildered—I hope you will forgive me. I have been thirty-two year at the bar, sir, and I should be confounded were I called upon to defend these people. Let you consider, now— *(to Proctor and the others)* And I bid you all do likewise. In an ordinary crime, how does one defend the accused? One calls up witnesses to prove his innocence. But witchcraft is *ipso facto*, on its face and by its nature, an invisible crime, is it not? Therefore, who may possibly be witness to it? The witch and the victim. None other. Now we cannot hope the witch will accuse herself; granted? Therefore, we must rely upon her victims—and they do testify, the children certainly do testify. As for the witches, none will deny that we are most eager for all their confessions. Therefore, what is left for a lawyer to bring out? I think I have made my point. Have I not?

> How effective is Danforth's logic with the others?

HALE But this child claims the girls are not truthful, and if they are not—

DANFORTH That is precisely what I am about to consider, sir. What more may you ask of me? Unless you doubt my probity?

HALE *(defeated)* I surely do not, sir. Let you consider it, then.

DANFORTH And let you put your heart to rest. Her deposition, Mr. Proctor.

Proctor hands it to him. Hathorne rises, goes beside Danforth, and starts reading. Parris comes to his other side. Danforth looks at John Proctor, then proceeds to read. Hale gets up, finds position near the judge, reads too. Proctor glances at Giles. Francis prays silently, hands pressed together. Cheever waits placidly, the sublime official, dutiful. Mary Warren sobs once. John Proctor touches her head reassuringly. Presently Danforth lifts his eyes, stands up, takes out a kerchief and blows his nose. The others stand aside as he moves in thought toward the window.

> How does Miller create a special sense of suspense through detailed stage directions at this critical moment?

PARRIS *(hardly able to contain his anger and fear)* I should like to question—

DANFORTH—*(his first real outburst, in which his contempt for Parris is clear)* Mr. Parris, I bid you be silent! *(He stands in silence, looking out the window. Now, having established that he will set the gait.)* Mr. Cheever, will you go into the court and bring the children here? *(Cheever gets up and goes out upstage. Danforth now turns to Mary.)* Mary Warren, how came you to this turnabout? Has Mr. Proctor threatened you for this deposition?

MARY WARREN No, sir.

DANFORTH Has he ever threatened you?

MARY WARREN *(weaker)* No, sir.

DANFORTH *(sensing a weakening)* Has he threatened you?

MARY WARREN No, sir.

DANFORTH Then you tell me that you sat in my court, callously lying, when you knew that people would hang by your evidence? *(She does not answer.)* Answer me!

MARY WARREN *(almost inaudibly)* I did, sir.

DANFORTH How were you instructed in your life? Do you not know that God damns all liars? *(She cannot speak.)* Or is it now that you lie?

MARY WARREN No, sir—I am with God now.

DANFORTH You are with God now.

MARY WARREN Aye, sir.

DANFORTH *(containing himself)* I will tell you this—you are either lying now, or you were lying in the court, and in either case you have committed perjury and you will go to jail for it. You cannot lightly say you lied, Mary. Do you know that?

MARY WARREN I cannot lie no more. I am with God, I am with God.

But she breaks into sobs at the thought of it, and the right door opens, and enter Susanna Walcott, Mercy Lewis, Betty Parris, and finally Abigail. Cheever comes to Danforth.

CHEEVER Ruth Putnam's not in the court, sir, nor the other children.

DANFORTH These will be sufficient. Sit you down, children. *(Silently they sit.)* Your friend, Mary Warren, has given us a deposition. In which she swears that she never saw familiar spirits, apparitions, nor any manifest of the Devil. She claims as well that none of you

> How does the diametrically opposed testimony of the two girls sharpen the importance of the showdown?

THE CRUCIBLE 331

have seen these things either. *(slight pause)* Now, children, this is a court of law. The law, based upon the Bible, and the Bible, writ by Almighty God, forbid the practice of witchcraft, and describe death as the penalty thereof. But likewise, children, the law and Bible damn all bearers of false witness. *(slight pause)* Now then. It does not escape me that this deposition may be devised to blind us; it may well be that Mary Warren has been conquered by Satan, who sends her here to distract our sacred purpose. If so, her neck will break for it. But if she speak true, I bid you now drop your guile and confess your pretense, for a quick confession will go easier with you. *(pause)* Abigail Williams, rise. *(Abigail slowly rises.)* Is there any truth in this?

ABIGAIL No, sir.

DANFORTH *(thinks, glances at Mary, then back to Abigail)* Children, a very augur bit will now be turned into your souls until your honesty is proved. Will either of you change your positions now, or do you force me to hard questioning?

ABIGAIL I have naught to change, sir. She lies.

DANFORTH *(to Mary)* You would still go on with this?

MARY WARREN *(faintly)* Aye, sir.

DANFORTH *(turning to Abigail)* A poppet were discovered in Mr. Proctor's house, stabbed by a needle. Mary Warren claims that you sat beside her in the court when she made it, and that you saw her make it and witnessed how she herself stuck the needle into it for safe-keeping. What say you to that?

ABIGAIL *(with a slight note of indignation)* It is a lie, sir.

DANFORTH *(after a slight pause)* While you worked for Mr. Proctor, did you see poppets in that house?

ABIGAIL Goody Proctor always kept poppets.

PROCTOR Your Honor, my wife never kept no poppets. Mary Warren confesses it was her poppet.

CHEEVER Your Excellency.

DANFORTH Mr. Cheever.

CHEEVER When I spoke with Goody Proctor in that house, she said she never kept no poppets. But she said she did keep poppets when she were a girl.

PROCTOR She has not been a girl these fifteen years, Your Honor.

HATHORNE But a poppet will keep fifteen years, will it not?

PROCTOR It will keep if it is kept, but Mary Warren swears she never saw no poppets in my house, nor anyone else.

PARRIS Why could there not have been poppets hid where no one ever saw them?

PROCTOR *(furious)* There might also be a dragon with five legs in my house, but no one has ever seen it.

PARRIS We are here, Your Honor, precisely to discover what no one has ever seen. *Is there any humor in this line?*

PROCTOR Mr. Danforth, what profit this girl to turn herself about? What may Mary Warren gain but hard questioning and worse?

DANFORTH You are charging Abigail Williams with a marvelous cool plot to murder, do you understand that?

PROCTOR I do, sir. I believe she means to murder.

DANFORTH *(pointing at Abigail, incredulously)* This child would murder your wife?

PROCTOR It is not a child. Now hear me, sir. In the sight of the congregation she were twice this year put out of this meetin' house for laughter during prayer.

DANFORTH *(shocked, turning to Abigail)* What's this? Laughter during—!

PARRIS Excellency, she were under Tituba's power at that time, but she is solemn now.

GILES Aye, now she is solemn and goes to hang people!

DANFORTH Quiet, man.

HATHORNE Surely it have no bearing on the question, sir. He charges contemplation of murder.

DANFORTH Aye. *(He studies Abigail for a moment, then:)* Continue, Mr. Proctor.

PROCTOR Mary. Now tell the Governor how you danced in the woods.

PARRIS *(instantly)* Excellency, since I come to Salem this man is blackening my name. He—

> What part does Parris take during the questioning of the girls, and why?

DANFORTH In a moment, sir. *(to Mary Warren, sternly, and surprised)* What is this dancing?

MARY WARREN I—*(She glances at Abigail, who is staring down at her remorselessly. Then, appealing to Proctor)* Mr. Proctor—

PROCTOR *(taking it right up)* Abigail leads the girls to the woods, Your Honor, and they have danced there naked—

PARRIS Your Honor, this—

PROCTOR *(at once)* Mr. Parris discovered them himself in the dead of night! There's the "child" she is!

DANFORTH —*(It is growing into a nightmare, and he turns, astonished, to Parris.)* Mr. Parris—

PARRIS I can only say, sir, that I never found any of them naked, and this man is—

DANFORTH But you discovered them dancing in the woods? *(Eyes on Parris, he points at Abigail.)* Abigail?

HALE Excellency, when I first arrived from Beverly, Mr. Parris told me that.

DANFORTH Do you deny it, Mr. Parris?

PARRIS I do not, sir, but I never saw any of them naked.

DANFORTH But she have *danced*?

PARRIS *(unwillingly)* Aye, sir.

Danforth, as though with new eyes, looks at Abigail.

HATHORNE Excellency, will you permit me? *(He points at Mary Warren.)*

DANFORTH *(with great worry)* Pray, proceed.

HATHORNE You say you never saw no spirits, Mary, were never threatened or afflicted by any manifest of the Devil or the Devil's agents.

MARY WARREN *(very faintly)* No, sir.

HATHORNE *(with a gleam of victory)* And yet, when people accused of witchery confronted you in court, you would faint, saying their spirits came out of their bodies and choked you—

> Why would Hathorne want to shake Mary Warren's version of the events? What does he now have at stake?

MARY WARREN That were pretense, sir.

DANFORTH I cannot hear you.

MARY WARREN Pretense, sir.

PARRIS But you did turn cold, did you not? I myself picked you up many times, and your skin were icy. Mr. Danforth, you—

DANFORTH I saw that many times.

PROCTOR She only pretended to faint, Your Excellency. They're all marvelous pretenders.

HATHORNE Then can she pretend to faint now?

PROCTOR Now?

PARRIS Why not? Now there are no spirits attacking her, for none in this room is accused of witchcraft. So let her turn herself cold now, let her pretend she is attacked now, let her faint. *(He turns to Mary Warren.)* Faint!

MARY WARREN Faint?

PARRIS Aye, faint. Prove to us how you pretended in the court so many times.

MARY WARREN *(looking to Proctor)* I—cannot faint now, sir.

PROCTOR *(alarmed, quietly)* Can you not pretend it?

MARY WARREN I— *(She looks about as though searching for the passion to faint.)* I—have no *sense* of it now, I—

> There is unconscious and ironic truth in Mary's admission that she cannot faint on command because she has no "sense" of it at the moment. What makes up the proper "sense" to allow hallucination and hysteria?

DANFORTH Why? What is lacking now?

MARY WARREN I—cannot tell, sir, I—

DANFORTH Might it be that here we have no afflicting spirit loose, but in the court there were some?

MARY WARREN I never saw no spirits.

PARRIS Then see no spirits now, and prove to us that you can faint by your own will, as you claim.

MARY WARREN *(stares, searching for the emotion of it, and then shakes her head)* I—cannot do it.

PARRIS Then you will confess, will you not? It were attacking spirits made you faint!

MARY WARREN No, sir, I—

The girls under interrogation, from the Lincoln Center production.

PARRIS Your Excellency, this is a trick to blind the court!

MARY WARREN It's not a trick! *(She stands.)* I—I used to faint because I—I thought I saw spirits.

DANFORTH *Thought* you saw them!

MARY WARREN But I did not, Your Honor.

HATHORNE How could you think you saw them unless you saw them?

MARY WARREN I—I cannot tell how, but I did. I—I heard the other girls screaming, and you, Your Honor, you seemed to believe them, and I—It were only sport in the beginning, sir, but then the whole world cried spirits, spirits, and I—I promise you, Mr. Danforth, I only thought I saw them but I did not.

Danforth peers at her.

PARRIS *(smiling, but nervous because Danforth seems to be struck by Mary Warren's story)* Surely Your Excellency is not taken by this simple lie.

DANFORTH *(turning worriedly to Abigail)* Abigail. I bid you now search your heart and tell me this—and beware of it, child, to God every soul is precious and His vengeance is terrible on them that take life without cause. Is it possible, child, that the spirits you have seen are illusion only, some deception that may cross your mind when—

ABIGAIL Why, this—this—is a base question, sir.

DANFORTH Child, I would have you consider it—

ABIGAIL I have been hurt, Mr. Danforth; I have seen my blood runnin' out! I have been near to murdered every day because I done my duty pointing out the Devil's people—and this is my reward? To be mistrusted, denied, questioned like a—

DANFORTH *(weakening)* Child, I do not mistrust you—

ABIGAIL *(in an open threat)* Let *you* beware, Mr. Danforth. Think you to be so mighty that the power of Hell may not turn *your* wits? Beware of it! There is— *(Suddenly, from an accusatory attitude, her face turns, looking into the air above—it is truly frightened.)*

DANFORTH *(apprehensively)* What is it, child?

Abigail tries to gain the upper hand with Danforth—at least temporarily. To what does she appeal in his thinking to win his trust in her?

ABIGAIL *(looking about in the air, clasping her arms about her as though cold)* I—I know not. A wind, a cold wind, has come. *(Her eyes fall on Mary Warren.)*

MARY WARREN *(terrified, pleading)* Abby!

MERCY LEWIS *(shivering)* Your Honor, I freeze!

PROCTOR They're pretending!

HATHORNE *(touching Abigail's hand)* She is cold, Your Honor, touch her!

MERCY LEWIS *(through chattering teeth)* Mary, do you send this shadow on me?

MARY WARREN Lord, save me!

SUSANNA WALCOTT I freeze, I freeze!

ABIGAIL *(shivering visibly)* It is a wind, a wind!

MARY WARREN Abby, don't do that!

DANFORTH *(himself engaged and entered by Abigail)* Mary Warren, do you witch her? I say to you, do you send your spirit out?

With a hysterical cry Mary Warren starts to run. Proctor catches her.

MARY WARREN *(almost collapsing)* Let me go, Mr. Proctor, I cannot, I cannot—

ABIGAIL *(crying to Heaven)* Oh, Heavenly Father, take away this shadow!

Without warning or hesitation, Proctor leaps at Abigail and, grabbing her by the hair, pulls her to her feet. She screams in pain. Danforth, astonished, cries, "What are you about?" and Hathorne and Parris call, "Take your hands off her!" and out of it all comes Proctor's roaring voice.

PROCTOR How do you call Heaven! Whore! Whore!

Herrick breaks Proctor from her.

HERRICK John!

DANFORTH Man! Man, what do you—

PROCTOR *(breathless and in agony)* It is a whore!

DANFORTH *(dumfounded)* You charge—?

ABIGAIL Mr. Danforth, he is lying!

PROCTOR Mark her! Now she'll suck a scream to stab me with, but—

DANFORTH You will prove this! This will not pass!

PROCTOR *(trembling, his life collapsing about him)* I have known her, sir. I have known her.

DANFORTH You—you are a lecher?

FRANCIS *(horrified)* John, you cannot say such a—

PROCTOR Oh, Francis, I wish you had some evil in you that you might know me! *(to Danforth)* A man will not cast away his good name. You surely know that.

DANFORTH *(dumfounded)* In—in what time? In what place?

To confess oneself an adulterer was a very serious matter in Puritan New England, for it charged oneself with violating both civil and church laws.

PROCTOR (*his voice about to break, and his shame great*) In the proper place—where my beasts are bedded. On the last night of my joy, some eight months past. She used to serve me in my house, sir. (*He has to clamp his jaw to keep from weeping.*) A man may think God sleeps, but God sees everything. I know it now. I beg you, sir, I beg you—see her what she is. My wife, my dear good wife, took this girl soon after, sir, and put her out on the highroad. And being what she is, a lump of vanity, sir— (*He is being overcome.*) Excellency, forgive me, forgive me. (*Angrily against himself, he turns away from the Governor for a moment. Then, as though to cry out is his only means of speech left.*) She thinks to dance with me on my wife's grave! And well she might, for I thought of her softly. God help me, I lusted, and there is a promise in such sweat. But it is a whore's vengeance, and you must see it; I set myself entirely in your hands. I know you must see it now.

DANFORTH (*blanched, in horror, turning to Abigail*) You deny every scrap and tittle of this?

ABIGAIL If I must answer that, I will leave and I will not come back again!

Danforth seems unsteady.

PROCTOR I have made a bell of my honor! I have rung the doom of my good name—you will believe me, Mr. Danforth! My wife is innocent, except she knew a whore when she saw one!

ABIGAIL (*stepping up to Danforth*) What look do you give me? (*Danforth cannot speak.*) I'll not have such looks! (*She turns and starts for the door.*)

DANFORTH You will remain where you are! (*Herrick steps into her path. She comes up short, fire in her eyes.*) Mr. Parris, go into the court and bring Goodwife Proctor out.

PARRIS (*objecting*) Your Honor, this is all a—

DANFORTH (*sharply to Parris*) Bring her out! And tell her not one word of what's been spoken here. And let you knock before you enter. (*Parris goes out.*) Now we shall touch the bottom of this swamp. (*to Proctor*) Your wife, you say, is an honest woman.

PROCTOR In her life, sir, she have never lied. There are them that cannot sing, and them that cannot weep—my wife cannot lie. I have paid much to learn it, sir.

DANFORTH And when she put this girl out of your house, she put her out for a harlot?

PROCTOR Aye, sir.

DANFORTH And knew her for a harlot?

PROCTOR Aye, sir, she knew her for a harlot.

DANFORTH Good then. (*to Abigail*) And if she tell me, child, it were for harlotry, may God spread His mercy on you! (*There is a knock. He calls to the door.*) Hold! (*to Abigail*) Turn your back. Turn your back. (*to Proctor*) Do likewise. (*Both turn their back—Abigail with indignant slowness.*) Now let neither of you turn to face Goody Proctor. No one in this room is to speak one word, or raise a gesture aye or nay. (*He turns toward the door, calls*) Enter! (*The door opens. Elizabeth enters with*

Proctor's shocking confession of lechery threatens to topple the credibility of the government's star witness. Thus, the tension rises to fever pitch here.

Parris. Parris leaves her. She stands alone, her eyes looking for Proctor.) Mr. Cheever, report this testimony in all exactness. Are you ready?

CHEEVER Ready, sir.

DANFORTH Come here, woman. *(Elizabeth comes to him, glancing at Proctor's back.)* Look at me only, not at your husband. In my eyes only.

ELIZABETH *(faintly)* Good, sir.

DANFORTH We are given to understand that at one time you dismissed your servant, Abigail Williams.

ELIZABETH That is true, sir.

DANFORTH For what cause did you dismiss her? *(Slight pause. Then Elizabeth tries to glance at Proctor.)* You will look in my eyes only and not at your husband. The answer is in your memory and you need no help to give it to me. Why did you dismiss Abigail Williams?

ELIZABETH *(not knowing what to say, sensing a situation, wetting her lips to stall for time)* She—dissatisfied me. *(pause)* And my husband.

DANFORTH In what way dissatisfied you?

ELIZABETH She were—*(She glances at Proctor for a cue.)*

DANFORTH Woman, look at me? *(Elizabeth does.)* Were she slovenly? Lazy? What disturbance did she cause?

ELIZABETH Your Honor, I—in that time I were sick. And I—My husband is a good and righteous man. He is never drunk as some are, nor wastin' his time at the shovelboard, but always at his work. But in my sickness—you see, sir, I were a long time sick after my last baby, and I thought I saw my husband somewhat turning from me. And this girl— *(She turns to Abigail.)*

DANFORTH Look at me.

ELIZABETH Aye, sir. Abigail Williams— *(She breaks off.)*

DANFORTH What of Abigail Williams?

ELIZABETH I came to think he fancied her. And so one night I lost my wits, I think, and put her out on the highroad.

DANFORTH Your husband—did he indeed turn from you?

ELIZABETH *(in agony)* My husband—is a goodly man, sir.

DANFORTH Then he did not turn from you.

ELIZABETH *(starting to glance at Proctor)* He—

DANFORTH *(reaches out and holds her face, then)* Look at me! To your own knowledge, has John Proctor ever committed the crime of lechery? *(In a crisis of indecision she cannot speak.)* Answer my question! Is your husband a lecher!

ELIZABETH *(faintly)* No, sir.

DANFORTH Remove her, Marshal.

PROCTOR Elizabeth, tell the truth!

DANFORTH She has spoken. Remove her!

PROCTOR *(crying out)* Elizabeth, I have confessed it!

ELIZABETH Oh, God! *(The door closes behind her.)*

PROCTOR She only thought to save my name!

HALE Excellency, it is a natural lie to tell; I beg you, stop now before another is condemned! I may shut my conscience to it no more —private vengeance is working through this testimony! From the beginning this man has struck me true. By my oath to Heaven, I believe him now, and I pray you call back his wife before we—

DANFORTH She spoke nothing of lechery, and this man has lied!

HALE I believe him! *(pointing at Abigail)* This girl has always struck me false! She has—

Again, Hale's new-found "truth" does not help.

Abigail, with a weird, wild, chilling cry, screams up to the ceiling.

ABIGAIL You will not! Begone! Begone, I say!

DANFORTH What is it, child? *(But Abigail, pointing with fear, is now raising up her frightened eyes, her awed face, toward the ceiling—the girls are doing the same—and now Hathorne, Hale, Putnam, Cheever, Herrick, and Danforth do the same. What's there? He lowers his eyes from the ceiling, and now he is frightened; there is real tension in his voice.)* Child! *(She is transfixed—with all the girls, she is whimpering open-mouthed, agape at the ceiling.)* Girls! Why do you—?

MERCY LEWIS *(pointing)* It's on the beam! Behind the rafter!

DANFORTH *(looking up)* Where!

ABIGAIL Why—? *(She gulps.)* Why do you come, yellow bird?

PROCTOR Where's a bird? I see no bird!

ABIGAIL *(to the ceiling)* My face? My face?

PROCTOR Mr. Hale—

DANFORTH Be quiet!

PROCTOR *(to Hale)* Do you see a bird?

DANFORTH Be quiet!!

ABIGAIL *(to the ceiling, in a genuine conversation with the "bird" as though trying to talk it out of attacking her)* But God made my face; you cannot want to tear my face. Envy is a deadly sin, Mary.

MARY WARREN *(on her feet with a spring, and horrified, pleading)* Abby!

ABIGAIL —*(unperturbed, continuing to the "bird")* Oh, Mary, this is a black art to change your shape. No, I cannot, I cannot stop my mouth; it's God's work I do.

MARY WARREN Abby, I'm *here*!

PROCTOR *(frantically)* They're pretending, Mr. Danforth!

ABIGAIL *(Now she takes a backward step, as though in fear the bird will swoop down momentarily.)* Oh, please, Mary! Don't come down.

SUSANNA WALCOTT Her claws, she's stretching her claws!

PROCTOR Lies, lies.

ABIGAIL *(backing further, eyes still fixed above)* Mary, please don't hurt me!

MARY WARREN *(to Danforth)* I'm not hurting her!

DANFORTH *(to Mary Warren)* Why does she see this vision?

MARY WARREN She sees nothin'!

ABIGAIL (*now staring full front as though hypnotized, and mimicking the exact tone of Mary Warren's cry*) She sees nothin'!

MARY WARREN (*pleading*) Abby, you mustn't!

ABIGAIL AND ALL THE GIRLS (*all transfixed*) Abby, you mustn't!

MARY WARREN (*to all the girls*) I'm here, I'm here!

GIRLS I'm here, I'm here!

DANFORTH (*horrified*) Mary Warren! Draw back your spirit out of them!

MARY WARREN Mr. Danforth!

GIRLS (*cutting her off*) Mr. Danforth!

DANFORTH Have you compacted with the Devil? Have you?

MARY WARREN Never, never!

GIRLS Never, never!

DANFORTH (*growing hysterical*) Why can they only repeat you?

PROCTOR Give me a whip—I'll stop it!

MARY WARREN They're sporting. They—!

GIRLS They're sporting!

MARY WARREN (*turning on them all hysterically and stamping her feet*) Abby, stop it!

GIRLS (*stamping their feet*) Abby, stop it!

MARY WARREN Stop it!

GIRLS Stop it!

MARY WARREN (*screaming it out at the top of her lungs, and raising her fists*) Stop it!!

GIRLS (*raising their fists*) Stop it!!

Mary Warren, utterly confounded, and becoming overwhelmed by Abigail's—and the girls'—utter conviction, starts to whimper, hands half raised, powerless, and all the girls begin whimpering exactly as she does.

DANFORTH A little while ago you were afflicted. Now it seems you afflict others; where did you find this power?

MARY WARREN (*staring at Abigail*) I—have no power.

GIRLS I have no power.

PROCTOR They're gulling you, Mister!

DANFORTH Why did you turn about this past two weeks? You have seen the Devil, have you not?

HALE (*indicating Abigail and the girls*) You cannot believe them!

MARY WARREN I—

PROCTOR (*sensing her weakening*) Mary, God damns all liars!

DANFORTH (*pounding it into her*) You have seen the Devil, you have made compact with Lucifer, have you not?

PROCTOR God damns liars, Mary!

> What visual and sound effects add to the horror of this episode?

Mary utters something unintelligible, staring at Abigail, who keeps watching the "bird" above.

DANFORTH I cannot hear you. What do you say? *(Mary utters again unintelligibly.)* You will confess yourself or you will hang! *(He turns her roughly to face him.)* Do you know who I am? I say you will hang if you do not open with me!

PROCTOR Mary, remember the angel Raphael—do that which is good and—

ABIGAIL *(pointing upward)* The wings! Her wings are spreading! Mary, please, don't, don't—!

HALE I see nothing, Your Honor!

DANFORTH Do you confess this power! *(He is an inch from her face.)* Speak!

ABIGAIL She's going to come down! She's walking the beam!

DANFORTH Will you speak!

MARY WARREN *(staring in horror)* I cannot!

GIRLS I cannot!

PARRIS Cast the Devil out! Look him in the face! Trample him! We'll save you, Mary, only stand fast against him and—

ABIGAIL *(looking up)* Look out! She's coming down!

She and all the girls run to one wall, shielding their eyes. And now, as though cornered, they let out a gigantic scream, and Mary, as though infected, opens her mouth and screams with them. Gradually Abigail and the girls leave off, until only Mary is left there, staring up at the "bird," screaming madly. All watch her, horrified by this evident fit. Proctor strides to her.

PROCTOR Mary, tell the Governor what they— *(He has hardly got a word out, when, seeing him coming for her, she rushes out of his reach, screaming in horror.)*

MARY WARREN Don't touch me—don't touch me! *(at which the girls halt at the door)*

PROCTOR *(astonished)* Mary!

MARY WARREN *(pointing at Proctor)* You're the Devil's man!

He is stopped in his tracks.

PARRIS Praise God!

GIRLS Praise God!

PROCTOR *(numbed)* Mary, how—?

MARY WARREN I'll not hang with you! I love God, I love God.

DANFORTH *(to Mary)* He bid you do the Devil's work?

MARY WARREN *(hysterically, indicating Proctor)* He come at me by night and every day to sign, to sign, to—

DANFORTH Sign what?

PARRIS The Devil's book? He come with a book?

MARY WARREN *(hysterically, pointing at Proctor, fearful of him)* My

> Except to accuse Proctor, what recourse does Mary have at this point?

THE CRUCIBLE **341**

name, he want my name. "I'll murder you," he says, "if my wife hangs! We must go and overthrow the court," he says!

Danforth's head jerks toward Proctor, shock and horror in his face.

PROCTOR *(turning, appealing to Hale)* Mr. Hale!

MARY WARREN *(her sobs beginning)* He wake me every night, his eyes were like coals and his fingers claw my neck, and I sign, I sign . . .

HALE Excellency, this child's gone wild!

PROCTOR *(as Danforth's wide eyes pour on him)* Mary, Mary!

MARY WARREN *(screaming at him)* No, I love God; I go your way no more. I love God, I bless God. *(Sobbing, she rushes to Abigail.)* Abby, Abby, I'll never hurt you more! *(They all watch, as Abigail, out of her infinite charity, reaches out and draws the sobbing Mary to her, and then looks up to Danforth.)*

> Note the characters' movements. What are the groupings on stage of the characters now, as compared to an earlier scene in this act when the other girls are first brought in to confront Mary?

DANFORTH *(to Proctor)* What are you? *(Proctor is beyond speech in his anger.)* You are combined with anti-Christ, are you not? I have seen your power; you will not deny it! What say you, Mister?

HALE Excellency—

DANFORTH I will have nothing from you, Mr. Hale! *(to Proctor)* Will you confess yourself befouled with Hell, or do you keep that black allegiance yet? What say you?

PROCTOR *(his mind wild, breathless)* I say—I say—God is dead!

PARRIS Hear it, hear it!

PROCTOR *(laughs insanely, then)* A fire, a fire is burning! I hear the boot of Lucifer, I see his filthy face! And it is my face, and yours, Danforth! For them that quail to bring men out of ignorance, as I have quailed, and as you quail now when you know in all your black hearts that this be fraud—God damns our kind especially, and we will burn, we will burn together.

> What is the full meaning of Proctor's final denunciation of the situation in Salem?

DANFORTH Marshal! Take him and Corey with him to the jail!

HALE *(starting across to the door)* I denounce these proceedings!

PROCTOR You are pulling Heaven down and raising up a whore!

HALE I denounce these proceedings, I quit this court! *(He slams the door to the outside behind him.)*

> Why is it significant that Hale storms out of the room? Is this a turning point for him?

DANFORTH *(calling to him in a fury)* Mr. Hale! Mr. Hale!

The curtain falls.

ACT IV

A cell in Salem jail, that fall.

At the back is a high barred window; near it, a great, heavy door. Along the walls are two benches.

The place is in darkness but for the moonlight seeping through the bars. It appears empty. Presently footsteps are heard coming down a corridor beyond the wall, keys rattle, and the door swings open. Marshal Herrick enters with a lantern.

He is nearly drunk, and heavy-footed. He goes to a bench and nudges a bundle of rags lying on it.

HERRICK Sarah, wake up! Sarah Good! *(He then crosses to the other bench.)*

SARAH GOOD *(rising in her rags)* Oh, Majesty! Comin', comin'! Tituba, he's here, His Majesty's come!

HERRICK Go to the north cell; this place is wanted now. *(He hangs his lantern on the wall. Tituba sits up.)*

TITUBA That don't look to me like His Majesty; look to me like the marshal.

HERRICK *(taking out a flask)* Get along with you now, clear this place. *(He drinks, and Sarah Good comes and peers up into his face.)*

SARAH GOOD Oh, is it you, Marshal! I thought sure you be the devil comin' for us. Could I have a sip of cider for me goin'-away?

HERRICK *(handing her the flask)* And where are you off to, Sarah?

TITUBA *(as Sarah drinks)* We goin' to Barbados, soon the Devil gits here with the feathers and the wings.

HERRICK Oh? A happy voyage to you.

SARAH GOOD A pair of bluebirds wingin' southerly, the two of us! Oh, it be a grand transformation, Marshal! *(She raises the flask to drink again.)*

HERRICK *(taking the flask from her lips)* You'd best give me that or you'll never rise off the ground. Come along now.

TITUBA I'll speak to him for you, if you desires to come along, Marshal.

HERRICK I'd not refuse it, Tituba; it's the proper morning to fly into Hell.

TITUBA Oh, it be no Hell in Barbados. Devil, him be pleasureman in Barbados, him be singin' and dancin' in Barbados. It's you folks —you riles him up 'round here; it be too cold 'round here for that Old Boy. He freeze his soul in Massachusetts, but in Barbados he just as sweet and— *(A bellowing cow is heard, and Tituba leaps up and calls to the window.)* Aye, sir! That's him, Sarah!

SARAH GOOD I'm here, Majesty! *(They hurriedly pick up their rags as Hopkins, a guard, enters.)*

HOPKINS The Deputy Governor's arrived.

HERRICK *(grabbing Tituba)* Come along, come along.

TITUBA *(resisting him)* No, he comin' for me. I goin' home!

HERRICK *(pulling her to the door)* That's not Satan, just a poor old cow with a hatful of milk. Come along now, out with you!

TITUBA *(calling to the window)* Take me home, Devil! Take me home!

SARAH GOOD *(following the shouting Tituba out)* Tell him I'm goin', Tituba! Now you tell him Sarah Good is goin' too!

In the corridor outside Tituba calls on—"Take me home, Devil; Devil take me home!" and Hopkins' voice orders her to move on. Herrick returns and begins to push old rags and straw into a corner. Hearing footsteps, he turns, and enter Danforth and Judge Hathorne. They are in greatcoats and wear hats against the bitter cold. They are followed in by Cheever, who carries a dispatch case and a flat wooden box containing his writing materials.

How does Miller suggest that a sense of moral degeneration has overtaken these once upright Puritan citizens?

How do we know that several months have passed between the events of Act IV and those before?

THE CRUCIBLE 343

HERRICK Good morning, Excellency.

DANFORTH Where is Mr. Parris?

HERRICK I'll fetch him. *(He starts for the door.)*

DANFORTH Marshal. *(Herrick stops.)* When did Reverend Hale arrive?

HERRICK It were toward midnight, I think.

DANFORTH *(suspiciously)* What is he about here?

HERRICK He goes among them that will hang, sir. And he prays with them. He sits with Goody Nurse now. And Mr. Parris with him.

DANFORTH Indeed. That man have no authority to enter here, Marshal. Why have you let him in?

HERRICK Why, Mr. Parris command me, sir. I cannot deny him.

DANFORTH Are you drunk, Marshal?

HERRICK No, sir; it is a bitter night, and I have no fire here.

DANFORTH *(containing his anger)* Fetch Mr. Parris.

HERRICK Aye, sir.

DANFORTH There is a prodigious stench in this place.

HERRICK I have only now cleared the people out for you.

DANFORTH Beware hard drink, Marshal.

HERRICK Aye, sir. *(He waits an instant for further orders. But Danforth, in dissatisfaction, turns his back on him, and Herrick goes out. There is a pause. Danforth stands in thought.)*

HATHORNE Let you question Hale, Excellency; I should not be surprised he have been preaching in Andover lately.

DANFORTH We'll come to that; speak nothing of Andover. Parris prays with him. That's strange. *(He blows on his hands, moves toward the window, and looks out.)*

HATHORNE Excellency, I wonder if it be wise to let Mr. Parris so continuously with the prisoners. *(Danforth turns to him, interested.)* I think, sometimes, the man has a mad look these days.

DANFORTH Mad?

HATHORNE I met him yesterday coming out of his house, and I bid him good morning—and he wept and went his way. I think it is not well the village sees him so unsteady.

DANFORTH Perhaps he have some sorrow.

CHEEVER *(stamping his feet against the cold)* I think it be the cows, sir.

DANFORTH Cows?

CHEEVER There be so many cows wanderin' the highroads, now their masters are in the jails, and much disagreement who they will belong to now. I know Mr. Parris be arguin' with farmers all yesterday—there is great contention, sir, about the cows. Contention make him weep, sir; it were always a man that weep for contention. *(He turns, as do Hathorne and Danforth, hearing someone coming up the corridor. Danforth raises his head as Parris enters. He is gaunt, frightened, and sweating in his greatcoat.)*

PARRIS *(to Danforth, instantly)* Oh, good morning, sir, thank you for coming. I beg your pardon wakin' you so early. Good morning, Judge Hathorne.

DANFORTH Reverend Hale have no right to enter this—

PARRIS Excellency, a moment. *(He hurries back and shuts the door.)*

HATHORNE Do you leave him alone with the prisoners?

DANFORTH What's his business here?

PARRIS *(prayerfully holding up his hands)* Excellency, hear me. It is a providence. Reverend Hale has returned to bring Rebecca Nurse to God.

DANFORTH *(surprised)* He bids her confess?

PARRIS *(sitting)* Hear me. Rebecca have not given me a word this three month since she came. Now she sits with him, and her sister and Martha Corey and two or three others, and he pleads with them, confess their crimes and save their lives.

> What is Hale's chief reason for wanting the condemned women to confess and save themselves from death?

DANFORTH Why—this is indeed a providence. And they soften, they soften?

PARRIS Not yet, not yet. But I thought to summon you, sir, that we might think on whether it be not wise, to— *(He dares not say it.)* I had thought to put a question, sir, and I hope you will not—

DANFORTH Mr. Parris, be plain, what troubles you?

PARRIS There is news, sir, that the court—the court must reckon with. My niece, sir, my niece—I believe she has vanished.

DANFORTH Vanished!

PARRIS I had thought to advise you of it earlier in the week, but—

DANFORTH Why? How long is she gone?

PARRIS This be the third night. You see, sir, she told me she would stay a night with Mercy Lewis. And next day, when she does not return, I send to Mr. Lewis to inquire. Mercy told him she would sleep in *my* house for a night.

DANFORTH They are both gone?!

PARRIS *(in fear of him)* They are, sir.

DANFORTH *(alarmed)* I will send a party for them. Where may they be?

PARRIS Excellency, I think they be aboard a ship. *(Danforth stands agape.)* My daughter tells me how she heard them speaking of ships last week, and tonight I discover my—my strongbox is broke into. *(He presses his fingers against his eyes to keep back tears.)*

HATHORNE *(astonished)* She have robbed you?

PARRIS Thirty-one pound is gone. I am penniless. *(He covers his face and sobs.)*

DANFORTH Mr. Parris, you are a brainless man! *(He walks in thought, deeply worried.)*

> What might be said now about Abigail and Mercy Lewis? Does their "escape" confirm the basis of support for Danforth's death sentences? Why has Abigail left?

PARRIS Excellency, it profit nothing you should blame me. I cannot think they would run off except they fear to keep in Salem any more.

(*He is pleading.*) Mark it, sir, Abigail had close knowledge of the town, and since the news of Andover has broken here—

DANFORTH Andover is remedied. The court returns there on Friday, and will resume examinations.

PARRIS I am sure of it, sir. But the rumor here speaks rebellion in Andover, and it—

DANFORTH There is no rebellion in Andover!

PARRIS I tell you what is said here, sir. Andover have thrown out the court, they say, and will have no part of witchcraft. There be a faction here, feeding on that news, and I tell you true, sir, I fear there will be riot here.

HATHORNE Riot! Why at every execution I have seen naught but high satisfaction in the town.

PARRIS Judge Hathorne—it were another sort that hanged till now. Rebecca Nurse is no Bridget that lived three year with Bishop before she married him. John Proctor is not Isaac Ward that drank his family to ruin. (*to Danforth*) I would to God it were not so, Excellency, but these people have great weight yet in the town. Let Rebecca stand upon the gibbet and send up some righteous prayer, and I fear she'll wake a vengeance on you.

HATHORNE Excellency, she is condemned a witch. The court have—

DANFORTH (*in deep concern, raising a hand to Hathorne*) Pray you. (*to Parris*) How do you propose, then?

PARRIS Excellency, I would postpone these hangin's for a time.

DANFORTH There will be no postponement.

PARRIS Now Mr. Hale's returned, there is hope, I think—for if he bring even one of these to God, that confession surely damns the others in the public eye, and none may doubt more that they are all linked to Hell. This way, unconfessed and claiming innocence, doubts are multiplied, many honest people will weep for them, and our good purpose is lost in their tears.

DANFORTH (*after thinking a moment, then going to Cheever*) Give me the list.

Cheever opens the dispatch case, searches.

PARRIS It cannot be forgot, sir, that when I summoned the congregation for John Proctor's excommunication there were hardly thirty people come to hear it. That speak a discontent, I think, and—

DANFORTH (*studying the list*) There will be no postponement.

PARRIS Excellency—

DANFORTH Now, sir—which of these in your opinion may be brought to God? I will myself strive with him till dawn. (*He hands the list to Parris, who merely glances at it.*)

PARRIS There is not sufficient time till dawn.

DANFORTH I shall do my utmost. Which of them do you have hope for?

PARRIS (*not even glancing at the list now, and in a quavering voice, quietly*) Excellency—a dagger— (*He chokes up.*)

A reaction against the witch hunts appears underway in neighboring communities. What inner criteria have been in operation for the death sentences, according to the remarks by Hathorne and Parris here?

Why does Parris suggest a postponement?

DANFORTH What do you say?

PARRIS Tonight, when I open my door to leave my house—a dagger clattered to the ground. *(Silence. Danforth absorbs this. Now Parris cries out.)* You cannot hang this sort. There is danger for me. I dare not step outside at night!

Reverend Hale enters. They look at him for an instant in silence. He is steeped in sorrow, exhausted, and more direct than he ever was.

DANFORTH Accept my congratulations, Reverend Hale; we are gladdened to see you returned to your good work.

HALE *(coming to Danforth now)* You must pardon them. They will not budge.

Herrick enters, waits.

DANFORTH *(conciliatory)* You misunderstand, sir; I cannot pardon these when twelve are already hanged for the same crime. It is not just.

PARRIS *(with failing heart)* Rebecca will not confess?

HALE The sun will rise in a few minutes. Excellency, I must have more time.

DANFORTH Now hear me, and beguile yourselves no more. I will not receive a single plea for pardon or postponement. Them that will not confess will hang. Twelve are already executed; the names of these seven are given out, and the village expects to see them die this morning. Postponement now speaks a floundering on my part; reprieve or pardon must cast doubt upon the guilt of them that died till now. While I speak God's law, I will not crack its voice with whimpering. If retaliation is your fear, know this—I should hang ten thousand that dared to rise against the law, and an ocean of salt tears could not melt the resolution of the statutes. Now draw yourselves up like men and help me, as you are bound by Heaven to do. Have you spoken with them all, Mr. Hale?

HALE All but Proctor. He is in the dungeon.

DANFORTH *(to Herrick)* What's Proctor's way now?

HERRICK He sits like some great bird; you'd not know he lived except he will take food from time to time.

DANFORTH *(after thinking a moment)* His wife—his wife must be well on with child now.

HERRICK She is, sir.

DANFORTH What think you, Mr. Parris? You have closer knowledge of this man; might her presence soften him?

PARRIS It is possible, sir. He have not laid eyes on her these three months. I should summon her.

DANFORTH *(to Herrick)* Is he yet adamant? Has he struck at you again?

HERRICK He cannot, sir, he is chained to the wall now.

DANFORTH *(after thinking on it)* Fetch Goody Proctor to me. Then let you bring him up.

HERRICK Aye, sir. *(Herrick goes. There is silence.)*

What is the true reason for Parris' alarm?

Danforth's regard for consistency supersedes his concern for individual human life. Paraphrase Danforth's speech and explain how it bears on the theme of the play.

HALE Excellency, if you postpone a week and publish to the town that you are striving for their confessions, that speak mercy on your part, not faltering.

DANFORTH Mr. Hale, as God have not empowered me like Joshua to stop this sun from rising, so I cannot withhold from them the perfection of their punishment.

> Note Danforth's imagery in this passage. He sees his judgment as ordained by God, like the rising sun.

HALE *(harder now)* If you think God wills you to raise rebellion, Mr. Danforth, you are mistaken!

DANFORTH *(instantly)* You have heard rebellion spoken in the town?

HALE Excellency, there are orphans wandering from house to house; abandoned cattle bellow on the highroads, the stink of rotting crops hangs everywhere, and no man knows when the harlots' cry will end his life—and you wonder yet if rebellion's spoke? Better you should marvel how they do not burn your province!

DANFORTH Mr. Hale, have you preached in Andover this month?

HALE Thank God they have no need of me in Andover.

DANFORTH You baffle me, sir. Why have you returned here?

HALE Why, it is all simple. I come to do the Devil's work. I come to counsel Christians they should belie themselves. *(His sarcasm collapses.)* There is blood on my head! Can you not see the blood on my head!!

> What does Hale mean by "blood on my head"?

PARRIS Hush! *(For he has heard footsteps. They all face the door. Herrick enters with Elizabeth. Her wrists are linked by heavy chain, which Herrick now removes. Her clothes are dirty; her face is pale and gaunt. Herrick goes out.)*

DANFORTH *(very politely)* Goody Proctor. *(She is silent.)* I hope you are hearty?

ELIZABETH *(as a warning reminder)* I am yet six months before my time.

DANFORTH Pray be at your ease, we come not for your life. We— *(uncertain how to plead, for he is not accustomed to it)* Mr. Hale, will you speak with the woman?

HALE Goody Proctor, your husband is marked to hang this morning.

> What type of "wilderness" does Hale refer to?

Pause

ELIZABETH *(quietly)* I have heard it.

HALE You know, do you not, that I have no connection with the court? *(She seems to doubt it.)* I come of my own, Goody Proctor. I would save your husband's life, for if he is taken I count myself his murderer. Do you understand me?

ELIZABETH What do you want of me?

HALE Goody Proctor, I have gone this three month like our Lord into the wilderness. I have sought a Christian way, for damnation's doubled on a minister who counsels men to lie.

HATHORNE It is no lie, you cannot speak of lies.

HALE It is a lie! They are innocent!

DANFORTH I'll hear no more of that!

HALE *(continuing to Elizabeth)* Let you not mistake your duty as I mistook my own. I came into this village like a bridegroom to his beloved, bearing gifts of high religion; the very crowns of holy law I brought, and what I touched with my bright confidence, it died; and where I turned the eye of my great faith, blood flowed up. Beware, Goody Proctor—cleave to no faith when faith brings blood. It is mistaken law that leads you to sacrifice. Life, woman, life is God's most precious gift; no principle, however glorious, may justify the taking of it. I beg you, woman, prevail upon your husband to confess. Let him give his lie. Quail not before God's judgment in this, for it may well be God damns a liar less than he that throws his life away for pride. Will you plead with him? I cannot think he will listen to another.

ELIZABETH *(quietly)* I think that be the Devil's argument.

> Note the irony of this moment: an ordained minister now is begging for the prisoners to lie to the authorities.

HALE *(with a climactic desperation)* Woman, before the laws of God we are as swine! We cannot read His will!

ELIZABETH I cannot dispute with you, sir; I lack learning for it.

DANFORTH *(going to her)* Goody Proctor, you are not summoned here for disputation. Be there no wifely tenderness within you? He will die with the sunrise. Your husband. Do you understand it? *(She only looks at him.)* What say you? Will you contend with him? *(She is silent.)* Are you stone? I tell you true, woman, had I no other proof of your unnatural life, your dry eyes now would be sufficient evidence that you delivered up your soul to Hell! A very ape would weep at such calamity! Have the devil dried up any tear of pity in you? *(She is silent.)* Take her out. It profit nothing she should speak to him!

ELIZABETH *(quietly)* Let me speak with him, Excellency.

PARRIS *(with hope)* You'll strive with him? *(She hesitates.)*

DANFORTH Will you plead for his confession or will you not?

ELIZABETH I promise nothing. Let me speak with him.

> How have her terrible experiences made Elizabeth more canny now?

A sound—the sibilance of dragging feet on stone. They turn. A pause. Herrick enters with John Proctor. His wrists are chained. He is another man, bearded, filthy, his eyes misty as though webs had overgrown them. He halts inside the doorway, his eye caught by the sight of Elizabeth. The emotion flowing between them prevents anyone from speaking for an instant. Now Hale, visibly affected, goes to Danforth and speaks quietly.

HALE Pray, leave them, Excellency.

DANFORTH *(pressing Hale impatiently aside)* Mr. Proctor, you have been notified, have you not? *(Proctor is silent, staring at Elizabeth.)* I see light in the sky, Mister; let you counsel with your wife, and may God help you turn your back on Hell. *(Proctor is silent, staring at Elizabeth.)*

HALE *(quietly)* Excellency, let—

Danforth brushes past Hale and walks out. Hale follows. Cheever stands and follows, Hathorne behind. Herrick goes. Parris, from a safe distance, offers:

PARRIS If you desire a cup of cider, Mr. Proctor, I am sure I— *(Proctor turns an icy stare at him, and he breaks off. Parris raises his palms toward Proctor.)* God lead you now. *(Parris goes out.)*

THE CRUCIBLE

Alone. Proctor walks to her, halts. It is as though they stood in a spinning world. It is beyond sorrow, above it. He reaches out his hand as though toward an embodiment not quite real, and as he touches her, a strange soft sound, half laughter, half amazement, comes from his throat. He pats her hand. She covers his hand with hers. And then, weak, he sits. Then she sits, facing him.

PROCTOR The child?

ELIZABETH It grows.

PROCTOR There is no word of the boys?

ELIZABETH They're well. Rebecca's Samuel keeps them.

PROCTOR You have not seen them?

ELIZABETH I have not. *(She catches a weakening in herself and downs it.)*

PROCTOR You are a—marvel, Elizabeth.

ELIZABETH You—have been tortured?

PROCTOR Aye. *(Pause. She will not let herself be drowned in the sea that threatens her.)* They come for my life now.

ELIZABETH I know it.

Pause.

PROCTOR None—have yet confessed?

ELIZABETH There be many confessed.

PROCTOR Who are they?

ELIZABETH There be a hundred or more, they say. Goody Ballard is one; Isaiah Goodkind is one. There be many.

Why is Proctor interested in who has or has not confessed to witchcraft in Salem?

PROCTOR Rebecca?

ELIZABETH Not Rebecca. She is one foot in Heaven now; naught may hurt her more.

PROCTOR And Giles?

ELIZABETH You have not heard of it?

PROCTOR I hear nothin', where I am kept.

ELIZABETH Giles is dead.

He looks at her incredulously.

PROCTOR When were he hanged?

ELIZABETH *(quietly, factually)* He were not hanged. He would not answer aye or nay to his indictment; for if he denied the charge they'd hang him surely, and auction out his property. So he stand mute, and died Christian under the law. And so his sons will have his farm. It is the law, for he could not be condemned a wizard without he answer the indictment, aye or nay.

PROCTOR Then how does he die?

ELIZABETH *(gently)* They press him, John.

PROCTOR Press?

ELIZABETH Great stones they lay upon his chest until he plead aye or nay. *(with a tender smile for the old man)* They say he give them but two words. "More weight," he says. And died.

The crude politics of death is introduced here. If a person admits to sorcery, his properties are forfeited to the state, thus disinheriting his offspring. But if a person denies the accusation of the indictment, then he can be tried and found guilty—never innocent in these particular trials. Giles chooses to remain silent, however, which means an agonizing death by being crushed beneath boulders heaped on his body, one at a time. But at least this way he dies a Christian, neither indicted nor convicted of any crime, and his lands remain in his family.

Do the words "more weight" have

350   ARTHUR MILLER

PROCTOR *(numbed—a thread to weave into his agony)* "More weight."

ELIZABETH Aye. It were a fearsome man, Giles Corey.

Pause.

PROCTOR *(with great force of will, but not quite looking at her)* I have been thinking I would confess to them, Elizabeth. *(She shows nothing.)* What say you? If I give them that?

ELIZABETH I cannot judge you, John.

Pause

PROCTOR *(simply—a pure question)* What would you have me do?

ELIZABETH As you will, I would have it. *(slight pause)* I want you living, John. That's sure.

PROCTOR *(pauses, then with a flailing of hope)* Giles' wife? Have she confessed?

ELIZABETH She will not.

Pause

PROCTOR It is a pretense, Elizabeth.

ELIZABETH What is?

PROCTOR I cannot mount the gibbet like a saint. It is a fraud. I am not that man. *(She is silent.)* My honesty is broke, Elizabeth; I am no good man. Nothing's spoiled by giving them this lie that were not rotten long before.

ELIZABETH And yet you've not confessed till now. That speak goodness in you.

PROCTOR Spite only keeps me silent. It is hard to give a lie to dogs. *(Pause, for the first time he turns directly to her.)* I would have your forgiveness, Elizabeth.

ELIZABETH It is not for me to give, John, I am—

PROCTOR I'd have you see some honesty in it. Let them that never lied die now to keep their souls. It is pretense for me, a vanity that will not blind God nor keep my children out of the wind. *(pause)* What say you?

ELIZABETH *(upon a heaving sob that always threatens)* John, it come to naught that I should forgive you, if you'll not forgive yourself. *(Now he turns away a little, in great agony.)* It is not my soul, John, it is yours. *(He stands, as though in physical pain, slowly rising to his feet with a great immortal longing to find his answer. It is difficult to say, and she is on the verge of tears.)* Only be sure of this, for I know it now: Whatever you will do, it is a good man does it. *(He turns his doubting, searching gaze upon her.)* I have read my heart this three month, John. *(pause)* I have sins of my own to count. It needs a cold wife to prompt lechery.

PROCTOR *(in great pain)* Enough, enough—

ELIZABETH *(now pouring out her heart)* Better you should know me!

PROCTOR I will not hear it! I know you!

ELIZABETH You take my sins upon you, John—

PROCTOR *(in agony)* No, I take my own, my own!

Elizabeth (Martha Henry) and John Proctor (Robert Foxworth).

ELIZABETH John, I counted myself so plain, so poorly made, no honest love could come to me! Suspicion kissed you when I did; I never knew how I should say my love. It were a cold house I kept! (*In fright, she swerves, as Hathorne enters.*)

HATHORNE What say you, Proctor? The sun is soon up.

Proctor, his chest heaving, stares, turns to Elizabeth. She comes to him as though to plead, her voice quaking.

ELIZABETH Do what you will. But let none be your judge. There be no higher judge under Heaven than Proctor is! Forgive me, forgive me, John—I never knew such goodness in the world! (*She covers her face, weeping.*)

Proctor turns from her to Hathorne; he is off the earth, his voice hollow.

PROCTOR I want my life.

HATHORNE (*electrified, surprised*) You'll confess yourself?

PROCTOR I will have my life.

HATHORNE (*with a mystical tone*) God be praised! It is a providence!

What level of the two-fold plot is being resolved in this encounter?

(He rushes out the door, and his voice is heard calling down the corridor.) He will confess! Proctor will confess!

PROCTOR *(with a cry, as he strides to the door)* Why do you cry it? *(In great pain he turns back to her.)* It is evil, is it not? It is evil.

ELIZABETH *(in terrror, weeping)* I cannot judge you, John, I cannot!

PROCTOR Then who will judge me? *(suddenly clasping his hands)* God in Heaven, what is John Proctor, what is John Proctor? *(He moves as an animal, and a fury is riding in him, a tantalized search.)* I think it is honest, I think so; I am no saint. *(As though she had denied this he calls angrily at her.)* Let Rebecca go like a saint; for me it is fraud!

Voices are heard in the hall, speaking together in suppressed excitement.

ELIZABETH I am not your judge, I cannot be. *(as though giving him release)* Do as you will, do as you will!

PROCTOR Would you give them such a lie? Say it. Would you ever give them this? *(She cannot answer.)* You would not; if tongs of fire were singeing you you would not! It is evil. Good, then—it is evil, and I do it!

Hathorne enters with Danforth, and, with them, Cheever, Parris, and Hale. It is a businesslike, rapid entrance, as though the ice had been broken.

DANFORTH *(with great relief and gratitude)* Praise to God, man, praise to God; you shall be blessed in Heaven for this. *(Cheever has hurried to the bench with pen, ink, and paper. Proctor watches him.)* Now then, let us have it. Are you ready, Mr. Cheever?

PROCTOR *(with a cold, cold horror at their efficiency)* Why must it be written?

DANFORTH Why, for the good instruction of the village, Mister; this we shall post upon the church door! *(to Parris, urgently)* Where is the marshal?

PARRIS *(runs to the door and calls down the corridor)* Marshal! Hurry!

DANFORTH Now, then, Mister, will you speak slowly, and directly to the point, for Mr. Cheever's sake. *(He is on record now, and is really dictating to Cheever, who writes.)* Mr. Proctor, have you seen the Devil in your life? *(Proctor's jaws lock.)* Come, man, there is light in the sky; the town waits at the scaffold; I would give out this news. Did you see the Devil?

PROCTOR I did.

PARRIS Praise God!

DANFORTH And when he come to you, what were his demand? *(Proctor is silent. Danforth helps.)* Did he bid you to do his work upon the earth?

PROCTOR He did.

DANFORTH And you bound yourself to his service? *(Danforth turns, as Rebecca Nurse enters, with Herrick helping to support her. She is barely able to walk.)* Come in, come in, woman!

REBECCA *(brightening as she sees Proctor)* Ah, John! You are well, then, eh?

Proctor turns his face to the wall.

> Why does Proctor seem so anxious in wishing to do evil here? What does this tell us about his self-regard?

> How may Proctor's answers to these questions be construed? Where has he *really* seen the devil at work?

> Why does Rebecca Nurse's presence cause Proctor immense spiritual agony? What does she stand for which erases Proctor's rationalizations about his lying?

THE CRUCIBLE 353

DANFORTH Courage, man, courage—let her witness your good example that she may come to God herself. Now hear it, Goody Nurse! Say on, Mr. Proctor. Did you bind yourself to the Devil's service?

REBECCA *(astonished)* Why, John!

PROCTOR *(through his teeth, his face turned from Rebecca)* I did.

DANFORTH Now, woman, you surely see it profit nothin' to keep this conspiracy any further. Will you confess yourself with him?

REBECCA Oh, John—God send his mercy on you!

DANFORTH I say, will you confess yourself, Goody Nurse?

REBECCA Why, it is a lie, it is a lie; how may I damn myself? I cannot, I cannot.

DANFORTH Mr. Proctor. When the Devil came to you did you see Rebecca Nurse in his company? *(Proctor is silent.)* Come, man, take courage—did you ever see her with the Devil?

PROCTOR *(almost inaudibly)* No.

Danforth, now sensing trouble, glances at John and goes to the table, and picks up a sheet—the list of condemned.

DANFORTH Did you ever see her sister, Mary Easty, with the Devil?

PROCTOR No, I did not.

DANFORTH *(His eyes narrow on Proctor.)* Did you ever see Martha Corey with the Devil?

PROCTOR I did not.

DANFORTH *(realizing, slowly putting the sheet down)* Did you ever see anyone with the Devil?

PROCTOR I did not.

DANFORTH Proctor, you mistake me. I am not empowered to trade your life for a lie. You have most certainly seen some person with the Devil. *(Proctor is silent.)* Mr. Proctor, a score of people have already testified they saw this woman with the Devil.

PROCTOR Then it is proved. Why must I say it?

DANFORTH Why "must" you say it! Why, you should rejoice to say it if your soul is truly purged of any love for Hell!

PROCTOR They think to go like saints. I like not to spoil their names.

DANFORTH *(inquiring, incredulous)* Mr. Proctor, do you think they go like saints?

PROCTOR *(evading)* This woman never thought she done the Devil's work.

DANFORTH Look you, sir. I think you mistake your duty here. It matters nothing what she thought—she is convicted of the unnatural murder of children, and you for sending your spirit out upon Mary Warren. Your soul alone is the issue here, Mister, and you will prove its whiteness or you cannot live in a Christian country. Will you tell me now what persons conspired with you in the Devil's company? *(Proctor is silent.)* To your knowledge was Rebecca Nurse ever—

> Why does Proctor now respond as he does to this second series of questions?

PROCTOR I speak my own sins; I cannot judge another. *(crying out, with hatred)* I have no tongue for it.

HALE *(quickly to Danforth)* Excellency, it is enough he confess himself. Let him sign it, let him sign it.

PARRIS *(feverishly)* It is a great service, sir. It is a weighty name; it will strike the village that Proctor confess. I beg you, let him sign it. The sun is up, Excellency!

DANFORTH *(considers; then with dissatisfaction)* Come, then, sign your testimony. *(to Cheever)* Give it to him. *(Cheever goes to Proctor, the confession and a pen in hand. Proctor does not look at it.)* Come, man, sign it.

> Why does Danforth relent, reluctantly contenting himself with only Proctor's signed confession?

PROCTOR *(after glancing at the confession)* You have all witnessed it—it is enough.

DANFORTH You will not sign it?

PROCTOR You have all witnessed it; what more is needed?

DANFORTH Do you sport with me? You will sign your name or it is no confession, Mister! *(His breast heaving with agonized breathing, Proctor now lays the paper down and signs his name.)*

PARRIS Praise be to the Lord!

Proctor has just finished signing when Danforth reaches for the paper. But Proctor snatches it up, and now a wild terror is rising in him, and a boundless anger.

DANFORTH *(perplexed, but politely extending his hand)* If you please, sir.

PROCTOR No.

DANFORTH *(as though Proctor did not understand)* Mr. Proctor, I must have—

PROCTOR No, no. I have signed it. You have seen me. It is done! You have no need for this.

PARRIS Proctor, the village must have proof that—

PROCTOR Damn the village! I confess to God, and God has seen my name on this! It is enough!

DANFORTH No, sir, it is—

PROCTOR You came to save my soul, did you not? Here! I have confessed myself; it is enough!

> Proctor calls the bluff of the officials who claim to want to save souls, while their actions indicate political motives instead

DANFORTH You have not con—

PROCTOR I have confessed myself! Is there no good penitence but it be public? God does not need my name nailed upon the church! God sees my name; God knows how black my sins are! It is enough!

DANFORTH Mr. Proctor—

PROCTOR You will not use me! I am no Sarah Good or Tituba, I am John Proctor! You will not use me! It is no part of salvation that you should use me!

DANFORTH I do not wish to—

PROCTOR I have three children—how may I teach them to walk like men in the world, and I sold my friends?

DANFORTH You have not sold your friends—

PROCTOR Beguile me not! I blacken all of them when this is nailed to the church the very day they hang for silence!

DANFORTH Mr. Proctor, I must have good and legal proof that you—

PROCTOR You are the high court, your word is good enough! Tell them I confessed myself; say Proctor broke his knees and wept like a woman; say what you will, but my name cannot—

DANFORTH *(with suspicion)* It is the same, is it not? If I report it or you sign to it?

> A key concern for Miller—a man's name, i.e., his self-esteem and reputation—shows up here, as it does in most of his dramas.

PROCTOR *(He knows it is insane.)* No, it is not the same! What others say and what I sign to is not the same!

DANFORTH Why? Do you mean to deny this confession when you are free?

PROCTOR I mean to deny nothing!

DANFORTH Then explain to me, Mr. Proctor, why you will not let—

PROCTOR *(with a cry of his whole soul)* Because it is my name! Because I cannot have another in my life! Because I lie and sign myself to lies! Because I am not worth the dust on the feet of them that hang! How may I live without my name? I have given you my soul; leave me my name!

DANFORTH *(pointing at the confession in Proctor's hand)* Is that document a lie? If it is a lie I will not accept it! What say you? I will not deal in lies, Mister! *(Proctor is motionless.)* You will give me your honest confession in my hand, or I cannot keep you from the rope. *(Proctor does not reply.)* Which way do you go, Mister?

His breast heaving, his eyes staring, Proctor tears the paper and crumples it, and he is weeping in fury, but erect.

DANFORTH Marshal!

PARRIS *(hysterically, as though the tearing paper were his life)* Proctor, Proctor!

HALE Man, you will hang! You cannot!

PROCTOR *(his eyes full of tears)* I can. And there's your first marvel, that I can. You have made your magic now, for now I do think I see some shred of goodness in John Proctor. Not enough to weave a banner with, but white enough to keep it from such dogs. *(Elizabeth, in a burst of terror, rushes to him and weeps against his hand.)* Give them no tear! Tears pleasure them! Show honor now, show a stony heart and sink them with it! *(He has lifted her, and kisses her now with great passion.)*

> What is the effect of the play's resolution on the people involved and on the community?

REBECCA Let you fear nothing! Another judgment waits us all!

DANFORTH Hang them high over the town! Who weeps for these, weeps for corruption! *(He sweeps out past them. Herrick starts to lead Rebecca, who almost collapses, but Proctor catches her, and she glances up at him apologetically.)*

REBECCA I've had no breakfast.

HERRICK Come, man.

Herrick escorts them out, Hathorne and Cheever behind them. Elizabeth stands staring at the empty doorway.

PARRIS *(in deadly fear, to Elizabeth)* Go to him, Goody Proctor! There is yet time!

From outside a drumroll strikes the air. Parris is startled. Elizabeth jerks about toward the window.

PARRIS Go to him! *(He rushes out the door, as though to hold back his fate.)* Proctor! Proctor!

Again, a short burst of drums.

HALE Woman, plead with him! *(He starts to rush out the door, and then goes back to her.)* Woman! It is pride, it is vanity. *(She avoids his eyes, and moves to the window. He drops to his knees.)* Be his helper!—What profit him to bleed? Shall the dust praise him? Shall the worms declare his truth? Go to him, take his shame away!

ELIZABETH *(supporting herself against collapse, grips the bars of the window, and with a cry)* He have his goodness now. God forbid I take it from him!

The final drumroll crashes, then heightens violently. Hale weeps in frantic prayer, and the new sun is pouring in upon her face, and the drums rattle like bones in the morning air.

The curtain falls.

> Why is the dawn sunlight a fitting visual equivalent for the play's conclusion?

ECHOES DOWN THE CORRIDOR

Not long after the fever died, Parris was voted from office, walked out on the highroad, and was never heard of again.

The legend has it that Abigail turned up later as a prostitute in Boston.

Twenty years after the last execution, the government awarded compensation to the victims still living, and to the families of the dead. However, it is evident that some people still were unwilling to admit their total guilt, and also that the factionalism was still alive, for some beneficiaries were actually not victims at all, but informers.

Elizabeth Proctor married again, four years after Proctor's death.

In solemn meeting, the congregation rescinded the excommunications—this in March 1712. But they did so upon orders of the government. The jury, however, wrote a statement praying forgiveness of all who had suffered.

Certain farms which had belonged to the victims were left to ruin, and for more than a century no one would buy them or live on them.

To all intents and purposes, the power of theocracy in Massachusetts was broken.

POSTVIEW: THEME

Like most well-written plays, *The Crucible* has a main theme which provides focus and cohesiveness to the action.

1. What is the theme of this play?
2. Where do the crucial issues in the theme first emerge?
3. What associated theme, constructed on a highly personal basis, complements and is bonded to the principal, more general topic?
4. Who carries the weight of the more intimate theme?

5. Who constitute the two main antagonistic factions as the play develops?
6. How would one best characterize Proctor? Parris? Giles Corey? Danforth? Rebecca Nurse? Hathorne?
7. What special role is reserved for Reverend Hale? For instance, what was his opinion of witchcraft and witch trials at the beginning, the middle, and the end of the play?
8. Why might Hale be considered a variation of the Chorus figure?

A popular topic of Miller's plays is that of the individual who evaluates his worth accurately and then insists on his rightful status in society. (See the general introduction preceding *The Crucible*.)

9. Why does Proctor paradoxically harbor serious doubts regarding his worth?
10. How does Elizabeth Proctor's treatment of her husband in the early stages of the play reinforce his uncertainty of himself?
11. What does Proctor salvage of his self-esteem by refusing to confess officially to sorcery charges at the end of the drama?
12. What are some different uses of the term "name," as Proctor employs this word in his final self-debate in Act IV?

Although *The Crucible* is a period play, replete with a setting in the past, costumes from a past age, and strange speech patterns and customs, yet it pertains to our modern world.

13. Based on Miller's commentaries, what are the similarities between the Salem witch hunts and the McCarthy hearings of the early 1950s?
14. Why is the title appropriate for the events of the drama?
15. Why can we still learn today from *The Crucible* with its examples of peer pressures? Of mob psychology? Of lying for self-protection? Of assuming guilt by association? Of fearing self-serving authority figures?

INTRODUCTION
A *RAISIN IN THE SUN*

Lorraine Hansberry

A *RAISIN IN THE SUN* was a resounding critical success at its New York premiere in March of 1959. Its dramatization of a struggling black family in Chicago won for its young author, Lorraine Hansberry, the New York Drama Critics' Circle Award for the 1958–59 season. Nor has the play's popularity diminished appreciably in subsequent years. A successful motion picture has been made from the work, and a New York musical stage version, called simply *Raisin,* won a Tony Award in 1974.

A Raisin in the Sun gained immediate acceptance on the American stage, for it captured within the confines of a single setting the central social matters facing the United States during the last half of the twentieth century. In a balanced plot, Hansberry develops the issues of civil rights and materialism as a personal as well as a national obsession; of the generation gap resulting from fundamental differences in values between parents and offspring; of imperialism, the Third World, growth of minority self-awareness; of sexism, and even of abortion. *A Raisin in the Sun* is a social drama, and it is comparable to those of other masterful social commentators, such as Ibsen and Miller.

Lorraine Hansberry's life (1930–1965) clarifies the multifaceted achievement of her drama. Born in Chicago of wealthy black parents, she lived through much the same process of moving as does the Younger family in the play. Her family purchased a home in a white neighborhood and then, allied with the NAACP, fought successfully all the way to the Supreme Court for the right to live there. Educated in painting and writing at the Chicago Art Institute, the University of Wisconsin, and the University of Guadalajara in Mexico, Hansberry moved to New York City in 1950, where she married music publisher Robert Nemiroff and became involved in social movements. She was active on behalf of minority causes and she helped edit Paul Robeson's monthly journal, *Freedom*.

Her second play, *The Sign in Sidney Brustein's Window* (1964), also treated social problems, including prejudices against Jews and homosexuals in modern society. Although it received a few good reviews, this play never was as popular as *A Raisin in the Sun*. Sadly and ironically, *The Sign in Sidney Brustein's Window* closed after 101 performances on the night that Hansberry died of cancer. At the time of her death, she left unfinished another full-length play, *Les Blancs*. Her ex-husband Robert Nemiroff (they were divorced shortly before her death), however, continued to be active on her behalf. He adapted excerpts from her letters, dramas, and novels to construct and produce *To Be Young, Gifted and Black* (1969), a biographical play, and he completed *Les Blancs*. A less than successful production of this latter drama was given in New York in 1970.

In all her dramas, Lorraine Hansberry probed the faults of societies which lacked tolerance and fairness. Her plays document the dynamics of people thwarted in attaining their dreams of the good life. Frustration at being trapped in a deprived social setting constitutes the chief subject matter of her works, as her characters seek the means for achieving material success. The lines from Langston Hughes's poem "Montage of a Dream Deferred" furnish Hansberry not only the title for *A Raisin in the Sun*, but also the hint that explosions could result when hopes have been frustrated. (See the Preview section following the text of this play.) *A Raisin in the Sun*, then, explores the dynamic process involved when one's hopes have been dashed.

Beneath the militancy seething in her plays, Hansberry revealed genuine artistic talent by transcending the simple emotional possibilities of social drama. She considers individuals *as* individuals, caught in a world not of their making. *A Raisin in the Sun* cannot be viewed merely as a black family learning to "cope." There are *real* people in the play: Lena Younger, the warm, selfless mother devoted to improving her family's situation; Walter, the young black man who cannot assume his total manhood in a context which forbids him to act like a man; Ruth, a simple but dedicated wife who recognizes that much that goes on in the world is beyond her comprehension; and Beneatha, the gifted, bright sister who, because of her intelligence and education, understands both the oppressiveness of the ghetto and the white society's open-ended possibilities for success.

The most remarkable feature of Miss Hansberry's play, consequently, is her ability to make us care for her characters as *people,* not just as blacks or the poor or the downtrodden.

PREVIEW: STRUCTURE

Exposition in a play can be developed simultaneously on several levels, including the establishment of a particular mood in the setting. Throughout her drama, Hansberry uses stage descriptions to convey both a visual and atmospheric nature for the action.

1. In the opening description of the setting, what suggests the quality of worn-out furnishings?
2. Why is the change in appearance of the Younger apartment helpful as exposition at the beginning of Act II, scene ii?

Because Lorraine Hansberry is skilled at characterizing her protagonists, we can ascertain the vocational roles and the unique individual personalities of the major figures early in the play.

3. What does Walter do for a living?
4. Why is Walter's job particularly frustrating to him, in view of his aspirations for the future?
5. What stereotyped role does Ruth fall into from the outset of the drama?
6. Who heads the Younger household? How do we know?

The complications in the plot surface early on several planes of action.

7. Why is Walter so excessively concerned with "the" check?
8. How do Walter's friends contribute to the tension between Walter and Ruth?
9. Why do Beneatha's future career plans constitute a threat to Walter?
10. Why is Mama's decision to buy a house a blow to Walter's plans?

By gradually developing additional complications during the play, Hansberry increases the conflicting encounters among the characters to provide suspense.

11. What complicating element is introduced near the end of the first act when Ruth admits to having visited a doctor? What kind of "doctor" did she see and why?
12. What is the relationship between Beneatha and George? Between Beneatha and Asagai?
13. How does the location of Mama's newly purchased house add to the tension?
14. Why does Karl Lindner's visit in the third scene of Act II become a source of dramatic tension?
15. Why does Bobo's news precipitate a crisis situation for the Youngers?

When Willy runs away with the Youngers' money, he has set the stage for the climax of the play.

16. What is Walter's initial attitude and behavior after discovering that he had been cheated?
17. How does Walter decide to recoup the lost money early in the final act?
18. Why is the play's climax parallel to the climactic development of Walter's spirit and character?

Hansberry arranges for an ideal showdown scene in the last act which leads to the resolution.

19. Why does Lindner's second visit to the Youngers provide the ingredients for a resolution of the major dilemmas?
20. Whose crucial decision is involved in the resolution, and what is it?

Following Walter's commitment on behalf of the family, only a few lines of dialogue are left in the play for the presentation of any denouement.

21. Is there a promise in the air that everything has been perfectly resolved and that all the Youngers' problems are over for good? How do we know?
22. Why do Mama's wordless actions on stage, as the play concludes, constitute a recognizable denouement? What does she indicate when she seizes her favorite plant before leaving the apartment forever?

Quoted immediately before the original published text of Hansberry's play is a portion of a poem by Langston Hughes, "Harlem: What happens to a dream deferred?" The section used by Miss Hansberry as her inscription is as follows:

Harlem

What happens to a dream deferred?
   Does it dry up
   like a raisin in the sun?
   Or fester like a sore—
   And then run?
   Does it stink like rotten meat?
   Or crust and sugar over—
   like a syrupy sweet?

Maybe it just sags
like a heavy load.

Or does it explode?

The dream motif mentioned in Hughes' poem plays a key part in Hansberry's drama, as well. While reading the play, be aware of this crucial element of frustrated dreams.

A RAISIN IN THE SUN

Lorraine Hansberry

CHARACTERS

Ruth Younger
Travis Younger
Walter Lee Younger (Brother)
Beneatha Younger
Lena Younger (Mama)
Joseph Asagai
George Murchison
Karl Lindner
Bobo
Moving Men

The action of the play is set in Chicago's Southside, sometime between World War II and the present.

Act I
Scene i. Friday morning.
Scene ii. The following morning.

Act II
Scene i. Later, the same day.
Scene ii. Friday night, a few weeks later.
Scene iii. Moving day, one week later.

Act III
An hour later.

ACT I

SCENE I

The Younger living room would be a comfortable and well-ordered room if it were not for a number of indestructible contradictions to this state of being. Its furnishings are typical and undistinguished and their primary feature now is that they have clearly had to accommodate the living of too many people for too many years—and they are tired. Still, we can see that at some time, a time probably no longer remembered by the family (except perhaps for Mama) the furnishings of this room were actually selected with care and love and even hope—and brought to this apartment and arranged with taste and pride.

That was a long time ago. Now the once loved pattern of the couch upholstery has to fight to show itself from under acres of crocheted doilies and couch covers which have themselves finally come to be more important than the upholstery. And here a table or a chair has been moved to disguise the worn places in the carpet; but the carpet has fought back by showing its weariness, with depressing uniformity, elsewhere on its surface.

Weariness has, in fact, won in this room. Everything has been polished, washed, sat on, used, scrubbed too often. All pretenses but living itself have long since vanished from the very atmosphere of this room.

Moreover, a section of this room, for it is not really a room unto itself, though the landlord's lease would make it seem so, slopes backward to provide a small kitchen area, where the family prepares the meals that are

---

The author takes care in her opening description of the Youngers' apartment to communicate the "indestructible contradictions" of the "state of being" presented by the setting. The furnishings are to appear run-down, thus conveying the economic status of the tenants. But those living here obviously *care*, as evidenced by the "care and love and even hope" that once went into the selection of the now-worn furniture.

What details of the setting convey a sense of congested living?

eaten in the living room proper, which must also serve as dining room. The single window that has been provided for these "two" rooms is located in this kitchen area. The sole natural light the family may enjoy in the course of a day is only that which fights its way through this little window.

At left, a door leads to a bedroom which is shared by Mama and her daughter, Beneatha. At right, opposite, is a second room (which in the beginning of the life of this apartment was probably a breakfast room) which serves as a bedroom for Walter and his wife, Ruth.

Time: Sometime between World War II and the present.

Place: Chicago's Southside.

At Rise: It is morning dark in the living room. Travis is asleep on the make-down bed at center. An alarm clock sounds from within the bedroom at right, and presently Ruth enters from that room and closes the door behind her. She crosses sleepily toward the window. As she passes her sleeping son she reaches down and shakes him a little. At the window she raises the shade and a dusky Southside morning light comes in feebly. She fills a pot with water and puts it on to boil. She calls to the boy, between yawns, in a slightly muffled voice.

Ruth is about thirty. We can see that she was a pretty girl, even exceptionally so, but now it is apparent that life has been little that she expected, and disappointment has already begun to hang in her face. In a few years, before thirty-five even, she will be known among her people as a "settled woman."

She crosses to her son and gives him a good, final, rousing shake.

RUTH Come on now, boy, it's seven thirty! *(Her son sits up at last, in a stupor of sleepiness.)* I say hurry up, Travis! You ain't the only person in the world got to use a bathroom! *(The child, a sturdy, handsome little boy of ten or eleven, drags himself out of the bed and almost blindly takes his towels and "today's clothes" from drawers and a closet and goes out to the bathroom, which is in an outside hall and which is shared by another family or families on the same floor. Ruth crosses to the bedroom door at right and opens it and calls in to her husband.)* Walter Lee! . . . It's after seven thirty! Lemme see you do some waking up in there now! *(She waits.)* You better get up from there, man! It's after seven thirty I tell you. *(She waits again.)* All right, you just go ahead and lay there and next thing you know Travis be finished and Mr. Johnson'll be in there and you'll be fussing and cussing round here like a mad man! And be late too! *(She waits, at the end of patience.)* Walter Lee—it's time for you to get up!

She waits another second and then starts to go into the bedroom, but is apparently satisfied that her husband has begun to get up. She stops, pulls the door to, and returns to the kitchen area. She wipes her face with a moist cloth and runs her fingers through her sleep-disheveled hair in a vain effort and ties an apron around her housecoat. The bedroom door at right opens and her husband stands in the doorway in his pajamas, which are rumpled and mismated. He is a lean, intense young man in his middle thirties, inclined to quick nervous movements and erratic speech habits—and always in his voice there is a quality of indictment.

WALTER Is he out yet?

RUTH What you mean *out?* He ain't hardly got in there good yet.

WALTER *(wandering in, still more oriented to sleep than to a new day)* Well, what was you doing all that yelling for if I can't even get in there yet? *(stopping and thinking)* Check coming today?

What does the expression a "settled woman" mean?

How does the dialogue aid the stage description in conveying the Youngers' tight living quarters?

Hansberry quickly establishes Walter's principal concern. What is it, and how do we learn that it has long been his main preoccupation?

364   LORRAINE HANSBERRY

RUTH They *said* Saturday and this is just Friday and I hopes to God you ain't going to get up here first thing this morning and start talking to me 'bout no money—'cause I 'bout don't want to hear it.

WALTER Something the matter with you this morning?

RUTH No—I'm just sleepy as the devil. What kind of eggs you want?

WALTER Not scrambled. (*Ruth starts to scramble eggs.*) Paper come? (*Ruth points impatiently to the rolled up* Tribune *on the table, and he gets it and spreads it out and vaguely reads the front page.*) Set off another bomb yesterday.

RUTH (*maximum indifference*) Did they?

WALTER (*looking up*) What's the matter with you?

RUTH Ain't nothing the matter with me. And don't keep asking me that this morning.

WALTER Ain't nobody bothering you. (*reading the news of the day absently again*) Say Colonel McCormick is sick.

RUTH (*affecting tea-party interest*) Is he now? Poor thing.

WALTER (*sighing and looking at his watch*) Oh, me. (*He waits.*) Now what is that boy doing in that bathroom all this time? He just going to have to start getting up earlier. I can't be being late to work on account of him fooling around in there.

RUTH (*turning on him*) Oh, no he ain't going to be getting up no earlier no such thing! It ain't his fault that he can't get to bed no earlier nights 'cause he got a bunch of crazy good-for-nothing clowns sitting up running their mouths in what is supposed to be his bedroom after ten o'clock at night . . .

WALTER That's what you mad about, ain't it? The things I want to talk about with my friends just couldn't be important in your mind, could they?

He rises and finds a cigarette in her handbag on the table and crosses to the little window and looks out, smoking and deeply enjoying this first one.

RUTH (*almost matter of factly, a complaint too automatic to deserve emphasis*) Why you always got to smoke before you eat in the morning?

WALTER (*at the window*) Just look at 'em down there . . . Running and racing to work . . . (*He turns and faces his wife and watches her a moment at the stove, and then, suddenly*) You look young this morning, baby.

RUTH (*indifferently*) Yeah?

WALTER Just for a second—stirring them eggs. It's gone now—just for a second it was—you looked real young again. (*then, drily*) It's gone now—you look like yourself again.

RUTH Man, if you don't shut up and leave me alone.

WALTER (*looking out to the street again*) First thing a man ought to learn in life is not to make love to no colored woman first thing in the morning. You all some evil people at eight o'clock in the morning.

Travis appears in the hall doorway, almost fully dressed and quite wide awake now, his towels and pajamas across his shoulders. He opens the door and signals for his father to make the bathroom in a hurry.

One of the chief aims of dramatic realism is to capture natural speech. What special dialect patterns, here and elsewhere, create a realistic depiction of a poor black household?

What intimate, realistic details here suggest the "old hat" quality of Walter and Ruth's marriage?

TRAVIS *(watching the bathroom)* Daddy, come on!

Walter gets his bathroom utensils and flies out to the bathroom.

RUTH Sit down and have your breakfast, Travis.

TRAVIS Mama, this is Friday. *(gleefully)* Check coming tomorrow, huh?

RUTH You get your mind off money and eat your breakfast.

TRAVIS *(eating)* This is the morning we supposed to bring the fifty cents to school.

RUTH Well, I ain't got no fifty cents this morning.

TRAVIS Teacher say we have to.

RUTH I don't care what teacher say. I ain't got it. Eat your breakfast, Travis.

TRAVIS I *am* eating.

RUTH Hush up now and just eat!

The boy gives her an exasperated look for her lack of understanding, and eats grudgingly.

TRAVIS You think Grandmama would have it?

RUTH No! And I want you to stop asking your grandmother for money, you hear me?

TRAVIS *(outraged)* Gaaaleee! I don't ask her, she just gimme it sometimes!

RUTH Travis Willard Younger—I got too much on me this morning to be—

TRAVIS Maybe Daddy—

RUTH Travis!

The boy hushes abruptly. They are both quiet and tense for several seconds.

TRAVIS *(presently)* Could I maybe go carry some groceries in front of the supermarket for a little while after school then?

RUTH Just hush, I said. *(Travis jabs his spoon into his cereal bowl viciously, and rests his head in anger upon his fists.)* If you through eating, you can get over there and make up your bed.

The boy obeys stiffly and crosses the room, almost mechanically, to the bed and more or less carefully folds the covering. He carries the bedding into his mother's room and returns with his books and cap.

TRAVIS *(sulking and standing apart from her unnaturally)* I'm gone.

RUTH *(looking up from the stove to inspect him automatically)* Come here. *(He crosses to her and she studies his head.)* If you don't take this comb and fix this here head, you better! *(Travis puts down his books with a great sigh of oppression, and crosses to the mirror. His mother mutters under her breath about his "slubbornness.")* 'Bout to march out of here with that head looking just like chickens slept in it! I just don't know where you get your slubborn ways . . . And get your jacket, too. Looks chilly out this morning.

TRAVIS *(with conspicuously brushed hair and jacket)* I'm gone.

The word "slubborn" is not found in any dictionary. In light of the context, what does it probably mean and what word does it come from? Ruth's fussing over Travis reinforces what earlier impression about the Youngers' attitude toward themselves and life?

366 LORRAINE HANSBERRY

RUTH Get carfare and milk money—*(waving one finger)*—and not a single penny for no caps, you hear me?

TRAVIS *(with sullen politeness)* Yes'm.

He turns in outrage to leave. His mother watches after him as in his frustration he approaches the door almost comically. When she speaks to him, her voice has become a very gentle tease.

RUTH *(mocking; as she thinks he would say it)* Oh, Mama makes me so mad sometimes, I don't know what to do! *(She waits and continues to his back as he stands stock-still in front of the door.)* I wouldn't kiss that woman good-bye for nothing in this world this morning! *(The boy finally turns around and rolls his eyes at her, knowing the mood has changed and he is vindicated; he does not, however, move toward her yet.)* Not for nothing in this world! *(She finally laughs aloud at him and holds out her arms to him and we see that it is a way between them, very old and practiced. He crosses to her and allows her to embrace him warmly but keeps his face fixed with masculine rigidity. She holds him back from her presently and looks at him and runs her fingers over the features of his face. With utter gentleness—)* Now—whose little old angry man are you?

TRAVIS *(the masculinity and gruffness start to fade at last.)* Aw gaalee—Mama . . .

RUTH *(mimicking)* Aw—gaaaaalleeeee, Mama! *(She pushes him, with rough playfulness and finality, toward the door.)* Get on out of here or you going to be late.

TRAVIS *(in the face of love, new aggressiveness)* Mama, could I *please* go carry groceries?

RUTH Honey, it's starting to get so cold evenings.

WALTER *(coming in from the bathroom and drawing a make-believe gun from a make-believe holster and shooting at his son)* What is it he wants to do?

RUTH Go carry groceries after school at the supermarket.

WALTER Well, let him go . . .

TRAVIS *(quickly, to the ally)* I *have* to—she won't gimme the fifty cents . . .

WALTER *(to his wife only)* Why not?

RUTH *(simply, and with flavor)* 'Cause we don't have it.

WALTER *(to Ruth only)* What you tell the boy things like that for? *(reaching down into his pants with a rather important gesture)* Here, son—

He hands the boy the coin, but his eyes are directed to his wife's. Travis takes the money happily.

TRAVIS Thanks, Daddy.

He starts out. Ruth watches both of them with murder in her eyes. Walter stands and stares back at her with defiance, and suddenly reaches into his pocket again on an afterthought.

WALTER *(without even looking at his son, still staring hard at his wife)* In fact, here's another fifty cents . . . Buy yourself some fruit today—or take a taxicab to school or something!

> Hansberry creates here a specific, personal scene of affectionate home life. At the same time, she captures familial love in a universal way.

TRAVIS Whoopee—

He leaps up and clasps his father around the middle with his legs, and they face each other in mutual appreciation; slowly Walter Lee peeks around the boy to catch the violent rays from his wife's eyes and draws his head back as if shot.

WALTER You better get down now—and get to school, man.

TRAVIS *(at the door)* O.K. Good-bye.

He exits.

WALTER *(after him, pointing with pride)* That's *my* boy. *(She looks at him in disgust and turns back to her work.)* You know what I was thinking 'bout in the bathroom this morning?

> Why is Walter so sensitive about his son having spending money?

RUTH No.

WALTER How come you always try to be so pleasant!

RUTH What is there to be pleasant 'bout!

WALTER You want to know what I was thinking 'bout in the bathroom or not!

RUTH I know what you thinking 'bout.

WALTER *(ignoring her)* 'Bout what me and Willy Harris was talking about last night.

RUTH *(immediately—a refrain)* Willy Harris is a good-for-nothing loud mouth.

WALTER Anybody who talks to me has got to be a good-for-nothing loud mouth, ain't he? And what you know about who is just a good-for-nothing loud mouth? Charlie Atkins was just a "good-for-nothing loud mouth" too, wasn't he! When he wanted me to go in the dry-cleaning business with him. And now—he's grossing a hundred thousand a year. A hundred thousand dollars a year! You still call *him* a loud mouth!

> What does this dialogue tell us about Walter and Ruth's relationship?

RUTH *(bitterly)* Oh, Walter Lee . . .

She folds her head on her arms over the table.

WALTER *(rising and coming to her and standing over her)* You tired, ain't you? Tired of everything. Me, the boy, the way we live—this beat-up hole—everything. Ain't you? *(She doesn't look up, doesn't answer.)* So tired—moaning and groaning all the time, but you wouldn't do nothing to help, would you? You couldn't be on my side that long for nothing, could you?

RUTH Walter, please leave me alone.

WALTER A man needs for a woman to back him up . . .

RUTH Walter—

> A point of continuous friction between Ruth and Walter emerges here, stemming from his insecurity and her weariness with a hopeless existence.

WALTER Mama would listen to you. You know she listen to you more than she do me and Bennie. She think more of you. All you have to do is just sit down with her when you drinking your coffee one morning and talking 'bout things like you do and—*(He sits down beside her and demonstrates graphically what he thinks her methods and tone should be.)*—you just sip your coffee, see, and say easy like that you been thinking 'bout that deal Walter Lee is so interested in, 'bout the store and all, and sip more coffee, like what you saying

LORRAINE HANSBERRY

ain't really that important to you—And the next thing you know, she be listening good and asking you questions and when I come home—I can tell her the details. This ain't no fly-by-night proposition, baby. I mean we figured it out, me and Willy and Bobo.

RUTH *(with a frown)* Bobo?

WALTER Yeah. You see, this little liquor store we got in mind cost seventy-five thousand and we figured the initial investment on the place be 'bout thirty thousand, see. That be ten thousand each. Course, there's a couple of hundred you got to pay so's you don't spend your life just waiting for them clowns to let your license get approved—

RUTH You mean graft?

WALTER *(frowning impatiently)* Don't call it that. See there, that just goes to show you what women understand about the world. Baby, don't *nothing* happen for you in this world 'less you pay *somebody* off!

RUTH Walter, leave me alone! *(She raises her head and stares at him vigorously—then says, more quietly.) Eat* your eggs, they gonna be cold.

WALTER *(straightening up from her and looking off)* That's it. There you are. Man say to his woman: I got me a dream. His woman say: Eat your eggs. *(sadly, but gaining in power)* Man say: I got to take hold of this here world, baby! And a woman will say: Eat your eggs and go to work. *(passionately now)* Man say: I got to change my life, I'm choking to death, baby! And his woman say—*(in utter anguish as he brings his fists down on his thighs)*—Your eggs is getting cold!

RUTH *(softly)* Walter, that ain't none of our money.

WALTER *(not listening at all or even looking at her)* This morning, I was lookin' in the mirror and thinking about it . . . I'm thirty-five years old; I been married eleven years and I got a boy who sleeps in the living room—*(very, very quietly)*—and all I got to give him is stories about how rich white people live . . .

RUTH Eat your eggs, Walter.

WALTER *Damn my eggs . . . damn all the eggs that ever was!*

RUTH Then go to work.

WALTER *(looking up at her)* See—I'm trying to talk to you 'bout myself—*(shaking his head with the repetition)*—and all you can say is eat them eggs and go to work.

RUTH *(wearily)* Honey, you never say nothing new. I listen to you every day, every night and every morning, and you never say nothing new *(shrugging)* So you would rather be Mr. Arnold than be his chauffeur. So—I would *rather* be living in Buckingham Palace.

WALTER That is just what is wrong with the colored woman in this world . . . Don't understand about building their men up and making 'em feel like they somebody. Like they can do something.

RUTH *(drily, but to hurt)* There *are* colored men who do things.

WALTER No thanks to the colored woman.

RUTH Well, being a colored woman, I guess I can't help myself none.

Audiences soon recognize the speech patterns meant to portray the Youngers as poor blacks. What features recreate such dialect?

What are the two sides of the stalemated, running argument between Ruth and Walter?

A RAISIN IN THE SUN

She rises and gets the ironing board and sets it up and attacks a huge pile of rough-dried clothes, sprinkling them in preparation for the ironing and then rolling them into tight fat balls.

WALTER *(mumbling)* We one group of men tied to a race of women with small minds.

His sister Beneatha enters. She is about twenty, as slim and intense as her brother. She is not as pretty as her sister-in-law, but her lean, almost intellectual face has a handsomeness of its own. She wears a bright-red flannel nightie, and her thick hair stands wildly about her head. Her speech is a mixture of many things; it is different from the rest of the family's insofar as education has permeated her sense of English—and perhaps the Midwest rather than the South has finally—at last—won out in her inflection; but not altogether, because over all of it is a soft slurring and transformed use of vowels which is the decided influence of the Southside. She passes through the room without looking at either Ruth or Walter and goes to the outside door and looks, a little blindly, out to the bathroom. She sees that it has been lost to the Johnsons. She closes the door with a sleepy vengeance and crosses to the table and sits down a little defeated.

BENEATHA I am going to start timing those people.

WALTER You should get up earlier.

BENEATHA *(Her face in her hands. She is still fighting the urge to go back to bed.)* Really—would you suggest dawn? Where's the paper?

> What does Beneatha's different manner of speaking say about her?

WALTER *(pushing the paper across the table to her as he studies her almost clinically, as though he has never seen her before)* You a horrible-looking chick at this hour.

BENEATHA *(drily)* Good morning, everybody.

WALTER *(senselessly)* How is school coming?

BENEATHA *(in the same spirit)* Lovely. Lovely. And you know, biology is the greatest. *(looking up at him)* I dissected something that looked just like you yesterday.

WALTER I just wondered if you've made up your mind and everything.

BENEATHA *(gaining in sharpness and impatience)* And what did I answer yesterday morning—and the day before that?

RUTH *(from the ironing board, like someone disinterested and old)* Don't be so nasty, Bennie.

BENEATHA *(still to her brother)* And the day before that and the day before that!

WALTER *(defensively)* I'm interested in you. Something wrong with that? Ain't many girls who decide—

> Why is Walter "interested" in his sister's educational plans?

WALTER and **BENEATHA** *(in unison)* —"to be a doctor."

Silence

WALTER Have we figured out yet just exactly how much medical school is going to cost?

RUTH Walter Lee, why don't you leave that girl alone and get out of here to work?

BENEATHA *(exits to the bathroom and bangs on the door)* Come on out of there, please!

She comes back into the room.

WALTER *(looking at his sister intently)* You know the check is coming tomorrow.

> The check is mentioned again, marking the crucial motif that dominates the first act.

BENEATHA *(turning on him with a sharpness all her own)* That money belongs to Mama, Walter, and it's for her to decide how she wants to use it. I don't care if she wants to buy a house or a rocket ship or just nail it up somewhere and look at it. It's hers. Not ours—*hers.*

WALTER *(bitterly)* Now ain't that fine! You just got your mother's interest at heart, ain't you, girl? You such a nice girl—but if Mama got that money she can always take a few thousand and help you through school too—can't she?

BENEATHA I have never asked anyone around here to do anything for me!

WALTER No! And the line between asking and just accepting when the time comes is big and wide—ain't it!

BENEATHA *(with fury)* What do you want from me, Brother—that I quit school or just drop dead, which!

WALTER I don't want nothing but for you to stop acting holy 'round here. Me and Ruth done made some sacrifices for you—why can't you do something for the family?

> Though laudatory in the abstract, Beneatha's aspirations raise friction in the family. Why?

RUTH Walter, don't be dragging me in it.

WALTER You are in it—Don't you get up and go work in somebody's kitchen for the last three years to help put clothes on her back?

RUTH Oh, Walter—that's not fair . . .

WALTER It ain't that nobody expects you to get on your knees and say thank you, Brother; thank you, Ruth; thank you, Mama—and thank you, Travis, for wearing the same pair of shoes for two semesters—

> How do the aspirations of the people in this drama compare with those of the people in O'Neill's *A Touch of the Poet*?

BENEATHA *(dropping to her knees)* Well—I *do*—all right?—thank everybody . . . and forgive me for ever wanting to be anything at all . . . forgive me, forgive me!

RUTH Please stop it! Your mama'll hear you.

WALTER Who the hell told you you had to be a doctor? If you so crazy 'bout messing 'round with sick people—then go be a nurse like other women—or just get married and be quiet . . .

BENEATHA Well—you finally got it said. It took you three years but you finally got it said. Walter, give up; leave me alone—it's Mama's money.

WALTER He was my father, too!

BENEATHA So what? He was mine, too—and Travis' grandfather—but the insurance money belongs to Mama. Picking on me is not going to make her give it to you to invest in any liquor stores—*(underbreath, dropping into a chair)*—and I for one say, God bless Mama for that!

> The explicit "bone of contention," brought into the open here, establishes the source of many conflicting issues.

A RAISIN IN THE SUN

WALTER *(to Ruth)* See—did you hear? Did you hear!

RUTH Honey, please go to work.

WALTER Nobody in this house is ever going to understand me.

BENEATHA Because you're a nut.

WALTER Who's a nut?

BENEATHA You—you are a nut. Thee is mad, boy.

WALTER *(looking at his wife and his sister from the door, very sadly)* The world's most backward race of people, and that's a fact.

BENEATHA *(turning slowly in her chair)* And then there are all those prophets who would lead us out of the wilderness—*(Walter slams out of the house.)*—into the swamps!

RUTH Bennie, why you always gotta be pickin' on your brother? Can't you be a little sweeter sometimes? *(Door opens. Walter walks in.)*

WALTER *(to Ruth)* I need some money for carfare.

RUTH *(looks at him, then warms; teasing, but tenderly)* Fifty cents? *(She goes to her bag and gets money.)* Here, take a taxi.

Walter exits. Mama enters. She is a woman in her early sixties, full-bodied and strong. She is one of those women of a certain grace and beauty who wear it so unobtrusively that it takes a while to notice. Her dark-brown face is surrounded by the total whiteness of her hair, and, being a woman who has adjusted to many things in life and overcome many more, her face is full of strength. She has, we can see, wit and faith of a kind that keep her eyes lit and full of interest and expectancy. She is, in a word, a beautiful woman. Her bearing is perhaps most like the noble bearing of the women of the Hereros of Southwest Africa—rather as if she imagines that as she walks she still bears a basket or a vessel upon her head. Her speech, on the other hand, is as careless as her carriage is precise—she is inclined to slur everything —but her voice is perhaps not so much quiet as simply soft.

> Why is this comparison appropriate?

MAMA Who that 'round here slamming doors at this hour?

She crosses through the room, goes to the window, opens it, and brings in a feeble little plant growing doggedly in a small pot on the window sill. She feels the dirt and puts it back out.

RUTH That was Walter Lee. He and Bennie was at it again.

MAMA My children and they tempers. Lord, if this little old plant don't get more sun than it's been getting it ain't never going to see spring again. *(She turns from the window.)* What's the matter with you this morning, Ruth? You looks right peaked. You aiming to iron all them things? Leave some for me. I'll get to 'em this afternoon. Bennie honey, it's too drafty for you to be sitting 'round half dressed. Where's your robe?

> Watch for later references to Mama's plant and its lack of sunlight.

BENEATHA In the cleaners.

MAMA Well, go get mine and put it on.

BENEATHA I'm not cold, Mama, honest.

MAMA I know—but you so thin . . .

BENEATHA *(irritably)* Mama, I'm not cold.

MAMA *(seeing the make-down bed as Travis has left it)* Lord have mercy, look at that poor bed. Bless his heart—he tries, don't he?

She moves to the bed Travis has sloppily made up.

RUTH No—he don't half try at all 'cause he knows you going to come along behind him and fix everything. That's just how come he don't know how to do nothing right now—you done spoiled that boy so.

MAMA Well—he's a little boy. Ain't supposed to know 'bout house-keeping. My baby, that's what he is. What you fix for his breakfast this morning?

RUTH *(angrily)* I feed my son, Lena!

MAMA I ain't meddling—*(underbreath; busy-bodyish)* I just noticed all last week he had cold cereal, and when it starts getting this chilly in the fall a child ought to have some hot grits or something when he goes out in the cold—

RUTH *(furious)* I gave him hot oats—is that all right!

MAMA I ain't meddling. *(pause)* Put a lot of nice butter on it? *(Ruth shoots her an angry look and does not reply.)* He likes lots of butter.

RUTH *(exasperated)* Lena—

MAMA *(To Beneatha. Mama is inclined to wander conversationally sometimes.)* What was you and your brother fussing 'bout this morning?

BENEATHA It's not important, Mama.

She gets up and goes to look out at the bathroom, which is apparently free, and she picks up her towels and rushes out.

MAMA What was they fighting about?

RUTH Now you know as well as I do.

MAMA *(shaking her head)* Brother still worrying hisself sick about that money?

RUTH You know he is.

MAMA You had breakfast?

RUTH Some coffee.

MAMA Girl, you better start eating and looking after yourself better. You almost thin as Travis.

RUTH Lena—

MAMA Un hunh?

RUTH What are you going to do with it?

MAMA Now don't you start, child. It's too early in the morning to be talking about money. It ain't Christian.

RUTH It's just that he got his heart set on that store—

MAMA You mean that liquor store that Willy Harris want him to invest in?

RUTH Yes—

MAMA We ain't no business people, Ruth. We just plain working folks.

> How does Mama's early dialogue sketch the essentials of her character? How is she similar to Nora in *A Touch of the Poet*?

> How is Ruth fulfilling her husband's suggestion?

RUTH Ain't nobody business people till they go into business. Walter Lee say colored people ain't never going to start getting ahead till they start gambling on some different kinds of things in the world—investments and things.

MAMA What done got into you, girl? Walter Lee done finally sold you on investing.

RUTH No. Mama, something is happening between Walter and me. I don't know what it is—but he needs something—something I can't give him any more. He needs this chance, Lena.

MAMA *(frowning deeply)* But liquor, honey—   *Another still-unverbalized cause of tension is coming into view regarding Walter. Can you make it out?*

RUTH Well—like Walter say—I spec people going to always be drinking themselves some liquor.

MAMA Well—whether they drinks it or not ain't none of my business. But whether I go into business selling it to 'em *is,* and I don't want that on my ledger this late in life. *(stopping suddenly and studying her daughter-in-law)* Ruth Younger, what's the matter with you today? You look like you could fall over right there.

RUTH I'm tired.

MAMA Then you better stay home from work today.

RUTH I can't stay home. She'd be calling up the agency and screaming at them, "My girl didn't come in today—send me somebody! My girl didn't come in!" Oh, she just have a fit . . .

MAMA Well, let her have it. I'll just call her up and say you got the flu—

RUTH *(laughing)* Why the flu?

MAMA 'Cause it sounds respectable to 'em. Something white people get, too. They know 'bout the flu. Otherwise they think you been cut up or something when you tell 'em you sick.

RUTH I got to go in. We need the money.

MAMA Somebody would of thought my children done all but starved to death the way they talk about money here late. Child, we got a great big old check coming tomorrow.

RUTH *(sincerely, but also self-righteously)* Now that's your money. It ain't got nothing to do with me. We all feel like that—Walter and Bennie and me—even Travis.

MAMA *(thoughtfully, and suddenly very far away)* Ten thousand dollars—

RUTH Sure is wonderful.

MAMA Ten thousand dollars.

RUTH You know what you should do, Miss Lena? You should take yourself a trip somewhere. To Europe or South America or someplace—

MAMA *(throwing up her hands at the thought)* Oh, child!

RUTH I'm serious. Just pack up and leave! Go on away and enjoy yourself some. Forget about the family and have yourself a ball for once in your life—   *Does this idea suggest a hidden desire of Ruth's?*

MAMA (*drily*) You sound like I'm just about ready to die. Who'd go with me? What I look like wandering 'round Europe by myself?

RUTH Shoot—these here rich white women do it all the time. They don't think nothing of packing up they suitcases and piling on one of them big steamships and—swoosh!—they gone, child.

MAMA Something always told me I wasn't no rich white woman.

RUTH Well—what are you going to do with it then?

MAMA I ain't rightly decided. (*Thinking. She speaks now with emphasis.*) Some of it got to be put away for Beneatha and her schoolin'—and ain't nothing going to touch that part of it. Nothing. (*She waits several seconds, trying to make up her mind about something, and looks at Ruth a little tentatively before going on.*) Been thinking that we maybe could meet the notes on a little old two-story somewhere, with a yard where Travis could play in the summertime, if we use part of the insurance for a down payment and everybody kind of pitch in. I could maybe take on a little day work again, few days a week—

RUTH (*studying her mother-in-law furtively and concentrating on her ironing, anxious to encourage without seeming to*) Well, Lord knows, we've put enough rent into this here rat trap to pay for four houses by now . . .

> Why is Ruth afraid to openly express her support of Mama's plan?

MAMA (*looking up at the words "rat trap" and then looking around and leaning back and sighing—in a suddenly reflective mood—*) "Rat trap"—yes, that's all it is. (*smiling*) I remember just as well the day me and Big Walter moved in here. Hadn't been married but two weeks and wasn't planning on living here no more than a year. (*She shakes her head at the dissolved dream.*) We was going to set away, little by little, don't you know, and buy a little place out in Morgan Park. We had even picked out the house. (*chuckling a little*) Looks right dumpy today. But Lord, child, you should know all the dreams I had 'bout buying that house and fixing it up and making me a little garden in the back—(*She waits and stops smiling.*) And didn't none of it happen.

Dropping her hands in a futile gesture

RUTH (*keeps her head down, ironing*) Yes, life can be a barrel of disappointments, sometimes.

MAMA Honey, Big Walter would come in here some nights back then and slump down on that couch there and just look at the rug, and look at me and look at the rug and then back at me—and I'd know he was down then . . . really down. (*After a second very long and thoughtful pause, she is seeing back to times that only she can see.*) And then, Lord, when I lost that baby—little Claude—I almost thought I was going to lose Big Walter too. Oh, that man grieved hisself! He was one man to love his children.

> In these reminiscences about the past, Mama gives us information which continues to have a bearing on the thinking of those in the present.

RUTH Ain't nothin' can tear at you like losin' your baby.

> There is foreshadowing irony in Ruth's remark about losing a baby.

MAMA I guess that's how come that man finally worked hisself to death like he done. Like he was fighting his own war with this here world that took his baby from him.

A RAISIN IN THE SUN 375

RUTH He sure was a fine man, all right. I always liked Mr. Younger.

MAMA Crazy 'bout his children! God knows there was plenty wrong with Walter Younger—hard-headed, mean, kind of wild with women—plenty wrong with him. But he sure loved his children. Always wanted them to have something—be something. That's where Brother gets all these notions, I reckon. Big Walter used to say, he'd get right wet in the eyes sometimes, lean his head back with the water standing in his eyes and say, "Seem like God didn't see fit to give the black man nothing but dreams—but He did give us children to make them dreams seem worth while." *(She smiles.)* He could talk like that, don't you know.

> Despite some acknowledged personality deficiencies in the deceased Mr. Younger, why has Mama continued to love and appreciate him?

RUTH Yes, he sure could. He was a good man, Mr. Younger.

MAMA Yes, a fine man—just couldn't never catch up with his dreams, that's all.

> What are the full implications of Mama's remark, "just couldn't never catch up with his dreams"?

Beneatha comes in, brushing her hair and looking up to the ceiling, where the sound of a vacuum cleaner has started up.

BENEATHA What could be so dirty on that woman's rugs that she has to vacuum them every single day?

RUTH I wish certain young women 'round here who I could name would take inspiration about certain rugs in a certain apartment I could also mention.

BENEATHA *(shrugging)* How much cleaning can a house need, for Christ's sakes.

MAMA *(not liking the Lord's name used thus)* Bennie!

RUTH Just listen to her—just listen!

BENEATHA Oh, God!

MAMA If you use the Lord's name just one more time—

BENEATHA *(a bit of a whine)* Oh, Mama—

RUTH Fresh—just fresh as salt, this girl!

BENEATHA *(drily)* Well—if the salt loses its savor—

MAMA Now that will do. I just ain't going to have you 'round here reciting the scriptures in vain—you hear me?

BENEATHA How did I manage to get on everybody's wrong side by just walking into a room?

RUTH If you weren't so fresh—

BENEATHA Ruth, I'm twenty years old.

MAMA What time you be home from school today?

BENEATHA Kind of late. *(with enthusiasm)* Madeline is going to start my guitar lessons today.

Mama and Ruth look up with the same expression.

MAMA Your *what* kind of lessons?

BENEATHA Guitar.

RUTH Oh, Father!

MAMA How come you done taken it in your mind to learn to play the guitar?

BENEATHA I just want to, that's all.

MAMA (*smiling*) Lord, child, don't you know what to do with yourself? How long it going to be before you get tired of this now—like you got tired of that little play-acting group you joined last year? (*looking at Ruth*) And what was it the year before that?

RUTH The horseback-riding club for which she bought that fifty-five-dollar riding habit that's been hanging in the closet ever since!

MAMA (*to Beneatha*) Why you got to flit so from one thing to another, baby?

BENEATHA (*sharply*) I just want to learn to play the guitar. Is there anything wrong with that?

MAMA Ain't nobody trying to stop you. I just wonders sometimes why you has to flit so from one thing to another all the time. You ain't never done nothing with all that camera equipment you brought home—

> How does the interplay of question and answer between Beneatha and her mother capture the well-publicized notion of "generation gap"?

BENEATHA I don't flit! I—I experiment with different forms of expression—

RUTH Like riding a horse?

BENEATHA —People have to express themselves one way or another.

MAMA What is it you want to express?

BENEATHA (*angrily*) Me! (*Mama and Ruth look at each other and burst into raucous laughter.*) Don't worry—I don't expect you to understand.

> Point out some instances of bantering humor in this section.

MAMA (*to change the subject*) Who you going out with tomorrow night?

BENEATHA (*with displeasure*) George Murchison again.

MAMA (*pleased*) Oh—you getting a little sweet on him?

RUTH You ask me, this child ain't sweet on nobody but herself—(*underbreath*) Express herself!

> What use (or misuse) of words provides a laugh or two here for audiences? How are Beneatha's expectations of life and men similar to those of Sara in *A Touch of the Poet*?

They laugh.

BENEATHA Oh—I like George all right, Mama. I mean I like him enough to go out with him and stuff, but—

RUTH (*for devilment*) What does *and stuff* mean?

BENEATHA Mind your own business.

MAMA Stop picking at her now, Ruth. (*a thoughtful pause, and then a suspicious sudden look at her daughter as she turns in her chair for emphasis*) What *does* it mean?

> Why does Mama's "double-take" (i.e., a casual glance at someone or something, followed by a second, more intense look) produce a light moment?

BENEATHA (*wearily*) Oh, I just mean I couldn't ever really be serious about George. He's—he's so shallow.

RUTH Shallow—what do you mean he's shallow? He's *Rich!*

MAMA Hush, Ruth.

BENEATHA I know he's rich. He knows he's rich, too.

RUTH Well—what other qualities a man got to have to satisfy you, little girl?

BENEATHA You wouldn't even begin to understand. Anybody who married Walter could not possibly understand.

MAMA *(outraged)* What kind of way is that to talk about your brother?

BENEATHA Brother is a flip—let's face it.

MAMA *(to Ruth, helplessly)* What's a flip?

RUTH *(glad to add kindling)* She's saying he's crazy.

BENEATHA Not crazy. Brother isn't really crazy yet—he—he's an elaborate neurotic.

Does Mama Younger become insulted at Beneatha's description of Walter because she understands what "an elaborate neurotic" is, or because the expression just sounds dreadful?

MAMA Hush your mouth!

BENEATHA As for George. Well. George looks good—he's got a beautiful car and he takes me to nice places and, as my sister-in-law says, he is probably the richest boy I will ever get to know and I even like him sometimes—but if the Youngers are sitting around waiting to see if their little Bennie is going to tie up the family with the Murchisons, they are wasting their time.

RUTH You mean you wouldn't marry George Murchison if he asked you someday? That pretty, rich thing? Honey, I knew you was odd—

BENEATHA No I would not marry him if all I felt for him was what I feel now. Besides, George's family wouldn't really like it.

MAMA Why not?

BENEATHA Oh, Mama—The Murchisons are honest-to-God-real-live-rich colored people, and the only people in the world who are more snobbish than rich white people are rich colored people. I thought everybody knew that. I've met Mrs. Murchison. She's a scene!

Is Beneatha's reluctance to take George Murchison seriously just youthful stubbornness or evidence of something more thoughtful in her character?

MAMA You must not dislike people 'cause they well off, honey.

BENEATHA Why not? It makes just as much sense as disliking people 'cause they are poor, and lots of people do that.

RUTH *(A wisdom-of-the-ages manner. To Mama)* Well, she'll get over some of this—

BENEATHA Get over it? What are you talking about, Ruth? Listen, I'm going to be a doctor. I'm not worried about who I'm going to marry yet—if I ever get married.

MAMA and **RUTH** If!

How does the "If!" exclaimed by both Mama and Ruth indicate their attitude toward the institution of marriage for a girl?

MAMA Now, Bennie—

BENEATHA Oh, I probably will . . . but first I'm going to be a doctor, and George, for one, still thinks that's pretty funny. I couldn't be bothered with that. I am going to be a doctor and everybody around here better understand that!

Beneatha is trying to surmount two traditional barriers—one racial, the other sexist. Has she received consistent encouragement from her family or from her boyfriends?

MAMA *(kindly)* 'Course you going to be a doctor, honey, God willing.

BENEATHA *(drily)* God hasn't got a thing to do with it.

MAMA Beneatha—that just wasn't necessary.

BENEATHA Well—neither is God. I get sick of hearing about God.

MAMA Beneatha!

BENEATHA I mean it! I'm just tired of hearing about God all the time. What has He got to do with anything? Does he pay tuition?

MAMA You 'bout to get your fresh little jaw slapped!

RUTH That's just what she needs, all right!

BENEATHA Why? Why can't I say what I want to around here, like everybody else?

MAMA It don't sound nice for a young girl to say things like that—you wasn't brought up that way. Me and your father went to trouble to get you and Brother to church every Sunday.

BENEATHA Mama, you don't understand. It's all a matter of ideas, and God is just one idea I don't accept. It's not important. I am not going out and be immoral or commit crimes because I don't believe in God. I don't even think about it. It's just that I get tired of Him getting credit for all the things the human race achieves through its own stubborn effort. There simply is no blasted God—there is only man and it is he who makes miracles!

Mama absorbs this speech, studies her daughter and rises slowly and crosses to Beneatha and slaps her powerfully across the face. After, there is only silence and the daughter drops her eyes from her mother's face, and Mama is very tall before her.

MAMA Now—you say after me, in my mother's house there is still God. (*There is a long pause and Beneatha stares at the floor wordlessly. Mama repeats the phrase with precision and cool emotion.*) In my mother's house there is still God.

BENEATHA In my mother's house there is still God.

A long pause

MAMA (*Walking away from Beneatha, too disturbed for triumphant posture. Stopping and turning back to her daughter*) There are some ideas we ain't going to have in this house. Not long as I am at the head of this family.

BENEATHA Yes, ma'am.

Mama walks out of the room.

RUTH (*almost gently, with profound understanding*) You think you a woman, Bennie—but you still a little girl. What you did was childish—so you got treated like a child.

BENEATHA I see. (*quietly*) I also see that everybody thinks it's all right for Mama to be a tyrant. But all the tyranny in the world will never put a God in the heavens!

She picks up her books and goes out.

RUTH (*goes to Mama's door*) She said she was sorry.

MAMA (*coming out, going to her plant*) They frightens me, Ruth. My children.

RUTH You got good children, Lena. They just a little off sometimes—but they're good.

MAMA No—there's something come down between me and them

How does this explosive moment establish who runs the household? Have we suspected it before? In what scenes?

A RAISIN IN THE SUN 379

that don't let us understand each other and I don't know what it is. One done almost lost his mind thinking 'bout money all the time and the other done commence to talk about things I can't seem to understand in no form or fashion. What is it that's changing, Ruth?

RUTH *(soothingly, older than her years)* Now . . . you taking it all too seriously. You just got strong-willed children and it takes a strong woman like you to keep 'em in hand.

MAMA *(looking at her plant and sprinkling a little water on it)* They spirited all right, my children. Got to admit they got spirit—Bennie and Walter. Like this little old plant that ain't never had enough sunshine or nothing—and look at it . . .

She has her back to Ruth, who has had to stop ironing and lean against something and put the back of her hand to her forehead.

What connection does Mama make between her children and her plant?

RUTH *(trying to keep Mama from noticing)* You . . . sure . . . loves that little old thing, don't you? . . .

MAMA Well, I always wanted me a garden like I used to see sometimes at the back of the houses down home. This plant is close as I ever got to having one. *(She looks out of the window as she replaces the plant.)* Lord, ain't nothing as dreary as the view from this window on a dreary day, is there? Why ain't you singing this morning, Ruth? Sing that "No Ways Tired." That song always lifts me up so—*(She turns at last to see that Ruth has slipped quietly into a chair, in a state of semiconsciousness.)* Ruth! Ruth honey—what's the matter with you . . . Ruth!

Why is this action at the conclusion of the scene so effective as a curtain-closer?

Curtain

SCENE ii

It is the following morning; a Saturday morning, and house cleaning is in progress at the Youngers'. Furniture has been shoved hither and yon and Mama is giving the kitchen-area walls a washing down. Beneatha, in dungarees, with a handkerchief tied around her face, is spraying insecticide into the cracks in the walls. As they work, the radio is on and a Southside disk-jockey program is inappropriately filling the house with a rather exotic saxophone blues. Travis, the sole idle one, is leaning on his arms, looking out of the window.

Why is the family indifferent to the spraying of strong insecticide in the flat?

TRAVIS Grandmama, that stuff Bennie is using smells awful. Can I go downstairs, please?

MAMA Did you get all them chores done already? I ain't seen you doing much.

TRAVIS Yes'm—finished early. Where did Mama go this morning?

MAMA *(looking at Beneatha)* She had to go on a little errand.

TRAVIS Where?

MAMA To tend to her business.

TRAVIS Can I go outside then?

MAMA Oh, I guess so. You better stay right in front of the house, though . . . and keep a good lookout for the postman.

TRAVIS Yes'm. *(He starts out and decides to give his Aunt Beneatha a good swat on the legs as he passes her.)* Leave them poor little old cockroaches alone, they ain't bothering you none.

LORRAINE HANSBERRY

He runs as she swings the spray gun at him both viciously and playfully. Walter enters from the bedroom and goes to the phone.

MAMA Look out there, girl, before you be spilling some of that stuff on that child!

TRAVIS *(teasing)* That's right—look out now!

He exits.

BENEATHA *(drily)* I can't imagine that it would hurt him—it has never hurt the roaches.

MAMA Well, little boys' hides ain't as tough as Southside roaches.

WALTER *(into phone)* Hello—Let me talk to Willy Harris.

MAMA You better get over there behind the bureau. I seen one marching out of there like Napoleon yesterday.

WALTER Hello, Willy? It ain't come yet. It'll be here in a few minutes. Did the lawyer give you the papers?

BENEATHA There's really only one way to get rid of them, Mama—

MAMA How?

BENEATHA Set fire to this building.

WALTER Good. Good. I'll be right over.

BENEATHA Where did Ruth go, Walter?

WALTER I don't know.

He exits abruptly.

> Walter obviously is preoccupied. What is he thinking about?

BENEATHA Mama, where did Ruth go?

MAMA *(looking at her with meaning)* To the doctor, I think.

BENEATHA The doctor? What's the matter? *(They exchange glances.)* You don't think—

MAMA *(with her sense of drama)* Now I ain't saying what I think. But I ain't never been wrong 'bout a woman neither.

> To what is Mama specifically referring?

The phone rings.

BENEATHA *(at the phone)* Hay-lo . . . *(pause, and a moment of recognition)* Well—when did you get back! . . . And how was it? . . . Of course I've missed you—in my way . . . This morning? No . . . house cleaning and all that and Mama hates it if I let people come over when the house is like this . . . You *have?* Well, that's different . . . What is it— Oh, what the hell, come on over . . . Right, see you then.

She hangs up.

MAMA *(who has listened vigorously, as is her habit)* Who is that you inviting over here with this house looking like this? You ain't got the pride you was born with!

BENEATHA Asagai doesn't care how houses look, Mama—he's an intellectual.

MAMA Who?

BENEATHA Asagai—Joseph Asagai. He's an African boy I met on campus. He's been studying in Canada all summer.

MAMA What's his name?

BENEATHA Asagai, Joseph. Ah-sah-guy . . . He's from Nigeria.

MAMA Oh, that's the little country that was founded by slaves way back . . .

BENEATHA No, Mama—that's Liberia.

MAMA I don't think I never met no African before.

BENEATHA Well, do me a favor and don't ask him a whole lot of ignorant questions about Africans. I mean, do they wear clothes and all that—

MAMA Well, now, I guess if you think we so ignorant 'round here maybe you shouldn't bring your friends here—

What does this interchange suggest about the relationship of American blacks and Third World Africans?

BENEATHA It's just that people ask such crazy things. All anyone seems to know about when it comes to Africa is Tarzan—

MAMA (*indignantly*) Why should I know anything about Africa?

BENEATHA Why do you give money at church for the missionary work?

MAMA Well, that's to help save people.

BENEATHA You mean save them from *heathenism*—

MAMA (*innocently*) Yes.

BENEATHA I'm afraid they need more salvation from the British and the French.

What is meant by Beneatha's reference to the British and French? How does it provide a time frame for the play?

Ruth comes in forlornly and pulls off her coat with dejection. They both turn to look at her.

RUTH (*dispiritedly*) Well, I guess from all the happy faces —everybody knows.

BENEATHA You pregnant?

MAMA Lord have mercy, I sure hope it's a little old girl. Travis ought to have a sister.

Beneatha and Ruth give her a hopeless look for this grandmotherly enthusiasm.

BENEATHA How far along are you?

RUTH Two months.

BENEATHA Did you mean to? I mean did you plan it or was it an accident?

MAMA What do you know about planning or not planning?

BENEATHA Oh, Mama.

RUTH (*wearily*) She's twenty years old, Lena.

BENEATHA Did you plan it, Ruth?

RUTH Mind your own business.

BENEATHA It is my business—where is he going to live, on the roof?(*There is silence following the remark as the three women react to the sense of it.*) Gee—I didn't mean that, Ruth, honest. Gee, I don't feel like that at all. I—I think it is wonderful.

RUTH *(dully)* Wonderful.

BENEATHA Yes—really.

MAMA *(looking at Ruth, worried)* Doctor say everything going to be all right?

RUTH *(far away)* Yes—she says everything is going to be fine . . .

MAMA *(immediately suspicious)* "She"— What doctor you went to?

Ruth folds over, near hysteria.

MAMA *(worriedly hovering over Ruth)* Ruth honey—what's the matter with you—you sick?

Ruth has her fists clenched on her thighs and is fighting hard to suppress a scream that seems to be rising in her.

BENEATHA What's the matter with her, Mama?

MAMA *(working her fingers in Ruth's shoulder to relax her)* She be all right. Women gets right depressed sometimes when they get her way. *(speaking softly, expertly, rapidly)* Now you just relax. That's right . . . just lean back, don't think 'bout nothing at all . . . nothing at all—

RUTH I'm all right . . .

The glassy-eyed look melts and then she collapses into a fit of heavy sobbing. The bell rings.

BENEATHA Oh, my God—that must be Asagai.

MAMA *(to Ruth)* Come on now, honey. You need to lie down and rest awhile . . . then have some nice hot food.

They exit, Ruth's weight on her mother-in-law. Beneatha, herself profoundly disturbed, opens the door to admit a rather dramatic-looking young man with a large package.

ASAGAI Hello, Alaiyo—

BENEATHA *(holding the door open and regarding him with pleasure)* Hello . . . *(long pause)* Well—come in. And please excuse everything. My mother was very upset about my letting anyone come here with the place like this.

ASAGAI *(coming into the room)* You look disturbed too . . . Is something wrong?

BENEATHA *(still at the door, absently)* Yes . . . we've all got acute ghetto-itis. *(She smiles and comes toward him, finding a cigarette and sitting.)* So—sit down! How was Canada?

ASAGAI *(a sophisticate)* Canadian.

BENEATHA *(looking at him)* I'm very glad you are back.

ASAGAI *(looking back at her in turn)* Are you really?

BENEATHA Yes—very.

ASAGAI Why—you were quite glad when I went away. What happened?

BENEATHA You went away.

ASAGAI Ahhhhhhhh.

What kind of "doctor" does Mama suspect the unnamed woman to be?

Most audiences recognize that Ruth's depression results from a desperate concern—how to provide for another member of the family.

Would Beneatha's wisecrack about her family's "ghetto-itis" be understood by today's audiences? What does she mean?

A RAISIN IN THE SUN 383

BENEATHA Before—you wanted to be so serious before there was time.

ASAGAI How much time must there be before one knows what one feels?

BENEATHA (*Stalling this particular conversation. Her hands pressed together, in a deliberately childish gesture*) What did you bring me?

ASAGAI (*handing her the package*) Open it and see.

BENEATHA (*eagerly opening the package and drawing out some records and the colorful robes of a Nigerian woman*) Oh, Asagai! . . . You got them for me! . . . How beautiful . . . and the records too! (*She lifts out the robes and runs to the mirror with them and holds the drapery up in front of herself.*)

ASAGAI (*coming to her at the mirror*) I shall have to teach you how to drape it properly. (*He flings the material about her for the moment and stands back to look at her.*) A—Oh-pay-gay-day, oh-ghah-mu-shay. (*a Yoruba exclamation for admiration*) You wear it well . . . very well . . . mutilated hair and all.

BENEATHA (*turning suddenly*) My hair—what's wrong with my hair?

ASAGAI (*shrugging*) Were you born with it like that?

BENEATHA (*reaching up to touch it*) No . . . of course not.

She looks back to the mirror, disturbed.

ASAGAI (*smiling*) How then?

BENEATHA You know perfectly well how . . . as crinkly as yours . . . that's how.

ASAGAI And it is ugly to you that way?

BENEATHA (*quickly*) Oh, no—not ugly . . . (*more slowly, apologetically*) But it's so hard to manage when it's, well—raw.

ASAGAI And so to accommodate that—you mutilate it every week?

BENEATHA It's not mutilation!

ASAGAI (*laughing aloud at her seriousness*) Oh . . . please! I am only teasing you because you are so very serious about these things. (*He stands back from her and folds his arms across his chest as he watches her pulling at her hair and frowning in the mirror.*) Do you remember the first time you met me at school? . . . (*He laughs.*) You came up to me and you said—and I thought you were the most serious little thing I had ever seen—you said: (*He imitates her.*) "Mr. Asagai—I want very much to talk with you. About Africa. You see, Mr. Asagai, I am looking for my *identity!*"

He laughs.

BENEATHA (*turning to him, not laughing*) Yes—

Her face is quizzical, profoundly disturbed.

ASAGAI (*still teasing and reaching out and taking her face in his hands and turning her profile to him*) Well . . . it is true that this is not so much a profile of a Hollywood queen as perhaps a queen of the Nile—(*a mock dismissal of the importance of the question*) But what does it matter? Assimilationism is so popular in your country.

> Asagai here first broaches the subject of hair styles worn by blacks in the United States. What is his point?

> To assimilate means to absorb and incorporate as one's own. What racial and social process is Asagai alluding to here?

384   LORRAINE HANSBERRY

BENEATHA *(wheeling, passionately, sharply)* I am not an assimilationist!

ASAGAI *(The protest hangs in the room for a moment and Asagai studies her, his laughter fading.)* Such a serious one. *(There is a pause.)* So—you like the robes? You must take excellent care of them—they are from my sister's personal wardrobe.

BENEATHA *(with incredulity)* You—you sent all the way home—for me?

ASAGAI *(with charm)* For you—I would do much more . . . Well, that is what I came for. I must go.

BENEATHA Will you call me Monday?

ASAGAI Yes . . . We have a great deal to talk about. I mean about identity and time and all that.

BENEATHA Time?

ASAGAI Yes. About how much time one needs to know what one feels.

BENEATHA You never understood that there is more than one kind of feeling which can exist between a man and a woman—or, at least, there should be.

ASAGAI *(shaking his head negatively but gently)* No. Between a man and a woman there need be only one kind of feeling. I have that for you . . . Now even . . . right this moment . . .

BENEATHA I know—and by itself—it won't do. I can find that anywhere.

ASAGAI For a woman it should be enough.

BENEATHA I know—because that's what it says in all the novels that men write. But it isn't. Go ahead and laugh—but I'm not interested in being someone's little episode in America or—*(with feminine vengeance)*—one of them! *(Asagai has burst into laughter again.)* That's funny as hell, huh!

ASAGAI It's just that every American girl I have known has said that to me. White—black—in this you are all the same. And the same speech, too!

BENEATHA *(angrily)* Yuk, yuk, yuk!

ASAGAI It's how you can be sure that the world's most liberated women are not liberated at all. You all talk about it too much!

Mama enters and is immediately all social charm because of the presence of a guest

BENEATHA Oh—Mama—this is Mr. Asagai

MAMA How do you do?

ASAGAI *(total politeness to an elder)* How do you do, Mrs. Younger. Please forgive me for coming at such an outrageous hour on a Saturday.

MAMA Well, you are quite welcome. I just hope you understand that our house don't always look like this. *(chatterish)* You must come again. I would love to hear all about—*(not sure of the name)*—your country. I think it's so sad the way our American Negroes don't

Although Asagai urges Beneatha to break one general stereotype concerning blacks, he perpetuates what other long-standing attitude about women?

know nothing about Africa 'cept Tarzan and all that. And all that money they pour into these churches when they ought to be helping you people over there drive out them French and Englishmen done taken away your land.

The mother flashes a slightly superior look at her daughter upon completion of the recitation.

ASAGAI *(taken aback by this sudden and acutely unrelated expression of sympathy)* Yes . . . yes . . .

MAMA *(smiling at him suddenly and relaxing and looking him over)* How many miles is it from here to where you come from?

ASAGAI Many thousands.

MAMA *(looking at him as she would Walter)* I bet you don't half look after yourself, being away from your mama either. I spec you better come 'round here from time to time and get yourself some decent homecooked meals . . .

ASAGAI *(moved)* Thank you. Thank you very much. *(They are all quiet, then—)* Well . . . I must go. I will call you Monday, Alaiyo.

MAMA What's that he call you?

ASAGAI Oh—"Alaiyo." I hope you don't mind. It is what you would call a nickname, I think. It is a Yoruba word. I am a Yoruba.

MAMA *(looking at Beneatha)* I—I thought he was from—

ASAGAI *(understanding)* Nigeria is my country. Yoruba is my tribal origin—

BENEATHA You didn't tell us what Alaiyo means . . . for all I know, you might be calling me Little Idiot or something . . .

ASAGAI Well . . . let me see . . . I do not know how just to explain it . . . The sense of a thing can be so different when it changes languages.

BENEATHA You're evading.

ASAGAI No—really it is difficult . . . *(thinking)* It means . . . it means One for Whom Bread—Food—Is Not Enough. *(He looks at her.)* Is that all right?

According to Asagai's definition of "Alaiyo," why is that name appropriate for Beneatha?

BENEATHA *(understanding, softly)* Thank you.

MAMA *(looking from one to the other and not understanding any of it)* Well . . . that's nice . . . You must come see us again—Mr.—

ASAGAI Ah-sah-guy . . .

MAMA Yes . . . Do come again.

ASAGAI Good-bye.

He exits.

MAMA *(after him)* Lord, that's a pretty thing just went out here! *(insinuatingly, to her daughter)* Yes, I guess I see why we done commence to get so interested in Africa 'round here. Missionaries my aunt Jenny!

She exits.

BENEATHA Oh, Mama! . . .

She picks up the Nigerian dress and holds it up to her in front of the mirror again. She sets the headdress on haphazardly and then notices her hair again and clutches at it and then replaces the headdress and frowns at herself. Then she starts to wriggle in front of the mirror as she thinks a Nigerian woman might. Travis enters and regards her.

TRAVIS You cracking up?

BENEATHA Shut up.

She pulls the headdress off and looks at herself in the mirror and clutches at her hair again and squinches her eyes as if trying to imagine something. Then, suddenly, she gets her raincoat and kerchief and hurriedly prepares for going out.

MAMA *(coming back into the room)* She's resting now. Travis, baby, run next door and ask Miss Johnson to please let me have a little kitchen cleanser. This here can is empty as Jacob's kettle.

TRAVIS I just came in.

MAMA Do as you told. *(He exits and she looks at her daughter.)* Where you going?

BENEATHA *(halting at the door)* To become a queen of the Nile!

She exits in a breathless blaze of glory. Ruth appears in the bedroom doorway.

MAMA Who told you to get up?

RUTH Ain't nothing wrong with me to be lying in no bed for. Where did Bennie go?

MAMA *(drumming her fingers)* Far as I could make out—to Egypt. *(Ruth just looks at her.)* What time is it getting to?

RUTH Ten twenty. And the mailman going to ring that bell this morning just like he done every morning for the last umpteen years.

Travis comes in with the cleanser can.

TRAVIS She say to tell you that she don't have much.

MAMA *(angrily)* Lord, some people I could name sure is tight-fisted! *(directing her grandson)* Mark two cans of cleanser down on the list there. If she that hard up for kitchen cleanser, I sure don't want to forget to get her none!

RUTH Lena—maybe the woman is just short on cleanser—

MAMA *(not listening)*—Much baking powder as she done borrowed from me all these years, she could of done gone into the baking business!

The bell sounds suddenly and sharply and all three are stunned—serious and silent—mid-speech. In spite of all the other conversations and distractions of the morning, this is what they have been waiting for, even Travis, who looks helplessly from his mother to his grandmother. Ruth is the first to come to life again.

RUTH *(to Travis)* Get down them steps, boy!

Travis snaps to life and flies out to get the mail.

MAMA *(her eyes wide, her hand to her breast)* You mean it done really come?

Beneatha's comical remark about becoming "queen of the Nile," though lost on her mother, is understood by audiences. What is Beneatha thinking about at this point?

RUTH *(excited)* Oh, Miss Lena!

MAMA *(collecting herself)* Well . . . I don't know what we all so excited about 'round here for. We known it was coming for months.

RUTH That's a whole lot different from having it come and being able to hold it in your hands . . . a piece of paper worth ten thousand dollars . . . *(Travis bursts back into the room. He holds the envelope high above his head, like a little dancer, his face is radiant and he is breathless. He moves to his grandmother with sudden slow ceremony and puts the envelope into her hands. She accepts it, and then merely holds it and looks at it.)* Come on! Open it . . . Lord have mercy, I wish Walter Lee was here!

TRAVIS Open it, Grandmama!

MAMA *(staring at it)* Now you all be quiet. It's just a check.

RUTH Open it . . .

MAMA *(still staring at it)* Now don't act silly . . . We ain't never been no people to act silly 'bout no money—

RUTH *(swiftly)* We ain't never had none before—open it!

Mama finally makes a good strong tear and pulls out the thin blue slice of paper and inspects it closely. The boy and his mother study it raptly over Mama's shoulders.

MAMA Travis! *(She is counting off with doubt.)* Is that the right number of zeros?

TRAVIS Yes'm . . . ten thousand dollars. Gaalee, Grandmama, you rich.

MAMA *(She holds the check away from her, still looking at it. Slowly her face sobers into a mask of unhappiness.)* Ten thousand dollars. *(She hands it to Ruth.)* Put it away somewhere, Ruth. *(She does not look at Ruth; her eyes seem to be seeing something somewhere very far off.)* Ten thousand dollars they give you. Ten thousand dollars.

TRAVIS *(to his mother, sincerely)* What's the matter with Grandmama—don't she want to be rich?

RUTH *(distractedly)* You go on out and play now, baby. *(Travis exits. Mama starts wiping dishes absently, humming intently to herself. Ruth turns to her, with kind exasperation.)* You've gone and got yourself upset.

MAMA *(not looking at her)* I spec if it wasn't for you all . . . I would just put that money away or give it to the church or something.

RUTH Now what kind of talk is that. Mr. Younger would just be plain mad if he could hear you talking foolish like that.

MAMA *(stopping and staring off)* Yes . . . he sure would. *(sighing)* We got enough to do with that money, all right. *(She halts then, and turns and looks at her daughter-in-law hard; Ruth avoids her eyes and Mama wipes her hands with finality and starts to speak firmly to Ruth.)* Where did you go today, girl?

RUTH To the doctor.

MAMA *(impatiently)* Now, Ruth . . . you know better than that. Old Doctor Jones is strange enough in his way but there ain't nothing 'bout him make somebody slip and call him "she"—like you done this morning.

RUTH Well, that's what happened—my tongue slipped.

MAMA You went to see that woman, didn't you?

RUTH *(defensively, giving herself away)* What woman you talking about?

MAMA *(angrily)* That woman who—

Walter enters in great excitement.

WALTER Did it come?

MAMA *(quietly)* Can't you give people a Christian greeting before you start asking about money?

WALTER *(to Ruth)* Did it come? *(Ruth unfolds the check and lays it quietly before him, watching him intently with thoughts of her own. Walter sits down and grasps it close and counts off the zeros.)* Ten thousand dollars—*(He turns suddenly, frantically to his mother and draws some papers out of his breast pocket.)* Mama—look. Old Willy Harris put everything on paper—

MAMA Son—I think you ought to talk to your wife . . . I'll go on out and leave you alone if you want—

WALTER I can talk to her later— Mama, look—

MAMA Son—

WALTER WILL SOMEBODY PLEASE LISTEN TO ME TODAY!

MAMA (quietly) I don't 'low no yellin' in this house, Walter Lee, and you know it—*(Walter stares at them in frustration and starts to speak several times.)* And there ain't going to be no investing in no liquor stores. I don't aim to have to speak on that again.

A long pause

WALTER Oh—so you don't aim to have to speak on that again? So *you* have decided . . . *(crumpling his papers)* Well, *you* tell that to my boy tonight when you put him to sleep on the living-room couch . . . *(turning to Mama and speaking directly to her)* Yeah—and tell it to my wife, Mama, tomorrow when she has to go out of here to look after somebody else's kids. And tell it to *me,* Mama, every time we need a new pair of curtains and I have to watch *you* go out and work in somebody's kitchen. Yeah, you tell me then!

Walter starts out.

RUTH Where you going?

WALTER I'm going out!

RUTH Where?

WALTER Just out of this house somewhere—

RUTH *(getting her coat)* I'll come too.

WALTER I don't want you to come!

RUTH I got something to talk to you about, Walter.

WALTER That's too bad.

What does Ruth want to talk with her husband about?

A RAISIN IN THE SUN

MAMA *(still quietly)* Walter Lee—*(She waits and he finally turns and looks at her.)* Sit down.

WALTER I'm a grown man, Mama.

MAMA Ain't nobody said you wasn't grown. But you still in my house and my presence. And as long as you are—you'll talk to your wife civil. Now sit down.

RUTH *(suddenly)* Oh, let him go on out and drink himself to death! He makes me sick to my stomach! *(She flings her coat against him.)*

WALTER *(violently)* And you turn mine too, baby! *(Ruth goes into their bedroom and slams the door behind her.)* That was my greatest mistake—

MAMA *(still quietly)* Walter, what is the matter with you?

WALTER Matter with me? Ain't nothing the matter with *me*!

MAMA Yes there is. Something eating you up like a crazy man. Something more than me not giving you this money. The past few years I been watching it happen to you. You get all nervous acting and kind of wild in the eyes—*(Walter jumps up impatiently at her words.)* I said sit there now, I'm talking to you!

WALTER Mama—I don't need no nagging at me today.

MAMA Seem like you getting to a place where you always tied up in some kind of knot about something. But if anybody ask you 'bout it you just yell at 'em and bust out the house and go out and drink somewheres. Walter Lee, people can't live with that. Ruth's a good, patient girl in her way—but you getting to be too much. Boy, don't make the mistake of driving that girl away from you.

WALTER Why—what she do for me?

MAMA She loves you.

WALTER Mama, I'm going out. I want to go off somewhere and be by myself for a while.

MAMA I'm sorry 'bout your liquor store, son. It just wasn't the thing for us to do. That's what I want to tell you about—

WALTER I got to go out, Mama—

He rises.

MAMA It's dangerous, son.

WALTER What's dangerous?

MAMA When a man goes outside his home to look for peace.

WALTER *(beseechingly)* Then why can't there never be no peace in this house then?

MAMA You done found it in some other house?

WALTER No—there ain't no woman! Why do women always think there's a woman somewhere when a man gets restless. *(coming to her)* Mama—Mama—I want so many things . . .

MAMA Yes, son—

WALTER I want so many things that they are driving me kind of crazy . . . Mama—look at me.

> Hansberry calls attention to the menacing undercurrents in Walter's nature, alerting us to watch him closely as the play develops.

MAMA I'm looking at you. You a good-looking boy. You got a job, a nice wife, a fine boy and—

WALTER A job. *(looks at her)* Mama, a job? I open and close car doors all day long. I drive a man around in his limousine and I say, "Yes, sir; no, sir; very good, sir; shall I take the Drive, sir?" Mama, that ain't no kind of job . . . that ain't nothing at all. *(very quietly)* Mama, I don't know if I can make you understand.

MAMA Understand what, baby?

WALTER *(quietly)* Sometimes it's like I can see the future stretched out in front of me—just plain as day. The future, Mama. Hanging over there at the edge of my days. Just waiting for me—a big, looming blank space—full of *nothing*. Just waiting for *me*. *(pause)* Mama—sometimes when I'm downtown and I pass them cool, quiet-looking restaurants where them white boys are sitting back and talking 'bout things . . . sitting there turning deals worth millions of dollars . . . sometimes I see guys don't look much older than me—

MAMA Son—how come you talk so much 'bout money?

WALTER *(with immense passion)* Because it is life, Mama!

MAMA *(quietly)* Oh—*(very quietly)* So now it's life. Money is life. Once upon a time freedom used to be life—now it's money. I guess the world really do change . . .

WALTER No—it was always money, Mama. We just didn't know about it.

MAMA No . . . something has changed. *(She looks at him.)* You something new, boy. In my time we was worried about not being lynched and getting to the North if we could and how to stay alive and still have a pinch of dignity too . . . Now here come you and Beneatha—talking 'bout things we ain't never even thought about hardly, me and your daddy. You ain't satisfied or proud of nothing we done. I mean that you had a home; that we kept you out of trouble till you was grown; that you don't have to ride to work on the back of nobody's streetcar— You my children—but how different we done become.

WALTER You just don't understand, Mama, you just don't understand.

MAMA Son—do you know your wife is expecting another baby? *(Walter stands, stunned, and absorbs what his mother has said.)* That's what she wanted to talk to you about. *(Walter sinks down into a chair.)* This ain't for me to be telling—but you ought to know. *(She waits.)* I think Ruth is thinking 'bout getting rid of that child.

WALTER *(slowly understanding)* No — no — Ruth wouldn't do that.

MAMA When the world gets ugly enough—a woman will do anything for her family. *The part that's already living.*

WALTER You don't know Ruth, Mama, if you think she would do that.

Ruth opens the bedroom door and stands there a little limp.

RUTH *(beaten)* Yes I would too, Walter. *(pause)* I gave her a five-dollar down payment.

Exactly what does Walter mean when he says that life "was always money"?

Mama refers to the migration, over the past one hundred years, as poor blacks and whites from the South moved to the northern urban areas, in hopes of finding a better livelihood and life. Is Mama relatively happy about the results in her case? Is Walter satisfied?

There is total silence as the man stares at his wife and the mother stares at her son.

MAMA *(presently)* Well — *(tightly)* Well — son, I'm waiting to hear you say something . . . I'm waiting to hear how you be your father's son. Be the man he was . . . *(pause)* Your wife say she going to destroy your child. And I'm waiting to hear you talk like him and say we a people who give children life, not who destroys them—*(She rises.)* I'm waiting to see you stand up and look like your daddy and say we done give up one baby to poverty and that we ain't going to give up nary another one . . . I'm waiting.

WALTER Ruth—

MAMA If you a son of mine, tell her! *(Walter turns, looks at her and can say nothing. She continues, bitterly.)* You . . . you are a disgrace to your father's memory. Somebody get me my hat.

Curtain

> Mama's lines ending Act 1 gain effect from its irony. What other figure had almost stormed out of the apartment only a few minutes earlier in anger, frustration, and disappointment?

ACT II

SCENE i

Time: Later the same day.
At rise: Ruth is ironing again. She has the radio going. Presently Beneatha's bedroom door opens and Ruth's mouth falls and she puts down the iron in fascination.

RUTH What have we got on tonight!

BENEATHA *(emerging grandly from the doorway so that we can see her thoroughly robed in the costume Asagai brought)* You are looking at what a well-dressed Nigerian woman wears—*(She parades for Ruth, her hair completely hidden by the headdress; she is coquettishly fanning herself with an ornate oriental fan, mistakenly more like Butterfly than any Nigerian that ever was.)* Isn't it beautiful? *(She promenades to the radio and, with an arrogant flourish, turns off the good loud blues that is playing.)* Enough of this assimilationist junk! *(Ruth follows her with her eyes as she goes to the phonograph and puts on a record and turns and waits ceremoniously for the music to come up. Then, with a shout—)*
OCOMOGOSIAY!

> During this episode, the audience is offered a relief from the serious complications laid out in Act I.

Ruth jumps. The music comes up, a lovely Nigerian melody. Beneatha listens, enraptured, her eyes far away—"back to the past." She begins to dance. Ruth is dumfounded.

RUTH What kind of dance is that?

BENEATHA A folk dance.

RUTH *(Pearl Bailey)* What kind of folks do that, honey?

> What are the implications of Ruth acting like Pearl Bailey, the popular black songstress?

BENEATHA It's from Nigeria. It's a dance of welcome.

RUTH Who you welcoming?

BENEATHA The men back to the village.

RUTH Where they been?

BENEATHA How should I know—out hunting or something. Anyway, they are coming back now . . .

> How much does Beneatha *really* know about African ways ("out hunting or something")?

RUTH Well, that's good.

BENEATHA (with the record)
Alundi, alundi
Alundi alunya
Jop pu a jeepua
Ang gu sooooooooooo

Ai yai yae . . .
Ayehaye—alundi . . .

Walter comes in during this performance; he has obviously been drinking. He leans against the door heavily and watches his sister, at first with distaste. Then his eyes look off—"back to the past"—as he lifts both his fists to the roof, screaming.

WALTER YEAH . . . AND ETHIOPIA STRETCH FORTH HER HANDS AGAIN! . . .

RUTH (drily, looking at him) Yes—and Africa sure is claiming her own tonight. (She gives them both up and starts ironing again.)

WALTER (all in a drunken, dramatic shout) Shut up! . . . I'm digging them drums . . . them drums move me! . . . (He makes his weaving way to his wife's face and leans in close to her.) In my heart of hearts—(He thumps his chest.)—I am much warrior!

RUTH (without even looking up) In your heart of hearts you are much drunkard.

WALTER (coming away from her and starting to wander around the room, shouting) Me and Jomo . . . (Intently, in his sister's face. She has stopped dancing to watch him in this unknown mood.) That's my man, Kenyatta. (shouting and thumping his chest) FLAMING SPEAR! HOT DAMN! (He is suddenly in possession of an imaginary spear and actively spearing enemies all over the room.) OCOMOGOSIAY . . . THE LION IS WAKING . . . OWIMOWEH! (He pulls his shirt open and leaps up on a table and gestures with his spear. The bell rings. Ruth goes to answer.)

BENEATHA (to encourage Walter, thoroughly caught up with this side of him) OCOMOGOSIAY, FLAMING SPEAR!

WALTER (On the table, very far gone, his eyes pure glass sheets. He sees what we cannot, that he is a leader of his people, a great chief, a descendant of Chaka, and that the hour to march has come.) Listen, my black brothers—

BENEATHA OCOMOGOSIAY!

WALTER —Do you hear the waters rushing against the shores of the coastlands—

BENEATHA OCOMOGOSIAY!

WALTER —Do you hear the screeching of the cocks in yonder hills beyond where the chiefs meet in council for the coming of the mighty war—

BENEATHA OCOMOGOSIAY!

WALTER —Do you hear the beating of the wings of the birds flying low over the mountains and the low places of our land—

Ruth opens the door. George Murchison enters.

BENEATHA OCOMOGOSIAY!

WALTER —Do you hear the singing of the women, singing the war songs of our fathers to the babies in the great houses . . . singing the sweet war songs? OH, DO YOU HEAR, MY BLACK BROTHERS!

BENEATHA *(completely gone)* We hear you, Flaming Spear—

WALTER Telling us to prepare for the greatness of the time—*(to George)* Black Brother!

He extends his hand for the fraternal clasp.

GEORGE Black Brother, hell!

RUTH *(having had enough, and embarrassed for the family)* Beneatha, you got company—what's the matter with you? Walter Lee Younger, get down off that table and stop acting like a fool . . .

Walter comes down off the table suddenly and makes a quick exit to the bathroom.

RUTH He's had a little to drink . . . I don't know what her excuse is.

GEORGE *(to Beneatha)* Look honey, we're going *to* the theatre—we're not going to be *in* it . . . so go change, huh?

RUTH You expect this boy to go out with you looking like that?

BENEATHA *(looking at George)* That's up to George. If he's ashamed of his heritage—

GEORGE Oh, don't be so proud of yourself, Bennie—just because you look eccentric.

BENEATHA How can something that's natural be eccentric?

GEORGE That's what being eccentric means—being natural. Get dressed.

BENEATHA I don't like that, George.

RUTH Why must you and your brother make an argument out of everything people say?

BENEATHA Because I hate assimilationist Negroes!

RUTH Will somebody please tell me what assimila-who-ever means!

GEORGE Oh, it's just a college girl's way of calling people Uncle Toms—but that isn't what it means at all.

RUTH Well, what does it mean?

BENEATHA *(cutting George off and staring at him as she replies to Ruth)* It means someone who is willing to give up his own culture and submerge himself completely in the dominant, and in this case, *oppressive* culture!

GEORGE Oh, dear, dear, dear! Here we go! A lecture on the African past! On our Great West African Heritage! In one second we will hear all about the great Ashanti empires; the great Songhay civilizations; and the great sculpture of Bénin—and then some poetry in the Bantu—and the whole monologue will end with the word *heritage!* *(nastily)* Let's face it, baby, your heritage is nothing but a bunch of raggedy-assed spirituals and some grass huts!

BENEATHA *Grass huts! (Ruth crosses to her and forcibly pushes her toward the bedroom.)* See there . . . you are standing there in your splendid

---

With the help of alcoholic encouragement, Walter joins in with the African tribal dance charades. Does he genuinely feel any kinship with African blacks? Why?

Would Asagai accept George's definition?

There is a stark contrast between Ruth and Beneatha. In what central ways are they different persons in their viewpoints about life, and why?

How does George's description coincide with Walter's just completed mock heroics?

ignorance talking about people who were the first to smelt iron on the face of the earth! *(Ruth is pushing her through the door.)* The Ashanti were performing surgical operations when the English—*(Ruth pulls the door to, with Beneatha on the other side, and smiles graciously at George. Beneatha opens the door and shouts the end of the sentence defiantly at George.)*—were still tatooing themselves with blue dragons . . . *(She goes back inside.)*

RUTH Have a seat, George. *(They both sit, Ruth folds her hands rather primly on her lap, determined to demonstrate the civilization of the family.)* Warm, ain't it? I mean for September. *(pause)* Just like they always say about Chicago weather: If it's too hot or cold for you, just wait a minute and it'll change. *(She smiles happily at this cliché of clichés.)* Everybody say it's got to do with them bombs and things they keep setting off. *(pause)* Would you like a nice cold beer?

> In an attempt to calm the situation, Ruth chats with George in a manner which utterly reveals her own uneducated upbringing. How?

GEORGE No, thank you. I don't care for beer. *(He looks at his watch.)* I hope she hurries up.

RUTH What time is the show?

GEORGE It's an eight-thirty curtain. That's just Chicago, though. In New York standard curtain time is eight forty.

He is rather proud of this knowledge.

RUTH *(properly appreciating it)* You get to New York a lot?

GEORGE *(offhand)* Few times a year.

RUTH Oh—that's nice. I've never been to New York.

Walter enters. We feel he has relieved himself, but the edge of unreality is still with him.

WALTER New York ain't got nothing Chicago ain't. Just a bunch of hustling people all squeezed up together—being "Eastern."

He turns his face into a screw of displeasure.

GEORGE Oh—you've been?

WALTER *Plenty* of times.

RUTH *(shocked at the lie)* Walter Lee Younger!

WALTER *(staring her down)* Plenty! *(pause)* What we got to drink in this house? Why don't you offer this man some refreshment. *(to George)* They don't know how to entertain people in this house, man.

GEORGE Thank you I don't really care for anything.

> Is George being snobbish here? How do we know?

WALTER *(feeling his head; sobriety coming)* Where's Mama?

RUTH She ain't come back yet.

WALTER *(looking Murchison over from head to toe, scrutinizing his carefully casual tweed sports jacket over cashmere V-neck sweater over soft eyelet shirt and tie, and soft slacks, finished off with white buckskin shoes)* Why all you college boys wear them fairyish-looking white shoes?

> White buckskin shoes were the campus fashion in the 1950s. Some, like Walter, who never went to college considered such affected styles sissy.

RUTH Walter Lee!

George Murchison ignores the remark.

WALTER *(to Ruth)* Well, they look crazy as hell—white shoes, cold as it is.

A RAISIN IN THE SUN

RUTH (*crushed*) You have to excuse him—

WALTER No he don't! Excuse me for what? What you always excusing me for! I'll excuse myself when I needs to be excused! (*a pause*) They look as funny as them black knee socks Beneatha wears out of here all the time.

RUTH It's the college *style*, Walter.

WALTER Style, hell. She looks like she got burnt legs or something!

RUTH Oh, Walter—

WALTER (*an irritable mimic*) Oh, Walter! Oh, Walter! (*to Murchison*) How's your old man making out? I understand you all going to buy that big hotel on the Drive? (*He finds a beer in the refrigerator, wanders over to Murchison, sipping and wiping his lips with the back of his hand, and straddling a chair backwards to talk to the other man.*) Shrewd move. Your old man is all right, man. (*tapping his head and half winking for emphasis*) I mean he knows how to operate. I mean he thinks *big*, you know what I mean, I mean for a *home*, you know? But I think he's kind of running out of ideas now. I'd like to talk to him. Listen, man, I got some plans that could turn this city upside down. I mean I think like he does. *Big*. Invest big, gamble big, hell, lose *big* if you have to, you know what I mean. It's hard to find a man on this whole Southside who understands my kind of thinking—you dig? (*He scrutinizes Murchison again, drinks his beer, squints his eyes and leans in close, confidential, man to man.*) Me and you ought to sit down and talk sometimes, man. Man, I got me some ideas . . .

MURCHISON (*with boredom*) Yeah—sometimes we'll have to do that, Walter.

WALTER (*understanding the indifference, and offended*) Yeah—well, when you get the time, man. I know you a busy little boy.

RUTH Walter, please—

WALTER (*bitterly, hurt*) I know ain't nothing in this world as busy as you colored college boys with your fraternity pins and white shoes . . .

RUTH (*covering her face with humiliation*) Oh, Walter Lee—

WALTER I see you all all the time—with the books tucked under your arms—going to your (*British A—a mimic*) "clahsses." And for what! What the hell you learning over there? Filling up your heads—(*counting off on his fingers*)—with the sociology and the psychology—but they teaching you how to be a man? How to take over and run the world? They teaching you how to run a rubber plantation or a steel mill? Naw—just to talk proper and read books and wear white shoes . . .

GEORGE (*looking at him with distaste, a little above it all*) You're all wacked up with bitterness, man.

WALTER (*intently, almost quietly, between the teeth, glaring at the boy*) And you—ain't you bitter, man? Ain't you just about had it yet? Don't you see no stars gleaming that you can't reach out and grab? You happy?—You contented son-of-a-bitch—you happy? You got it made? Bitter? Man, I'm a volcano. Bitter? Here I am a giant—surrounded by ants! Ants who can't even understand what it is the giant is talking about.

A tug-of-war develops over George, Beneatha's wealthy boyfriend. Each combatant—Ruth and Walter—manages to alienate George before they are through.

RUTH *(passionately and suddenly)* Oh, Walter—ain't you with nobody!

WALTER *(violently)* No! 'Cause ain't nobody with me! Not even my own mother!

RUTH Walter, that's a terrible thing to say!

Beneatha enters, dressed for the evening in a cocktail dress and earrings.

GEORGE Well—hey, you look great.

BENEATHA Let's go, George. See you all later.

RUTH Have a nice time.

GEORGE Thanks. Good night. *(to Walter, sarcastically)* Good night, Prometheus.

Beneatha and George exit.

WALTER *(to Ruth)* Who is Prometheus?

RUTH I don't know. Don't worry about it.

WALTER *(in fury, pointing after George)* See there—they get to a point where they can't insult you man to man—they got to go talk about something ain't nobody never heard of!

RUTH How do you know it was an insult? *(to humor him)* Maybe Prometheus is a nice fellow.

WALTER Prometheus! I bet there ain't even no such thing! I bet that simple-minded clown—

RUTH Walter—

She stops what she is doing and looks at him.

WALTER *(yelling)* Don't start!

RUTH Start what?

WALTER Your nagging! Where was I? Who was I with? How much money did I spend?

RUTH *(plaintively)* Walter Lee—why don't we just try to talk about it . . .

WALTER *(not listening)* I been out talking with people who understand me. People who care about the things I got on my mind.

RUTH *(wearily)* I guess that means people like Willy Harris.

WALTER Yes, people like Willy Harris.

RUTH *(with a sudden flash of impatience)* Why don't you all just hurry up and go into the banking business and stop talking about it!

WALTER Why? You want to know why? 'Cause we all tied up in a race of people that don't know how to do nothing but moan, pray and have babies!

The line is too bitter even for him and he looks at her and sits down.

RUTH Oh, Walter . . . *(softly)* Honey, why can't you stop fighting me?

WALTER *(without thinking)* Who's fighting you? Who even cares about you?

This line begins the retardation of his mood.

Prometheus, a Titan in Greek mythology, helped create mankind out of clay and then furnished men with fire (an emblem for both power and knowledge), despite the attempts of the god Zeus to wipe out all men. Thus Prometheus symbolizes an omniscient, paternal savior of the human species. Why does George call Walter by that name?

RUTH Well—*(She waits a long time, and then with resignation starts to put away her things.)* I guess I might as well go on to bed . . . *(more or less to herself)* I don't know where we lost it . . . but we have . . . *(then, to him)* I—I'm sorry about this new baby, Walter. I guess maybe I better go on and do what I started . . . I guess I just didn't realize how bad things was with us . . . I guess I just didn't really realize—*(She starts out to the bedroom and stops.)* You want some hot milk?

WALTER Hot milk?

RUTH Yes—hot milk.

WALTER Why hot milk?

RUTH 'Cause after all that liquor you come home with you ought to have something hot in your stomach.

WALTER I don't want no milk.

RUTH You want some coffee then?

WALTER No, I don't want no coffee. I don't want nothing hot to drink. *(almost plaintively)* Why you always trying to give me something to eat?

RUTH *(standing and looking at him helplessly)* What else can I give you, Walter Lee Younger?

She stands and looks at him and presently turns to go out again. He lifts his head and watches her going away from him in a new mood which began to emerge when he asked her "Who cares about you?".

WALTER It's been rough, ain't it, baby? *(She hears and stops but does not turn around and he continues to her back.)* I guess between two people there ain't never as much understood as folks generally thinks there is. I mean like between me and you—*(She turns to face him.)* How we gets to the place where we scared to talk softness to each other. *(He waits, thinking hard himself.)* Why you think it got to be like that? *(He is thoughtful, almost as a child would be.)* Ruth, what is it gets into people ought to be close?

RUTH I don't know, honey. I think about it a lot.

WALTER On account of you and me, you mean? The way things are with us. The way something done come down between us.

RUTH There ain't so much between us, Walter . . . Not when you come to me and try to talk to me. Try to be with me . . . a little even.

WALTER *(total honesty)* Sometimes . . . sometimes . . . I don't even know how to try.

RUTH Walter—

WALTER Yes?

RUTH *(coming to him, gently and with misgiving, but coming to him)* Honey . . . life don't have to be like this. I mean sometimes people can do things so that things are better . . . You remember how we used to talk when Travis was born . . . about the way we were going to live . . . the kind of house . . . *(She is stroking his head.)* Well, it's all starting to slip away from us . . .

Mama enters, and Walter jumps up and shouts at her.

> Ruth's question sums up her disenchantment with life, just as had Walter's own prior outbursts. What precisely does Ruth mean by her question?

> How are Ruth's dreams similar to those articulated earlier by Mama?

WALTER Mama, where have you been?

MAMA My—them steps is longer than they used to be. Whew! *(She sits down and ignores him.)* How you feeling this evening, Ruth?

Ruth shrugs, disturbed some at having been prematurely interrupted and watching her husband knowingly.

WALTER Mama, where have you been all day?

MAMA *(still ignoring him and leaning on the table and changing to more comfortable shoes)* Where's Travis?

RUTH I let him go out earlier and he ain't come back yet. Boy, is he going to get it!

WALTER Mama!

MAMA *(as if she has heard him for the first time)* Yes, son?

WALTER Where did you go this afternoon?

MAMA I went downtown to tend to some business that I had to tend to.

> Note how Mama stalls by ignoring Walter's questions about where she has been that day.

WALTER What kind of business?

MAMA You know better than to question me like a child, Brother.

WALTER *(rising and bending over the table)* Where were you, Mama? *(bringing his fists down and shouting)* Mama, you didn't go do something with that insurance money, something crazy?

The front door opens slowly, interrupting him, and Travis peeks his head in, less than hopefully.

TRAVIS *(to his mother)* Mama, I—

RUTH "Mama I" nothing! You're going to get it, boy! Get on in that bedroom and get yourself ready!

TRAVIS But I—

MAMA Why don't you all never let the child explain hisself.

RUTH Keep out of it now, Lena.

Mama clamps her lips together, and Ruth advances toward her son menacingly.

RUTH A thousand times I have told you not to go off like that—

MAMA *(holding out her arms to her grandson)* Well—at least let me tell him something. I want him to be the first one to hear . . . Come here, Travis. *(The boy obeys, gladly.)* Travis— *(She takes him by the shoulder and looks into his face.)*—you know that money we got in the mail this morning?

TRAVIS Yes'm—

MAMA Well—what you think your grandmama gone and done with that money?

> In terms of dramatic blocking on stage—the positioning of the characters—how does Hansberry frame Mama's decision to buy a house as her guarantee to improve the future welfare of her brood? Where is each figure standing?

TRAVIS I don't know, Grandmama.

MAMA *(putting her finger on his nose for emphasis)* She went out and she bought you a house! *(The explosion comes from Walter at the end of the revelation and he jumps up and turns away from all of them in a fury. Mama continues, to Travis.)* You glad about the house? It's going to be yours when you get to be a man.

A RAISIN IN THE SUN   399

TRAVIS Yeah—I always wanted to live in a house.

MAMA All right, gimme some sugar then—*(Travis puts his arms around her neck as she watches her son over the boy's shoulder. Then, to Travis, after the embrace)* Now when you say your prayers tonight, you thank God and your grandfather—'cause it was him who give you the house—in his way.

RUTH *(taking the boy from Mama and pushing him toward the bedroom)* Now you get out of here and get ready for your beating.

TRAVIS Aw, Mama—

RUTH Get on in there—*(closing the door behind him and turning radiantly to her mother-in-law)* So you went and did it!

MAMA *(quietly, looking at her son with pain)* Yes, I did.

RUTH *(raising both arms classically)* Praise God! *(Looks at Walter a moment, who says nothing. She crosses rapidly to her husband.)* Please, honey—let me be glad . . . you be glad too. *(She has laid her hands on his shoulders, but he shakes himself free of her roughly, without turning to face her.)* Oh, Walter . . . a home . . . a home. *(She comes back to Mama.)* Well—where is it? How big is it? How much it going to cost?

MAMA Well—

RUTH When we moving?

MAMA *(smiling at her)* First of the month.

RUTH *(throwing back her head with jubilance)* Praise God!

MAMA *(tentatively, still looking at her son's back turned against her and Ruth)* It's—it's a nice house too . . . *(She cannot help speaking directly to him. An imploring quality in her voice, her manner, makes her almost like a girl now.)* Three bedrooms—nice big one for you and Ruth. . . . Me and Beneatha still have to share our room, but Travis have one of his own—and *(with difficulty)* I figure if the—new baby—is a boy, we could get one of them double-decker outfits . . . And there's a yard with a little patch of dirt where I could maybe get to grow me a few flowers . . . And a nice big basement . . .

RUTH Walter honey, be glad—

MAMA *(still to his back, fingering things on the table)* 'Course I don't want to make it sound fancier than it is . . . It's just a plain little old house—but it's made good and solid—and it will be *ours*. Walter Lee—it makes a difference in a man when he can walk on floors that belong to *him* . . .

RUTH Where is it?

MAMA *(frightened at this telling)* Well—well—it's out there in Clybourne Park—

Ruth's radiance fades abruptly, and Walter finally turns slowly to face his mother with incredulity and hostility.

RUTH Where?

MAMA *(matter-of-factly)* Four o six Clybourne Street, Clybourne Park.

RUTH Clybourne Park? Mama, there ain't no colored people living in Clybourne Park.

The intersection of divergent dreams here presents a powerful dramatic moment on stage. Why is the women's joy tempered, however?

Does it seem plausible that Mama's decision to buy a house was partly precipitated by news of the baby?

In the late 1950s, when *A Raisin the the Sun* was written, racially integrated neighborhoods were rare in this country. To move into an all-white residential area, consequently, would be a daring act on the part of the Youngers.

MAMA *(almost idiotically)* Well, I guess there's going to be some now.

WALTER *(bitterly)* So that's the peace and comfort you went out and bought for us today!

MAMA *(raising her eyes to meet his finally)* Son—I just tried to find the nicest place for the least amount of money for my family.

RUTH *(trying to recover from the shock)* Well—well—'course I ain't one never been 'fraid of no crackers, mind you—but—well, wasn't there no other houses nowhere?

MAMA Them houses they put up for colored in them areas way out all seem to cost twice as much as other houses. I did the best I could.

RUTH *(Struck senseless with the news, in its various degrees of goodness and trouble, she sits a moment, her fists propping her chin in thought, and then she starts to rise, bringing her fists down with vigor, the radiance spreading from cheek to cheek again.)* Well—well!—All I can say is—if this is my time in life—*my time*—to say good-bye—*(and she builds with momentum as she starts to circle the room with an exuberant, almost tearfully happy release)*—to these Goddamned cracking walls!—*(She pounds the walls.)*—and these marching roaches!—*(She wipes at an imaginary army of marching roaches.)*—and this cramped little closet which ain't now or never was no kitchen! . . . then I say it loud and good, Hallelujah! and goodbye misery . . . I don't never want to see your ugly face again! *(She laughs joyously, having practically destroyed the apartment, and flings her arms up and lets them come down happily, slowly, reflectively, over her abdomen, aware for the first time perhaps that the life therein pulses with happiness and not despair)* Lena?

MAMA *(moved, watching her happiness)* Yes, honey?

RUTH *(looking off)* Is there—is there a whole lot of sunlight?

MAMA *(understanding)* Yes, child, there's a whole lot of sunlight.

Long pause

RUTH *(collecting herself and going to the door of the room Travis is in)* Well—I guess I better see 'bout Travis. *(to Mama)* Lord, I sure don't feel like whipping nobody today!

She exits.

MAMA *(The mother and son are left alone now and the mother waits a long time, considering deeply, before she speaks.)* Son—you—you understand what I done, don't you? *(Walter is silent and sullen.)* I—I just seen my family falling apart today . . . just falling to pieces in front of my eyes . . . We couldn't of gone on like we was today. We was going backwards 'stead of forwards—talking 'bout killing babies and wishing each other was dead . . . When it gets like that in life—you just got to do something different, push on out and do something bigger . . . *(She waits.)* I wish you say something, son . . . I wish you'd say how deep inside you you think I done the right thing—

WALTER *(crossing slowly to his bedroom door and finally turning there and speaking measuredly)* What you need me to say you done right for? *You* the head of this family. You run our lives like you want to. It was your money and you did what you wanted with it. So what you need for me to say it was all right for? *(bitterly, to hurt her as deeply as he knows is possible)* So you butchered up a dream of mine—you —who always talking 'bout your children's dreams . . .

In your opinion, what would the situation be like today?

The term "crackers" refers to white bigots.

The basis of Mama's and Walter's disagreement concerning money and life values is clear. Why does each say what he does at this point?

A RAISIN IN THE SUN 401

MAMA Walter Lee—

He just closes the door behind him. Mama sits alone, thinking heavily.

Curtain

SCENE ii

Time: Friday night. A few weeks later.

At rise: Packing crates mark the intention of the family to move. Beneatha and George come in, presumably from an evening out again.

GEORGE O.K. . . . O.K., whatever you say . . . *(They both sit on the couch. He tries to kiss her. She moves away.)* Look, we've had a nice evening; let's not spoil it, huh? . . .

He again turns her head and tries to nuzzle in and she turns away from him, not with distaste but with momentary lack of interest; in a mood to pursue what they were talking about.

BENEATHA I'm *trying* to talk to you.

GEORGE We always talk.

BENEATHA Yes—and I love to talk.

GEORGE *(exasperated; rising)* I know it and I don't mind it sometimes . . . I want you to cut it out, see—The moody stuff, I mean. I don't like it. You're a nicelooking girl . . . all over. That's all you need, honey, forget the atmosphere. Guys aren't going to go for the atmosphere—they're going to go for what they see. Be glad for that. Drop the Garbo routine. It doesn't go with you. As for myself, I want a nice—*(groping)*—simple *(thoughtfully)*—sophisticated girl . . . not a poet—O.K.?

She rebuffs him again and he starts to leave.

BENEATHA Why are you angry?

GEORGE Because this is stupid! I don't go out with you to discuss the nature of "quiet desperation" or to hear all about your thoughts —because the world will go on thinking what it thinks regardless—

BENEATHA Then why read books? Why go to school?

GEORGE *(with artificial patience, counting on his fingers)* It's simple. You read books—to learn facts—to get grades—to pass the course —to get a degree. That's all—it has nothing to do with thoughts.

A long pause

BENEATHA I see. *(a longer pause as she looks at him)* Good night, George.

George looks at her a little oddly, and starts to exit. He meets Mama coming in.

GEORGE Oh—hello, Mrs. Younger.

MAMA Hello, George, how you feeling?

GEORGE Fine—fine, how are you?

MAMA Oh, a little tired. You know them steps can get you after a day's work. You all have a nice time tonight?

GEORGE Yes—a fine time. Well, good night.

How do the crates visually inform audiences of the passing of time since the last scene?

Where in literature does one find the phrase "lives of quiet desperation"?

Hansberry does not mean to indicate that George is unintelligent, but here she establishes him as a superficial and cynical young man. How?

MAMA Good night. *(He exits. Mama closes the door behind her.)* Hello, honey. What you sitting like that for?

BENEATHA I'm just sitting.

MAMA Didn't you have a nice time?

BENEATHA No.

MAMA No? What's the matter?

BENEATHA Mama, George is a fool—honest. *(She rises.)*

MAMA *(Hustling around unloading the packages she has entered with. She stops.)* Is he, baby?

BENEATHA Yes.

Beneatha makes up Travis' bed as she talks.

MAMA You sure?

BENEATHA Yes.

MAMA Well—I guess you better not waste your time with no fools.

Beneatha looks up at her mother, watching her put groceries in the refrigerator. Finally she gathers up her things and starts into the bedroom. At the door she stops and looks back at her mother.

BENEATHA Mama—

MAMA Yes, baby—

BENEATHA Thank you.

MAMA For what?

BENEATHA For understanding me this time.

She exits quickly and the mother stands, smiling a little, looking at the place where Beneatha just stood. Ruth enters.

RUTH Now don't you fool with any of this stuff, Lena—

MAMA Oh, I just thought I'd sort a few things out.

The phone rings. Ruth answers.

RUTH *(at the phone)* Hello—Just a minute. *(goes to door)* Walter, it's Mrs. Arnold. *(Waits. Goes back to the phone. Tense)* Hello. Yes, this is his wife speaking . . . He's lying down now. Yes . . . well, he'll be in tomorrow. He's been very sick. Yes—I know we should have called, but we were so sure he'd be able to come in today. Yes—yes, I'm very sorry. Yes . . . Thank you very much. *(She hangs up Walter is standing in the doorway of the bedroom behind her.)* That was Mrs. Arnold.

WALTER *(indifferently)* Was It?

RUTH She said if you don't come in tomorrow that they are getting a new man . . .

WALTER Ain't that sad—ain't that crying sad.

RUTH She said Mr. Arnold has had to take a cab for three days . . . Walter, you ain't been to work for three days! *(This is a revelation to her.)* Where you been, Walter Lee Younger? *(Walter looks at her and starts to laugh.)* You're going to lose your job.

WALTER That's right . . .

Why do you think Mama is being so solicitous with Ruth about putting away groceries and cleaning up the apartment?

RUTH Oh, Walter, and with your mother working like a dog every day—

WALTER That's sad too— Everything is sad.

MAMA What you been doing for these three days, son?

WALTER Mama—you don't know all the things a man what got leisure can find to do in this city . . . What's this—Friday night? Well—Wednesday I borrowed Willy Harris' car and I went for a drive . . . just me and myself and I drove and drove . . . Way out . . . way past South Chicago, and I parked the car and I sat and looked at the steel mills all day long. I just sat in the car and looked at them big black chimneys for hours. Then I drove back and I went to the Green Hat. *(pause)* And Thursday—Thursday I borrowed the car again and I got in it and I pointed it the other way and I drove the other way—for hours—way, way up to Wisconsin, and I looked at the farms. I just drove and looked at the farms. Then I drove back and I went to the Green Hat. *(pause)* And today—today I didn't get the car. Today I just walked. All over the Southside. And I looked at the Negroes and they looked at me and finally I just sat down on the curb at Thirty-ninth and South Parkway and I just sat there and watched the Negroes go by. And then I went to the Green Hat. You all sad? You all depressed? And you know where I am going right now—

Ruth goes out quietly.

MAMA Oh, Big Walter, is this the harvest of our days?

WALTER You know what I like about the Green Hat? *(He turns the radio on and a steamy, deep blues pours into the room.)* I like this little cat they got there who blows a sax . . . He blows. He talks to me. He ain't but 'bout five feet tall and he's got a conked head and his eyes is always closed and he's all music—

MAMA *(rising and getting some papers out of her handbag)* Walter—

WALTER And there's this other guy who plays the piano . . . and they got a sound. I mean they can work on some music . . . They got the best little combo in the world in the Green Hat . . . You can just sit there and drink and listen to them three men play and you realize that don't nothing matter worth a damn, but just being there—

MAMA I've helped do it to you, haven't I, son? Walter, I been wrong.

WALTER Naw—you ain't never been wrong about nothing, Mama.

MAMA Listen to me, now. I say I been wrong, son. That I been doing to you what the rest of the world been doing to you. *(She stops and he looks up slowly at her and she meets his eyes pleadingly.)* Walter—what you ain't never understood is that I ain't got nothing, don't own nothing, ain't never really wanted nothing that wasn't for you. There ain't nothing as precious to me . . . There ain't nothing worth holding on to, money, dreams, nothing else—if it means—if it means it's going to destroy my boy. *(She puts her papers in front of him and he watches her without speaking or moving.)* I paid the man thirty-five hundred dollars down on the house. That leaves sixty-five hundred dollars. Monday morning I want you to take this money and take three thousand dollars and put it in a savings account for Beneatha's medical schooling. The rest you put in a checking account—with your name on it. And from now on any penny

> Walter has found a way to retaliate against his mother and wife because they used the money for their purposes, not his. What has he been doing instead of going to work?

that come out of it or that go in it is for you to look after. For you to decide. *(She drops her hands a little helplessly.)* It ain't much, but it's all I got in the world and I'm putting it in your hands. I'm telling you to be the head of this family from now on like you supposed to be.

WALTER *(stares at the money)* You trust me like that, Mama?

MAMA I ain't never stop trusting you. Like I ain't never stop loving you.

She goes out, and Walter sits looking at the money on the table as the music continues in its idiom, pulsing in the room. Finally, in a decisive gesture, he gets up, and, in mingled joy and desperation, picks up the money. At the same moment, Travis enters for bed.

TRAVIS What's the matter, Daddy? You drunk?

WALTER *(sweetly, more sweetly than we have ever known him)* No, Daddy ain't drunk. Daddy ain't going to never be drunk again. . . .

TRAVIS Well, good night, Daddy.

The father has come from behind the couch and leans over, embracing his son.

WALTER Son, I feel like talking to you tonight.

TRAVIS About what?

WALTER Oh, about a lot of things. About you and what kind of man you going to be when you grow up. . . . Son—son, what do you want to be when you grow up?

TRAVIS A bus driver.

WALTER *(laughing a little)* A what? Man, that ain't nothing to want to be!

TRAVIS Why not?

WALTER 'Cause, man—it ain't big enough—you know what I mean.

TRAVIS I don't know then. I can't make up my mind. Sometimes Mama asks me that too. And sometimes when I tell you I just want to be like you—she says she don't want me to be like that and sometimes she says she does. . . .

WALTER *(gathering him up in his arms)* You know what, Travis? In seven years you going to be seventeen years old. And things is going to be very different with us in seven years, Travis. . . . One day when you are seventeen I'll come home—home from my office downtown somewhere—

TRAVIS You don't work in no office, Daddy.

WALTER No—but after tonight. After what your daddy gonna do tonight, there's going to be offices—a whole lot of offices. . . .

TRAVIS What you gonna do tonight, Daddy?

WALTER You wouldn't understand yet, son, but your daddy's gonna make a transaction . . . a business transaction that's going to change our lives. . . . That's how come one day when you 'bout seventeen years old I'll come home and I'll be pretty tired, you know what I mean, after a day of conferences and secretaries getting things wrong the way they do . . . 'cause an executive's life is hell, man—*(The more he talks the farther away he gets.)* And I'll pull the car

> Mrs. Younger's selfless nature emerges with her announced decision to give Walter some of the money. What does she acknowledge about Walter's earlier complaint that she now wants to make amends for?

> Walter finally will have a chance to try out his plans for making money; he believes that his dreams now will come true.

A RAISIN IN THE SUN   405

up on the driveway . . . just a plain black Chrysler, I think, with white walls—no—black tires. More elegant. Rich people don't have to be flashy . . . though I'll have to get something a little sportier for Ruth—maybe a Cadillac convertible to do her shopping in. . . . And I'll come up the steps to the house and the gardener will be clipping away at the hedges and he'll say, "Good evening, Mr. Younger." And I'll say, "Hello, Jefferson, how are you this evening?" And I'll go inside and Ruth will come downstairs and meet me at the door and we'll kiss each other and she'll take my arm and we'll go up to your room to see you sitting on the floor with the catalogues of all the great schools in America around you. . . . All the great schools in the world! And—and I'll say, all right son—it's your seventeenth birthday, what is it you've decided? . . . Just tell me where you want to go to school and you'll *go.* Just tell me, what it is you want to be—and you'll *be* it. . . . Whatever you want to be—Yessir! *(He holds his arms open for Travis.)* You just name it, son . . . *(Travis leaps into them.)* and I hand you the world!

Walter's voice has risen in pitch and hysterical promise and on the last line he lifts Travis high. Blackout.

Walter's dreams of an ideal future rest on what kinds of things?

SCENE iii

Time: Saturday, moving day, one week later.

Before the curtain rises, Ruth's voice, a strident, dramatic church alto, cuts through the silence.

It is, in the darkness, a triumphant surge, a penetrating statement of expectation: "Oh, Lord, I don't feel no ways tired! Children, oh, glory hallelujah!"

As the curtain rises we see that Ruth is alone in the living room, finishing up the family's packing. It is moving day. She is nailing crates and tying cartons. Beneatha enters, carrying a guitar case, and watches her exuberant sister-in-law.

RUTH Hey!

BENEATHA *(putting away the case)* Hi.

RUTH *(pointing at a package)* Honey—look in that package there and see what I found on sale this morning at the South Center. *(Ruth gets up and moves to the package and draws out some curtains.)* Lookahere—hand-turned hems!

BENEATHA How do you know the window size out there?

RUTH *(who hadn't thought of that)* Oh— Well, they bound to fit something in the whole house. Anyhow, they was too good a bargain to pass up. *(Ruth slaps her head, suddenly remembering something.)* Oh, Bennie—I meant to put a special note on that carton over there. That's your mama's good china and she wants 'em to be very careful with it.

BENEATHA I'll do it.

Beneatha finds a piece of paper and starts to draw large letters on it.

RUTH You know what I'm going to do soon as I get in that new house?

BENEATHA What?

RUTH Honey—I'm going to run me a tub of water up to here . . .

(*with her fingers practically up to her nostrils*) And I'm going to get in it—and I am going to sit . . . and sit . . . and sit in that hot water and the first person who knocks to tell *me* to hurry up and come out—

BENEATHA Gets shot at sunrise.

RUTH (*laughing happily*) You said it, sister! (*noticing how large Beneatha is absent-mindedly making the note*) Honey, they ain't going to read that from no airplane.

BENEATHA (*laughing herself*) I guess I always think things have more emphasis if they are big, somehow.

RUTH (*looking up at her and smiling*) You and your brother seem to have that as a philosophy of life. Lord, that man—done changed so 'round here. You know—you know what we did last night? Me and Walter Lee?

BENEATHA What?

RUTH (*smiling to herself*) We went to the movies. (*looking at Beneatha to see if she understands*) We went to the movies. You know the last time me and Walter went to the movies together?

BENEATHA No.

RUTH Me neither. That's how long it been. (*smiling again*) But we went last night. The picture wasn't much good, but that didn't seem to matter. We went—and we held hands.

BENEATHA Oh, Lord!

RUTH We held hands—and you know what?

BENEATHA What?

RUTH When we come out of the show it was late and dark and all the stores and things was closed up . . . and it was kind of chilly and there wasn't many people on the streets . . . and we was still holding hands, me and Walter.

BENEATHA You're killing me.

Walter enters with a large package. His happiness is deep in him; he cannot keep still with his new-found exuberance. He is singing and wiggling and snapping his fingers. He puts his package in a corner and puts a phonograph record, which he has brought in with him, on the record player. As the music comes up he dances over to Ruth and tries to get her to dance with him. She gives in at last to his raunchiness and in a fit of giggling allows herself to be drawn into his mood and together they deliberately burlesque an old social dance of their youth.

BENEATHA (*regarding them a long time as they dance, then drawing in her breath for a deeply exaggerated comment which she does not particularly mean*) Talk about—olddddddddddd-fashioneddddddd—Negroes!

WALTER (*stopping momentarily*) What kind of Negroes?

He says this in fun. He is not angry with her today, nor with anyone. He starts to dance with his wife again.

BENEATHA Old-fashioned.

WALTER (*as he dances with Ruth*) You know, when these *New Negroes* have their convention—(*pointing at his sister*)—that is going to be the chairman of the Committee on Unending Agitation. (*He goes on danc-*

> Why does Ruth emphasize her intention to take a leisurely bath, once they have moved to their own home?

A RAISIN IN THE SUN

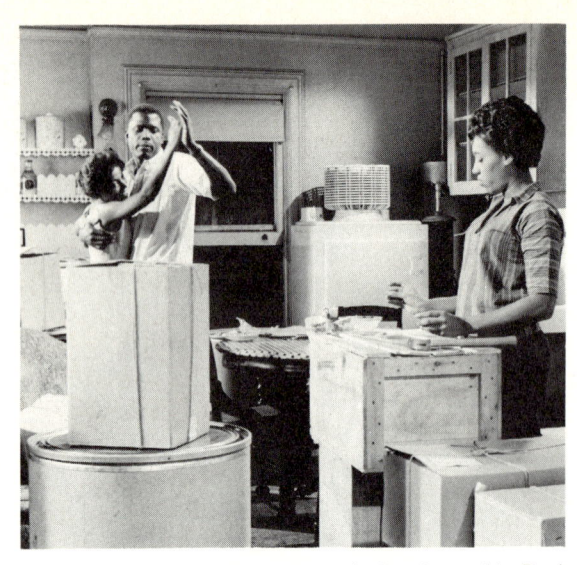

Walter (Sidney Poitier) dancing with Ruth (Ruby Dee) in the kitchen, from the motion picture, A Raisin in the Sun.

ing, then stops.) Race, race, race! . . . Girl, I do believe you are the first person in the history of the entire human race to successfully brainwash yourself. *(Beneatha breaks up and he goes on dancing. He stops again, enjoying his tease.)* Damn, even the N double A C P takes a holiday sometimes! *(Beneatha and Ruth laugh. He dances with Ruth some more and starts to laugh and stops and pantomimes someone over an operating table.)* I can just see that chick someday looking down at some poor cat on an operating table before she starts to slice him, saying . . . *(pulling his sleeves back maliciously)* "By the way, what are your views on civil rights down there? . . ."

He laughs at her again and starts to dance happily. The bell sounds.

BENEATHA Sticks and stones may break my bones but . . . words will never hurt me!

Beneatha goes to the door and opens it as Walter and Ruth go on with the clowning. Beneatha is somewhat surprised to see a quiet-looking middle-aged white man in a business suit holding his hat and a briefcase in his hand and consulting a small piece of paper.

MAN Uh—how do you do, miss. I am looking for a Mrs.—*(He looks at the slip of paper.)* Mrs. Lena Younger?

BENEATHA *(smoothing her hair with slight embarrassment)* Oh—yes, that's my mother. Excuse me *(She closes the door and turns to quiet the other two.)* Ruth! Brother! Somebody's here. *(Then she opens the door. The man casts a curious quick glance at all of them.)* Uh—come in please.

MAN *(coming in)* Thank you.

BENEATHA My mother isn't here just now. Is it business?

MAN Yes . . . well, of a sort.

How do Walter's remarks correspond to the overall mood of this scene?

408 LORRAINE HANSBERRY

WALTER *(freely, the Man of the House)* Have a seat. I'm Mrs. Younger's son. I look after most of her business matters.

Ruth and Beneatha exchange amused glances.

MAN *(regarding Walter, and sitting)* Well—My name is Karl Lindner . . .

WALTER *(stretching out his hand)* Walter Younger. This is my wife—*(Ruth nods politely.)*—and my sister.

LINDNER How do you do.

WALTER *(amiably, as he sits himself easily on a chair, leaning with interest forward on his knees and looking expectantly into the newcomer's face)* What can we do for you, Mr. Lindner!

LINDNER *(some minor shuffling of the hat and briefcase on his knees)* Well—I am a representative of the Clybourne Park Improvement Association—

> What kind of "improvement" is meant by this term in the title of Lindner's group? Can you make up a title which more precisely describes the function of this organization?

WALTER *(pointing)* Why don't you sit your things on the floor?

LINDNER Oh—yes. Thank you. *(He slides the briefcase and hat under the chair.)* And as I was saying—I am from the Clybourne Park Improvement Association and we have had it brought to our attention at the last meeting that you people—or at least your mother—has bought a piece of residential property at—*(He digs for the slip of paper.)*—four o six Clybourne Street . . .

WALTER That's right. Care for something to drink? Ruth, get Mr. Lindner a beer.

LINDNER *(upset for some reason)* Oh—no, really. I mean thank you very much, but no thank you.

RUTH *(innocently)* Some coffee?

LINDNER Thank you, nothing at all.

Beneatha is watching the man carefully.

LINDNER Well, I don't know how much you folks know about our organization. *(He is a gentle man; thoughtful and somewhat labored in his manner.)* It is one of these community organizations set up to look after—oh, you know, things like block upkeep and special projects and we also have what we call our New Neighbors Orientation Committee . . .

> More sophisticated than the others in her family, Beneatha is the first to sense the potential menace in Karl Lindner's visit. What, in the name of Lindner's organization, gives the audience a clue about his coming to the Youngers?

BENEATHA *(drily)* Yes—and what do they do?

LINDNER *(turning a little to her and then returning the main force to Walter)* Well—it's what you might call a sort of welcoming committee, I guess. I mean they, we, I'm the chairman of the committee—go around and see the new people who move into the neighborhood and sort of give them the lowdown on the way we do things out in Clybourne Park.

BENEATHA *(with appreciation of the two meanings, which escape Ruth and Walter)* Un-huh.

LINDNER And we also have the category of what the association calls—*(He looks elsewhere.)*—uh—special community problems . . .

BENEATHA Yes—and what are some of those?

WALTER Girl, let the man talk.

A RAISIN IN THE SUN

LINDNER *(with understated relief)* Thank you. I would sort of like to explain this thing in my own way. I mean I want to explain to you in a certain way.

WALTER Go ahead.

LINDNER Yes. Well. I'm going to try to get right to the point. I'm sure we'll all appreciate that in the long run.

BENEATHA Yes.

WALTER Be still now!

LINDNER Well—

RUTH *(still innocently)* Would you like another chair—you don't look comfortable.

LINDNER *(more frustrated than annoyed)* No, thank you very much. Please. Well—to get right to the point I—*(A great breath, and he is off at last.)* I am sure you people must be aware of some of the incidents which have happened in various parts of the city when colored people have moved into certain areas—*(Beneatha exhales heavily and starts tossing a piece of fruit up and down in the air.)* Well—because we have what I think is going to be a unique type of organization in American community life—not only do we deplore that kind of thing—but we are trying to do something about it.*(Beneatha stops tossing and turns with a new and quizzical interest to the man.)* We feel—*(gaining confidence in his mission because of the interest in the faces of the people he is talking to)*—we feel that most of the trouble in this world, when you come right down to it—*(He hits his knee for emphasis.)*—most of the trouble exists because people just don't sit down and talk to each other.

RUTH *(nodding as she might in church, pleased with the remark)* You can say that again, mister.

LINDNER *(more encouraged by such affirmation)* That we don't try hard enough in this world to understand the other fellow's problem. The other guy's point of view.

RUTH Now that's right.

Beneatha and Walter merely watch and listen with genuine interest.

LINDNER Yes—that's the way we feel out in Clybourne Park. And that's why I was elected to come here this afternoon and talk to you people. Friendly like, you know, the way people should talk to each other and see if we couldn't find some way to work this thing out. As I say, the whole business is a matter of *caring* about the other fellow. Anybody can see that you are a nice family of folks, hard working and honest I'm sure. *(Beneatha frowns slightly, quizzically, her head tilted regarding him.)* Today everybody knows what it means to be on the outside of *something*. And of course, there is always somebody who is out to take the advantage of people who don't always understand.

WALTER What do you mean?

LINDNER Well—you see our community is made up of people who've worked hard as the dickens for years to build up that little community. They're not rich and fancy people; just hard-working, honest people who don't really have much but those little homes

---

Ruth is the last to understand Lindner's true mission, as shown by her totally innocent reactions to his statements.

Lindner here is describing families just like Mama's. Why is it ironic in this context?

and a dream of the kind of community they want to raise their children in. Now, I don't say we are perfect and there is a lot wrong in some of the things they want. But you've got to admit that a man, right or wrong, has the right to want to have the neighborhood he lives in a certain kind of way. And at the moment the overwhelming majority of our people out there feel that people get along better, take more of a common interest in the life of the community, when they share a common background. I want you to believe me when I tell you that race prejudice simply doesn't enter into it. It is a matter of the people of Clybourne Park believing, rightly or wrongly, as I say, that for the happiness of all concerned that our Negro families are happier when they live in their *own* communities.

BENEATHA (*with a grand and bitter gesture*) This, friends, is the Welcoming Committee!

WALTER (*dumfounded, looking at Lindner*) Is this what you came marching all the way over here to tell us?

LINDNER Well, now we've been having a fine conversation. I hope you'll hear me all the way through.

WALTER (*tightly*) Go ahead, man.

LINDNER You see—in the face of all things I have said, we are prepared to make your family a very generous offer . . .

BENEATHA Thirty pieces and not a coin less!

WALTER Yeah?

LINDNER (*putting on his glasses and drawing a form out of the briefcase*) Our association is prepared, through the collective effort of our people, to buy the house from you at a financial gain to your family.

RUTH Lord have mercy, ain't this the living gall!

WALTER All right, you through?

LINDNER Well, I want to give you the exact terms of the financial arrangement—

WALTER We don't want to hear no exact terms of no arrangements. I want to know if you got any more to tell us 'bout getting together?

LINDNER (*taking off his glasses*) Well—I don't suppose that you feel . . .

WALTER Never mind how I feel—you got any more to say 'bout how people ought to sit down and talk to each other? . . . Get out of my house, man.

He turns his back and walks to the door.

LINDNER (*looking around at the hostile faces and reaching and assembling his hat and briefcase*) Well—I don't understand why you people are reacting this way. What do you think you are going to gain by moving into a neighborhood where you just aren't wanted and where some elements—well—people can get awful worked up when they feel that their whole way of life and everything they've ever worked for is threatened.

WALTER Get out.

LINDNER (*at the door, holding a small card*) Well—I'm sorry it went like this.

How has Lindner's visit added to the complications of the play?

Beneatha's allusion to "thirty pieces" refers to money paid for Jesus Christ's betrayal.

Does Hansberry need to clarify Lindner's (and Clybourne Park's) viewpoint about having a black family move into an all-white area? Why?

A RAISIN IN THE SUN   411

WALTER Get out.

LINDNER *(almost sadly regarding Walter)* You just can't force people to change their hearts, son.

He turns and put his card on a table and exits. Walter pushes the door to with stinging hatred, and stands looking at it. Ruth just sits and Beneatha just stands. They say nothing. Mama and Travis enter.

MAMA Well—this all the packing got done since I left out of here this morning. I testify before God that my children got all the energy of the dead. What time the moving men due?

BENEATHA Four o'clock. You had a caller, Mama.

She is smiling, teasingly.

MAMA Sure enough—who?

BENEATHA *(her arms folded saucily)* The Welcoming Committee.

Walter and Ruth giggle.

MAMA *(innocently)* Who?

BENEATHA The Welcoming Committee. They said they're sure going to be glad to see you when you get there.

WALTER *(devilishly)* Yeah, they said they can't hardly wait to see your face.

Laughter

MAMA *(sensing their facetiousness)* What's the matter with you all?

WALTER Ain't nothing the matter with us. We just telling you 'bout the gentleman who came to see you this afternoon. From the Clybourne Park Improvement Association.

MAMA What he want?

RUTH *(in the same mood as Beneatha and Walter)* To welcome you, honey.

WALTER He said they can't hardly wait. He said the one thing they don't have, that they just *dying* to have out there is a fine family of colored people! *(to Ruth and Beneatha)* Ain't that right!

RUTH and **BENEATHA** *(mockingly)* Yeah! He left his card in case—

They indicate the card, and Mama picks it up and throws it on the floor—understanding and looking off as she draws her chair up to the table on which she has put her plant and some sticks and some cord.

MAMA Father, give us strength. *(knowingly—and without fun)* Did he threaten us?

BENEATHA Oh—Mama—they don't do it like that any more. He talked Brotherhood. He said everybody ought to learn how to sit down and hate each other with good Christian fellowship.

She and Walter shake hands to ridicule the remark.

MAMA *(sadly)* Lord, protect us . . .

RUTH You should hear the money those folks raised to buy the house from us. All we paid and then some.

BENEATHA What they think we going to do—eat 'em?

How does Mrs. Younger interpret the news of Lindner's visit?

412 LORRAINE HANSBERRY

RUTH No, honey, marry 'em.

MAMA (shaking her head) Lord, Lord, Lord . . .

RUTH Well—that's the way the crackers crumble. Joke.

BENEATHA (laughingly noticing what her mother is doing) Mama, what are you doing?

MAMA Fixing my plant so it won't get hurt none on the way . . .

BENEATHA Mama, you going to take *that* to the new house?

MAMA Un-huh—

BENEATHA That raggedy-looking old thing?

MAMA (stopping and looking at her) It expresses *me*.

RUTH (with delight, to Beneatha) So there, Miss Thing!

Walter comes to Mama suddenly and bends down behind her and squeezes her in his arms with all his strength. She is overwhelmed by the suddenness of it and, though delighted, her manner is like that of Ruth with Travis.

MAMA Look out now, boy! You make me mess up my thing here!

WALTER (His face lit, he slips down on his knees beside her, his arms still about her.) Mama . . . you know what it means to climb up in the chariot?

MAMA (gruffly, very happy) Get on away from me now . . .

RUTH (near the gift-wrapped package, trying to catch Walter's eye) Psst—

WALTER What the old song say, Mama . . .

RUTH Walter— Now?

She is pointing at the package.

WALTER (speaking the lines, sweetly, playfully, in his mother's face)

    I got wings . . . you got wings . . .
    All God's Children got wings . . .

MAMA Boy—get out of my face and do some work . . .

WALTER

    When I get to heaven gonna put on my wings,
    Gonna fly all over God's heaven . . .

BENEATHA (teasingly, from across the room) Everybody talking 'bout heaven ain't going there!

WALTER (to Ruth, who is carrying the box across to them) I don't know, you think we ought to give her that . . . Seems to me she ain't been very appreciative around here.

MAMA (eying the box, which is obviously a gift) What is that?

WALTER (taking it from Ruth and putting it on the table in front of Mama) Well—what you all think? Should we give it to her?

RUTH Oh—she was pretty good today.

MAMA I'll good you—

She turns her eyes to the box again.

BENEATHA Open it, Mama.

She stands up, looks at it, turns and looks at all of them, and then presses her hands together and does not open the package.

WALTER (*sweetly*) Open it, Mama. It's for you. (*Mama looks in his eyes. It is the first present in her life without its being Christmas. Slowly she opens her package and lifts out, one by one, a brand-new sparkling set of gardening tools. Walter continues, prodding.*) Ruth made up the note —read it . . .

MAMA (*picking up the card and adjusting her glasses*) "To our own Mrs. Miniver—Love from Brother, Ruth and Beneatha." Ain't that lovely . . .

> Mrs. Miniver was the chief figure in a movie of the same name shown during the 1940s. In it, Mrs. Miniver kept up her courage and her gardening during the bombing of Great Britain in World War II. She sustained her family and brought them all back together.

TRAVIS (*tugging at his father's sleeve*) Daddy, can I give her mine now?

WALTER All right, son. (*Travis flies to get his gift.*) Travis didn't want to go in with the rest of us. Mama. He got his own. (*somewhat amused*) We don't know what it is . . .

TRAVIS (*racing back in the room with a large hatbox and putting it in front of his grandmother*) Here!

MAMA Lord have mercy, baby. You done gone and bought your grandmother a hat?

TRAVIS (*very proud*) Open it!

She does and lifts out an elaborate, but very elaborate, wide gardening hat, and all the adults break up at the sight of it.

RUTH Travis, honey, what is that?

TRAVIS (*who thinks it is beautiful and appropriate*) It's a gardening hat! Like the ladies always have on in the magazines when they work in their gardens.

BENEATHA (*giggling fiercely*) Travis—we were trying to make Mama Mrs. Miniver—not Scarlett O'Hara!

MAMA (*indignantly*) What's the matter with you all! This here is a beautiful hat! (*absurdly*) I always wanted me one just like it!

> Scarlett O'Hara was the lead character in *Gone With The Wind*, a novel and then a movie set in the deep South during the American Civil War. Scarlett, a beautiful and impetuous woman, wore some large, flamboyant hats in the film.

She pops it on her head to prove it to her grandson, and the hat is ludicrous and considerably oversized.

RUTH Hot dog! Go, Mama!

WALTER (*doubled over with laughter*) I'm sorry, Mama—but you look like you ready to go out and chop you some cotton sure enough!

> In terms of pacing in the action, note the relatively lighthearted mood following Lindner's hasty departure.

They all laugh except Mama, out of deference to Travis' feelings.

MAMA (*gathering the boy up to her*) Bless your heart—this is the prettiest hat I ever owned— (*Walter, Ruth and Beneatha chime in*—*noisily, festively and insincerely congratulating Travis on his gift.*) What are we all standing around here for? We ain't finished packin' yet. Bennie, you ain't packed one book.

The bell rings.

BENEATHA That couldn't be the movers . . . it's not hardly two good yet—

Beneatha goes into her room. Mama starts for door.

WALTER (*turning, stiffening*) Wait—wait—I'll get it.

> How is the audience alerted that something menacing is in store?

He stands and looks at the door.

MAMA You expecting company, son?

WALTER *(just looking at the door)* Yeah—yeah . . .

Mama looks at Ruth, and they exchange innocent and unfrightened glances.

MAMA *(not understanding)* Well, let them in, son.

BENEATHA *(from her room)* We need some more string.

MAMA Travis—you run to the hardware and get me some string cord.

Mama goes out and Walter turns and looks at Ruth. Travis goes to a dish for money.

RUTH Why don't you answer the door, man?

WALTER *(suddenly bounding across the floor to her)* 'Cause sometimes it hard to let the future begin! *(stooping down in her face)*

I got wings! You got wings!
All God's children got wings!

(He crosses to the door and throws it open. Standing there is a very slight little man in a not too prosperous business suit and with haunted frightened eyes and a hat pulled down tightly, brim up, around his forehead. Travis passes between the men and exits. Walter leans deep in the man's face, still in his jubilance.)

When I get to heaven gonna put on my wings,
Gonna fly all over God's heaven . . .

(The little man just stares at him.)

Heaven—

(Suddenly he stops and looks past the little man into the empty hallway.) Where's Willy, man?

BOBO He ain't with me.

WALTER *(not disturbed)* Oh—come on in. You know my wife.

BOBO *(dumbly, taking off his hat)* Yes—h'you, Miss Ruth.

RUTH *(quietly, a mood apart from her husband already, seeing Bobo)* Hello, Bobo.

WALTER You right on time today . . . Right on time. That's the way! *(He slaps Bobo on his back.)* Sit down . . . lemme hear.

Ruth stands stiffly and quietly in back of them, as though somehow she senses death, her eyes fixed on her husband.

BOBO *(his frightened eyes on the floor, his hat in his hands)* Could I please get a drink of water, before I tell you about it, Walter Lee?

Walter does not take his eyes off the man. Ruth goes blindly to the tap and gets a glass of water and brings it to Bobo.

WALTER There ain't nothing wrong, is there?

BOBO Lemme tell you—

WALTER Man—didn't nothing go wrong?

BOBO Lemme tell you—Walter Lee. *(looking at Ruth and talking to her*

Do any of the Younger women suspect anything unusual from Walter's expected guest? How does the playwright reveal their frame of mind?

In the description of Bobo, what leads the reader to dislike and fear him from the start?

more than to Walter) You know how it was. I got to tell you how it was. I mean first I got to tell you how it was all the way . . . I mean about the money I put in, Walter Lee . . .

WALTER *(with taut agitation now)* What about the money you put in?

BOBO Well—it wasn't much as we told you—me and Willy—*(He stops.)* I'm sorry, Walter. I got a bad feeling about it. I got a real bad feeling about it . . .

WALTER Man, what you telling me about all this for? . . . Tell me what happened in Springfield . . .

BOBO Springfield.

RUTH *(like a dead woman)* What was supposed to happen in Springfield?

BOBO *(to her)* This deal that me and Walter went into with Willy—Me and Willy was going to go down to Springfield and spread some money 'round so's we wouldn't have to wait so long for the liquor license . . . That's what we were going to do. Everybody said that was the way you had to do, you understand, Miss Ruth?

WALTER Man—what happened down there?

BOBO *(a pitiful man, near tears)* I'm trying to tell you, Walter.

WALTER *(screaming at him suddenly)* THEN TELL ME, GODDAMMIT . . . WHAT'S THE MATTER WITH YOU?

BOBO Man . . . I didn't go to no Springfield, yesterday.

WALTER *(halted, life hanging in the moment)* Why not?

BOBO *(the long way, the hard way to tell)* 'Cause I didn't have no reasons to . . .

WALTER Man, what are you talking about!

BOBO I'm talking about the fact that when I got to the train station yesterday morning—eight o'clock like we planned . . . Man—*Willy didn't never show up.*

WALTER Why . . . where was he . . . where is he?

BOBO That's what I'm trying to tell you . . . I don't know . . . I waited six hours . . . I called his house . . . and I waited . . . six hours . . . I waited in that train station six hours . . . *(breaking into tears)* That was all the extra money I had in the world . . . *(looking up at Walter with the tears running down his face)* Man, Willy is gone.

WALTER Gone, what you mean Willy is gone? Gone where? You mean he went by himself. You mean he went off to Springfield by himself—to take care of getting the license—*(turns and looks anxiously at Ruth)* You mean maybe he didn't want too many people in on the business down there? *(looks to Ruth again, as before)* You know Willy got his own ways. *(looks back to Bobo)* Maybe you was late yesterday and he just went on down there without you. Maybe—maybe—he's been callin' you at home tryin' to tell you what happened or something. Maybe—maybe—he just got sick. He's somewhere—he's got to be somewhere. We just got to find him—me and you got to find him. *(grabs Bobo senselessly by the collar and starts to shake him)* We got to!

Springfield, the capital of Illinois, is where official state licenses could be arranged for and granted.

Why is Walter frantically grasping at straws in trying to explain Willy's absence?

416 LORRAINE HANSBERRY

BOBO *(in sudden angry, frightened agony)* What's the matter with you, Walter! When a cat take off with your money he don't leave you no maps!

WALTER *(turning madly, as though he is looking for Willy in the very room)* Willy! . . . Willy . . . don't do it . . . Please don't do it . . . Man, not with that money . . . Man, please, not with that money . . . Oh, God . . . Don't let it be true . . . *(He is wandering around, crying out for Willy and looking for him or perhaps for help from God.)* Man . . . I trusted you . . . Man, I put my life in your hands . . . *(He starts to crumple down on the floor as Ruth just covers her face in horror. Mama opens the door and comes into the room, with Beneatha behind her.)* Man . . . *(He starts to pound the floor with his fists, sobbing wildly.)* That money is made out of my father's flesh . . .

BOBO *(standing over him helplessly)* I'm sorry, Walter . . . *(Only Walter's sobs reply. Bobo puts on his hat.)* I had my life staked on this deal, too . . .

He exits.

MAMA *(to Walter)* Son—*(She goes to him, bends down to him, talks to his bent head.)* Son . . . Is it gone? Son, I gave you sixty-five hundred dollars. Is it gone? All of it? Beneatha's money too?

WALTER *(lifting his head slowly)* Mama . . . I never . . . went to the bank at all . . .

MAMA *(not wanting to believe him)* You mean . . . your sister's school money . . . you used that too . . . Walter? . . .

WALTER Yessss! . . . All of it . . . It's all gone . . .

There is total silence. Ruth stands with her face covered with her hands; Beneatha leans forlornly against a wall, fingering a piece of red ribbon from the mother's gift. Mama stops and looks at her son without recognition and then, quite without thinking about it, starts to beat him senselessly in the face. Beneatha goes to them and stops it.

BENEATHA Mama!

Mama stops and looks at both of her children and rises slowly and wanders vaguely, aimlessly away from them.

MAMA I seen . . . him . . . night after night . . . come in . . . and look at that rug . . . and then look at me . . . the red showing in his eyes . . . the veins moving in his head . . . I seen him grow thin and old before he was forty . . . working and working and working like somebody's old horse . . . killing himself . . . and you—you give it all away in a day . .

BENEATHA Mama—

MAMA Oh, God . . . *(She looks up to Him.)* Look down here—and show me the strength.

BENEATHA Mama—

MAMA *(folding over)* Strength . . .

BENEATHA *(plaintively)* Mama . . .

MAMA Strength!

Curtain

The theme of betrayal resurfaces, as it had with Lindner's "deal" and Walter's opinion of Mama's earlier treatment of him, before she gave him the money. Now, not only has Willy betrayed Walter, but Walter has betrayed his sister, too, by using her share of the money for his "transaction."

Who is the "him" haunting Mama's memories here?

Why does Mama's repetition of the word "strength" offer a fitting close to this climactic scene?

A RAISIN IN THE SUN

ACT III

An hour later.

At curtain, there is a sullen light of gloom in the living room, gray light not unlike that which began the first scene of Act One. At left we can see Walter within his room, alone with himself. He is stretched out on the bed, his shirt out and open, his arms under his head. He does not smoke, he does not cry out, he merely lies there, looking up at the ceiling, much as if he were alone in the world.

In the living room Beneatha sits at the table, still surrounded by the now almost ominous packing crates. She sits looking off. We feel that this is a mood struck perhaps an hour before, and it lingers now, full of the empty sound of profound disappointment. We see on a line from her brother's bedroom the sameness of their attitudes. Presently the bell rings and Beneatha rises without ambition or interest in answering. It is Asagai, smiling broadly, striding into the room with energy and happy expectation and conversation.

> Why do the stage directions which describe Walter have special correlation with the spirit of the moment?

ASAGAI I came over . . . I had some free time. I thought I might help with the packing. Ah, I like the look of packing crates! A household in preparation for a journey! It depresses some people . . . but for me . . . it is another feeling. Something full of the flow of life, do you understand? Movement, progress . . . It makes me think of Africa.

BENEATHA Africa!

ASAGAI What kind of a mood is this? Have I told you how deeply you move me?

BENEATHA He gave away the money, Asagai . . .

ASAGAI Who gave away what money?

BENEATHA The insurance money. My brother gave it away.

ASAGAI Gave it away?

BENEATHA He made an investment! What a man even Travis wouldn't have trusted.

ASAGAI And it's gone?

BENEATHA Gone!

ASAGAI I'm very sorry . . . And you, now?

BENEATHA Me? . . . Me? . . . Me I'm nothing . . . Me. When I was very small . . . we used to take our sleds out in the wintertime and the only hills we had were the ice-covered stone steps of some houses down the street. And we used to fill them in with snow and make them smooth and slide down them all day . . . and it was very dangerous you know . . . far too steep . . . and sure enough one day a kid named Rufus came down too fast and hit the sidewalk . . . and we saw his face just split open right there in front of us . . . And I remember standing there looking at his bloody open face thinking that was the end of Rufus. But the ambulance came and they took him to the hospital and they fixed the broken bones and they sewed it all up . . . and the next time I saw Rufus he just had a little line down the middle of his face . . . I never got over that . . .

Walter sits up, listening on the bed. Throughout this scene it is important that we feel his reaction at all times, that he visibly respond to the words of his sister and Asagai.

418 LORRAINE HANSBERRY

ASAGAI What?

BENEATHA That that was what one person could do for another, fix him up—sew up the problem, make him all right again. That was the most marvelous thing in the world . . . I wanted to do that. I always thought it was the one concrete thing in the world that a human being could do. Fix up the sick, you know—and make them whole again. This was truly being God . . .

ASAGAI You wanted to be God?

BENEATHA No—I wanted to cure. It used to be so important to me. I wanted to cure. It used to matter. I used to care. I mean about people and how their bodies hurt . . .

ASAGAI And you've stopped caring?

BENEATHA Yes—I think so.

ASAGAI Why?

Walter rises, goes to the door of his room and is about to open it, then stops and stands listening, leaning on the door jamb.

BENEATHA Because it doesn't seem deep enough, close enough to what ails mankind—I mean this thing of sewing up bodies or administering drugs. Don't you understand? It was a child's reaction to the world. I thought that doctors had the secret to all the hurts. . . . That's the way a child sees things—or an idealist.

ASAGAI Children see things very well sometimes—and idealists even better.

BENEATHA I know that's what you think. Because you are still where I left off—you still care. This is what you see for the world, for Africa. You with the dreams of the future will patch up all Africa —you are going to cure the Great Sore of colonialism with Independence——

ASAGAI Yes!

BENEATHA Yes—and you think that one word is the penicillin of the human spirit: "Independence!" But then what?

ASAGAI That will be the problem for another time. First we must get there.

BENEATHA And where does it end?

ASAGAI End? Who even spoke of an end? To life? To living?

BENEATHA An end to misery!

ASAGAI *(smiling)* You sound like a French intellectual.

BENEATHA No! I sound like a human being who just had her future taken right out of her hands! While I was sleeping in my bed in there, things were happening in this world that directly concerned me—and nobody asked me, consulted me—they just went out and did things—and changed my life. Don't you see there isn't any real progress, Asagai, there is only one large circle that we march in, around and around, each of us with our own little picture—in front of us—our own little mirage that we think is the future.

ASAGAI That is the mistake.

BENEATHA What?

What is the basis for Beneatha's new disillusionment with medicine and with life generally?

A RAISIN IN THE SUN

ASAGAI What you just said—about the circle. It isn't a circle—it is simply a long line—as in geometry, you know, one that reaches into infinity. And because we cannot see the end—we also cannot see how it changes. And it is very odd but those who see the changes are called "idealists"—and those who cannot, or refuse to think, they are the "realists." It is very strange, and amusing too, I think.

How is Asagai's vision of man similar to Mama's? How is it dissimilar?

BENEATHA You—you are almost religious.

ASAGAI Yes . . . I think I have the religion of doing what is necessary in the world—and of worshipping man—because he is so marvelous, you see.

BENEATHA Man is foul! And the human race deserves its misery!

ASAGAI You see: *you* have become the religious one in the old sense. Already, and after such a small defeat, you are worshipping despair.

Why does Asagai believe that Beneatha is "worshipping despair"?

BENEATHA From now on, I worship the truth—and the truth is that people are puny, small and selfish. . . .

ASAGAI Truth? Why is it that you despairing ones always think that only you have the truth? I never thought to see *you* like that. You! Your brother made a stupid, childish mistake—and you are grateful to him. So that now you can give up the ailing human race on account of it. You talk about what good is struggle; what good is anything? Where are we all going? And why are we bothering?

BENEATHA *And you cannot answer it!* All your talk and dreams about Africa and Independence. Independence and then what? What about all the crooks and petty thieves and just plain idiots who will come into power to steal and plunder the same as before—only now they will be black and do it in the name of the new Independence— You cannot answer that.

ASAGAI *(shouting over her)* I live the answer! *(pause)* In my village at home it is the exceptional man who can even read a newspaper . . . or who ever sees a book at all. I will go home and much of what I will have to say will seem strange to the people of my village . . . But I will teach and work and things will happen, slowly and swiftly. At times it will seem that nothing changes at all . . . and then again . . . the sudden dramatic events which make history leap into the future. And then quiet again. Retrogression even. Guns, murder, revolution. And I even will have moments when I wonder if the quiet was not better than all that death and hatred. But I will look about my village at the illiteracy and disease and ignorance and I will not wonder long. And perhaps . . . perhaps I will be a great man . . . I mean perhaps I will hold on to the substance of truth and find my way always with the right course . . . and perhaps for it I will be butchered in my bed some night by the servants of empire . . .

BENEATHA *The martyr!*

ASAGAI . . . or perhaps I shall live to be a very old man, respected and esteemed in my new nation . . . And perhaps I shall hold office and this is what I'm trying to tell you, Alaiyo; perhaps the things I believe now for my country will be wrong and outmoded, and I will not understand and do terrible things to have things my way or merely to keep my power. Don't you see that there will be young men and women, not British soldiers then, but my own black countrymen . . . to step out of the shadows some evening and slit my

Asagai's commentary extends far beyond simple rebellion against colonialism. It leads to the very nature of revolt against any inhibiting factors in the operations of a country. How do Asagai's remarks take into account a natural and continuing evolution of a sovereign state?

From the Tony Award-winning Broadway musical, Raisin!

then useless throat? Don't you see they have always been there . . . that they always will be. And that such a thing as my own death will be an advance? They who might kill me even . . . actually replenish me!

BENEATHA Oh, Asagai, I know all that.

ASAGAI Good! Then stop moaning and groaning and tell me what you plan to do.

BENEATHA Do?

ASAGAI I have a bit of a suggestion.

BENEATHA What?

ASAGAI *(rather quietly for him)* That when it is all over—that you come home with me—

BENEATHA *(slapping herself on the forehead with exasperation born of misunderstanding)* Oh—Asagai—at this moment you decide to be romantic!

ASAGAI *(quickly understanding the misunderstanding)* My dear, young creature of the New World—I do not mean across the city—I mean across the ocean; home—to Africa.

BENEATHA *(slowly understanding and turning to him with murmured amazement)* To—to Nigeria?

ASAGAI Yes! . . . *(smiling and lifting his arms playfully)* Three hundred years later the African Prince rose up out of the seas and swept the maiden back across the middle passage over which her ancestors had come—

Is Asagai afraid of any on-going revolutionary process in his homeland, even when it may mean his own overthrow?

A RAISIN IN THE SUN 421

BENEATHA *(unable to play)* Nigeria?

ASAGAI Nigeria. Home. *(coming to her with genuine romantic flippancy)* I will show you our mountains and our stars; and give you cool drinks from gourds and teach you the old songs and the ways of our people—and, in time, we will pretend that—*(very softly)*—you have only been away for a day—

She turns her back to him, thinking. He swings her around and takes her full in his arms in a long embrace which proceeds to passion.

BENEATHA *(pulling away)* You're getting me all mixed up—

ASAGAI Why?

BENEATHA Too many things—too many things have happened today. I must sit down and think. I don't know what I feel about anything right this minute.

She promptly sits down and props her chin on her fist.

ASAGAI *(charmed)* All right, I shall leave you. No—don't get up. *(touching her, gently, sweetly)* Just sit awhile and think . . . Never be afraid to sit awhile and think. *(He goes to door and looks at her.)* How often I have looked at you and said, "Ah—so this is what the New World hath finally wrought . . ."

He exits. Beneatha sits on alone. Presently Walter enters from his room and starts to rummage through things, feverishly looking for something. She looks up and turns in her seat.

> Asagai's premise concerning Beneatha and all American blacks seems to be that they simply are an extension in time and space of old-world Negro races.

BENEATHA *(hissingly)* Yes—just look at what the New World hath wrought! . . . Just look! *(She gestures with bitter disgust.)* There he is! *Monsieur le petit bourgeois noir*—himself! There he is—Symbol of a Rising Class! Entrepreneur! Titan of the system! *(Walter ignores her completely and continues frantically and destructively looking for something and hurling things to floor and tearing things out of their place in his search. Beneatha ignores the eccentricity of his actions and goes on with the monologue of insult.)* Did you dream of yachts on Lake Michigan, Brother? Did you see yourself on that Great Day sitting down at the Conference Table, surrounded by all the mighty bald-headed men in America? All halted, waiting, breathless, waiting for your pronouncements on industry? Waiting for you—Chairman of the Board? *(Walter finds what he is looking for—a small piece of white paper—and pushes it in his pocket and puts on his coat and rushes out without ever having looked at her. She shouts after him.)* I look at you and I see the final triumph of stupidity in the world!

> "*Monsieur le petit bourgeois noir*" means "Mister Middle-class Black Businessman." Why does Beneatha's epithet for Walter have such sting?
>
> In Greek myth Titan was a giant god—hence here the top man in the business enterprise system.

The door slams and she returns to just sitting again. Ruth comes quickly out of Mama's room.

RUTH Who was that?

BENEATHA Your husband.

RUTH Where did he go?

BENEATHA Who knows—maybe he has an appointment at U.S. Steel.

RUTH *(anxiously, with frightened eyes)* You didn't say nothing bad to him, did you?

BENEATHA Bad? Say anything bad to him? No—I told him he was a sweet boy and full of dreams and everything is strictly peachy keen, as the ofay kids say!

Mama enters from her bedroom. She is lost, vague, trying to catch hold, to make some sense of her former command of the world, but it still eludes her. A sense of waste overwhelms her gait; a measure of apology rides on her shoulders. She goes to her plant, which has remained on the table, looks at it, picks it up and takes it to the window sill and sits it outside, and she stands and looks at it a long moment. Then she closes the window, straightens her body with effort and turns around to her children.

MAMA Well—ain't it a mess in here, though? *(a false cheerfulness, a beginning of something)* I guess we all better stop moping around and get some work done. All this unpacking and everything we got to do. *(Ruth raises her head slowly in response to the sense of the line; and Beneatha in similar manner turns very slowly to look at her mother.)* One of you all better call the moving people and tell 'em not to come.

RUTH Tell 'em not to come?

MAMA Of course, baby. Ain't no need in 'em coming all the way here and having to go back. They charges for that too. *(She sits down, fingers to her brow, thinking.)* Lord, ever since I was a little girl, I always remembers people saying, "Lena—Lena Eggleston, you aims too high all the time. You needs to slow down and see life a little more like it is. Just slow down some." That's what they always used to say down home—"Lord, that Lena Eggleston is a high-minded thing. She'll get her due one day!"

RUTH No, Lena . . .

MAMA Me and Big Walter just didn't never learn right.

RUTH Lena, no! We gotta go. Bennie—tell her . . . *(She rises and crosses to Beneatha with her arms outstretched. Beneatha doesn't respond.)* Tell her we can still move . . . the notes ain't but a hundred and twenty-five a month. We got four grown people in this house—we can work . . .

MAMA *(to herself)* Just aimed too high all the time—

RUTH *(turning and going to Mama fast—the words pouring out with urgency and desperation)* Lena—I'll work . . . I'll work twenty hours a day in all the kitchens in Chicago . . . I'll strap my baby on my back if I have to and scrub all the floors in America and wash all the sheets in America if I have to—but we got to move . . . We got to get out of here . . .

Mama reaches out absently and pats Ruth's hand.

MAMA No—I sees things differently now. Been thinking 'bout some of the things we could do to fix this place up some. I seen a second-hand bureau over on Maxwell Street just the other day that could fit right there. *(She points to where the new furniture might go. Ruth wanders away from her.)* Would need some new handles on it and then a little varnish and then it look like something brand-new. And—we can put up them new curtains in the kitchen . . . Why this place be looking fine. Cheer us all up so that we forget trouble ever came . . . *(to Ruth)* And you could get some nice screens to put up in your room round the baby's bassinet . . . *(She looks at both of them, plead-*

"Ofay" is a deprecating term used by some blacks to refer to some whites.

How is Lena Younger's total capitulation indicated to the audience?

Why is it so crucial that the Youngers move at this time?

ingly.) Sometimes you just got to know when to give up some things . . . and hold on to what you got.

Walter enters from the outside, looking spent and leaning against the door, his coat hanging from him.

MAMA Where you been, son?

WALTER *(breathing hard)* Made a call.

MAMA To who, son?

WALTER To The Man.

MAMA What man, baby?

WALTER The Man, Mama. Don't you know who The Man is?

RUTH Walter Lee?

WALTER *The Man.* Like the guys in the streets say—The Man. Captain Boss—Mistuh Charley . . . Old Captain Please Mr. Bossman . . .

BENEATHA *(suddenly)* Lindner!

WALTER That's right! That's good. I told him to come right over.

BENEATHA *(fiercely, understanding)* For what? What do you want to see him for!

WALTER *(looking at his sister)* We going to do business with him.

MAMA What you talking 'bout, son?

WALTER Talking 'bout life, Mama. You all always telling me to see life like it is. Well—I laid in there on my back today . . . and I figured it out. Life just like it is. Who gets and who don't get. *(He sits down with his coat on and laughs.)* Mama, you know it's all divided up. Life is. Sure enough. Between the takers and the "tooken." *(He laughs.)* I've figured it out finally. *(He looks around at them.)* Yeah. Some of us always getting "tooken." *(He laughs.)* People like Willy Harris, they don't never get "tooken." And you know why the rest of us do? 'Cause we all mixed up. Mixed up bad. We get to looking 'round for the right and the wrong; and we worry about it and cry about it and stay up nights trying to figure out 'bout the wrong and the right of things all the time . . . And all the time, man, them takers is out there operating, just taking and taking. Willy Harris? Shoot—Willy Harris don't even count. He don't even count in the big scheme of things. But I'll say one thing for old Willy Harris . . . he's taught me something. He's taught me to keep my eye on what counts in this world. Yeah—*(shouting out a little)* Thanks, Willy!

RUTH What did you call that man for, Walter Lee?

WALTER Called him to tell him to come on over to the show. Gonna put on a show for the man. Just what he wants to see. You see, Mama, the man came here today and he told us that them people out there where you want us to move—well they so upset they willing to pay us not to move out there. *(He laughs again.)* And—and oh, Mama—you would of been proud of the way me and Ruth and Bennie acted. We told him to get out . . . Lord have mercy! We told the man to get out. Oh, we was some proud folks this afternoon, yeah. *(He lights a cigarette.)* We were still full of that old-time stuff . . .

> In current colloquial usage, "The Man" means the man in charge. Who does Walter mean specifically?

> "Mistuh Charley" is a black expression for a white man.

RUTH (*coming toward him slowly*) You talking 'bout taking them people's money to keep us from moving in that house?

WALTER I ain't just talking 'bout it, baby—I'm telling you that's what's going to happen.

BENEATHA Oh, God! Where is the bottom! Where is the real honest-to-God bottom so he can't go any farther!

WALTER See—that's the old stuff. You and that boy that was here today. You all want everybody to carry a flag and a spear and sing some marching songs, huh? You wanna spend your life looking into things and trying to find the right and the wrong part, huh? Yeah. You know what's going to happen to that boy someday—he'll find himself sitting in a dungeon, locked in forever—and the takers will have the key! Forget it, baby! There ain't no causes—there ain't nothing but taking in this world, and he who takes most is smartest—and it don't make a damn bit of difference *how*.

MAMA You making something inside me cry, son. Some awful pain inside me.

WALTER Don't cry, Mama. Understand. That white man is going to walk in that door able to write checks for more money than we ever had. It's important to him and I'm going to help him . . . I'm going to put on the show, Mama.

MAMA Son—I come from five generations of people who was slaves and sharecroppers—but ain't nobody in my family never let nobody pay 'em no money that was a way of telling us we wasn't fit to walk the earth. We ain't never been that poor. (*raising her eyes and looking at him*) We ain't never been that dead inside.

BENEATHA Well—we are dead now. All the talk about dreams and sunlight that goes on in this house. All dead.

WALTER What's the matter with you all! I didn't make this world! It was give to me this way! Hell, yes, I want me some yachts someday! Yes, I want to hang some real pearls 'round my wife's neck. Ain't she supposed to wear no pearls? Somebody tell me—tell me, who decides which women is suppose to wear pearls in this world. I tell you I am a *man*—and I think my wife should wear some pearls in this world!

This last line hangs a good while and Walter begins to move about the room. The word "Man" has penetrated his consciousness; he mumbles it to himself repeatedly between strange agitated pauses as he moves about.

MAMA Baby, how you going to feel on the inside?

WALTER Fine! . . . Going to feel fine . . . a man . . .

MAMA You won't have nothing left then, Walter Lee.

WALTER (*coming to her*) I'm going to feel fine, Mama. I'm going to look that son-of-a-bitch in the eyes and say—(*He falters.*)—and say, "All right, Mr. Lindner—(*He falters even more.*)—that's your neighborhood out there. You got the right to keep it like you want. You got the right to have it like you want. Just write the check and—the house is yours." And, and I am going to say—(*His voice almost breaks.*) And you—you people just put the money in my hand and you won't have to live next to this bunch of stinking niggers! . . . (*He

After much brooding, Walter has arrived at fresh conclusions about the best way to get along in life. What are his basic points, according to his searing dialogue?

Walter's innermost turmoil grows out of his urgent need to prove himself a man. What does his mother warn him about, with respect to the cost of such proof according to Walter's definition of a man?

A RAISIN IN THE SUN   425

straightens up and moves away from his mother, walking around the room.) Maybe—maybe I'll just get down on my black knees . . . *(He does so; Ruth and Bennie and Mama watch him in frozen horror.)* Captain, Mistuh, Bossman. *(He starts crying.)* A-hee-hee-hee! *(wringing his hands in profoundly anguished imitation)* Yasssssuh! Great White Father, just gi' ussen de money, fo' God's sake, and we's ain't gwine come out deh and dirty up yo' white folks neighborhood . . .

He breaks down completely, then gets up and goes into the bedroom.

BENEATHA That is not a man. That is nothing but a toothless rat.

MAMA Yes—death done come in this here house. *(She is nodding, slowly, reflectively.)* Done come walking in my house. On the lips of my children. You what supposed to be my beginning again. You—what supposed to be my harvest. *(to Beneatha)* You—you mourning your brother?

BENEATHA He's no brother of mine.

MAMA What you say?

BENEATHA I said that that individual in that room is no brother of mine.

> Ironically, Beneatha fails to see the correlation between her repudiation of her brother and the disciples' denial of Jesus Christ during moments of crisis.

MAMA That's what I thought you said. You feeling like you better than he is today? *(Beneatha does not answer.)* Yes? What you tell him a minute ago? That he wasn't a man? Yes? You give him up for me? You done wrote his epitaph too—like the rest of the world? Well, who give you the privilege?

BENEATHA Be on my side for once! You saw what he just did, Mama! You saw him—down on his knees. Wasn't it you who taught me—to despise any man who would do that. Do what he's going to do.

MAMA Yes—I taught you that. Me and your daddy. But I thought I taught you something else too . . . I thought I taught you to love him.

BENEATHA Love him? There is nothing left to love.

MAMA There is always something left to love. And if you ain't learned that, you ain't learned nothing. *(looking at her)* Have you cried for that boy today? I don't mean for yourself and for the family 'cause we lost the money. I mean for him; what he been through and what it done to him. Child, when do you think is the time to love somebody the most; when they done good and made things easy for everybody? Well then, you ain't through learning—because that ain't the time at all. It's when he's at his lowest and can't believe in hisself 'cause the world done whipped him so. When you starts measuring somebody, measure him right, child, measure him right. Make sure you done taken into account what hills and valleys he come through before he got to wherever he is.

> According to Mrs. Younger's view of life, what is more important: pride in one's self or love for others?

Travis bursts into the room at the end of the speech, leaving the door open.

TRAVIS Grandmama—the moving men are downstairs! The truck just pulled up.

MAMA *(turning and looking at him)* Are they, baby? They downstairs?

She sighs and sits. Lindner appears in the doorway. He peers in and knocks lightly, to gain attention, and comes in. All turn to look at him.

426 LORRAINE HANSBERRY

LINDNER *(hat and briefcase in hand)* Uh—hello . . .

Ruth crosses mechanically to the bedroom door and opens it and lets it swing open freely and slowly as the lights come up on Walter within, still in his coat, sitting at the far corner of the room. He looks up and out through the room to Lindner.

RUTH He's here.

A long minute passes and Walter slowly gets up.

LINDNER *(coming to the table with efficiency, putting his briefcase on the table and starting to unfold papers and unscrew fountain pens)* Well, I certainly was glad to hear from you people. *(Walter has begun the trek out of the room, slowly and awkwardly, rather like a small boy, passing the back of his sleeve across his mouth from time to time.)* Life can really be so much simpler than people let it be most of the time. Well—with whom do I negotiate? You, Mrs. Younger, or your son here? *(Mama sits with her hands folded on her lap and her eyes closed as Walter advances. Travis goes close to Lindner and looks at the papers curiously.)* Just some official papers, sonny.

RUTH Travis, you go downstairs.

MAMA *(opening her eyes and looking into Walter's)* No. Travis, you stay right here. And you make him understand what you doing, Walter Lee. You teach him good. Like Willy Harris taught you. You show where our five generations done come to. Go ahead, son—

WALTER *(Looks down into his boy's eyes. Travis grins at him merrily and Walter draws him beside him with his arm lightly around his shoulders.)* Well, Mr. Lindner. *(Beneatha turns away.)* We called you—*(There is a profound, simple groping quality in his speech.)*—because, well, me and my family *(He looks around and shifts from one foot to the other.)* Well—we are very plain people . . .

LINDNER Yes—

WALTER I mean—I have worked as a chauffeur most of my life—and my wife here, she does domestic work in people's kitchens. So does my mother. I mean—we are plain people . . .

LINDNER Yes, Mr. Younger—

WALTER *(really like a small boy, looking down at his shoes and then up at the man)* And—uh—well, my father, well, he was a laborer most of his life.

LINDNER *(absolutely confused)* Uh, yes—

WALTER *(looking down at his toes once again)* My father almost beat a man to death once because this man called him a bad name or something, you know what I mean?

LINDNER No, I'm afraid I don't.

WALTER *(finally straightening up)* Well, what I mean is that we come from people who had a lot of pride. I mean—we are very proud people. And that's my sister over there and she's going to be a doctor—and we are very proud—

LINDNER Well—I am sure that is very nice, but—

WALTER *(starting to cry and facing the man eye to eye)* What I am telling

Why does Mama insist that Travis remain to witness Walter's talk with Lindner? How does it set the stage for the ultimate climax of the drama? What is at stake for everyone?

A RAISIN IN THE SUN   427

Mama (Claudia McNeil) listens as Mr. Lindner speaks, from the motion picture.

you is that we called you over here to tell you that we are very proud and that this is—this is my son, who makes the sixth generation of our family in this country, and that we have all thought about your offer and we have decided to move into our house because my father—my father—he earned it. *(Mama has her eyes closed and is rocking back and forth as though she were in church, with her head nodding the amen yes.)* We don't want to make no trouble for nobody or fight no causes—but we will try to be good neighbors. That's all we got to say. *(He looks the man absolutely in the eyes.)* We don't want your money.

He turns and walks away from the man.

LINDNER *(looking around at all of them)* I take it then that you have decided to occupy.

BENEATHA That's what the man said.

LINDNER *(to Mama in her reverie)* Then I would like to appeal to you, Mrs. Younger. You are older and wiser and understand things better I am sure . . .

MAMA *(rising)* I am afraid you don't understand. My son said we was going to move and there ain't nothing left for me to say. *(shaking her head with double meaning)* You know how these young folks is nowadays, mister. Can't do a thing with 'em. Good-bye.

It is ironic that Mama refuses to override Walter's decision to move into their new home. What has Walter proven, in the eyes of the family?

428   LORRAINE HANSBERRY

LINDNER *(folding up his materials)* Well—if you are that final about it . . . There is nothing left for me to say. *(He finishes. He is almost ignored by the family, who are concentrating on Walter Lee. At the door Lindner halts and looks around.)* I sure hope you people know what you're doing.

He shakes his head and exits.

RUTH *(looking around and coming to life)* Well, for God's sake—if the moving men are here—LET'S GET THE HELL OUT OF HERE!

MAMA *(into action)* Ain't it the truth! Look at all this here mess. Ruth, put Travis' good jacket on him . . . Walter Lee, fix your tie and tuck your shirt in, you look just like somebody's hoodlum. Lord have mercy, where is my plant? *(She flies to get it amid the general bustling of the family, who are deliberately trying to ignore the nobility of the past moment.)* You all start on down . . . Travis child, don't go empty-handed . . . Ruth, where did I put that box with my skillets in it? I want to be in charge of it myself . . . I'm going to make us the biggest dinner we ever ate tonight . . . Beneatha, what's the matter with them stockings? Pull them things up, girl . . .

The family starts to file out as two moving men appear and begin to carry out the heavier pieces of furniture, bumping into the family as they move about.

BENEATHA Mama, Asagai—asked me to marry him today and go to Africa—

MAMA *(in the middle of her getting-ready activity)* He did? You ain't old enough to marry nobody—*(seeing the moving men lifting one of her chairs precariously)* Darling, that ain't no bale of cotton, please handle it so we can sit in it again. I had that chair twenty-five years . . .

The movers sigh with exasperation and go on with their work.

BENEATHA *(girlishly and unreasonably trying to pursue the conversation)* To go to Africa, Mama—be a doctor in Africa . . .

MAMA *(distracted)* Yes, baby—

WALTER Africa! What he want you to go to Africa for?

BENEATHA To practice there . . .

WALTER Girl, if you don't get all them silly ideas out your head! You better marry yourself a man with some loot . . .

BENEATHA *(angrily, precisely as in the first scene of the play)* What have you got to do with who I marry!

WALTER Plenty. Now I think George Murchison—

He and Beneatha go out yelling at each other vigorously; Beneatha is heard saying that she would not marry George Murchison if he were Adam and she were Eve, etc. The anger is loud and real till their voices diminish. Ruth stands at the door and turns to Mama and smiles knowingly.

MAMA *(fixing her hat at last)* Yeah—they something all right, my children . . .

RUTH Yeah—they're something. Let's go, Lena.

MAMA *(stalling, starting to look around at the house)* Yes—I'm coming. Ruth—

Has Hansberry improved the personalities of her characters by the end of the play? Why would such a transformation ring false?

Mama (Claudia McNeil) and her plant.

RUTH Yes?

MAMA (*quietly, woman to woman*) He finally come into his manhood today, didn't he? Kind of like a rainbow after the rain . . .

RUTH (*biting her lip lest her own pride explode in front of Mama*) Yes, Lena.

Walter's voice calls for them raucously.

MAMA (*waving Ruth out vaguely*) All right, honey—go on down. I be down directly.

Ruth hesitates, then exits. Mama stands, at last alone in the living room, her plant on the table before her as the lights start to come down. She looks around at all the walls and ceilings and suddenly, despite herself, while the children call below, a great heaving thing rises in her and she puts her fist to her mouth, takes a final desperate look, pulls her coat about her, pats her hat and goes out. The lights dim down. The door opens and she comes back in, grabs her plant, and goes out for the last time. Curtain.

What is the audience to infer from Mama's final silent look around the apartment at the play's end?

An astute viewer of *A Raisin in the Sun* will recognize that the play's theme grows out of the source for its title, Langston Hughes' poem, "Montage of a Dream Deferred." If we re-read that poem (see the "Preview" section for this play), we will see that Hughes concludes the poem with the suggestion that the dream might explode.

POSTVIEW: THEME

1. Why can the play be seen as a study in deferred dreams? Who in the drama tells of his (her) dreams for the future?

2. Why is the purchase of a house symbolic of a long-sought dream for generations of people like Lena and Ruth, trapped in a low socioeconomic position?
3. What will the realization of a house of their own mean to each member of the Younger family?
4. Why does the move into a middle-class white neighborhood signify an act of "revolt" on the part of the Youngers?

Complicating the Youngers' attempt to make their dream come true is the matter of racial prejudice, which arises as a corrolated theme.

5. Who serves as the play's focal point for the white community's discrimination?
6. Is Hansberry's treatment of the white people's attitudes in Clybourne Park wholly one-sided?
7. Does the Youngers' struggle for their dreams result exclusively from their status as a racial minority in Chicago? Could certain white families also encounter similar hurdles in attaining their objectives in life? How?

Although *A Raisin in the Sun* was first performed in early 1959, it portrays many present-day social matters.

8. Why can Beneatha be considered a "women's lib" figure?
9. How does Asagai personify the present emphasis on increased black awareness of their heritage?
10. How does Asagai's insistence on an "Afro/natural" hair style and African clothes fit in with the black desire to create a separate, unique racial identity? Does George Murchison agree with Asagai's theories? Why, in your opinion?
11. Why can Asagai be considered a "male chauvinist"?
12. How does the issue of God enter into the generation gap that has developed between Beneatha and her mother?
13. Where in the play do we encounter debate over abortion?

Hansberry's drama intertwines many social themes of topical importance. Additionally, the play involves the issue of one's character, particularly when it is placed under stress.

14. How does Mrs. Younger's strength of character serve to substantiate the matriarchal family design, frequently alleged to exist in poor black households?
15. What is Walter's most fervent desire in life? How does his goal relate to his sense of manhood?
16. Has Hansberry characterized Walter as a profound thinker and outstanding young man, or as an ordinary human being? Why is such a person most appropriate for conveying her theme?
17. How do Beneatha's two suitors serve as allegorical alternatives for the life ahead of her? Does the play insist that either one's path in life is exactly correct for Beneatha?
18. What is the thematic significance of the plant Mrs. Younger takes with her to the new home?

CATALOGUE OF RESOURCES

Euripides, *Medea*

SOME HELPFUL BOOKS AND ESSAYS:

Bates, William N. *Euripides: A Student of Human Nature.* New York: Russell & Russell, 1969.

Conacher, D. J. *Euripidean Drama.* Toronto: University of Toronto Press, 1967.

Decharme, Paul. *Euripides and the Spirit of His Dramas.* Translated by James Loeb. Port Washington, N.Y.: Kennikat Press, 1968.

Kitto, H. D. F. *Greek Tragedy.* 3d. rev. ed. New York: Barnes & Noble, 1966.

Lucas, F. L. *Euripides and His Influence.* New York: Gordon Press, 1923.

Melchinger, Siegfried. *Euripides.* Translated by Samuel R. Rosenbaum. New York: Frederick Ungar, 1973.

RECORDING OF THE PLAY:

Medea, featuring Judith Anderson and Anthony Quayle (2 disks). Caedmon S-302. Also, consider any of the several recordings of Cherubini's opera *Medea.*

FILM VERSION OF THE PLAY:

Medea (1971) in Italian with English subtitles was directed by Paolo Pasolini and stars Maria Callas. It is available through New Line Cinema, 235 Second Avenue, New York, N.Y. 10003.

Shakespeare, *Twelfth Night*

SOME HELPFUL BOOKS AND ESSAYS:

Barber, C. L. *Shakespeare's Festive Comedy.* Princeton: Princeton University Press, 1959.

Draper, John W. *The Twelfth Night of Shakespeare's Audience.* Stanford: Stanford University Press, 1950.

Hotson, John Leslie. *The First Night of "Twelfth Night."* New York: Macmillan, 1961.

King, Walter N., ed. *Twentieth Century Interpretations of "Twelfth Night": A Collection of Critical Essays.* Englewood Cliffs, N.J.: Prentice-Hall, 1968.

Leech, Clifford. *"Twelfth Night" and Shakespearian Comedy.* Oxford University Press, 1965.

Palmer, David J., ed. *Shakespeare: "Twelfth Night": A Casebook.* London: Macmillan, 1972.

Salingar, L. G. "The Design of *Twelfth Night,*" *Shakespeare Quarterly* 9 (1958): 117-139.

RECORDINGS OF THE PLAY:

Twelfth Night, Marlowe Society (3 disks). Argo ZPR-186/8.

Twelfth Night, featuring Paul Scofield (3 disks). Caedmon SRS-S-213.

Also, consider the rock musical based on *Twelfth Night: Your Own Thing.* RCA LOC-1148.

FILM VERSIONS OF THE PLAY:

Twelfth Night (1956) in Russian with English subtitles was directed by Yakov Fried and stars Klara Luchko. It is available through Twyman Films, Inc., 329 Salem Avenue, Dayton, Ohio 45401.

Twelfth Night—An Introduction (1969), selected scenes from the play (23 minutes), was produced by Seaben. It is available through Bailey Film Association, 2211 Michigan Avenue, Santa Monica, California 90404.

Ibsen, *An Enemy of the People*

SOME HELPFUL BOOKS AND ESSAYS:

Downs, Brian W. *Ibsen: The Intellectual Background.* New York: Octagon Books, 1969.

Knight, G. Wilson. *Henrik Ibsen.* New York: Grove Press, 1962.

Lyons, Charles R. *Henrik Ibsen: The Divided Consciousness*. Carbondale: Southern Illinois University Press, 1972.

McFarlane, James, ed. *Henrik Ibsen*. Penguin Critical Anthologies. Baltimore: Penguin Books, 1970.

Mayer, Michael L. *Ibsen: A Biography*. Garden City, N.Y.: Doubleday, 1971.

Sprinchorn, Evert, ed. *Letters and Speeches*. New York: Hill & Wang, 1964.

RECORDING OF THE PLAY:

There is no recording of Ibsen's drama available, but Arthur Miller's adaptation of the work, also titled *An Enemy of the People*, is available as performed by the Lincoln Center Repertory Theatre (3 disks). Caedmon S-TRS-349.

O'Neill, *A Touch of the Poet*

SOME HELPFUL BOOKS AND ESSAYS:

Bogard, Travis. *Contour in Time: The Plays of Eugene O'Neill*. New York: Oxford University Press, 1972.

Frenz, Horst. *Eugene O'Neill*. Translated by Helen Sebba. New York: Ungar, 1971.

Gassner, John. *Eugene O'Neill*. Minneapolis: Univ. of Minnesota Press, 1965.

Gassner, John, ed. *O'Neill: A Collection of Critical Essays*. Englewood Cliffs, N.J.: Prentice-Hall, 1964.

Gelb, Arthur and Barbara. *O'Neill*. rev. ed. New York: Harper and Row, 1974.

Leech, Clifford. *Eugene O'Neill*. New York: Grove Press, 1963.

Marcus, Mordecai. "Eugene O'Neill's Debt to Thoreau in *A Touch of the Poet*." *Journal of English and Germanic Philology* 62 (1963): 270-279.

Roy, Emil. "The Archetypal Unity of Eugene O'Neill's Drama." *Comparative Drama* 3 (1969-1970): 263-274.

Miller, *The Crucible*

SOME HELPFUL BOOKS AND ESSAYS:

Corrigan, Robert. "The Achievement of Arthur Miller." *Comparative Drama* 3 (1968): 141-160.

Fender, Stephen. "Precision and Pseudo Precision in *The Crucible*." *Journal of American Studies* 1 (1967): 87-98.

Hill, Philip. "*The Crucible*: A Structural View." *Modern Drama* 10 (1967): 312-317.

Hogan, Robert. *Arthur Miller*. Minneapolis: University of Minnesota Press, 1964.

Moss, Leonard. *Arthur Miller*. New York: Twayne, 1967.

Popkin, Henry. "Arthur Miller's *The Crucible*." *College English* 26 (1964): 139-146.

Weales, Gerald, ed. *The Crucible: Text and Criticism*. New York: Viking Press, 1971.

In addition, consider the opera adapted from Miller's play, also titled *The Crucible*, written by Robert Ward with libretto by Bernard Stambler. It is available through Galaxy Music Corporation, Highgate Press, New York, N.Y.

RECORDINGS OF THE PLAY:

There is no recording of the complete drama. There is, however, a one-disk version of excerpts from Miller's *The Crucible*. Spoken Arts 704.

Also, there is a recording of Robert Ward's opera version of *The Crucible* (2 disks), featuring Bible and Ludgin. Composers Recordings, Inc. (CRI) S-168.

Hansberry, *A Raisin in the Sun*

SOME HELPFUL BOOKS AND ESSAYS:

Abramson, Doris. *Negro Playwrights in the American Theatre 1925-1959*. New York: Columbia University Press, 1969.

Bontemps, Arna. "The New Black Renaissance." *Negro Digest*, November, 1961.

Isaacs, Harold R. Five Writers and Their African Ancestors. *Phylon*, 21 (1960), 243-65.

Nemiroff, Robert, ed. *Les Blancs: The Collected Last Plays of Lorraine Hansberry*. New York: Random House, 1972.

Nemiroff, Robert, adapter. *To Be Young, Gifted, and Black*. Englewood Cliffs, N.J.: Prentice-Hall, 1969.

RECORDINGS OF THE PLAY:

A Raisin in the Sun featuring Ruby Dee (3 disks). Caedmon 355.

Also, consider the recording of the musical drama adapted from *A Raisin in the Sun*, which is titled *Raisin* and which earned several Tony Awards for its stage version in 1973 and 1974. Columbia Records KS-32754.

FILM VERSION OF THE PLAY:

A Raisin in the Sun (Columbia Pictures, 1961) was directed by Daniel Petrie and stars Sidney Poitier, Claudia McNeil, and Ruby Dee. It is available for rental through Twyman Films, Inc., 329 Salem Avenue, Dayton, Ohio 45401.

INDEX OF KEY TERMS AND DEFINITIONS

action
    falling, 5
    rising, 5
antagonist, 7
Aristotle
    definition of drama, 3, 6
    See also *Poetics*, by Aristotle
aside, 91
blocking (for performance), 8, 399
box set, 117
characters, 4, 6
characterization, 122
chorus, 7
    in classical Greek drama, 21–22, 31
climax, 5
complications, 5
coryphaeus, 14. *See also* Greek drama
crisis, 5
cultural assimilation, 206, 384
denouement, 5, 58, 119
deus ex machina, 49
development, 5, 118
dialogue, 7
    of realism, 128
dithyramb, 14. *See also* Greek drama
domestic tragedy, 271
double-take, 377
dramatic irony, 137
eccyclema, 49. *See also* Greek drama
Euripides, 12–16
exposition, 5, 57, 118, 360
expressionism, 195
First Folio, 55. *See also* William Shakespeare
foreshadowing, 21, 90–91, 375
Greek drama (classical), 12–16
groundlings, 55
Hansberry, Lorraine, 359–360
"Harlem" (poem), by Langston Hughes, 362

Ibsen, Henrik, 115–117
kinetic movement, 4
language, 7
    use of dialects, 199, 298, 365, 369
Miller, Arthur, 270–272
modern drama, 116–117, passim
    drama of ideas, 116
    problem plays, 116
    social drama, 116, 360
O'Neill, Eugene, 194–196
orchestra, 15. *See also* Greek drama
parados, 15. *See also* Greek drama
plot, 4
Poetics, by Aristotle, 3
proscenium stage, 117
proskenion, 15. *See also* Greek drama
protagonist, 7
pun, 59
raisonneur, 7
realism, 116–117, 119–120, 128
representationalism, 195
resolution, 5
satire, 15
Shakespeare, William, 54–55
    fools in the works of, 85
    use of language in, 64–65
    theater conventions during lifetime of, 55, 59, 60
skene, 15. *See also* Greek drama
soliloquy, 7, 72
stage business, 302
stage directions, 7
    introduced in dialogue, 161
    to parallel action of plot, 165, 166, 208
stichomythia, 26, 33
theatron, 15. *See also* Greek drama
theme, 4, 52
well-made play, 5–6

PICTURE CREDITS

Medea
Page 16, Bettmann Archive, Inc.; p. 17, Greek National Tourist Office; p. 47, Culver Pictures, Inc.; p. 52, Greek National Tourist Office.

Twelfth Night
Page 54, Folger Shakespeare Library, Courtesy the Vicar and Churchwardens of Holy Trinity Church; p. 56, Bettmann Archive, Inc.; p. 57, Bettmann Archive, Inc.; p. 82, Theatre Collection, The New York Public Library at Lincoln Center—Astor, Lenox, and Tilden Foundations; p. 88, Friedman-Abeles; p. 110, Theatre Collection, The New York Public Library at Lincoln Center—Astor, Lenox, and Tilden Foundations; p. 113, Theatre Collection, The New York Public Library at Lincoln Center—Astor, Lenox, and Tilden Foundations/Bert Andrews.

An Enemy of the People
Page 115, Bettmann Archive, Inc.; p. 134, Culver Pictures, Inc.; p. 162, Theatre Collection, The New York Public Library at Lincoln Center—Astor, Lenox, and Tilden Foundations; p. 168, Theatre Collection, The New York Public Library at Lincoln Center—Astor, Lenox, and Tilden Foundations.

A Touch of the Poet
Page 194, photograph by Muray, The Bettmann Archive, Inc.; p. 196, George E. Joseph; p. 233, George E. Joseph; p. 251, Culver Pictures, Inc.; p. 263, George E. Joseph.

The Crucible
Page 270, Friedman-Abeles; p. 272, Bettmann Archive, Inc.; p. 301, Martha Swope; p. 334, Theatre Collection, The New York Public Library—Astor, Lenox, and Tilden Foundations; p. 352, Martha Swope.

A Raisin in the Sun
Page 359, Springer/Bettmann Film Archive; p. 408, Culver Pictures, Inc.; p. 421, Martha Swope; p. 429, Friedman-Abeles; p. 430, Friedman-Abeles.